Abbatial Authority and the Writing of History in the Middle Ages

Abbatial Authority and the Writing of History in the Middle Ages

BENJAMIN POHL

OXFORD
UNIVERSITY PRESS

Great Clarendon Street, Oxford, OX2 6DP,
United Kingdom

Oxford University Press is a department of the University of Oxford.
It furthers the University's objective of excellence in research, scholarship,
and education by publishing worldwide. Oxford is a registered trade mark of
Oxford University Press in the UK and in certain other countries

© Benjamin Pohl 2023

The moral rights of the author have been asserted

All rights reserved. No part of this publication may be reproduced, stored in
a retrieval system, or transmitted, in any form or by any means, without the
prior permission in writing of Oxford University Press, or as expressly permitted
by law, by licence or under terms agreed with the appropriate reprographics
rights organization. Enquiries concerning reproduction outside the scope of the
above should be sent to the Rights Department, Oxford University Press, at the
address above

You must not circulate this work in any other form
and you must impose this same condition on any acquirer

Published in the United States of America by Oxford University Press
198 Madison Avenue, New York, NY 10016, United States of America

British Library Cataloguing in Publication Data
Data available

Library of Congress Control Number: 2023940940

ISBN 978–0–19–879537–7

DOI: 10.1093/oso/9780198795377.001.0001

Printed and bound by
CPI Group (UK) Ltd, Croydon, CR0 4YY

Links to third party websites are provided by Oxford in good faith and
for information only. Oxford disclaims any responsibility for the materials
contained in any third party website referenced in this work.

For Leah and Anneli

Acknowledgements

The motivation for writing this book came from a place of curiosity, of *not* knowing. When researching the work of Robert of Torigni, celebrated abbot-historian of Mont-Saint-Michel, I increasingly found myself wondering how common (or not) it was for the heads of medieval monasteries to play an active part in historical writing, be that by putting their own pen to parchment or by commissioning, facilitating, resourcing, and managing the historiographical endeavours of others inside and outside their communities. I found, to my surprise, that little scholarly attention had been paid to the subject beyond the level of individual case studies, and except for an article-length survey written in German some ten years ago—and still virtually unknown in the anglophone academy—no attempt had been made to study systematically the important relationship between abbatial authority and the writing of history in the Middle Ages. In attending to this desideratum, I have incurred debts that no honest man can pay. Funding was provided by, in the first instance, the British Academy (Mid-Career Fellowship, 2019–21; Neil Ker Memorial Fund, 2018), with further fellow-/scholarships from the Faculty of Theology, University of Fulda/ *Bibliotheca Fuldensis* (Gangolf Schrimpf Visiting Fellowship, 2019), Durham University (Lendrum Priory Residential Research Library Fellowship, 2019), Fordham University, New York (Faculty Visiting Fellowship, 2019), and the Newberry Library, Chicago (Center for Renaissance Studies Faculty Fellowship, 2019). My home institution, the University of Bristol, granted me research leave, a Seedcorn Research Grant from the Centre for Material Texts (2020), a Conference/Workshop Grant from the Bristol Institute for Research in the Humanities and Arts (2018), a Next Generation Visiting Professorship (to host Scott Bruce, 2023), an Arts Faculty Visiting Fellowship (to host Nicholas Paul, 2018), and a Benjamin Meaker Visiting Professorship (to host Steven Vanderputten, 2017). The monastic community of Downside Abbey, Somerset (now the Community of St Gregory the Great at Southgate House, Devon) proved an invaluable partner in my endeavours, and I am grateful to them for their collaboration and hospitality. I also thank Downside's Director of Heritage, Simon Johnson, and former Outreach Officer, Steven Parsons, for their support and advice. Others whose judicious counsel and kind encouragement were instrumental to this book's completion, and who are deserving of special mention, include Liesbeth van Houts, Scott Bruce, Tessa Webber, Laura Gathagan, Brendan Smith, Jamie Doherty, Simon Parsons, Rick Sowerby, and Richard Allen, who read drafts of this book (or parts thereof) and helped chaperone it through to completion.

Samu Niskanen, Lauri Leinonen, and Olli-Pekka Kasurinen granted me advance access to the database of their ERC-funded project *Medieval Publishing from c.1000–1500*. My former PhD students, Dan Booker and Alice Morrey, acted as research assistants during the COVID-19 pandemic, whilst María Abellán, a former postgraduate student on Bristol's MA Medieval Studies, contributed to the related online exhibition via a work placement (https://historyandcommunity.com/). Those who kindly advised me on specific topics and/or provided drafts of their own work prior to publication include Marie Bisson, James Clark, Laura Cleaver, Stephen Church, Margaret Connolly, Coraline Coutant, Julia Crick, Coraline Daydé, David Ganz, Véronique Gazeau, John Gillingham, Bernd Goebel, Sarah Greer, Martin Heale, Johanna Jebe, Jesse Keskiaho, Stéphane Lecouteux, Graham Loud, Rosamond McKitterick, Gert Melville, Carolyn Muessig, Thomas O'Donnell, Fabien Paquet, Nicholas Paul, Alison Ray, Pascal Rideau, Levi Roach, Charlie Rozier, Winfried Rudolf, Kathryn Rudy, Francesco Siri, Alessandra Sorbello Staub, Johannes Staub, Dominique Stutzmann, Jonathan Turnock, Jan Vandeburie, Steven Vanderputten, Nicholas Vincent, Björn Weiler, Joshua Westgard, Beth Williamson, Ulrich Winzer, Harald Wolter-von dem Knesebeck, David Zettl, and Miha Zor. One person whose guidance and friendship over the years have contributed more than anyone's to setting me on the scholarly path, but who sadly will not witness the publication of this book, is Christoph Houswitschka—Du fehlst mir, mein lieber Freund und Lehrer. Thanks are due also to the many libraries and archives (and their staff) who granted me access to their collections, supplied photographs, and gave permission for their reproduction (cf. List of Figures and Bibliography). Finally, I want to thank my loving wife and learned companion, Leah. Without her, this book would not exist. During the years it took to conduct and write up my research, her faith and reassurance brought me back from the brink of desperation and defeat more times than I can remember; her patience and sacrifice enabled me to continue even in challenging times; and her love keeps empowering me to do what I could not do—and to be who I could not be—on my own. It is to her and our amazing daughter, Anneli, that this book is dedicated.

Contents

List of Abbreviations	xi
List of Figures	xiii
Introduction	1
1. Abbatial Authorship	14
1.1 Introduction	14
1.2 Writing with Authority	20
1.3 Historical Writing as Self-Fashioning	45
1.4 Abbess-Historians—An Exceptionalism?	73
1.5 Conclusions	88
2. Abbatial Patronage	91
2.1 Introduction	91
2.2 Abbatial Patronage—A Case Apart?	99
2.3 Resistance and Reinforcement	112
2.4 Commission, Competition, and Quality Control	127
2.5 Obscured and Concealed Patronage	141
2.6 Architects of Memory	151
2.7 Conclusions	167
3. Abbatial Book Provision and Library Building	169
3.1 Introduction	169
3.2 Book Production and Procurement	177
3.3 Books as Commemorative Currency	192
3.4 Resourcing and Collaboration	218
3.5 'Interlibrary Loans'	233
3.6 Conclusions	250
4. 'In studio abbatis'	252
4.1 Introduction	252
4.2 Abbatial Workplaces	263
4.3 Private Collections	280
4.4 Custodianship, Inheritance, and Bequest	297
4.5 Conclusions	313
Conclusion	316
Appendix: The Abbots of Flavigny and Their Deeds (*Series abbatum Flaviniacensium*)	325
Bibliography	333
Index	399

List of Abbreviations

AASS	*Acta Sanctorum*, ed. by Société des Bollandistes, 68 vols. (Paris: Palm., 1643–1940).
BBM	*Bibliotheca Belgica manuscripta*, ed. by Antonius Sanderus, 2 vols. (Lille: Insulis, 1641–3).
BMF	*Bibliothèques médiévales de France: Répertoire des catalogues, inventaires, listes diverses de manuscrits médiévaux (VIIIe–XVIIIe siècles)*, http://www.libraria.fr/BMF/.
CALMA	*Compendium Auctorum Latinorum Medii Aevi*, ed. by Michael Lapidge et al., 38 vols. (Florence: SISMEL-Edizioni del Galluzzo, 2000–21).
CGM	*Catalogue général des manuscrits des bibliothèques publiques de France: Départements*, 52 vols. (Paris: Plon, 1886–1960).
CHLBI	*The Cambridge History of Libraries in Britain and Ireland*, ed. by Elizabeth Leedham-Green et al., 3 vols. (Cambridge: Cambridge University Press, 2006).
CHMMLW	*The Cambridge History of Medieval Monasticism in the Latin West*, ed. by Alison I. Beach and Isabelle Cochelin, 2 vols. (Cambridge: Cambridge University Press, 2020).
CMBLC	*Corpus of Medieval British Library Catalogues*, ed. by Richard Sharpe et al., 16 vols. (London: British Library, 1990–).
GB	*Germania Benedictina*, ed. by Ulrich Faust et al., 12 vols. (St. Ottilien: EOS, 1970–2014).
MBKDS	*Mittelalterliche Bibliothekskataloge Deutschlands und der Schweiz*, ed. by Paul Lehmann et al., 4 vols. (Munich: Beck, 1918–2009).
MBKÖ	*Mittelalterliche Bibliothekskataloge Österreichs*, ed. by Theodor Gottlieb et al., 5 vols. (Vienna: Österreichische Akademie der Wissenschaften, 1915–71).
MGH	*Monumenta Germaniae Historica*,
Epp.	*Epistolae (in Quart)*
Epp. sel.	*Epistolae selectae*
Poetae	*Poetae Latini medii aevi*
SS	*Scriptores (in Folio)*
SS rer. Germ.	*Scriptores rerum Germanicarum in usum scholarum separatim editi*
SS rer. Lang.	*Scriptores rerum Langobardicarum et Italicarum*
SS rer. Merov.	*Scriptores rerum Merovingicarum*
MLGB3	*Medieval Libraries of Great Britain*, http://mlgb3.bodleian.ox.ac.uk/.
PL	*Patrologia Latina*, ed. by Jean-Paul Migne, 221 vols. (Paris: Garnier, 1841–55).
RB	*The Rule of St Benedict*, ed./tr. by Bruce L. Venarde (Cambridge, MA: Harvard University Press, 2011).

List of Figures

Cover image Karlsruhe, Badische Landesbibliothek, Cod. Lichtenthal 20, fol. 184r, reproduced with permission.

1.1 Hildegard of Bingen/Rupertsberg and her *amanuensis*, Volmar. Heidelberg, Universitätsbibliothek, MS Cod. Sal. X.16, fol. 3v, reproduced under Creative Commons licence CC BY-SA 4.0.   34

1.2a Miniature depicting Jerome. Avranches, Bibliothèque patrimoniale, MS 159, fol. 4r, reproduced with permission.   35

1.2b Miniature depicting Eusebius. Avranches, Bibliothèque patrimoniale, MS 159, fol. 7v, reproduced with permission.   35

1.2c Miniature depicting Robert of Torigni and his personal scribe, Adam(?). Avranches, Bibliothèque patrimoniale, MS 159, fol. 70r, reproduced with permission.   36

1.2d Miniature depicting Robert of Torigni and Henry of Huntingdon. Avranches, Bibliothèque patrimoniale, MS 159, fol. 174v, reproduced with permission.   36

1.3 Stephen of Saint-Airy and his scribe. Verdun, Bibliothèque d'étude du Grand Verdun, MS 8, fol. 1v © CAGV, all rights reserved, reproduced with permission.   38

1.4a Rupert of Deutz and his scribal assistant. Munich, Bayerische Staatsbibliothek, MS Clm. 14355, fol. 1r, reproduced under Creative Commons licence CC BY-NC-SA 4.0.   40

1.4b Rupert of Deutz as scribe. Munich, Bayerische Staatsbibliothek, MS Clm. 14355, fol. 1v, reproduced under Creative Commons licence CC BY-NC-SA 4.0.   41

1.5 Hugh of Flavigny's 'anti-dedicatory' poem. Berlin, Staatsbibliothek zu Berlin–Preußischer Kulturbesitz, MS Phill. 1870, fol. 7r, public domain, reproduced with permission in accordance with the German Copyright Act (UrhG).   55

2.1 Leonas of Casauria and Pope Adrian IV. Paris, Bibliothèque nationale de France, MS Lat. 5411, fol. 253r, reproduced with permission.   99

2.2 Alan de Nesse holding a book. Oxford, Bodleian Library, MS Bodley 39, fol. 169r, reproduced under Creative Commons licence CC BY-NC 4.0.   111

2.3 William of Tournai writing in his bed. Paris, Institut de France–Bibliothèque Mazarine, MS 753, fol. ix, reproduced under Creative Commons licence CC BY-NC 3.0.   117

xiv   LIST OF FIGURES

2.4   The 'Sturmius-pillar' in the crypt of St Michael's Church, Fulda.
      Michaelskirche–Bistum Fulda, reproduced with permission.   158

2.5   Eigil of Fulda's (empty) grave in the crypt of St Michael's Church,
      Fulda. Michaelskirche–Bistum Fulda, reproduced with permission.   159

2.6   Andreas Lang's portrait in the *Fasciculus abbatum*. Bamberg,
      Staatsbibliothek, MS RB. Msc. 49, fol. 54v, photo: Gerald Raab, reproduced
      under Creative Commons licence CC BY-SA 4.0.   164

3.1   Desiderius of Montecassino and his books. Vatican, Biblioteca Apostolica
      Vaticana, MS Vat. lat. 1202, fol. 2r, reproduced with permission.   191

3.2a Berthold of Weingarten's book list. Stuttgart, Württembergische
      Landesbibliothek, MS HB I 240, fol. 43r, public domain, reproduced
      with permission in accordance with the German Copyright Act (UrhG).   197

3.2b Berthold of Weingarten's *gesta*. Stuttgart, Württembergische
      Landesbibliothek, MS HB I 240, fol. 44r, public domain, reproduced
      with permission in accordance with the German Copyright Act (UrhG).   198

3.3   Warin of St Albans and his books. London, British Library, MS Cotton
      Claudius E IV, fol. 125v © British Library Board 02/02/2023, reproduced
      with permission.   202

3.4   Paul of Caen and his books. London, British Library, MS Cotton Nero
      D VII, fol. 13v © British Library Board 02/02/2023, reproduced with
      permission.   203

3.5   Robert de Lindsey presenting the *Peterborough Psalter*. Cambridge,
      Fitzwilliam Museum, MS 12, fol. 139v © The Fitzwilliam Museum,
      Cambridge, reproduced with permission.   205

3.6   Hitda of Meschede presenting the *Hitda Codex*. Darmstadt, Universitäts-
      und Landesbibliothek, MS 1640, fol. 6r, reproduced under Creative
      Commons licence CC0.   207

3.7   Kunigunde of Prague, her nuns, and her two scribes, Colda and Beneš.
      Prague, National Library of the Czech Republic, MS XIV A 17, fol. 1v,
      reproduced with permission.   209

3.8   Frowin of Engelberg and his scribe, Richene. Engelberg, Stiftsbibliothek,
      MS Cod. 5, fol. 1r, reproduced with permission.   213

3.9a Reinher's inventory in the *Fasciculus abbatum*. Bamberg, Staatsbibliothek,
      MS RB. Msc. 49, fol. 57r, photo: Gerald Raab, reproduced under Creative
      Commons licence CC BY-SA 4.0.   214

3.9b Nonnosus's inventory in the *Fasciculus abbatum*. Bamberg, Staatsbibliothek,
      MS RB. Msc. 49, fol. 57v, photo: Gerald Raab, reproduced under Creative
      Commons licence CC BY-SA 4.0.   215

3.10 Faritius of Abingdon holding a book. London, British Library, MS Cotton
      Claudius C IX, fol. 144r © British Library Board 02/02/2023, reproduced
      with permission.   224

4.1 Nineteenth-century portrait of Robert of Torigni in his private study. Édouard de Bergevin, 1889, public domain (out of copyright). 254

4.2 Wibald of Corvey's(?) writing desk. Berlin, Staatsbibliothek zu Berlin–Preußischer Kulturbesitz, MS lat. fol. 252, fol. 1v, public domain, reproduced with permission in accordance with the German Copyright Act (UrhG). 275

4.3 Ansbert of Saint-Wandrille and his book chest. Le Havre, Bibliothèque municipale Armand Salacrou, MS 332, fol. 41v, reproduced with permission. 294

4.4 Simon of St Albans and his book chest. London, British Library, MS Cotton Claudius E IV, fol. 124r © British Library Board 02/02/2023, reproduced with permission. 295

4.5 Hamelin of Gloucester(?) receiving a charter from King Henry II. Kew, National Archives, C 150/1, stamped fol. 18 © The National Archives, reproduced with permission. 308

Permissions were obtained from the relevant copyright holders under the licensing terms indicated above.

Introduction

From 11–13 June 1480, the Abbey of SS Peter and Paul in Erfurt played host to the General Chapter of the Bursfelde Congregation, a confederation of reformed Benedictine monasteries founded in the early fifteenth century and named after Bursfelde Abbey in present-day Lower Saxony.[1] Twenty-seven heads of house had travelled to Erfurt at the invitation of Theoderic of Homborch, Bursfelde's then abbot (1469–85) and president of the Congregation, with twenty-three sending deputies or apologies.[2] As was customary, Mass was celebrated by those in attendance and a homily delivered by the host, Gunther of Nordhausen, Erfurt's ruling abbot (1458–1501).[3] The subject chosen by Gunther was one that could be expected to ruffle some feathers amongst his peers. Provisionally titled *De historia sermo claustralis*, the homily was committed to writing in January 1481 with the more programmatic title *De historiae studio et utilitate*, and it is to this written version made for publication and circulation that we owe our knowledge of this important text today.[4] Judging from *De historiae*, Gunther began his verbal address with an elaborate parable: he who compares history with the sun ('historiam cum sole comparaverit') will find that just as the sun invigorates all life on Earth, history underpins the entire monastic lifestyle ('historia vitam, fidem, auctoritatem et stabilimentum donat omnibus rebus in vita communi'). There is

---

[1] Pius Engelbert, 'Die Bursfelder Kongregation: Werden und Untergang einer benediktinischen Reformbewegung', in *925 Jahre Kloster Bursfelde–40 Jahre Geistliches Zentrum Kloster Bursfelde*, ed. by Rüdiger Krause and Thomas Kaufmann (Göttingen: Wallstein, 2020), pp. 83–101; Walter Ziegler, 'Die Bursfelder Kongregation', in *Die Reformverbände und Kongregationen der Benediktiner im deutschen Sprachraum*, ed. by Ulrich Faust and Franz Quartal (St Ottilien: Eos, 1999), pp. 315–407. On the General Chapter, see Paulus Volk, *Die Generalkapitel der Bursfelder Benediktiner-Kongregation* (Münster: Aschendorff, 1928).

[2] The General Chapter convened at Erfurt on over twenty occasions, second only to Bursfelde itself; see Ziegler, 'Kongregation', pp. 367–72; Matthias Eifler, *Die Bibliothek des Erfurter Petersklosters im späten Mittelalter: Buchkultur und Literaturrezeption im Kontext der Bursfelder Klosterreform*, 2 vols. (Cologne: Böhlau, 2017), I, 96–7.

[3] The Chapter's procedure is set out in Paulus Volk, *Die Generalkapitels-Rezesse der Bursfelder Kongregation*, Vol. I: *1458–1530* (Siegburg: Respublica, 1955), pp. 186–90.

[4] Edited in Barbara Frank, *Das Erfurter Peterskloster im 15. Jahrhundert* (Göttingen: Vandenhoeck and Ruprecht, 1973), pp. 382–7 [hereafter *De historiae*]; Frank's view of this text as an early draft of a speech intended for delivery at the General Chapter of 1485 is unconvincing, and *De historiae* almost certainly represents an authorial revision of the 1480 homily made for dissemination. Gunther's autograph is lost, and the sole copy (Melk, Stiftsbibliothek, MS 20, pp. 207–13) produced by Oliver Legipont in the early eighteenth century is printed in *Antiquitates Bursfeldenses*, ed. by Johann G. Leuckfeld (Leipzig: Freytag, 1713), pp. 183–90; Leuckfeld's transcription contains many errors, however, some of which are repeated by Frank, which is why citations hereafter will refer, in the first instance, to Legipont's manuscript.

no light without the sun, and no community without history. Without history, man is not man and monks are not monks ('Sine historia homo non est homo. Sine ea non sumus monachi').[5] Moving on to address his audience directly, Gunther expresses great astonishment 'that the study of history [. . .] should be treated so uncaringly, poorly, and improperly—if indeed it is treated at all—in our cloisters'.[6] To rectify the situation, a 'doctus historiarum magister' should be appointed in every monastery for the instruction of its monks, even the most senior of whom ('seniores') are but children ('infantes sunt') in their historical studies.[7] The term 'seniores' here refers to both advanced age and seniority of office, the insinuation being that even the highest-ranking individuals in these monasteries—the abbots—were often very ignorant of the past ('omnium rerum antiquarum ignorantissimi'). 'I was baffled', Gunther continues, 'that when I asked the abbots of our order about their predecessors and the founders of their monasteries ('de fundatoribus et antecessoribus monasteriorum suorum'), I would find them dumbstruck like fish ('magis mutos deprehendi quam pisces') with nothing to respond ('[n]ihil enim, plane nihil respondere sciebant')'.[8] As far as Gunther was concerned, knowledge of the past was a moral imperative,[9] and ignorance of it inexcusable in a monastic superior. Reiterating his earlier point about history's centrality to the monastic enterprise, he cautions his audience to shun this dreadful monster ('monstrum horrendum'),[10] whose lack of historical knowledge makes him the beastliest of beasts ('bestia bestialior erit'),[11] and who is therefore unfit to govern a religious community with authority.

The relationship between abbatial authority and the writing of history portrayed with great conviction and pathos in *De historiae* is the subject of this

---

[5] MS Melk 20, pp. 207–8 and 211; *De historiae*, ed. Frank, pp. 382–3 and 385.

[6] MS Melk 20, p. 208: 'Quod cum ita sit, miror sane demirorque, religiosi sacrae congregationis patres, studium historicum, sine quo nullus solide erudiri potest, adeo frigide, ieiune et inepte—si tractetur—in monasteriis nostris passim tractari'; *De historiae*, ed. Frank, p. 383.

[7] MS Melk 20, p. 208; *De historiae*, ed. Frank, p. 383.

[8] MS Melk 20, p. 208; *De historiae*, ed. Frank, p. 383.

[9] On this moral imperative, cf. Sigbjørn O. Sønnesyn, *William of Malmesbury and the Ethics of History* (Woodbridge: Boydell, 2012); Georgia Henley, 'Geoffrey of Monmouth and the Conventions of History Writing in Early 12th-Century England', in *A Companion to Geoffrey of Monmouth*, ed. by Georgia Henley and Joshua B. Smith (Leiden: Brill, 2020), pp. 291–314 (p. 296).

[10] MS Melk 20, p. 208: 'Fugite posthac monstrum istud horrendum, cui lumen rationis ademptum, ignorantiam scilicet historiarum'; *De historiae*, ed. Frank, p. 383.

[11] MS Melk 20, p. 212; *De historiae*, ed. Frank, p. 386. Gunther was not the first to describe humans ignorant of the past as irrational beasts. In his *Historia Anglorum*, Henry of Huntingdon had similarly distinguished rational creatures ('rationabiles') from brutes ('brutis') on the basis that the latter, be they humans ('homines') or beasts ('animalia'), refuse to learn about the past; *Henry of Huntingdon: Historia Anglorum–The History of the English People*, ed./tr. by Diana E. Greenway (Oxford: Oxford University Press, 1996), pp. 4–5. For further examples, see Antonia Gransden, 'Prologues in the Historiography of Twelfth-Century England', in *England in the Twelfth Century*, ed. by Daniel Williams (Woodbridge: Boydell, 1990), pp. 55–81; Matthew Kempshall, *Rhetoric and the Writing of History, 400–1500* (Manchester: Manchester University Press, 2011), pp. 260–1. On boundaries between humans and animals in medieval thought, see Ian P. Wei, *Thinking about Animals in Thirteenth-Century Paris: Theologians on the Boundary between Humans and Animals* (Cambridge: Cambridge University Press, 2020).

book, and dwelling on Gunther's arguments—and their reception amongst contemporaries—a little longer serves to introduce the various lines of enquiry I will be pursuing in and across its individual chapters. To begin with, there is the expectation that no monastic community, whether large or small, should be exempt from the duty to record its history in writing. The reason for this, we are told, is that even the lowliest and most obscure house ('vilissimum et obscurissimum omnium') has a story worth preserving for posterity. Who were the founders, what were their intentions, and what did they give? Who were the abbots and abbesses, how long did they hold the office, and what good and bad things did they do? How did the community's fortunes wax and wane under their abbatial leadership?[12] These, Gunther explains, are questions *every* monastic superior must be able to answer, and failure to do so constitutes a violation of abbatial leadership and duty of care.

A strikingly similar expectation was voiced some thirty years earlier by Sophia of Stolberg (*fl.* 1451), abbess of Helfta and author of her community's *Libellus de fundatione*. In a letter addressed to her peer, the abbot of Halberstadt, Sophia reminds—and perhaps implicitly reprimands—her correspondent that it would be absurd not to know the history of one's own monastery and the names of those through whose pious deeds and donations it was permitted to thrive in this world ('valde absurdum esset ignorare eos, per quos ad talem proventum felicitatem pervenimus'), which is why Sophia led by example and spent day and night ('die noctuque') gathering sources from near and far ('de diversis mundi partibus in unum collecti') to write her history of the abbey's foundation and its benefactors ('disposui scribere libellum [. . .] primo de inchoatione claustri nostri [et] nomina ac genus fundatorum nostrorum') for the education of its present and future inhabitants ('[a]d profectum et utilitatem tam presentium quam futurorum').[13] Whether Sophia's words were meant primarily to justify her own historiographical activity or apply some peer-pressure on Halberstadt's abbot to do the same for his community, not every monastic superior would have been in a position to follow her example and meet these high expectations, subsequently reiterated by Gunther, even if he/she were thus inclined.

In fact, there is evidence that Gunther's emphatic appeal to the 1480 General Chapter was met with some reservation on the part of his audience. The subject of

---

[12] MS Melk 20, p. 210; *De historiae*, ed. Frank, pp. 384–5: 'An non fundatorem seu fundatricem habuit? Quis vel quaenam ille seu illa? Quae familia, vita et intentio utriusque fuit? Quae et quanta donatio claustri? Quae privilegia? Quae series et successio praelatorum seu praelatarum? Quamdiu sedit? Quid quisve seu quaeve bene vel male egit? Quomodo de saeculo in saeculum monasterium crevit et decrevit? Ex quibus occasionibus et circumstantiis?'.

[13] Hanover, Niedersächsisches Landesarchiv, Dep. 76, C 113; edited in *Urkundenbuch der Klöster der Grafschaft Mansfeld*, ed. by Max Krühne (Halle: Hendel, 1888), pp. 223–6 (p. 223) (= no. 148); also cf. Hans Patze, 'Klostergründung und Klosterchronik', *Blätter für deutsche Landesgeschichte* 113 (1977), 89–121, repr. in *Ausgewählte Aufsätze von Hans Patze*, ed. by Peter Johanek et al. (Stuttgart: Thorbecke, 2002), pp. 251–84 (p. 278); Charlotte Woodford, *Nuns as Historians in Early Modern Germany* (Oxford: Oxford University Press, 2002), pp. 185–6.

the abbots' scepticism and Gunther's response to it are both reflected in *De historiae*, which includes a short dialogue that may well resemble the heated conversations that had ensued following—or even during—the homily's delivery:

> You say: where is an abbot supposed find time for this [the writing of history] when he must take care of [the monastery's] sacred and economic business? [To this I, Gunther, respond:] If indeed he cannot—or does not want to—undertake this work personally, is there not someone else suitable within the monastery to whom he can delegate it by appointment? And if there is none, there will be someone elsewhere who could be approached to execute the work well.[14]

The message is clear: the apprehensions of his peers notwithstanding, Gunther insists that the responsibility for the writing of history inside a monastery lies ultimately with the abbot, who cannot render his community a greater service than through historical education, the reward of which outweighs all the silver and gold in this world ('nec auro vel argento comparandum').[15] What could be more advantageous, therefore, than if the General Chapter were to pass a statute ('statutum') obliging every abbot to take personal responsibility for committing his monastery's history to writing ('ut quilibet praelatus de conscribendis annalibus vel historia monasterii sui sollicitus esse debeat')? Better still, what if the pope were to issue a mandate ('universale mandatum') compelling all monasteries and bishoprics to demonstrate the same zeal ('studium') and care ('curam') in compiling its domestic annals ('colligendis annalibus suis')? Perhaps the emperor would consider adding a similar command ('suum adderet praeceptum') and oblige his magnates to imitate their ecclesiastical counterparts by promoting the writing of history in their secular territories ('quisque in suo territorio')?[16] This remained wishful thinking. No pope or emperor issued a decree formally prescribing the writing of history, nor did the Congregation respond to Gunther's fervent call to action with official legislation. The question, however, is whether his arguments concerning the abbot's principal role in the writing of history were so unrealistic as to be dismissed out of hand, or whether they were informed, at least partially, by historical precedent and practice. We already saw one precedent in the *Libellus de fundatione monasterii in Helfta* written by Sophia of Stolberg thirty

---

[14] MS Melk 20, p. 209: 'Dicis: Unde otium abbati, qui curam debet habere rei sacrae et oeconomicae? Licet ipse nec velit nec possit hunc laborem in se suscipere, ac non in conventu idoneus aliquis, quem ad hoc opus deligere et constitutere valeat? At desit, aliunde petendus erit qui bonum opus perficiat'; *De historiae*, ed. Frank, p. 384.

[15] MS Melk 20, pp. 208-9: 'Curate igitur, sacrae congregationis antistites, ut hoc studium [. . .] in scholis nostris vigeat, floreat, crescat fructusque ferat mortali et perenni vita dignos [. . .] Nemo poterit certius et iustius admirari providentiam Divinam in regenda navicula ecclesiae, suae quam hoc modo, si origines et progressum cuiuslibet in particulari attentius legat'; *De historiae*, ed. Frank, pp. 383-4.

[16] MS Melk 20, p. 209; *De historiae*, ed. Frank, p. 384. It is not implausible that Gunther's suggestion took its inspiration from the precedent of Charlemagne's famous *Epistola de litteris colendis*.

years prior to the publication of *De historiae*, but just how far can we trace this tradition of abbots and abbesses acting as their communities' historians, and just how widespread was it?

In 1496, sixteen years after Gunther had delivered his homily at Erfurt, the Bursfelde General Chapter again provided a platform for a similar appeal. The speaker designated to address the prelates gathered at Reinhardsbrunn was Johannes Trithemius, then abbot of Sponheim (1483–1506), though his words were read out *in absentia* by his colleague, Andreas Lang, abbot of Michelsberg in Bamberg (1483–1502).[17] Sponheim and Bamberg had joined the Bursfelde Congregation in 1417 and 1467, respectively, and their representatives claimed considerable authority in its assemblies.[18] Trithemius used this authority to revive Gunther's cause and reprimand his fellow abbots for having allowed the standard of literacy and scribal expertise to decline dramatically within their communities, to the detriment of historiography.[19] This was not a new gripe for Trithemius, who just a few years before had published a treatise in praise of monastic scribes.[20] At Reinhardsbrunn, he doubled down on his arguments by reproaching his peers for neglecting not only their own education, but also, and worse still, that of their monks ('quod gravis est, monachis suis studium legendi interdicunt').[21] Quick to name and shame, Trithemius singled out the abbots of Hirsau for having disregarded their community's long historiographical tradition ever since the fateful regime of Wigand (1369–80). Unlike his predecessors—who, as discussed later in this book, had championed the writing of history and occasionally even served as scribes themselves—Wigand is said to have misled his monks by encouraging them to revel in their ignorance and refusing to read or write about the past.[22]

Exaggerated though this portrayal of Wigand might be, its significance lies in the fact that the abbots who followed his example by neglecting the writing of history in their monasteries are presented as breaking with historical tradition. To Trithemius, Gunther, and Sophia, their behaviour stood in sharp contrast with

---

[17] Barbara Frank, 'Ein Entwurf zu einer Kapitelsansprache des Abtes Johannes Trithemius aus dem Jahr 1496', *Studien und Mitteilungen zur Geschichte des Benediktinerordens und seiner Zweige* 80 (1969), 145–204 (p. 146).

[18] Ziegler, 'Kongregation', pp. 376–407.

[19] *De duodecim excidiis observantiae regularis*, edited in Frank, 'Entwurf', pp. 158–204 [hereafter *De duodecim excidiis*], with side-by-side versions of the author's draft (Oldenburg, Landesbibliothek, MS 99i) and the final published version.

[20] *Johannes Trithemius: In Praise of Scribes (De laude scriptorum)*, ed./tr. by Klaus Arnold and Roland Berendt (Lawrence, KS: Coronado, 1974); cf. Klaus Arnold, 'Von Trittenheim nach Sponheim und Würzburg: Zu Leben und Werk des Büchersammlers Johannes Trithemius (1462-1516)', in *Johannes Trithemius (1462-1516): Abt und Büchersammler, Humanist und Geschichtsschreiber*, ed. by Klaus Arnold and Franz Fuchs (Würzburg: Königshausen & Neumann, 2019), pp. 19–34 (pp. 26–8).

[21] *De duodecim excidiis*, ed. Frank, p. 179.

[22] *Chronicon Hirsaugiense*, in *Johannes Trithemius: Opera historica, quotquot hactenus reperiri potuerunt omnia*, ed. by Marquard Freher, 2 vols. (Frankfurt a. M.: Marne & Aubry, 1601; repr. Minerva, 1966), II, 1–235 (p. 230): 'Aiunt enim: Quid nobis scire, conducere potest fundationis monasteriorum nostrorum antiquitas?'; Noel L. Brann, *The Abbot Trithemius (1462-1516): The Renaissance of Monastic Humanism* (Leiden: Brill, 1981), pp. 309–12.

a 'golden age' in which monastic superiors took regular charge of their communities' historiographical production, not just at Hirsau, but across the European map. Was this 'golden age' a product of their imagination and nostalgia, or is there evidence to corroborate the notion that abbots and abbesses were instrumental to the writing of history in the Middle Ages? And if there is, then how did they use their abbatial authority and resources to enable historical writing within their monasteries in addition—or as an alternative—to putting their pen to parchment? Answering these questions, and others related to them, is the objective of this book.

Studying the relationship between abbatial authority and historical writing in the millennium known as the European Middle Ages (c.500–1500) is no small task, and one that requires consideration, however brief, of what history was/is, why it was written in medieval religious communities, by whom, and with whose authorization. Fortunately, these considerations do not have to start from scratch, but on the contrary can build on a long and prolific tradition of scholarship that is, if anything, too substantial to be reviewed in full here. Beginning with the fundamental question of *what* can—and, by implication, what cannot—be considered 'history', 'historical writing', and, in a broader sense, 'historical culture', much ink has been spilled by proponents of both inclusive and exclusive definitions, from meta-level surveys to comparative perspectives and forensic case studies of individual authors and texts.[23] The definition adopted here is an all-encompassing one that transcends boundaries of language, form, and 'genre' to include a wide range of historical narratives—that is, texts that present the past, or a version thereof, in various narrative formats—from Latin to vernacular writings; from prose to poetry; from books (and their fragments) to inscriptions and visual depictions; from annals, chronicles, and *gesta* to the narrative contents of charters, cartularies, and letters; from local, domestic, and institutional narratives

---

[23] Recent examples of such broader and comparative studies include John H. Arnold, *What Is Medieval History?* 2nd ed. (Medford, MA: Polity, 2021); Björn Weiler, 'Historical Writing in Europe, c.1100–1300', in *The Chronicles of Medieval Wales and the March: New Contexts, Studies, and Texts*, ed. by Ben Guy et al. (Turnhout: Brepols, 2020), pp. 33–67; *How the Past was Used: Historical Cultures, c.750–2000*, ed. by Peter Lambert and Björn Weiler (Oxford: Oxford University Press, 2018); *Medieval Historical Writing: Britain and Ireland, 500–1500*, ed. by Jennifer Jahner et al. (Cambridge: Cambridge University Press, 2019); *The Oxford History of Historical Writing*, Vol. 2: *400–1400*, ed. by Sarah Foot and Chase F. Robinson (Oxford: Oxford University Press, 2015); see also the titles published since 2015 in the 'Writing History in the Middle Ages' series, https://boydellandbrewer.com/writing-history-in-the-middle-ages/. Works that remain fundamental to the subject include Hans-Werner Goetz, *Geschichtsschreibung und Geschichtsbewußtsein im hohen Mittelalter* (Berlin: De Gruyter, 2008); Patrick J. Geary, *Phantoms of Remembrance: Memory and Oblivion at the End of the First Millennium* (Princeton, NJ: Princeton University Press, 1994); Franz-Josef Schmale, *Funktion und Formen mittelalterlicher Geschichtsschreibung* (Darmstadt: Wissenschaftliche Buchgesellschaft, 1985); Herbert Grundmann, *Geschichtsschreibung im Mittelalter: Gattungen, Epochen, Eigenart*, 3rd ed. (Göttingen: Vandenhoeck & Ruprecht, 1978). Needless to say, this list is not exhaustive and inevitably reflects the author's own training and specific interests.

to so-called 'universal' histories; from first-hand recollections of recent events to collective memories and imaginations of the distant past; from the deeds of the living (including autobiographies) to those of the dead; and from narratives that record the imitable accomplishments of one's contemporaries and forebears to those celebrating the exemplary if ultimately unattainable achievements of saints and other larger-than-life personae traditionally classified as 'hagiography'.[24]

The advantage of such an approach is not only that it reflects an increasing consensus in scholarship formed by conversations across the historical disciplines,[25] but also that it resonates with medieval discourse on the subject. We need only look to Gunther's *De historiae* for a conception of historical writing that defies modern preoccupations with literary form and genre. To Gunther, writing history is part of the human condition, something that is as natural to man as flying is to birds and swimming to fish.[26] People of all ages, genders, and ranks take delight in it ('omnis aetas, omnis sexus, omnis homo, seu magnus vel parvus ille sit, delectatur historia'). From the peasants in the alehouses ('rustici in cauponis inter se confabulantur') to the mother soothing her crying child to sleep ('ad somnum reduxit mater plorantem infantiam'), every man, woman, and child turns to history for reassurance, protection, and comfort.[27] What do the prophets relate if not histories ('Quid prophetae ad unum omnes enarrant, nisi historias')? What are the holy Gospels if not a history book ('Quid sanctissima evangelia, quam liber historiarum')? Scripture is pure history ('historia et amplius nihil') written with God's own pen ('stilo divino conscripta'). Moses and the Evangelists are writers of histories ('historiarum scriptores fuerunt'), and he who seeks an accurate understanding of the world must combine knowledge of sacred and profane history ('sacra et profana historia coniugenda est'). Of all subjects taught and studied in a monastery, history is the queen who reigns

---

[24] The relationship between 'history'/'historical writing' and 'hagiography' is a subject of continuing discussion and debate; cf. Samantha K. Herrick, 'Introduction', in *Hagiography and the History of Latin Christendom, 500–1500*, ed. by Samantha K. Herrick (Leiden: Brill, 2019), pp. 1–10; Felice Lifshitz, 'Beyond Positivism and Genre: "Hagiographical" Texts as Historical Narrative', *Viator* 25 (1994), 95–113; now also Felice Lifshitz, 'Still Useless after All These Years: The Concept of "Hagiography" in the Twenty-First Century', in *Writing Normandy: Stories of Saints and Rulers*, ed. by Felice Lifshitz (London: Routledge, 2020), pp. 26–46; recent case studies include Victoria Hodgson, 'History and Hagiography: The *Vita Sancti Servani* and the Foundation of Culross Abbey', *Downside Review* 139 (2021), 65–81.

[25] For example, Jennifer Jahner et al., 'General Introduction', in *Medieval Historical Writing: Britain and Ireland, 500–1500*, ed. by Jennifer Jahner et al. (Cambridge: Cambridge University Press, 2019), pp. 1–15; Laura Cleaver and Andrea Worm, 'Introduction: Making and Reading History Books in the Anglo-Norman World', in *Writing History in the Anglo-Norman World: Manuscripts, Makers and Readers, c.1066–1250*, ed. by Laura Cleaver and Andrea Worm (Woodbridge: York Medieval Press, 2018), pp. 1–6; Robert F. Berkhofer III, *Forgeries and Historical Writing in England, France, and Flanders, 900–1200* (Woodbridge: Boydell 2022).

[26] MS Melk 20, p. 210: 'Ad hunc enim nati sumus, ut volucres coeli ad volandum et pisces ad natandum'; *De historiae*, ed. Frank, p. 385.

[27] MS Melk 20, pp. 207–8: 'Seu terreas secures et impios, seu consoleris pavidos et tristes, seu confortes fideles in fide et persecutionibus, historia opus est, et sine hac nihil unquam efficies' (ibid., p. 207); *De historiae*, ed. Frank, p. 383.

supreme ('historia triumphat et imperat, ut regina a Deo nobis data').[28] Gunther's vision of history and its place at the centre of monastic life and learning owed substantially to the influence of fifteenth-century humanism and reform,[29] and aspects of it might well have struck earlier medieval audiences as somewhat unusual, if not altogether unrecognizable. Still, it provides a useful reminder that for the period covered in this book, and the legacy of Isidore of Seville's definition of *historia* notwithstanding,[30] history was written in various guises and recognized as such, and which shape it took depended as much on authorial preference as it did on local custom, tradition, and circumstance.

This brings us to our second consideration, the question of *why* history was written in medieval monasteries. Much work has been done on this subject, though rather than rehearsing what can reasonably be considered *communis opinio*, I would like to address one model of interpretation that has gained ground as a 'go-to view' of monastic historiographical activity to a degree that seems excessive and difficult to justify, and which actually risks having a reductionist effect on our understanding of history's role in religious communities. Rather than seeing the writing of history as an inherent and integral part of communal life, it has now become something of a commonplace to present the monastic historian's work as a utilitarian exercise in which the decision to commit the past to writing results primarily from internal crises or conflicts with external forces (kings, bishops, monastic rivals, etc.). The fact that some histories were indeed written in response to communal crisis and trauma or in defence against infringement and alienation must not give rise to the assumption that monastic historians typically and by default operated on the back foot,[31] and the increasing tendency

---

[28] MS Melk 20, pp. 207–10; *De historiae*, ed. Frank, pp. 382–5.

[29] Kaspar Elm, 'Monastische Reformen zwischen Humanismus und Reformation', in *900 Jahre Kloster Bursfelde: Reden und Vorträge zum Jubiläum 1993*, ed. by Lothar Perlitt (Göttingen: Vandenhoeck and Ruprecht, 1994), pp. 59–111; Klaus Schreiner, 'Erneuerung durch Erinnerung: Reformstreben, Geschichtsbewußtsein und Geschichtsschreibung im benediktinischen Mönchtum Südwestdeutschlands an der Wende vom 15. zum 16. Jahrhundert', in *Historiographie am Oberrhein im späten Mittelalter und in der frühen Neuzeit*, ed. by Kurt Andermann (Sigmaringen: Thorbecke, 1988), pp. 35–87; Paul Joachimsen, *Geschichtsauffassung und Geschichtsschreibung in Deutschland unter dem Einfluss des Humanismus* (Stuttgart: Teubner, 1910; repr. 1968); Hermann Herbst, 'Niedersächsische Geschichtsschreibung unter dem Einfluss der Bursfelder Reform', *Jahrbuch des Braunschweigischen Geschichtsvereins* 5 (1933), 74–94.

[30] Jamie Wood, 'Isidore of Seville as an Historian', in *A Companion to Isidore of Seville*, ed. by Andrew T. Fear and Jamie Wood (Leiden: Brill, 2019), pp. 153–81; also cf. David Ganz, '*Historia*: Some Lexicographical Considerations', in *Medieval Cantors and Their Craft: Music, Liturgy and the Shaping of History, 800–1500*, ed. by Margot E. Fassler et al. (Woodbridge: Boydell, 2017), pp. 8–22; Robert F. Berkhofer III, 'Rewriting the Past: Monastic Forgeries and Plausible Narratives', in *Rewriting History in the Central Middle Ages, 900–1300*, ed. by Emily A. Winkler and Christopher P. Lewis (Turnhout: Brepols, 2022), pp. 151–67.

[31] Steffen Patzold, *Konflikte im Kloster: Studien zu Auseinandersetzungen in monastischen Gemeinschaften des ottonisch-salischen Reichs* (Husum: Matthiesen, 2000); Markus Krumm, *Herrschaftsumbruch und Historiographie: Zeitgeschichtsschreibung als Krisenbewältigung bei Alexander von Telese und Falco von Benevent* (Berlin: De Gruyter, 2021); Klaus Krönert, 'La production hagiographique en Germanie à l'époque de Louis le Pieux: Productivité littéraire et crises, mais quel rapport?', in *Politische Kultur und Textproduktion unter Ludwig dem Frommen/Culture politique et*

to search for catalysts has led some scholars 'to wonder whether the model which sees communities turn to the pen to record their history and identity in moments of crisis can lead to historians creating or exaggerating crises solely to provide an explanation for why groups of religious wrote'.[32] Perhaps a more helpful position from which to approach the writing of history in a monastic context was outlined in a plenary lecture delivered in 2014 by the then president of the *Monumenta Germaniae Historica*, Rudolf Schieffer, who encourages us to understand the preservation of knowledge about one's origins as a basic socio-anthropological constant that is common to all human life, but which acquires additional significance in communities whose very existence and identity depend on a sense of tradition.[33] For monastic communities, history thus was (and is) a natural and necessary part of life, and writing it a means of self-assurance and, ultimately, survival.

History's vital function as a community-building and identity-affirming life-force means that writing history was a communal activity that involved various agents within and sometimes without the monastery, which finally brings us to the question of *who* participated in—and, importantly, *who* authorized—monastic historiographical production in the Middle Ages. Beginning with the former, there is now a growing recognition in scholarship that focusing primarily on the (named) authors of monastic histories only generates a partial picture of this collaborative mode of production, and that viewing the full panorama requires consideration of other contributors such as scribes and copyists, assistants and *amanuenses*, librarians and archivists, commissioners and patrons, all of whom had significant agency in the process and therefore need to be included in our investigation. Some important work has been done in this respect,[34] including in recent years,[35] but we are yet to witness a breakthrough in scholars' preoccupation with individual authors to disrupt the pervasive view of monastic historians as

---

production littéraire sous Louis le Pieux, ed. by Martin Gravel and Sören Kaschke (Ostfildern: Thorbecke, 2019), pp. 269–373; Alison I. Beach, *The Trauma of Monastic Reform: Community and Conflict in Twelfth-Century Germany* (Cambridge: Cambridge University Press, 2017).

[32] Daniel Talbot, 'Review of Charles C. Rozier, *Writing History in the Community of St Cuthbert, c.700-1130: From Bede to Symeon of Durham*', *History* 106 (2021), 477–8 (p. 478).

[33] This lecture has been published as Rudolf Schieffer, 'Von der Geschichte der Äbte und der Klöster zur Geschichte des Ordens: Grundlinien benediktinischer Historiographie im Mittelalter', in *Benediktiner als Historiker*, ed. by Andreas Sohn (Bochum: Winkler, 2016), pp. 23–39.

[34] For example, Matthew N. Fisher, *Scribal Authorship and the Writing of History in Medieval England* (Columbus, OH: Ohio State University Press, 2012); Monique-Cécile Garand, *Guibert de Nogent et ses secretaires* (Turnhout: Brepols, 1995); Elspeth Kennedy, 'The Scribe as Editor', in *Mélanges de langue et de littérature du Moyen Age et de la Renaissance offerts à Jean Frappier*, 2 vols. (Paris: Minard, 1970), I, 523–31; David W. Rollason, 'Symeon of Durham's *Historia de regibus Anglorum et Dacorum* as a Product of Twelfth-Century Historical Workshops', in *The Long Twelfth-Century View of the Anglo-Saxon Past*, ed. by Martin Brett and David A. Woodman (Farnham: Routledge, 2015), pp. 95–112.

[35] Jeffrey F. Hamburger, *The Birth of the Author: Pictorial Prefaces in Glossed Books of the Twelfth Century* (Toronto: Pontifical Institute of Mediaeval Studies, 2021); Ad van Els, *A Man and His Manuscripts: The Notebooks of Ademar of Chabannes (989-1034)* (Turnhout: Brepols, 2020); *Medieval Publishing from c.1000–1500*, ERC-funded research project (2017-22) at the University of Helsinki led by Samu Niskanen, https://www.helsinki.fi/en/researchgroups/medieval-publishing.

celebrated soloists and instead allow them to be appreciated as members of an orchestra. No orchestra can work without a conductor, and whilst the writing of history in a monastery was a communal and collaborative exercise, it was not a democratic one. Certain individuals wielded greater agency and authority than others by virtue of the offices they held in their communities, but not all have had scholarship devoted to them. Considerable, and perhaps disproportionate, attention has been paid to cantors/precentors, whose increasingly formalized association with the provision and care of books offered them privileged access to resources indispensable for historiographical production and publication.[36] This may help explain why several cantors acted as historians themselves,[37] though the absence of a systematic enquiry beyond the level of individual case studies precludes the identification of a causal link between the role and the activity. The same caveat also applies to other monastic historians in roles of responsibility and institutional leadership, few of whom have had their historiographical activity contextualized specifically against the backdrop of their respective offices—a desideratum that, if attended to, would offer insights into their potential interconnectivity that could be transformative for our understanding of how history was written in medieval monasteries.

This book aims to address this desideratum for the office whose rank and authority within the monastic community were second to none: the abbot. Seeking to understand the operational dynamics of a monastery without considering the abbot is rather like trying to figure out the internal workings of the human body without studying the head, and the writing of history constitutes no exception here. And yet, our knowledge so far rests on provisional foundations provided by, on the one hand, unconnected case studies of individual abbots and their historiographical activity without wider comparison or contextualization,[38] and, on

---

[36] See principally Margot E. Fassler, 'The Office of the Cantor in Early Western Monastic Rules and Customaries: A Preliminary Investigation', *Early Music History* 5 (1985), 29–51; also cf. the more recent contributions to *Medieval Cantors and Their Craft: Music, Liturgy and the Shaping of History, 800–1500*, ed. by Margot E. Fassler et al. (Woodbridge: Boydell, 2017).

[37] For example, Samu Niskanen, 'William of Malmesbury as Librarian: The Evidence of His Autographs', in *Discovering William of Malmesbury*, ed. by Rodney M. Thomson et al. (Woodbridge: Boydell, 2019), pp. 117–27; Paul A. Hayward, 'William of Malmesbury as a Cantor-Historian', in *Medieval Cantors and Their Craft: Music, Liturgy and the Shaping of History, 800–1500*, ed. by Margot E. Fassler et al. (Woodbridge: Boydell, 2017), pp. 222–39; Alison I. Beach, 'Shaping Liturgy, Shaping History: A Cantor-Historian from Twelfth-Century Peterhausen', in *Medieval Cantors and Their Craft: Music, Liturgy and the Shaping of History, 800–1500*, ed. by Margot E. Fassler et al. (Woodbridge: Boydell, 2017), pp. 297–309; Charles C. Rozier, 'Symeon of Durham as Cantor and Historian at Durham Cathedral Priory c.1090–1129', in *Medieval Cantors and Their Craft: Music, Liturgy and the Shaping of History, 800–1500*, ed. by Margot E. Fassler et al. (Woodbridge: Boydell, 2017), pp. 190–206; Charles C. Rozier, 'Orderic Vitalis as Librarian and Cantor of Saint-Evroul', in *Orderic Vitalis: Life, Works and Interpretations*, ed. by Charles C. Rozier et al. (Woodbridge: Boydell, 2016), pp. 61–77.

[38] For example, Erika S. Dorrer, *Angelus Rumpler, Abt von Formbach (1501–1513) als Geschichtsschreiber: Ein Beitrag zur klösterlichen Geschichtsschreibung in Bayern am Ausgang des Mittelalters* (Kallmünz: Lassleben, 1965); Klaus Schreiner, 'Abt Johannes Trithemius (1462–1516) als Geschichtsschreiber des Klosters Hirsau: Überlieferungsgeschichtliche und quellenkritische

the other, an article-length survey of about eighty cases by German historian Norbert Kersken.[39] Published in 2013, Kersken's pioneering study seems largely to have eluded scholars' notice, at least in the anglophone academy, and though its focus is primarily, and perhaps necessarily, a quantitative one, the data it generates allows for some important qualitative observations that are discussed later in this book. These works apart, the role of medieval abbots—and, even more so, that of medieval abbesses—in the writing of history has received little specific treatment to date. Scholarship on the history and development of the abbatial office tends to gloss over it,[40] and studies of the histori(ographi)cal culture of specific communities rarely devote more than a few sentences to the principal involvement of their superiors.[41] What is more, whenever abbots *are* mentioned, however cursorily, in the context of monastic historiographical activity, they appear almost exclusively in the capacity of authors. Even Kersken focuses explicitly and entirely on abbots who personally *wrote* works of history during their tenure, thereby excluding from his survey the various ways in which they and their peers facilitated historical writing in their communities without picking up the pen themselves, a key dimension of abbatial authority and leadership that, as we saw above, was recognized as having at least equal significance as abbatial authorship, and which is thus equally deserving of investigation. By approaching the subject holistically, this study aims to uncover the true extent, and the many different facets, of the historiographical activity of medieval monastic superiors and

Bemerkungen zu den "Annales Hirsaugienses"', *Rheinische Vierteljahrsblätter* 31 (1966/7), 72–138; Piotr Górecki, 'Rhetoric, Memory, and Use of the Past: Abbot Peter of Henrykow as Historian and Advocate', *Citeaux* 48 (1997), 261–94; Arend Mindermann, 'Abt Albert von Stade: Ein Chronist des 13. Jahrhunderts', in *Stupor Saxoniae inferioris: Ernst Schubert zum 60. Geburtstag*, ed. by Wiard Hinrichs et al. (Göttingen: Duehrkohp & Radicke, 2001), pp. 51–8; Benjamin Pohl, '*Abbas qui et scriptor*? The Handwriting of Robert of Torigni and His Scribal Activity as Abbot of Mont-Saint-Michel (1154–1186)', *Traditio* 69 (2014), 45–86; Laura Cleaver, '"A Most Studious Man, a Researcher and Collector of Sacred and Profane Books": Robert of Torigni and the Making of the Mont-Saint-Michel Chronicle (Avranches Bibliothèque Municipale MS 159)', in *Mapping New Territories in Art and Architectural Histories: Essays in Honour of Roger Stalley*, ed. by Niamh NicGhabhann and Danielle O'Donovan (Turnhout: Brepols, 2022), pp. 327–39.

[39] Norbert Kersken, 'Äbte als Historiker: Klöster als Zentren der Geschichtsschreibung im Mittelalter', in *Chronicon Aulae regiae–Die Königsaaler Chronik: Eine Bestandsaufnahme*, ed. by Stefan Albrecht (Frankfurt a. M.: Peter Lang, 2013), pp. 11–62.

[40] For example, Franz J. Felten, 'Herrschaft des Abtes', in *Herrschaft und Kirche: Beiträge zur Entstehung und Wirkungsweise episkopaler und monastischer Organisationsformen*, ed. by Friedrich Prinz (Stuttgart: Hiersemann, 1988), pp. 147–296; Pierre Salmon, *L'abbé dans la tradition monastique: Contribution à l'histoire du caractère perpétuel des supérieurs religieux en Occident* (Paris: Sirey, 1992); Martina Wiech, *Das Amt des Abtes im Konflikt: Studien zu den Auseinandersetzungen um Äbte früh- und hochmittelalterlicher Klöster unter besonderer Berücksichtigung des Bodenseegebiets* (Siegburg: Schmitt, 1999); Martin Heale, *The Abbots and Priors of Late Medieval and Renaissance England* (Oxford: Oxford University Press, 2016).

[41] See, for example, the chapters in *Écrire son histoire: Les communautés régulières face à leur passé*, ed. by Nicole Bouter (Saint-Étienne: Publications de l'Université de Saint-Étienne, 2005). Notable exceptions include Janneke Raaijmakers, *The Making of the Monastic Community of Fulda, c.744–c.900* (Cambridge: Cambridge University Press, 2012).

showcase its importance for our understanding of how, why, and by whom history was written in medieval monasteries.

This book is organized into four major chapters, each of which is then divided into several sub-chapters to facilitate navigation and cross-referencing. The rationale for this design is that each chapter can be read both as a thematic unit in its own right, complete with an introduction and conclusion, and as part of an overarching argument that builds gradually across the entire book and culminates in the overall Conclusion at the end. The first three chapters each consider one major facet of the abbot's role in the writing of history. Chapter 1 continues where Kersken and others have left off with a conceptual investigation of abbatial authorship. It commences with a review of the scholarly *état présent* (1.1) before examining the relationship between authorial composition and authority (1.2), historiography as a strategic means of abbatial self-fashioning (1.3), and the significance of female abbatial authorship (1.4), a subject too often glossed over in previous scholarship. Chapter 2 then turns to patronage as another principal mode of abbatial historiographical involvement. Introduced by a series of case studies (2.1), it situates abbatial sponsorship within other forms of patronage (2.2) before considering ways in which monastic authors sought to subvert and undermine the authority of abbatial patrons, and the consequences they faced for doing so (2.3), external commission, competition, and quality control (2.4), cases of obscured and/or concealed patronage (2.5), and the role of abbots as architects of memory (2.6). Chapter 3 completes the picture by studying the abbatial facilitation of historiographical activity through book provision and library building. Following a review of the evidence provided by monastic rules and customaries (3.1), it discusses various modes of production and procurement (3.2), books as commemorative currency (3.3), resourcing and collaboration (3.4), and the importance of library networks and interlibrary loans (3.5). Chapter 4 has a different remit than the preceding chapters in that it focuses on the practicalities of historiographical production by taking us into the physical workplaces inhabited by medieval abbot- and abbess-historians. Following an introductory case study (4.1), it provides a survey of abbatial writing and study spaces (4.2) before discussing the private collection of books (4.3) and their custodianship, inheritance, and bequest (4.4). This discussion brings the book full circle by showing us the spaces in which many of the activities studied in Chapters 1–3 took place and how the availability of private workplaces influenced the processes of historiographical production.

Unless otherwise specified, the word *abbatial* in this book refers equally to abbots and abbesses. Apart from Chapter 1 that, for reasons explained there, dedicates a separate discussion to female authorship (1.4), most arguments developed in this study concern male and female forms of abbatial authority alike, and the two will be considered together without categorical distinction. The period covered by this book is c.500–1500 with a concentration on the high Middle Ages (c.1000–1250), and the main geographical focus is on north-western (Latin) Europe with some forays into the wider medieval world. This wide angle is not intended to conceal or gloss over chronological developments or geographical differences, and the emphasis on the continuity of abbatial authority as a conceptual factor in the writing of history across time and space will be considered carefully against the backdrop of social, political, and economic change in specific localities and across the map. Rather than prioritizing, as some studies of monastic culture do, normative texts such as monastic rules and customaries, the evidence analysed in this book is gathered from a wide range of narrative, documentary, visual, and material sources, including previously unedited/unpublished materials, from chronicles and other narrative texts to charters and wills, account books and inventories, personal letters and memoirs, reports and visitation records, book lists and library catalogues, inscriptions and engravings, paintings and manuscript illuminations, buildings, and other forms of art and architecture. Studying these sources together and in context will generate new insights into the expectations and realities of abbatial authority in the medieval period, whilst the book's broad chronological and geographical remit will help reveal this authority's role in the writing of history with unprecedented clarity and detail.

1
Abbatial Authorship

1.1 Introduction

At the Bursfelde General Chapter of 1480, Gunther of Nordhausen voiced the expectation that every monastery should have a written account of its history, an expectation which he then reiterated in writing the very next year. One way to satisfy this expectation was for monastic superiors to lead by example and commit their communities' histories to writing personally. As seen above (Introduction), this was met with some opposition from Gunther's peers, some of whom protested that they did not have the time and resources, nor perhaps the skills and inclination, to act as their abbeys' historiographers. Unmoved by such apprehensions, Gunther reminded his critics that abbots unable—or unwilling—to provide this crucial service to their monks are obliged all the same to know the history of their monastery and must be able, when called upon, to give a full and accurate account of it as if they had written it with their own pen. The implication, of course, was that they might as well do the writing themselves by endowing these historical narratives with their official authorship and *auctoritas*.

We do not know whether Gunther's ideal(ized) vision of the consummate abbot-historian was informed by specific individuals, and even if he had concrete role models in mind, he did not disclose their identities. Either way, his cause was soon vindicated thanks to two abbatial appointments made in 1483, two years after the publication of *De historiae*. One was that of Johannes Trithemius, abbot of Sponheim (1483–1506) and subsequently Würzburg (1506–16), who would channel the spirit of Gunther's vision in his own address to the General Chapter of 1496. Trithemius not only wrote history for the communities over which he presided, but he also offered his historical expertise—and his pen—to the abbots of other monasteries, and even to Emperor Maximilian I (1508–19).[1] His oeuvre includes monastic histories of Sponheim (*Chronicon Sponheimense*), Würzburg (*Compendium breve fundationis et reformationis monasterii sancti Iacobi in*

---

[1] Klaus Arnold, *Johannes Trithemius (1462–1516)*, 2nd ed. (Würzburg: Schöningh, 1991), pp. 240–6. Besides monastic chronicles and *historiae fundationum*, Trithemius's historiographical oeuvre comprises dynastic histories and *origo gentis* narratives (*Compendium de origine gentis Francorum; Chronicon successionis ducum Bavariae et comitum Palatinorum*), saints' lives (*Vita beati Rabani Mauri; Vita beati Maximi episcopi Moguntini*), biographical-bibliographical catalogues (*Catalogus illustrium virorum Germaniae; De viris illustribus ordinis sancti Benedicti; De scriptoribus ecclesiasticis*), and a history of the Carmelite Order (*De origine, progressu et laudibus ordinis fratrum Carmelitarum*). On Trithemius's work for Maximilian I, see Brann, *Trithemius*, pp. 91–8.

suburbio Herbipolensi), and Hirsau (*Annales Hirsaugienses* and *Chronicon Hirsaugiense*), all of which survive as autographs.² Elected in the same year as Trithemius, Gunther's second champion was Andreas Lang, abbot-historian of Michelsberg (1483–1502). Though Andreas's profile and reputation as a writer of history could not rival Trithemius's, he, too, embodied Gunther's vision and even helped promote it by reading out Trithemius's *De duodecim excidiis* at Reinhardsbrunn.³ And just like Trithemius, Andreas practised what he preached by producing a portfolio of historical narratives that included the history of his predecessors in two redactions (*Catalogus abbatum* and *Fasciculus abbatum*), an episcopal chronicle and catalogue (*Chronica episcoporum Babenbergensium* and *Catalogus Bambergensis ecclesiae pontificum*), a catalogue of saints (*Catalogus sanctorum ordinis sancti Benedicti*), and two *vitae* of Bamberg's venerated bishop-saint, Otto (1102–39).⁴ If Gunther's critics at Erfurt had declared it all but impossible to take on the role of monastic historian in addition to that of abbot, they were surely humbled by two abbatial authors whose historiographical resourcefulness must have made such scepticism seem, if not altogether unjustified, then at least exaggerated. The question is, however, whether cases such as theirs resemble an exception or a practice that can be observed more widely across the medieval European map?

To answer this question, we luckily do not have to start from scratch. In an important study published in 2013, Norbert Kersken identifies just over eighty abbots who authored works of history between *c*.500 and *c*.1500, with a notable concentration in the twelfth and fifteenth centuries, each of which accounts for nearly a quarter of the cases in his survey. The majority (>80%) were active after *c*.1100, with Kersken noting just half a dozen cases in the eleventh century and fewer than ten across the previous five centuries.⁵ This sizeable catalogue can be expanded further, and the total number of cases taken well into the triple digits, by

---

² A list of Trithemius's authorial writings is provided by Arnold, *Trithemius*, pp. 228–52. Autographs of the *Chronicon Sponheimense* and the Würzburg *Compendium* survive in Würzburg, Universitätsbibliothek, MS ch. f. 126; those of the *Annales Hirsaugienses* and *Chronicon Hirsaugiensis* are Munich, Bayerische Staatsbibliothek, MSS Clm. 703 and 704; Vatican City, Biblioteca Apostolica Vaticana, Pal. lat. 929. On this manuscript tradition, see Schreiner, 'Bemerkungen', pp. 75–95.

³ See above (Introduction).

⁴ On the *Catalogus* and *Fasciculus abbatum*, see below (2.6); on Andreas's historiographical activity, cf. Franz Machilek, 'Geschichtsschreibung im und über das Kloster Michaelsberg unter besonderer Berücksichtigung der Memoria Bischof Ottos des Heiligen', in *Im Schutz des Engels: 1000 Jahre Kloster Michaelsberg Bamberg, 1015–2015*, ed. by Norbert Jung and Holger Kempkens (Petersberg: Imhof, 2015), pp. 306–25 (p. 314); Jürgen Petersohn, 'Fragmente einer unbekannten Fassung der Ottoviten-Kompilationen des Michelsberger Abtes Andreas Lang', *Deutsches Archiv für Erforschung des Mittelalters* 67 (2011), 593–608.

⁵ The earliest case listed by Kersken is Eugippius, abbot (*c*.492–540) of the island monastery in the Bay of Naples known as Castellum Lucullanum and author of a *vita* dedicated to its patron saint, St Severin; see Kersken, 'Äbte', p. 41; *Eugippius: Vita Sancti Severini–Das Leben des heiligen Severin*, ed./tr. by Theodor Nüßlein (Stuttgart: Reclam, 2004); on Eugippius's life and abbacy, including his supposed authorship of the *Regula Eugippii*, see Abigail K. Gometz, 'Eugippius of Lucullanum: A Biography' (unpublished PhD dissertation, University of Leeds, 2008).

inserting individuals who slipped through Kersken's net, especially for the period pre-1100, and by incorporating certain groups (or 'types') of writers that are excluded, explicitly and implicitly, from his otherwise commendably comprehensive overview.[6] Two such groups/types that are acknowledged yet omitted by Kersken are those whose historiographical activity preceded or postdated their abbatial tenure and monastic superiors who instead of putting their own pen to parchment used their authority to commission and patronize works of history from authors both inside and outside their monastic communities, and who, as shown below (2.2–2.5), acted as powerful *auctores* in their own right.[7] A third group that is absent from Kersken's survey is that of medieval abbesses, an absence which—unlike that of the previous groups—remains unacknowledged and unexplained. One is left to wonder whether there simply were no cases of abbess-historians for Kersken to report, or whether their involvement in the writing of history differed so profoundly from that of their male counterparts that discussing the two in a single article may have seemed unviable. Part of the present book (1.4) is thus dedicated specifically to reflections on female abbatial authorship and its relationship with the more prominent male equivalent, including the crucial question as to whether or not the former constituted a case apart.

The above is not intended as criticism of Kersken's work, which thanks to its robust data and analysis has proved a valuable foundation, and a useful point of departure, for the research presented in this book. We should appreciate, moreover, that there will have been conceptual limitations to the scope and detail that Kersken—or anyone—could have accommodated realistically within the remit of an article-length publication, and he even acknowledges these limitations by suggesting some omitted subjects for the attention of future research.[8] In a sense, therefore, this study picks up where Kersken left off with a contextual discussion of abbatial authorship that focuses less on the quantitative picture and more on the practical conditions and consequences of this historiographical phenomenon. Before we can commence this discussion, however, we must return briefly to Kersken's article and review its main quantitative and qualitative

---

[6] Early medieval examples omitted by Kersken include Adomnán, abbot (627–704) of Iona and author of a *vita* of his relative and Iona's founder, St Columba, as well as Eigil, abbot-historian (818–22) of Fulda, on whom cf. below (2.6); *Adamnan: Das Leben des heiligen Columba von Iona-Vitae S. Columbae*, tr. by Theodor Klüppel (Stuttgart: Hiersemann, 2010). The identification of these and other cases is now facilitated by searchable online databases such as *CALMA* and *Geschichtsquellen des deutschen Mittelalters*, the latter of which is based on the *Repertorium fontium historiae Medii Aevi* published 1962–2007, https://www.geschichtsquellen.de; not yet publicly available is the database developed at the University of Helsinki by the ERC-funded (2017–22) project *Medieval Publishing from c.1000–1500* based on the core data in Richard Sharpe, *A Handlist of the Latin Writers of Great Britain and Ireland before 1540, with Additions and Corrections* (Turnhout: Brepols, 2001). I am grateful to Samu Niskanen and his team, specifically Lauri Leinonen and Olli-Pekka Kasurinen, for kindly providing me with advance access to their database.

[7] See Kersken, 'Äbte', pp. 15–18.   [8] Kersken, 'Äbte', p. 62.

findings. Even in the face of our expanded and diversified corpus of case studies, the overarching trends and distribution patterns identified by Kersken remain accurate, albeit with a somewhat larger proportion of cases from the centuries pre-1100. In terms of geographical distribution, the two main areas of concentration are the medieval German(-speaking) and Frankish/French territories and polities, which together account for just about half the corpus, followed by the Low Countries, the British Isles, the Mediterranean (specifically Italy), and central/eastern Europe. In terms of their religious and institutional affiliations, the dominant majority of medieval abbot-/abbess-historians (between two-thirds and three-quarters) belong to monastic communities that for ease of reference, yet in full recognition of the term's inherent difficulties, can best be described as 'Benedictine', both before and after the formation of the Benedictine Order proper in the high Middle Ages, with their Cistercian counterparts taking a distant second place.[9] This comes as no surprise, given that amongst the major traditions of medieval monasticism—or, to adopt the terminology of a recent study, monasticisms—the Benedictines were generally the most historiographically prolific by some margin, though new research into the writing of history by other religious orders and their members has produced compelling evidence to suggest that some of them, specifically the Cistercians, were not as unproductive as traditionally assumed.[10]

How, then, do we interpret this quantitative data and its relative distribution across medieval Europe? On a macro level, we would do well to heed Kersken's advice not to delineate the phenomenon of abbatial authorship chronologically or geographically ('das Phänomen der Geschichte schreibenden Äbte weder zeitlich noch räumlich einzuengen'), but to adopt a broad pan-European view.[11] As Kersken demonstrates, the writing of history by monastic superiors constituted, if not a formal convention as such, then a notably widespread practice that, whilst subject to some ebb and flow, can be witnessed throughout the Middle Ages, and which thus evades granular periodization.[12] Indeed, the general distribution

---

[9] Kersken, 'Äbte', p. 20. On the difficulties of terminology, see Alison I. Beach and Isabelle Cochelin, 'General Introduction', in *The Cambridge History of Medieval Monasticism in the Latin West*, ed. by Alison I. Beach and Isabelle Cochelin, 2 vols. (Cambridge: Cambridge University Press, 2020), I, 1–15 (p. 5); also cf. Steven Vanderputten, *Medieval Monasticisms: Forms and Experiences of the Monastic Life in the Latin West* (Berlin: De Gruyter, 2020).

[10] For an overview of medieval Benedictine historiography, see Schieffer, 'Grundlinien'. Two important reassessments of the writing of history by medieval Cistercians are Richard Allen, 'History, Memory and Community in Cistercian Normandy (12th–13th Centuries)', *Downside Review* 139 (2021), 44–64; Hodgson, 'History', *passim*. Examples of *historiae fundationum* and *gesta abbatum* survive from the Cistercian houses at Aduard, Kamp, Bloemkamp, Egmond, and various others; see Jaap J. van Moolenbroek, 'De abtenkroniek van Aduard: Geleerdheid en devocie in een overgangstijd', in *De abtenkroniek van Aduard: Studies, editie en vertaling*, ed. by Jaap J. van Moolenbroek et al. (Hilversum: Verloren, 2010), pp. 21–52 (pp. 22–3). Also cf. Elizabeth Freeman, *Narratives of a New Order: Cistercian Historical Writing in England, 1150–1220* (Turnhout: Brepols, 2002).

[11] Kersken, 'Äbte', p. 15.

[12] Kersken, 'Äbte', p. 20: '[E]ine Periodisierung des Typus des geschichtsschreibenden Abtes drängt sich nicht auf'.

patterns articulated by Kersken and corroborated by the research in this study would seem to conform to broader trends and developments of historiographical production in the Latin West, which, as frequently noted, increased substantially in the context of the so-called 'Twelfth-Century Renaissance' and in the hundred or so years that preceded the Reformation.[13] Considering the proportionally higher loss rates of texts and manuscripts in earlier medieval centuries, the numbers referenced here offer evidence that monastic superiors operated regularly as writers of history, and that their collective contribution to the corpus of both extant and lost medieval historiography followed very similar trajectories as that of other 'types' of historians.[14]

More than a third of the abbots studied by Kersken exclusively wrote domestic history, that is, history concerned primarily, and explicitly, with the traditions, memories, and identities of their own institutions, whereas the others also, and sometimes exclusively, authored histories whose temporal and geographical horizons significantly transgressed the boundaries of the monastic communities from which they emanated.[15] From about the early twelfth century, we can see monastic superiors engage with increasing frequency in the writing of universal histories and 'world chronicles', though as Kersken points out, this 'trend' was already in

---

[13] For a general overview, see still Max Manitius, *Geschichte der lateinischen Literatur des Mittelalters*, 3 vols. (Munich: Beck, 1923–31); also cf. the chapters on periodization(s) in *The Oxford Handbook of Medieval Latin Literature*, ed. by Ralph Hexter and David Townsend (Oxford: Oxford University Press, 2012). On historical writing specifically, see the chapters in *Handbuch Chroniken des Mittelalters*, ed. by Gerhard Wolf and Norbert H. Ott (Berlin: De Gruyter, 2016). On the rise of vernacular historiography during the twelfth century, see Peter Damian-Grint, *The New Historians of the Twelfth-Century Renaissance: Inventing Vernacular Authority* (Woodbridge: Boydell, 1999); Brian Stock, *The Implications of Literacy: Written Language and Models of Interpretation in the 11th and 12th Centuries* (Princeton, NJ: Princeton University Press, 1983).

[14] Thomas Haye, *Verlorenes Mittelalter: Ursachen und Muster der Nichtüberlieferung mittellateinischer Literatur* (Leiden: Brill, 2016), p. 481 suspects that most early medieval Latin literature has been lost ('dass sich die Literatur des frühen Mittelalters zu großen Teilen nicht erhalten hat'); the loss/survival of medieval literature from six major European vernacular traditions (English, French, German, Dutch, Irish, and Icelandic) is the subject of two recent interdisciplinary studies that use so-called 'unseen species models' in an attempt to address 'survivorship bias' in pre-modern manuscript culture(s); Mike Kestemont et al., 'Forgotten Books: The Application of Unseen Species Models to the Survival of Culture', *Science* 375 (2022), 765–9, with estimated survival rates ranging from 4.9% (English) to 19.2% (Irish); Mike Kestemont and Folgert Karsdorp, 'Estimating the Loss of Medieval Literature with an Unseen Species Model from Ecodiversity', *CEUR Workshop Proceedings* 2723 (2020), 44–55. Also cf. Eltjo Buringh, *Medieval Manuscript Production in the Latin West: Explorations with a Global Database* (Leiden: Brill, 2011), pp. 203–4, who estimates a loss rate of −31% (Buringh's 'L_1' = 'geometric average'; see ibid., pp. 54–7) in the tenth-century Latin West, compared to −19%, −24%, and −26% during the eleventh, twelfth, and thirteenth centuries, respectively. Note, though, that the statistical estimates generated by these studies and the methodologies on which they are based have attracted some justified criticism amongst medieval (book) historians and ought to be used with caution; see, for example, the detailed response to Buringh's work by Marilena Maniaci, 'Quantificare la produzione manoscritta del passato: Ambizioni, rischi, illusioni di una "bibliometria storica globale"', *IASLonline* (2013), http://www.iaslonline.de/index.php?vorgang_id=3567, whose principal reservations can also be applied to the more recent studies by Kestemont et al.

[15] Kersken, 'Äbte', pp. 45–6 and 61–2.

decline by the late thirteenth century.¹⁶ Other types or 'genres' of history written by abbots and abbesses with a primary focus outside their own communities include dynastic chronicles, national histories and *origo gentis* narratives, and histories of bishoprics, courts, and, less frequently, municipalities.¹⁷ One of the best-known examples of this is the chronicle of northern Germany and Livonia, commonly known as the *Chronica Slavorum*, by Arnold, the first abbot (1177–1211/14) of St John's Abbey in Lübeck, a principal source for the German Crusade of 1197–8 that has been dubbed 'the most ambitious and sophisticated' historical narrative to survive from thirteenth-century Germany.¹⁸ The *Chronica* was not Abbot Arnold's only literary endeavour, as he also translated Hartmann von Aue's poem *Gregorius* from the original Middle High German into Latin.¹⁹ With the exception of *gesta episcoporum*, the momentum gathered by these kinds of histories during the eleventh and twelfth centuries largely seems to have subsided by the early fourteenth century. Domestic historiography, by contrast, continued to be a subject of first-hand abbatial involvement throughout the entire Middle Ages, most notably in the shape of annalistic records, house chronicles, *historiae fundationum*, local saints' lives and *historiae translationum*, and, with an intrinsic focus on the abbatial office, *gesta abbatum/ abbatissarum*. This is not to suggest, of course, that producing these kinds of histories was the prerogative of abbots and abbesses, much less a formal prerequisite of their abbatial tenure, however much Gunther of Nordhausen and his reform-minded associates may have wished for this. Whilst no exclusive privilege or obligation, the phenomenon of abbatial authorship is, as my discussion will

---

[16] Kersken, 'Äbte', p. 49. On the proliferation of universal histories, see Michael I. Allen, 'Universal History 300–1000: Origins and Western Developments', in *Historiography in the Middle Ages*, ed. by Deborah M. Deliyannis (Leiden: Brill, 2003), pp. 17–42; Roman Deutinger, 'Lateinische Weltchronistik des Hochmittelalters', in *Handbuch der Chroniken des Mittelalters*, ed. by Gerhard Wolf and Nobert H. Ott (Berlin: De Gruyter, 2016), pp. 77–103; Fabian Schwarzbauer, *Geschichtszeit: Über Zeitvorstellungen in den Universalchroniken Frutolfs von Michelsberg, Honorius' Augustodunensis und Ottos von Freising* (Berlin: Akademie Verlag, 2005); *Universal Chronicles in the High Middle Ages*, ed. by Michele Campopiano and Henry Bainton (Woodbridge: York Medieval Press, 2017).

[17] Cf. Leah Shopkow, 'Dynastic History', in *Historiography in the Middle Ages*, ed. by Deborah M. Deliyannis (Leiden: Brill, 2003), pp. 217–48; Norbert Kersken, 'High and Late Medieval National Historiography', in *Historiography in the Middle Ages*, ed. by Deborah M. Deliyannis (Leiden: Brill, 2003), pp. 181–216; Alheydis Plassmann, *Origo gentis: Identitäts- und Legitimitätsstiftung in früh- und hochmittelalterlichen Herkunftserzählungen* (Berlin: Akademie Verlag, 2006).

[18] *The Chronicle of Arnold of Lübeck*, tr. by Graham A. Loud (London: Routledge, 2019), p. 1, with a discussion of Arnold's career and his likely appointment as episcopal treasurer (*custos*) (ibid., pp. 2–4). Arnold's chronicle continues the earlier work of Helmold of Bosau (and, by extension, that of Adam of Bremen), and it has been proposed that his reason for writing might have been to produce something akin to a history of kings ('historia regum')—a view that, however, has failed to attract much support in scholarship; cf. Bernd U. Hucker, 'Die Chronik Arnolds von Lübeck als "Historia regum"', *Deutsches Archiv für Erforschung des Mittelalters* 44 (1988), 98–119; Volker Scior, 'Zwischen *terra nostra* und *terra sancta*: Arnold von Lübeck als Geschichtsschreiber', in *Die Chronik Arnolds von Lübeck: Neue Wege zu ihrem Verständnis*, ed. by Bernd Schütte and Stephan Freund (Frankfurt a. M.: Peter Lang, 2008), pp. 149–74.

[19] *Chronicle*, tr. Loud, pp. 6–7, with the relevant references. Loud considers Adam not only a sophisticated historian, but also 'an accomplished versifier' (ibid., p. 7).

show, fundamental for our understanding of monastic historiographical culture. Establishing where, when, why, and what kinds of histories abbots wrote in the Middle Ages is important, and Kersken's survey remains invaluable in this respect. Arguably more important, however, is to establish what difference it made if the author of a historical narrative was him/herself an abbot/abbess, and it is this question that forms the core driver of the following investigation.

1.2 Writing with Authority

Except for inherently autocentric historical narratives such as autobiographies, memoirs, and *apologiae*, cases of which are discussed later in this book (1.3), histories written by abbots generally distinguish themselves less through subject matter than by their intrinsic sense of authority. Theirs is a very special kind of authority, one that is unique within the monastic historiographical *milieu* and manifest not only in the texts themselves, but equally, and perhaps more significantly, in the broader context of their production and reception. Examining these manifestations requires us to consider the abbot as a figure of authority inside and outside the monastery, and to assess how this *ex officio* authority was negotiated with and accommodated by medieval concepts of authorship. As we will see, the abbot's principal *auctoritas* as head of a religious community and his power and lordship (*potestas/dominium*) within society more widely were determining—and distinguishing—factors for the writing of history and its legacy in the Middle Ages and beyond.

By putting their names and abbatial titles to historical narratives, monastic superiors effectively transferred authority onto them, meaning that the texts themselves and the material artefacts in which they are preserved—typically manuscripts, but also inscriptions and forms of visual art—became at once powerful reifications of their authors' rank within the institution, commanding media of communal memory, and official status symbols that were recognized far beyond the monastic walls within which they originated. We can see this clearly in how works of history written by abbots were received and remembered on both the inside and the outside of their authors' own communities. A good example of the former is the work of Eigil, the fourth abbot (818–22) of Fulda, to whose pen we owe the *Life* of the monastery's founding abbot, Sturmius (744–79).[20] The reasons why Eigil personally took on the task of writing the *Vita Sturmi* are complex and have been explored elsewhere, so a summary will suffice here.[21]

---

[20] *Die Vita Sturmi des Eigil von Fulda: Literarkritisch-historische Untersuchung und Edition*, ed. by Pius Engelbert (Marburg: Elwert, 1968).

[21] See now Benjamin Pohl, '*Locus memoriae–locus historiae*: Die Fuldaer Michaelskirche im Zentrum der monastischen Geschichts- und Erinnerungslandschaft im frühen und hohen Mittelalter', *Archiv für mittelrheinische Kirchengeschichte* (2023), forthcoming.

Not only was Sturmius one of the community's foundational figures (besides his contemporary, St Boniface) and a powerful anchor of its collective memory, as well as Eigil's kinsman, but the composition of his abbatial biography marked a crucial moment—indeed a watershed—in the institution's historical tradition. Four generations into its existence, Fulda's monastery had suffered painful conflicts under Sturmius's successors, Baugulph (779–802) and Ratger (802–17), the latter of whom, Eigil's predecessor, had caused something of a communal identity crisis that led to his removal from office.[22] Faced with this difficult legacy, Eigil, who had been a ringleader of the internal opposition that forced Ratger's deposition, used his abbatial authority to launch an ambitious historiographical and architectural campaign aimed at restoring a sense of unity and promoting historical continuity.[23] Eigil's *Vita Sturmi* was the keystone of a narrative arc that positioned Eigil as Sturmius's direct heir, and which, as argued below (2.6), was designed as an authoritative model and point of departure for a serial abbatial history or *gesta abbatum* continued at Eigil's initiative by Fulda's monks, one of whom, Brun Candidus, later wrote Eigil's *vita* at the initiative of his successor, Rabanus Maurus (822–42).[24] By forging the first and formative link in a historiographical chain that also includes the *Vita Baugulphi*, *Vita Ratgarii*, and *Vita Aegil*, Eigil used the authority inherent in abbatial authorship to 're-boot' Fulda's histori(ographi)cal tradition after a period of trauma with an official account of the community's past; or rather, a version of the past that he as abbot decided to be official.

Cases of abbots who, like Eigil, wrote histories of/for their communities or *vitae/gesta* of their revered predecessors are documented across medieval Europe, such as at Farfa, Corbie, Cluny, Saint-Denis, Vabres, Andres, Tournai, Lobbes, Saint Trond, Oudenburg, Metz, Deutz, Bamberg, Scheyern, Vornbach, Niederaltaich, Żagań, Kłodzko, Zbraslav, Oliva/Gdańsk, Meaux, and St Albans, to name but a few prominent examples.[25] In addition, there is evidence of monastic superiors who relied not on their own authority, but on that of their peers for the production of these important official narratives. In the first quarter of the eleventh century, Fridebold, abbot (1020–30) of SS Ulrich and Afra in Augsburg, thus approached the abbot of Reichenau, Bern (1008–48), to request from him an authoritative re-writing of the *Vita* of one of Augsburg's venerated

---

[22] See Steffen Patzold, 'Konflikte im Kloster Fulda zur Zeit der Karolinger', *Fuldaer Geschichtsblätter* 76 (2000), 69–162; Raaijmakers, *Fulda*, pp. 99–131.

[23] Raaijmakers, *Fulda*, pp. 132–74; Johanna Jebe, 'Reform als Bedrohung? Diagnosen aus der Fuldaer Mönchsgemeinschaft im Spiegel des *Supplex libellus* und der *Vita Sturmi*', in *Les communautés menacées au haut Moyen Âge (vie–xie siècles)*, ed. by Geneviève Bührer-Thierry et al. (Turnhout: Brepols, 2021), pp. 57–79.

[24] Edited as *Vita Aegil abbatis Fuldensis a Candido ad modestum edita prosa et versibus: Ein Opus geminum des IX. Jahrhunderts-Einleitung und kritische Edition*, ed. by Gereon Becht-Jördens (Marburg: self-published, 1994). The *Vita Baugulphi* and *Vita Ratgarii* are lost.

[25] See Kersken, 'Äbte', pp. 21–47 for further examples and references.

patron saints, St Ulrich.[26] Almost five centuries later, the abbot of Hirsau, Blasius (1484–1503), made a similar request to Johannes Trithemius, then abbot of Sponheim and later Würzburg, 'urging' him to compose two 'enormous books of histories or annals' ('ingentes codices historiarum sive annalium') of his monastery known as the *Annales Hirsaugienses*.[27] Blasius passed away before the work's completion, and his successor, John (1503–24), showed himself less than enthusiastic about the historiographical project whose patronage he had just inherited. Communications between John and Trithemius broke down over questions of remuneration, causing the project to stall for over half a decade before Trithemius, having renegotiated his payment, finally resumed writing in 1509, by which point he had moved from Sponheim to Würzburg.[28] In 1511, he despatched the presentation copy of the *Annales*'s first volume to Hirsau, followed by the second volume in 1514, both of which (Munich, Bayerische Staatsbibliothek, MSS Clm. 703 and 704) Trithemius had prepared personally, and which are written entirely in his recognizable hand.[29] What makes the examples of Fridebold/Bern and Blasius/John/Trithemius particularly significant is that in both cases the rationale for entrusting the writing of the monasteries' official histories to an external abbot was not a lack of domestic resources or expertise, but the superior reputation and authority of the particular individuals and communities approached. Both Hirsau and Augsburg were prolific sites of monastic book production during the high and later Middle Ages, the latter even with its own printing workshop, and their prominent position within the reformed congregations of Melk, Bursfelde, and, of course, Hirsau itself offered them wide-ranging connections and influence.[30] Still, the status claimed either institutionally by the abbots of Reichenau, a leading centre of historical writing and book culture from the Carolingian period onwards, or individually by

---

[26] Bern's *Vita sancti Uodalrici* has been edited by Dieter Blume, *Bern von Reichenau (1008–1048): Abt, Gelehrter, Biograph* (Ostfildern: Thorbecke, 2008), pp. 196–265; on the context of composition, see also Dieter Blume, 'Abt Berns von der Reichenau "Vita (III) S. Uodalrici": Ein frühes Zeugnis des Reformwillens in der Reichskirche?', in *Scripturus vitam: Lateinische Biographie von der Antike bis zur Gegenwart*, ed. by Dorothea Walz (Heidelberg: Mattes, 2002), pp. 833–40.

[27] Johannes Trithemius: *Annales Hirsaugienses*, 2 vols. (St. Gall: Schlegel, 1690), II, 5; in the work's preface, Trithemius recalls to have accepted the commission 'at Abbot Blasius's urging' ('[a]d preces Blasii abbatis Hirsaugiensis Chronicon eiusdem coenobii scribere adorsus maiorem partem complevi'; ibid., n.p. (= 'Praefatio ad lectorem')).

[28] Arnold, *Trithemius*, p. 150; Schreiner, 'Trithemius', p. 76.   [29] See below (4.1).

[30] Felix Heinzer, 'Buchkultur und Bibliotheksgeschichte Hirsaus', in *Klosterreform und mittelalterliche Buchkultur im deutschen Südwesten*, ed. by Felix Heinzer (Leiden: Brill, 2008), pp. 85–167; Klaus Schreiner, 'Geschichtsschreibung im Interesse der Reform: Die "Hirsauer Jahrbücher" des Johannes Trithemius (1462–1516)', in *Hirsau St. Peter und Paul 1091–1991*, ed. by Klaus Schreiner, 2 vols. (Stuttgart: Theiss, 1991), II, 297–324; Karl-Georg Pfändtner, 'Die Klosterreform von St. Ulrich und Afra in Augsburg im Spiegel der illuminierten Handschriften', in *Reformen vor der Reformation: Sankt Ulrich und Afra*, ed. by Gisela Drossbach and Klaus Wolf (Berlin: De Gruyter, 2018), pp. 239–54; on SS Ulrich and Afra's printing workshop, see Günter Hägele, 'Melker Reform und Buchdruck: Zur Druckerei im Augsburger Benediktinerkloster St. Ulrich und Afra', in *Reformen vor der Reformation: Sankt Ulrich und Afra*, ed. by Gisela Drossbach and Klaus Wolf (Berlin: De Gruyter, 2018), pp. 187–204.

Trithemius, whose reputation as a writer of history radiated far beyond and overshadowed the relatively humble spheres of influence of his successive home monasteries, was such that their authorship was recognized widely as a desirable mark of authority.[31]

This desirability and cross-institutional recognition of abbatial authority can be seen not only in the authorship of historical narratives, but also in their dedication and patronage, cases of which will are discussed elsewhere in this study (2.2). To mention but one example here, when in the eleventh century Rodulfus Glaber wrote his monumental five-volume history of his age, sometimes known by the non-contemporary title *Historiarum libri quinque*, he not only sought to imbue this work with an abbot's authority through its dedication, but he also distinguished carefully between the different degrees of authority that certain potential abbatial dedicatees would be able to bestow upon it.[32] In the work's preface, Rodulfus reports to have been commissioned by Odilo, abbot (994–1049) of Cluny, yet in his *Vita domni Willelmi abbatis* composed some years earlier, he recalls conversely that the initial request to produce the *Historia* had come from that work's dedicatee and Rodulfus's own former abbot at Saint-Bénigne de Dijon, William of Volpiano (989/90–1031).[33] The evidence provided by an early manuscript copy of the *Historia* (Paris, Bibliothèque nationale de France, MS Lat. 10912) that is either a partial autograph or extremely close to one—perhaps the author's working copy or a presentation copy—suggests that both assertions may carry some truth, and that Rodulfus changed his mind concerning his preferred abbatial patron at some point in the composition process.[34] Palaeographical and codicological examination reveals the manuscript's opening quire to be an addition, the contents of which, including the *Historia*'s first book and prologue with the (re-)dedication to Abbot Odilo, were edited and partially revised, probably by Rodulfus himself, since their original composition and initial codification. Indeed, there is every reason to believe the *Vita*'s proclamation that when Rodulfus

---

[31] On Trithemius's reputation and the reception of his historical writings, see Anna C. Nierhoff, 'Die Hirsauer Ruhmesliste und ihre Rezeption: Zum "Chronicon Hirsaugiense" und zu den "Annales Hirsaugienses" des Johannes Trithemius', in *Johannes Trithemius (1462-1516): Abt und Büchersammler, Humanist und Geschichtsschreiber*, ed. by Klaus Arnold and Franz Fuchs (Würzburg: Königshausen & Neumann, 2019), pp. 59–96.

[32] *Rodulfus Glaber: Historiarum libri quinque*, in *Rodulfus Glaber Opera*, ed./tr. by John France et al. (Oxford: Clarendon, 1989), pp. 1–253; the modern title goes back to that first given to the work in *Historiae Francorum scriptores coaetanei*, ed. by André Duchesne, 5 vols. (Paris: Cramoisy, 1636-49), IV, 1–58.

[33] See *Rodulfus Glaber: Vita domni Willelmi abbatis*, in *Rodulfus Glaber Opera*, ed./tr. by John France et al. (Oxford: Clarendon, 1989), pp. 254–99 (p. 294). A more recent edition/translation is included in *Guillaume de Volpiano: Un réformateur en son temps (962-1031)-Vita domni Willelmi de Raoul Glaber: Texte, traduction, commentaire*, ed./tr. by Veronique Gazeau and Monique Goullet (Caen: Publications du CRAHM, 2008).

[34] *Opera*, ed./tr. France et al., pp. xxxiv–xlv and lxxxii–lxxxvi; I owe this information to Samu Niskanen, who very kindly pointed me to this manuscript and its significance for the *Historia*'s patronage.

commenced the project and drafted the original version (now assumed lost) of the *Historia*'s first book at Dijon, he did so at the order of his then abbot, William. By the time he completed the project, however, circumstances had changed considerably. Following William's death in 1131, Rodulfus relocated first to Cluny and then to Saint-Germain d'Auxerre, where he re-wrote the *Historia*'s beginning and credited its composition to the abbot who had welcomed him to Cluny, Odilo. The reason for this decision may well have been that Odilo's reputation and authority as a monastic leader and reformer—and, importantly, as an abbot-historian: Odilo authored the abbatial *Vita* of his predecessor, Majolus (964–94), as well as a panegyric biography of his relative, the Empress Adelheid (962–99), which he dedicated to the abbot of San Salvatore in Pavia—were unrivalled in the Latin West and outstripped even the memory of Rodulfus's previous patron and celebrated reformer of Burgundy, Lorraine, and Normandy.[35] To Rodulfus's mind, associating the *Historia* with Odilo rather than William might therefore have seemed the more promising and attractive option.

An abbot's historiographical activity and the considerable authority and prestige associated with it did not have to be confined to the period of his tenure, and there are cases of individuals who wrote history both during and before/after their abbacies. One such case comes from Saint-Germain d'Auxerre, the very abbey to which Rodulfus Glaber moved for the final stage of his career, and where he re-dedicated his *Historia* to Odilo of Cluny. About two centuries later, the community's then abbot, Jean de Joceval (1250–78), tasked a local monk called Guy with the production of a cartulary-chronicle, and the same Guy later became abbot himself (1285–1313) and, in this capacity, wrote a new history of the monastery.[36] Other abbots whose authorship of historical narratives extended beyond their years of office include Simon, continuator of the *Chronicon Sithiense/Gesta abbatum Sithiensium* and briefly abbot of Saint-Bertin (1131–6), whom we will meet again below (1.3), and whose continuous historiographical work 'radically shaped the memory of more than a century of the communal past [at Saint-Bertin]' before, during, and after his abbacy.[37] They also include Ekkehard, who had begun his famous continuation of Frutolf's *Chronicon universale* as a monk of Michelsberg, then continued it at Würzburg, and revised it several times during

---

[35] Neithard Bulst, *Untersuchungen zu den Klosterreformen Wilhelms von Dijon (962–1031)* (Bonn: Röhrscheid, 1973); Jacques Hourlier, *Saint Odilon, abbé de Cluny* (Louvain: Bibliothèque de l'Université, 1964); Scott G. Bruce, 'Local Sanctity and Civic Typology in Early Medieval Pavia: The Example of the Cult of Abbot Maiolus of Cluny', in *Cities, Texts, and Social Networks 400–1500*, ed. by Caroline J. Goodson et al. (Farnham: Routledge, 2010), pp. 177–92.

[36] Noëlle Deflou-Leca, 'L'élaboration d'un cartulaire au XIIIe siècle: Le cas de Saint-Germain d'Auxerre', *Revue Mabillon* 8 (1997), 183–207; Anne Heath, 'Elevating Saint Germanus of Auxerre: Architecture, Politics, and Liturgy in the Reclaiming of Monastic Identity', *Speculum* 90 (2015), 60–113.

[37] Steven Vanderputten, *Monastic Reform as Process: Realities and Representations in Medieval Flanders, 900–1100* (Ithaca, NY: Cornell University Press, 2013), p. 16.

his tenure as the first abbot (1108–25) of Aura.[38] Lampert of Hersfeld wrote all of his histories (*Annales*; *Libellus de institutione Hersveldensis ecclesiae*; *Vita Lulli archiepiscopi Moguntiacensis*) prior to his short-lived abbacy at Hasungen (1081 × 85), and the same is true of the *Vita* and *Miracula* of Archbishop Heribert of Cologne written by another Lambert (or Lantpert) who only later became abbot of Liège (1060–9),[39] as well as of Berthold of Zwiefalten, whose *Libellus de constructione monasterii Zwivildensis* predates his various abbatial (re-) appointments and resignations in 1139 × 69.[40] Abbots who predominantly (or even exclusively) wrote history after their tenures had come to an end or witnessed a temporary hiatus include Herman, who wrote his *Liber de restauratione monasterii sancti Martini Tornacensis* following his resignation as abbot of Tournai (1127–36), Albert of Stade, whose *Annales Stadenses* postdate his institutional transfer from the Benedictine abbey where he had been abbot (1232–40) to a local Franciscan convent, and several more.[41]

Many abbot-historians, however, indeed the majority, wrote history *whilst* in post. Besides the examples studied above and later in this book, these include Baldric, whose historiographical activity falls squarely, and virtually exclusively, within his abbacy at Saint-Pierre de Bourgueil (1077–1106), rather than his subsequent archiepiscopacy (1108–30). Baldric was highly educated, having studied at Angers under one 'Master Hubert', and extremely well connected, having been an eyewitness of the foundation of Fontevraud, whose founder, Robert of Arbrissel, he knew personally, and whose *Life* he composed at the commission of Petronilla de Chemillé, the first abbess of Fontevraud.[42] Balderic's early oeuvre primarily comprises compositions in verse, including his famous poem to Countess Adela,[43] followed by works of hagiography and, as the culmination of

---

[38] Thomas J. McCarthy, *The Continuations of Frutolf of Michelsberg's Chronicle* (Wiesbaden: Harrassowitz, 2018), pp. 58–80; Roman Deutinger, 'From Lake Constance to the Elbe: Rewriting a Reichenau World Chronicle from the Eleventh to the Thirteenth Century', in *Rewriting History in the Central Middle Ages, 900–1300*, ed. by Emily A. Winkler and Christopher P. Lewis (Turnhout: Brepols, 2022), pp. 39–65.

[39] *Lantbert von Deutz: Vita Heriberti–Miracula Heriberti–Gedichte–Liturgische Texte*, ed. by Bernhard Vogel [= *MGH SS rer. Germ.* LXXIII] (Hanover: Hahn, 2001); see also Bernhard Vogel, 'Das hagiographische Werk Lantberts von Deutz über Heribert von Köln', in *Hagiographie im Kontext: Wirkungsweisen und Möglichkeiten historischer Auswertung*, ed. by Dieter R. Bauer and Klaus Herbers (Stuttgart: Steiner, 2000), pp. 117–29.

[40] For further examples, see Kersken, 'Äbte', pp. 16–17.

[41] Kersken, 'Äbte', pp. 17–18 with the relevant references.

[42] See *Les Deux vies de Robert d'Arbrissel, fondateur de Fontevraud: Légendes, écrits et témoignages–The Two Lives of Robert of Arbrissel, Founder of Fontevraud: Legends, Writings, and Testimonies*, ed. by Jacques Dalarun et al. (Turnhout: Brepols, 2006), pp. 130–87. On Baldric's career and his works, see *The Historia Ierosolimitana of Baldric of Bourgueil*, ed. by Steven Biddlecombe (Woodbridge: Boydell & Brewer, 2014), pp. xi–xxiv; on his contacts, see Petra Aigner, 'Poetry and Networking in High Medieval France (ca. 1100): Baudri de Bourgueil and His Scholarly Contacts', in *Networks of Learning: Perspectives on Scholars in Byzantine East and Latin West*, ed. by Sita Steckel et al. (Berlin: De Gruyter, 2015), pp. 33–56.

[43] *Baudri de Bourgueil: Poèmes*, ed./tr. by Jean-Yves Tilliette, 2 vols. (Paris: Les Belles Lettres, 1998–2002), II, 1–43 (= no. 134): Monika Otter, 'Baudri of Bourgueil, "To Countess Adela"', *Journal*

his authorial portfolio, historiography in the strictest sense, in addition to various extant letters. The same is true of consummate abbot-historian William of Andres, whose 'motivation for writing [the history of his abbey] came from the monks of Andres's desire to establish the right to choose their own abbot[,] rather than be governed by Charroux-imposed ones',[44] as well as of William Malvern (also known as William Parker), the final abbot (1515–39) of Gloucester, who halfway through his tenure authored a monumental poem on the monastery's history and foundation with no fewer than one hundred and fifty-four lines (seven per stanza), which he had inscribed prominently, and in its entirety, in the north aisle of the nave of Gloucester's abbey church as a powerful medium of the community's collective memory and a memento of his own abbacy, the last before the monastery's dissolution in 1540.[45] In the poem's final stanza, the author identifies himself as 'Will[el]m Malverne, Abbot of this Monastery, Whome God preserve in long life & prosperity, And after death him graunt Eternall Felicity',[46] probably with the dual intention of facilitating the salvation of his own soul and imbuing the preceding poetic historical narrative with the official authority that only an abbot could provide.

That such declarations of abbatial authorship were not empty gestures is shown in the way that histories written by abbots were received by their contemporaries and remembered by posterity. We can see this in the memory of the work of Robert of Torigni, abbot-historian (1154–86) of Mont-Saint-Michel, whom we will meet again shortly. The colophon of a historiographical compendium (Paris, Bibliothèque nationale de France, MS fr. 10468) produced at Mont-Saint-Michel at the command of Robert's fifteenth-century successor and namesake, Robert Jolivet (1411–44), in 1436 emphasizes the fact that the extracts it contains of Robert's *Chronica* were written whilst he was abbot.[47] Robert's contemporary and fellow historian working in London, Ralph of Diceto, refers to the same text and its author in his voluminous handlist of chroniclers whom he—and, we may presume, his audiences—deemed authoritative and worthy of memory. In two of the earliest and most important manuscript copies of Ralph's list (London,

---

of Medieval Latin 11 (2001), 61–141 (66–99); Benjamin Pohl and Elisabeth M. C. van Houts, 'History and Memory', in *The Cambridge Companion to the Age of William the Conqueror*, ed. by Benjamin Pohl (Cambridge: Cambridge University Press, 2022), pp. 244–71 (p. 263).

[44] *William of Andres: The Chronicle of Andres*, tr. by Leah Shopkow (Washington, D.C.: Catholic University of America Press, 2017); a new edition of the text is also being prepared by Shopkow; quote from Elisabeth M. C. van Houts, 'Review of *William of Andres: The Chronicle of Andres*, tr. by Leah Shopkow', *Church History and Religious Culture* 99 (2019), 6–7 (p. 6).

[45] Extant in Cambridge, Gonville and Caius College, MS 391, pp. 63–8; printed in *Robert of Gloucester's Chronicle*, ed. by Thomas Hearne, 2 vols. (Oxford: Theater, 1724), II, 578–85 (= Appendix). Also cf. Julian M. Luxford, *The Art and Architecture of English Benedictine Monasteries, 1300–1540* (Woodbridge: Boydell, 2012), p. 11.

[46] *Chronicle*, ed. Hearne, II, 584.

[47] *Colophons de manuscrits occidentaux des origines au XVIe siècle*, Vol. 5: *Colophons signés P–Z (14889–18951)*, ed. by Bénédictins du Bouveret (Fribourg: Éditions universitaires, 1979), p. 242 (= no. 16660).

British Library, MSS Add. 40007 and Cotton Claudius E III), Robert's name is the penultimate entry, succeeded only by that of Ralph himself (in an act of unapologetic self-promotion), and both entries explicitly and unambiguously refer to him as 'Robertus abbas'.[48] Whether we look to Robert's historiographical colleagues or to his abbatial successors, both were eager to remind themselves and others that the great history Robert wrote in imitation of Sigebert had been produced (or at least most of it) whilst he was abbot and thus benefited from a special kind of authority; to their minds, and to those of others, this made an important difference.

Another aspect of historiographical production in which the abbot's authority manifests itself is the preparation of authorial manuscripts and working copies. As discussed below (3.2), in a medieval monastery the assignment of copyists—and the allocation of time and resources in support of their scribal labour—was ultimately subject to the abbot's approval and authorization, even if in everyday practice this process was often streamlined and involved the devolution and delegation of authority amongst senior monastic officers such as the prior, the sacristan, and, perhaps most frequently, the cantor/*armarius*. This institutionalized sense of hierarchy with the abbot at the top and various dependant agents operating under his command—a corporeal metaphor for the Church that places the abbot *in loco Christi*—provided the basic operational framework for the monastic life and routine, and the writing of history was no exception. Without the abbot's licence, nobody in the monastery was at liberty to commit (a) history to writing or instruct others to do so on their behalf, though as we will see later in this study (2.3), monastic historians sometimes tried to evade this obligation, albeit with varying degrees of success, and always at the risk of facing severe repercussions. In principle, however, the superior's authorization was a *conditio sine qua non* for the composition and codification of historical narratives within a monastic community. By the same principle, the monastic superior had unparalleled and, at least in theory, unrestricted access to a community's material and human resources, and abbots who were themselves writers of history could exercise their *auctoritas* to assemble a scribal workforce to assist them with their historiographical projects as and when required provided the relevant expertise was available locally or could be brought in at short notice with the resources at the abbot's disposal. Some abbot-historians availed themselves so regularly of this *ex officio* privilege that they rarely (or never) physically laid hands on the

---

[48] Benjamin Pohl, 'The Memory of Robert of Torigni: From the Twelfth Century to the Present Day', in *Maîtriser le temps et façonner l'histoire: Les historiens normands aux époques médiévale et moderne*, ed. by Fabien Paquet (Caen: Presses universitaires de Caen, 2022), pp. 111–34 (pp. 124–5), with photographic reproductions of both these manuscripts (ibid., p. 125); also cf. Laura Cleaver, *Illuminated History Books in the Anglo-Norman World, 1066–1272* (Oxford: Oxford University Press, 2018), pp. 201–2.

manuscripts which preserve their historiographical compositions, including those that can be identified confidently as author drafts or working copies.

A perfect example of this is provided by the authorial manuscripts of Robert of Torigni, who following a brief tenure as claustral prior (and possibly *armarius*) of Le Bec (*c.*1149–54), the monastery which he had joined as a young man in 1128, became abbot of Mont-Saint-Michel.[49] Robert's authorial oeuvre encompasses a range of genres with a notable focus on historiography/chronography and administrative documentation, and the two works that earned him particular fame amongst medieval and modern readers are his redaction of William of Jumièges's *Gesta Normannorum ducum* and his continuation of Sigebert of Gembloux's *World Chronicle*, the second of which is commonly known as the *Chronica* and constitutes the more 'original' of the two projects.[50] It survives in more than twenty manuscripts, one of which (Avranches, Bibliothèque patrimoniale, MS 159) is of particular interest here as it preserves the author's 'working copy'.[51] The project that would eventually become the *Chronica* was begun during the later 1140s—a decade or so after Robert's redaction of William's *Gesta* had been brought to a first state of completion (barring later additions) *c.*1139, and about half a decade before his abbatial appointment—and it has recently been suggested that one portion of the manuscript (that which is based most closely on and incorporates a copy of Sigebert's work) may have been prepared at Le Bec and was brought to Mont-Saint-Michel in 1154.[52] This is implausible, however, and the codicological evidence gives no reason to doubt the established consensus that the entire manuscript as it survives today was produced at Mont-Saint-Michel during the period of Robert's abbacy, the *terminus post quem* being 1156, and that whatever preliminary copies or drafts he may have made at Le Bec have since been lost.[53]

---

[49] On Robert's life and monastic career, see Benjamin Pohl, 'Robert of Torigni and Le Bec: The Man and the Myth', in *A Companion to the Abbey of Le Bec in the Central Middle Ages (11th–13th Centuries)*, ed. by Benjamin Pohl and Laura L. Gathagan (Leiden: Brill, 2017), pp. 94–124; also cf. *The Chronography of Robert of Torigni*, ed./tr. by Thomas N. Bisson, 2 vols. (Oxford: Oxford University Press, 2020), I, xxvi–xlvii [hereafter *RT*].

[50] Some of Robert's authorial works are edited alongside the *Chronica* in *RT*, ed./tr. Bisson, *passim*. On his continuation of the *GND*, see *The Gesta Normannorum Ducum of William of Jumièges, Orderic Vitalis and Robert of Torigni*, ed./tr. by Elisabeth M. C. van Houts, 2 vols. (Oxford: Oxford University Press, 1992–5), I, cxxxvi–cxxviii [hereafter *GND*]. On Robert's administrative writings, cf. Pohl, 'Pragmatic Literacy', *passim*.

[51] *RT*, ed./tr. Bisson, I, lvii–lxxxvi. Bisson's remarks on MS Avranches 159 (= Bisson's MS A*; ibid., pp. lxi–lxiii) and his proposed manuscript stemma (p. xcv) must be used with caution, however. For more comprehensive discussions of this manuscript, see Gabriele Passabì, 'Robert of Torigni's *Liber Chronicorum*: The Chronography as a Textual Project in Avranches, Bibliothèque patrimoniale, MS 159', *Tabularia* (2021), https://doi.org/10.4000/tabularia.5475; Pohl, '*Abbas*', pp. 54–70.

[52] See *RT*, ed./tr. Bisson, I, lxi–lxii, who contrary to *communis opinio* argues that part of MS Avranches 159 (fols. 4r–206v) was 'undertaken in Le Bec probably about 1152, [and] is written in a single hand as far as 1156', a chronology that seems confused as a manuscript supposedly produced in 1152 surely cannot contain an annalistic entry for the year 1156.

[53] See most recently Passabì, '*Liber Chronicorum*', pp. 6–17, whose meticulous study of the manuscript cements the established dating by concluding that 'the first portion of the manuscript [= fols. 4r–206v] was completed shortly after 1157' (ibid., p. 10), and that 'the Bec exemplar of the chronography [= *Chronica*] is now lost' (p. 6) but was based on an extant manuscript which Robert had

The production of the *Chronica*'s working copy at Mont-Saint-Michel was a concerted and collaborative undertaking that involved more than a dozen copyists, some of whom worked in parallel, whereas others copied their allocated sections of the text sequentially or in intervals.[54] Notably, Robert was not one of them, though the fact that short yet essential corrections and annotations in his own hand feature sporadically, and in an authoritative capacity, throughout the entire manuscript shows that the process took place under his personal supervision. Details and concrete examples of Robert's scribal contributions to the *Chronica*'s working copy and other manuscripts used by and/or produced for him are available elsewhere, but what is most striking about them, and thus warrants repeating here, is not only that they are marked by a distinctive sense of authority which is superior to the dependent agency of Robert's anonymous collaborators and places him at the very top of the operational hierarchy, but also—and perhaps conversely—that the levels of formality and skill exhibited by most specimens of Robert's handwriting are inferior to those of the copyists working under his abbatial supervision.[55] As explored elsewhere, the second observation may be explained by a range of factors that include a possible lack of formative calligraphic training due to Robert's secular upbringing and initial career path, the absence of regular formal writing practice later on in his career due to his other abbatial duties, and, not least, his advanced age (born in 1106, Robert was eighty years old when he put the finishing touches to the *Chronica* in the year of his death).[56] I return to this below.

As for the first observation, a strikingly similar *modus operandi* marked by the same sense of hierarchy and authority can be observed in the preparation of a second manuscript that is also closely connected with Robert's historiographical activity, but which unlike the *Chronica*'s working copy was produced not at Mont-Saint-Michel, but at Le Bec.[57] Like the *Chronica*, this authorial manuscript of Robert's redaction of the *Gesta Normannorum ducum* consists of two parts, the second of which mainly contains a copy of Geoffrey of Monmouth's *Historia regum Britanniae/De gestis Brittonum*, though unlike the previous case these two did not constitute a codicological unit from the beginning and were only bound

---

borrowed from the bishop of Beauvais (Paris, Bibliothèque nationale de France, MS Lat. 17545); previously *Chronique de Robert de Torigni, abbé du Mont-Saint-Michel*, ed. by Léopold Delisle, 2 vols. (Rouen: Le Brument, 1872–73), I, li–lii.

[54] Pohl, '*Abbas*', pp. 54–8; Passabì, '*Liber Chronicorum*', pp. 6–7; Cleaver, 'Studious Man', *passim*.

[55] See the analysis in Pohl, '*Abbas*', *passim*. Some of the conclusions of this analysis have been challenged by Thomas N. Bisson, 'The Scripts of Robert of Torigni: Some Notes of Conjectural History', *Tabularia* (2019), https://doi.org/10.4000/tabularia.3938, though this challenge fails to compel; see Benjamin Pohl, 'Review of Thomas N. Bisson, *The Chronography of Robert of Torigni*', *History* 106 (2021), 293–8, https://doi.org/10.1111/1468-229X.13109.

[56] Pohl, '*Abbas*', pp. 75–8; Pohl, 'Robert and Le Bec', pp. 112–14.

[57] *GND*, ed./tr. van Houts, I, cix–cx; Julia C. Crick, *The* Historia regum Britanniae *of Geoffrey of Monmouth*, Vol. 3: *A Summary Catalogue of the Manuscripts* (Woodbridge: D. S. Brewer, 1989), pp. 124–6.

into a single codex c.1163. Just like the *Chronica*, the text of the *Gesta*'s redaction was copied by a team of scribes working under Robert's close supervision without substantive contributions in his own hand. Again, Robert's scribal interventions are limited to occasional corrections and annotations, most of which are additions and/or emendations of historical dates, personal/places names, regnal years, or dynastic relationships, exactly as they are in the *Chronica*.[58] Despite recent suggestions to the contrary, these annotations were all made *after* the composite codex obtained its present form in the early/mid-1160s.[59] The fact that they run across both parts of the combined manuscript, and that these constituent parts are identified as 'in uno volumine' in a library inventory from Le Bec produced in or after 1163 that survives on the opening sheets of the *Chronica*'s working copy alongside another Le Bec book list—both of which were, as shown below (3.5), drawn up at Robert's abbatial behest and for his personal reference—strongly suggests either that Robert inserted these glosses during a visit to Le Bec or, perhaps more likely, that he used his abbatial authority to borrow the book from his former home so he could read and revise it at Mont-Saint-Michel.[60] As we will see later in this study, this was a common practice amongst medieval monastic superiors, many of whom used their authority to borrow books in support of their historiographical projects or those undertaken by others at their abbatial commission.

The domestic copyists from Le Bec at work in Robert's manuscript of the *Gesta Normannorum ducum* are fewer in number than those who later copied out his *Chronica* at Mont-Saint-Michel, but their work follows a similar pattern. In both cases, the scribes copied the text prepared by Robert, presumably on wax tablets or in the shape of rough drafts, at the same time as leaving blank spaces for later additions and parts of the narrative that were still work-in-progress, which once completed were inserted into these spaces by whoever was at hand, but never by Robert himself.[61] In fact, some of the hands that copied Robert's redaction of the *Gesta* are extremely similar to those who prepared the *Chronica*, to the point that they might belong to the same individual(s). If correct, this would further cement the suggestion that Robert upon his abbatial appointment relocated some of the scribes with whom he had been working at Le Bec to Mont-Saint-Michel, possibly

---

[58] See Pohl, 'Abbas', pp. 55–7 (MS Avranches 159) and 60–1 (MS Leiden BPL 20).

[59] *RT*, ed./tr. Bisson, I, lxxxiv argues that some of these annotations were made prior to 1154, but the evidence presented in support of this suggestion does not hold up to scrutiny. The traditional *terminus post quem* of 1163 is cemented by Jenny Weston, 'Manuscripts and Book Production at Le Bec', in *A Companion to the Abbey of Le Bec in the Central Middle Ages (11th–13th Centuries)*, ed. by Benjamin Pohl and Laura L. Gathagan (Leiden: Brill, 2017), pp. 144–70 (p. 168).

[60] For a study and critical edition of this inventory, see Laura Cleaver, 'The Monastic Library at Le Bec', in *A Companion to the Abbey of Le Bec in the Central Middle Ages (11th–13th Centuries)*, ed. by Benjamin Pohl and Laura L. Gathagan (Leiden: Brill, 2017), pp. 171–205 (p. 203).

[61] Cf. *GND*, ed./tr. van Houts, I, cix.

permanently.⁶² Such a relocation would not have been possible, of course, without the consent of Le Bec's abbot, Roger (1149–54), though given that Roger had facilitated Robert's appointment as claustral prior in 1149 and generally seems to have been supportive of Robert's subsequent promotion—in fact, he even assisted Rouen's archbishop in performing Robert's abbatial benediction on 22 July 1154—he may well have permitted his trusted second-in-command to take a selection of scribes with him when departing for his new home of Mont-Saint-Michel that same year.⁶³ By the same token, it would have been impossible for Robert to adopt the aforesaid working model and use a team of scribes for the codification of the *Gesta*'s redaction in 1139—a decade before his appointment as prior under Abbot Roger—unless he had been authorized to do so by the latter's predecessor(s), Letardus (1139–49) and, depending on just how long the manuscript took to complete, possibly also Theobald (1136–8).⁶⁴ As we will see below (3.4), abbots could and did make available substantial resources and scribal workforces to domestic historiographers to facilitate the timely production of their writing projects, particularly (but not exclusively) if they themselves had played a part in commissioning and patronizing these histories, and it is not unreasonable to suspect that the early twelfth-century abbots of Le Bec may have done likewise to support their in-house historian(s).⁶⁵ The *modus operandi* that characterizes the preparation of the *Chronica*'s authorial working copy was one which Robert had likely learnt to cultivate at Le Bec with the permission and authorization of his abbot(s), and one which in his later career as abbot-historian of Mont-Saint-Michel he continued to use regularly, and at an even larger scale, by the power of his own abbatial *auctoritas*.

As indicated above, Robert was not the only abbot-historian who used his official authority to assemble, resource, and personally supervise a scribal workshop in pursuit of historiographical projects. A few examples will suffice here, and more will be presented later in this study (3.2). They include Robert's near-contemporary peer Geoffrey I, abbot (1093–1132) of Vendôme, whom Stéphane Lecouteux identifies as the probable initiator of the *Annales Vindocinenses*, a local continuation of a later eleventh-century chronicle from Angers that, as per Lecouteux, had been brought to Vendôme by Abbot Geoffrey himself with the

---

⁶² Patricia D. Stirnemann, 'Two Twelfth-Century Bibliophiles and Henry of Huntingdon's *Historia Anglorum*', *Viator* 24 (1993), 121–42 (p. 137); Weston, 'Manuscripts', pp. 148–52.

⁶³ Pohl, 'Robert and Le Bec', pp. 117–18; Véronique Gazeau, *Normannia monastica (Xe–XIIe siècle)*, 2 vols. (Caen: Publications du CRAHM, 2007), II, 21.

⁶⁴ Gazeau, *Normannia monastica*, II, 18–21.

⁶⁵ See Elisabeth M. C. van Houts, 'The Writing of History at Le Bec', in *A Companion to the Abbey of Le Bec in the Central Middle Ages (11th–13th Centuries)*, ed. by Benjamin Pohl and Laura L. Gathagan (Leiden: Brill, 2017), pp. 125–43; Benjamin Pohl, 'Who Wrote Paris, BnF, Latin 2342? The Identity of the *Anonymus Beccensis* Revisited', in *France et Angleterre: Manuscrits médiévaux entre 700 et 1200*, ed. by Charlotte Denoël and Francesco Siri (Turnhout: Brepols, 2020), pp. 153–89.

specific intention of continuing it in-house.⁶⁶ Vendôme's annals are extant in a single manuscript (Oxford, Bodleian Library, MS Bodley 309, fols. 111r–131v) that was produced by a team of scribes working collaboratively, each with his own tasks and responsibilities. One of them acts more or less exclusively in the capacity of an annotator and corrector, which combined with the fact that his hand can also be traced in several other manuscripts produced during Geoffrey's abbacy (and likely used by him) leads Lecouteux to identify him tentatively, yet compellingly, as Geoffrey.⁶⁷ Another example, and one directly contemporary with Robert of Torigni's work, is that of Hildegard, abbess of Disibodenberg (1136–50), Rupertsberg (1150–79), and Eibingen (1165–79), who is, of course, better known as Hildegard of Bingen. At Disibodenberg, a community which she herself had founded, Hildegard established a scriptorium 'with its own set of surviving manuscripts, and a distinctive style of script practiced by multiple scribes'.⁶⁸ The latter included not just Volmar, Hildegard's *secretarius* and *amanuensis*, but also several of the community's nuns and some copyists whose gender and identify cannot be determined with certainty, one of whom Margot Fassler detects in at least four manuscripts from the 'Trilogy' of Hildegard's authorial oeuvre (*Scivias*; *Liber vitae meritorum*; *Liber divinorum operum*) copied at Rupertsberg.⁶⁹ Similar to Robert's workforce at Mont-Saint-Michel, some of the scribes who worked under Hildegard at Rupertsberg had followed her there from Disibodenberg, including Volmar, who, it has been suggested compellingly, had previously produced the *Disibodenberg Chronicle* (Frankfurt, Universitätsbibliothek, MS Barth. 104) at Hildegard's abbatial instruction.⁷⁰

The presence of experienced *amanuenses* and abbatial secretaries such as Volmar amongst the scribal workshops assembled by monastic superiors can be traced across the Middle Ages, for example, at later medieval Bamberg, where abbot-historian Andreas Lang (1483–1502) of Michelsberg appointed his trusted chaplain, Nonnosus, to copy out the first redaction of his voluminous *Catalogus abbatum* composed in 1487 before producing an authorial abbreviation known as

---

⁶⁶ Stéphane Lecouteux, 'L'abbé Geoffroy de Vendôme (1093–1132), initiateur des Annales de Vendôme?', *Cahiers de Civilisation Médiévale* 52 (2009), 37–43.

⁶⁷ See Lecouteux, 'Geoffroy', pp. 40–2; Stéphane Lecouteux, 'L'Archétype et le stemma des annales angevines et vendômoises', *Revue d'histoire des textes* 3 (2008), 229–61 (pp. 250–1).

⁶⁸ Margot E. Fassler, 'Hildegard of Bingen and Her Scribes', in *The Cambridge Companion to Hildegard of Bingen*, ed. by Jennifer Bain (Cambridge: Cambridge University Press, 2021), pp. 280–305 (p. 280), with reference to the standard literature on the subject (ibid., p. 280 n. 1).

⁶⁹ This scribe, known as 'Scribe A', remains anonymous and may have been a man or a woman; see Fassler, 'Hildegard', pp. 291–8, with a list of manuscripts (p. 300). On medieval *secretarii*, see Véronique Gazeau, 'Du *secretarius* au secretaire: Remarques sur un office médiéval méconnu', in *Faire lien: Aristocratie, réseaux et échanges compétitifs*, ed. by Laurent Jégou et al. (Paris: Publications de la Sorbonne, 2015), pp. 63–72.

⁷⁰ Margot E. Fassler, 'Volmar, Hildegard, and St. Matthias', in *Medieval Music in Practice: Studies in Honor of Richard Crocker*, ed. by Judith A. Pereino (Middleton, WI: American Institute of Musicology, 2013), pp. 85–112; Anna M. Silvas, *Jutta and Hildegard: The Biographical Sources* (University Park, PA: Pennsylvania State University Press, 1999), pp. 46–50.

the *Fasciculus abbatum* in 1494, the codification of which he assigned to Reinher, a local monk-scribe who may have held a similar office under Andreas, and who after the latter's death in 1502 would compete with Nonnosus over the privilege to be remembered as the late abbot's 'go-to copyist'.[71] As with the writings of Robert and Andreas, Hildegard's hand seems conspicuously absent from the authorial manuscripts copied and decorated under her abbatial supervision, suggesting that she habitually delegated the task of copying to scribes whilst she herself 'apparently wrote exclusively on wax tablets[,] rather than on parchment'.[72] Visual evidence of this can be found in the manuscripts that preserve Hildegard's compositions with miniatures of her using wax tablets to note down words received by divine inspiration before passing them on to a scribe who then commits them to the more durable medium of parchment. The three most striking examples of this are the illustrated frontispieces of the *Scivias-Codex* produced at Rupertsberg under Hildegard's personal supervision (Wiesbaden, Hochschul- und Landesbibliothek RheinMain, MS 1, fol. 1r; original lost but preserved through photographs and a faithful twentieth-century copy), a late twelfth-/early thirteenth-century copy of the *Scivias* (Heidelberg, Universitätsbibliothek, MS Cod. Sal. X.16, fol. 3v), and an early thirteenth-century copy of the *Liber divinorum operum* (Lucca, Biblioteca Statale, MS 1942, fol. 1v), all of which depict Hildegard with a wax tablet and stylus alongside Volmar, who is portrayed with a book (and, in two cases, a quill and penknife) ready to produce a copy at the abbess's command and under her authorization (Fig. 1.1).[73]

Hildegard's vivid author portraits have parallels elsewhere, including at Mont-Saint-Michel. Returning to Robert of Torigni's working copy of the *Chronica*, we can see no fewer than four such portraits throughout the manuscript, all of which were executed by domestic artists at the abbot's command and, presumably, with specific instructions as to their design. Some of these miniatures have attracted more scholarly attention than others, but so far they have never, to my knowledge, been discussed as an ensemble.[74] The first (MS Avranches 159, fol. 4r) shows the

---

[71] On Andreas, Nonnosus, and Reinher, see below (2.6 and 4.3).

[72] Fassler, 'Hildegard', p. 288, emphasizing that '[n]o one has argued for the possibility that one of the many Rupertsberg hands may be that of Hildegard herself', at the same time as cautioning that 'the possibility that her hand is present among the scribes cannot be utterly denied'.

[73] Cf. *Hildegard von Bingen: Scivias–Die Miniaturen vom Rupertsberg*, ed. by Hildegard Schönfeld and Wolfgang Podehl (Bingen: Pennrich, 1979), pp. 16–17; Kimberley Benedict, *Empowering Collaborations: Writing Partnerships between Religious Women and Scribes in the Middle Ages* (New York, NY: Routledge, 2014), pp. 19 and 71–81; Katrin Graf, 'Les portraits d'auteur de Hildegarde de Bingen: Une étude iconographique', *Scriptorium* 55 (2001), 179–96; *Hildegard von Bingen: Liber scivias–Rüdesheimer Codex aus der Benediktinerinnenabtei St. Hildegard* (Graz: Akademische Druck- und Verlagsanstalt, 2013). Most recently Margot E. Fassler, *Cosmos, Liturgy, and the Arts in the Twelfth Century: Hildegard's Illuminated Scivias* (Philadelphia, PA: University of Pennsylvania Press, 2022), pp. 63–8.

[74] For example, in Benjamin Pohl, 'When Did Robert of Torigni First Receive Henry of Huntingdon's *Historia Anglorum*, and Why Does It Matter?', *Haskins Society Journal* 26 (2015), 143–67 (pp. 150–2); Cleaver, *History Books*, pp. 29–32.

Fig. 1.1 Hildegard of Bingen/Rupertsberg and her *amanuensis*, Volmar. Heidelberg, Universitätsbibliothek, MS Cod. Sal. X.16, fol. 3v.

famous Bible translator and historian, St Jerome, crouched over a writing desk with a long parchment scroll, pen, and an ink pot (Fig. 1.2a). The second (fol. 7v) is of influential bishop-historian and theologian Eusebius, who is depicted in a similar pose and with identical writing equipment and a folded sheet (or quire?) of parchment (Fig. 1.2b). The third (fol. 70r), which is the one of primary interest here, shows an abbot—tonsured and holding his abbatial staff—dictating to a scribe, but this time the figure's identity is more difficult to establish (Fig. 1.2c). Unlike in the previous cases in which the miniatures closely match the authors of the text(s) they accompany, namely Eusebius's *Chronicle* with Jerome's preface, this time the author of the adjacent text, Sigebert, never held an abbacy and therefore cannot be identified with the abbot depicted in the image.[75]

---

[75] A miniature with similar iconography survives in a compendium of chronicles from Christ Church, Canterbury (Cambridge, Corpus Christi College, MS 51, p. 1), which shows Jerome relying on the service of a tonsured *amanuensis* whose writing he 'directs' by guiding the tip of the quill with his index finger.

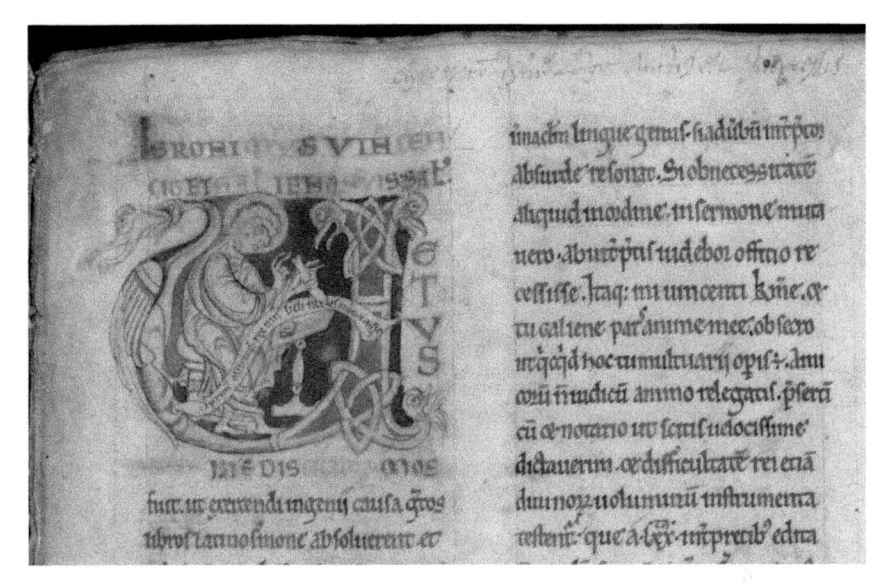

Fig. 1.2a Miniature depicting Jerome. Avranches, Bibliothèque patrimoniale, MS 159, fol. 4r.

Fig. 1.2b Miniature depicting Eusebius. Avranches, Bibliothèque patrimoniale, MS 159, fol. 7v.

Fig. 1.2c Miniature depicting Robert of Torigni and his personal scribe, Adam(?). Avranches, Bibliothèque patrimoniale, MS 159, fol. 70r.

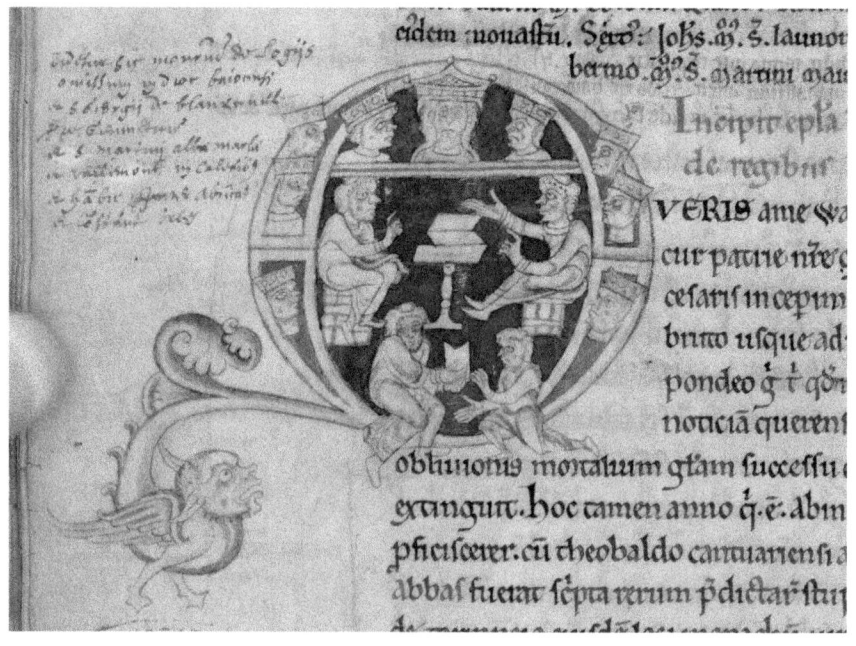

Fig. 1.2d Miniature depicting Robert of Torigni and Henry of Huntingdon. Avranches, Bibliothèque patrimoniale, MS 159, fol. 174v.

If the abbot depicted in the company of a scribal assistant in the third miniature of Robert's personal manuscript of the *Chronica* is not Sigebert, then who is he? The answer is, I contend, provided by the fourth miniature (fol. 174v), the iconography of which has been examined elsewhere (Fig. 1.2d).[76] It depicts two male figures—in fact, two historians—in lively conversation over an open book, one of whom is Henry of Huntingdon, author of the *Historia Anglorum*, and the other Robert, and the book they discuss is Le Bec's copy of Geoffrey of Monmouth's *Historia regum Britanniae/De gestis Brittonum*, which Robert made available to Henry upon the latter's expedition to Rome via Normandy in 1139. Visually, one of these identifiable figures, the one with a tonsure, Robert, is a near-perfect match for the enigmatic character in the previous miniature, except for his lack of the latter's abbatial insignia. We will recall, however, that when Henry came to Le Bec Robert was still a 'simple monk', and his promotion to abbot (via the rank of prior) was almost two decades away, meaning that the miniaturist of Mont-Saint-Michel responsible for both these images had every reason to depict Robert as a monk here but as an abbot elsewhere in the same manuscript, especially considering that he was working under Robert's personal instruction and thus would have been briefed carefully as to which miniature corresponded to the latter's respective career stages. I propose, therefore, that the miniature that marks the beginning of Sigebert's work in the *Chronica*'s authorial working copy portrays not him, but his self-styled continuator, the abbot-historian Robert, whose use of personal scribes for the preparation of his authorial manuscripts discussed above corresponds precisely to what we see depicted in this image. Similar iconography characterizes the authorial portrait on the frontispiece of the *Vita sancti Agerici per abbatem Stephanum*, a life of St Agericus composed by Stephen, the third abbot (1069–84) of Saint-Airy, that survives in four manuscripts, the oldest of which (Verdun, Bibliothèque d'étude du Grand Verdun, MS 8) was produced at Saint-Airy during the author's abbacy.[77] The miniature's lower half shows the abbot ('Stephanus abbas') enthroned with a square nimbus, a book in his hand and his left index finger extended to instruct the facing scribe ('scriba'), whose quill and penknife are resting on the blank page atop his writing desk in anticipation of the abbot's command to write (Fig. 1.3).

The examples discussed so far are not intended to suggest that the use of copyists and scribal assistants was the only *modus operandi* available to medieval abbot- and abbess-historians, nor that it was available to every monastic superior

---

[76] Pohl, 'When Did Robert', p. 151.

[77] *Écriture et enluminure en Lorraine au Moyen Âge*, ed. by Simone Collin-Roset et al. (Nancy: Société Thierry Alix, 1984), pp. 170–1 (= no. 117). The three other copies are Montpellier, Bibliothèque interuniversitaire–Bibliothèque universitaire historique de médecine, MS H 151 and Paris, Bibliothèque nationale de France, MSS Lat. 11757 and 14651, from the thirteenth and fifteenth century, respectively; on Saint-Airy's abbots, see *Pouillé du diocèse de Verdun*, ed. by Nicolas Robinet et al., 4 vols. (1888–1910), I, 228–34.

Fig. 1.3 Stephen of Saint-Airy and his scribe. Verdun, Bibliothèque d'étude du Grand Verdun, MS 8, fol. 1v.

as a matter of course, nor indeed that it was everyone's preference. In fact, there is good evidence of abbots who used scribal workforces for the codification of some of their authorial writings but chose to rely on the service of their own pen and quill for others, as well as of abbots who, as far as we know, only ever released their historiographical projects in the form of auto- or holographs. The former group includes Rupert, abbot (1120–9) of Saint-Heribert in Deutz/Cologne, whose substantial oeuvre comprises not only influential works of theology and a commentary on the *Rule of St Benedict*, but also a piece of contemporary historiography concerning the devastating fire in his own monastery in 1128, a (fragmentary) history of the church of Liège known as the *Libellus*, a range of saintly and non-saintly biographies such as his *Vita Cunonis abbatis Sigebergensis*, a *Life* of St Augustine, a redaction of Lambert's *Vita sancti Heriberti archiepiscopi Coloniensis* written prior to Rupert's abbacy at the instruction of his predecessor, Abbot Marquard (1110/13–20), and even his own autobiography.[78] Some of these writings Rupert committed to the page himself whilst abbot, whereas others he entrusted to his scribal assistant(s). Both working methods are depicted in exquisite miniatures found on adjacent pages in the authorial manuscript of Rupert's *Liber de Divinis officiis* (Munich, Bayerische Staatsbibliothek, MS Clm. 14355) that was produced at Deutz, almost certainly under his supervision and possibly with his first-hand participation, and dedicated to Bishop Kuno of Regensburg in c.1127. The first miniature (fol. 1r) shows Rupert presenting the completed work (in two volumes?) to his episcopal patron in the company of his scribal assistant, who likewise carries two books (Fig. 1.4a). All three figures have identifying rubrics, but unlike Rupert's ('ROUDPERTUS ABBAS') and Kuno's ('CHUNO EPISCOPUS'), the scribe's rubric is written in minuscule as a sign of his inferior status and identifies him as Stephen ('Stephanus'). Below Stephen's rubric used to be another short word that has since been erased, but what remains legible ('au - - r?') may suggest that the miniature had originally designated him as the 'maker' ('au(c)t(h)or') of the manuscript(s), and that this qualifier was then removed at a later point for reasons unknown, perhaps to avoid confusion between the different meanings carried by the medieval Latin terminology *auctor/author/actor* and identify Rupert unequivocally as the 'maker' (in the modern sense of 'author') of the *Liber* as a *text*, if not the *liber* as the *physical book(s)* in which it is preserved.[79]

[78] See John H. van Engen, 'Rupert von Deutz und das sogenannte *Chronicon sancti Laurentii Leodiensis*: Zur Geschichte des Investiturstreites in Lüttich', *Deutsches Archiv für Erforschung des Mittelalters* 35 (1979), 33–81; Walter Berschin, '*Os meum aperui*: Die Autobiographie Ruperts von Deutz (†um 1130)', *Studien und Mitteilungen zur Geschichte des Benediktinerordens und seiner Zweige* 119 (2008), 69–121.

[79] Jan-Dirk Müller, '*Auctor–Actor–Author*: Einige Anmerkungen zum Verständnis vom Autor in lateinischen Schriften des frühen und hohen Mittelalters', in *Der Autor im Dialog: Beiträge zu Autorität und Autorschaft*, ed. by Felix P. Ingold and Wener Wunderlich (St Gall: UVK, 1995), pp. 17–31; Marie-Dominique Chenu, 'Auctor, actor, autor', *Archivum latinitatis medii aevi* 3 (1927), 81–86, repr. in *Studi di lessicografia filosofica medievale*, ed. by Marie-Dominique Chenu and Giacinta Spinosa (Florence: Olschki, 2001), pp. 51–6.

Fig. 1.4a Rupert of Deutz and his scribal assistant. Munich, Bayerische Staatsbibliothek, MS Clm. 14355, fol. 1r.

Such confusion or ambiguity could well have been caused by the presence of four books in the dedication scene—two carried by Rupert and two by Stephen—though these may in fact have been intended to signify the same two volumes produced by Stephen under Rupert's supervision, rather than four separate items. By contrast, the second miniature painted on the reverse of the same page (fol. 1v) shows Abbot Rupert ('ROUDPERTUS ABBAS') in his alternative mode of authorial manuscript production: unaccompanied by Stephen or any other *amanuenses*, he sharpens his own quill with a penknife ready to fill the pages of the book that rests on his lap with his own writing (Fig. 1.4b).

Fig. 1.4b Rupert of Deutz as scribe. Munich, Bayerische Staatsbibliothek, MS Clm. 14355, fol. 1v.

Some abbot-historians of the Middle Ages never seem to have bothered with copyists but relied exclusively on their own penmanship for the codification of their authorial works. This was the case with, for example, Guibert, the abbot-historian of Nogent-sous-Coucy whom we will meet again soon, who reports never to have drafted his narratives on wax for others to copy on his behalf, but to have written them straight onto parchment *manu propria*.[80] As will be discussed below (2.3), this was a practice Guibert had cultivated before his abbacy out of necessity rather than choice—namely when writing without abbatial authorization and trying to keep his work hidden from his then abbot, Garnier—but one which he continued after his promotion in 1104 despite the fact that from that point onwards he surely would have had the resources (and the authority) to delegate these tasks to some of his monks, even within a community as small and humble as Nogent.[81] In fact, we know that as abbot Guibert used assistants for various other writing tasks, for example, the drafting of a charter that records his own 'anniversary donations' of c.1121, and the important work of Monique-Cécile Garand shows beyond doubt that this was the case throughout Guibert's abbacy (1104–25) for most quotidian and administrative written assignments.[82] He even seems to have had a 'go-to *amanuensis*' or personal secretary, William the Subdeacon ('Guillelmus subdiaconus'), whose hand can be traced in multiple documents issued in Guibert's name, as well as another regular assistant who remains anonymous but is known as 'Scribe B'.[83] When it came to his authorial writing projects, by contrast, Guibert stuck to his own pen whenever and for as long as he could, and only as his eyesight and fine motor skills increasingly failed him with advanced age did he eventually succumb to having his works penned by others on his behalf, but never without a discernible sense of reluctance and even embarrassment—the most striking expression of which occurs in the preface of the *Tropologia in Osee* completed during the final years of his abbacy, c.1121–4 (Paris, Bibliothèque nationale de France, MS Lat.

---

[80] Guibert describes this working method on two occasions, namely in his *Monodiae* and in the *Dei gesta per Francos*; for the respective references and discussion, see below (2.3).

[81] According to Guibert and another contemporary source, the community's initial endowments had been just about sufficient to provide for half a dozen monks—half the number envisaged in the *Rule of St Benedict*. Even by the time Guibert assumed its governance in December 1104, almost half a century after its foundation, the number of monks is still reported to have been no more than nine. When the monastery was dissolved in 1789, only five monks remained; *Guibert de Nogent: Autobiographie*, ed./tr. by Edmond-René Labande (Paris: Les Belles Lettres, 1981), p. 226; Nicholas of Saint-Crépin, 'Vita sancti Godefredi Ambianensis episcopi', in *Acta sanctorum*, ed. by Société des Bollandistes, 68 vols., 3rd ed. (Antwerp et al.: Société des Bollandistes, 1643–1940), LXV (= November III), 905–44 (p. 912); Georges Bourgin, *Guibert de Nogent: Histoire de sa vie (1053–1124)* (Paris: Picard, 1907), p. ix; Maximilien Melleville, *Histoire de la ville et des sires de Coucy-le-chateau* (Laon: Journal de l'Aisne, 1848), p. 277.

[82] Garand, *Guibert*, passim; Monique-Cécile Garand, 'Le scriptorium de Guibert de Nogent', *Scriptorium* 31 (1977), 3–29.

[83] Garand, *Guibert*, pp. 71–7; Garand, 'Scriptorium', pp. 13–19.

2502, fols. 1r–2v).[84] It is clear, therefore, that for Guibert the use of scribal assistants was a conscious choice, one that he was much more willing to make for certain kinds (or 'genres') of writings than for others. Whenever he *did* make that choice, however, whether out of practicability (as he did with administrative chores) or because his physical impairment left him no real alternative, he could always rely on his abbatial authority to provide him with a suitable workforce within the walls of his monastery, and perhaps beyond.

Another abbot whose historiographical activity is treated in greater detail below (1.3), and one who, like Guibert, preferred to commit his work to writing personally, is Hugh of Flavigny. In Hugh's case, as in Guibert's, this habit dates to before his short-lived abbacy (1096–1101) at Flavigny(-sur-Ozerain). Hugh's major work, the *Chronicon*, which he began before, continued during, and completed after his abbatial tenure, survives exclusively in autograph form with no traces of scribal collaborators or contributions by hands other than Hugh's, making it a holograph or *Vollautograph*. This was not Hugh's first or only historiographical involvement, though. Both before and alongside the *Chronicon*'s extended process of composition and re-imagination, Hugh wrote history under Abbot Rodulf of Saint-Vanne—the *Chronicon*'s original commissioner, if not its eventual patron or dedicatee—and possibly also under Jarento, the abbot of Saint-Bénigne de Dijon. Indeed, there is evidence that Hugh served as the latter's personal *amanuensis* and *cancellarius*. At Saint-Vanne and Dijon, Hugh had direct access to historical narratives and documents from the monasteries' respective libraries and archives that he used liberally with the permission of their abbots and, on occasion, even made corrections and annotations to them. Whilst at Dijon, Hugh read and annotated in his own hand a historical dossier (Montpellier, Bibliothèque interuniversitaire–Bibliothèque universitaire historique de médecine, MS H 151) that contains, amongst other writings, the *Annals* of Flodoard of Reims and Abbot Stephen of Saint-Airy's *Vita Agerici* introduced earlier, and which, as shown by Lecouteux, constituted an integral source for the *Chronicon*, providing important insights into the working methods that Hugh first formed at Saint-Vanne and Dijon and then adopted (and adapted) during his abbacy at Flavigny.[85] The manuscript is a composite codex, parts of which were produced at Saint-Bénigne and others at Saint-Vanne, whence they had been brought to Dijon during the community's exile (on which more below). At least

---

[84] The preface is edited by Robert B. C. Huygens, *La tradition manuscrite de Guibert de Nogent* (Steenbrugge: In Abbatia S. Petri, 1991), pp. 110–13, with the relevant passage on pp. 112–13: 'Hactenus enim [...] erubesco'; also cf. Garand, *Guibert*, pp. 27–8, with a discussion of the *Tropologia*'s likely date of completion (ibid., p. 24).

[85] See the comprehensive analysis in Stéphane Lecouteux, 'Les Annales de Flodoard de Reims (919–66) dans la tradition historiographique du Moyen Âge: Travail de l'annaliste et de l'historien, perception et maîtrise du temps (VIIIe–XIIe siècles)' (unpublished Master's thesis, École Pratique des Hautes Études, 2010–11), pp. 43–5 and 54–68, which concludes that '[c]e manuscrit est donc d'un grand intérêt [...] pour comprendre la méthode de travail d'Hugues de Flavigny' (ibid., p. 55).

one of the copyists from Dijon was a contemporary of Hugh's, and unlike Hugh's later projects the two men appear to have been collaborating closely in sections of this manuscript, with Hugh's hand being especially prominent in the third *libellus* (fols. 27r–88r).[86] This teamwork and collaboration during the formative years of Hugh's training as a monastic historian—his historical apprenticeship, so to speak—marks a notable contrast to the solitary and exclusive enterprise that was the first-hand codification of his historiographical *magnum opus*.

Similar though the cases of Hugh of Flavigny and Guibert of Nogent may be in some respects, they are separated by one important difference: Guibert's habit from early on had been to act as his own copyist and this remained so throughout his abbacy for the works closest to his heart—specifically his historiographical projects, which he would not entrust to anyone else's pen if he could avoid it. As abbot, though, he regularly, and readily, handed over various non-authorial writing tasks to his secretary William and others within the monastery, possibly as a means of freeing up precious writing time for himself to concentrate on his authorial works. Hugh's custom, by contrast, seems to have developed almost in reverse. As a monk-historian writing for Abbots Rodulf and Jarento and a team member of their respective workforces at Saint-Vanne and Dijon, Hugh had started out by habitually collaborating with other copyists, as he did in the historical dossier mentioned above, whilst as abbot he increasingly adopted a more insular and self-reliant working method. Rather than using his abbatial authority and resources to draft in helping hands, Hugh appears to have employed the new freedoms and decision-making powers invested in him *ex officio* to make space for writing in his own schedule that enabled him to continue and even accelerate the historiographical pursuit he had begun prior to his abbacy, the completion of which would eventually take several more decades. As we will see later in this book (4.1), though, such single-mindedness could cause friction and sometimes lead to serious conflicts between abbot-historians and their communities, especially if the latter felt their superiors were spending more time writing than they did managing, and that their historiographical projects led them to neglect their other abbatial responsibilities. In the end, therefore, adopting the right working method for the codification of authorial works was not simply a matter of personal preference, but one of institutional consensus and, ultimately, communal politics, thus obliging abbots and abbesses to consider their duties and recognition within the monastic community as much as their own egos and recognition as writers of history in society more widely.

Provided their monasteries had the domestic personnel and/or the resources to buy in external expertise—for example, by 'outsourcing' scribal assignments to affiliated communities or by hiring professional scribes, a practice that, as will be

---

[86] Lecouteux, 'Annales', pp. 63–4 and 67–8.

discussed below (2.4), was not uncommon during the high and later Middle Ages—abbot-historians principally had a choice whether to commit their authorial compositions to writing *manu propria* or delegate this scribal labour to others inside and, if required, outside their communities. The fact that in a monastery the assignment of human resources (scribes/copyists), material provisions (writing materials, etc.), and, importantly, writing time took place at the abbot's final discretion and was subject to his official approval put abbots/abbesses who were themselves writers of history in a privileged position, one that was both unparalleled within the monastic historiographical *milieu* and linked intrinsically with their superlative authority as institutional superiors. This set them apart from other monastic historiographers, be they simple monks/nuns or so-called cantor-historians, all of whom depended, directly or indirectly, on the abbot's authorization for the composition and codification of their works. Whether they wanted to put their own pens to parchment or request the assistance of copyists, neither, but especially not the latter, could be enacted and sustained without abbatial licence. The choice as to who wrote history in a monastery was ultimately the abbot's, and a substantial number of medieval abbots (and, as we will see, quite a few abbesses) chose themselves for the task. In doing so, they enjoyed freedoms and decision-making powers that were not available, or barely available, to other writers of history. Besides the authority to carve out writing time for themselves (4.2) and assemble scribal workforces (3.2) for the preparation of manuscripts, another important prerogative of monastic superiors writing history was the ability to write themselves prominently into these histories and, as the next part of this study will demonstrate, even use them as vehicles of abbatial self-fashioning.

1.3 Historical Writing as Self-Fashioning

One major advantage that historiographical authorship offered to monastic superiors was the ability to write history as a means of abbatial self-fashioning. Some used this opportunity strategically, to align themselves with, or distance themselves from, the memory of their institutional predecessors by stressing elements of continuity or change between their tenures. Celebrated examples include Abbot Suger of Saint-Denis (1122–51), who produced a flattering account of his own abbatial government in his authorial writings, most notably in his *De administratione*, and Henry of Blois, abbot of Glastonbury (1126–71), who in addition to commissioning the foundation history known as *De antiquitate Glastoniensis ecclesiae* from William of Malmsbury authored a first-person account of his monastery's more recent history.[87] Whether the theme was one

---

[87] On Suger's self-referential historiography, see below (2.5); on Henry of Blois and his writing, see N. E. Stacy, 'Henry of Blois and the Lordship of Glastonbury', *English Historical Review* 114 (1999),

of (invented) tradition or reform—expressed and justified, respectively, through imitation or criticism of one's forebears—these strategies depended fundamentally on the explicit juxtaposition, comparison, and contrast of the author's autobiographical persona with the lives and deeds of those who had held the same office previously, even if the resulting narratives would then culminate, as many of them do, in an account of the author's own accomplishments and their benefits for the community that overshadowed and outweighed earlier achievements. A few took this self-fashioning one step further by intentionally foregrounding their own role in the history of their communities to the detriment of their predecessors, whom they relegated to the margins of the historical record or removed altogether whilst inserting themselves in pre-eminent positions. It was not just this strategic positioning of the authorial self in relation to the most prominent past and present members of a monastic community that could form the focus of histories written by abbots, however, but also the showcasing of personal relationships, amicable and inimical, with individuals and groups external to the monastery. This was the case especially where abbatial authors could claim to have won themselves—and, by extension, their communities—the friendship and support of powerful political allies and benefactors (princes, kings, emperors, popes, etc.), or to have triumphed over formidable adversaries and institutional rivals (usually bishops) following historical periods of personal struggle and collective hardship.

A striking example of this last category is the *Chronicon* of Hugh, abbot of Flavigny (1096–1101).[88] As discussed in greater detail below, Hugh wrote, expanded, revised, and—importantly—re-imagined his *Chronicon* over several decades, which means that only a relatively small but, as I will demonstrate here, transformative part of the extended composition process fell within the period of his abbatial tenure. In its final form, the work is marked by a strong sense of vindication that can best be described as Hugh's personal reckoning with Bishop Norgaud of Autun (1098–1111/12), who is presented as a sower of discord between Hugh and his monastic community and the primary architect of the abbot's repeated banishment and eventual downfall. In fact, the *Chronicon* resembles something of an *apologia* on the part of its author, with Hugh ostensibly

---

1–33 (p. 2); Nicholas Karn, 'Introduction to the Foundation Narrative', in *Foundation Documents from St Mary's Abbey, York 1085–1137*, ed. by Richard Sharpe et al. (Woodbridge: Boydell, 2022), pp. 339–78 (pp. 364–5).

[88] In the autograph manuscript (Berlin, Staatsbibliothek–Preußischer Kulturbesitz, MS Phill. 1870), the only surviving medieval witness, Hugh's work is transmitted without a title, but it is usually referred to in scholarship as either the *Chronicon Virdunense* (after Saint-Vanne de Verdun, the monastery of Hugh's original monastic profession) or the *Chronicon Flaviniacense* (after the monastery over which he came to preside as abbot). It has been edited as Hugh of Flavigny, 'Chronicon', in *Chronica et gesta aevi Salici*, ed. by Georg H. Pertz [= *MGH SS* VIII] (Hanover: Hahn, 1848), pp. 288–502. A revised version of Pertz's edition was prepared and published online by Mathias Lawo, https://www.mgh.de/de/mgh-digital/digitale-angebote-zu-mgh-abteilungen#flavigny, which is the one cited here unless otherwise indicated.

at pains to justify and style himself as a victim of the drawn-out and ever more acrimonious conflict with Norgaud that prevented him from governing his monastery effectively and, as a result, left his abbatial *auctoritas* in tatters.[89] This was not how Hugh had envisaged and conceptualized the *Chronicon* from the beginning, however, and to appreciate how and why his work adopted its eventual outlook, we must recapitulate, in brief, the key stages of its composition and re-imagination over the course of Hugh's life and career with a specific focus on his role as abbot and how this determined the way in which he wrote and re-wrote history in a self-fashioning capacity.

The beginnings of Hugh's historiographical activity predated his abbacy by several years, with most scholars now in agreement that he began the work which eventually would become the *Chronicon* c.1085 × 92.[90] At that point, Hugh was still technically a monk of Saint-Vanne in Verdun, where he had professed himself and begun his education under Abbot Rodulf (1076–99/1100), though earlier in 1085 the monastic community had been forced to leave Verdun following mounting tensions with its diocesan bishop, Theoderic (1047–89), who sided with Emperor Henry IV in the ecclesio-political power conflicts better known as the 'Investiture Controversy'.[91] Hugh would subsequently refer to this collective exile as an act of pilgrimage ('peregrinatio').[92] Having abandoned their home monastery, Rodulf and his monks sojourned briefly at their dependent priory of Flavigny-sur-Moselle before continuing their journey—via Saint-Blin and Langres—to Saint-Bénigne de Dijon at the invitation of its then abbot, Jarento (1076–1113). After some deliberation and disagreement about how to accommodate the forty or so newcomers and integrate them into the hosting community, Hugh and his fellow exiles are reported to have re-professed themselves, albeit many of them reluctantly, as monks of Saint-Bénigne.[93] It was there, at their 'home away from home', and perhaps *en route*, that Hugh began to commit the

---

[89] Hugh's conflicts with Norgaud are studied in detail by Mathias Lawo, *Studien zu Hugo von Flavigny* (Hanover: Hahn, 2010), pp. 17–33; also cf. Patrick Healy, *The Chronicle of Hugh of Flavigny: Reform and the Investiture Contest in the Late Eleventh Century* (Aldershot: Ashgate, 2006), pp. 77–81.

[90] On the *Chronicon*'s likely *terminus a quo* and the scholarly debates surrounding it, see Healy, *Chronicle*, pp. 91–3.

[91] Ian S. Robinson, *Authority and Resistance in the Investiture Contest: The Polemical Literature of the Late Eleventh Century* (Manchester: Manchester University Press, 1978), pp. 153–6; Charles West, *Reframing the Feudal Revolution: Political and Social Transformation between Marne and Moselle, c.800–c.1100* (Cambridge: Cambridge University Press, 2013), pp. 213–21. On Bishop Theoderic and his relationship with Saint-Vanne, see Mechthild Sandmann, 'Theoderich von Verdun und die religiösen Gemeinschaften seiner Diözese', in *Person und Gemeinschaft im Mittelalter: Festschrift für Karl Schmid zum fünfundsechzigsten Geburtstag*, ed. by Gerd Althoff et al. (Sigmaringen: Thorbecke, 1988), pp. 315–44.

[92] Hugh of Flavigny, 'Chronicon', ed. Pertz and rev. Lawo, p. 468; 'Annales sancti Benigni Divionensis, a. 564–1285', ed. by Georg Waitz, in *Annales et chronica aevi Salici*, ed. by Georg H. Pertz [= *MGH SS* V] (Hanover: Hahn, 1844), pp. 37–50 (p. 43); Michael Borgolte, 'Fiktive Gräber in der Historiographie: Hugo von Flavigny und die Sepultur der Bischöfe von Verdun', in *Fälschungen im Mittelalter*, 5 vols. (Hanover: Hahn, 1988), I, 205–40 (pp. 216–17).

[93] On this secondary profession (*Zweitprofess*), see Lawo, *Studien*, pp. 10–11.

history of Verdun to writing at Rodulf's abbatial request with a dual-focus on the monastic community of Saint-Vanne and the diocesan episcopate that had forced it into exile. When Rodulf and his monks could finally return home in 1092, some chose to remain at Saint-Bénigne, including Hugh, who spent the next half a decade as Abbot Jarento's assistant and *amanuensis* (see below) before being appointed, with Jarento's endorsement, to the abbacy of Flavigny in 1096.[94] It was during this interim period at Dijon (1092–6) that the *Chronicon* was subjected to its first re-imagination and conceptual re-design which bears the hallmark of Jarento, who at this point likely took over from Rodulf as the work's main patron. Instead of concentrating on Verdun and its ecclesio-political landscape, the *Chronicon*'s focus shifted to the history of Saint-Bénigne and its abbots, the archbishopric of Lyon, the church reforms under Pope Gregory VII, and the Investiture Controversy.[95] When leaving Dijon for Flavigny, Hugh was accompanied by a group of Dijonnaise monks ('[f]ratres quoque nostros Divionenses') who had been ordered by Jarento to assist him in mastering the challenges of his appointment ('qui mihi ad solatium laboris et ordinis custodiam dati fuerant'), though the next years proved more burdensome than either he or Jarento could have anticipated.[96] Within a few years of his arrival at Flavigny, Abbot Hugh found himself embroiled in conflict with Autun's episcopate that soon took their toll on the community and his authority as abbot. These conflicts have been studied in detail elsewhere,[97] so a summary with a specific focus on their impact on Hugh's historiographical activity as abbot will suffice here.

According to Hugh's recollection, the initial bone of contention had been his absence from Norgaud's episcopal election on 6 May 1098.[98] Norgaud's late predecessor, Hagano (†25 June 1097), had been on favourable terms with Hugh, having supported (and perhaps initiated) his abbatial appointment at Flavigny and recommended him personally as an agent in the reform of its monastic church.[99] The relationship with Norgaud, by contrast, seemed ill-fated from the moment Hugh sent a delegate to Autun to cast the election vote in his place ('vicem nostram suppleret'), a 'vote by proxy' which Norgaud is said to have deemed such an affront that even Hugh's presence at the subsequent consecration followed by his personal invitation to host and entertain Norgaud and his

---

[94] As shown by Healy, *Chronicle*, p. 75, the most likely date of Hugh's abbatial election is 22 November 1096; Lawo, *Studien*, pp. 4–5 favours the same date.

[95] Lawo, *Studien*, pp. 79–80; Healy, *Chronicle*, p. 3; see also Patrick Healy, 'Hugh of Flavigny and Canon Law as Polemic in the Investiture Contest', *Zeitschrift der Savigny-Stiftung für Rechtsgeschichte: Kanonistische Abteilung* 91 (2005), 17–58.

[96] Hugh of Flavigny, 'Chronicon', ed. Pertz and rev. Lawo, p. 478.

[97] See Lawo, *Studien*, pp. 17–33.

[98] Hugh of Flavigny, 'Chronicon', ed. Pertz and rev. Lawo, pp. 477–9; on Norgaud's election, see Healy, *Chronicle*, p. 76; Lawo, *Studien*, p. 22.

[99] Hagano strongly recommends Hugh in a letter to the archbishop of Lyon; Hugh of Flavigny, 'Chronicon', ed. Pertz and rev. Lawo, p. 475.

entourage at one of Flavigny's dependent priories could not assuage him.[100] Norgaud now accused the monks of Flavigny—and, by implication, their abbot—to have assaulted him during an episcopal visitation.[101] Despite Hugh's protestations to the contrary, Norgaud made quick use of his episcopal *potestas* by placing the abbot—and, by extension, his monks—under an interdict that prevented them from administering the sacraments (including marriages and funeral rites) on behalf of the local community.[102] He reportedly went one step further by threatening to excommunicate all churches affiliated to Flavigny, but was prevented from doing so by whatever influence Hugh had left within Autun's cathedral chapter.[103] Despite paying no fewer than seven visits to Autun in as many months, Hugh's attempts to (re-)gain the bishop's favour failed until another seven months later, when he and Norgaud came to an agreement, at least for the time being, and celebrated the feast of St Nazarius on 28 July 1099. Whether this public display of their renewed *concordia* and *amicitia* was genuine or merely performative in nature is difficult to know, but it seems telling that the interdict placed upon Hugh's abbey the previous year was lifted not by Norgaud, but by Archbishop Hugh of Lyon (1082–1106; previously bishop of Die, 1073–82), which may well indicate a certain reluctance and disingenuity on Norgaud's part.[104] As far as Hugh's domestic position at Flavigny was concerned, the damage had been done in any case, and he had to withdraw himself from the community at Flavigny's daughter house at Couches, the very priory where he had entertained Bishop Norgaud the previous summer.[105]

According to Hugh, his own monks had not just advised, but practically ordered him to leave Flavigny and go to Couches ('[d]ederunt enim mihi verba, non consilia, ut Colticas irem'), and during his absence some of them closed ranks by forming a coalition with Norgaud.[106] Having appealed unsuccessfully to papal legate Archbishop Hugh of Lyon, Hugh found a mediator in Jarento, his old mentor and abbot of Saint-Bénigne de Dijon, who was appointed to arbitrate

---

[100] See Hugh of Flavigny, 'Chronicon', ed. Pertz and rev. Lawo, p. 477. Healy, *Chronicle*, p. 77 suggests that Hugh's absence might have been motivated by accusations of simony faced by Norgaud that would have jeopardized Hugh's own abbatial election, though this must remain conjecture.

[101] Hugh of Flavigny, 'Chronicon', ed. Pertz and rev. Lawo, p. 477.

[102] Hugh of Flavigny, 'Chronicon', ed. Pertz and rev. Lawo, pp. 477–8; Lawo, *Studien*, p. 18 n. 94 sees this interdict as an act short of excommunication aimed not at Hugh personally, but the community in its entirety. As bishop, Norgaud's *potestas* consisted of his jurisdictional power (*potestas iurisdictionis* or *potestas regiminis*), his sacramentary power and the right to perform ordinations (*potestas ordinis* or *potestas ministerii*), and his spiritual power in teaching the orthodox faith (*potestas magisterii*); cf. Benjamin Pohl, 'The Problem of Cluniac Exemption', in *A Companion to the Abbey of Cluny in the Middle Ages*, ed. by Scott G. Bruce and Steven Vanderputten (Leiden: Brill, 2021), pp. 288–305.

[103] Hugh of Flavigny, 'Chronicon', ed. Pertz and rev. Lawo, p. 478.

[104] Hugh of Flavigny, 'Chronicon', ed. Pertz and rev. Lawo, p. 479.

[105] When Couches was subjected to Flavigny by Walter, bishop of Autun (977–1018) in an act dated 1018 that survives in Flavigny's cartulary, it was referred to as a 'little monastery' ('coenobiolum') inhabited by no monks or canons, home only to one priest; *The Cartulary of Flavigny, 717–1113*, ed. by Constance B. Bouchard (Cambridge, MA: Medieval Academy of America, 1991), pp. 109–12 (= no. 43).

[106] Hugh of Flavigny, 'Chronicon', ed. Pertz and rev. Lawo, p. 484.

between the two rival factions at Flavigny.[107] Those who sided with Norgaud renounced their obedience to Hugh in every regard ('in omnibus mihi [= Hugh] abrenunciantes'), even denying him entry into his own monastery, which they instead promised, along with their loyalty, to Norgaud ('domno episcopo filiationem per legatos eius offerentes').[108] Taking up residence at Saint-Bénigne once more, Hugh sent two letters to Norgaud between late October and early November 1099 demanding his unconditional restoration as abbot, both of which he copied verbatim in his *Chronicon*.[109] As the conflict dragged on, Hugh, still in exile, composed another letter in August 1100 addressed to Flavigny's monks and their prior, Gerard, inviting 'all those who profess themselves children of the church of Flavigny' ('omnibus qui se profitentur filios ecclesiae Flaviniacensis') to a synod convened at Valence the following month, where 'we shall present our case with the Lord's protection [...] to listen, respond, and be judged. May all the accusers, slanderers, and witnesses come [forth], everyone who has a case against us, all of you who conspired in our exile and robbery, debased yourselves with such unheard-of injury, and despised those who could be persuaded to come to their senses'.[110] Referring to himself as 'the banished abbot of Flavigny' ('Flaviniacensis expulsus abbas'), Hugh at the time of writing had been absent from his community at Flavigny for about ten months. To make matters worse for him, Norgaud used his absence to obtain a strategically highly significant privilege from Pope Paschal II that confirmed Norgaud and his successors their *potestas* to anathematize wrongdoers and exclude them from the community of the faithful in precisely the way that Norgaud had penalized Hugh and his monks in the summer of 1098.[111]

Faced with such threats to his abbatial authority, Hugh's appeal at the highest judicial level by bringing the case before the Council of Valence seems a logical choice, and one that shows his desperation. Initially, this paid dividends: the council ruled in his favour, and the papal legates issued a letter to Flavigny's monks ordering them to reinstate him immediately as their rightful abbot and renew their obedience to him, lest they suffered the penalty of the pope's interdict.

---

[107] On Hugh of Lyons, cf. Uta-Renate Blumenthal, 'Hugh of Die and Lyons, Primate and Papal Legate', in *Scripturus vitam: Lateinische Biographie von der Antike bis in die Gegenwart. Festgabe für Walter Berschin zum 65. Geburtstag*, ed. by Dorothea Walz (Heidelberg: Mattes, 2002), pp. 487–95; Kriston R. Rennie, *Law and Practice in the Age of Reform: The Legatine Work of Hugh of Die (1073–1106)* (Turnhout: Brepols, 2010).

[108] Hugh of Flavigny, 'Chronicon', ed. Pertz and rev. Lawo, p. 485.

[109] Hugh of Flavigny, 'Chronicon', ed. Pertz and rev. Lawo, pp. 486–7.

[110] Hugh of Flavigny, 'Chronicon', ed. Pertz and rev. Lawo, p. 488: 'Nos enim concilio nos praesentabimus, Deo protectore, [...] parati cum Dei adiutorio audire, respondere et iudicari canonice. Veniant igitur accusatores, criminatores et testes, quicumque erga nos causam habent, qui expulsioni et spoliationi nostrae consensistis, qui inauditum, indempnatum abiecistis, et ammoniti resipiscere despexistis'.

[111] A copy of Paschal II's privilege for Norgaud dated 10 April 1100 survives in the medieval cartulary of Autun; *Cartulaire de l'église d'Autun*, ed. by Anatole de Charmasse, 2 vols. (Paris: Pédone, 1865–1900; repr. Geneva: Mégariotis, 1978), I, 2–4 (= no. II).

However, when Hugh returned to Flavigny triumphantly and personally read out a copy of this letter to the monks in the chapter house ('in capitulo'), it became clear that any hopes he might have entertained for things to return to normal were about be frustrated. Those who had opposed him previously still showed no humility in word or deed ('[i]n verbis vero eorum et factis nulla inventa est humilitas'), and they had no intention to honour the synod's ruling ('aut erga statuta concilii obedientia')—a powerful reminder of the difference between legal theory and practice, and that between normative/prescriptive texts and everyday lived realities.[112] Authoritative and encouraging though the outcome at Valences may have been, from Hugh's point-of-view at least, its implementation at Flavigny (located almost 300 km from Valences as the crow flies) was a different matter altogether, and the reluctance of his domestic opponents to obey the legates' instructions left Hugh with little choice but to withdraw to Couches again and prepare another appeal for presentation at the Council of Poitiers on 18 November 1100.[113] However, when Hugh stopped over at Flavigny *en route* to Poitiers, he was assaulted by a group of monks headed by Prior Gerard, violently stripped of his abbatial insignia (including his staff), and robbed of the synodal letter issued to him at Valence, which he presumably had intended to present at Poitiers as a crucial piece of evidence.[114] Norgaud was sentenced and excommunicated at Poitiers but reinstated by the archbishop of Lyon the following year, allowing him to remain in office for another decade. Hugh, by contrast, was unable to resume his abbacy, with Norgaud installing Gerard, Flavigny's prior and ringleader of the internal opposition against Hugh, in his place. To add insult to injury, even Hugh's long-standing ally, Abbot Jarento of Saint-Bénigne, turned against him and placed him under excommunication. Whether he obtained a different abbacy in the diocese of Verdun—and if he did, exactly where—has long been a subject of conjecture and debate that cannot be resolved here, but he probably died not long after 1114.[115]

The reason why it is useful and necessary to recapitulate in some detail these stages in Hugh's conflict with Bishop Norgaud and his allies is that they were instrumental to the *Chronicon*'s second re-imagination (the first being the work's

---

[112] Hugh of Flavigny, 'Chronicon', ed. Pertz and rev. Lawo, p. 489.

[113] Besides Valence and Poitiers, the only other papal synod held in 1100—and the only one attended in person by Pope Paschal II, rather than by his legates—was that convened at Melfi in mid-October; cf. Georg Gresser, *Die Syonden und Konzilien in der Zeit des Reformpapsttums in Deutschland und Italien von Leo IX. bis Calixt II., 1049–1123* (Paderborn: Schöningh, 2006), pp. 335–6; Uta-Renate Blumenthal, *The Early Councils of Pope Paschal II, 1100–1110* (Toronto: Pontifical Institute of Mediaeval Studies, 1978), pp. 7–11; Hans-Werner Goetz, 'Kirchenfest und weltliches Alltagsleben im früheren Mittelalter', *Mediaevistik* 2 (1989), 123–71 (p. 148).

[114] Hugh of Flavigny, 'Chronicon', ed. Pertz and rev. Lawo, pp. 489–90. As argued compellingly by Lawo, *Studien*, p. 30, the 'Valentinensis investitura concilii' that Gerard took from Hugh by force upon his arrival at Flavigny can be identified with the letter issued by Cardinals John of Saint-Anastasia and Benedict of Saint-Pudenziana at Valence.

[115] See Lawo, *Studien*, pp. 33–6 for discussion of these matters.

shift of focus under the patronage of Abbot Jarento of Saint-Bénigne in 1092–6) that occurred in the period of Hugh's short but eventful abbacy. It was likely completed in or around 1103, though again it seems highly plausible that Hugh drafted substantial parts of this text as the events unfolded and his abbacy unravelled, meaning that he, too, must be considered an abbatial author for most of this key stage in the *Chronicon*'s history of composition. This second re-imagination—unlike the previous writing stages undertaken at the instigation of Rodulf and Jarento, respectively—did not depend on the commission and authorization of an abbatial patron, but instead was driven and sustained by Hugh's own authority as abbot of Flavigny, an authority that applied even during the author's repeated exile at Couches. As a result of this new-found and self-contained (if short-lived) *auctoritas*, Flavigny's abbots took centre-stage in Hugh's historiographical vision, though none more so than himself. We can see concrete palaeographical and codicological evidence of this conceptual change of direction in the *Chronicon*'s autograph, to which I return below. The presence of a distinct series of marginalia and paratextual notes written on inserted slips of parchment in what has been identified as Hugh's personal handwriting, and which relate to Flavigny's abbots and their accomplishments, shows that Hugh went back systematically over the earlier versions of the *Chronicon* not long after his abbatial appointment to insert information about the deeds of his predecessors.[116] The first two insertions (fols. 36v and 37v) both concern Flavigny's foundation and the appointment of its first abbot, Magoald (719–32);[117] these are followed by notes about his successors up to Zacho (793/4–96/7) (fols. 51r–60^{bis}r).[118]

As noted by Eduard Hlawitschka, most of Hugh's insertions about the abbots of Flavigny have equivalents in a short text known as the *Series abbatum Flaviniacensium*, a full translation of which is provided in the Appendix of this book.[119] Once part of the *Chronicon*'s autograph manuscript (where it would have

---

[116] See Eduard Hlawitschka, 'Textkritisches zur Series abbatum Flaviniacensium', in *Landschaft und Geschichte: Festschrift für Franz Petri zu seinem 65. Geburtstag*, ed. by Georg Droege et al. (Bonn: Röhrscheid, 1970), pp. 250–65 (pp. 258–61). Lawo, *Studien*, p. 75 refers to the *Chronicon*'s autograph as a 'in der Entstehung konserviertes Original, sozusagen als "work in progress"'; on Hugh's handwriting, cf. Lecouteux, 'Annales', pp. 162–3, with photographical reproductions of various samples (ibid., p. 195 = Planche V).

[117] Hugh of Flavigny, 'Chronicon', ed. Pertz and rev. Lawo, pp. 322–4.

[118] The abbots of Flavigny who form the subjects of Hugh's marginalia in MS Berlin Phill. 1870 are: Magoald (fol. 51r: death); Widerard (fol. 51v: ordination; fol. 51v: death); Geruin (fol. 51v: appointment and death); Manasses (fol. 52r: ordination; fol. 59v: ordination, translation of the remains of St Praejectus the Martyr to Flavigny, death; fol. 60v: receives exemption privileges from Charlemagne; fol. 60^{bis}r: translation of St Praejectus); Adalbert (fol. 59v: ordination; fol. 60^{bis}r: death); Zacho (fol. 60^{bis}r: appointment). Further to the marginalia on fol. 37v, Widerard is said to have 'ruled [Flavigny] for twelve years' ('praefuit XII · annos'; ibid., fol. 51r) after the death of Magoald.

[119] The *Series abbatum Flaviniacensium* was first edited in *Nova bibliotheca manuscriptorum librorum sive specimen antiquarum lectionum latinarum et graecarum*, ed. by Philippe Labbé, 2 vols. (Paris: Henault, 1657), I, 791–3; when Pertz then printed it from this edition in Hugh of Flavigny, 'Chronicon', ed. Pertz and rev. Lawo, pp. 502–3, he adopted various errors and omissions that are rectified/reconstructed in Hlawitschka, 'Textkritisches'.

preceded the calendar/necrology on fols. 1r–3v), the *Series abbatum* records the names and memorable deeds of Flavigny's abbots from Magoald to Elmuin (*c.*1096), albeit with omissions.[120] The account thus terminates right before Hugh's abbatial appointment in the winter of 1096, leading Hlawitschka to suspect that it might have been Hugh himself who composed the *Series abbatum*.[121] Recent doubts and objections notwithstanding,[122] the solid evidence produced by Hlawitschka in support of Hugh's probable authorship remains compelling on balance. The *Chronicon*'s insertions and marginalia are more elaborate and offer a greater level of detail than the *Series abbatum*, whose 'raw data' (names, dates, etc.) is shared, moreover, with the aforementioned calendar/necrology that it preceded in the original manuscript, and which can be identified securely as Hugh's own work.[123] Indeed, it has been suggested plausibly, and on multiple occasions, that this calendar/necrology was most likely made not for communal purposes, but specifically for Hugh's personal use.[124] Having adopted the calendar/necrology's basic structure from a mid-eleventh-century model made at Saint-Pierre de Bèze near Dijon (Dijon, Bibliothèque municipale, MS 448, fols. 88r–92v), Hugh added several new layers of information—or data—that showcase both his re-focused interests as a historian and Flavigny's abbatial tradition following Hugh's appointment.[125] The first of these layers comprises more than a hundred obits for individuals that range widely from Hugh's personal acquaintances and members of his family to powerful secular and ecclesiastical rulers, many of whom figure prominently in the *Chronicon*'s narrative.[126] At the same time, Hugh inserted the names of saints and martyrs venerated in the localities that constitute the *Chronicon*'s evolving geographical and political foci, specifically the two dioceses of Verdun and Autun. The second layer of data that Abbot Hugh added to his monastery's calendar/necrology—the one that is of primary

---

[120] See below (Appendix). [121] Hlawitschka, 'Textkritisches', pp. 259–61 and 264–5.

[122] Lawo, *Studien*, pp. 152–4 argues that the text might have been commissioned by Bishop Hagano of Autun early in 1096, thus prior to Hugh's abbacy, and that a copy might have been presented to Hugh upon his appointment. This must remain conjecture.

[123] The most detailed study of this calendar/necrology, which establishes Hugh's authorship beyond reasonable doubt, remains Ulrich Winzer, 'Studien zum Kalender Hugos von Flavigny' (unpublished PhD dissertation, University of Münster, 1979). I am thankful to Ulrich Winzer for kindly providing me with a copy of his dissertation. See further Eckhard Freise, 'Kalendarische und annalistische Grundformen der Memoria', in *'Memoria': Der geschichtliche Zeugniswert des liturgischen Gedenkens im Mittelalter*, ed. by Karl Schmid and Joachim Wollasch (Munich: Fink, 1984), pp. 441–577.

[124] See Freise, 'Grundformen', p. 557, referring to it as Hugh's 'privater Merkkalender'; Borst, *Reichskalender*, I, 281 calls it a 'persönliches Merkbuch eines Historikers'; and Borgolte, 'Gräber', p. 230 describes it as 'für Hugos persönlichen Gebrauch bestimmt'.

[125] Arno Borst, *Der karolingische Reichskalender und seine Überlieferung bis ins 12. Jahrhundert*, 3 vols. (Hanover: Hahn, 2001), I, 276–8. Like Saint-Bénigne de Dijon, and based partially on its archives, the monks of Saint-Pierre de Bèze produced an elaborate cartulary during the first quarter of the twelfth century; *The Cartulary-Chronicle of St-Pierre of Bèze*, ed. by Constance B. Bouchard (Toronto: University of Toronto Press, 2019).

[126] A full catalogue of these individuals is provided by Winzer, 'Studien', pp. 57–131. On the different stages of redaction ('Redaktionsstufen'), see Freise, 'Grundformen', pp. 554–6.

interest here—is even more specific than the first and deals almost exclusively with Flavigny's abbots and their rivals, the bishops of Autun.[127] Completed in the winter months of 1099/1100, this second layer reveals close textual links with the information found in both the *Series abbatum* and the *Chronicon*'s notes concerning the lives and deeds of Hugh's abbatial predecessors, and a systematic comparison of the three texts (see Appendix) reveals that their sequence of composition almost certainly began with the 'raw data' contained in the expanded calendar/necrology before giving rise, successively, to the *Series abbatum* and the second re-imagination of the *Chronicon*.[128]

This also explains why from the point of Hugh's abbatial appointment, the main text of the *Chronicon* extant in his autograph is concerned primarily with the events of his own tenure, specifically his escalating conflict with Norgaud as summarized above.[129] Hugh's appointment thanks to the intervention of Abbot Jarento and Bishop Hagano is in fact the manuscript's first (and only) concrete reference (fol. 137r) to Flavigny and its history prior to the insertion of the marginalia, with no more than casual mention of the seven-year vacancy after Abbot Rainald's death in 1090.[130] Everything pertaining to the period prior to November 1096, by contrast, takes the shape of marginalia or subsequently inserted pages. This major chronological-codicological *caesura* serves to confirm that an account of Flavigny's institutional history told through the sequential achievements of its abbots had not been part of the *Chronicon*'s original outlook as commissioned by Rodulf of Saint-Vanne, nor of its first re-imagination under Jarento of Saint-Bénigne post-1092. The insertion of the material lifted from the calendar/necrology and *Series abbatum*—and, if Hugh was indeed the author, the fact of the latter's very composition—casts Hugh's personal enmity with Norgaud as part of a long-standing tradition of hostilities between Flavigny's abbots and the bishops of Autun. Systematically and fundamentally re-working the *Chronicon* during the period of his abbatial tenure and exile, Hugh (re-)constructed a narrative according to which Autun's bishops had for centuries been enemies of the monastic church of Flavigny and the papacy.[131] In the *Chronicon*'s first re-imagination of 1092–6, the position of 'arch-simonist' had been reserved for Pope Gregory VII's declared opponent, Emperor Henry IV,[132] though Hugh in 1099/1100 re-assigned this role to his own personal nemesis, Bishop Norgaud. In the many years of crisis that followed his appointment as Flavigny's abbot, writing

---

[127] Freise, 'Grundformen', p. 556.
[128] On the calendar/necrology's *terminus post quem*, see Winzer, 'Studien', pp. 55–6.
[129] As noted also by Hlawitschka, 'Textkritisches', p. 258.
[130] Hugh of Flavigny, 'Chronicon', ed. Pertz and rev. Lawo, p. 475; on this episode, see Lawo, *Studien*, p. 152.
[131] For a similar interpretation, see Anatole de Charmasse, 'Flavigny et les évêques d'Autun', *Mémoires de la Société Eduenne* 46 (1929/31), 159–71, 269–91, and 342–53 (pp. 166–70).
[132] Cf. Healy, *Chronicle*, p. 9.

history for Hugh became at once an effective medium of abbatial self-fashioning and a powerful 'weapon' aimed at his most formidable enemy.

Nowhere do we see clearer evidence of this 'weaponization' than in a short poem that Hugh inserted *manu propria* into what is now the opening quire of the *Chronicon*'s autograph and authorial working copy (fol. 7r; Fig. 1.5). Consisting of four elegiac couplets, this poem—evidently Hugh's own composition—was inserted into a space which, as Mathias Lawo argues convincingly, had been left blank deliberately for a dedicatory epistle or similar to be included upon the *Chronicon*'s completion and publication.[133] A far cry from a flattering panegyric composed in praise of his erstwhile abbatial patron(s), the poem that Hugh, disillusioned by the turn of events he reports at great length in the narrative, ended up inserting in this space forms virtually the perfect antithesis to a dedicatory letter: it is a vitriolic and deeply personal attack channelling years of built-up frustration by an abbot and historiographer who after many uphill battles, and despite some minor and short-lived victories, was stripped of his office, humbled, humiliated, and forced to concede defeat. Assuming the identity of the book held in the reader's hands ('qui manibus teneor'), Hugh makes it his—that is, the *Chronicon*'s—avowed case ('hec causa') to caution against the evil deeds ('res mala

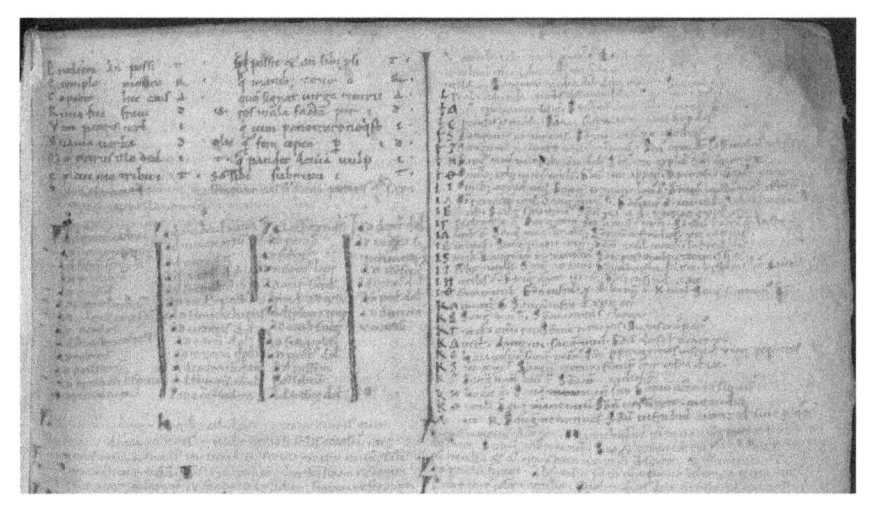

Fig. 1.5 Hugh of Flavigny's 'anti-dedicatory' poem. Berlin, Staatsbibliothek zu Berlin– Preußischer Kulturbesitz, MS Phill. 1870, fol. 7r.

---

[133] See Lawo, *Studien*, pp. 44–5 and 47–8: 'Das kann eigentlich nur bedeuten, dass der Lagenanfang absichtsvoll leergelassen wurde, und zwar für einen Widmungsbrief, den Hugo erwartungsgemäß erst nach Vollendung des Werkes schreiben wollte'; extended discussion in Mathias Lawo, 'Hugo von Flavigny und die lateinische Dichtkunst', in *Latin Culture in the Eleventh Century*, ed. by Michael W. Herren et al., 2 vols. (Turnhout: Brepols, 2002) II, 34–50 (pp. 47–50), who also provides a transcription and translation of the poem (ibid., pp. 48 and 50), though the latter differs somewhat from the interpretation presented here.

facta') and deceit ('fraus') of an unnamed enemy designated by a curved staff ('quem signat virga recurva'), a Peter ('Petrus ille') whose violence consisted not of physical attacks, but of words ('verba') that were sometimes sweet ('svavia'), sometimes savage ('fera'), but always words of treachery ('verba doli'). As noted by Lawo, the poem's addressee is undoubtedly a prelate (abbot or bishop) whose official insignia included a pastoral staff ('virga recurva'),[134] but rather than embracing his identification of this enigmatic prelate with Abbot Jarento of Saint-Bénigne, who, as we will recall, had been Hugh's supporter for most of his career and only turned against him at the very end, a more plausible suggestion must be the man who had machinated relentlessly against Hugh from the beginning, and whose appointment of the defiant Prior Gervase as Flavigny's new abbot in the end forced Hugh to surrender his monastery for good: Bishop Norgaud of Autun. In fact, the thinly veiled allusion to Hugh's malefactor as 'that Peter' ('Petrus ille') makes precious little sense when applied to an abbot, but perfect sense when referring to a bishop and successor of St Peter—an allusion that surely would have been easily recognizable to Hugh's medieval readership. Set originally within the chronographical framework of a 'world chronicle', Hugh of Flavigny's *Chronicon* in effect remained a work of local (or at best regional) historiography, even if the specific localities that provided its primary points of reference shifted and changed as a consequence of its repeated re-imagination over the course of the author's monastic life and career.[135] For central parts of the narrative, this focus then narrows down further to what is in essence, and unapologetically, a history of the author's own tribulations projected onto the historical tradition of Flavigny's abbatial succession, and a key source of both individual and collective abbatial self-fashioning.

Another well-known case of autobiographical history written by an abbot that, as shall be seen, can usefully be set in relation to Hugh of Flavigny's *Chronicon* is provided by the *Monodiae* written by Guibert of Nogent. As with Hugh, it is precisely because Guibert and his work have received so much attention in scholarship that revisiting them in the rarely explored context of abbatial self-fashioning holds promise. As noted before, Guibert's appointment as abbot of Nogent-sous-Coucy (1104–25) marked an important milestone in both his career and historical vision, with Jay Rubenstein concluding that Guibert's 'evolving, increasingly ironic sense of life begins with his election as abbot'.[136] In a modification of Rubenstein's oft-quoted assessment, I am suggesting here an alternative

---

[134] Lawo, 'Hugo', p. 48.

[135] Elisabeth M. C. van Houts, *Local and Regional Chronicles* (Turnhout: Brepols, 1995). As observed by Borgolte, 'Gräber', p. 216, '[o]bwohl seine [Hughs] Chronik als Weltgeschichte angelegt war, stellt sie weitgehend die Geschichte der Bischofe von Verdun und des Klosters S. Vanne dar'; Healy, *Chronicle*, p. 2 likewise refers to the *Chronicon* as 'a local history of reform and its consequences in Lotharingia and Burgundy'.

[136] Jay Rubenstein, *Guibert of Nogent: Portrait of a Medieval Mind* (New York, NY: Routledge, 2002), p. 87.

model of interpretation in which this change of outlook brought about by Guibert's abbacy manifested itself less in an autocentric or autotelic approach to histor(iograph)y, and more in the *Monodiae*'s re-orientation towards a communal and institutional sense of the past. Often referred to in scholarship as Guibert's 'memoirs',[137] the *Monodiae* in actual fact do not fit neatly into any one category of literary and historiographical production. Rather than pigeonholing it unduly, we would do better to recognize it as a text that transgresses and defies, quite possibly deliberately, our notions of genre. The work's title itself might well have been inspired by Guibert's reading of Isidore of Seville's *Etymologiae*, which explains that 'when one person sings ('canere'), it is called a *monodia* in Greek, a *sicinium* in Latin; when two sing, it is called *bicinium*; when many [sing], [it is called] a choir ('chorus')'.[138] This was not the only occasion upon which Guibert borrowed from Isidore in the context of his historiographical activity as abbot. In fact, arguably the most striking and instructive expression of this Isidorean debt, the significance of which has often been passed over in scholarship,[139] manifests itself in Guibert's historical consciousness, more specifically in his performative self-fashioning as a historian in the preface of the crusading narrative known as the *Gesta Dei per Francos*. Anticipating scepticism on the part of the *Gesta*'s readership, Guibert admits that he, unlike some other crusade chroniclers, was no eyewitness to the events he reports. Rather than denying or concealing the second-hand nature of his testimony, Guibert declares to have heard about these events from trustworthy witnesses, which, as he assures his readers, is almost as reliable as seeing them oneself. This statement probably forms a defensive response to the *Etymologies*'s famous definition of history ('De historia') with its categorical demotion of secondary witnesses ('Melius enim oculis quae fiunt deprehendimus, quam quae auditione colligimus. Quae enim videntur, sine mendacio proferuntur'), which remained a familiar staple with historiographers and their audiences throughout the Middle Ages.[140]

---

[137] Most notably perhaps in the titles of modern translations such as *A Monk's Confession: The Memoirs of Guibert of Nogent*, tr. by Paul J. Archambault (University Park, PA: Pennsylvania State University Press, 1996); *Guibert of Nogent: Monodiae–'Einzelgesänge': Bekenntnisse und Memoiren eines Abtes aus Nordfrankreich*, ed./tr. by Reinhold Kaiser and Anne Liebe, 2 vols. (Freiburg i. B.: Herder, 2019).
[138] Cited from *The Etymologies of Isidore of Seville*, tr. by Stephen A. Barney et al. (Cambridge: Cambridge University Press, 2006), p. 147.
[139] Notable exceptions are *The Deeds of God through the Franks: A Translation of Guibert de Nogent's 'Gesta Dei per Francos'*, tr. by Robert Levine (Woodbridge: Boydell, 1997), pp. 6–8; Elizabeth Lapina, '"Nec signis nec testibus creditur…": The Problem of Eyewitnesses in the Chronicles of the First Crusade', *Viator* 38 (2007), 117–39 (p. 134); Bernard Guenée, *Histoire et culture historique dans l'Occident medieval* (Paris: Aubier-Montaigne, 1980), p. 78.
[140] *Guibert de Nogent: Dei gesta per Francos et cinq autres textes*, ed. by Robert B. C. Huygens (Turnhout: Brepols, 1996), pp. 81–2; *Etymologies*, tr. Barney et al., p. 67: 'Indeed, among the ancients no one would write a history unless he had been present and had seen what was to be written down, for we grasp with our eyes things that occur better than what we gather with our hearing'; for discussion, see Ganz, 'Historia', pp. 14–15.

If Guibert could not claim to be an eyewitness to the First Crusade and the events related in his *Gesta*, he certainly had, by contrast, first-hand knowledge and experience of the history which forms the subject of his *Monodiae*, including those sections of the narrative that pertain to the institutional history of Nogent's monastic community and Guibert's accomplishments as abbot, which are of primary interest here. Elected in 1104, Guibert was only the third abbot of Nogent, and at that point the community had not yet cultivated a historiographical tradition or a written account of its collective memory.[141] This means that for the period between the monastery's foundation in *c.*1059 and the commencement of Guibert's abbatial tenure, these communal memories had been circulating primarily within a 'synchronic space of memory' whose horizon was determined (and limited) by the shared experiences of individuals belonging to the same or adjacent generational cohorts.[142] After three generations—an important and widely recognized threshold for the codification of memory through acts of 'cultural formation'[143]—Guibert first furnished these memories with a 'diachronic axis' that offered sustainability and, thanks to his abbatial authorship, *authority*. The result was what Aleida Assmann calls 'tradition'.[144] At the centre of this tradition, and acting as its foundational artefact, was the written history of Nogent and its abbots—the first of its kind—in Guibert's *Monodiae*. When approached from this perspective, the *Monodiae*'s second book—or rather what little survives of it today—can be revealed as potentially much more significant for the work's overall conceptual outlook than allowed for in scholarship to date, which typically has paid comparatively little attention to this 'shortest, least coherent, and for most the least satisfying of the [*Monodiae*'s] three books'.[145]

---

[141] On the medieval abbots of Nogent, see still *Gallia Christiana in provincias ecclesiasticas distributa*, ed. by Denys de Sainte-Marthe et al., 13 vols. (Paris: Ex Typographia regia, 1715–1877), IX, 604–10.

[142] On this phenomenon on 'generational location' (*Generationslagerung*), see Karl Mannheim, 'The Problem of Generations', in *Essays on the Sociology of Knowledge*, ed. by Karl Mannheim and Paul Kecskemeti (London: Routledge, 1952, repr. 1972), pp. 276–322 (pp. 288–90). The translation of Mannheim's terminology into English continues to prove difficult, which is why recourse to the original German essay is strongly recommended; Karl Mannheim, 'Das Problem der Generationen', in *Wissenssoziologie: Auswahl aus dem Werk*, ed. by Karl Mannheim and Kurt H. Wolff (Berlin: Luchterhand, 1964), pp. 509–65 (pp. 524–7).

[143] See Jan Assmann, 'Communicative and Cultural Memory', in *Cultural Memory Studies: An International and Interdisciplinary Handbook*, ed. by Astrid Erll et al. (Berlin: De Gruyter, 2008), pp. 109–18 (p. 111). For further examples of 'cultural formation(s)', see below (2.6).

[144] See Aleida Assmann, *Zeit und Tradition: Kulturelle Strategien der Dauer* (Cologne: Böhlau, 1999), p. 64; partly translated into English in Jan Assmann: 'Introduction: What Is Cultural Memory?', in *Religion and Cultural Memory: Ten Studies*, ed./tr. by Jan Assmann and Rodney Livingstone (Stanford, CA: Stanford University Press, 2006), pp. 1–30 (p. 8): 'Tradition [according to Aleida Assmann] can be understood as a special case of communication in which information is not exchanged reciprocally and horizontally, but is transmitted vertically through the generations'. Jan Assmann adds that '[i]f we think of the typical three-generation cycle of communicative memory as a synchronic memory space, then cultural memory, with its traditions reaching far back into the past, forms the diachronic axis' (ibid., p. 8).

[145] Rubenstein, *Guibert*, p. 61.

Most published research on Guibert and his *Monodiae* prioritizes either the autobiographical account of Guibert's early life (Book I) or, especially those with an interest in his conceptual relationship with the writing of history (or so-called 'pseudo-history'), Guibert's report on the ecclesio-political conflicts within the diocese and commune of Laon (Book III).[146] Book II, by contrast, so far has not been understood fully as a conceptual unit in its own right. This may be due, to some extent, to the work's manuscript tradition. Today, the *Monodiae* (or parts thereof) survive in various copies, redactions, and fragments, with the most complete text preserved in a seventeenth-century copy (Paris, Bibliothèque nationale de France, MS Baluze 42, fols. 30r–107v).[147] As demonstrated by Rubenstein and others, the version that has come down to us is incomplete and originally would have contained a narrative account (now lost) of Guibert's abbatial *gesta*, be that in the shape of a separate book or—and I, like Rubenstein, consider this more plausible—as an integral part of Book II.[148] This erstwhile presence and subsequent loss/removal of a report of Guibert's abbatial deeds and achievements on behalf of Nogent's monastic community not only explains the notable imbalance in length between Book II in its current form and the two longer books either side of it, but it also makes perfect sense from a conceptual point of view. Combined with Guibert's accounts of the monastery's distant origins and the deeds of its previous abbots—that is, his two predecessors—the events pertaining to Guibert's own abbatial election and tenure would have constituted the basic framework of a monastic foundation history (*historia fundationis*) and *gesta abbatum* written at the decisive moment (c.1115) when, as we saw above, the community's memory tradition had reached a watershed at which it was either codified in writing or surrendered to oblivion.[149]

---

[146] Book III forms a subject of investigation in, for example, Bernard Monod, 'De la méthode historique chez Guibert de Nogent', *Revue Historique* 84 (1904), 51–70; Jacques Chaurand, 'La conception de l'histoire de Guibert de Nogent (1053–1124)', *Cahiers de civilisation médiévale* 31/2 (1965), 381–95; Jonathan Kantor, 'A Pseudo-Historical Source: The Memoirs of Abbot Guibert of Nogent', *Journal of Medieval History* 2 (1976), 281–304; more recently Heather F. Blurton, 'Guibert of Nogent and the Subject of History', *Exemplaria* 15 (2003), 111–31. These studies dedicated to Guibert's historical consciousness do not take into account the role of his primary communal environment at the time of writing, the monastic community of Nogent.

[147] The most recent and comprehensive discussion of the manuscripts is that in *Monodiae*, ed./tr. Reinhold and Liebe, pp. 98–101. Previously Bourgin, *Guibert*, pp. xxxviii–xlv; François Dolbeau, 'Deux nouveaux manuscrits des "Mémoires" de Guibert de Nogent', *Sacris Erudiri* 26 (1983), 155–76. On MS Baluze 42, see *Monodiae*, ed./tr. Labande, pp. xxiii–xxv.

[148] Rubenstein, *Guibert*, p. 61. Whether these sections of Book II were lost accidentally or purposefully removed by Guibert himself or someone with access to his lost autograph is impossible to know. On the possible existence of a fourth book, as suggested by the thirteenth-century necrology of Laon Cathedral, see *Monodiae*, ed./tr. Reinhold and Liebe, pp. 47–9. Reinhold and Liebe's speculative reconstruction of a four-book structure corresponding to its author's four life stages (*infantia/pueritia–adolescentia–iuventus–senectus*) is intriguing but ultimately fails to convince (ibid., p. 49).

[149] On the date of composition, see *Monodiae*, ed./tr. Reinhold and Liebe, pp. 26–8, where the possible influence of the monastic *historiae fundationum* tradition on Guibert's *Monodiae* is acknowledged in passing (ibid., p. 40).

If this was indeed the work's original outlook, and knowing what we know (due, not least, to Guibert's own account in Book III) about the historically difficult relationship between the monks/abbots of Nogent and their diocesan bishops of Laon, then this would enable the further possibility that the *Monodiae*, and particularly Book II, were intended not merely as a domestic *gesta abbatum*, but also—in a way not dissimilar from Hugh of Flavigny's *Chronicon*—as an 'anti-gesta episcoporum' in support of Nogent's monastic exemption and emancipation from Laon's episcopate.[150] In the surviving narrative, Guibert thus takes aim not just at the bishops of Laon and their attempts to restrict the monastery's liberties, but also, and importantly, at his abbatial predecessors, especially his direct precursor, Abbot Godfrey (c.1085–1104), who subsequently became bishop of Amiens.[151] Guibert is at pains to stress that he, unlike Godfrey, became abbot by free election independent of the bishop's *potestas*.[152] Indeed, the *Monodiae* contain several episodes that provide commentary, implicitly and explicitly, on the history of Nogent's monastic emancipation. For example, Guibert's narration of the deeds and misdeeds (with an emphasis on the latter) of Laon's eleventh- and early twelfth-century prelates as the opening of Book III jumps from Adalbero (977–1030) straight to Elinand (1052–98), thereby omitting—deliberately—over two decades' worth of events and two bishops who governed the diocese in the interim, Gébuin (1030–49) and Liétry (1049–52).[153] The parallels with Hugh of Flavigny's selective treatment of the past are striking and can be explained through similar authorial strategies. As with Hugh's *Chronicon*, the absence of these bishops from Guibert's *Monodiae* creates a *caesura* that serves to underscore the presence of their direct successor, Elinand, who is presented by Guibert as a key agent in the abbey's foundation and exemption. After all, it was Elinand who in 1059 had issued the monastic community with its first foundation/exemption charter and secured the subsequent confirmation of its privileges *regiae auctoritatis sigillo* at the request ('ad praeces') of Alberic of Coucy.[154]

---

[150] Indeed, in MS Baluze 42 the work is titled 'Libri tres de vita sua, et de episcoporum Laudunensium gestis' (fol. 28r).

[151] John S. Ott, 'Writing Godfrey of Amiens: Guibert of Nogent and Nicholas of Saint-Crépin between Sanctity, Ideology, and Society', *Mediaeval Studies* 67 (2005), 317–65, noting that Guibert and Godfrey 'were close contemporaries whose lives and careers, up to a point, followed a similar trajectory' (ibid., p. 321).

[152] As also noted by Rubenstein, *Guibert*, pp. 87–95.

[153] The deeds of both bishops are attested in multiple charters *Actes des évêques de Laon: Des origines à 1151*, ed. by Annie Dufour-Malbezin (Paris: Éditions du CNRS, 2001), pp. 91–7 (= nos. 17–23).

[154] The original charter dated 3 December 1059 is lost, as is its thirteenth-century copy in the medieval cartulary of Nogent; however, the text has been preserved in later copies, which include Paris, Bibliothèque nationale de France, MS Lat. 12681, fols. 83r–84r and 95v–97r (= cartae XXXIII and XXXIII[a]); Paris, Bibliothèque nationale de France, Coll. Picardie 233, fol. 186r-v; Paris, Bibliothèque nationale de France, Coll. Picardie 268, fol. 1r; Laon, Archives départementales de l'Aisne, H 325, fols. 220r–222v; cf. *Catalogue des actes d'Henri Ier, roi de France, 1031–1060*, ed. by Frédéric Soehnée (Paris: Champion, 1907), p. 122; Anne Prache and Dominique Barthélémy, 'Notre-Dame de Nogent-sous-Coucy, une abbaye bénédictine disparue', *Bulletin Monumental* 140 (1982), 7–14 (p. 13 n. 2).

Beginning with Elinand and through to the end of the *series episcoporum* covered by the *Monodiae*, each of Laon's subsequent bishops played a part in the development of Nogent's monastic fortunes and misfortunes, which seems to have secured each of them a space, if not necessarily a positive portrayal, in Guibert's work. Elinand's immediate successor, Enguerrand (1098/9–1104), was included mainly because of his political involvement with his namesake, Enguerrand I of Boves, lord of Coucy, whose son and successor, Thomas Marle, provided the monks of Nogent with his own exemption charter under Guibert's abbacy (1117 × 30).[155] Though Guibert began writing the *Monodiae* at least two years before Thomas's confirmation charter was issued, it is not implausible that this charter contributed but one piece to a larger mosaic, thereby forming the final episode—and, from the monks' perspective, the triumphant conclusion— within a long chain of historical events re-imagined in Guibert's teleological narrative. It is surely significant, in this context, that when King Philip I of France issued his confirmation charter to the monastery in 1095, he did so on the insistence ('ad instantiam') of Thomas's father, Enguerrand.[156] Issued at Coucy, the royal charter validated the monastery's exemption from episcopal and secular influence, and its witnesses included both Bishop Enguerrand and Guibert's abbatial predecessor, Godfrey (c.1085–1104) ('S[ignum] Godefridi abbatis eiusdem loci'), alongside a long list of secular and ecclesiastical magnates. As with Elinand, Guibert could therefore easily, and convincingly, present Enguerrand as a key agent in the recent history not just of Laon, but also, and crucially, of Nogent and its monastery. Enguerrand's successor, Bishop Gaudry (1106–12), Lord Chancellor of England who was appointed after a two-year interregnum, probably owes his prominence in the *Monodiae* to Guibert's personal involvement in his nomination, whereas his successor, Hugh, whose tenure lasted only months, is hardly mentioned at all.[157] Bartholomew (1113–51), by contrast, the last bishop of Laon to figure in the *Monodiae*, can again be related

---

[155] Though regularly referred to as lost even in some of the most recent scholarship, the original privilege issued by Thomas of Marles to the monks of Nogent in fact survives in a dossier of eleventh- to eighteenth-century charters (dated c.1086–1786) from Nogent, Saint-Nicolas-au-Bois, and Montreuil (Paris, Bibliothèque nationale de France, Coll. Picardie 291, no 6); Dominique Barthélemy, *Les deux ages de la seigneurie banale: Pouvoir et société dans la terre des sires de Coucy (milieu XIe–milieu XIIIe siècle)* (Paris: Publications de la Sorbonne, 1984), pp. 248 n. 50, 364–5, and 498–9. Copies survive in Laon, Archives départementales de l'Aisne, H 325 and Paris, Bibliothèque nationale de France, MS Lat. 17775, pp. 200–2 (= carta VII); Paris, Bibliothèque nationale de France, MS Lat. 12681, fols. 87r-v and 92r-v (= cartae VII and VIIª).

[156] Paris, Bibliothèque nationale de France, MS Lat. 12681, fols. 89r and 93 (= cartae XXXV and XXXVª); also cf. *Recueil des actes de Philippe Ier, roi de France, 1059–1108*, ed. by Maurice Prou (Paris: Imprimerie Nationale, 1908), pp. 340–1 (= no. CXXXIV).

[157] On Gaudry (or Waldric), cf. Henry W. C. Davis, 'Waldric, the Chancellor of Henry I', *English Historical Review* 26 (1911) 84–8; Charles Johnson, 'Waldric, the Chancellor of Henry I', *English Historical Review* 51 (1936), 103. Guibert merely states that Hugh's appointment took place without election ('nulla electione praemissa'); see *Monodiae*, ed./tr. Labande, pp. 394–5; ed./tr. Reinhold and Liebe, pp. 572–3.

closely to Nogent, and indeed to Guibert personally. Not only was he the named dedicatee of one of Guibert's early authorial compositions, the *Moralia Geneseos* discussed below (2.3), but he, too, issued a confirmation charter to Guibert corroborating Thomas of Marle's earlier exemption privileges.

Taken together, the evidence gathered here from the *Monodiae*'s third book and the no-longer-extant sections of its second book strongly suggest that the work, whilst difficult to classify, was intended by its author and abbot-historiographer Guibert to serve as, amongst other purposes, a *gesta abbatum*, *historia fundationis*, and, importantly, *historia libertatis* of Guibert's monastic community of Nogent-sous-Coucy written three generations after its foundation. In doing so, it foregrounds Guibert's own achievements as abbot, especially his involvement in maintaining Nogent's exemption and emancipation from the episcopal authority of Laon. Composed in an autobiographical mode, the *Monodiae* tell the story not only of Guibert's life, but equally, and crucially, of his abbatial *potestas* and *auctoritas*. What is more, Guibert tells this story from a position that is neither autocentric nor autotelic, but, as argued here, shaped by a historical consciousness that is profoundly communal in its orientation.

A rather more subtle but no less effective case of abbatial self-fashioning can be found in a narrative that records the respective achievements and, in at least one instance, shortcomings of the first four abbots of La Trinità della Cava in southern Italy, known amongst scholars as the *Vitae quatuor primorum abbatum Cavensium*.[158] Contrary to the erroneous attribution on the part of their twentieth-century editor, the *Vitae abbatum* were almost certainly authored by a former monk of Cava named Peter, who prior to writing the work had been made abbot (*c.*1141–56) of Venosa.[159] Though the work's preface is addressed to Cava's monks collectively, with Peter recalling that his former brethren had asked him to write about the lives and miracles of their monastery's venerable fathers and other religious brothers ('quam etiam audientium profectibus invitatus, venerabilium patrum Alferii videlicet, Leonis, Petri atque Constabilie abbatum Cavensium, et item quorundam religiosorum fratrum eiusdem monasterii vitae atque miracula scribere proposui'), the more plausible version of events is that Peter had been tasked to do so either by his erstwhile superior and current peer, Abbot Falco (1141–6), or by the latter's successor, Marinus (1146–70).[160] As Graham Loud demonstrates, Abbot Peter (II)'s account of the lives of Falco's

---

[158] *Vitae quatuor primorum abbatum Cavensium Alferii, Leonis, Petri et Constabilis auctore Hugone abbate Venusino*, ed. by Leone M. Cerasoli (Bologna: Zanichelli 1941).

[159] On this identification, see Hubert Houben, 'L'autore delle "Vitae quatuor priorum abbatum Cavensium"', *Studi medievali* 26 (1985), 871–9; now also Graham A. Loud, 'The Posthumous Reputation of Abbot Peter of Cava', in *Medioevo e Mediterraneo: Incontri, scambi e confronti. Studi per Salvatore Fodale*, ed. by Patrizia Sardina et al. (Palermo: Palermo University Press, 2020), pp. 389–403 (p. 393).

[160] Cf. Graham A. Loud, *The Social World of the Abbey of Cava, c.1020–1300* (Woodbridge: Boydell, 2021), pp. 234–5, with a handlist of Cava's abbots in the period *c.*1020–1300 (p. xix).

predecessors—Alferius (c.1020–50), Leo I (1050–79), Peter I (1079–1123), and Constable (1123–4)—was considered, and likely intended as, the 'official' narrative of Cava's early abbatial succession, making it all the more probable that the *Vitae abbatum* were a product of abbatial authorship as well as abbatial patronage.[161] As observed by Loud, the author had known and remembered two of his subjects personally, namely Constable and his namesake Peter, and it is the latter's deeds—or rather his misdeeds—that receive particularly extensive treatment in the text and take up nearly as much space as the other three *vitae* combined.[162] What makes Abbot Peter of Venosa's writing on Abbot Peter I of Cava especially significant to the present discussion of abbatial self-fashioning is that it is ripe with implicit and, on occasion, explicit criticism of the latter's leadership, criticism that offers a cautionary tale for future generations of abbots at Cava and Venosa, and which, by way of implied contrast, serves to cast the respective abbacies of the author and his patron in a positive light.

The main subject of Peter II's criticism in Cava's *Vitae abbatum* is his namesake's reported propensity for violence in ways that by far exceeded the *Rule of St Benedict*'s recommendation that the abbot's conduct towards his monks should combine fatherly kindness with strictness,[163] and which, we are told, even extended beyond the grave. In life, he showed himself unforgiving towards those who confessed their sins to him, subjecting them to merciless punishment and ferocious flogging even when they were already at death's door.[164] In death, he then returned to haunt those who spoke ill of him, persecuting them in their dreams and leaving their bodies with signs of torture on awakening. Thus when Sergius, the monastery's librarian ('monachus et monasterii armarius'), spat on the dead abbot's tomb to spite him ('contra viri Dei sepulchrum expuit'), Peter exacted his vengeance from beyond the grave by disfiguring the monk's face, breaking his bones, and turning him into an invalid.[165] So bad was the abbot's reputation for violence that it soon spread to communities outside Cava, and when he died in 1123, certain members of Cava's dependent priories apparently refused categorically to celebrate his memory ('laudatoribus patris [...] resistere vehementer cepit'), insisting that his love for punishment be remembered instead ('non sua merita, sed correctionis sue amaritudinem memoraret'). Again, though, Peter would not let such criticism go unpunished, so he appeared to Ursinus, the monk who had opposed his memory most vehemently, in a dream and flogged him until he woke up crying in anguish with bruises across his upper body.[166] Peter I of Cava was, to borrow Loud's words, 'a very

---

[161] Loud, 'Reputation', pp. 393–4; also cf. the discussion by Jean-Marie Sansterre, 'Figures abbatiales et distribution des rôles dans les *Vitae Quatuor Priorum Abbatum Cavensium* (milieu du XIIe siècle)', *Mélanges de l'école française de Rome, Moyen Âge* 111 (1999), 61–104.
[162] Loud, 'Reputation', p. 395.   [163] *RB*, ed./tr. Venarde, pp. 20–7.
[164] *Vitae*, ed. Cerasoli, pp. 21–4, with discussion in Loud, 'Reputation', p. 400.
[165] *Vitae*, ed. Cerasoli, pp. 26–8.   [166] *Vitae*, ed. Cerasoli, pp. 26–7.

unpopular abbot',[167] and one who understood how to silence his critics. If we ask why Peter II of Venosa chose to disregard the proverbial dictum not to speak ill of the dead by reporting Peter I's repeated acts of violence in the pages of his *Vitae abbatum*—even putting himself in harm's way by incurring the latter's posthumous wrath and risking punishment like Sergius and Ursinus—the answer must be because this was not how he and his patron(s) wished to be remembered by posterity. Peter I was, in a sense, the perfect antithesis of the kind of abbot that Peter II had found in his superiors whilst still a monk at Cava, and on whose positive role model he, having advanced to abbatial rank himself by the time of writing, fashioned his own identity and memory.

Whilst not all abbatial historiographers were quite as vocal about their internal and external opponents as Guibert of Nogent and Hugh of Flavigny, with some, such as Peter II of Venosa, opting for more subtle and implicit ways of criticizing those who stood against them and their communities, others, by contrast, went one step further by making these conflicts an integral element in their histories' conceptual outlook. One particularly instructive example of this that, until recently, has lacked a critical edition and systematic study, and which therefore has often eluded scholars' attention (including Kersken), is the short but detailed monastic foundation narrative by Stephen of Whitby, first abbot (after 1078–1112) and self-proclaimed 'founding father' of St Mary's Abbey, York.[168] Transmitted without a title in the two earliest manuscripts from the second half of the twelfth century (London, British Library, MS Additional 38816, fols. 29v–34v; Cambridge, Corpus Christi College, MS 139, fols. 152r–154r) but commonly referred to as the *Historia fundationis abbatiae sanctae Mariae Eboracensis*,[169] the text's preface leaves little doubt as to Stephen's authorial intentions. Addressing the community's present and future members, he promises not only an account of the monastery's foundation ('qualiter ecclesia sancte Marie Eboracensis [...] fundata sit') and the key persons involved in it ('qui vel quales huius nostre ecclesie fuerint fundatores'), but also a record of how he came to hold the office of abbot by unanimous consent between God and his monks ('Dei gratia fratrumque meorum unanimi mihi faciendum electione abbas constitutus, qualiter ad hunc gradum pervenerim') and, more specifically, a memento of the many troubles that he and the monastery thus placed under his governance had to endure at the hands of the malevolent ('quantas invidorum turbinibus impulsa sustinuerit pertubationes'), and which in the end were overcome thanks to his stewardship.[170] Framing a monastic history explicitly in terms of endured and

---

[167] Loud, 'Reputation', p. 398.
[168] Now expertly edited and translated by Nicholas Karn, 'The Foundation Narrative', in *Foundation Documents from St Mary's Abbey, York 1085–1137*, ed. by Richard Sharpe et al. (Woodbridge: Boydell, 2022), pp. 379–407.
[169] On the *Historia*'s manuscript tradition, see Karn, 'Introduction', pp. 370–6.
[170] *Historia*, ed./tr. Karn, 'Foundation Narrative', pp. 380–1.

overcome hardship was not Stephen's invention, of course. But unlike histories that were written at the commission or authorization of a superior—say, the famous *Casus sancti Galli* begun by Ratpert in the ninth century and continued by Ekkehard and an anonymous monk in the eleventh and thirteenth centuries, respectively, which in their most recent translation have been dubbed *Fortune and Misfortune at Saint Gall*[171]—the *Historia* from St Mary's, York sets itself apart through an autobiographical focus that is owed to, and made possible by, a single distinguishing factor: its author was himself an abbot writing from an official position of authority.

As the *Historia*'s recent editor has observed, the text is, in essence, a narrative of continuous personal and collective hardship, in which Stephen describes 'a mass of disputes with different persons, some long-running and with different stages to them, which are often reported incompletely', at the same time as maintaining '[a] tendency to place himself at the centre of events, so that other contributions are passed by'.[172] Throughout this selective account, Stephen emerges as the 'prime mover' of the events surrounding the foundation and early history of his embryonic community, a history that may well have been more complicated than that of many monasteries established at that time,[173] but which, as forensic documentary research by the late Richard Sharpe (published posthumously) has shown, in reality was very much a collective achievement that involved, and indeed necessitated, the support of various ecclesiastical and secular magnates.[174] Besides Stephen, these *dramatis personae* were, first and foremost, Count Alan ('Rufus') of Brittany, King William I ('the Conqueror'), and the latter's son and successor, King William II ('Rufus'), each of whom granted a separate dwelling place to Stephen and his monks, but also families from the ranks of the local aristocracy, as well as, in an adversarial position, York's successive archbishops and, playing the role of arch-villain, Baron William de Percy.[175] The basic timeline of events reconstructed from Stephen's narrative and other sources now conveniently gathered and edited alongside it in a volume published by the Surtees Society can be summarized as follows:[176] originally established at Whitby on a piece of land granted by William de Percy and led by one Renfrid (under whom Stephen entered the monastic life), the community subsequently (following Stephen's

---

[171] *Ratpert: St Galler Klostergeschichten* (Casus sancti Galli), ed./tr. by Hannes Steiner [= MGH SS rer. Germ. LXXV] (Hanover: Hahn, 2002); *Ekkehart IV.: St Galler Klostergeschichten* (Casus sancti Galli), ed./tr. by Hans F. Haefele and Ernst Tremp [= MGH SS rer. Germ. LXXXII] (Hanover: Hahn, 2020); *Ekkehard IV: Fortune and Misfortune at Saint Gall*, tr. by Emily Albu and Natalia Lozovsky (Cambridge, MA: Harvard University Press, 2021).

[172] Karn, 'Introduction', p. 340.   [173] Karn, 'Introduction', p. 339.

[174] Richard Sharpe, 'The Foundation of the Abbey: A Material Perspective', in *Foundation Documents from St Mary's Abbey, York 1085–1137*, ed. by Richard Sharpe et al. (Woodbridge: Boydell, 2022), pp. 11–119, quote on p. 12. As Sharpe points out, 'the would-be abbot of York formed a series of alliances through which he achieved his aspiration' (ibid., p. 14).

[175] Cf. Sharpe, 'Foundation', pp. 17–21; Karn, 'Introduction', pp. 341–57.

[176] *Foundation Documents*, ed. Sharpe et al., *passim*.

election as its abbot and Renfrid's departure) relocated to the site of a former yet abandoned monastery at Lastingham that was provided by King William I. It then moved location again to St Olaf's Church outside York thanks to an endowment by Count Alan of Brittany that was enabled by William I and confirmed by William II, only to find its next and final home inside the city boundaries to the west of York Minster. Written between 1093 × 1112, possibly as early as 1094,[177] the account in Stephen's *Historia* recounts all but the last of these moves, and from the beginning it is Stephen himself who confidently assumes the role of history's main architect. Consequently, he has little to say on Renfrid's early governance at Whitby or the rivalries that existed between them, rivalries that should continue to characterize the relationship between the community that would eventually settle at York under Stephen's abbatial leadership and that which traced its history to the same origins but would then evolve into St Peter's Abbey, Whitby (via an interlude at Hackness). As pointed out elsewhere, Stephen's silence on these matters was deliberate, and it is mirrored, moreover, in the works of Whitby's domestic historians, who—in a case of 'tit for tat'—do not mention Stephen in relation to their community's early history, but instead focus on their own contestant for the role of founding figure, Renfrid.[178]

As a result of this silence, the haters ('invidi') first referred to in the *Historia*'s preface and then again later in the text are not the enemies Stephen faced within his community, but those who, whilst dwelling outside the monastery's walls, were intrinsically connected with it, first William de Percy and then, during the time spent at Lastingham and St Olaf's Church, the archbishops of York.[179] The details of these confrontations are analysed elsewhere, so suffice to say here that a major bone of contention, and the likely reason for the enduring enmity between Stephen and William de Percy, were the abbot's repeated attempts to style himself and his election—and, by implication, all future abbatial elections amongst his successors—as independent of William and his heirs, instead claiming dependence directly and exclusively from the crown, as well as, in strictly spiritual matters, from York's archiepiscopal see.[180] Even when reporting how William's continuous aggressions following the relocation to Lastingham forced the community's second move to St Olaf's Church, Stephen is at pains to emphasize that the donation providing him and his monks with this new (temporary) home was secured thanks to his long-standing personal friendship with Count Alan that even preceded his conversion to the monastic life ('cum essem in seculo familiariter mihi in amicitiis coniunctus').[181] In reality, though, this grant, just like the

---

[177] This is the date proposed by Karn, 'Introduction', p. 367. Based on the text's limited length, Karn sees 'no need to assume that it would have taken a long time to produce'.
[178] Sharpe, 'Foundation', pp. 18–19; Karn, 'Introduction', p. 345.
[179] For example, *Historia*, ed./tr. Karn, 'Foundation Narrative', pp. 400–1.
[180] *Historia*, ed./tr. Karn, 'Foundation Narrative', pp. 388–91; see also Sharpe, 'Foundation', p. 19.
[181] *Historia*, ed./tr. Karn, 'Foundation Narrative', pp. 394–5.

previous one at Lastingham, was very much subject to King William I's authority and likely motivated by his own political machinations.[182] The events enabling the third and final move from St Olaf's Church to the site of St Mary's are rather convoluted and need not be unravelled here, not least considering that the *Historia* does not disclose them either, but the plausible version of events reconstructed by Nicholas Karn again suggests that Stephen 'was not party to these [...] transactions, but appeared primarily as an object of the king's action rather than as an independent actor',[183] though it seems unlikely that Stephen would have thought of himself, let alone presented himself to his readers, in such an auxiliary capacity. Might this be why he remained largely silent about these particular episodes from the monastery's most recent history despite the fact that he was an eyewitness? We may speculate, but we cannot know for certain.

We also do not know what physical form Stephen's *Historia* took upon its completion around 1094. Did the self-assured abbot-historian commit the relatively short narrative to parchment himself, or did he have it copied out by assistant scribes and *amanuenses* as some of his peers preferred to do? Did it take the shape of an independent, stand-alone book or booklet, or was it part of a textual ensemble gathered between the boards of a single codex? Was it kept in the abbey's library or *armarium*, used for communal reading, or perhaps locked away in the abbot's private quarters so as to facilitate personal study and reference (4.3)? In the absence of an autograph or contemporary working copy, questions like these must remain open. What we do know, though, is that within a hundred or so years of its publication, whichever format this may originally have taken, the *Historia* was copied not only at St Mary's, where it was sandwiched between the *Rule of St Benedict* and various documents (charters, a confraternity list, etc.) in a 'foundation book',[184] but also beyond its place of origin, quite possibly (but not certainly) at Durham, where it became part of a compendium of (extracts of) historical works that include, amongst various others, Regino of Prüm's *Chronicon*, the *Historia Brittonum*, William of Malmesbury's *Gesta regum Anglorum*, Symeon of Durham's *Historia regum*, Richard of Hexham's continuation of Symeon's work and his own *De gestis regis Stephani*, Ælred of Rievaulx's *Relatio de standardo*, and Serlo of Wilton's poem on the same subject.[185] In these twelfth-century manuscripts, Stephen's *Historia* sits comfortably not only

---

[182] See Sharpe, 'Foundation', pp. 21-31.   [183] Karn, 'Introduction', p. 357.

[184] MS BL Add. 38816; on this manuscript, see the detailed discussion by Michael Gullick, 'A Foundation Book? Three Twelfth-Century Booklets', in *Foundation Documents from St Mary's Abbey, York 1085-1137*, ed. by Richard Sharpe et al. (Woodbridge: Boydell, 2022), pp. 1-10, with the section containing Abbot Stephen's *Historia fundationis* (Gullick's 'Part 4') on pp. 5-7. Gullick's codicological analysis reveals that these texts 'were originally sewn into distinct volumes' and 'all five parts [...] have been separated from their original context' (ibid., p. 1); also cf. Karn, 'Introduction', p. 371 (= MS A).

[185] MS CCCC 139; see Karn, 'Introduction', pp. 371-3 (= MS B), with references to previous scholarship dedicated to this manuscript.

amongst the most authoritative sources for the history of his own monastery, but also alongside the single most authoritative text for the communal religious life and some of the most authoritative works of history of the day. For a text that, unlike the major dynastic and universal chronicles which it accompanies, relates the foundation story of a single institution—one that, at the time of composition, and even at the time of copying, was relatively young if extraordinarily well patronized—this is remarkable. The reason why Stephen's work could claim this privileged position is likely to be complex, but it may well have to do with the fact that the author was the abbot—indeed, the self-fashioned founding abbot!—of what should become one of the most important abbeys in England whose superiors held considerable authority until the end of the Middle Ages. One of them is widely held to have provided the source of inspiration for the infamous 'ryche abbot [...] of Seynt Mari Abbey' who, in a role reversal of the relationship between Abbot Stephen and his nemesis William de Percy in the *Historia*, acts as the cloaked hero's arch-rival in the Middle English *Gest of Robyn Hode*.[186]

To conclude this discussion of historiographical authorship as a medium of abbatial self-fashioning, let us consider the intriguing case of an abbot who, unlike the various examples examined so far, did *not* give an account of himself or his achievements in the *gesta abbatum* which he wrote for his community, even though he described the respective lives and deeds of both his predecessor(s) and direct successor. Conceived and presented as a continuation of the work produced by Folcuin in *c.*962, the *Chronicon Sithiense sive gesta abbatum Sithiensium* authored by Abbot Simon of Saint-Bertin (1131–6), also known as 'Simon of Ghent' after his birth- and deathplace, is a text that, after decades of relative indifference, has drawn renewed interest in recent scholarship.[187] Having entered the community of Saint-Bertin as a child and professed himself to Abbot Lambert (1095–1123), Simon was appointed abbot of Auchy-lès-Hesdin (1127–31) before he was placed in charge of his home monastery in 1131 following a reported stint as Lambert's official deputy and '*de facto* abbot' owing to the latter's increasing incapacitation (see below). What renders the *Chronicon* of special interest to us is that Simon began writing it prior to his abbatial appointment(s), likely continued it during his tenure, and returned to it briefly after his abbacy at Saint-Bertin had come to an early end (Simon resigned from

---

[186] Cited after '*A Gest of Robyn Hode*', in *Robin Hood and Other Outlaw Tales*, ed. by Stephen Knight and Thomas Ohlgren, 2nd ed. (Kalamazoo, MI: Medieval Institute Publications, 2000), pp. 80–168 (p. 96, ll. 215–16). John R. Madicott, 'Birth and Setting of the Ballads', *English Historical Review* 93 (1978), 276–99, repr. in *Robin Hood: An Anthology of Scholarship and Criticism*, ed. by Stephen Knight (Woodbridge: Brewer, 1999), pp. 233–55 (pp. 239–41) identifies the probable role model as Abbot Thomas de Multon (1332–59) with his reputation as a money lender.

[187] 'Simonis gesta abbatum sancti Bertini Sithiensium', ed. by Oswald Holder-Egger, in *Supplementa tomorum I-XII, pars I* [= *MGH SS* XIII] (Hanover: Hahn, 1881), pp. 635–63. The most detailed discussion of the text and its context is that by Steven Vanderputten, *Reform as Process*, pp. 14–30; more recently David Defries, *From Sithiu to Saint-Bertin: Hagiographic Exegesis and Collective Memory in the Early Medieval Cults of Omer and Bertin* (Turnhout: Brepols, 2019), pp. 251–7.

office and left the community in 1136, but he did not cease adding to the narrative until c.1145 at the earliest, possibly still writing as late as 1148, the year of his death). He almost certainly had commenced the initial project by 1116, over a decade before his first abbatial appointment at Auchy, at the commission of his then abbot, Lambert. Though technically a continuation of Folcuin's *Gesta abbatum*, Simon's *Chronicon* does not in fact pick up where Folcuin had left off at the end of Adalolf's (961–2) short abbacy, but rather omits six whole decades (962–1021) from the community's history that comprised six (really seven) subsequent abbacies, from Hildebrand (962–4/971) to Hemfrid (1007–21), thus only resuming the chronology with Abbot Roderic's (1021–42) tenure.[188] As the *Chronicon*'s prologue explains, Simon did not ignore these abbots, their deeds, and the events that had marked their respective tenures because there was no information about them, nor because he lacked access to sources from the abbey's library and archives, but rather because the community's collective memories and written records contained, in his opinion, 'nothing memorable' ('nihil memorabile') that would have been worthy of inclusion.[189]

Different explanations have been put forward for this rather remarkable omission. Steven Vanderputten argues that the reason why Simon chose not to make use of or reference to the 'diplomatic notices, hagiographic narratives, dedications, and colophons in manuscripts, inscriptions, and other written and material artifacts' that would have offered evidence of the persons and events in question—and which, as Vanderputten shows, were definitely available *in situ* at Saint-Bertin—was that '[h]is principal concern was the shaping of a collective historical identity for the monks, not an objective exploration of the communal past'.[190] According to Vanderputten, this choice was rooted in the difficult situation in which the community found itself at the time of writing, a situation that necessitated a new historical narrative of decline and reform which Simon projected onto an 'invented past', and which 'had no use for discussions concerning the abbey's history between 961/62 and 1021'.[191] Following this logic, when Simon mined the community's records for quotable evidence of decline under his patron's abbatial predecessors but could not find any—worse still, the evidence he found suggested that these abbots had in fact been capable leaders under whose governance the community had prospered—he opted to ignore it entirely lest it jeopardized his depiction of Lambert as the shining light of reform that had led Saint-Bertin's monks out of the darkness inflicted upon them by his late

---

[188] Vanderputten, *Reform as Process*, p. 17; a handlist of Saint-Bertin's abbots during the period 982–1123 is provided in ibid., pp. 197–9.

[189] 'Simonis gesta abbatum', ed. Holder-Egger, p. 635.

[190] Vanderputten, *Reform as Process*, pp. 19–24, who further argues that 'Simon had made a conscious decision to remove the period before 1021 entirely from the monks' collective past'.

[191] Vanderputten, *Reform as Process*, p. 27.

tenth- and early eleventh-century precursors.[192] An alternative, if not altogether incompatible, interpretation is offered by David Defries, who considers the *Chronicon*'s selective use of the past 'more sophisticated and artful than a narratological analysis can reveal', and who, *contra* Vanderputten, argues that Simon 'actually did have evidence for the abbey's decline—the fire and the plague'.[193] According to Defries, then, the motivation for Simon's deliberate omission of the period 962–1021 and the existing evidence testifying to it was owed, on the one hand, to 'Richard of Saint-Vanne's condemnation of the community', and, on the other, to the fact that 'ideals [of reform] imported from tenth-century English Benedictine reformers put Odbert's community at odds with [the] contemporary Lotharingian reformers' from whom both Roderic and Lambert took their cue.[194] Following this explanation, the issue was not that the evidence available locally did not suit Simon's plan of painting a picture of decline under Lambert's precursors—on the contrary, the various documented misfortunes experienced by the monks under their leadership would have offered concrete evidence of God's judgement and disapproval—but that their leadership had been, from Simon's perspective, inspired by the wrong kind of reform agendas.[195] Drawing on biblical allegory and terminology that he lifted from, amongst others, Isidore's *Etymologiae*, especially in his account of Abbot Bovo (1042–65), Simon, according to Defries, deliberately created the narrative *caesura* between the abbacies of Adalolf and Roderic to cast a shroud of silence over the community's tenth-century reforms, reforms that had been influenced by movements across the English Channel and clashed with the Continental-inspired reform endeavours of the *Chronicon*'s abbatial patron.[196]

Whichever interpretation we choose to embrace—in fact, the basic arguments put forward by Defries and Vanderputten are not strictly speaking mutually exclusive—the fact remains that Simon, when first setting out to write the *Chronicon* at the commission of Abbot Lambert, deliberately passed over the

---

[192] Vanderputten, *Reform as Process*, p. 27: 'Presenting evidence from the latter decades of the tenth century would only have cluttered the [*Chronicon*'s] narrative's central argument, as there were indications that the abbey had flourished and that monastic leadership had been strong and decisive. In order to present the reform of 1021 as a new departure for abbatial leadership, he [Simon] needed to incorporate in his account the suggestion of decline. When he failed to find any substantial evidence to corroborate this claim or when he discovered, as he probably did, a far more complex historical reality than suited his discourse, he simply stated the decline as fact'.

[193] Defries, *From Sithiu to Saint-Bertin*, p. 253.

[194] Quotes from Defries, *From Sithiu to Saint-Bertin*, pp. 251 and 253.

[195] Defries, *From Sithiu to Saint-Bertin*, p. 253, who argues that in the minds of Simon and his patron, '[m]isfortunes, not practices, were the real evidence for decline'.

[196] See Defries, *From Sithiu to Saint-Bertin*, p. 257: 'Over the period that Simon consigned to oblivion, Saint-Bertin seems to have developed significant ties to English monastic reformers', reformers whose 'idiosyncracies may have influenced Saint-Bertin's monastic practice in a way that clashed with Richard's version of monasticism'. According to Vanderputten, by contrast, Simon in his *Chronicon* depicts the abbacies of Roderic (1021–42), Bovo (1042–65), and Heribert (1065–81) 'as if they belong to a different era, with events and practices alien to Simon's own experience', and in a 'tone [that] is sympathetic but overall fairly neutral'; see Vanderputten, *Reform as Process*, p. 23.

vita et gesta of six/seven former abbots not because he sought to criticize them individually or erase them from the community's collective memory in an act of *damnatio memoriae*, but because the story he wanted (or was instructed) to tell demanded it, whether this was a tale of decline or one of two contrasting reform movements. Meanwhile, another fact that has attracted less comment in scholarship, but which is of equal if not indeed greater significance to the present discussion, is that there is yet another abbacy which Simon passes over in silence in the *Chronicon*: his own. In its original form, the text seems to have consisted of one book (*liber*) (plus prologue?) that spanned three-quarters of a century and comprised the abbacies of Roderic (1021–42), Bovo (1042–65), Heribert (1065–82), and John (1082–95), to which Simon then added a second and considerably longer book (almost three times the length of book one) that was dedicated exclusively to the period of Lambert's twenty-eight-year tenure (1095–1123).[197] We do not know exactly when this second book was completed and committed to parchment, nor how long its composition took Simon, though its publication cannot have preceded Lambert's death in 1123. Whilst it is possible, and perhaps plausible, that certain sections had been drafted whilst Lambert was still alive, there is every chance that the process of producing the polished final version and appending it to the existing manuscript (now lost but transcribed during the eighteenth century, see below) extended into Simon's abbacy at Auchy, if not into the early months/years of his time as Lambert's eventual successor at Saint-Bertin. Better established is the fact that at some point after 1145, nearly a decade after Simon had resigned from Saint-Bertin and withdrawn to his native Ghent where he would die in 1148, he returned to the text once more to add a third book, the shortest by some margin, on the deeds of his abbatial successor, Leo (1137–45).[198] The result of Simon's final intervention was a history that, though up-to-date on Saint-Bertin's abbatial succession, had a glaring *lacuna* in the shape of his very own abbacy, and only at an unknown later point did an anonymous continuator append a short summary of Simon's *vita*—but not, conspicuously, his *gesta*—to the end of the second book, at the same time as inserting a brief note about Simon's death alongside a verse epitaph to the end of book three before continuing the narrative with an account of the more recent events and abbacies post-1145.[199]

As the continuator's additions make explicit, Simon had been part of Saint-Bertin's monastic community from boyhood ('a puero nutritum in eodem coenobio') and, having been sent to gain experience at other Flemish communities at his abbot's command ('iussu eiusdem patris per nonnulla coeonobia Flandrie

---

[197] 'Simonis gesta abbatum', ed. Holder-Egger, pp. 636–43 and 643–61, respectively.
[198] 'Simonis gesta abbatum', ed. Holder-Egger, pp. 661–3.
[199] Edited as 'Gesta abbatum s[ancti] Bertini continuatio', ed. by Oswald Holder-Egger, in *Supplementa tomorum I–XII, pars I* [= *MGH SS* XIII] (Hanover: Hahn, 1881), pp. 663–73.

ordinem correxerit'), was initially assigned as Lambert's deputy—perhaps even acting abbot—during the latter's incapacitating illness ('eidem infirmanti vicarius huius loci substitutus est'). He was then appointed and consecrated as abbot of Auchy, but after nearly four troublesome years of governance was recalled to Saint-Bertin to take over officially from the late abbot ('Quam ecclesiam cum per quattuor fere annos strenue gubernasset [...] huc adductus est anno 1131 et in sede principali abbatis sollemniter collocatus'), an office which he held for almost five years ('sed vix quinquiennio post haec abbatizavit') before he had to resign once again, thus spelling the end of his abbatial career.[200] No further details are provided by the continuator as to why Simon was unable to hold on to either of his abbacies for more than a few years, though we are offered some brief yet thought-provoking details about his person. Most pertinent to the present discussion is the statement that Simon was, from an early age, a devout and noble man who was well versed in letters ('vir religiosus, nobilis et bene litteratus') but afflicted by a speech impediment ('sed impeditioris linguae'). As his death note makes clear, however, this impediment did not stop Simon from both writing and, intriguingly, dictating to others (presumably copyists) the work of history he himself had authored ('Symon, quondam abbas huius loci, qui etiam haec omnia a tempore domni Roderici abbatis conscripsit atque dictavit').[201] From the time he was first commissioned to write history by Abbot Lambert, and continuing during and beyond the time of his abbatial tenure, Simon thus seems to have put his own pen to parchment—indeed, the *Chronicon*'s continuator specifies that, to the best of his knowledge, Simon had personally transcribed his *Gesta abbatum* 'with [his] skilled pen' ('huc gesta abbatum erudito, ut apparet, descripsit stilo')—at the same time as availing himself of *amanuenses* who would put into writing whatever he dictated to them.[202]

As shown above and discussed in greater detail later in this book (3.1), the provision of monastic copyists and assistant scribes generally required the authorization of a community's superior. As Lambert's appointed historiographer, *vicarius*, and eventual successor, Simon thus would have had the authority and the resources at his disposal to undertake the writing project *manu propria* with the help of scribal support staff, whose role may well have become more instrumental than before, and perhaps indispensable for the project's timely completion, once Simon advanced to the office of abbot himself and thus had to negotiate his historiographical activity with the various duties and expectations that came with this appointment. By the same token, the composition of the *Chronicon*'s third book c.1145–8 presumably could not have benefited from the same kind of resources and in-house support, given that the author had long since left the

---

[200] 'Simonis gesta abbatum', ed. Holder-Egger, p. 661.
[201] 'Simonis gesta abbatum', ed. Holder-Egger, p. 663.
[202] 'Gesta abbatum continuatio', ed. Holder-Egger, p. 663.

monastery and retired to Ghent. In fact, this change of circumstance might help explain why Simon himself did not provide an account of his own abbacy to bridge the evident narrative chasm between his predecessor Lambert and his successor Leo in the *Chronicon*, but instead had to consign this to the pen of a future continuator. One possibility is that Simon was lacking the resource and opportunity to write history in earnest outside the walls of his former monastery, meaning that the best he could muster was the short and cursory account of Leo's abbatial deeds that constitutes book three and fills fewer than two pages in the modern edition, whereas a more extensive and detailed *gesta* for himself was out of the question under these isolated conditions. Another possibility is that Simon *did* manage to write his autobiographical deeds following his withdrawal in 1136 and sent them to Saint-Bertin alongside the Leo-continuation prior to his death in the later 1140s, but that the monks' collective memory of his abbacy and the undisclosed circumstances that had led to his resignation were still strong, or at least strong enough that whoever appended book three to the *Chronicon*'s original manuscript—which we must assume Simon had left behind upon his departure for Ghent—decided not to do the same with Simon's memoires, perhaps precisely because they jarred with the community's memory. Unfortunately, the fact that this autograph/working copy was lost not long after it was transcribed in the eighteenth century (St-Omer, Bibliothèque d'Agglomération, MS 815), and, moreover, that the earliest extant copy (Boulogne-sur-Mer, Bibliothèque Municipale, MS 146A) is awash with later interpolations, erasures, and textual replacements,[203] means we cannot ascertain which possibility is the more likely. What is certain, however, is that once Simon was no longer abbot himself nor benefiting from the patronage and authority of Saint-Bertin's superior as he had done under Lambert, he could no longer use the *Chronicon*'s historical narrative to fashion his own identity and memory.

1.4 Abbess-Historians—An Exceptionalism?

It is time to return to a subject introduced above (1.1) by addressing the question why previous studies of monastic historical writing have, by and large, eschewed the topic of female abbatial authorship. Were there no abbess-historians in the Middle Ages, or did their writing of history differ so fundamentally from that of their male counterparts that it must be viewed as a case apart? As we will see, the first possibility can be discarded fairly easily due to some well-documented examples of abbesses writing history in various parts of the medieval Latin West that could, without too much difficulty, have been treated alongside cases of male

---

[203] Vanderputten, *Reform as Process*, p. 17 n. 15.

superiors in surveys such as Kersken's. The question must be, therefore, why they have typically been excluded from the conversation, and how we can ensure to include them more regularly and meaningfully in the future. Whilst it is useful briefly to review some of the broader discourses that have shaped scholarly thinking to date, we ultimately can only speculate as to the first part of the question, though we can—and indeed I will—propose an alternative approach to guide the discussion developed in this book and, hopefully, in future scholarship more generally.

One factor that seems to have played a bigger part than most in discouraging scholarship on abbatial historiography from engaging more fully with the role(s) of abbesses is the problematic yet persistent notion that medieval women, and specifically religious/monastic women, were somehow less invested in history (and the writing thereof) than men/monks. Despite important challenges, pessimistic assessments such as that famously expressed by Eileen Power in her ground-breaking 1922 study on the nunneries of late medieval England still exercise considerable influence even on some recently published work. To Power, the early medieval, pre-Conquest period had been 'the only one during which English nuns were at all conspicuous for learning', whereas the eleventh to thirteenth centuries marked a time when 'we have no trace of women occupying themselves with the copying and illumination of manuscripts'.[204] Focusing on the writing of chronicles, which Power considered 'the most notable contribution of the [male] monastic houses to learning from the eleventh to the fourteenth centuries', she saw proof of monastic women's lack of historical interest in that 'no nunnery produced a chronicle', even though many of them, especially the larger and wealthier communities, 'received many visitors and must have heard much that was worth recording, besides the humbler annals of their own houses. But they recorded nothing'.[205] Power's rather gloomy judgement on the state of female monastic historiography has since been revisited and revised, thanks in no small part to David Bell's crucial work on the book collections and reading habits of English women's convents.[206] The fact remains, though, that the historiographical

---

[204] See Eileen Power, *Medieval English Nunneries, c.1275 to 1535* (Cambridge: Cambridge University Press, 1922), p. 237.

[205] Power, *Nunneries*, pp. 237–8, with the further conclusion that '[w]hile the monks composed chronicles, the nuns embroidered copes; and those who sought the gift of a manuscript from the monasteries, sought only the gift of needlework from the nunneries' (ibid., p. 238).

[206] David N. Bell, *What Nuns Read: Books and Libraries in Medieval English Nunneries* (Kalamazoo, MI: Cistercian Publications, 1995); more recently David N. Bell, 'What Nuns Read: The State of the Question', in *The Culture of Medieval English Monasticism*, ed. by James G. Clark (Woodbridge: Boydell & Brewer, 2007), pp. 113–33, with reference to other key works of scholarship available at the time (pp. 114–15 n. 6). Published the same year as Bell's *status quaestionis* is Diane Watt, *Medieval Women's Writing: Works by and for Women in England, 1100–1500* (Cambridge: Polity, 2007), with introductory remarks on women's authorship as a category of analysis (pp. 7–13). Also cf. the more extensive discussion on the same subject by Jennifer Summit, 'Women and Authorship', in *The Cambridge Companion to Medieval Women's Writing*, ed. by Carolyn Dinshaw and David Wallace (Cambridge: Cambridge University Press, 2003), pp. 91–108.

outputs of women religious surviving from England are fairly modest when compared to those produced by their contemporaries on the Continent, whose scribal and authorial prolificity continues to be showcased by a fast-growing body of international and interdisciplinary scholarship.[207] As Bell reminds us, however, such simplified comparisons can be 'perilous' at times, 'useless' even, not least considering that 'the actual number of surviving books which, in England, can be traced with certainty or high probability to any particular house tells us virtually nothing about the size of its library'.[208]

Bell's cautionary words ring true not only with regard to histories collected and read by the members—and indeed the leaders—of medieval female religious communities, but surely also, *mutatis mutandis*, in respect of histories which they wrote themselves. As we will recall, the estimated survival rate for texts and manuscripts from medieval England, specifically those composed in the English vernacular(s), proposed by recent interdisciplinary studies is the lowest (4.9%) in north-western Europe, with other regions and languages such as German(y) (14.5%) registering noticeably higher rates.[209] A similar, if slightly less stark, ratio between average loss rates in high and late medieval England *vis-à-vis* the rest of the Latin West, irrespective of linguistic classification, has been proposed elsewhere, with England recording losses of −22%, −28%, −37%, and −39% in the twelfth, thirteenth, fourteenth, and fifteenth centuries, respectively (average −31.5%), compared to −24%, −26%, −32%, and −32% across the entire Latin West (average: −28.5%).[210] Broken down further, these figures suggest a marked difference in the estimated loss rates of England's so-called 'non-suppressed institutions', that is, non-monastic cathedrals and churches that survived the Dissolution/Reformation, and which according to the same study averaged −26% across the Middle Ages, *vis-à-vis* those of 'suppressed institutions', that is, monastic communities, which across the same time period reached −39% on average.[211] Needless to say, such statistics and quantitative

---

[207] Some pioneering contributions to this field published prior to 2007 are referenced by Bell, 'What Nuns Read', p. 121 n. 42 and ibid., pp. 121–2 n. 43. Since then, a considerable body of work has been generated, including the proceedings of three international and interdisciplinary 'dialogues' on nuns' literacies in a comparative, pan-European perspective published in 2013–17; *Nuns' Literacies in Medieval Europe: The Hull Dialogue*, ed. by Virginia Blanton et al. (Turnhout: Brepols, 2013); *Nuns' Literacies in Medieval Europe: The Kansas City Dialogue*, ed. by Virginia Blanton et al. (Turnhout: Brepols, 2015); *Nuns' Literacies in Medieval Europe: The Antwerp Dialogue*, ed. by Virginia Blanton et al. (Turnhout: Brepols, 2017). More recently Martha W. Driver, 'Medieval Women Writers and What They Read, c.1000–c.1500', in *The Edinburgh History of Reading: Early Readers*, ed. by Mary Hammond (Edinburgh: Edinburgh University Press, 2020), pp. 54–73. A particularly instructive example of interdisciplinarity between the Humanities and STEM subjects is Anita Radini et al., 'Medieval Women's Early Involvement in Manuscript Production Suggested by Lapis Lazuli Identification in Dental Calculus', *Science Advances* 5 (2019), 1–8.
[208] Bell, 'What Nuns Read', p. 117. [209] Kestemont et al., 'Forgotten Books', p. 769.
[210] Buringh, *Manuscript Production*, pp. 194 and 204, who considers the loss rates 'in the rest of the Latin West to be somewhat lower than those calculated for England'.
[211] Buringh, *Manuscript Production*, p. 199, with a further breakdown into individual institutions (where applicable) in ibid., pp. 479–523 (= 'Annex L–N').

estimates must always be treated with caution, and the distribution patterns and chronological 'trends' they suggest demand corroboration—and, not infrequently, correction—through a careful combination of specific case studies and broader historical contextualization, which at the time of writing remains a desideratum for several geographical regions and literary traditions.

For Latin—the single most prolific and pre-eminent language of historiographical production in medieval Europe—the broader contexts and principal drivers of textual losses are discussed by Thomas Haye in his study *Verlorenes Mittelalter*. Haye's qualitative analysis distinguishes not only between chronological periods and geographical areas, but also between various 'genres' (including historiography) and *milieux* of production (including monastic settings), and it thus provides a helpful contextualization and, in certain respects, corrective for the quantitative estimates cited above. As Haye shows, Latin historical writing suffered substantial (if not disproportionate) losses in the Middle Ages, including a surprisingly large corpus of now-lost monastic historiography in the form of domestic chronicles, foundation narratives, and *gesta abbatum*, especially amongst the Benedictines who, as noted above (1.1), remained the most historiographically prolific of the major monastic orders.[212] Haye, too, notes major loss rates in England in the centuries following the Norman Conquest, though unlike Bell he encourages comparisons with the Continent, especially with France, which he views as largely inseparable from England in terms of their development during the thirteenth and fourteenth centuries.[213] Though he offers no dedicated discussion of female literary and historiographical production—in fact, the two dozen case studies that conclude his book are exclusively male—Haye's analysis broadly confirms what the numbers have suggested: that we are likely dealing with a considerable corpus of historical writing (predominantly in Latin) produced in monastic communities across medieval Europe which have left little or no trace today; that these losses include, with remarkable regularity, narratives which were instrumental to the articulation of a community's historical consciousness and the preservation of its collective memories; that the situation in England was, if probably more pronounced, still broadly comparable to that seen elsewhere, including on the Continent; and, crucially, that absence of evidence does not equal evidence of absence. This is before we even begin to consider the elephant in the room that is anonymity of textual production and transmission, a phenomenon which, as others have noted, seems disproportionately to have affected medieval women's writings, with anonymous works being attributed routinely to men/abbots without even considering the possibility that they may just as well

---

[212] See Haye, *Verlorenes Mittelalter*, pp. 250–5 and 449–52, with case studies of individual monasteries in ibid., pp. 314–78; also cf. Doyle, 'Publication', p. 111.

[213] Haye, *Verlorenes Mittelalter*, pp. 481–6.

have been written by women/abbesses.²¹⁴ These observations are important for the purposes of the present investigation, and they must apply to female monastic and abbatial authorship as much as they do to histories written by monks and abbots, even if—or perhaps precisely because—the latter survive in much larger, though far from complete, numbers.

Another argument against the idea that female abbatial authorship should be viewed as an exception(alism) is that its overall quantitative and qualitative trends closely resemble those established for its male equivalent, albeit on a smaller scale. Again, most recorded cases come from the medieval German and Frankish/French lands, with the Low Countries in second place and England/the British Isles trailing in the distance alongside other regions including the Mediterranean. Like their male peers, a sizeable proportion—in fact, the majority—of abbess-historians lived and wrote in the twelfth and fifteenth centuries, with fewer cases from the periods in-between and prior to *c*.1100. Most of them were Benedictines, though there is also evidence of historical writing by the heads of female Cistercian, Dominican, and Carmelite houses. Whilst a full survey would be beyond the scope of this study, it is worth discussing a selection of cases to reveal their differences and similarities with the male authors studied so far. One of the earliest examples—perhaps even *the* earliest—of an abbess writing history in the Latin West is that of Heilwig, abbess (*c*.825–after 833) and historian of Chelles. Heilwig's predecessors included Gisela (*c*.800–10), Charlemagne's sister, whom we will meet again below (2.4) as a sponsor and patroness of historical writing. In fact, it was the very work Gisela had commissioned during her abbacy—the *Annales Mettenses priores*—that prompted Heilwig to pick up the pen and author a continuation which emphasizes the life and deeds of her own daughter, Judith, empress and second wife of Louis the Pious.²¹⁵ As abbess, Heilwig can thus be seen as acting in the double capacity of domestic chronicler for Chelles's monastic

---

[214] A good case in point is Abbot Godfrey of Admont (1137–65), who, as observed by Alison Beach, since the eighteenth century has been credited unduly with the authorship of several writings that, upon (Beach's) closer inspection, exhibit conspicuous signs of female authorship and scribal work conducted in collaboration with male scribes under Abbot Irimbert (1172–6), who prior to his appointment had been the nuns' preacher; Alison I. Beach, 'Listening for the Voices of Admont's Twelfth-Century Nuns', in *Voices in Dialogue: Reading Women in the Middle Ages*, ed. by Linda Olson and Kathryn Kerby-Fulton (Notre Dame, IN: University of Notre Dame Press) pp. 187–98 (pp. 187 and 196–7 n. 2). Bell, 'What Nuns Read', pp. 122–3 considers it 'eminently probable that more was written by women than we know, and the desire for (or imposition of) anonymity [...] has resulted in the names of many female authors being irretrievably lost' (p. 123). For broader discussion, see Mary Swan, 'Authorship and Anonymity', in *A Companion to Anglo-Saxon Literature*, ed. by Phillip Pulsiano and Elaine Treharne (Oxford: Wiley, 2001), pp. 71–83.

[215] Stuart Airlie, *Making and Unmaking the Carolingians, 751–888* (London: Bloomsbury Academic, 2021), pp. 260 and 266–7; Janet L. Nelson, 'Carolingian Royal Funerals', in *Rituals of Power from Late Antiquity to the Early Middle Ages*, ed. by Frans Theuws and Janet L. Nelson (Leiden: Brill, 2000), pp. 131–84 (p. 154 n. 90); on Heilwig's abbacy, see also Janet L. Nelson, 'Gender and Genre in Women Historians of the Early Middle Ages', in *L'historiographie médiévale en Europe*, ed. by Jean-Philippe Genet (Paris: Éditions du CNRS, 1999), pp. 149–63; repr. in *The Frankish World, 750–900*, ed. by Janet L. Nelson (London: Bloomsbury Academic, 1993), pp. 183–98 (pp. 191–4); Irene Crusius, 'Im Dienst

community and dynastic historian in the service of her own kin, and calling her continuation of the *Annals of Metz* a 'mini-biography of Judith' risks downplaying Heilwig's personal and official commitment to recording the history of the religious women placed under her care for the communal good.[216]

A good example from the high Middle Ages is provided by Petronilla de Chemillé, first abbess (1115–49) of Fontevraud, who was appointed personally by the community's founder, Robert d'Arbrissel, and who continued/expanded the so-called *Statutes*—really a kind of rudimentary *gesta* and foundational narrative—produced by Robert prior to his death. Like Heilwig's, Patronilla's work also served a twofold purpose by providing the young community with an identity-affirming account of its founder's vision at the same time as cementing the abbatial authority of the author and her successors over the monastery and over a dozen of its daughter houses.[217] The extent of Petronilla's investment in the writing of her abbey's history was not exhausted by her continuation of Robert's *Statutes*. In addition, and perhaps as part of a larger historiographical campaign, she used her *auctoritas* to order the making of Fontevraud's *Grand cartulaire* and commission the earliest known *Vita* of Robert to which we owe much of our knowledge about his life, the latter of which was written by Baldric, archbishop of Dol and sometime abbot-historian of Saint-Pierre de Bourgueil.[218] In his prologue, Baldric identifies Petronilla as the work's initiator, though he complains that the abbess provided him with little more than a few notes about Robert's life even though he knew next to nothing about it.[219] Disappointed with the outcome of Baldric's best but ill-equipped endeavours, Petronilla then ordered Andreas, one of her abbey's lay brothers(?) and Robert's former chaplain, to write a second *Vita* that conformed more to her expectations. Considerably longer than Baldric's work, this second *Vita Roberti* focuses almost exclusively on Robert's final years, and its detailed account suggests that Petronilla had supplied Andreas with more

---

der Königsherrschaft: Königinnen, Königswitwen und Prinzessinnen als Stifterinnen und Äbtissinnen von Frauenstiften und -klöstern', in *Nonnen, Kanonissen und Mystikerinnen: Religiöse Frauengemeinschaften in Süddeutschland*, ed. by Eva Schlotheuber et al. (Göttingen: Vandenhoeck & Ruprecht, 2008), pp. 59-77 (pp. 72-3). It has been argued that Gisela was not formally an abbess; see Martina Hartmann, '*Concubina vel regina*: Zu einigen Ehefrauen und Konkubinen der karolingischen Könige', *Deutsches Archiv für Erforschung des Mittelalters* 63 (2007), 545-68 (pp. 548-50).

[216] See Elizabeth F. Ward, 'The Career of the Empress Judith, 819–43' (unpublished PhD dissertation, King's College, University of London, 2002), p. 70, who further suggests that '[t]he appointment of Heilwig at Chelles may have been part of Judith's plans for her future retirement as royal widow' (ibid., pp. 101–2).

[217] See Bruce L. Venarde, 'Making History at Fontevraud: Abbess Petronilla de Chemillé and Practical Literacy', in *Nuns' Literacies in Medieval Europe: The Hull Dialogue*, ed. by Virginia Blanton et al. (Turnhout: Brepols, 2013), pp. 19–31. On the foundation and early history of Fontevraud, see Michel Melot, *Histoire de l'abbaye de Fontevraud-Notre-Dame-des-pleurs, 1101–1793* (Paris: CNRS Éditions, 2022), pp. 39–81.

[218] Venarde, 'Making History', pp. 24–6, who believes that '[t]he statutes and the cartulary were part of an internal campaign, so to speak, to preserve Robert's unusual spiritual vision and emphasize that Petronilla was seeing to its continued realization' (ibid., p. 25).

[219] *Deux vies*, ed. Dalarun et al., pp. 136–7.

detailed information, probably based on her personal memory, and perhaps even had a hand in the work's composition, which technically would make her co-author.[220]

Petronilla's authorship of the *Statutes*' continuation and her possible co-authorship of Andreas's *Vita* leave no doubt that she, like many abbesses before and after her, was literate, even if the extent of her literacy—or more to the point, the context(s) in which she deployed it during her abbatial tenure—has been the subject of some debate. Bruce Venarde suggests that Petronilla's Latinity may have been sufficient to enable her to perform pragmatic tasks pertaining to the monastery's governance and administration, but perhaps not quite advanced enough to permit more substantial and original literary composition (such as historiography).[221] Venarde's arguments concerning Petronilla's 'pragmatic literacy' could help explain why she chose not to write the *Lives* of her monastery's venerated founding father herself, but instead enlisted the help of two highly trained writers whom she furnished with her personal notes, probably on wax tablets or perhaps by means of oral dictation. We should note, however, that Andreas's prior appointment as chaplain indicates that his literacy, too, could be pragmatic at times, and if he could switch between pragmatic and literary modes of writing, then there seems little reason to doubt that Petronilla could do likewise. Perhaps, therefore, Petronilla's decision to delegate the actual task of composition—and, we may assume, that of codification, though the lack of the original manuscript(s) means we cannot know whether these *Vitae* were autographs or the work of copyists—had less to do with her own literacy and qualification than with the time that she was (un)able to commit to the task in amongst her various abbatial responsibilities, or maybe it was simply a matter of personal preference. I return to this below.

Whatever the extent and circumstances of Petronilla's historiographical immersion, there were other abbesses in the eleventh and twelfth centuries who could—and did—find the time and inclination to write history. One was her near-contemporary Beatrice, abbess (c.1080s–1116) of St Mary, Überwasser, the likely author of a house chronicle that survives appended to a Gospel book where it is succeeded by a detailed description of the oaths Überwasser's abbesses had to swear upon their appointment.[222] Beatrice was not the only abbess-historian

---

[220] This second *Vita Roberti* is edited in *Deux vies*, ed. Dalarun et al., pp. 190–298. Also cf. Venarde, 'Making History', p. 27, who likewise concludes that 'Petronilla's guiding hand is evident' in Andreas's work.

[221] Venarde, 'Making History', pp. 29 and 31, who is 'inclined to doubt that Robert would have chosen as abbess someone who knew no Latin', but thinks it 'possible that she [Petronilla] was literate only to the extent necessary to carry out her executive duties'.

[222] Edeltraud Klueting, 'Fromme Frauen als Chronistinnen und Historikerinnen', in *Fromme Frauen als gelehrte Frauen: Bildung, Wissenschaft und Kunst im weiblichen Religiosentum des Mittelalters und der Neuzeit*, ed. by Edeltraud Klueting and Harm Klueting (Cologne: Erzbischöfliche Diözesan- und Dombibliothek, 2010), pp. 217–30 (pp. 226–7).

of her community. Her fifteenth-century successor, Sophia Dobbers, has left us with a short historical narrative written in the first person that emphasizes her instrumental role in accomplishing the reform agenda initiated under her predecessor(s), specifically the abbey's affiliation to the Bursfelde Congregation and the resulting adoption of the *Caeremoniae Bursfeldenses* in 1483.[223] Sophia's work—and to a degree Beatrice's, too—exhibits unmistakable signs of strategic abbatial self-fashioning and memory-making very similar to those encountered in the works of male abbot-historians. Unlike in the works of, say, Hugh of Flavigny and Guibert of Nogent, however, the abbess' authorial and autobiographical persona rarely occupies the narrative focus for very long, let alone takes over entirely, and even in Sophia's case the emphasis returns to and remains with the monastic community. This is not to say, of course, that abbesses did not find ways of incorporating detailed records of their own achievements when writing histories of and for their communities. Two instructive examples of this are provided by the writings of Sophia's late fifteenth-/early sixteenth-century contemporaries, Ursula Pfaffinger and Caritas Pirckheimer.

As abbess (1494–1509) of Frauen-Chiemsee, Ursula continued the communal 'history book' (*Gschicht Büech*) that had been commissioned by her late predecessor, Magdalena, and copied (but left unfinished) by her notary and *secretarius*, Peter.[224] Much of Peter's text is dedicated to Magdalena's achievements on behalf of the community in the years 1467–77, which he and his patron might have intended as an example or mirror (*speculum*) for future abbesses. Ursula's continuation of the *Gschicht Büech* maintains this personal focus. Unlike Magdalena, however, Ursula did not delegate the task to an *amanuensis*, but personally produced a detailed account (*Rechenschaftsbericht*) of her abbatial *gesta* that commences with her abbatial election in 1494 and continues with more than a hundred examples of her accomplishments whilst in office, accomplishments which, as is emphasized consistently, were aimed at the communal benefit.[225] Caritas Pirckheimer went one step further. As abbess (1524–7) of St Clare in Nuremberg, she, too, wrote a detailed, first-hand account (in Latin) of what she had achieved for the community during her comparatively short tenure, which she had then translated into German by one of the sisters to facilitate its reception inside the cloister, as well as, presumably, to promote her own abbatial

---

[223] *Caeremoniae Bursfeldenses*, ed. by Marcel Albert (Siegburg: Schmitt, 2002). See Klueting, 'Fromme Frauen', p. 228 n. 36, with the relevant references.

[224] Gisela Brandt, 'Textsorten weiblicher Chronistik: Beobachtungen an den chronikalischen Aufzeichnungen von Agnes Sampach (–1406/07), Elisabeth Kempf (um 1470), Ursula Pfaffinger (1494–1509) und Caritas Pirckheimer (1524–1527)', in *Textsortentypologien und Textallianzen von der Mitte des 15. bis zur Mitte des 16. Jahrhunderts*, ed. by Franz Simmler and Claudia Wich-Reif (Berlin: Weidler, 2004), pp. 217–42 (p. 230).

[225] They include Ursula's extensive architectural campaigns, acquisitions of external donations, settlements of legal disputes on behalf of the community, etc.; see the helpful summary table in Brandt, 'Textsorten', pp. 231–2.

memoria.²²⁶ Like several examples of male abbatial self-fashioning studied above (1.3), Caritas also wrote history in the shape of episodic and experience-based narratives, thereby inseparably linking her authorial voice with the collective memory and identity of the women placed under her authority, a voice which, in Caritas's case, seems to have been at its most powerful not in the original language of composition, but in the vernacular.²²⁷

The power of the vernacular as a medium of monastic historiography, particularly in the later Middle Ages, is shown also by a historiographical compendium made *c*.1470 at the order of Elisabeth Kempf, then prioress (1469–85) of Unterlinden (Dominican). A 'composite chronicle' for the community founded in 1232, the manuscript (Wolfenbüttel, Herzog August Bibliothek, MS. Cod. 164.1 Extrav.) contains a *historia fundationis*, a history of events up to 1430, and Elisabeth's translation of the *Vitae sororum* (also known as *Liber de vitis primarum sororum de Subtilia in Columbaria*) written in the first quarter of the fourteenth century by her predecessor, Prioress Katharina of Gebersweiler. Just like Caritas half a century later, Elisabeth infused her historical narrative with her personal experiences and oral memories, and she, too, evidently recognized the value of history in translation.²²⁸ That the use of Latin and/or the vernacular was not mutually exclusive can be seen in the work of Agnès de Thieuville, abbess (1482–91) of La Trinité de Caen. Similar to Beatrice of Überwasser and Ursula of Frauen-Chiemsee, Agnès authored a detailed narrative account of her own election (London, British Library, MS Harley 3661; probably dictated by Agnès herself and copied by a member of her community) that is written in a mixture of (mostly) French and Latin. The purpose of Agnès's work was to bridge a gap in her community's *series abbatissarum* that had been caused by the unusual conditions surrounding the appointment of her late predecessor, Catherine Ire de Blangy de Saint-Hilaire (1470–82). Contrary to established practice, Catherine had been appointed personally to the abbatial office by her predecessor, Blanche d'Auberville (1441–70), without free election on the part of their nuns, whose role had been reduced to that of mere approval and approbation. As Agnès stresses in her account, neither human memory nor written record ('nest point de memore par homme our par quelque escripture') knew of any precedent for this, which is why she, unlike her predecessor, insisted on being elected

---

²²⁶ Andrea Stieldorf, 'Frauenbildung in der Vormoderne', in *Doch plötzlich jetzt emanzipiert will die Wissenschaft sie treiben: Frauen an der Universität Bonn (1818–2018)*, ed. by Andrea Stieldorf et al. (Göttingen: Vandenhoeck & Ruprecht, 2018), pp. 11–30 (p. 20). Caritas's fourteenth-century predecessor, Catherine, acted as compiler—and copyist—of a multi-volume hagiographical-historiographical compendium commonly known as the 'St. Klara-Buch' (Bamberg, Staatsbibliothek, MSS Msc. Hist. 146–7); see Kurt Ruh, 'Das "St. Klara Buch"', *Wissenschaft und Weisheit* 46 (1983), 192–206.

²²⁷ Brandt, 'Textsorten', pp. 236–9, who refers to Caritas's work as 'erlebte und mitgestaltete Geschichte' (ibid., p. 239).

²²⁸ Brandt, 'Textsorten', p. 226.

freely and unanimously by the nuns in keeping with their monastery's tradition and recorded history.[229]

Attempting to quantify the phenomenon of female abbatial authorship and scale it across the medieval Latin West is difficult, though it might just be possible to gauge its extent and geographical spread with the help of quantitative research on the writing of history in women's religious communities in the early modern world. Focusing on central Europe in the period c.1500–1800, Stefan Benz identifies about eleven hundred and sixty female monasteries that existed long enough (at least ninety years/three generations) to be able to cultivate a communal memory and historiographical tradition.[230] Based on a representative sample of some fifty-nine communities, Benz notes that just over half (51%) have left no evidence of historiographical activity, whereas more than a third (41%) produced written records in the shape of annals, chronicles, and other kinds of historical narratives. Projected onto the entire corpus, this would suggest that about four hundred and eighty of the communities considered by Benz may have engaged with historical writing, and that nearly two hundred and seventy (56%) were home to female authors, whereas the others had their respective histories committed to writing by male authors who worked *within* the communities and were able to represent the women's internal perspectives.[231] These numbers are remarkable, especially in comparison with the much lower percentage of female historians outside the monastic *milieu*, who at the time formed just one hundred and forty (6.5%) of the two thousand one hundred and thirty-six historians counted by Benz.[232] Even more remarkable is the fact that no more than a handful (less than 2%) of Benz's female monastic historiographers seem to have held a position of institutional leadership at the time of writing. They include Elisabeth Herold, abbess (1599–1657) of Oberschönenfeld, who wrote a history of her community from its foundation in 1211 to 1633; Anna Maria von Mellin, abbess (1759–67) and domestic historian of Himmelpforten; Sabina Barbara Lutzin, prioress (1613–79) of Würzburg's Dominican convent of St Marx, who chronicled the history of her community after it burnt down in the Thirty Years' War; and

---

[229] MS BL Harley 3661, fol. 2r. I am grateful to Laura Gathagan for bringing this manuscript to my attention, and for generously sharing her knowledge of Abbess Agnès with me.

[230] Stefan Benz, 'Geschichtsschreibung der Frauenklöster Zentraleuropas im 18. Jahrhundert', in *Between Revival and Uncertainty: Monastic and Secular Female Communities in Central Europe in the Long Eighteenth Century*, ed. by Veronika Čapská et al. (Opava: Silesian University, 2012), pp. 214–65, who describes the geographical parameters of his dataset as 'zwischen Mähren im Osten, Tirol im Süden, Flandern sowie dem Elsass im Westen und fließenden, konfessionellen Grenzen im Norden' (p. 244). For comparison, see the recent case study of historical writing and forgery at Bouxières Abbey by Steven Vanderputten, *Dismantling the Medieval: Early Modern Perceptions of a Female Convent's Past* (Turnhout: Brepols, 2021).

[231] Benz, 'Geschichtsschreibung', p. 245.

[232] See Benz, 'Geschichtsschreibung', p. 246. The historians identified by Benz were all born between 1570 and 1689.

Cornelia Melyn, abbess (?–1648) and historiographer of the Carmelite Sisters in Antwerp, though she only wrote history after her resignation from office.[233]

Insightful though Benz's quantitative analysis of female monastic historiography in the early modern period may be, its findings cannot easily be transposed onto the centuries that form the focus of the present study, nor is it sensible to assume that the numbers generated from his geographically circumscribed (if commendably wide-ranging) testbed are representative of the entire Latin West. Still, Benz's work is helpful to our investigation in that it shows us the later stages (if not quite the 'end point') of a long-term historical development that did not begin *ex nihilo* sometime around the year 1500, but which had its roots in medieval cultures of female literacy and monastic historiographical production. Even when conceding, as we must, that this development lacked uniformity and rarely (if ever) adhered to linear trajectories, and that the advent of print in the West acted as something of a catalyst, it seems implausible—not to say impossible—for just shy of five hundred female communities to have produced works of history in the period *c.*1500–1800, more than half by domestic authors, unless there had been an established tradition of writing history (in manuscript) by the members of medieval women's convents.[234] Even a conservative estimate that allows for a major increase in the later fifteenth and early sixteenth centuries with more irregular and incremental growth during earlier periods, including phases of no growth or even decrease, projected tentatively across the European map would suggest hundreds of cases by the later Middle Ages, with at least several dozen in the early and high medieval centuries subject to regional and local circumstances. Such estimates may seem optimistic given the extremely limited corpus of extant medieval historiography known to have been authored by women, specifically by monastic women; and yet, when set against the total number of monasteries (male, female, and 'unisex') in the medieval Latin West and the many thousands of texts they produced, many (if not indeed most) of which are lost or only attested indirectly (if at all), they are not altogether unrealistic.[235] Add to this the comparatively high loss rate of works by or

---

[233] Benz, 'Geschichtsschreibung', pp. 247–9 with the relevant references.

[234] On the cataclysmic effect of the printing press, see Andrew Pettegree, *Brand Luther: 1517, Printing, and the Making of the Reformation* (London: Penguin, 2015).

[235] See the table in Buringh, *Manuscript Production*, p. 90 (= Table 2.14), which gives the cumulative number of monasteries in the Latin West as 1,193 (sixth century), 2,094 (seventh century), 3,168 (eighth century), 4,385 (ninth century), 6,343 (tenth century), 12,485 (eleventh century), 20,125 (twelfth century), 23,794 (thirteenth century), 23,489 (fourteenth century), and 22,551 (fifteenth century). The use of the term 'unisex' with reference to monastic communities that housed both men and women (sometimes known as 'double monasteries') has been adopted from Albrecht Diem, 'The Gender of the Religious: Wo/Men and the Invention of Monasticism', in *The Oxford Handbook of Women and Gender in Medieval Europe*, ed. by Judith Bennett and Ruth M. Karras (Oxford: Oxford University Press, 2013) pp. 432–47; also cf. Alison I. Beach, 'The Double Monastery as a Historiographical Problem (Fourth to Twelfth Century)', in *The Cambridge History of Medieval Monasticism in the Latin West*, ed. by Alison I. Beach and Isabelle Cochelin, 2 vols. (Cambridge: Cambridge University Press, 2020), I, 561–78.

attributed to medieval women that scholarship has linked to number of factors—for example, their habitual exclusion from the literary and historiographical 'canon' and the (forced) adoption of anonymity or pseudonymity already alluded to—and there can be no doubt that the examples of abbess-historians discussed so far are but the tip of an iceberg whose true volume we may never be able to grasp fully.[236]

Slimmer chances of transmission and higher average loss rates only take us so far in explaining why there were far fewer, in both relative and absolute terms, abb*ess*-historians than there were abb*ot*-historians in medieval Europe. In absolute terms, this gender(ed) imbalance needs little explanation, if only because of the larger overall number of male communities that over the centuries naturally, and unsurprisingly, led to a larger number of male superiors, and thus to a larger pool of prospective abbot-historians, even if only a small proportion picked up the pen.[237] In relative terms, however, the uneven ratio between medieval abbess- and abbot-historians—judging from the evidence collated during the research that underpins this study, 1:10 may be erring on the side of optimism—requires further comment and contextualization, even if at this point we can but speculate as to its probable causes. Fortunately, some explanations can be discarded relatively easily. For example, we may confidently reject any suggestion that seeks to explain the relatively small number of identifiable female monastic historians, and specifically abbess-historians, through an alleged lack of education and literacy on their part.[238] Equally uncompelling is the notion that medieval monastic women

---

[236] See Katharina M. Wilson, 'Introduction', in *Medieval Women Writers*, ed. by Katharina M. Wilson (Athens, GA: University of Georgia Press, 1984), pp. vii–xxix (p. xix); *The Writings of Medieval Women: An Anthology*, ed./tr. by Marcelle Thiébaux, 2nd ed. (Abingdon: Routledge, 1994), pp. xvii–xviii.

[237] This is true virtually across the medieval European map. To give but one example, the ratio between female and male communities in post-Conquest England (*c*.1066–1540) ranges from about 1:4 in the mid-eleventh century to 1:6 in the later thirteenth and early fourteenth centuries; see the summary table in David Knowles and R. Neville Hadcock, *Medieval Religious Houses: England and Wales*, 2nd ed. (London: Longman, 1971), p. 494. Power, *Nunneries*, p. 1 counts some one hundred and thirty-eight nunneries for the period *c*.1270–1536, with a summary table in ibid., pp. 685–92 (= 'Appendix IV'), which, as an average, matches the cumulative numbers given by Knowles and Hadcock.

[238] As research into the literacy of medieval (religious) women has shown, the educational standards amongst female monastic superiors were comparatively high across the board and remained thus throughout the Middle Ages, subject to some variation, with many abbesses boasting levels of literary and linguistic training that rivalled, and frequently outperformed, those of their male peers. For England, see Power, *Nunneries*, pp. 237–84. For a comparison between England and the Continent, see Veronica O'Mara, 'The Late Medieval English Nun and Her Scribal Activity: A Complicated Quest', in *Nuns' Literacies in Medieval Europe: The Hull Dialogue*, ed. by Virginia Blanton et al. (Turnhout: Brepols, 2013), pp. 69–93. Also cf. Lisa M. Weston, 'Conceiving the Word(s): Habits of Literacy among Earlier Anglo-Saxon Monastic Women', in *Nuns' Literacies in Medieval Europe: The Hull Dialogue*, ed. by Virginia Blanton et al. (Turnhout: Brepols, 2013), pp. 149–67, with discussion of early medieval English abbesses based on Bede and other contemporary sources. There is ample evidence from across the European map that abbesses led by example to set up centres of education, literary composition, and book production within their communities; see Alison I. Beach, *Women as Scribes: Book Production and Monastic Reform in Twelfth-Century Bavaria* (Cambridge: Cambridge University Press, 2004); Rosamond McKitterick, 'Nun's Scriptoria in England and Francia in the Eighth Century', *Francia* 19 (1992), 1–35; Katrinette Bodarwé, Sanctimoniales litteratae: *Schriftlichkeit und*

were interested primarily, or even exclusively, in the production of liturgical books and devotional literature, a notion that remains oddly pervasive despite overwhelming evidence to the contrary.[239] In fact, they were very much interested—and deeply invested—in history. As Elisabeth van Houts and others have shown, women were amongst the principal carriers of memory in medieval society, and their work as historians—if not necessarily historio*graphers*—of families, extended kin groups, and widely connected aristocratic and dynastic networks had its equivalent in the life within the monastic walls.[240] We only have to look to the monastic *memoria* to see abbesses play a regular and instrumental role in the preservation and codification of historical knowledge on behalf of their *familia* very similar to what we can see happening outside the cloister.[241] This did not have to involve putting one's own pen to parchment.

It is this last point that sets us on the right path towards a plausible explanation as to why the number of medieval abbesses who *wrote* history remains small compared to that of their male equivalents. With accidents of transmission and qualificational disparities (literacy, education, historical interest, etc.) excluded from the catalogue of probable causes, the question must be whether we might in fact be dealing with a difference in *quality* rather than quantity. This is not intended as a value judgement, nor do I wish to imply that the historiographical involvement of abbesses was in any way inferior to that of abbots. Instead, I posit that both groups/genders engaged regularly with the writing of history, and that

Bildung in den ottonischen Frauenkommunitäten Gandersheim, Essen und Quedlinburg (Münster: Aschendoff, 2004). The arguments about the early medieval women of Kitzingen by Felice Lifshitz, *Religious Women in Early Carolingian Francia: A Study of Manuscript Transmission and Monastic Culture* (New York, NY: Fordham University Press, 2014) are intriguing, but they must remain conjecture; cf. my comments in Benjamin Pohl, 'Review of *Religious Women in Early Carolingian Francia*', *Reviews in History* (2015), https://reviews.history.ac.uk/review/1844.

[239] For critical discussion, see Bell, *What Nuns Read*; Julie Hotchin, '*Reformatrices* and Their Books: Religious Women and Reading Networks in Fifteenth-Century Germany', in *Communities of Learning: Networks and the Shaping of Intellectual Identity in Europe, 1100–1500*, ed. by Constant J. Mews and John N. Crossley (Turnhout: Brepols, 2011), pp. 251–91; Stieldorf, 'Frauenbildung', p. 12.

[240] Elisabeth M. C. van Houts, *Memory and Gender in Medieval Europe, 900–1200* (London: Palgrave, 1999); Matthew J. Innes, 'Keeping It in the Family: Women and Aristocratic Memory, 700–1200', in *Medieval Memories: Men, Women and the Past, 700–1300*, ed. by Elisabeth M. C. van Houts (London: Harlow, 2001), pp. 17–35; now also Laura L. Gathagan, 'Family and Kinship', in *The Cambridge Companion to the Age of William the Conqueror*, ed. by Benjamin Pohl (Cambridge: Cambridge University Press, 2022), pp. 143–62, with particular reference to Cecilia, daughter of William the Conqueror and Matilda, and second abbess (1113–27) of her mother's foundation of La Trinité de Caen.

[241] For example, the production of mortuary rolls (*rouleaux mortuaires/funeraires*) such as that made under (and perhaps by?) Matilda, first abbess (*c.*1059/66–1113) of La Trinité de Caen; *Rouleaux des morts du IXe au XVe siècle*, ed. by Léopold Delisle (Paris: Renouard, 1866), pp. 178–278. For context and discussion, see Monique Goullet, 'Poésie et mémoire des morts: Le rouleau funèbre de Mathilde, abbesse de la Sainte-Trinité de Caen (†1113)', in *'Ad libros': Mélanges offerts à Denise Angers et Joseph-Claude Poulin*, ed. by Jean-François Cottier et al. (Montreal: Presses de l'Université de Montréal, 2010), pp. 163–98; Monique Goullet, 'De Normandie en Angleterre: Enquête sur la poétique de trois rouleaux mortuaires', *Tabularia* (2016), 217–78, http://journals.openedition.org/tabularia/2782. Even where abbesses were not strictly speaking the authors of these *rouleaux* and the *tituli* they contain, they were typically the authorities behind them.

neither one was by default any more qualified to do so or better at it than the other, but that there are differences in their respective approaches and implementations which mean that the work of abbesses is typically less visible than that of abbots. I further suggest that this lack of visibility may not be accidental, nor does it seem to result from the systematic suppression of female voices seen in other areas of medieval literary and historical culture, but rather from what we could describe as a renunciation of the authorial self in favour of collective identities and communal authorship models that must be distinguished from anonymity. Such strategies of self-renunciation and communal authorship stand in contrast to the presence typically claimed by male authorial personae and their more aggressive assertions of authority, examples of which we saw above (1.3), but are especially common in the work of abbesses who regularly operated with their communities at the front and centre—indeed, at the heart—of their historiographical endeavours, including the cases studied here. Could one explanation for the perceived difference between female and male abbatial historiography, and the reason why the latter tends to dominate our perception, be that abbesses were, for some reason, predisposed towards prioritizing communal benefit over individual advancement, thus institutionally (and perhaps intuitively) enabling and facilitating the historiographical writing talents within their communities over and above their own?

This suggestion chimes well with the important observations made by Edeltraud Klueting and Gisela Brandt in their studies of female monastic historiography in later medieval and early modern Germany, studies which have received little attention in anglophone scholarship, but whose conclusions are in fact highly pertinent to our discussion. According to Klueting, what distinguishes many of the histories written by and for cloistered women is that they tend to be aimed at communal purposes ('dem Gemeinschaftszweck zugeordnet') and thus promote the writing of history as a collective exercise and responsibility.[242] This did not have to exclude elements of abbatial self-fashioning, and the examples of Petronilla de Chemillé, Beatrice of Überwasser, Caritas Pirckheimer, and Agnès de Thieuville show that the two could go hand in hand. Still, the fact that the orientation of these histories ultimately remained a communal one means they do not lend themselves naturally to notions of authorship that focus on individuals. This may also help explain Klueting's observation that these histories typically remained physically confined to their places of origin, with little evidence of external transmission and reception. As Klueting notes, they often had their home not in the monastic library, but rather in the communal archive.[243] This practice can be traced across the medieval Latin West, such as at Caen, where the abbesses of La Trinité kept their community's most valuable charters and foundation narratives together under lock and key.[244] Whilst not exclusive to women's

---

[242] Klueting, 'Fromme Frauen', p. 230.   [243] Klueting, 'Fromme Frauen', pp. 217–18.
[244] See below (4.4).

communities, this close proximity—conceptual and physical—between historiography and documentary culture leads Klueting to argue that both should be understood as a form of 'pragmatic literacy', an argument that gains support from Brandt's description of Ursula's *Gschicht Büech* as written 'in chancery style' ('im Stil der Kanzlei'), and which resembles Venarde's interpretation of Petronilla's work.[245] Evidence of pragmatic literacy is not unique to women's historical writing, however, but has also been identified in the work of abbot-historians such as Robert of Torigni.[246] Viewed in this context, female authorship as characterized by Klueting and Brandt does not constitute an example of exceptionalism, nor does it stand in opposition to its male equivalent. It is simply a different calibration of the same exercise, albeit one whose propensity for inclusivity and communal involvement has rendered it ultimately less conspicuous.

A full appreciation of female abbatial historiography requires more than can be covered in this study. The discussion offered here provides food for thought, but more remains to be done. Nevertheless, the evidence presented here clearly shows that unpacking the historiographical involvement of medieval abbesses and making it visible in the sources means rethinking some basic categories of analysis. These include not only notions of authorship, which, as I have suggested here, need to be broadened to include both individuals and communities, but also questions of historiographical 'genre'. The contributions of abbesses are often overlooked in scholarship simply because definitions of historiography *stricto sensu* tend to prioritize annals, chronicles, etc. over historical narratives composed in other formats such as 'hagiography', visions, or letters, all of which are formats frequently employed—and perhaps preferred—by abbesses, including luminaries like Heloïse and Hildegard of Bingen.[247] Some of these letters constitute 'micro

---

[245] Klueting, 'Fromme Frauen', pp. 219 and 230; Brandt, 'Textsorten', p. 240. Also cf. Marilyn Oliva, 'Rendering Accounts: The Pragmatic Literacy of Nuns in Late Medieval England', in *Nuns' Literacies in Medieval Europe: The Hull Dialogue*, ed. by Virginia Blanton et al. (Turnhout: Brepols, 2013), pp. 51–68. The scholarly literature on medieval forms of pragmatic literacy (*pragmatische Schriftlichkeit* in German; *écriture pragmatique* in French; *scrittura pragmatica* in Italian) is substantial; for an overview, see *Pragmatic Literacy, East and West, 1200–1330*, ed. by Richard H. Britnell (Woodbridge, Boydell, 1997); *Pragmatische Schriftlichkeit im Mittelalter: Erscheinungsformen und Entwicklungsstufen*, ed. by Hagen Keller et al. (Munich: Fink, 1992); *L'écriture pragmatique: Un concept d'histoire médiévale à l'échelle européenne* (2012) [= *Cahiers électroniques d'histoire textuelle du LAMOP* V], https://archive-2013-2016.lamop.fr/spip.php%3Farticle772.html; Dominique Stutzmann and Sébastien Barret, 'L'écriture pragmatique: (1) Objet historique et problématique; (2) Italie; (3) Allemagne, Suisse, Autriche; (4) Angleterre; (5) France; (6) Perspectives et nouveaux concepts', *Paléographie médiévale* (2012), https://ephepaleographie.wordpress.com/2012/04/18/; Paul Bertrand, *Les écritures ordinaires: Sociologie d'un temps de révolution documentaire (1250–1350)* (Paris: Publications de la Sorbonne, 2015); translated as *Documenting the Everyday in Medieval Europe: The Social Dimensions of a Writing Revolution, 1250–1350* (Turnhout: Brepols, 2019).

[246] See Benjamin Pohl, 'Robert of Torigni's "Pragmatic Literacy": Some Theoretical Considerations', *Tabularia* (2022), 1–29, https://journals.openedition.org/tabularia/5576; Pohl, '*Abbas*', passim.

[247] Birgit Kochskämper, 'Die germanistische Mediävistik und das Geschlechterverhältnis: Forschungen und Perspektiven', in *Germanistische Mediävistik*, ed. by Volker Honemann and Tomas Tomasek (Münster: LIT, 2000), pp. 309–52 (p. 343); Albrecht Classen, '... und sie schrieben

histories' in their own right, such as the *Libellus de fundatione monasterii in Helfta* by Sophia of Stolberg, abbess of Helfta, the autograph of which has survived amongst Sophia's official correspondence. Written in 1451, the *Libellus* was no private literary pursuit aimed at personal gratification, but, as we saw in the Introduction, an expression of the abbess's duty towards her community. And yet, Sophia belongs to a minority of abbesses who explicitly attached their own names to the historiography of their communities. Accessing the work of the majority that did not needs a different approach. Diane Watt pertinently observes that 'only an understanding of medieval textual production as *collaborative* enables us to grasp the nature and extent of women's engagement with and contribution to literary culture',[248] and the present study will substantiate this statement with plenty of evidence of abbesses who used their authority to enable and facilitate the writing of history by means other than simply putting pen to parchment.

1.5 Conclusions

The evidence discussed here leaves little doubt that abbots—and indeed abbesses—contributed substantially, and often in an authorial capacity, to the historiographical corpora of their communities. Theirs was a special kind of authorship, one that carried a unique sense of authority both inside and outside the monastery and therefore must be differentiated from that claimed by other monastic authors whose freedom to write history depended fundamentally on their institutional superior's authorization. If abbot- and abbess-historians did not necessarily distinguish themselves through *what* they wrote, they were certainly set apart by *how* they wrote thanks to the autonomy and resources at their disposal. As we saw, this enabled them not only to carve out precious writing time for themselves to pursue historiographical projects in addition to—albeit sometimes in perceived conflict with—their managerial duties, not infrequently over extended periods of time, but also to draft in assistants and assemble scribal workforces for the codification of their authorial works. Naturally, not all abbatial authors had the same human and material resources available to them locally, with some having access to much more extensive domestic funds and expertise than others, nor did all of them avail themselves equally of these means. In fact, some seem to have preferred to adopt and maintain a more insular and self-sufficient *modus operandi* through choice rather than necessity, which saw them

---

doch: Frauen als Schriftstellerinnen im deutschen Mittelalter', *Wirkendes Wort* 44 (1994), 7–24; Steven Vanderputten, '"Against the Custom": Hagiographical Rewriting and Female Abbatial Leadership at Mid-Eleventh-Century Remiremont', *Journal of Medieval Monastic Studies* 10 (2021), 41–66.

[248] Watt, *Medieval Women's Writing*, p. 2.

operating either in continuity with or in a departure from the working methods they had cultivated prior to their abbatial appointments. We saw examples of abbots whose historiographical involvement pre- and/or post-dated their period of office, whereas others only engaged first-hand with the writing of history during their tenure. In both cases, the histories they wrote *whilst* abbots enjoyed a distinctive authority and reputation, one that made them 'official' in a way that few (if any) histories written within the monastic *milieu* could claim to be. Abbatial authorship and the authority it imbued upon historical narratives formed a mark of distinction that was recognized and considered desirable not only by contemporaries, but equally by subsequent generations of readers, copyists, and continuators, who would place great emphasis on the fact that a given text had been written in an official capacity by an abbot or abbess, thereby perpetuating both the authority of the texts themselves and the legacy of their authors.

This concern with official memory and legacy was made visible not only in the reception and transmission of histories authored by abbots and abbesses, but also in the presence that some of these authors claimed within the narratives. In fact, if we wanted to identify one way in which abbot-historians differed from other historiographers within their communities because of *what* they wrote, this probably would be their ability—and authority—to 'write themselves into' their monastery's official histories in such a way as to link the monks'/nuns' communal sense of the past intrinsically, and sometimes inseparably, with the memory of their own lives and deeds. Such abbatial self-fashioning did not have to run contrary to communal interests, and we saw various cases in which the two went hand in hand to the point of being virtually indistinguishable from each other. In some instances, though, it led to an imbalance in which the authorial persona took centre-stage to such an extent as to relegate the monastic community to the margins or even make it disappear from the narrative altogether. These cases constitute a minority, however, and on the whole the historiographical involvement of monastic superiors should be seen in service of their communities and for their collective benefit, to the point that some abbot-historians chose to step out of the limelight by concealing their authorial identity in favour of communal models of authorship or by delegating the lead role of historian to others whom they would support from the background with the means at their disposal. As we will see, delegation, facilitation, and resourcing were fundamental aspects of monastic historiographical production that are key to our understanding of abbatial authority just as much as—if not more than—authorial writing. What is more, studying these aspects will show us the true extent of the historical work done by medieval abbesses, whose authorial involvement quantitatively falls behind that of their male peers both in absolute terms (that is, the overall number of abbesses known to have authored histories) and in relative terms (the proportion of abbess-historians amongst the total number of abbesses), but who—as I will show in the following chapters—were just as active as patrons, commissioners, and promoters of historical narratives inside and outside their communities, and who for the remainder of this book will therefore be discussed alongside and without distinction from their male counterparts.

2
Abbatial Patronage

2.1 Introduction

As my discussion of abbatial authorship has shown, abbots and abbesses of the Middle Ages regularly acted as writers of history. Their authorial compositions range from histories aimed primarily at internal and communal usage such as domestic annals, house chronicles, foundation histories, and *gesta abbatum/abbatissarum* to (auto)biographies and historical narratives whose scope extends beyond the cloister walls. Abbot- and abbess-historians held a special position thanks to, on the one hand, their superior authority within their own communities, and, on the other, their considerable power in the personal and socio-political networks that linked these communities with the wider medieval world. This combination of institutional *auctoritas* and lordly *potestas* was a decisive factor in why and how they wrote history, and one that set them apart from—and above—other authors inside as well as outside their monasteries. Authorial composition only constitutes one aspect of monastic historiographical production, however, and to appreciate the instrumental role of monastic superiors in the writing of history we need to broaden our notion of the medieval historian and his/her craft by extending the focus to other aspects—and agents—in this collaborative and communal exercise.[1] As I will show, one of the most effective means by which abbots and abbesses facilitated the writing of history without putting pen to parchment was patronage.

Some of the best-known works of history written in the Middle Ages were produced at the commission of abbatial patrons. The early-ninth-century *Gesta abbatum* of Saint-Wandrille, considered by some the 'oldest Western monastic history', are a perfect case in point.[2] The fact that the last abbot to have his deeds

---

[1] It has even been argued that the label 'historian' as typically understood today 'conveys such unhelpful assumptions about their projects, and such dangerous temptations to cosy identification, that we should avoid the term altogether' with regard to medieval writers; Bernard Gowers, 'Review of Edward Roberts, *Flodoard of Rheims and the Writing of History in the Tenth Century*', *The Medieval Review* (2021), https://scholarworks.iu.edu/journals/index.php/tmr/article/view/32206/36018.

[2] *Chronique des abbés de Fontenelle (Saint-Wandrille)*, ed./tr. by Pascal Pradié (Paris: Les Belles Lettres, 1999); quote from John Howe, 'The Hagiography of Saint-Wandrille (Fontenelle) (Province of Haute-Normandie)', in *L'hagiographie du haut Moyen Âge en Gaule du Nord: Manuscrits, textes et centres de production*, ed. by Martin Heinzelmann (Stuttgart: Thorbecke, 2001), pp. 127–92 (p. 190). See also Ian N. Wood, 'Saint-Wandrille and Its Hagiography', in *Church and Chronicle in the Middle Ages: Essays Presented to John Taylor*, ed. by Ian N. Wood and Graham A. Loud (London: Bloomsbury Academic, 2003), pp. 1–14.

memorialized in the *Gesta abbatum Fontanellensium* is Ansegis (823–33) has led some to suspect that he must have been the work's patron, whereas others have proposed a collective, multi-generational patronage model that also involved his predecessors, Gervold (787–806), Trasaire (806–17), Hildebert II (817–18), and the lay abbot Einhard (817–23), Charlemagne's courtier and biographer.[3] The *Gesta*'s anonymous author(s) must have had access to a sizeable corpus of sources that included various annals, the *Liber pontificalis*, and key documents from the monastic archives.[4] Written in the first quarter of the ninth century at the order of either Trasaire or Hildebert II, the *Life* of Saint-Wandrille's third abbot, Ansbert (678–90), reports that these archives held thousands of charters at the time of writing,[5] which matches the *Gesta*'s claim that under Ansegis their holdings had outgrown the monastery's available storage facilities, prompting the abbot to authorize the construction of a 'charter house' outside the monks' dormitory ('domus cartarum [...] ante dormitorium sita') in addition to a new 'book house' outside the refectory ('domus qua librorum copia conservaretur [...] ante refectorium') whose roof tiles were reinforced, at Ansegis's orders, with iron nails ('tegulas ferreis clavis configere iussit') for better protection from the elements and thieves.[6] Access to these maximum-security facilities would have been subject to the abbot's special permission, and the authors of the *Gesta abbatum* and the *Vita Ansberti* benefited from this privilege courtesy of their abbatial patrons.

Predating these histories from Saint-Wandrille by the best part of a century, and extant today in over one hundred and sixty manuscript copies, is the

[3] Michel Sot, *Gesta episcoporum, gesta abbatum* (Turnhout: Brepols, 1981), pp. 34–5; Pascal Pradié, 'L'historiographie à Fontenelle au temps d'Eginhard: Une lecture des *Gesta Abbatum*, l'histoire sainte de Fontenelle', in *Einhard: Leben und Werk*, ed. by Hermann Schefers, 2 vols. (Regensburg: Schnell & Steiner, 1997–2019), II, 62–74 (pp. 64–5); Matthias Becher, 'Die Chronologie der Äbte von Saint-Wandrille in der ersten Hälfte des 8. Jahrhunderts: Studien zu den *Gesta abbatum Fontanellensium*', in *Vielfalt der Geschichte: Lernen, Lehren und Erforschen vergangener Zeiten*, ed. by Sabine Happ and Ulrich Nonn (Berlin: WVB, 2004), pp. 25–47 (p. 27).

[4] *Chronique*, ed./tr. Pradié, pp. lv–lxx; also cf. Becher, 'Chronologie', pp. 29–30; Howe, 'Hagiography', p. 128; Rosamond McKitterick, *Rome and the Invention of the Papacy: The* Liber pontificalis (Cambridge: Cambridge University Press, 2020), p. 172.

[5] 'Vita Ansberti episcopi Rotomagensis', in *Passiones vitaeque sanctorum aevi Merovingici*, Vol. 3, ed. by Bruno Krusch and Wilhelm Levison [= *MGH SS rer. Merov.* V] (Hanover: Hahn, 1910), pp. 613–43 (p. 628): '[Q]uae cuncta curiosus lector, inspectis testamentis seu largitionibus eorundem fidelium, facile repperiet. Quae etiam, ut multis liquido patet, multimodam millenarii numeri effecerunt summam'. The *Vita*'s author, Aigrad(us), explicitly indebts himself to his abbatial patron in the work's preface (ibid., p. 618). This expansion of the abbey's archives supports John Howe's view of the early ninth century as 'a time of relatively intense literary activity at Saint-Wandrille'; see Howe, 'Hagiography', p. 191, who rejects the 'backdating [of] many surviving texts' from Saint-Wandrille by Felice Lifshitz, *The Norman Conquest of Pious Neustria: Historiographic Discourse and Saintly Relics, 684–1090* (Toronto: Pontifical Institute of Mediaeval Studies, 1995). Note that Wood, 'Saint-Wandrille', pp. 2–3 dates the *Vita Ansberti* shortly before 811, which would suggest that the original commission came from Trasaire.

[6] *Chronique*, ed./tr. Pradié, pp. 170–1. On domestic book production at Saint-Wandrille, cf. Pascal Pradié, 'Un fragment de manuscrit inédit du IXe siècle découvert à l'abbaye Saint-Wandrille', *Tabularia* 4 (2004), 131–42, https://doi.org/10.4000/tabularia.1381.

prodigious *Historia ecclesiastica gentis Anglorum* composed by Bede from sources available at Wearmouth-Jarrow and further afield.[7] Though the work was dedicated to King Ceolwulf of Northumbria (729–37) and personally presented to him on two occasions, the preface explicitly credits it to the initiative of Albinus, abbot of St Augustine's, Canterbury (709/10–32). Bede calls Albinus the *Historia*'s foremost facilitator and sponsor ('auctor ante omnes atque adiutor opusculi huius'),[8] and he even gives concrete examples of how the abbot exercised his patronage in support of the writing project. Perhaps most crucially, Albinus supplied Bede with books from St Augustine's well-stocked monastic library, which he arranged to be copied at Canterbury and delivered to Wearmouth-Jarrow by Nothelm, a priest who in 735 would become Canterbury's next archbishop, and for whom Bede would later compose *In regum librum XXX quaestiones* and, possibly, *De VIII quaestionibus*.[9] On at least one occasion, Albinus sent Nothelm as far as Rome to copy certain documents from the papal archives ('perscrutato eiusdem sanctae ecclesiae Romanae scrinio'), which Nothelm then carried across England to Northumbria so Bede could use them for his *Historia*. Having benefited from such service, it is no surprise to see Bede indebting himself repeatedly to Albinus ('Albini consilio'; 'Albini abbatis industria') and his faithful assistant ('Nothelmo perferente'), who enabled him to compose substantial parts of his *magnum opus* without leaving the comfort of his home.[10] The most explicit acknowledgement of Albinus as Bede's abbatial patron occurs not in the *Historia*'s preface, though, but in a letter addressed to Albinus that accompanied the finished work upon its initial presentation—that is, before the subsequent presentation(s) to Ceolwulf. The letter's authenticity is above suspicion,[11] and in it Bede stresses the abbot's integral agency throughout the project, from its conception to the provision of resources. He thus recalls that Albinus had urged him to write in the

---

[7] The most comprehensive list of extant manuscripts is provided by Joshua A. Westgard, 'Dissemination and Reception of Bede's *Historia ecclesiastica gentis Anglorum* in Germany, c.731–1500: The Manuscript Evidence' (unpublished PhD dissertation, University of North Carolina at Chapel Hill, 2005), pp. 135–41; I am grateful to Joshua Westgard for sharing a copy of his dissertation with me. On the sources available to Bede locally, see still David P. Kirby, 'Bede's Native Sources for the *Historia Ecclesiastica*', *Bulletin of the John Rylands Library* 48 (1965/6), 341–71; repr. in *Anglo-Saxon History: Basic Readings*, ed. by David A. E. Pelteret (New York, NY: Garland, 2000), pp. 55–81.

[8] *Bede's Ecclesiastical History of the English People*, ed./tr. by Bertram Colgrave and Roger A. B. Mynors (Oxford: Clarendon, 1969), p. 2 [hereafter *HEGA*]. On Albinus, see Marios Costambeys, 'Albinus (*d.* 732)', in *Oxford Dictionary of National Biography* (Oxford: Oxford University Press, 2004), https://doi.org/10.1093/ref:odnb/285. Recently Richard Shaw, *How, When and Why Did Bede Write His Ecclesiastical History?* (London: Routledge, 2022), p. 14 who refers to Albinus as 'crucial in initiating and probably commissioning the project'.

[9] *HEGA*, ed./tr. Colgrave and Mynors, p. 4; Shaw, *How, When and Why*, pp. 57–60 and 81–9; William Hunt and Henry Mayr-Harting, 'Nothhelm (Nothelm) (*d.* 739)', *Oxford Dictionary of National Biography* (Oxford: Oxford University Press, 2004), https://doi.org/10.1093/ref:odnb/20368.

[10] *HEGA*, ed./tr. Colgrave and Mynors, p. 4.

[11] The letter's authenticity is reaffirmed by the discovery of two previously unknown twelfth-century copies; Joshua A. Westgard, 'New Manuscripts of Bede's Letter to Albinus', *Revue bénédictine* 120 (2010), 208–15, with a critical edition and translation (ibid., pp. 214–15).

first place ('historia ad quam me scribendam iam dudum instigaveras'), that he had frequently sent him tokens of affection ('munuscula dilectionis') via Nothelm—no doubt an allusion to the many copies and transcriptions Nothelm had been asked to produce and hand-deliver to his abbot's protégé over the years—and that he had readily offered guidance and support along the way ('creber adiuvare atque instituere curasti').[12] This was more than just lip-service. What Bede describes here is not passive sponsorship by an abbot who lent his name to a historiographical project purely as a token of his authority, but (pro) active and sustained patronage that offered unparalleled levels of support and access to resources without which works like Bede's monumental history of the English Church would have been virtually unthinkable.

Bede was not the only monastic historian of the Middle Ages to reap these benefits of abbatial patronage. Other prominent beneficiaries include Symeon, monk-historian of Durham Cathedral Priory and author of the *Libellus de exordio*.[13] Described as 'the fullest example of a historiographical prologue written in the community of St Cuthbert before *c*.1130',[14] the work's preface refers to Symeon writing 'maiorum auctoritate iussus', a phrase which we may interpret as referring to the patronage of Durham's then superior, Turgot (1087–1109), or his successor, Algar (1109–38), or even both, given the use of the plural.[15] The composition of the *Libellus*'s preface is usually dated to the first or second decade of the twelfth century, and William Aird's suggestion that the work may reflect the monastic community's concerted historiographical response to the mounting political pressure and increasing taxation from Ranulf Flambard, King William II's courtier who was appointed Durham's new bishop in 1099, would make Turgot the more plausible instigator of the work.[16] That said, it is not impossible that Symeon intended to indebt himself to both superiors, one of whom had instigated the work and the other seen it to completion. As David Rollason has shown, Symeon did not produce his historical works in isolation, but collaboratively as part of a 'historical workshop' connecting Durham with other centres of historical writing such as Worcester, Malmesbury, and Canterbury, whose

---

[12] Westgard, 'New Manuscripts', p. 214.

[13] *Symeon of Durham: Libellus de exordio atque procursu istius, hoc est Dunhelmensis, ecclesie*, ed./tr. by David W. Rollason (Oxford: Oxford University Press, 2000).

[14] Quote from Charles C. Rozier, *Writing History in the Community of St Cuthbert, c.700–1130: From Bede to Symeon of Durham* (Woodbridge: York Medieval Press, 2020), p. 6. The standard reference work on Symeon and his writings remains the volume of essays *Symeon of Durham: Historian of Durham and the North*, ed. by David W. Rollason (Stamford: Tyas, 1999).

[15] *Libellus*, ed./tr. Rollason, pp. 2–3; this identification is adopted by Rozier, *History*, p. 6.

[16] William M. Aird, 'The Political Context of the *Libellus de Exordio*', in *Symeon of Durham: Historian of Durham and the North*, ed. by David W. Rollason (Stamford: Tyas, 1999), pp. 32–45 (pp. 42–5); David W. Rollason, 'Symeon of Durham's *Historia de regibus Anglorum et Dacorum* as a Product of Twelfth-Century Historical Workshops', in *The Long Twelfth-Century View of the Anglo-Saxon Past*, ed. by Martin Brett and David A. Woodman (Farnham: Routledge, 2015), pp. 95–112 (p. 98); Rozier, *History*, p. 1 dates the preface's composition broadly to *c*.1104 × 15.

superiors likewise acted as patrons of historical narratives.[17] I return to Canterbury (2.3) and Malmesbury (2.5) below. At Worcester, a monk named John oversaw the production of a chronicle that, as per Orderic Vitalis, had been ordered by the head of the community, the monk-bishop Wulfstan II (1062–95) ('iussu [...] Vulfstani pontificis et monachi').[18] John's chronicle was not the only history patronized by Wulfstan, who also had a commissioning hand in Worcester's cartulary-chronicle penned by a scribe called Hemming (London, British Library, MS Cotton Tiberius A xiii; also known as the *Hemming Cartulary*).[19] A generation later, the founding abbess of Fontevraud, Petronilla de Chemillé (1115–49), commissioned the writing of her community's *Grand cartulaire* almost immediately upon her election.[20] And another few generations later, Peter, abbot (1162–82) of Saint-Rémi in Reims, encouraged visiting English historian and polymath John of Salisbury to compose his *Historia pontificalis* whilst sojourning at his monastery.[21] Peter was himself a prolific writer, and the *Historia*'s preface recalls that John commenced the project at the explicit demand of his abbatial host ('voluntati tue, dominorum amicorumque karissime, libentius acquiescens').[22]

Some 1,500 km south of Reims, Leo Marsicanus (also known as Leo of Ostia) produced his monastic history of Montecassino (*Chronica monasterii sancti Benedicti Casinensis*) around 1099, having previously authored a series of shorter historical narratives that might well have served as 'prefatory studies' (*Vorstudien*) for this *magnum opus*.[23] The *Chronica*'s dedicatory letter is addressed to Leo's abbatial patron, Oderisius I (1087–1105), and it sets out with notable clarity the author's motivation for chronicling the community's history.[24] According to Leo, Oderisius had

---

[17] Rollason, '*Historia*', pp. 100–11; Martin Brett, 'John of Worcester and His Contemporaries', in *The Writing of History in the Middle Ages: Essays Presented to Richard William Southern*, ed. by Ralph H. C. Davis and John M. Wallace-Hadrill (Oxford: Clarendon, 1981), pp. 106–26; on Durham's connections with Malmesbury, see Stanislav Mereminskiy, 'William of Malmesbury and Durham: The Circulation of Historical Knowledge in Early Twelfth-Century England', in *Discovering William of Malmesbury*, ed. by Rodney M. Thomson et al. (Woodbridge: Boydell, 2019), pp. 107–16.

[18] *The Ecclesiastical History of Orderic Vitalis*, ed./tr. by Marjorie Chibnall, 6 vols. (Oxford: Oxford University Press, 1968–80), II, 186–7 [hereafter *HE*]; also cf. Cleaver, *History Books*, pp. 26 and 59.

[19] Brett, 'John', p. 102. See also the contributions in *Constructing History across the Norman Conquest: Worcester, c.1050–c.1150*, ed. by Francesca Tinti and D. A. Woodman (York: York Medieval Press, 2022).

[20] Venarde, 'Making History', pp. 24–5.   [21] Gransden, 'Prologues', p. 132.

[22] *John of Salisbury: Historia pontificalis–Memoirs of the Papal Court*, ed./tr. by Marjorie Chibnall (Oxford: Clarendon, 1986), p. 3; Clare Monagle, 'John of Salisbury and the Writing of History', in *A Companion to John of Salisbury*, ed. by Christophe Grellard and Frédérique Lachaud (Leiden: Brill, 2015), pp. 215–34 (p. 231).

[23] *Die Chronik von Montecassino–Chronica monasterii Casinensis*, ed. by Hartmut Hoffmann [= *MGH SS XXXIV*] (Hanover: Hahn, 1980), p. ix; William D. McCready, 'Leo of Ostia, the Montecassino Chronicle, and the *Dialogues* of Abbot Desiderius', *Mediaeval Studies* 62 (2000), 125–60. The *Chronica* was later continued by a series of other authors including Petrus Diaconus; see Hartmut Hoffmann, 'Studien zur Chronik von Montecassino', *Deutsches Archiv für Erforschung des Mittelalters* 29 (1973), 59–162 (pp. 138–52).

[24] The *Chronica*'s authorship continues to cause confusion in scholarship; see Graham A. Loud, 'Review of Kriston R. Rennie, *The Destruction and Recovery of Monte Cassino, 529–1964*', *Catholic Historical Review* 108 (2020), 602–3.

tasked him some time ago ('preceperat/iniunxerat michi iamdudum') with recording for the memory of posterity the deeds of his predecessor, Desiderius (1058–87), whom we shall meet again later in this book ('ut gloriosi predecessoris tui sancte memorie abbatis Desiderii [...] gloriosa ac magnifica gesta ad posterorum memoriam scribendi operam darem').[25] Reportedly, Oderisius's rationale for commissioning this work was that he refused to imitate the imprudent sloth of his elders ('[n]imis videlicet ineptum esse iudicans, loci huius veterum te desidiam imitari'), who had failed to record the deeds of previous abbots ('qui de tot abbatum gestis seu temporibus nichil fere litteris tradere studuerunt'), and even if by chance they had produced anything of the sort, it had been unsuitable and practically illegible due to its bad style ('si qua forte super hoc aliqui descripserunt, inepta prorsus, et rusticano stilo digesta fastidium potius quam scientiam aliquam legentibus conferunt').[26] Leo humbly obeyed the orders of his abbot ('tuo precepto parere potui'; 'debite obedientie famulatum'), though not without drawing attention to some existing historical narratives that, whilst not always of outstanding eloquence or wisdom, nevertheless provided him with useful information.[27]

One of these narratives was a certain 'chronica Iohannis abbatis qui prima in Capua nova monasterium nostrum construxit', which has been identified plausibly with the *Chronica monasterii sancti Benedicti Casinensis* (Montecassino, Archivio dell'Abbazia–Biblioteca Statale del Monumento Nazionale, MS Casin. 175, pp. 534–62), a historical compilation commissioned and perhaps part-authored by Abbot John I (915–34) of Montecassino.[28] It is not to John's chronicle that the codex owes its fame, however, but to its preservation of an illustrated copy of the *Rule of St Benedict* with the earliest known copy of Hildemar of Corbie's commentary. The book's frontispiece contains a full-page miniature of Abbot John opposite St Benedict and a female figure usually identified as the latter's sister, Scholastica, with the two men exchanging a book.[29] The conventional reading of this intriguing scene interprets this book as representing the *Rule* copied in the first part of the composite manuscript, with Benedict acting as its donor and John as its recipient, though a compelling case has been made in favour of reading it the other way around, that is, with John presenting the *Chronica* he himself had commissioned, and whose production he oversaw personally, to the abbey's venerated founder and patron saint.[30] This, then, was the model that Oderisius strove to imitate by commissioning Leo to write the

---

[25] *Chronik*, ed. Hoffmann, p. 3. Most extant copies have 'iniunxerat', whereas the primary manuscript made *c*.1100 and used by Hoffmann for his critical edition (A = Munich, Bayerische Staatsbibliothek, MS Clm. 4623, fol. 85r) has 'preceperat' in its place.

[26] *Chronik*, ed. Hoffmann, p. 3.   [27] *Chronik*, ed. Hoffmann, pp. 4–10.

[28] Edited as 'Chronica Sancti Benedicti Casinensis', in *Scriptores rerum Langobardicarum et Italicarum saec. VI–IX*, ed. by Georg Waitz [= *MGH SS rer. Lang.* I] (Hanover: Hahn, 1878), 468–88; see principally Walter Pohl, *Werkstätte der Erinnerung: Montecassino und die Gestaltung der langobardischen Vergangenheit* (Vienna: Oldenbourg, 2001), pp. 85–95.

[29] Pohl, *Werkstätte*, p. 80.

[30] See, for example, Giulia Orofino, *I codici decorati dell'Archivio di Montecassino*, 3 vols. (Rome: Istituto poligrafico e zecca dello Stato, 1994–2006), I, 52–7; for the traditional interpretation, see Hubert

Chronica monasterii sancti Benedicti Casinensis, thus fashioning himself as an abbatial patron of history following in his predecessor John's footsteps.

More spectacular still from a visual and conceptual perspective is the *Chronicon Casauriense* (sometimes known as the *Liber instrumentorum seu chronicorum monasterii Casauriensis*), a lavishly illustrated cartulary-chronicle from the Abbruzese Abbey of San Clemente a Casauria commissioned by Abbot Leonas (1152/55–82) that survives in the original presentation copy (Paris, Bibliothèque nationale de France, MS Lat. 5411).[31] Like the Montecassino chronicle, the *Chronicon Casauriense* is a compilation of existing and new historical narratives that together chart the monastery's history from its foundation in the 870s to Leonas's death in 1182, though the way in which the two organize and present their respective narratives differs notably. Unlike the fairly uniform *mise-en-page* of its counterpart, that of the *Chronicon Casauriense* exhibits significant variation throughout the manuscript. The main narrative sometimes occupies most of the available writing space, usually in multiple columns, but at other times constitutes more of a paratext relegated to the margins so as to frame another text placed in the centre of the page, typically that of a charter. All in all, the *Chronicon* incorporates copies of over two thousand charters from San Clemente's monastic archives, many of which are reproduced in their entirety with remarkably intricate drawings of their corroborative components (monograms, signatures, *rotae*, etc.). The production of this sophisticated 'hybrid text' required considerable scribal and diplomatic expertise, and it is no coincidence that Leonas chose a local monk called Giovanni Berardo for the task (not to be confused with the fifteenth-century archbishop and cardinal). Not only was this Giovanni an experienced writer who had entered the community as a child oblate and risen through the ranks of sacristan and then prior (c.1169–71), but he was also Leonas's trusted notary who regularly drafted legal and administrative documents that bear his name alongside the abbot's.[32] In this capacity, Giovanni enjoyed his abbot's special dispensation and support, and he was used to being given privileged access, by Leonas's permission, to his community's extensive archives.

Mordek, *Bibliotheca capitularium regum Francorum manuscripta: Überlieferung und Traditionszusammenhang der fränkischen Herrschererlasse* (Munich: Harrassowitz, 1995), pp. 270–3 (p. 271) (= Mc).

[31] Edited, with significant omissions, as 'Chronicon Casauriense, sive historia monasterii Casauriensis', in *Rerum Italicarum scriptores*, ed. by Lodovico A. Muratori, 25 vols. (Milan: Societas Palatina in Regia Curia, 1723–51), II.2, 775–1018. The most comprehensive study is Markus Späth, *Verflechtung von Erinnerung: Bildproduktion und Geschichtsschreibung im Kloster San Clemente a Casauria während des 12. Jahrhunderts* (Berlin: Akademie, 2007); also cf. Graham A. Loud, 'Monastic Chronicles in the Twelfth-Century Abruzzi', *Anglo-Norman Studies* 27 (2005), 101–31; previous studies include Cesare Manaresi, 'Il "Liber instrumentorum seu Chronicorum monasterii Casauriensis" della Nazionale di Parigi', *Istituto lombardo di scienze e lettere, rendiconti della Classe de lettere* 80 (1946/7), 29–62.

[32] See Loud, 'Chronicles', p. 105 n. 12, with references to some of these documents.

The product of this collaboration between Abbot Leonas and his right-hand man and house historian was 'a documentary history of the abbey [...] on an abbot by abbot basis',[33] one that combines a *historia fundationis* with an account of the community's possessions and privileges and a *gesta abbatum* that spans more than three centuries, from the 'praepositus' Celsus to the *Chronicon*'s abbatial patron, Leonas.[34] Adorning this narrative are no fewer than thirty-nine portraits of twenty-seven abbots, several of whom, including Leonas, are afforded multiple depictions.[35] The programme of illustration culminates with two large portraits of Leonas as cardinal (a position he held from about 1069) alongside Popes Adrian IV (fols. 253r–v) and Alexander III (fol. 258v–259r), respectively (Fig. 2.1).[36] Leonas is the only abbot whose two portraits are embellished with red pigment—surely a symbol of his patronage—whereas his predecessors have monochrome pen drawings, some of them flushed with ochre.[37] That this iconography was an integral part of Leonas's commission, rather than an expression of the illuminator's artistic license, is suggested by an intricate stone sculpture also commissioned by Leonas c.1172 for the main portal of San Clemente's abbey church that had been destroyed repeatedly during the tenth and eleventh centuries and rebuilt under his leadership. Like the *Chronicon*, this sculpture tells the origin story of the monastic community's foundation with carved figures accompanied by Latin *tituli*.[38] Leonas occupies the central position on the tympanum second only to the monastery's patron saint, Clemence, and he carries a miniature version of the restored church. Made for the same abbot and following a notably similar design, the sculpture and chronicle together form a vibrant text-image ensemble that reifies the abbey's institutional memory and deliberately showcases Leonas as the principal patron of its long and eminent history.

---

[33] Loud, 'Chronicles', p. 106.

[34] The prologue on MS BnF Lat. 5411, fols. 1r–v has the programmatic title 'Prologus in liber instrumentorum de possessionibus, rebus, sive dignitatibus quas Casauriense monasterium habuit, habet, vel habere debet', and its sets out the structure of the work as intended by its author and patron.

[35] These are, in the order of their appearance: Celsus: 118r; Beatus: fol. 120v; Aimeric: fol. 120v Lupus: fol. 122v; Itto: fol. 123v Alparius: fol. 125r; Ilderic: fol. 131r; Adam I: fols. 132v and 135r; John I: fol. 160v; Giselbert: fol. 167v; Grimoald I: fol. 168r; John II: fol. 172r; Ponzius: fol. 172v; Adam II: fol. 177v; Peter: fol. 178v; Stephen: fol. 179r; Wido: fols. 181v, 184v, and 185v; Franco: fol. 204v; Dominic: fols. 205v (two portraits), 208r, and 218v; Berard: fol. 226r; Trasemund: fol. 233v (two portraits); Adam III: fol. 235r; John III: fol. 236v; Grimoald II: fols. 237r and 238r; Alberic: fols. 242v and 243r; Giso: fols. 243v and 245r; Oldrius: fols. 246v and 248r; and Leonas: fols. 253r and 258v. Intriguingly, the community's first 'proper' abbot, Romanus, receives no portrait, though his successor, Beatus, does.

[36] The *Chronicon*'s final miniature shows Giovanni himself humbly presenting the finished book to the abbey's patron saint, St Clemence (fol. 272v).

[37] Examples of ink-flushed abbatial portraits include MS BnF Lat. 5411, fols. 122v (Lupus), 123r (Itto), and 125r (Alparius).

[38] For a detailed study of this stone sculpture and its iconography, see Laurent Feller, 'La foundation de San Clemente a Casauria et sa representation iconographique', *Mélanges de l'École française de Rome: Moyen-Age, Temps modernes* 94 (1982), 711–28, with an outline drawing of the figures on the tympanum/lintel and transcriptions of the *tituli* (ibid., p. 721).

Fig. 2.1 Leonas of Casauria and Pope Adrian IV. Paris, Bibliothèque nationale de France, MS Lat. 5411, fol. 253r.

Further examples could easily be added here,[39] but those introduced so far paint a sufficiently panoramic view of abbatial patronage that encompasses not just the initial order for the composition of historical narratives, but also, and importantly, the continuing facilitation and sustenance of historiographical projects through the provision of resources, the granting of privileged access to libraries and archives, and, as the case from Casauria demonstrates, the architectural and iconographical 'framing' of domestic chronicles, *gesta abbatum*, and other historiographical works within monastic memory landscapes. Exploring these aspects of abbatial patronage further will help us move the conversation towards a more systematic and holistic understanding of medieval abbots and abbesses as instrumental enablers and facilitators of historical writing.

2.2 Abbatial Patronage—A Case Apart?

Attempting to conceptualize the phenomenon of abbatial patronage quickly reveals itself as inherently more complex than it might at first appear. There was no single reason why medieval monastic superiors sponsored works of history, just as there was no single reason why some of them wrote such narratives themselves, nor can their historiographical sponsorship be mapped easily onto

---

[39] Including those listed by Kersken, 'Äbte', p. 20.

the matrix of secular and ecclesiastical patronage that characterized other areas of medieval literary and documentary culture.[40] Even without a systematic review of the various modes and manifestations of patronage in the Middle Ages, a task that lies beyond the remit of this study, it is possible—and necessary—to identify certain parameters that apply particularly, and perhaps uniquely, to the patronage of monastic superiors. Part of the problem is that, as observed in a recent study, '[p]atronage in the Middle Ages [...] seems, at first glance, to be a commonly understood concept', one that 'involve[s] the creation of a literary product in order to please a patron, often at his or her behest, and frequently in exchange for something of value, be that financial remuneration, status or influence'.[41] Attempting to reconcile such broad-brush definitions of patronage as a transactional relationship with the historiographical sponsorship of medieval abbots and abbesses generates difficulties. Unlike author-patron constellations that involve negotiating a consensus between two parties whose relationship is, if not on an equal footing, then based on a mutual recognition of autonomy—with the patron using his/her social, political, or economic capital to secure the author's services, who in turn can negotiate the terms of employment or turn it down if no agreement is reached—the dynamics of abbatial patronage were much more unilaterally defined. Especially when patronizing historians amongst the members of their own communities, monastic superiors did not have to offer them incentives in the form of financial gain, fame, or similar benefits. If nothing else, the strict prohibition of personal property, wealth, and privilege for individuals living communally in accordance with the *Rule of St Benedict* would have made this a practical impossibility.[42]

More significantly, though, the abbot's position as the community's supreme pastoral, spiritual, and administrative leader demanded a relationship that, in

---

[40] Recent challenges to traditional frameworks and terminologies of patronage, chiefly by philologists and literary scholars, include Deborah McGrady, 'Introduction: Rethinking the Boundaries of Patronage', *Digital Philology: A Journal of Medieval Cultures* 2 (2013), 145–54; Deborah McGrady, 'Challenging the Patronage Paradigm: Late-Medieval Francophone Writers and the Poet-Prince Relationship', in *The Oxford Handbook of Chaucer*, ed. by Suzanne C. Akbari and James Simpson (Oxford: Oxford University Press, 2020), pp. 270–85; Leah Tether, *Publishing the Grail in Medieval and Renaissance France* (Cambridge: D. S. Brewer, 2017), pp. 139–70; Elizabeth M. Tyler, *England in Europe: English Royal Women and Literary Patronage, c.1000–c.1150* (Toronto: University of Toronto Press, 2017).

[41] Tether, *Publishing*, p. 139, observing that 'for all the straightforwardness implied by this, it transpires to be difficult to find a scholarly source that states it as plainly. The reason for this', she suggests, 'is rooted in the existence of a conflation of identities that muddies the water' (ibid.).

[42] *RB*, ed./tr. Venarde, pp. 122–3. Thomas O'Donnell's suggestion that in a monastic context '[t]he image of a static, hierarchical relationship between patron and client must be discarded in favour of a model that recognizes medieval patronage as a vital exchange' primarily applies in cases of external patronage, but, for the various reasons discussed here, has little traction in the context of internal abbatial patronage; Thomas O'Donnell, '"The Ladies Have Made Me Quite Fat": Authors and Patrons at Barking Abbey', in *Barking Abbey and Medieval Literary Culture: Authorship and Authority in a Female Community*, ed. by Jennifer N. Brown and Donna A. Bussell (Woodbridge: Boydell, 2012), pp. 94–114 (p. 94).

principle, prevented favouritism and promoted equality (below the abbot himself) in exchange for the monks' total compliance ('oboedientia sine mora') and unquestioned submission with both body and mind ('nec corpora sua, nec voluntates licet habere in propria voluntate').[43] This total surrender of free will and the labour of one's hands combined with the renunciation of all personal property, both stipulated in the monastic rules and repeated in the vows of the professed, at once removed not only the need for the abbot to entice prospective domestic authors with promises of material or immaterial rewards, but also, and importantly, the monks' ability to refuse their abbot's commission.[44] In theory as well as in practice, abbatial patronage inside the monastery was governed not by the transactional laws of supply and demand, but by the fundamental and unnegotiable monastic principles of authority and obedience—authority that, whilst delegated and devolved, ultimately resided with the monastic superior alone, and obedience that was owed to him/her.[45] Whether medieval monks and nuns tasked with writing projects by their institutional superiors always delivered 'what [was] ordered without fear, delay, reluctance, grumbling, or refusal' ('quod iubetur non trepide, non tarde, non tepide aut cum murmurio vel cum responso nolentis efficiatur') is a different question entirely, of course.[46] Indeed, we will see examples of domestic historians showing remarkable ingenuity by interpreting their assignments creatively in their attempts to exercise some authorial autonomy without openly disobeying their commissioning abbot or abbess.

In principle, however, acceptance of an abbot's writing orders was a *fait accompli*, as is exemplified by the case of Caesarius of Heisterbach (†after 1240). A monk and prior of Heisterbach, Caesarius was a prolific author whose oeuvre includes an account of the life and violent death of Archbishop Engelbert of Cologne (1216-25), a continuation of the *Catalogus archiepiscoporum Coloniensium* for the years 1167-1238, a saintly biography of Elisabeth of Hungary (†1231) along with a sermon about the translation of her relics, and, his most famous work written c.1219-23, a compilation of miracles inspired by historical events known as the *Dialogus miraculorum*. In the prologue, Caesarius recalls that in his previous role as the monastery's novice master, he had been asked by many and with great resolve ('rogatus sum a quibusdam multis cum instancia multa') to put these

---

[43] *RB*, ed./tr. Venarde, pp. 20-7, 38-41, and 122-3. For discussion, cf. Adalbert de Vogüé, *Community and Abbot in the Rule of Saint Benedict* (Kalamazoo, MI: Cistercian Publications, 1979); Giles Constable, 'The Authority of Superiors in Religious Communities', in *La notion d'autorité au Moyen Âge: Islam, Byzance, Occident*, ed. by George Makdisi et al. (Paris: Presses universitaires de France, 1982), pp. 189-210, repr. in *Monks, Hermits and Crusaders in Medieval Europe*, ed. by Giles Constable (London: Variorum, 1988), no. III (pp. 189-210); Rembert Weakland, 'Obedience to the Abbot and the Community in the Monastery', *Cistercian Studies* 5 (1970), 309-16.

[44] *RB*, ed./tr. Venarde, pp. 160-3 and 186-91; M. Xavier McMonagle, 'Service of Authority: The Abbot in the Rule of Benedict', *Cistercian Studies* 17 (1982), 316-37.

[45] Elizabeth A. Lehfeldt, 'Authority and Agency: Women as Heads of Religious Houses', in *Medieval Women Religious, c.800-c.1500: New Perspectives*, ed. by Kimm Curran and Janet Burton (Woodbridge: Boydell, 2023), pp. 105-20 (pp. 105-15).

[46] *RB*, ed./tr. Venarde, pp. 40-1.

miraculous deeds ('miraculose gesta') to writing ('scripto perpetuare') for the instruction of posterity, lest they be consigned to oblivion ('[d]icebant enim irrecuperabile fore damnum, si ea perirent per oblivionem').[47] Conscious of his insufficient Latin and fearful of his fellow monks' envy—humility *topoi* found regularly in the prologues of medieval monastic historians—Caesarius turned down these requests for many years, but in the end was compelled by the command of his own abbot ('abbatis mei imperium') and the counsel of the abbot of Marienstatt ('et abbatis loci sanctae Mariae consilium'), two powerful patrons whose abbatial authority it was unlawful to disobey or contradict ('quibus contradicere licitum non est').[48]

The abbot's control over the spiritual and manual labour of those living under his care had important implications for monastic historiographical production and patronage. The *Rule of St Benedict* cautions abbots that 'there will have to be a trial in God's fearsome court', and that 'whatever use the father of the household finds lacking in the sheep will be blamed on the shepherd'.[49] This sense of accountability is present throughout the *Rule*, for example, in its stipulation that all tools should be issued by the abbot himself or at his behest, and that nothing may be distributed without the abbot's orders ('ne quis praesumat aliquid dare aut accipere sine iussionem abbatis'), 'no book, no wax tablets, no stylus, nothing whatsoever' ('neque codicem, neque tabulas, neque graphium, sed nihil omnino').[50] Economic considerations and safe-keeping apart, the reason for assigning the tools' custody to the head of the monastery was that he/she assumed ultimate responsibility for whatever was produced with them. Applied to the writing of history, this meant that monastic superiors were responsible for whatever was written by the members of their communities and could be held accountable for it in both this world and the next, making them *de facto* patrons not just of the histories they commissioned personally, but also of those whose patronage they assumed *ex officio*. Taking this notion of abbatial authority and accountability to its logical conclusion, no historical writing could take place officially in a

---

[47] *Caesarii Heisterbacensis monachi ordinis Cisterciensis Dialogus miraculorum*, ed. by Joseph Strange, 3 vols. (Cologne: Heberle, 1851–7), I, 1; translated as *Caesarius of Heisterbach: The Dialogue on Miracles*, tr. by Henry von Essen Scott and Charles C. Swinton Bland, 2 vols. (London: Routledge, 1929), I, 1. On the *Dialogus* as history, see Stefano Mula, 'Exempla and Historiography: Alberic of Trois-Fontaines's Reading of Caesarius's *Dialogus miraculorum*', in *The Art of Cistercian Persuasion in the Middle Ages and Beyond: Caesarius of Heisterbach's 'Dialogue on Miracles' and its Reception*, ed. by Victoria Smirnova et al. (Leiden: Brill, 2015), pp. 143–61.

[48] *Dialogus*, ed. Strange, I, 1–2; tr. von Essen Scott and Swinton Bland, I, 1.

[49] *RB*, ed./tr. Venarde, pp. 20–1: 'Memor semper abbas, quia doctrinae suae vel discipulorum oboedientiae utrarumque rerum in tremendo iudicio Dei facienda erit discussio. Sciatque abbas culpae pastoris incumbere, quidquid in obibus pater familias utilitatis minus potuerit inuenire'.

[50] *RB*, ed./tr. Venarde, pp. 120–1 and 122–3; also: 'Omnia vero necessaria a patre sperare monasterii, nec quicquam liceat habere quod abbas non dederit aut permiserit' (ibid.); for discussion, see below (3.1).

monastery without the principal endorsement—or at the very least the tacit approval—of its superior.[51]

It is impossible to imagine how many of the best-known and most-cited examples of medieval monastic historiography could realistically have been produced without the authorization of an abbot or abbess. And yet, this particular aspect of their production is rarely discussed in scholarship, which more often than not focuses on the authors and/or readers of these histories. A useful case in point is the colossal *Historia ecclesiastica* written over nearly three decades (*c.*1114–41) by Orderic Vitalis, the English-born chronicler of Saint-Évroult.[52] An important source for the history of eleventh- and twelfth-century Europe and a familiar staple with students and researchers, Orderic's work has traditionally been viewed as the product of one man's initiative and dedication to historical study, but little attention has been paid to the role of his abbatial patron(s).[53] Surely, though, the fact that in the *Historia*'s prologue Orderic refers to himself twice as having begun the project at the order of Abbot Roger (1091–1122) ('iubente Rogerio abbate'; 'hoc opus incepi venerandi senis Rogerii abbatis simplici precepto') is significant, as is the fact that after Roger's death Orderic then presented the text to his abbatial successor, Warin (1123–37) ('tibique pater Guarine, qui secundum ecclesie ritum ei legitime succedis, exhibeo').[54] What is more, Orderic even tells us what kind of history his abbot had requested of him. A far cry from the ambitious ecclesiastical history Orderic ended up writing, Roger's original commission had merely been for a (re-)foundation history of Saint-Évroult's monastery ('relatio de restauratione Uticensis coenobii').[55] Different motivations have been suggested for this, from Roger's veneration for his predecessors to an impending visit by King Henry I that created 'an urgent practical need to look into the charters and records of earlier gifts, and ascertain the history of properties that [...] had been temporarily lost to the house', and even 'a fatherly wish to enable one of his monks to make full use of his talents', a suggestion which, however, seems to owe more to wishful thinking than it does to concrete evidence.[56]

---

[51] As observed by A. Ian Doyle, 'Publication by Members of the Religious Orders', in *Book Production and Publishing in Britain, 1375-1475*, ed. by Jeremy Griffiths and Derek Pearsall (Cambridge: Cambridge University Press, 2007), pp. 109–23 (p. 110), within a monastic community 'writing for any purpose in principle required the command or permission of the religious superior', and the writing of history was no exception.

[52] According to the composition timeline in *Orderic Vitalis: Life, Works and Interpretations*, ed. by Charles C. Rozier et al. (Woodbridge: Boydell, 2016), p. xiv.

[53] Mention of Orderic's abbots has mostly been made in passing; cf. Hans Wolter, *Ordericus Vitalis: Ein Beitrag zur kluniazensischen Geschichtsschreibung* (Wiesbaden: Steiner, 1955), pp. 106–8; Gransden, 'Prologues', pp. 131–2; Marjorie Chibnall, *The World of Orderic Vitalis: Norman Monks and Norman Knights* (Woodbridge: Boydell, 2001), p. 40.

[54] *HE*, ed./tr. Chibnall, I, 130–1 and 132–3. On Abbots Roger and Warin of Saint-Évroult, see Gazeau, *Normannia monastica*, II, 281–5.

[55] *HE*, ed./tr. Chibnall, I, 130–1.   [56] *HE*, ed./tr. Chibnall, I, 31–2.

The historiographical patronage of abbots and abbesses did not have to be driven by such pragmatic, utilitarian, or philanthropic stimuli. Especially in the case of house chronicles and *historiae fundationum*, it could—and often did—reflect an intrinsic need to furnish one's community with an account of its history to serve as an anchor for collective memories and identities. If this was what Roger had in mind when appointing Orderic, he would have died believing his wish had been honoured. The earliest parts of the *Historia ecclesiastica* completed before Roger's death—those which eventually would become Book III (I)—fit the bill perfectly by treating, as per the abbot's instructions, the community's eleventh-century re-foundation and the events up to 1066.[57] Even the subsequent sections written in the later 1120s/early 1130s—Books IV (II), V (III), and VI (IV)—could just about be argued to meet this remit due to their focus on Saint-Évroult's benefactors. The material appended during the years 1130 × 33–41, by contrast, expanded the narrative to such an extent that the monastic community was gradually pushed into the background as different protagonists took centre-stage.[58] Though Roger did not live to witness this change of plan, it is implausible that Orderic could have got away with it without securing the permission of his new abbatial patrons, Warin, Richard (1137–40), and Ranulf (1140–before 1159).[59] After all, the project spanned nearly thirty years and would have consumed vast amounts of time and resources in the process. Any notion that Orderic acted autonomously, and that 'once Abbot Warin had given Orderic his head there was no holding him',[60] is at odds with the fact that as a life-long monk who from the age of ten (the age of his profession) was no longer master of his time and activities, Orderic's ability to write history depended fundamentally on the continuous support of his monastic community and—first and foremost—his abbots.[61]

---

[57] The timeline provided in *Orderic*, ed. Rozier at al., p. xiv dates the writing of Book III (I) to 1114–23/24, and that of Books IV (II), V (III), and VI (IV) to *c.*1125, *c.*1127, and *c.*1130–3 × 37, respectively; also cf. Chibnall, *World*, p. 37. Having suffered from ill health ('abbas aevo et aegritudine fractus'), Roger died in January 1126 after three years in retirement; *HE*, ed./tr. Chibnall, VI, 320–1 and 326–7.

[58] Amanda J. Hingst, *The Written World: Past and Place in the Work of Orderic Vitalis* (Notre Dame, IN: University of Notre Dame Press, 2009), pp. 70–91; Daniel Roach, 'Orderic Vitalis and the First Crusade', *Journal of Medieval History* 42 (2016), 177–201; Elisabeth Mégier, 'Jesus Christ, a Protagonist of Anglo-Norman History? History and Theology in Orderic Vitalis's *Historia ecclesiastica*', in *Orderic Vitalis: Life, Works and Interpretations*, ed. by Charles C. Rozier et al. (Woodbridge: Boydell, 2016), pp. 260–83. In its final form, Orderic's *Historia ecclesiastica* thus came to resemble a history of the Latin Church that encompassed not just Normandy and England, but also France, Southern Italy, and even the Holy Land.

[59] The sections of the *Historia* that Orderic wrote under Abbots Richard and Ranulf certainly include Books II, XII, XIII, and the Epilogue, as well as, possibly, sections of Books I and IX; *Orderic*, ed. Rozier at al., p. xiv; *HE*, ed./tr. Chibnall, I, 45–8.

[60] Chibnall, *World of Orderic*, p. 40.

[61] *HE*, ed./tr. Chibnall, III, 6–7: '[E]go de extremis Merciorum finibus decennis Angligena huc [Saint-Évroult] advectus'. Such notions of authorial autonomy form a paradox not just in the context of monastic historical writing, but also, as shown by Anne Leader, with regard to monastic artistic production; Anne Leader, *The Badia of Florence: Art and Observance in a Renaissance Monastery* (Bloomington, IN: Indiana University Press, 2012), pp. 55–97.

There are few sources that express this dependency better and more succinctly than Adam of Dryburgh's *Liber de quadripartito exercitio cellae* from the final quarter of the twelfth century. Adam was a Premonstratensian abbot (1184-8) who for several years had served as acting superior during the long incapacitation of his predecessor, Gerard (1177-84), before succeeding him officially in 1184. He left the community in 1188 and some years later joined, by special dispensation from his diocesan bishop, the Carthusian monastery of Witham where he remained for the rest of his life.[62] Produced *c*.1186/7 × before 1200—that is, either during Adam's comparatively short-lived abbacy at Dryburgh or, perhaps more plausibly, at Witham—*De quadripartito* calls upon religious men ('viri religiosi') who are literate ('qui [...] litterati sunt') and of able body and mind ('prout eis posse corporalis sanitas administrat') to participate in monastic book production ('libris utique vel praeparandis vel conficiendis vel ligandis vel emendandis vel ornandis vel illuminandis vel intitulandis vel iis quae ad ista pertinent ordinandis, faciendis et perficiendis sollicite intendere debent').[63] They must not do so of their own volition, however, but through the discretion and authority of their superiors ('non quidem prout eorum voluntas elegerit, magis autem sicut praesidentis auctoritas discreta et discretione authentica dictaverit').[64] The abbot's authorization is presented as obligatory for the production of books, and without it no book of any kind—including history books—must be prepared, completed, or even planned. Farfa's *Liber tramitis* written during the tenure, and possibly at the command, of Abbot Odilo of Cluny (994-1049) stipulates that monks writing by permission of their abbot ('per licentiam domni abbatis') may be excused from some liturgical duties, but *only* on the abbot's personal orders ('ipso iubente') and by his mandate ('domnus abbas praecipiet vel [...] mandaverit').[65] Similar regulations occur elsewhere, for example, in the later eleventh-century *Constitutiones Hirsaugienses*.[66] In the daily life of a monastery, the writing of history was an

---

[62] On Adam's career, cf. Peter Damian-Grint, 'Adam of Dryburgh', in *The History of Scottish Theology*, ed. by David Fergusson and Mark W. Elliott, 3 vols. (Oxford: Oxford University Press, 2019), I, 39-53; Christopher Holdsworth, 'Dryburgh, Adam of (*c*.1140-1212?)', *Oxford Dictionary of National Biography* (Oxford: Oxford University Press, 2004), https://doi.org/10.1093/ref:odnb/97.

[63] 'Liber de quadripartito exercitio cellae', in *Patrologia Latina*, ed. by Jean-Paul Migne, 221 vols. (Paris: Garnier, 1841-55), CLIII, 787-884 (p. 881) (= 'De opere manuum...').

[64] 'De quadripartito exercitio', ed. Migne, p. 881.

[65] Edited in *Liber tramitis aevi Odilonis abbatis*, ed. by Petrus Dinter (Siegburg: Schmitt, 1980), pp. 219 and 227. With the abbot's permission, monk-scribes were allowed to miss the morning and/or principal Mass ('missam matutinalem et principalem') if required, as well as the 'psalmi familiares', but not the litany, offerings, and the vigil for the dead ('non sunt illi dimittenda: laetania, offerenda et vigilia mortuorum') (ibid., p. 219). The hours of rest at midday ('meridianum') could also be foregone with the abbot's dispensation (ibid., p. 227). The abbot could also grant such exemptions when time was of the essence, for example, because he had borrowed the exemplar(s) from another monastery for a limited period ('[s]i domnus abbas aliquem librum de alio monasterio adquisierit et praefinito debet tempore reddere') (ibid.).

[66] 'S[ancti] Wilhelmi Constitutiones Hirsaugienses', in *Patrologia Latina*, ed. by Jean-Paul Migne, 221 vols. (Paris: Garnier, 1841-55), CL, 923-1146 (p. 1078). A more recent edition with facsimile is *Willehelmi Abbatis Constitutiones Hirsaugienses*, ed. by Pius Engelbert and Candida Elvert, 2 vols. (Siegburg: Schmitt, 2010), I, 68.

'activité secondaire',⁶⁷ one that was subordinate to an author's communal duties, and which was thus subject to special dispensation from the head of the community. Without its own designated timeslot in the closely circumscribed routine of *ora et labora* ('pray and work'), monastic historiographical production was an extraordinary event for which precious time needed to be carved out from amongst the monks' regular tasks, and any such redistribution and re-allocation of human and material resources required the abbot's approval. Without abbatial authorization, monastic historical writing—or any kind of writing—was thus a non-starter.

One writer who experienced this first-hand was the early medieval monk-historian Paul the Deacon, author of the *Historia Romana*, the *gesta* of the bishops of Metz, and, his best-known work, the *Historia Langobardorum*.⁶⁸ When after a long and prosperous career at court Paul professed himself as a monk at Montecassino, he soon found himself caught between the contesting authorities of two abbots. One was Adalard, the recently appointed abbot of Corbie (781–814 and 821–6) and later Corvey (822–6), who shortly after Paul's entry into the monastery asked him for a copy of his—or rather, his monastery's—collection of the letters of Gregory the Great. It was not until 782 × 86 that Paul complied with the request and sent the desired manuscript to Corbie accompanied by an apologetic letter in which he explains his sluggishness to Adalard. The problem, we are told, was less that Paul had been chained to his sickbed from September to just before Christmas ('a mense Septembrio pene usque ad diem nativitatis Domini lectulo detentus sim') than that no copyists had been made available to him ('desunt librarii') to expedite the work. Adding insult to injury, Paul's usual assistant had been forbidden from handling the inkwell ('nec licuerit clericulo illi [...] manum ad atramentarium mittere'), meaning that the labour fell to Paul himself.⁶⁹ Though Paul does not name and shame the person who had denied him copyists and supplies, it can only have been Montecassino's then abbot, Theodemar (777/8–96).⁷⁰ If Theodemar had indeed refused to endorse the project

---

⁶⁷ Guenée, *Histoire*, pp. 44–5. Also cf. Lars B. Mortensen, 'The Glorious Past: Entertainment, Example or History? Levels of Twelfth-Century Historical Culture', *Culture and History* 13 (1994), 57–71 (p. 66), observing that for most of the Middle Ages 'the study of the past was never a field in itself, with its own programme and curriculum'.

⁶⁸ On Paul the Deacon's career and his historiographical works, see Christopher Heath, *The Narrative Worlds of Paul the Deacon: Between Empires and Identities in Lombard Italy* (Amsterdam: Amsterdam University Press, 2017). On Paul's liturgical/theological work, see Zachary Guiliano, *The Homiliary of Paul the Deacon: Religious and Cultural Reform in Carolingian Europe* (Turnhout: Brepols, 2021).

⁶⁹ 'Paulus Adalhardo abbati Corbeiensi sanitate vix recuperata epistolas Gregorii papae a se ex parte emendatas mittit', in *Epistolae Karolini aevi II*, ed. by Ernst Dümmler [= *MGH Epp.* IV] (Berlin: Weidmann, 1895), pp. 508–9 (p. 509) (= no. 12).

⁷⁰ On Theodemar and his role in Montecassino's literary culture, cf. Sven Meeder, 'Monte Cassino's Network of Knowledge: The Earliest Manuscript Evidence', in *Writing the Early Medieval West: Studies in Honour of Rosamond McKitterick*, ed. by Elina Scree and Charles West (Cambridge: Cambridge University Press, 2018), pp. 131–45.

and perhaps prohibited it altogether, this might explain why Paul explicitly urges Adalard not to disseminate the book further ('sanctitati tuae suadeo, ne passim [...] puplicentur').[71] Perhaps the actual reason behind this request was not that certain passages might have caused confusion amongst less experienced readers ('propter aliqua, quae in eis minus idoneos latere magis quam scire convenit'), but rather the risk to Paul himself were the 'forbidden manuscript' produced without his abbot's permission—or even against Theodemar's orders— to enter into circulation beyond Corbie, alerting Theodemar to Paul's act of disobedience?[72]

Paul was not the only monastic author to have had his ability to write constrained by an unsupportive superior; some were even left incapable of writing altogether, at least temporarily. This was the case at Fulda, where Rabanus Maurus was prevented from writing by his abbot, Ratger (802–17), whom he should eventually succeed following the abbacy of Eigil (818–22). Rabanus laments this inhibition in a short poem addressed to Ratger ('ad Ratgerium abbatem suum'), in which he describes how the abbot had taken away his notebooks ('glosae parvique libelli') and even the parchment sheets ('foliis') he used for transcribing.[73] Of interest here are less the reasons behind this confiscation of writing materials, which remain undisclosed, than what Rabanus has to say about their provision in the first place. In his own words, they had been granted to him by the abbot's benevolence ('mihi concessit bonitas tua discere libros'). Just as servants rely on their masters for the provision of everything they have ('Servi quicquid habent, dominorum iure tenetur'), so monks rely on their abbots.[74] When towards the end of the poem Rabanus begs Ratger to return the writings he had taken and withheld from him by his abbatial right ('Sic ego quae scripsi, omnia iure tenes'), he does not act with insolence as if to demand his property ('Nec mihi ceu propria petulans haec vindico scripta'), but meekly defers to the abbot's ruling ('Desero sed vestro omnia iudicio') to decide whether they are returned to him or not ('Seu mihi haec tribuas, si non').[75] Given his appointment as a *magister* of Fulda's

---

[71] 'Epistolas', ed. Dümmler, p. 509.

[72] On the personal libraries of abbots and abbesses, including those of Corbie and Corvey, see below (4.3).

[73] 'Hrabani Mauri Carmina', in *Poetae Latini aevi Carolini (II)*, ed. by Ernst Dümmler [= MGH Poetae III] (Berlin: Weidmann, 1884), pp. 154–258 (pp. 185–6) (= no. XX); discussed and translated in Marc-Aeilko Aris, 'Hrabanus Maurus und die Bibliotheca Fuldensis', in *Hrabanus Maurus: Gelehrter, Abt von Fulda und Erzbischof von Mainz*, ed. by Franz J. Felten and Karl Lehmann (Mainz: Bistum Mainz, 2006), pp. 51–70 (pp. 57–9). Also cf. Sita Steckel, *Kulturen des Lehrens im Früh- und Hochmittelalter: Autorität, Wissenskonzepte und Netzwerke von Gelehrten* (Cologne: Böhlau, 2011), p. 386; Lutz E. V. Padberg and Thomas Klein, 'Hrabanus Maurus', in *Reallexikon der Germanischen Altertumskunde*, ed. by Heinrich Beck et al., 35 vols., 2nd ed. (Berlin: De Gryter, 1972–2008), XV, 139–46, who interpret Ratger's confiscation of Rabanus's books as a disciplinary measure ('aus disziplinären Gründen'; ibid., p. 140). James W. Thompson, *The Medieval Library* (New York, NY: Hafner, 1923), p. 68, goes further by suggesting that Ratger 'refused to let the monks have any time for writing'.

[74] 'Carmina', ed. Dümmler, p. 186.   [75] Ibid., p. 186.

monastic school and his personal contacts to Alcuin and Charlemagne's court, Rabanus presumably could have tried to resource notebooks and writing materials via alternative supply channels. That he seems not to have done so, instead pleading obsequiously with Ratger despite their increasingly acrimonious relationship, strongly suggests that Rabanus, like Paul the Deacon before him, was all too aware of the consequences of circumventing his abbot's authority by writing against his orders.

Further evidence that abbatial authorization was a *conditio sine qua non* for monastic historiographical activity—and that acting without it constituted a punishable offence—can be found in various regulations that instruct monastic superiors to reprimand, and even severely penalize, their monks and nuns for writing without a mandate or straying too far from their assignments. Instructive examples include the customary of Westminster Abbey compiled in the third quarter of the thirteenth century by Abbot Richard de Ware (1258–83) (London, British Library, MS Cotton Otho C. XI). Following the fundamental stipulation that nothing shall be written in the cloister unless it is beneficial to the community and the spiritual welfare of its members ('ne aliquid videlicet scribant nisi ad utilitatem ecclesiae et suarum profectum animarum'), the customary instructs the claustral prior ('prior claustri') and his invigilators ('claustri exploratores') to have an eye on the scribes at all times lest they keep their writings a secret from their superiors ('nec debet quisquam eorum aliquo modo, quod absit, ab ordinis custodibus celare quod scribit').[76] If any do so, they need to be punished severely ('si fecerint, acriter inde puniri debent') after being chastized in front of the entire chapter ('debet coram omnibus in capitulo acriter inde redargui'), and the forbidden fruit of their unauthorized labour should be taken away from them ('et quicquid scripserit a sua custodia funditus ammoveri').[77] Adding what may be considered a mechanism of collective enforcement and communal self-policing reminiscent of Foucault's principle of panopticism, the Westminster customary decrees that even those writing with the superior's knowledge and permission should do so, whenever possible, at times when the entire convent is physically present in the cloister, and only in exceptional circumstances—namely when writing a charter or document at the abbot's orders ('cartam aut aliquid huiuscemodi scriptum iussu superioris')—may they use the hours usually spent in the church, chapter, dormitory, or refectory.[78] Just as in the *Liber tramitis* and the *Constitutiones Hirsaugienses*, it is only with the superior's special dispensation—but *never* without it—that the monks are permitted to take time out of their regular day- and night-time routine in order to write.

---

[76] *Customary of the Benedictine Monasteries of Saint Augustine, Canterbury, and Saint Peter, Westminster*, ed. by Edward M. Thompson, 2 vols. (London: Henry Bradshaw Society, 1902–4), II, 161–2.

[77] *Customary*, ed. Thompson, II, 161.   [78] *Customary*, ed. Thompson, II, 162.

Stricter in tone than the *Consuetudines* of Westminster and harsher in the punishments they prescribe are the *Institutiones beati Gilberti et successorum eius*, a catalogue of statutes for the Order of Sempringham (also known as the Gilbertines) influenced strongly by Cistercian thought that survives in Oxford, Bodleian Library, MS Douce 136. Nestled under the stipulations concerning canons, novices, and lay brothers ('Capitula de canonicis et novicis [...] et laicis canonicis'), we find specific guidance for the punishment of scribes who write secretly ('De scriptoribus et poena occulte scribentium'): if anyone were to write something and show it to another to keep it hidden from their superior and other obedientiaries, they (both?) should do penance during chapter and eat by themselves for the next seven days; they should be given no more than a single meal per day, and bread and water on Fridays; and if they hold a rank of any kind within the community, they should be suspended from it for half a year.[79] Nobody within the community, the text continues, should take it upon themselves to write or commission books of any kind—including history books—without the superior's permission ('Nullus de nostris praesumat libros aliquos [...] scribere vel scribi facere sine assensu prioris domus'), nor should they hire and install scribes in the nuns' churches ('vel scriptores conducere et retinere in ecclesiis monialium').[80] Doing either will trigger a review and possible revocation of whatever rank or authority (if any) the offender holds ('Quod si aliquis contra hoc facere praesumpserit, ordinis vel potestatis suae, si officialis fuerit, periculo subiaceat'), and because of the severity of their disobedience they are to be subjected to corporal punishment by whipping ('et flagello gravioris culpae reatum luat'). Meanwhile, the superior will confiscate what was written without permission and re-distribute it for communal usage ('quod scriptum est ad voluntatem prioris domus in communes usus domus cedat').[81] Designed for communities of religious men and women living together under a single roof—with the nuns following the *Rule of St Benedict* and the male canons the *Rule of St Augustine*[82]—the

---

[79] The *Institutiones beati Gileberti* are edited in *Monasticon Anglicanum: A History of the Abbies and other Monasteries, Hospitals, Frieries, and Cathedral and Collegiate Churches, with their Dependencies, in England and Wales*, ed. by William Dugdale et al., 6 vols., new ed. (London: Longman, 1846-56), VI.2, *xix-*lviii (p. *xxxi) [hereafter *Institutiones*]: 'Si quis scripserit et alteri occulte demonstraverit, quod priori et caeteris maioribus celari voluerit, in capitulo culpam luat, et diebus septem in area refectorii comedat, uno contentus pulmento, et vi. feria in pane et aqua, et de ordine suo degradetur dimidii anni spacio, vel regulari disciplinae subiaceat'. On the *Institutiones*, their dating, and the historical context, cf. Katharine Sykes, *Inventing Sempringham: Gilbert of Sempringham and the Origins of the Role of the Master* (Zurich: LIT, 2011), pp. 22-3; more recently Nick Johnston, 'Vexatio Falsorum Fratrum: The Medieval Laybrother in the Order of Sempringham in Context' (unpublished PhD dissertation, University of Toronto, 2017), pp. 48-51, who advocates a later date.
[80] *Institutiones*, ed. Dugdale et al., p. *xxxi.   [81] Ibid., p. *xxxi.
[82] David Knowles, *The Monastic Order in England: A History of its Development from the Times of St Dunstan to the Fourth Lateran Council, 940-1216*, 2nd ed. (Cambridge: Cambridge University Press, 1966), pp. 205-7; Brian Golding, *Gilbert of Sempringham and the Gilbertine Order, 1130-1300* (Oxford: Clarendon, 1995).

Institutiones are an important reminder that historical writing was no male prerogative.[83] Most of its stipulations apply equally to both sexes or have equivalents aimed specifically at women, who, just like their male counterparts, faced removal from office and corporal punishment as a result of secretive and unauthorized writing.[84]

With the formation of the Benedictine Order and the advent of the 'new orders' in the high and later Middle Ages,[85] certain aspects of abbatial patronage were codified in monastic legislation, and in some cases the ultimate authority was transferred from individual heads of houses to overarching governing bodies such as the Provincial and General Chapters. The statutes of the General Chapter of the Benedictine province of Canterbury issued on 17 September 1277 and preserved today in a composite manuscript from St Mary's Abbey in York (Oxford, Bodleian Library, MS Bodley 39, fols. 52v-67r) state that without the abbot's dispensation, nobody in a monastery may write or illuminate a book of whatever format, nor task another person to do so ('[s]ine prelati sui licencia nullus librum magnum vel parvum scribat vel illuminet, vel scribi vel illuminari faciat').[86] In fact, it might not be coincidence that the monastic annals for the years 1258-1326 copied in the same codex (fols. 116r-215v) feature pen portraits of three abbots holding books: founding abbot Stephen of Whitby (c.1080-1112; fol. 117r), John de Gilling (1303-13; fol. 169r), and Alan de Nesse (1313-31; fol. 191v), the annals' patron and commissioning authority (Fig. 2.2).[87] The Cistercian General Chapter of 1134 introduced a remarkably similar kind of control mechanism that extended to the abbot's own literary activity by decreeing that no abbot, monk, or novice must write books without consent from the General Chapter ('[n]ulli liceat abbati, nec monacho, nec novitio libros facere, nisi forte cuiquam (id) in generali (abbatum) capitulo concessum fuerit'), a regulation that was reinforced first in

---

[83] Cf. Beach, *Women*, passim.

[84] The prohibitions for male canons, novices, and lay brothers are repeated word-for-word, with grammatical adjustments to reflect the female equivalents of monastic offices and titles, in the regulations for the chantress and her assistants ('De praecentrice et eius solatia [...] et libris sine licentia omnino non scribendis vel habendis'); *Institutiones*, ed. Dugdale et al., p. *l.

[85] James G. Clark, *The Benedictines in the Middle Ages* (Woodbridge: Boydell, 2011), pp. 50-8; Gert Melville, 'The Institutionalization of Religious Orders (Twelfth and Thirteenth Centuries)', in *The Cambridge History of Medieval Monasticism in the Latin West*, ed. by Alison I. Beach and Isabelle Cochelin, 2 vols. (Cambridge: Cambridge University Press, 2020), II, 783-802.

[86] Oxford, Bodleian Library, MS Bodley 39, fol. 58v; edited in *Documents Illustrating the Activities of the General and Provincial Chapters of the English Black Monks, 1215-1540*, ed. by William A. Pantin, 3 vols. (London: Royal Historical Society, 1931-7), I, 64-92 (p. 74) (= no. 28); *Illuminated Manuscripts in the Bodleian Library Oxford*, ed. by Otto Pächt and J. J. G. Alexander, 3 vols. (Oxford: Oxford University Press, 1966-73), II, 102-3 (= no. 1892).

[87] The monastic annals of St Mary are edited in *The Chronicle of St. Mary's Abbey, York, from Bodley MS. 39*, ed. by Herbert H. E. Craster and Mary E. Thornton (Durham, Andrews & Co., 1934). On the significance of books in illustrated abbatial portraits, see below (3.3).

Fig. 2.2 Alan de Nesse holding a book. Oxford, Bodleian Library, MS Bodley 39, fol. 169r.

the Cistercian Statutes of 1147, and then again in those of 1202.[88] Similar regulations were also introduced by the Dominicans and Franciscans.[89]

Just how effective were these regulations, though, and to what extent do they reflect actual practice? For a long time, monastic rules, customaries, statutes, etc. were used in a positivist manner and viewed optimistically as reflections of a *status quo*, with scholars treating them as *de*scriptive rather than *pre*scriptive accounts. As more recent scholarship has emphasized, however, they are better (and probably best) understood as inspirational—and, I would argue, aspirational—sources.[90] Succinctly put, '[n]orms never *depict* life'.[91] Their value to the historian lies less in their ability to satisfy Rankean notions of 'how it really was' than in what they can teach us about how things were *expected* to be. What they embody, therefore, are not fossilized realities, but dynamic processes shaped by negotiation and adjustment, and, as we will see now, by resistance and reinforcement.

2.3 Resistance and Reinforcement

The prospect of castigation and punishment sometimes did not prevent monastic authors from writing without their superiors' permission, and some went to remarkable lengths to keep their historiographical activity a secret. A good example is that of Eadmer, monk-historian of Christ Church, Canterbury, and author of the *Historia novorum in Anglia* and the *Vita Anselmi*—two works that had begun life as a single historiographical project. Eadmer was his community's foremost historian, though for the best part of his writing career he lacked a

---

[88] *Statuta Capitulorum Generalium ordinis Cisterciensis ab anno 1116 ad annum 1786*, ed. by Joseph-Marie Canivez, 8 vols. (Louvain: Bureaux de la Revue, 1933–41), I, 26; *Narrative and Legislative Texts from Early Citeaux*, ed. by Chrysogonus Waddell (Citeaux: Comentarii cistercienses, 1999), p. 351; *Libellus definitionum: La Codification Cistercienne de 1202 et son évolution ultérierure*, ed. by Bernard Lucet, (Rome: Editiones Cistercienses, 1964), p. 171.

[89] Klaus Schreiner, 'Verschriftlichung als Faktor monastischer Reform: Funktionen von Schriftlichkeit im Ordenswesen des hohen und späten Mittelalters', in *Pragmatische Schriftlichkeit im Mittelalter: Erscheinungsformen und Entwicklungsstufen*, ed. by Hagen Keller et al. (Munich: Funk, 1992), p. 37–75 (pp. 70–1).

[90] See Isabelle Cochelin, 'Customaries as Inspirational Sources', in *Consuetudines et Regulae: Sources for Monastic Life in the Middle Ages and the Early Modern Period*, ed. by Carolyn Marino Malone and Clark Maines (Turnhout: Brepols, 2014), pp. 27–72; Krijn Pansters, 'Medieval Rules and Customaries Reconsidered', in *A Companion to Medieval Rules and Customaries*, ed. by Krijn Pansters (Leiden: Brill, 2020), pp. 1–36.

[91] Albrecht Diem and Philip Rousseau, 'Monastic Rules (Fourth to Ninth Century)', in *The Cambridge History of Medieval Monasticism in the Latin West*, ed. by Alison I. Beach and Isabelle Cochelin, 2 vols. (Cambridge: Cambridge University Press, 2020), I, 162–94 (p. 191); the authors further observe that 'any attempt to reconstruct monastic practice on the basis of rules fails for two obvious reasons: we do not know to what extent a regulation, particularly a disciplinary measure, indicates a problem or points to a solution. Moreover, aside from incidentally providing elements of stage décor, monastic rules (and narratives similarly) leave out the consensual, everything that does not need to be regulated' (ibid., pp. 190–1).

formal patron and instead operated in the capacity of a 'self-publisher'.[92] His natural patrons would have been the community's superiors, first Anselm, who after a monastic career as prior (1063–78) and then abbot (1078–93) of Le Bec was made archbishop of Canterbury (1093–1109),[93] and then his successor, Ralph d'Escures (1114–22). Anselm initially appears to have been supportive of Eadmer's historiographical project, even correcting his work early on, but he subsequently withdrew his support and ordered the destruction of all existing drafts, an invasive use of the superior's authority that was usually reserved for the most controversial and scandalous cases.[94] Eadmer recalls this change of fortunes in the *Vita Anselmi*.[95] He reportedly had tried, to his superior's disapproval, to make a secret of the project from the beginning, but 'when I [Eadmer] had shown my desire to conceal the subject by silence rather than disclose it, he [Anselm] ordered me either to desist from what I had begun [...] or show him what I was writing' ('Cui cum rem magis silentio tegere quam detegere maluissem; praecepit quatinus aut coepto desistens aliis intenderem, aut quae scribebam sibi ostenderem').[96] When Anselm then commanded him 'to destroy entirely the quires in which I had gathered the work' ('praecepit, quatinus quaterniones in quibus ipsum opus congesseram penitus destruerem'), Eadmer found himself torn between his authorial pride and the obedience he owed to his monastic superior: 'I dared not entirely disobey his command, and yet I was not willing to lose altogether a work which I had put together with much labour' ('Non audens tamen ipsi precepto funditus inobediens esse, nec opus quod multo labore compegeram volens omnino perditum ire').[97] To escape this predicament, he decided to deceive Anselm by destroying the quires as instructed—thus ostensibly implementing the superior's orders—but only *after* he had secretly made copies that, as

---

[92] Benjamin Pohl and Leah Tether, 'Eadmer and His Books: A Case Study of Monastic Self-Publishing', in *Eadmer of Canterbury: Companion, Historian, Theologian*, ed. by Charles C. Rozier et al. (Leiden: Brill, 2022), in press; see also Richard Sharpe, 'Anselm as Author: Publishing in the Late Eleventh Century', *Journal of Medieval Latin* 19 (2009), 1–87.

[93] For summaries of Anselm's career, see *Letters of Anselm, Archbishop of Canterbury*, Vol. 1: *The Bec Letters*, ed./tr. by Samu Niskanen (Oxford: Clarendon, 2019), pp. xxv–lv; Richard W. Southern, *Saint Anselm and His Biographer: A Study of Monastic Life and Thought, 1059–c.1130* (Cambridge: Cambridge University Press, 1963), pp. 229–40.

[94] For example, an episcopal visitation of Thorney Abbey in 1345 revealed that Abbot Reynold (1323–47) had ordered the burning of a book made by the community's prior without his knowledge, which Reynold deemed scandalous; *English Benedictine Libraries: The Shorter Catalogues*, ed. by Richard Sharpe et al. [= *CBMLC* IV] (London: British Library, 1996), p. 598 (= B100).

[95] *Eadmeri monachi Cantuariensis vita sancti Anselmi archiepiscopi Cantuariensis–The Life of St Anselm, Archbishop of Canterbury by Eadmer*, ed./tr. by Richard W. Southern (Oxford: Clarendon, 1972), pp. 150–1 [hereafter *VA*]; for further discussion, see Pohl and Tether, 'Eadmer'; Southern, *Anselm*, pp. 277 and 314–16.

[96] *VA*, ed./tr. Southern, p. 150; Fisher, *Authorship*, pp. 172–5.

[97] Ibid., p. 150. Eadmer at that stage had transferred substantial parts of his work-in-progress from wax tablets onto parchment ('in cera dictaveram pergamenae magna ex parte tradidissem'); on Eadmer's autograph manuscripts, see Benjamin Pohl, 'The (Un)Making of a History Book: Revisiting the Earliest Manuscripts of Eadmer of Canterbury's *Historia novorum in Anglia*', *The Library* 20 (2019), 340–70.

far as we know, he kept hidden from Anselm as long as he was alive.[98] Eadmer knew full well he was behaving insubordinately; in fact, he tells us as much by admitting, sheepishly, to having carried out his superior's orders differently from how they had been intended ('aliter enim implevi praeceptum eius, ac illum intellexisse sciebam'), thereby knowingly committing the sin of disobedience ('inoboedientiae peccato').[99] Even with Ralph's succession, he did not gain a patron as such—Ralph seems to have been no more enthusiastic about Eadmer's writing project than his late predecessor—and there is evidence, analysed elsewhere, to suggest Eadmer might deliberately have timed the *Historia*'s initial release to fall within the long interregnum between Anselm's death in April 1109 and Ralph's installation in May 1114 specifically so as to avoid further confrontation with his superiors.[100]

Another monastic historian who rivals Eadmer's fame, and who initially also wrote without the knowledge and permission of his abbot, is Guibert, the later abbot of Nogent whom we met previously (1.3). Prior to composing the *Monodiae* and the *Dei gesta per Francos*, Guibert had tried his hand—and his pen—at other projects.[101] As a young monk of Saint-Germer-de-Fly, he set out, seemingly on his own initiative, to produce a commentary on the *Book of Genesis*, a principal history book found in any monastic library.[102] The abbot who had taken Guibert's profession, Garnier (1058–84), was unimpressed, however, repeatedly cautioning him to abort the task.[103] Realizing that Garnier could not be won over, Guibert continued to work secretly ('clam'). The fact that he tried to avoid both the abbot and anyone who might report his disobedience to him ('non solum eius, sed et omnium qui ad idipsum deferre poterant praesentias praecavendo') testifies to Guibert's guilty conscience, and it also serves to underline just how seriously

---

[98] *VA*, ed./tr. Southern, pp. 150–1: '[N]otatis verbis eius [Anselm's] quaterniones ipsos destruxi, iis quibus scripti erant aliis quaternionibus primo inscriptis'.

[99] Ibid., p. 151.

[100] Pohl, '(Un)Making', pp. 363–70; Pohl and Tether, 'Eadmer'; Martin Brett, 'Escures, Ralph d'', in *Oxford Dictionary of National Biography*, https://doi.org/10.1093/ref:odnb/23047.

[101] Cf. the dates of composition in Garand, *Guibert*, p. 25.

[102] We only need to recall the homily delivered by Abbot Gunther of Nordhausen at the Bursfelde General Chapter of 1480; *De historiae*, ed. Frank, pp. 282–3: 'Ipse Deus in sacrosanctis libris, quos vulgariter Biblia vocamus, praeter historiam nihil reliquit nobis. In toto v[etere] t[estamento] praeter psalmos Davidis, proverbia, canticum et Ecclesiastem, pura historia'. On the Bible as a history book *avant la lettre*, cf. Robert E. McNally, *The Bible in the Early Middle Ages* (Westminster: Newman, 1959), pp. 11–17; Jennifer A. Harris, 'The Bible and the Meaning of History in the Middle Ages', in *The Practice of the Bible in the Middle Ages: Production, Reception, and Performance in Western Christianity*, ed. by Susan Boynton and Diane J. Reilly (New York, NY: Columbia University Press, 2011), pp. 84–104.

[103] *Monodiae*, ed./tr. Labande, pp. 142–5; ed./tr. Reinhold and Liebe, I, 276–7: 'Cumque primum abbas meus sacrae illius historiae conspexisset adnotari capitulum, minus sano haec attendit intuit et, cum me plurima animadversione finem scriptis illis facere monuisset, videns quod non nisi spinas coepta talia oculis eius ingerebant, non solum eius, sed et omnium qui ad idipsum deferre poterant praesentias praecavendo, clam illud omne peregi'; note that Guibert refers to the Bible as 'sacra historia'. Garnier had been raised by Guibert's grandfather; ibid., pp. 108–9/I, 238–9: 'Abbas [...] avi mei alumnus'.

such disobedience was taken—and, if brought to light, punished—in medieval monasteries. The *Monodiae*'s narrative offers important insights into Garnier's authority over Guibert's literary activity. According to Guibert's own recollection, the initial encouragement for writing biblical commentaries had come from none other than Anselm, Eadmer's future superior at Canterbury who at that point was abbot of Le Bec and an acquaintance of Guibert's, possibly even his mentor.[104] Whilst lacking the support of his own abbot, Guibert thus would seem to have had a patron in the superior of one of the most important monasteries of the eleventh century.[105]

When it came to Saint-Germer-de-Fly and the historiographical activity of its monks, however, Anselm's intellectual mentorship would have been second to Garnier's institutional authority. Elsewhere in the *Monodiae*, Guibert recalls that Garnier had not always been unaccommodating of his writings and even encouraged his earliest compositions, albeit not entirely without reservation.[106] We are thus told that when the young and unsuspecting Guibert accompanied Garnier on a visitation of a nearby priory, he was asked to deliver an impromptu homily to its monks. Rising to the challenge, Guibert improvised a commentary on the *Book of Wisdom*, the reception of which was so positive that the prior later asked him to write it down so he could use it in his sermons ('familiariter a me exegit, ut id sibi scriberem, in quo materiam sumendi cuiuscumque sermonis acciperet').[107] Flattered though he was by this request, Guibert suspected that Garnier would object ('abbatem meum [...] aegre laturum scripta mea cognoveram'), and he only obtained the abbot's licence by reassuring him that he was merely following the wishes of a man whom he knew Garnier considered a friend ('ex latere quasi ex persona amici, et quasi talium minus studiosus precor').[108] The writing begun under slightly questionable pretence was none other than that which Garnier later ordered to be terminated, clearly having had a change of heart. Persevering against his abbot's orders, Guibert drafted the text not on wax tablets ('[o]puscula enim mea haec et alia nullis impressa tabulis dictando et screbendo'), but onto sheets of parchment ('scribenda etiam pariter commutando, immutabiliter

---

[104] *Monodiae*, ed./tr. Labande, pp. 138–9; ed./tr. Reinhold and Liebe, I, 270–1: 'In his praecipuum habui incentorem Beccensem abbatem Anselmum, postea Cantuariensem archiepiscopum'; Guibert's confident assertion that Anselm had first heard about him as prior and had been desperate to make his acquaintance probably owes more to wishful thinking than it does to reality, as does his statement that the only reason ('sola causa') for Anselm's regular visits to Saint-Germer-de-Fly both before and after his abbatial election in 1078 was to spend more time with Guibert (ibid., pp. 138–40/I, 268–75).

[105] On Le Bec's influence, see *A Companion to the Abbey of Le Bec in the Central Middle Ages (11th–13th Centuries)*, ed. by Benjamin Pohl and Laura L. Gathagan (Leiden: Brill, 2017).

[106] This episode is *Monodiae*, ed./tr. Labande, pp. 142–5; ed./tr. Reinhold and Liebe, I, 274–7; also cf. the discussions by Wanda Zemler-Cizewski, 'Guibert of Nogent's How to Preach a Sermon', *Theological Studies* 59 (1998), 406–19; Rubenstein, *Guibert*, pp. 27–8.

[107] *Monodiae*, ed./tr. Labande, pp. 142–3; ed./tr. Reinhold and Liebe, I, 274–5.

[108] Ibid., ed./tr. Labande, pp. 142–3; ed./tr. Reinhold and Liebe, I, 274–5.

paginis inferebam'),[109] which he stashed away so Garnier and the other monks would not find them. Unable to carve out much writing time during the day without the abbot's permission and ever careful not to raise suspicion, he resorted to working under his blanket at night whilst his brethren, who he thought envied him, were fast asleep—a *modus operandi* also embraced by a monk of Tournai called William, whose portrait features in a thirteenth-century codex (Paris, Bibliothèque Mazarine, MS 753) (Fig. 2.3).[110] Guibert did not complete the work until the abbatial vacancy following Garnier's resignation in 1084, and like Eadmer he, too, seems to have held off deliberately with its publication to avoid confrontation with his abbot.[111]

What emerges clearly from cases such as these is just how much power the presence of an unapproving superior had over a monk's historiographical activity, and the examples of Guibert and Eadmer provide us with instructive—and indeed emotive—illustrations of the human frustrations and anxieties that clandestine writing could cause. In both cases, the patron's withdrawal of support imposed significant limitations on the author's ability to complete their writing projects. At Garnier's Saint-Germer-de-Fly as much as at Anselm's Canterbury, the provision of materials and time for writing, both equally precious and almost always in limited supply, depended fundamentally on the continued support from the head of the community. Though Eadmer and Guibert both managed, with varying degrees of success, to continue their projects in secret by sacrificing sleep and social interaction, neither dared to publish his work whilst the superior was in office. Without a patron, both historians bided their time and only released their works once an opportune moment for publication presented itself due to a vacancy of monastic leadership.

---

[109] Ibid., ed./tr. Labande, pp. 144–5; ed./tr. Reinhold and Liebe, I, 276–7; Guibert reports a similar working method in the preface or his other work of history, the *Dei gesta per Francos*, written after his promotion to abbot c.1106–9: 'nec ceris emendanda diligenter excepi, sed uti presto est fede delatrata membranis apposui'; *Dei gesta*, ed. Huygens, pp. 83–4; also cf. Garand, *Guibert*, pp. 26–9.

[110] *Monodiae*, ed./tr. Labande, pp. 112–13 and 126–7; ed./tr. Reinhold and Liebe, I, 242–3 and 256–7.

[111] Ibid., ed./tr. Labande, pp. 144–5; ed./tr. Reinhold and Liebe, I, 276–9; on the completion date(s), cf. again Garand, *Guibert*, p. 25. The manuscript tradition suggests that Guibert kept coming back to the work for another thirty years and later incorporated it into the *Moralia Geneseos*. The doubts of previous scholarship notwithstanding, Jay Rubenstein argues compellingly that when Guibert referred to his early commentary on the Hexameron as 'primus libellus' in the preface of the *Moralia Geneseos*, he was likely indicating that a re-worked version of this text—the 'rough draft' of which was copied in the later twelfth century and survives in Paris, Bibliothèque nationale de France, MS Lat. 529, fols. 1r–16v—had been re-cycled as the opening book of the expanded work (Paris, Bibliothèque nationale de France, MS Lat. 529, fols. 1r–256r; Guibert's partial autograph). Rubenstein concludes that '[i]n all probability, BN lat. 529 is a copy of the first draft of Guibert's commentary [on the Hexameron] before it was Book I of the *Moralia Geneseos*', and that 'Guibert examined (*tractavi*) the Hexameron, he attached (*pretexui*) the preacher's manual, and then he turned to work on the rest of the Genesis (*reliqua presumpsi*)'; Rubenstein, *Guibert*, pp. 28 and 211, with discussion of the manuscripts in ibid., pp. 209–12. Also cf. Huygens, *Tradition*, pp. 12–19; Garand, *Guibert*, pp. 34–62. The *Moralia Geneseos* are edited in *Patrologia Latina*, ed. by Jean-Paul Migne, 221 vols. (Paris: Garnier, 1841–55), CLVI, 19–338, with the passage in question on ibid., pp. 21–2.

Fig. 2.3 William of Tournai writing in his bed. Paris, Institut de France–Bibliothèque Mazarine, MS 753, fol. ix.

Intriguingly, not all monastic superiors were such vigilant enforcers of their patronal power, and some became themselves conspirators in clandestine writing projects by (ab)using their abbatial authority to solicit the services of literate monks and nuns under reciprocal vows of secrecy. In September 988, eleven years before his appointment to the papal throne whence he became Sylvester II, Gerbert of Aurillac wrote to the monk Rainard of Bobbio and urged him to copy several books for him ([a]ge ergo [...], ut michi scribantur [etc.]') without anyone's knowledge ('te solo conscio'), and he assured Rainard that he would keep their little arrangement under an oath of silence ('sub sancto silentio habebo').[112] The fact that Gerbert was abbot of Bobbio (982/3–99) at the time of writing,[113] which made Rainard one of his own monks, renders this a peculiar request. On the one hand, Gerbert explicitly couched his order in the terminology of domestic hierarchy by telling Rainard that complying with it would be seen as a case of worthy obedience ('laudabilem obędientiam'); on the other hand, he instructed Rainard to produce the requested books at his own cost ('ex tuis sumtpibus fac') and promised to reimburse him upon their receipt ('quicquid erogaveris cumulatum, remittam secundum tua scripta et quo tempore iusseris').[114] This was not Gerbert's standard *modus operandi* for ordering books, certainly not when dealing with monastic communities other than his own. When in 984/5 he approached Abbot Eberhard of Tours with a whole 'wish list' of books (now lost) he desired to have copied and sent to him, Gerbert agreed to provide both parchment and money upfront for Eberhard's scribes to fulfil this 'interlibrary request' at Tours ('[s]cribentibus membranas sumptusque necessarios ad vestrum imperium dirigemus').[115] What was different in 988, then, and why did Gerbert not do as many abbots did by appointing one (or more) of his own monks to make the books using domestic resources that he could have provided and approved *ex officio*? Why the need for financial reimbursement, and why the secrecy?

The most plausible explanation for the peculiar terms of Rainard's appointment is that Gerbert's abbacy at Bobbio had been marked by conflict and internal resistance from the beginning, which is why after a year or so of well-nigh constant infighting Gerbert left the monastery in 984 and for the next one and a half decades remained abbot in name only before being succeeded by Peter Aldus

---

[112] See *Die Briefsammlung Gerberts von Reims*, ed. by Fritz Weigle [= *MGH Briefe d. dt. Kaiserzeit* II] (Weimar: Böhlau, 1966), pp. 157–8 (p. 158) (= no. 130); *Gerbert d'Aurillac: Correspondence*, ed./tr. by Pierre Riché and Jean P. Callu, 2 vols. (Paris: Les Belles Lettres, 1993), II, 318–21 (= no. 130).

[113] The precise beginning of Gerbert's abbacy has caused no small amount of discussion; Pierre Riché, 'Gerbert d'Aurillac et Bobbio', in *Gerberto d'Aurillac da abate di Bobbio a papa dell'anno 1000*, ed. by Flavio G. Nuvolone (Bobbio: Associazione culturale Amici di Archivum bobiense, 2001), pp. 49–64 (p. 52) considers it beyond doubt that he was appointed in 982 ('sans doute en 982'), though for the benefit of doubt the more flexible date 982/3 will be maintained here.

[114] *Briefsammlung*, ed. Weigle, p. 158; *Correspondence*, ed. Riché and Callu, II, 320–1.

[115] *Briefsammlung*, ed. Weigle, pp. 72–3 (p. 73) (= no. 44); *Correspondence*, ed. Riché and Callu, I, 106–9 (= no. 44). On such 'interlibrary loans', see below (3.5).

(999–1014).¹¹⁶ When he reached out to Rainard in his letter, Gerbert had been away from Bobbio for four years with no apparent intention to return anytime soon. As 'abbot-in-exile' residing at his previous home of Reims, Gerbert therefore had every reason to instruct Rainard to keep his request a secret from the other monks, who presumably would have objected to spending their communal funds on books intended for an abbot whose nomination by Emperor Otto II (980–1002) they had rejected from day one, and one who at the time of writing had no real way of enforcing his authority from a distance of over 600 km as the crow flies. Gerbert's struggles with Bobbio's monks and his underhand dealings with Rainard provide an instructive example of the practical limitations of an abbot's authority, one which, however, underscores the general principle that monastic superiors were able—and entitled *ex officio*—to use the human and material resources placed at their disposal to commission (history) books domestically from their communities, even if in actual practice complicating factors such as communal resistance and physical absence could sometimes make it rather difficult for them to make full use of this prerogative. If this underlying principle was true for the reproduction of existing writings, then it must have applied also— if not more so—to the production of new historical narratives, especially those that pertained to a community's identity and sense of belonging. To understand better how this principle was applied, resisted, and reinforced within monastic author-patron relationships, we can look to the following case from the Abbey of Marchiennes.

At the close of the twelfth century, the monks of Marchiennes received a man called Simon as their new abbot (1199–1201/2). The details of Simon's career are uncertain, though it seems possible, and perhaps likely, that he had held a previous abbatial appointment elsewhere.¹¹⁷ Founded in the seventh century, the monastic community had seen its fair share of conflicts, controversies, and reforms.¹¹⁸ Marchiennes's first abbot was a certain Jona(tu)s, who has been identified with a

---

[116] See Hans-Henning Kortüm, 'Silvester II.', in *Neue Deutsche Biographie*, 28 vols. (Berlin: Duncker & Humblot, 1953–2023), XXIV, 415–16; Riché, 'Gerbert', pp. 61–2; Mathilde Uhlirz, 'Studien zu Gerbert von Aurillac, Teil 2: Die ottonischen Kaiserprivilegien für das Kloster Bobbio. Gerbert als Abt', *Archiv für Urkundenforschung* 13 (1935), 437–74.

[117] Charles-Antoine Fromentin, *Essai historique sur l'abbaye de Saint-Silvin d'Auchy-les-Moines* (Arras: Bradier, 1876), pp. 62–4 suggests that Simon came to Marchiennes from Saint-Silvin d'Auchy-les-Moines after having been abbot there for nearly a decade (1190–8), and so does Adolphe de Cardevacque, *Histoire de l'abbaye d'Auchy-les-Moines* (Arras: Sueur-Charruey, 1875), pp. 61 and 250. Jean-Pierre Gerzaguet, *L'abbaye de Marchiennes, milieu VII–début XIIIe siècle* (Turnhout: Brepols, 2022), p. 387 re-dates Simon's abbacy at Auchy to 1188–99. André-Joseph-Ghislain Le Glay, *Cameracum Christianum: Histoire ecclésiastique du diocèse de Cambrai* (Lille: Lefort, 1849), p. 208 places Simon at Saint-Médard de Soissons without mentioning a previous abbatial appointment. He is not identical with Abbot Simon of Anchin (1174–1201), though the two appear to have known each other; cf. Jean-Pierre Gerzaguet, *L'abbaye d'Anchin de sa foundation (1079) au XIVe siècle: Essor, vie et rayonnement d'une grande communauté bénédictine* (Lille: Presses Universitaires, 1997), pp. 31–2.

[118] Gerzaguet, *Marchiennes*, *passim*; see also Jean-Pierre Gerzaguet, 'Les communautés religieuses bénédictines de la vallée de la Scarpe (Saint-Vaast, Anchin, Marchiennes, Hasnon, Saint-Amand) du

sometime monk-historian of Bobbio and author of a *Vita* of St Columba.[119] Following the death of the community's founder, Adalbert I of Ostrevent, in *c.*652, Adalbert's widow, Rictrude, converted Marchiennes into a 'double monastery' for men and women and installed herself as its abbess (?–687/8) before being succeeded by her daughter, Clotsinda (687/8–703).[120] Generously endowed by the local aristocracy and even Frankish royalty, the community suffered the destruction of its demesne and, according to Hucbald of St Amand, its library and archives at the hands of Scandinavian raiders during the 880s.[121] Economic and intellectual recovery was slow, and Marchiennes for some time remained 'a low-profile community [...] living in the shadow of Saint-Amand'.[122] In 1024, however, Abbot Leduin of Saint-Vaast (1024–33) set out to reform and replace the community, which at that point was predominantly (if not exclusively) female, with a male congregation.[123] Later chroniclers would seek to justify his invasive reforms by polemically blaming the abbey's decline on its female inhabitants, thereby fuelling a gendered discourse of monastic identity politics that has been dubbed 'hagiographic warfare'.[124] These polemics notwithstanding, the re-founded monastery witnessed a long phase of stability under the auspices of Saint-Vaast—the recruiting ground of five more abbots after Leduin—that lasted throughout the eleventh century and only came to an end with the tenure of Fulcard (1103–15),[125] who was forced to resign in 1115 and had his disastrous government compared to a pigsty ('stabula porcorum') by a contemporary.[126] When nearly a century later Simon came to Marchiennes as yet another outsider

XIe au début du XIVe siècle: Travaux, recherches, perspectives' (unpublished habilitation, University of Lille, 2001); Karine Ugé, *Creating the Monastic Past in Medieval Flanders* (York: York Medieval Press, 2005), pp. 98–115.

[119] This identification was first proposed by Ileana Pagani, 'Ionas-Ionatus: a proposito della biografia di Giona di Bobbio', *Studi medievali* 29 (1988), 45–85; also cf. Ugé, *Past*, p. 107. Gerzaguet, *Marchiennes*, pp. 379–80 dates Jonatus's abbacy between *c.*640–90.

[120] Karine Ugé argues that Marchiennes might already have operated as a *de facto* 'double monastery' under Jona(tu)s; Ugé, *Past*, p. 108.

[121] See Ugé, *Past*, p. 99 n. 10. According to Steven Vanderputten, *Dark Age Nunneries: The Ambiguous Identity of Female Monasticism, 800–1050* (Ithaca, NY: Cornell University Press, 2018), p. 217 n. 101, Marchienne's estate during the later ninth century comprised around 4,200 ha, making it 'decidedly small compared to [its] male neighbors'. On Hucbald, see Julia M. H. Smith, 'A Hagiographer at Work: Hucbald and the Library at Saint-Amand', *Revue bénédictine* 106 (1996), 151–71.

[122] Ugé, *Past*, p. 97.

[123] See the helpful handlist of Flemish abbesses/abbots in Vanderputten, *Reform*, pp. 193–202, according to which Marchiennes's last attested abbess was Judith (*fl.* 970s) (ibid., p. 194).

[124] Vanderputten, *Reform*, p. 142.

[125] Ibid., pp. 194–5 associates Poppo with Stavelot, whereas Gerzaguet, *Marchiennes*, p. 382 and Ugé, *Past*, p. 113 also identify him as abbot of Saint-Vaast. On the recovery of the abbey's demesne post-1024, cf. ibid., pp. 130–6; Gerzaguet, *Marchiennes*, pp. 85–104.

[126] See Gualbert of Marchiennes's account in 'De patrocinio sancti Rictrudis', edited in *Acta Sanctorum Maii III* [= *AASS* XVI] (Paris: Palmé, 1866), pp. 139–53 (p. 149); also cf. Steven Vanderputten, 'Fulcard's Pigsty: Cluniac Reformers, Dispute Settlement and the Lower Aristocracy in Early-Twelfth-Century Flanders', *Viator* 38 (2007), 91–115 (p. 106); Gerzaguet, *Marchiennes*, pp. 104–11.

to take up his appointment, he probably knew relatively little about this troublesome series of events, which explains why upon his arrival he requested a written account of it, presumably so he could familiarize himself with the history of the monastery placed under his leadership and learn about/from the deeds of his predecessors—a commitment to historical study on the abbot's part that no doubt would have pleased the likes of Gunther of Nordhausen and his fifteenth-century contemporaries whom we met earlier in this book.

Much to his dismay, Simon was told that no such account existed, and that records about his abbatial predecessors were scarce.[127] To rectify the situation, he exercised his authority by commissioning a history of the monastery and its abbots from the monks. The result was the *Chronicon Marchianense*,[128] which in its preface gives a detailed account of Simon's request worth quoting in full:

> When one day during Lent after the mealtime reading the Lord Abbot Simon, the twenty-first abbot of this church of Marchiennes, had a conversation with certain brothers about the necessary things, he casually enquired whether we had a *gesta* or written catalogue of the abbots of this monastery. One [monk] responded to him that this did not exist in writing, but that he himself knew by some means or other—by heart, from the reports of the old [monks], or from certain chronicles and histories—about the original construction of the church, the arrival of the blessed Rictrude, the nuns' government, the burning of the monastery and the slaughter of its residents by the Normans, [who] at that time [were] pagans, the eviction of the nuns, and the reinstatement of the monks. And when he had reported for some time thereafter, the lord abbot in a gentle voice said to him who had spoken thus that it would have been more beneficial to the sons of this church if he had put these things in writing, rather than compiling the deeds of kings and the wars of emperors in chronicles. The same father kept asking for this to be done from dawn to dusk. Many amongst our brothers had come together and requested this same thing before, not urgently, but cautiously, still he [the monk] had been sluggish in the execution of the work. Following the venerable abbot's command, we will therefore speak, albeit in crude language, about the state of our church, yet we will also weave in something concerning the reigns of kings and write a few things about the lives of our principal saints. If

---

[127] The extant sources are discussed by Steven Vanderputten, 'Monastic Literary Practices in Eleventh- and Twelfth-Century Northern France', *Journal of Medieval History* 32 (2006), 101-26 (pp. 112-19).

[128] The best critical edition of the *Chronicon Marchianense* is that by Steven Vanderputten, 'Compilation et réinvention a la fin du douzieme siècle: André de Marchiennes, le *Chronicon Marchianense* et l'histoire primitive d'une abbaye bénédictine (édition et critique des sources)', *Sacris erudiri* 42 (2003), 403-36 (pp. 413-35). The historical context is discussed by Karl F. Werner, 'Andreas von Marchiennes und die Geschichtsschreibung von Anchin und Marchiennes in der zweiten Hälfte des 12. Jahrhunderts', *Deutsches Archiv für Erforschung des Mittelalters* 9 (1952), 402-63 (pp. 404-7); also cf. Steven Vanderputten, 'Benedictine Local Historiography from the Middle Ages and its Written Sources: Some Structural Observations', *Revue Mabillon* 76 (2004), 107-29 (pp. 107-9).

anyone should seize this rustic little work with a sceptical look or ridicule it, the author of this composition will pay little mind to this because he does not aim for praise or worry about vituperation, nor does he seek profit. What we write here we have assembled, first and foremost, from annals and chronicles, as well as from the deeds of saints and the acts of Cambrai's bishops. Finally, we have observed [some of these things] with our own eyes. And so, what the shrewdness of the venerable father has commanded must now be fulfilled by the obedience of the humble monk assisted by the favour of the Holy Spirit.[129]

The *Chronicon* leaves no doubt that the intellectual architect and driving force behind its composition was Simon, rather than the author who, judging from his own words, had been disinclined to take on the project, but succumbed to the authority of his new abbot—a case of abbatial patronage in action that brings to mind Caesarius's *Dialogus* discussed above (2.2). The author's lack of enthusiasm reverberates clearly from the preface, and rather than following Simon's assignment religiously, he interpreted it creatively to align more closely with his own historical interests. Despite the abbot's explicit instruction to exclude the deeds of kings and wars of emperors ('gesta regum et bella imperatorum') and focus exclusively on the monastery's own history and the deeds of its abbots ('abbatum huius monasterii gesta'), the strong-headed monk-historian nevertheless injected his work with a substantial amount of the former subject ('de temporibus regum aliquid interseremus'). Authorial 'window dressing' such as this was a risky business, however, and one that, if exposed, could subject monastic writers to accusations of disobedience that, as we saw above, could result in serious disciplinary measures, from the confiscation of drafts and writing materials to the withholding of food rations, loss of office, communal shaming, and even corporal punishment. Perhaps it was precisely the anticipation of such repercussions that made the author style himself a humble monk ('monachus humilis') who rendered obedience ('obedientia') to his abbatial patron—a proclamation that seems paradoxical considering how far he had strayed from his original assignment—in an attempt to pre-empt potential backlash from Simon? I return to this below.

The *Chronicon*'s author does not disclose his identity, though he is commonly identified as Andreas, one of the community's senior monks who had risen to the rank of prior.[130] Simon's decision to task this Andreas with writing the abbey's missing foundation history and *gesta abbatum* was no accident. Prior to Simon's arrival, Andreas had composed other historical narratives that include an account of the life and miracles of St Rictrude and, his *pièce de resistance*, the *Historia*

---

[129] My translation, based on the Latin edition in Vanderputten, 'Compilation', p. 413.

[130] On this identification, see Werner, 'Andreas', pp. 406–7; also cf. Ernst Sackur, 'Reise nach Nord-Frankreich im Frühjahr 1889', *Neues Archiv der Gesellschaft für ältere deutsche Geschichtskunde* 15 (1890), 437–73 (p. 453).

succincta de gestis et successione regum Francorum, the latter of which had been patronized by Bishop Peter of Arras (1184–1203).[131] Thanks to his advanced age and senior office, Andreas knew the monastery's library and archives better than most, and in the *Chronicon*'s preface he could thus boast to know much of the community's history by heart ('cordetenus'). In the first quarter of the twelfth century, an anonymous monk had laid the groundwork for him by appending the monastery's annals with a record of its estates and the succession of its abbots known as the *Poleticum Marceniensis cenobii*, which Andreas quotes verbatim in his preface.[132] Whoever the *Poleticum*'s author was, he would have long been dead when Simon arrived at Marchiennes in 1199, making Andreas the obvious—and perhaps the sole—candidate for the latter's assignment. As the preface informs us, Simon considered the *Chronicon*'s production a matter of priority and urgency, which is why he personally kept 'nagging' Andreas at all hours of the day ('hoc vespere, hoc mane facto idem pater secunda repetiit'). This sense of urgency also explains why Simon used his abbatial authority to do for Andreas what Theodemar of Montecassino had once refused to do for Paul the Deacon by assigning him (a) scribal assistant(s) to expedite the work's codification.

As shown elsewhere, this can be seen in the *Chronicon*'s sole surviving manuscript (Douai, Bibliothèque Marceline Desbordes-Valmore, MS 850), a composite codex penned by multiple hands, one of which has recently been identified as that of Andreas himself.[133] Unlike his collaborator(s), whose penmanship indicates experience and calligraphic training superior to Andreas's, Andreas did not pen much of the *Chronicon* first-hand but acted primarily as the project's supervisor and corrector—a *modus operandi* that can also be seen in the authorial manuscript of his *Historia succincta* (Arras, Bibliothèque municipale, MS 364 (453)),

---

[131] *Historiae Franco-Merovingicae synopsis seu historia succincta de gestis et successione regum Francorum*, ed. by Raphael de Beauchamps (Douai: Bogard, 1633), pp. 561–883; on the *Vita et miracula sanctae Rictrudis*, see Karine Ugé, 'The Legend of Saint Rictrude: Formation and Transformations (Tenth–Twelfth Century)', *Anglo-Norman Studies* 23 (2001), 281–97. Andreas's authorship of two other historiographical works, the *Genealogiae Aquicinctianae* and the *Continuatio Aquicinctina Sigeberti Gemblacensis*, cannot be established with certainty and remains contested; Werner, 'Andreas', pp. 407–14 and 423–52; refuted by Georges Despy, 'Review of K. F. Werner, Andreas von Marchiennes und die Geschichtsschreibung von Anchin und Marchiennes in der zweiten Hälfte des 12. Jahrhunderts', *Scriptorium* 9 (1955), 156–8; Vanderputten, 'Practices', p. 121 n. 124. Besides the bishop of Arras, Andreas's patrons also included the abbots of Anchin; Werner, 'Andreas', pp. 455–9; Lenka Jiroušková, *Der heilige Wikingerkönig Olav Haraldson und sein hagiographisches Dossier: Text und Kontext der 'Passio Olavi' (mit kritischer Edition)*, 2 vols. (Leiden: Brill, 2014), I, 313–16.

[132] *L'histoire-polyptyque de l'Abbaye de Marchiennes (1116–1121): Étude critique et édition*, ed. by Bernard Delmaire (Louvain-la-Neuve: Centre belge d'histoire rurale, 1985); Vanderputten, 'Compilation', pp. 406–7 and 408–11. The passage from the *Poleticum* quoted in the preface of the *Chronicon* is 'Quod si quisquam [...] lucrum inde requirit' (see above).

[133] For this identification, see Benjamin Pohl, 'A Reluctant Historian and His Craft: The Scribal Work of Andreas of Marchiennes Reconsidered', *Anglo-Norman Studies* 45 (2023), 141–61. A description of the manuscript is provided in *Histoire-polyptyque*, ed. Delmaire, pp. 3–9, albeit with erroneous folio references. See also *Catalogue général des manuscrits des bibliothèques publiques de France: Départements*, 52 vols. (Paris: Plon, 1886–1960) [hereafter *CGM*], VI, 596–8. Some of the manuscript's contents are printed by Sackur, 'Reise', pp. 455–73.

the codification of which was supported by at least two scribal assistants provided to Andreas by Simon's predecessor, Stephen (1193–9).[134] Two occasions upon which Andreas *did* put pen to parchment personally in the production of the *Chronicon* are in its final chapter and, of main interest here, in the preface, and it is in these sections that his relative lack of confidence—and perhaps competence—in contrast with his copyist(s) is most noticeable. As I argue elsewhere, though, this contrast may be exaggerated by an age-related impairment of Andreas's fine motor skills.[135] According to his contemporary and likely acquaintance, abbot-historian William of Andres (1211–34), Andreas lived past the age of eighty ('octogenarius et amplius existens'), putting him in at least his mid- to late seventies at the time of writing.[136] His age and possible impediment may help explain why Andreas was disinclined to discard his personal habits and historiographical preferences—epitomized by his *Historia succincta*—so as to observe the directives of a new abbot, especially one who was a stranger to Marchiennes and its history. An old dog refusing to learn new tricks, least of all from a new master, Andreas did the absolute minimum required to comply with his abbot's commission, and the product of his perfunctory labour cannot possibly have satisfied Simon's specific vision for the *Chronicon*.

Whilst delivering on Simon's request for an account of the monastery's foundation and early history that recapitulates, in tokenistic fashion, the effects of the Viking attacks and offers an ungenerous assessment of the women's regime,[137] Andreas's work ultimately fails to address its patron's fundamental demands. Completely glossing over the monastery's most recent history between Leduin's reform in 1024 and Simon's arrival in 1199, the *Chronicon*'s final chapter indulges unapologetically in secular and dynastic matters that Andreas had been ordered to avoid at all costs, and the entire narrative brazenly ignores the deeds of the community's abbots that had formed the single most crucial aspect of Simon's request—as we will recall, he had asked specifically for an 'abbatum huius monasterii gesta vel scriptum cathalogum'. It is difficult to imagine Andreas getting away with delivering a work to his abbatial patron that so obviously missed

---

[134] See Pohl, 'Historian'. Also cf. Werner, 'Andreas', pp. 455–9; *CGM*, IV, 148. On Abbot Stephen, cf. Gerzaguet, *Marchiennes*, p. 387.

[135] Pohl, 'Historian'.

[136] William notes that Andreas had 'spent nearly all his years carrying out religious duties and reading and narrating the deeds of illustrious men [...] following the example of the blessed Jerome'; 'Chronicon Andrense', ed. by Johannes Heller, in *Annales aevi Suevici: Supplementa tomorum XVI et XVII* [= *MGH SS* XXIV] (Hanover: Hahn, 1879), pp. 684–773 (p. 690): 'Vir vite venerabilis Andreas, [...] [q]ui, quoniam ad instar beati Hieronymi in diversis diversa legerat et, octogenarius et amplius existens, omnem fere etatem in religionis exercitiis et virorum illustrium gestis legendis et explicandis expleverat'. Translated in *Chronicle*, tr. Shopkow, pp. 37–8. Bernard Delmaire also entertains the possibility of 'un scribe peut-être agé ou conservateur'; *Histoire-polyptyque*, ed. Delmaire, p. 7. Andreas died not long after the *Chronicon*'s completion.

[137] These form the subject of MS Douai 850, fols. 118v–119r; cf. Vanderputten, 'Compilation', pp. 432–4.

the mark, especially considering that Simon had spared neither effort nor expense by making available precious writing time to Andreas, likely exempting him from some domestic duties to focus on the *Chronicon*'s composition, and even assigning him some well-trained support staff who likewise had to be relinquished from routine tasks around the monastery to assist with the work's codification. This was a major investment of human and material resources, and one for which Simon would have expected results.

As we saw above, Andreas may have tried to appease—or perhaps mislead— Simon by playing the humble monk and emphasizing his obedience to him in the work's preface, presumably in anticipation of the abbot's inevitable dissatisfaction when presented with an unsatisfactory text. Notably, the first half of the preface (MS Douai 850, fol. 104v, ll. 1–14) is written in the third person and copied by an anonymous assistant, whereas the second half including Andreas's duplicitous surrender to the authority of his abbatial patron (ibid., fols. 104v, l. 14–105r, l. 8) is composed in the first person and penned entirely in his own hand over an erasure.[138] The most plausible explanation for this is not that prefaces tend to be written last,[139] but rather that when the headstrong monk-historian put the finishing touches to the text before presenting it to Simon, he may have got cold feet and second-guessed his decision to have cast the abbot's directives to the wind. Attempting some last-minute damage control, Andreas erased half the existing preface prepared by an assistant and replaced it with words of deference written in his own hand—and in his own voice—that he hoped would appeal to Simon's mercy and ease the punishment he stood to receive for having taken such liberties with his abbot's orders, disregarding his patronal authority.[140]

Before we move on from Abbot Simon and his disobedient (if ultimately deferential) monk-historian, we must return briefly to the question of why Simon commissioned the *Chronicon Marchianense* in the first place and, more specifically, what plans he may have had for its use within the monastery. Key in this context is Andreas's recollection, again found in the preface, that the abbot made the request during Lent ('in diebus quadragesime'), a time of year that in monastic communities was marked by increased reading activity.[141] Andreas

---

[138] 'Igitur secundum abbatis [...] spiriti adiuvante gratia'. Photographic reproduction in Pohl, 'Historian', with further discussion.

[139] As observed by Richard Southern, *St Anselm: A Portrait in a Landscape* (Cambridge: Cambridge University Press, 1990), p. 415.

[140] Another possibility—though perhaps a less likely one—is that Andreas amended the preface *post*-presentation in response to, rather than in anticipation of, Simon's castigation.

[141] On the Lenten reading and book distribution, see Teresa Webber, 'Monastic and Cathedral Book Collections in the Late Eleventh and Twelfth Centuries', in *The Cambridge History of Libraries in Britain and Ireland*, Vol. 1: *To 1640*, ed. by Teresa Webber and Elizabeth Leedham-Green (Cambridge: Cambridge University Press, 2006), pp. 109–25 (pp. 120–2); Teresa Webber, 'Cantor, Sacrist or Prior? The Provision of Books in Anglo-Norman England', in *Medieval Cantors and Their Craft: Music, Liturgy and the Shaping of History, 800–1500*, ed. by Margot E. Fassler, Andrew B. Kraebel, and Katie A.-M. Bugyis (Woodbridge: Boydell, 2017), pp. 172–89 (pp. 185–9).

further recalls that the request was made immediately after the mealtime reading ('post lectionem collationis'), perhaps intimating that this was the context—and the refectory the place—in which Simon intended the work to be received. As we will see below, the *Chronicon* would not be the first history (nor indeed the last) written or commissioned by an abbot that was used for communal table reading. If that was indeed Simon's intention, this could help explain why he dismissed Andreas's *Historia succincta*, whose preoccupation with the exploits of secular princes made it unsuitable as a source of contemplation for the monks gathered around the table: rather than pondering worldly events, Simon wanted them to use the time in the refectory to consider their own institutional history.[142] This was an inward-looking mode of historical engagement that neither the *Historia succincta* nor the *Poleticum* could facilitate, so Simon ordered that they be supplemented with a history of the monastery and the *gesta* of its abbots.

The cases analysed here are instructive examples of abbatial patronage not just in theory, but in practice. They illustrate some of the ways in which an abbot's authority could be resisted and reinforced in the collaborative process of historiographical production, and they remind us that even the most determined and authoritative abbatial patron ultimately relied capable—and compliant—personnel. When Simon arrived at Marchiennes, he was fortunate to find there a historian who, with the appropriate support, was positioned ideally, at least in theory, to produce a monastic chronicle as a matter of urgency, even if in practice his personal preference lay with more secularly oriented kinds of historiography. Simon was even more fortunate that there was not one, but several skilled copyists amongst the abbey's inhabitants who could be deployed, at the abbot's discretion, to lend a hand in the *Chronicon*'s codification. The domestic conditions encountered by Simon upon his abbatial appointment thus combined to offer an environment favourable to historiographical activity, something that could not be taken for granted in any medieval monastery, and certainly not in one of Marchiennes's size, wealth, and status. Human resources apart, we should not assume that monastic superiors necessarily had the means to sponsor works of history even if they were so inclined. Many might well have been keen to commission histories as Simon did, especially histories of the communities placed under their authority, but not all were able to assemble the necessary writing materials, personnel, and historical expertise in-house. Some thus turned to external providers to furnish them with commissioned narratives, thereby significantly extending the scope of their sponsorship beyond the limits of their monasteries. The motivations behind internal and external acts of abbatial patronage

---

[142] Cf. Guenée, *Histoire*, pp. 25–33; Steven Vanderputten, 'Pourquoi les moines du Moyen Âge écrivaient-ils l'histoire? Une approche socio-constructiviste du problème', *Studi medievali* 42 (2001), 705–23 (p. 706).

might often have been similar, but their logistics and practicalities—and indeed their results—could differ significantly.

2.4 Commission, Competition, and Quality Control

When soliciting writers of history outside their own communities, abbots and abbesses had to depend not just on the authority they held by virtue of their monastic rank—which, though recognized widely in medieval society as a form of lordship, had different currency outside the monastery than it did on the inside— but equally, and crucially, on their wider socio-political networks, their families and kin, and, where applicable, their personal and/or institutional affiliations with the ruling elites. Some intuitively looked to members of other monastic communities, or to their leaders. Examples of monastic superiors commissioning historical narratives from their peers—in other words, abbots writing history for other abbots—include Blasius of Hirsau, who, as we saw above (1.2), urged Johannes Trithemius, then abbot of Sponheim, to produce a history of Hirsau from its distant beginnings up to the present (1495). Blasius's approach was no accident. Not only did Trithemius have a reputation as a writer, and sometimes forger, of history throughout Germany,[143] but Hirsau and Sponheim were both core members of the Bursfelde Congregation that, as seen in the Introduction, had placed particular emphasis on the writing of history, and whose General Chapter provided the occasion for the composition of Gunther of Nordhausen's *De historiae*.[144] At the time of Blasius's commission, neither he nor Trithemius could have foreseen the complications that should arise following Blasius's death when the patronage was transferred onto his successor, John, whose lack of enthusiasm and unwillingness to pay Trithemius's wages stymied progress for about half a decade.[145] At least initially, though, the cross-institutional arrangement must have been a productive one with every prospect of success and timely completion.

A similarly productive arrangement was agreed in the early 1160s between Laurence, abbot of Westminster (c.1158–73) and Ælred, abbot of Rievaulx (1147–67), with the former asking the latter to compose a new *Vita* of Edward

---

[143] On Trithemius's forgeries, see Nikolaus Staubach, 'Auf der Suche nach der verlorenen Zeit: Die historiographischen Fiktionen des Johannes Trithemius im Lichte seines wissenschaftlichen Selbstverständnisses', in *Fälschungen im Mittelalter*, 5 vols. (Hanover: Hahn, 1988), I, 263–316; Johannes Mötsch, 'Frühgeschichte, Fälschungen und Verwaltung des Klosters Sponheim zur Zeit des Trithemius', in *Johannes Trithemius (1462-1516): Abt und Büchersammler, Humanist und Geschichtsschreiber*, ed. by Klaus Arnold and Franz Fuchs (Würzburg: Königshausen & Neumann, 2019), pp. 121–31.

[144] Schreiner, 'Geschichtsschreibung', *passim*; Otto Herding, 'Johannes Trithemius (1462-1516) als Geschichtsschreiber des Klosters Hirsau', in *Beiträge zur südwestdeutschen Historiographie*, ed. by Otto Herding and Dieter Mertens (Stuttgart: Kohlhammer, 2005), pp. 63–9.

[145] See above (1.2).

the Confessor based on two eleventh-century texts that had since become 'outdated' (the *Vita Ædwardi* and Osbert de Clare's *Vita beati Eadwardi regis Anglorum*), copies of which Laurence made available personally to Ælred.[146] Given Edward's canonization in 1161 and the subsequent translation of his relics to Westminster in 1163, Laurence's timing of this assignment was apposite. We further learn from Ælred's own biography—which was written at the request of an abbot with the initial 'H.', who has been identified with Abbot Hugh of Revesby or Abbot Henry of Waverley, the heads of two of Rievaulx's dependencies in Lincolnshire and Surrey, respectively—that he produced his *Vita Edwardi regis et confessoris* 'at the request of his *kinsman* Laurence, the abbot of Westminster' ('haec scripsit rogatus a Laurencio abbate Westmonasterii *cognato* suo').[147] Having lived under Ælred's regime for seventeen years ('[d]ecem et septem annis vixi sub magisterio eius'),[148] the author of the *Vita Aelredi*, a monk of Rievaulx called Walter Daniel, is unlikely to be mistaken about his abbot's family connections. Influential though these kinship ties must have been in Laurence's decision as to whom to approach as prospective author of the new *Vita Edwardi*, they were not the only determining factor. At the point that Laurence commissioned him, Ælred had written a whole suite of historical narratives that include his *Genealogia regum Anglorum*, the *Eulogium Davidis regis Scotorum*, the *Relatio de standardo*, the *Vita Niniani*, the *De quodam miraculo mirabili*, and *De sanctis ecclesiae Haugustaldensis*, giving him the reputation of a 'historian amongst historians', to adopt the title bestowed upon Ælred by a modern scholar.[149] Outstripping these previous writings in popularity and dissemination, Ælred's *Vita Edwardi* survives in some thirty manuscript copies, and before long it was adapted by other writers and even translated into the vernacular.[150] Besides serving political agendas like the Plantagenets' legitimization as rulers by both

---

[146] 'Aelredi Rievallis Abbatis: Operum Pars Prima–Ascetica; Operum Pars Secunda–Historica', in *Patrologia Latina*, ed. by Jean-Paul Migne, 221 vols. (Paris: Garnier, 1841–55), CLXXXXV, 209–796 (pp. 739–40) (= 'Praefatio ad Laurentium abbatem Westmonasterii'). The traditional attribution of one of these eleventh-century *vitae* to Goscelin of Saint-Bertin has been rejected in favour of Folcard's authorship; Tom Licence, 'The Date and Authorship of the *Vita Ædwardi Regis*', *Anglo-Saxon England* 44 (2016), 259–85; Tom Licence, 'A New Source for the *Vita Ædwardi Regis*', *Journal of Medieval Latin* 29 (2019), 1–19; now also Moreed Arbabzadah, 'Word Order in Goscelin and Folcard: Implications for the Attribution of the *Vita Ædwardi regis* and Other Works', *Journal of Medieval Latin* 31 (2021), 191–218.

[147] *The Life of Ailred of Rievaulx*, ed. by Frederick M. Powicke (London: Nelson, 1950), pp. 41–2; my emphasis. The preface is addressed to '[v]irorum dolcissimo abbati H.' (ibid., p. 1), with the possible identifications discussed in ibid., p. xxxi.

[148] *Life*, ed. Powicke, p. 40.

[149] Elizabeth Freeman, 'Aelred as a Historian among Historians', in *A Companion to Aelred of Rievaulx (1110–1167)*, ed. Marsha Dutton (Leiden: Brill, 2017), pp. 113–46, who provides a summary discussion of Ælred's historical works and concludes that 'unless other evidence arises in the future, he [Ælred] remains the first known author of narrative histories among the English Cistercians' (ibid., p. 136). On Ælred as author, see above (1.3).

[150] Freeman, 'Aelred', pp. 140–2; Domenico Pezzini, 'Aelred of Rievaulx's *Vita Sancti Edwardi Regis et Confessoris*: Its Genesis and Radiation', *Cîteaux: Commentarii Cistercienses* 60 (2009), 27–77.

blood and conquest, the text seems to have had a communal purpose at its patron's home monastery at Westminster. This is suggested by Walter Daniel's passing remark that Laurence had in fact commissioned the *Vita* alongside an exposition on the Gospels that were to be read to the monks at the solemn vigils of the Confessor's feast day ('[d]einde evangelicam leccionem exposuit ad honorem eiusdem sancti et ad eam legendam in eius solempnitate ad vigilas').[151] It is therefore not impossible, and perhaps plausible, that the *Vita Edwardi* made by Laurence's abbatial peer at Rievaulx was also meant to be read or read out—either wholly or, more likely, episodically—in a similar setting.

What is particularly remarkable about the patronage agreement between Laurence and Ælred is not that they were both abbots, but that they were from two different monastic orders, with Westminster being Benedictine and Rievaulx Cistercian. Evidently, and for all the polemic exchanged between Benedictine and Cistercian writers during the twelfth century,[152] abbatial patronage and collaboration in the writing of history could easily transcend these kinds of boundaries, especially if assisted by connections of kinship. This was not the only boundary straddled habitually by abbatial patrons, and another—and equally important— one was that between the monastic and secular spheres. An early example of this is provided by St Hilda, founding abbess (657–80) of Whitby. According to Bede's *Historia ecclesiastica*, when one of Hilda's deputies charged with administering the abbey's demesne reported to her about a local herder called Cædmon who had a divine gift for composition even though he 'had lived in the secular habit until he was well advanced in age' ('in habitu saeculari usque ad tempora provectioris aetatis constitutus'), Hilda was quick to make Cædmon a lay brother so he could join her community, be educated, and, in return, offer his talents to the abbess and her nuns.[153] Details about Cædmon and his famous composition—'Cædmon's Hymn'—are preserved in Bede's history, which reports that his 'entry requirement' upon joining the community was to take a passage of sacred history ('sacrae historiae') read out to him and turn it into 'excellent verse' ('optimo carmine'). Witnessing Cædmon pass her challenge with flying colours, the abbess 'instructed him to renounce his secular habit and to take monastic vows' ('abbatissa [...] saecularem illum habitum relinquere et monachicum suscipere propositum

---

[151] *Life*, ed. Powicke, p. 41.

[152] *Le moine Idung et ses deux ouvrages: 'Argumentum super quatuor questionibus' et 'Dialogus duorum monachorum'*, ed. by Robert B. C. Huygens (Spoleto: Cento Italiano di studi sull'alto medioevo, 1972, repr. 1980); translation in *Idung of Prüfening: Cistercians and Cluniacs: The Case for Cîteaux. A Dialogue between Two Monks. An Argument on Four Questions*, tr. by Jeremiah F. O'Sullivan (Kalamazoo, MI: Cistercian Publications, 1977); see also Robert of Torigni's 'De immutatione ordinus monachorum–Concerning Change in the Order of Monks', in *The Chronography of Robert of Torigni*, ed./tr. by Thomas N. Bisson, 2 vols. (Oxford: Oxford University Press, 2020), II, 250–75.

[153] *HEGA*, ed. Colgrave and Mynors, pp. 414–21; also cf. the excellent analysis by Sarah Foot, 'Bede's Abbesses', in *Women Intellectuals and Leaders in the Middle Ages*, ed. by Kathryn Kerby-Fulton et al. (Cambridge: Brewer, 2020), pp. 261–76 (pp. 267–8).

docuit') and, gladly receiving him into her abbey, 'ordered that he should be instructed in the whole course of sacred history' ('iussitque illum seriem sacrae historiae doceri').[154] Though Bede does not say as much, it seems evident that as a consequence of the abbess's shrewd manoeuvre, a highly talented external writer—or, in Cædmon's case, singer—of history was 'converted' into an internal one and subjected, by formal vow, to Hilda's official authority and patronage as the community's superior. Hilda's successor, Ælfflæd (c.680–714), King Oswiu of Northumbria's daughter, exercised her abbatial authority to commission not only a biography of her predecessor and sometime mentor, but also, it would seem, the earliest *vita* of Pope Gregory I (590–604).[155] Because the latter was made anonymously, we do not know for certain whether its author was internal or external to Ælfflæd's community. If internal, and assuming that Ælfflæd was indeed the patron, then the author was most likely a nun, making her 'plausibly the earliest female historian in Britain'.[156] If external, then he/she could have been either a male or a female collaborator who was affiliated, in one way or another, with Ælfflæd and enjoyed her abbatial sponsorship.

An insightful example of just such a collaboration between an abbess-patron and an external historian is provided by Matilda, abbess of Essen (973–1011), and the English ealdorman Æthelweard, author of a chronicle that is at once a history of England spanning nearly half a millennium and a dynastic history for the sponsoring abbess and her extended kin.[157] When commissioning the *Chronicon* in the final quarter of the tenth century, Matilda could not—or perhaps did not wish to—assign the task to a member of her monastic community, but instead turned to Æthelweard, her kinsman and England's most senior ealdorman. (Æthelweard would later act as a patron for Ælfric, abbot of Eynsham (1005–10)). Æthelweard and Matilda both descended from Æthelwulf, father of Æthelred I and Alfred, and Matilda's grandmother was Eadgyth/Edith, Edward the Elder's daughter, who was sent across the English Channel to be married to the duke of Saxony and future emperor, Otto. The early death of her brother, Otto I of Swabia, made Matilda the sole surviving

---

[154] *HEGA*, ed. Colgrave and Mynors, pp. 418–19.

[155] Clare A. Lees, 'Gender and the Subjects of History in the Early Middle Ages', in *Medieval Historical Writing: Britain and Ireland, 500–1500*, ed. by Jennifer Jahner et al. (Cambridge: Cambridge University Press, 2019), pp. 299–318 (pp. 301–6), referring to the Gregory-*Vita* as '[t]he fullest and earliest evidence for the practice of writing hagiographic history within monastic communities that include women' (ibid., p. 303); see also Foot, 'Abbesses', p. 271.

[156] Lees, 'Gender', p. 300, who *contra* the text's editor observes rightly that 'anonymity is not necessarily synonymous with masculinity' (ibid.).

[157] *The Chronicle of Æthelweard*, ed./tr. by Alistair Campbell (London: Nelson, 1962); Aethelweard explicitly mentions Matilda's patronage on no fewer than four occasions (ibid., pp. 1–2, 15, 26, and 34); cf. Lees, 'Gender', pp. 306–12; Mechthild Gretsch, 'Historiography and Literary Patronage in Late Anglo-Saxon England: The Evidence of Æthelweard's *Chronicon*', *Anglo-Saxon England* 41 (2013), 205–48; Elisabeth M. C. van Houts, 'Women and the Writing of History in the Early Middle Ages: The Case of Abbess Matilda of Essen and Aethelweard', *Early Medieval Europe* 1 (1992), 53–68.

offspring from that high-profile marriage and the last living member of the family's 'English line' resident in Germany.¹⁵⁸ Compelling arguments are presented by Elisabeth van Houts to suggest that the production of Æthelweard's *Chronicon* at Matilda's abbatial command should be viewed in the context of a political rivalry between Ottonian Germany's great monasteries that saw Matilda's community at Essen pitched against other institutional 'heavyweights' like Quedlinburg, Nordhausen, and Gandersheim.¹⁵⁹ Building on this suggestion, Æthelweard's work can also be understood as part of a *historiographical competition* fought out on parchment between a group of contemporary—and often related—abbesses, all of whom decided, around the same time, to solicit major new works of history for their communities. Perhaps it was the act of historiographical production in and of itself that provided these powerful abbesses with valuable cultural capital and political currency, allowing them to showcase their respective patronage networks within a competitive environment. For a monastic superior as much as for any political and institutional leader, patronizing the writing of history was, after all, an exercise of authority, a show of status.

One of the women who thus competed with Matilda was her relative and namesake, Abbess Matilda of Quedlinburg (966–99). The daughter of Otto I and his second wife, Adelheid of Burgundy, this Matilda had served as regent for both her father and her brother on multiple occasions in the 960s/70s and 990s. As abbess of Quedlinburg, she commissioned the monk Widukind of Corvey to compose his influential *History of the Saxon People*.¹⁶⁰ Widukind acknowledges Matilda's patronage on no fewer than three separate occasions in the work's prologue, as well as in the prefaces of its individual books.¹⁶¹ Though Matilda was still in her teenage years, Widukind expected her—or perhaps she herself had proposed—to do more than simply endorse and 'rubberstamp' the history he wrote at her request, but to also exercise her patronage by engaging with and, if need be, amending the narrative presented to her. At the opening of the second book, Widukind states his hope that 'whatever in this is found less than suitable will be elevated by your [Matilda's] glorious mercy and kindness' ('quicquid in eo inventitur minus idoneum, glorisoa tuae clementiae lenitate sublevetur [spero]').¹⁶² And whilst it seems a step too far to present young Matilda as 'an

---

¹⁵⁸ See the genealogical table in van Houts, 'Women', p. 56.
¹⁵⁹ Van Houts, 'Women', p. 61; Gert Melville, *The World of Medieval Monasticism: Its History and Forms of Life* (Collegeville, MN: Cistercian Publications, 2016), pp. 42 and 51.
¹⁶⁰ *Die Sachsengeschichte des Widukind von Korvei*, ed. by Paul Hirsch and Hans-Eberhard Lohmann, 5th ed. [= *MGH SS rer. Germ.* LX] (Hanover: Hahn, 1935); translated as *Widukind of Corvey: Deeds of the Saxons*, tr. by Bernard S. Bachrach and David S. Bachrach (Washington, DC: Catholic University of America Press, 2014). See also Plassmann, *Origo*, pp. 265–89.
¹⁶¹ *Sachsengeschichte*, ed. Hirsch and Lohmann, pp. 1–2, 61, and 101–2.
¹⁶² *Sachsengeschichte*, ed. Hirsch and Lohmann, p. 61.

editor, or co-author, of the book',[163] she certainly was engaged actively, and from an early age, in the commemoration of her family and the curation of its dynastic *memoria*. One of the two *Vitae Mathildis reginae* produced at the female abbey of Nordhausen around the turn of the eleventh century reports how Matilda's grandmother—Queen Matilda, Otto I's mother and Quedlinburg's founder—had handed her a calendar with the names of deceased family members ('computarium, in quo erant nomina procerum scripta defunctorum') so Matilda would arrange for intercessory prayers, at the same time as commending to her the care of her own soul and that of her husband, Henry.[164] Matilda was not the only abbess of Quedlinburg—nor the only women in her family—to commission historical narratives. Her niece and successor, Adelheid I (999–1044), has been identified as the probable patron of the *Annales Quedlinburgenses* begun by one or more of the local nuns in *c*.1008–15 and completed in 1025 × 30.[165] Comparing the (re-)writing of history at Gandersheim and Quedlinburg, Sarah Greer proposes that these annals may well have been intended to curry favour with Empress Kunigunde, who following the death of her husband, Emperor Henry II, founded the monastic convent of Kaufungen in 1025,[166] again pointing strongly to a context in which the writing of history—and, importantly, its patronage—was seen as a marker of abbatial authority, prestige, and status. We can still see visual reflections of this in the earliest extant abbatial effigies from Quedlinburg dedicated to Abbesses Adelheid I (999–1044), Beatrix I (1044–61), and Adelheid II (1062–96), all three of whom are shown as carrying books which they clutch close to their chests—an iconography that also shapes the effigies and/or abbatial seals of no fewer than eleven of their twelfth- to fourteenth-century successors.[167]

---

[163] Karl F. Morrison, 'Widukind's Mirror for a Princess: An Exercise in Self-Knowledge', in *Forschungen zur Reichs-, Papst- und Landesgeschichte: Peter Herde zum 65. Gebertstag von Freunden, Schülern und Kollege dargebracht*, ed. by Karl Borchardt and Enno Bünz, 2 vols. (Stuttgart: Hiersemann, 1998), I, 49–71 (p. 49).

[164] 'Vita Mathildis reginae antiquior', in *Die Lebensbeschreibungen der Königin Mathilde*, ed. by Bernd Schütte [= *MGH SS rer. Germ.* LXVI] (Hanover: Hahn, 1994), pp. 107–42 (pp. 137–8); translated in *Queenship and Sanctity: The Lives of Mathilda and the Epitaph of Adelheid*, tr. by Sean Gilsdorf (Washington, DC: Catholic University of America Press, 2004), pp. 71–87 (pp. 85–6); van Houts, 'Women', p. 58 concludes that 'from an early age onwards [...] Matilda was told that it was her duty to commemorate the dead and to keep their memory alive'.

[165] *Die Annales Quedlinburgenses*, ed. by Martina Giese [= *MGH SS rer. Germ.* LXXII] (Hanover: Hahn, 2004), with discussion of the work's authorship (ibid., pp. 57–66); more recently Hartmut Hoffmann, 'Zu den Annales Quedlinburgenses', *Sachsen und Anhalt* 27 (2015), 139–78.

[166] Sarah Greer, *Commemorating Power in Early Medieval Saxony: Writing and Rewriting the Past at Gandersheim and Quedlinburg* (Oxford: Oxford University Press, 2021), pp. 168–71.

[167] Karen Blough, 'Abbatial Effigies and Conventual Identity at St. Servatius, Quedlinburg', in *A Companion to the Abbey of Quedlinburg in the Middle Ages*, ed. by Karen Blough (Leiden: Brill, 2023), pp. 181–222 (pp. 188–89), with photographic reproductions of these effigies. The effigy of Abbess Gertrude (1233–70) offers a variation of the same theme by depicting her with a large scroll. The seals of Quedlinburg's high and later medieval abbesses are reproduced in *Codex diplomaticus Quedlinburgensis*, ed. by Anton U. von Erath (Frankfurt a. M.: Moeller, 1764). Those that feature books belong to Abbesses Adelheid III (1161–84), Bertradis I (1226–30), Kunigunde (1230–1),

Other abbess-patrons whose sponsorship fits within this same context include Richburga of Nordhausen (c.962–1007), who probably instigated at least one (if not indeed both) of the two *Vitae* of Queen Matilda mentioned above.[168] Prior to her abbacy, Richburga had served as Matilda's chambermaid and was appointed personally by her as the first abbess for the royal monastic foundation at Nordhausen.[169] As abbess, she commissioned the *Vita(e)* of her former mistress from one of her own nuns with a dedication to the king and future emperor, Henry II, possibly to 'remind him of his obligations towards Nordhausen',[170] but also, and perhaps more significantly, to serve as an official *historia fundationis* for the fledgeling community similar to that provided to the nuns of Gandersheim by their abbess, Gerberga II (956–1001), Richburga's contemporary. A niece of Otto I and thus a relative of Matilda of Quedlinburg and Matilda of Essen, Abbess Gerberga of Gandersheim had received her formative education at St Emmeram and was made abbess shortly after her uncle's victory at the Battle of Lechfeld. A decade or so into her abbacy, she appointed one of her canonesses named Hrotsvitha to compose the *Gesta Ottonis*, a history in Latin verse that besides glorifying the deeds of her uncle and his son and successor, Otto II, pays particular attention to the female members of the dynasty.[171] Abbess Gerberga has been identified as the probable patron of another historical work authored by Hrotsvitha, the *Primordia coenobii Gandersheimensis*, a foundation history of Gandersheim's monastic community produced in close chronological proximity—and plausibly in deliberate conversation—with the first *Vita Mathildis* written at Nordhausen under Abbess Matilda and Widukind's *Res gestae Saxonicarum* written for Matilda of

---

Osterlinde (1231-3), Bertradis II (1270-1308), Jutta (1308-47), Luitgard (1347-53), Agnes III (1354-62), and Elisabeth I (1362-75). An interesting—and contemporary—parallel for this sphragistic iconography is provided by Stephen of Lexington, abbot of Savigny (1229-43), who broke with his predecessors' tradition (traceable from about 1165) by prominently including a book in his abbatial seal; see Richard Allen, 'The Abbey of Savigny (Manche) in Britain and Ireland in the 12th Century: Three Overlooked Documents', *Annales de Normandie* 68 (2018), 9–33 (p. 23).

[168] See van Houts, 'Women', p. 59, arguing that 'Richburga may well be the main source of inspiration behind the two lives, despite the fact that both were written at the request of two kings [Otto II and Henry II, respectively]'.

[169] Edited as 'Vita Mathildis reginae posterior', in *Die Lebensbeschreibungen der Königin Mathilde*, ed. by Bernd Schütte [= *MGH SS rer. Germ.* LXVI] (Hanover: Hahn, 1994), pp. 145–202; *Queenship*, tr. Gilsdorf, pp. 88–127; cf. Elisabeth M. C. van Houts, *Memory and Gender in Medieval Europe, 900–1200* (Basingstoke: Macmillan, 1999), pp. 49–50.

[170] Van Houts, *Memory*, p. 49.

[171] 'Gesta Ottonis', in *Hrosvit: Opera Omnia*, ed. by Walter Berschin (Munich: Saur, 2001), pp. 271–305; Hrotsvitha states in the *Gesta*'s preface that she wrote at Gerberga's abbatial orders ('vestra confectum [...] ex iussione'); translation in *Hrosvithae Liber Tertius*, tr. by Mary B. Bergman (Covington, KY: Sisters of St. Benedict Press, 1962), pp. 38–9; also *Hrotsvitha Gandeshemensis: Gesta Ottonis Imperatoris. Lotte, drammi e trionfi nel destino di un imperatore*, ed./tr. by Maria P. Pillolla (Firenze: Galluzzo, 2003), pp. 2–3; van Houts, 'Women', pp. 55–7; Peter Dronke, *Women Writers of the Middle Ages: A Critical Study of Texts from Perpetua (†203) to Marguerite Porete († 1310)* (Cambridge: Cambridge University Press, 1984), pp. 55–83.

Quedlinburg.[172] Unlike her peers at Quedlinburg and Essen, though, Gerberga did not have to search externally when patronizing works of history, but could use her abbatial authority and resources to solicit the services of a domestic historian—an 'epic historian', no less—with an imposing portfolio comprising eight saints' lives and multiple plays, several of which may have circulated at the Ottonian court.[173] Greer views Gerberga's/Hrotsvitha's (re-)writing of their community's foundation story as 'a political act', one that created 'a new literary memory of both the Ottonian family and her own monastic institution', and she concludes that '[s]tanding behind her [Hrotsvitha] throughout this process was her abbess, Gerberga'.[174] Contextualizing Gerberga's role as a patron with other examples of abbatial patronage amongst her peers in Germany and further afield, it is easy to appreciate how intrinsically connected authority and historiographical sponsorship were within medieval monastic culture(s). Combining institutional *auctoritas* with political *potestas*, these well-connected female leaders regularly enlisted not just members of their communities in historical writing projects, but also historians (male and female) outside the cloister. It is no coincidence, therefore, that when Æthelweard tells his patron, Matilda of Essen, that she is perfectly placed to support him actively in the writing of history, he justifies this by drawing attention to her family connections and—most crucially—her abundant *potestas* ('non solum affinitate, sed et potestate [...] obpleta').[175]

External and internal patronage were not mutually exclusive, of course, and some monastic superiors had the means and resources—and the connections—to commission historians both inside *and* outside their communities. A good example of this is provided by Mary, abbess of Barking (c.1173–5), who during her short tenure commissioned internal as well as external writers of history. Internally, Mary patronized a vernacular translation of the Latin *Vita* of St Catherine, which she had produced domestically by a nun called Clemence.[176] It has been speculated that this Clemence might also have written a vernacular biography of Edward the Confessor, but recent research has shown this to be unlikely, suggesting instead that this *Vie d'Edouard* was composed by an anonymous fellow-nun of Barking and quite possibly at the command of the same abbess-

---

[172] 'Primordia coenobii Gandeshemensis', in *Hrosvit: Opera Omnia*, ed. by Walter Berschin (Munich: Saur, 2001), pp. 306–29; tr. Bergman, pp. 86–113; van Houts, 'Women and the Writing of History', pp. 55–6; Greer, *Commemorating Power*, pp. 73–9, 90–6, and 100–2.

[173] See *The Writings of Medieval Women: An Anthology*, ed. by Marcelle Theibaux, 2nd ed. (New York, NY: Routledge, 2018), pp. 172–88, with the quotation as part of the chapter title ('Hagiographer, Playwright, Epic Historian'); also cf. Dronke, *Writers*, pp. 55–7.

[174] Greer, *Power*, p. 100.

[175] *Chronicle*, ed./tr. Campbell, p. 2, who simply translates 'potestas' as 'capacity'; see similarly van Houts, *Memory*, pp. 151–2.

[176] See Watt, *Writing*, pp. 71–81; Diane Auslander, 'Clemence and Catherine: The Life of St Catherine in its Norman and Anglo-Norman Context', in *Barking Abbey and Medieval Literary Culture: Authorship and Authority in a Female Community*, ed. by Jennifer N. Brown and Donna A. Bussell (Woodbridge: Boydell, 2012), pp. 164–82.

patron.[177] Extending her sponsorship beyond her convent, Mary commissioned a vernacular *Life* of Thomas Becket, her brother, from Garnier de Pont-Saint-Maxence, a wandering French clerk and poet whose literary pursuits had taken him across the English Channel.[178] As far as we know, Garnier's *Vie de saint Thomas le martyr* was the first biography of Thomas Becket in French and the earliest one in verse, and at the very end of the work the itinerant writer obliges himself explicitly to his abbess-patron. One of the earliest manuscripts (Paris, Bibliothèque nationale de France, MS fr. 13513, fols. 98r–v) preserves an epilogue that can be considered authorial, and which thanks 'the abbess, St Thomas's sister' ('L'abeesse suer saint Thomas') for her generous patronage.[179] According to this epilogue, Mary had provided Garnier with board and lodging, clothing, and even a horse, spurs and all, a kindness that the author vowed to repay 'by singing her praises everywhere and to everyone, high or low'.[180] It would be easy to dismiss this as an exaggeration on the historian's part, added for dramatic effect or to flatter his abbatial patron, or to consider it genuine but exceptional. And yet, there is evidence that Garnier's report is both truthful and broadly in line with the levels of support writers of history sponsored by medieval monastic superiors could reasonably expect. Later in the epilogue, Garnier thus recalls that before he commenced his 'writing retreat' at Barking, he had been shown comparable largesse by 'Odo, the good prior [1167/8–75] of Holy Trinity Canterbury', who together with his monks supported him in his historiographical pursuits by 'frequently giving me what was properly theirs and providing me with board and lodging over a number of years'.[181]

Just as Garnier came to enjoy the patronage and support of more than one monastic superior, Barking was home to more than one abbess who acted as a patron of historical writing. Mary's successor, Matilda (*c*.1175–*c*.1198), illegitimate daughter of King Henry II, tasked a certain Adgar/William—judging from this dual moniker, he was probably of mixed Anglo-Norman heritage—with translating just shy of fifty miracle stories from Latin exemplars, chief amongst them the works of William of Malmesbury, and combine them into a single text known as

---

[177] *La Vie d'Edouard le Confesseur, by a Nun of Barking Abbey*, tr. by Jane Bliss (Liverpool: Liverpool University Press, 2014); Jane Bliss, 'Who Wrote the Nun's Life of Edward?', *Reading Medieval Studies* 38 (2012), 77–98.

[178] See Michael Staunton, *Thomas Becket and His Biographers* (Woodbridge: Boydell, 2006), pp. 32–4.

[179] *Guernes de Pont-Sainte-Maxence: La Vie de Saint Thomas Becket*, ed. by Emmanuel Walberg (Paris: Champion, 1936), pp. 191–2; on the manuscript, see ibid., p. xiv; translated in *Guernes de Pont-Sainte-Maxence: A Life of Thomas Becket in Verse–La Vie de saint Thomas Becket*, tr. by Ian Short (Toronto: Pontifical Institute of Mediaeval Studies, 2013), pp. 176–7.

[180] *Vie*, ed. Walberg, p. 192: 'M'at doné palefrei e dras; n'i faillent nis li esperun. Ne getai pas mes dez sur as, quant to journai a sa meisun! Ne ele n'i ad mespris pas; de mei avra tel gueredun: E devent halz e devent bas par tut eschalcerai sun nun'; tr. Short, p. 176.

[181] *Vie*, ed. Walberg, p. 192; tr. Short, p. 177. See also Elisabeth M. C. van Houts, 'The Abbess, the Empress and the "Constitutions of Clarendon"', in *English Legal History and its Sources: Essays in Honour of Sir John Baker*, ed. by David Ibbetson et al. (Cambridge: Cambridge University Press, 2019), pp. 247–64 (pp. 247–9 and 251–4).

Le Gracial, possibly 'the oldest surviving vernacular miracle collection' from medieval Europe.[182] Around the turn of the fifteenth century, Sibyl de Felton (1394–1419) commissioned various devotional writings that all exhibit a historical focus.[183] This tradition of abbatial patronage at Barking can be traced back almost as far as the abbey's foundation. At its beginning stands Barking's second abbess, Hildelith (*c*.695–*c*.700), who sponsored her peer Aldhelm, abbot of Malmesbury (*c*.675–705), in the composition of *De virginitate*. At the same time as patronizing Aldhelm, Hildelith commissioned one—or perhaps several—of her own nuns to produce the 'Barking Abbey *Liber*', a now-lost narrative about the abbey's foundation and the deeds of Æthelburh, Hildelith's predecessor, founding abbess, and the community's joint patron saint.[184] This *Liber* provided an important source for Bede's *Historia ecclesiastica*,[185] and it has been suggested compellingly that Hildelith's patronage may have been motivated by, and timed carefully to coincide with, the translation of her predecessor's relics, thereby providing the historiographical framework for the monastic community's central *lieu de mémoire*.[186]

Whether Goscelin of Saint-Bertin's *Vitae* of Barking's abbesses (written *c*.1086 × 1100) were produced at the command of one of the abbey's late eleventh-century superiors is difficult to establish with certainty, but persuasive cases have been made for attributing the patronage of Goscelin's 'updated' *Lives* of Æthelburh and Wulfhild to Abbess Ælfgyva (1066 × 87), who shortly before, if not concurrently, commissioned shrines dedicated to Æthelburh for Barking's abbey church.[187] As observed by Thomas O'Donnell, Ælfgyva and her nuns were Goscelin's patrons 'in every practical sense', having 'provided him with the occasion for writing, supplied him with information, shaped his interpretation

---

[182] *Adgar: Le Gracial–Miracles de la Vierge*, tr. by Jean-Louis Benoit and Jerry Root (Turnhout: Brepols, 2021); Sarah Kay, *Courtly Contradictions: The Emergence of the Literary Object in the Twelfth Century* (Stanford, CA: Stanford University Press, 2001), pp. 183–90, with the quotation on p. 183; Emma Bérat, 'The Authority of Diversity: Communal Patronage in *Le Gracial*', in *Barking Abbey and Medieval Literary Culture: Authorship and Authority in a Female Community*, ed. by Jennifer N. Brown and Donna A. Bussell (Woodbridge: Boydell, 2012), pp. 210–32.

[183] Donna A. Bussell and Jennifer N. Brown, 'Barking's Lives, the Abbey and Its Abbesses', in *Barking Abbey and Medieval Literary Culture: Authorship and Authority in a Female Community*, ed. by Jennifer N. Brown and Donna A. Bussell (Woodbridge: Boydell, 2012), pp. 1–30 (pp. 14–17).

[184] Diane Watt, 'Lost Books: Abbess Hildelith and the Literary Culture of Barking Abbey', *Philological Quarterly* 91 (2012), 1–22 (p. 3), concluding that 'writing of this *liber* would in all likelihood have been commissioned by Abbess Hildelith, in order to foster the cult of Barking's foundress and thus to ensure the continuity of the monastery'.

[185] *HEGA*, ed. Colgrave and Mynors, pp. 356–7 and 364–5; Foot, 'Abbesses', pp. 270–1.

[186] Watt, 'Books', p. 6, who suggests that the abbess might even have had a hand in writing the *Liber*. This will have to remain conjecture, though.

[187] For example, 'Goscelin of St Bertin: Lives of the Abbesses at Barking (Extracts)', tr. by Vera Morton, in *Guidance for Women in Twelfth-Century Convents*, ed./tr. by Vera Morton and Jocelyn Wogan-Browne (Cambridge: Brewer, 2003), pp. 139–56 (pp. 139–40); Bussell and Brown, 'Lives', pp. 5–6; Katie A.-M. Bugyis, 'Dating the Translations of Barking's Abbess-Saints by Goscelin of Saint-Bertin and Abbess Ælfgifu', *Journal of Medieval Monastic Studies* 11 (2022), 97–130; on Ælfgyva, see *Heads of Religious Houses 1*, ed. Knowles et al., p. 208.

of events, and [...] received and preserved the works in their book collection'.[188] Like Garnier, Goscelin was also an outsider who resided at several monastic communities—including Canterbury, though unlike Garnier, he stayed at St Augustine's Abbey—and wrote history for their male and female superiors. The histories he produced at both Barking and Canterbury served a foundational purpose by facilitating the communal memory of their origins and founders in a way that 'married the nuns' [and monks'] "sense of the past" to the needs of the present'.[189] Similar to the cases from Ottonian Germany, it is worth noting that a fair number of Barking's abbess-patrons came from powerful aristocratic families or royal dynasties, and that many of them were appointed by the monarch and, from the later eleventh century, given 'quasi-baronial' rank with privileges and obligations very similar to those of major secular magnates.[190] Equipped with these connections and resources, Hildelith and her successors were in an ideal position to commission and help promote works of history.

The historiographical patronage of Barking's abbesses is remarkable but not without parallel. Further examples of abbesses sponsoring works of history include Charlemagne's sister Gisela, abbess of Chelles (c.800–10), who around 805/6 instigated the production of the *Annales Mettenses priores*.[191] Not only was Gisela an avid patron of historiography, but also a 'grande bâtisseuse' who ordered the construction of a new abbey church and several other buildings.[192] Two centuries earlier, Gisela's predecessor Dedimia had commissioned a female historian from the convent of Holy Cross in Poitiers named Baudonivia to compose a *vita* of St Radegund, Chelles's patron saint.[193] As Baudonivia recalls in the work's dedicatory epistle, the project had been 'imposed' upon her ('iniungitis mihi opus agere') by Abbess Dedimia and her convent, a commission which she humbly accepted as it resembled 'touching heaven with one's finger' ('quam sit digito caelum tangere').[194] As Yitzhak Hen has shown, abbesses were amongst the

---

[188] O'Donnell, 'Authors', p. 95.
[189] O'Donnell, 'Authors', pp. 96–7, with the quotation on p. 102.
[190] Bussell and Brown, 'Lives', pp. 7–8; Jocelyn Wogan-Browne, 'Barking and the Historiography of Female Community', in *Barking Abbey and Medieval Literary Culture: Authorship and Authority in a Female Community*, ed. by Jennifer N. Brown and Donna A. Bussell (Woodbridge: Boydell, 2012), pp. 283–96 (pp. 290–1).
[191] See Hartmut Hoffmann, *Untersuchungen zur karolingischen Annalistik* (Bonn: Röhrscheid, 1958), pp. 53–61; Rosamond McKitterick, 'Frauen und Schriftlichkeit im Frühmittelalter', in *Weibliche Lebensgestaltung im frühen Mittelalter*, ed. by Hans-Werner Goetz (Cologne: Böhlau, 1991), pp. 65–118 (p. 71); Rosamond McKitterick, *Charlemagne: The Formation of a European Identity* (Cambridge: Cambridge University Press, 2008), pp. 61–3.
[192] Anne-Marie Helvétius, 'Pour une biographie de Gisèle, sœur de Charlemagne, abbesse de Chelles', in *Splendor Reginae: Passions, genre et famille. Mélanges en l'honneur de Régine Le Jan*, ed. by Laurent Jégou et al. (Turnhout: Brepols, 2015), pp. 161–7 (p. 166).
[193] 'De vita s. Radegundis, Liber II.', in *Fredegarii et aliorum Chronica. Vitae sanctorum*, ed. by Bruno Krusch [= MGH SS rer. Merov. II] (Hanover: Hahn, 1888), pp. 377–95; *Writings*, ed. Theibaux, pp. 106–8; Jennifer C. Edwards, *Superior Women: Medieval Female Authority in Poitiers' Abbey of Sainte-Croix* (Oxford: Oxford University Press, 2019), pp. 30–1 and 76–7.
[194] 'Vita', ed. Krusch, p. 377.

foremost sponsors of early medieval saints' lives and *gesta abbatissarum*.[195] Besides Dedimia, they included Agnes, abbess of Nivelles, who c.670 ordered the composition of a *Vita* of her predecessor, Gertrude (c.628–58); Celsa, abbess of Arles, who commissioned Florentius of Tricastina to write a biography of her predecessor, Rusticula (c.556–632); Anstrudis, abbess of Laon, who acted as the driving force behind the anonymous *Vita* of Sadalberga (c.605–70), her mother and predecessor who had founded the community; and Julia, abbess of Pavilly, who patronized a *Life* of her predecessor, Austreberta (c.650–703).[196] These abbesses used their authority and resources to commission authors external or internal to their communities—and sometimes both—to compose an official biography of a predecessor who was typically the community's founding abbess and, frequently, a kinswoman. In doing so, they became at once patrons of their communities' histori(ographi)cal traditions and keepers of their dynastic and family memories.[197]

As is now clear, domestic patronage was not always an option. Their principal authority as institutional leaders notwithstanding, the ability of abbots and abbesses to have history written locally depended on a wide range of conditions that had to be brought into alignment before historiographical activity could commence in a medieval monastery. This was the exception, not the norm, and each act of composition consumed precious time and resource. For those in a position to commission histories domestically, this nevertheless seems to have constituted the preferred *modus operandi*. We saw several examples of this above, including the ecclesiastical history written by Orderic Vitalis under the patronage of four successive abbots of Saint-Évroult (2.2). As we will recall, this project was first commissioned by the elderly abbot Roger ('Rogerii abbatis senis [...] precepto') and then continued under his successors. As Orderic tells us, at least one, Warin, demanded to inspect the work-in-progress personally, 'delete what is superfluous, correct its infelicities, and reinforce the amended version with the authority of [his] wisdom' ('ut superflua delens incomposita corrigas, et emendata

---

[195] Yitzhak Hen, 'Gender and the Patronage of Culture in Merovingian Gaul', in *Gender in the Early Medieval World: East and West, 300–900*, ed. by Leslie Brubaker and Julia M. H. Smith (Cambridge: Cambridge University Press, 2004), pp. 217–33 (p. 225).

[196] *Sainted Women of the Dark Ages*, ed./tr. by Jo A. McNamara et al. (Durham, NC: Duke University Press, 1992); Paul Fouracre and Richard A. Gerberding, *Late Merovingian France: History and Hagiography, 640–720* (Manchester: Manchester University Press, 1996), pp. 306–7; on the *vitae* from Arles, see Luce Piétri, 'Les premières abbesses du monastère Saint-Jean d'Arles', in *Paul-Albert Février de l'Antiquité au Moyen Âge*, ed. by Michel Fixot (Aix-en-Provence: Publications de l'Université de Provence, 2003), pp. 73–86; on the *Vita Sadalbergae*, cf. Hans Hummer, 'Die merowingische Herkunft der *Vita Sadalbergae*', *Deutsches Archiv für Erforschung des Mittelalters* 59 (2003), 459–93; Michèle Gaillard, 'Les *Vitae* des saintes Salaberge et Anstrude de Laon, deux sources exceptionnelles pour l'étude de la construction hagiographique et du contexte socio-politique', *Revue du Nord* 391/2 (2011), 655–69.

[197] On religious women as 'memory keepers', cf. Katie A.-M. Bugyis, *The Care of Nuns: The Ministries of Benedictine Women in England during the Central Middle Ages* (Oxford: Oxford University Press, 2019), pp. 39–77; van Houts, *Memory*, pp. 65–92.

vestrae sagacitatis auctoritate munias').[198] The term 'auctoritas' serves a double purpose here. On the one hand, it refers to Warin's authority as the community's leader; on the other, it designates him as a man of letters who, like Matilda of Quedlinburg in her patronage of Widukind, could be expected—and perhaps had demanded—to play an active part in preparing the finished work for its official release and publication.

It was not uncommon for abbots and abbesses to act as reviewers and redactors of historical narratives written at their behest—and ultimately in their name—by authors inside and outside their own communities. Internally, such 'quality control' was yet another consequence of the superior's responsibility for what was produced by the community's members with the tools provided to them at his/her discretion. Externally, it was a means of safeguarding the patron's name—and, by extension, that of his/her community—from being brought into disrepute by a rogue author or a work that compromised their reputation and socio-political standing. Besides Warin of Saint-Évroult and Matilda of Quedlinburg, examples of this include Rabanus Maurus, who after two decades as abbot of Fulda (822–42) had been appointed as archbishop of Mainz (847–56) and, in this capacity, wrote to his abbatial successor, Hatto I (842–56), to request a copy of the *Liber de laudibus sanctae crucis* he himself had written c.810 and left behind at Fulda (Vatican, Biblioteca Apostolica Vaticana, MS Reg. lat. 124, with Rabanus's autograph corrections).[199] Though Rabanus was the *Liber's* author, his departure meant that the official authority over the book, its usage, and dissemination had passed to Hatto. This explains why Rabanus channelled his request through Hatto ('si cui commissum tibi opus ad rescribendum tradideris'), and why he asked him to make sure personally that the wording and layout were copied accurately, lest the work be corrupted and damage the authority of *both* its author and abbatial patron. In a similar vein, a letter written by Idung of Prüfening as a prologue for his *Dialogus duorum monachorum Cisterciensis et Cluniacensis* (c.1155) implores the addressee, Abbess Kunigunde of Niedermünster in Regensburg, to instruct the religious women under her authority to correct his composition and copy it out legibly, presumably for presentation and release ('ut legibiliter scribatur et diligenter emendetur ab aliquibus sororibus vestris').[200] Following a secular career as *magister*

---

[198] *HE*, ed./tr. Chibnall, I, 132–3.
[199] *Epistolae Karolini aevi III*, ed. by Ernst Dümmler [= *MGH Epp.* V] (Berlin: Weidmann, 1899), pp. 381–2 (= no. 1); Dümmler dates this letter to c.814 on the basis that it addresses Hatto as 'conlevita', which he considers proof that Rabanus must have written it before his ordination as priest on 23 December 814 (ibid., p. 381 n. 1); this is not imperative, though, and it seems more likely that Rabanus wrote from Mainz following Hatto's election in 842, and that he chose this salutation to remind his old friend of the days when they were had studied together at Tours; cf. Raaijmakers, *Fulda*, pp. 99 and 267. On the *Liber*, see Michael Embach, *Die Kreuzesschrift des Hrabanus Maurus 'De laudibus sanctae crucis'* (Trier: Paulinus, 2007); also Marc-Aeilko Aris and Regina Pütz, *Bibliotheca Fuldensis: Ausgewählte Handschriften und Handschriftenfragmente aus der mittelalterlichen Bibliothek des Klosters Fulda* (Fulda: Parzellers Buchverlag, 2010), pp. 112–13 (= no. 42).
[200] *Idung*, ed. Huygens, pp. 175–6; tr. O'Sullivan, pp. 21–2.

scholarum, Idung had joined Prüfening's Benedictine monks in the mid-1140s before embracing the Cistercian way of life. Prüfening was a prolific centre of book production in its own right, though rather than passing the authorial draft via its abbot, Erbo (1121–61)—whom we will meet again later as a book provider (3.3)—Idung submitted it to the abbess of a nearby monastery for correction.[201]

Mechanisms of quality assurance and reputational safeguarding were not limited to monastic superiors, but were used by the leaders of other institutions, too. In the first half of the ninth century, Frecul, bishop of Lisieux (*c*.822 × 25–50/2), thus went to some lengths to guarantee that a copy of Vegetius's *De re militari* which he had ordered to be produced by his cathedral canons from a corrupted exemplar ('vicio scriptorum ita erat depravatum') for presentation to King Charles the Bald was mended as much as possible by correcting it himself from scratch ('corrigere curavi sine exemplario'), an activity that is described in the dedication letter which accompanied the corrected manuscript to the royal court.[202] Frecul was an accomplished historiographer and author of a world chronicle in twelve books (*Historiarum libri XII*), and he would have appreciated the importance of clean copies—and the responsibility for their provision—in author-patron relationships like that between himself and the Frankish ruler.[203] Similarly, when *c*.1015 dynastic historian Dudo of Saint-Quentin sent a draft of his *Historia Normannorum* originally commissioned by Duke Richard I of Normandy (942–96) to Bishop Adalbero of Laon (977–1030) before presenting it to his late patron's son and successor, Duke Richard II (996–1026), the dedicatory epistle referred to Adalbero as an 'eminent corrector' ('egregius corrector'), with Dudo appealing to the bishop's authority to bring to light what was obscure ('ut quae in hoc codice suis tenebris obscura videntur, per te ad lucem referantur').[204] Consequently, credit ('laus') for the

---

[201] See Robert B. C. Huygens, 'Idungus', in *Die deutsche Literatur des Mittelalters–Verfasserlexikon*, ed. by Burghart Wachinger et al., 2nd rev. ed., 14 vols. (Berlin: De Gruyter, 1977–2008), IV, 362–4.

[202] Frecul's dedication letter is edited in *Epistolae III*, ed. Dümmler, pp. 618–19 (= no. 4); cf. Rosamond McKitterick, 'Charles the Bald (823–877) and His Library: The Patronage of Learning', *English Historical Review* 95 (1980), 28–47 (p. 31), with a possible identification of the presentation copy.

[203] The second part of Frecul's chronicle (produced during his episcopate) was dedicated to Charles the Bald's mother, Empress Judith. See Graeme Ward, *History, Scripture, and Authority in the Carolingian Empire: Frecul of Lisieux* (Oxford: Oxford University Press, 2022), pp. 4–5 and 21–24. Also cf. Steffen Patzold, *Episcopus: Wissen über Bischöfe im Frankenreich des späten 8. bis frühen 10. Jahrhunderts* (Ostfildern: Thorbecke, 2008), pp. 173–5; Werner Goez, 'Zur Weltchronik des Bischofs Frechulf von Lisieux', in *Festgabe für Paul Kirn zum 70. Geburtstag*, ed. by Ekkehard Kaufmann (Berlin: Schmidt, 1961), pp. 93–110; Graeme Ward, 'The Sense of an Ending in the Histories of Frecul of Lisieux', in *Historiography and Identity III: Carolingian Approaches*, ed. by Rutger Kramer et al. (Turnhout: Brepols, 2021), pp. 291–315; the work has been edited in *Frechulfi Lexoviensis episcopi opera omnia*, ed. by Michael I. Allen (Turnhout: Brepols, 2002), pp. 17–724, including the letter to Empress Judith (ibid., pp. 723–4).

[204] *De moribus et actis primorum Normanniae ducum*, ed. by Jules Lair (Caen: Le Blanc-Hardel, 1865), pp. 118–19 [hereafter *HN*]; translated in *Dudo of St Quentin: History of the Normans*, tr. by Eric Christiansen (Woodbridge: Boydell, 1998), pp. 5–6; Benjamin Pohl, *Dudo of Saint-Quentin's* Historia

finished work would go not just to Dudo as the author ('compositor'), but equally—and perhaps primarily—to Adalbero as the redactor ('corrector').[205]

If it were not for historiographical paratexts such as prefaces, dedications, and letters that accompanied authorial drafts and presentation copies, the vital aspects of abbatial patronage discussed here could easily escape our notice. The examples analysed above are instructive reminders that not all facets of a monastic superior's sponsorship are immediately obvious in the commissioned narratives themselves, and some must be made visible by other means, such as by scrutinizing the contexts of their production and the physical evidence of the manuscripts in which they are preserved. Such detective work is particularly challenging in cases where the identity of the abbatial patron is obscured inadvertently—for example, by accidents of transmission or because it was deemed self-evident by the author and his/her audience and therefore remained undisclosed—or concealed on purpose. Such obscured and concealed patronage is worthy of investigation as it teaches us not to limit our attention to what lies on the surface, but to drill deep into the evidence even—and especially—where this means questioning what authors and scribes would have us believe *prima facie*. This is not to suggest that we should adopt a cynical stance and read prologues, colophons, and dedications 'against the grain' as a matter of course, nor that we can expect to find an abbot or abbess behind every historiographical project if we look hard enough. That said, we need to be mindful that medieval authors acknowledged their patrons in various ways, some of which may seem more recognizable to us than others,[206] and some might have had good reasons for not disclosing their patrons' identities, examples of which are studied in the next part of this book.

2.5 Obscured and Concealed Patronage

Looking for examples of accidentally obfuscated or deliberately concealed patronage does not mean having to resort to obscure texts written in backwater communities with no circulation beyond the locality. On the contrary, a fresh look at

---

Normannorum: *Tradition, Innovation and Memory* (York: York Medieval Press, 2015), pp. 107–8. On Dudo's patrons, see also Leah Shopkow, 'The Man from Vermandois: Dudo of Saint-Quentin and his Patrons', in *Religion, Text, and Society in Medieval Spain and Northern Europe: Essays in Honor of J. N. Hillgarth*, ed. by Thomas E. Burman (Toronto: Pontifical Institute for Mediaeval Studies, 2002), pp. 302–18; a more comprehensive treatment of this important subject is currently being prepared by Lauri Leinonen at the University of Helsinki.

[205] *HN*, ed. Lair, p. 118: '[Q]uia non penuriosi et ingloriosi nomen compositoris, sed egregii correctoris laus acquiretur'; cf. *HN*, tr. Christiansen, p. 5, who also translates *compositor* as 'author'. Though Dudo's request was motivated, to some extent, by Adalbero's reputation as a writer of sophisticated verse, there can be no doubt that it was due equally to his authority as an ecclesiastical leader; see *Adalberon de Laon: Poème au roi Robert*, ed./tr. by Claude Carozzi (Paris: Belles Lettres, 1979).

[206] Cf. Tether, *Publishing*, pp. 63–107.

some of the best-known and most widely disseminated histories produced by men and women from medieval Europe's most powerful and resourceful monasteries reveals that they are just as likely—if not more so—to fall into this category. A good case in point is William of Malmesbury, widely considered one of 'the most learned historians of twelfth-century Europe, and, some would argue, the greatest historian of England since Bede'.[207] William's substantial oeuvre includes histories of kings and bishops (*Gesta regum Anglorum*; *Gesta pontificum Anglorum*), a history of recent events, a foundation history of Glastonbury Abbey, and various saints' lives.[208] A notion encountered regularly in scholarship is that William 'started to write history from personal choice',[209] and even that he 'considered himself as writing for anyone who wanted to know'.[210] As explained above with reference to William's contemporary, Orderic Vitalis (2.4), such notions of authorial autonomy are fundamentally incompatible with the structural and operational principles of monastic life in the medieval Latin West, which substituted individualism and self-determination with an institutional chain of command based on authority and obedience. However keen and/or gifted a historian William may have been, as a monk he was simply not in a position to write for just anyone—let alone initiate writing projects himself—without authorization from his superiors. And though William does not indebt himself explicitly to his abbots in his historical writings—his dedicatees do, however, include the abbot(s) of Glastonbury and Queen Matilda[211]—there is evidence to suggest that they played an instrumental role in their composition that effectively equates to patronage.

Born *c.*1090 and taking the habit before he turned ten, no schooling that William may have received prior to his oblation could have enabled him to 'hit the ground running' as a historian who, with his superiors' authorization, could be

---

[207] Emily A. Winkler and Emily Dolmans, 'Discovering William of Malmesbury: The Man and His Works', in *Discovering William of Malmesbury*, ed. by Rodney M. Thomson et al. (Woodbridge: Boydell, 2019), pp. 1–11 (p. 1).

[208] *William of Malmesbury: Gesta regum Anglorum–The History of the English Kings*, ed./tr. by Roger A. B. Mynors et al., 2 vols. (Oxford: Clarendon, 1998-9) [hereafter *GRA*]; *William of Malmesbury: Gesta pontificum Anglorum–The History of the English Bishops*, ed./tr. by Michael Winterbottom and Rodney M. Thomson, 2 vols. (Oxford: Clarendon, 2007); *William of Malmesbury: Historia Novella–The Contemporary History*, ed./tr. by Edmund King and Kenneth R. Potter (Oxford: Clarendon, 1998); *The Early History of Glastonbury: An Edition, Translation and Study of William of Malmesbury's 'De Antiquitate Glastonie Ecclesie'*, ed./tr. by John Scott (Woodbridge: Boydell, 1981); *William of Malmesbury: Saints' Lives. Lives of SS. Wulfstan, Dunstan, Patrick, Benignus and Indract*, ed./tr. by Michael Winterbottom and Rodney M. Thomson (Oxford: Clarendon, 2002). There is now a welcome consensus amongst scholars to treat William's saints' lives as historiographical works and abandon the label of 'hagiography'; cf. Anne E. Bailey, '*Gesta Pontificum Anglorum*: History of Hagiography?', in *Discovering William of Malmesbury*, ed. by Rodney M. Thomson et al. (Woodbridge: Boydell, 2019), pp. 13–26.

[209] Antonia Gransden, *Historical Writing in England*, 2 vols. (London: Routledge, 1974–82), I, 166–7.

[210] Winkler and Dolmans, 'William', p. 8.

[211] Jaakko Tahkokallio, *The Anglo-Norman Historical Canon: Publishing and Manuscript Culture* (Cambridge: Cambridge University Press, 2019), pp. 18–21.

excused from elementary communal duties to immerse himself in the monastic library and archives.²¹² There can no doubt, therefore, that he received his formative education at Malmesbury, where he was sponsored from early on by the abbot to whom he had professed himself, Godfrey (1084/7 × 91–1105/6).²¹³ Taking William under his wing, Godfrey entrusted him with activities that can be considered cornerstones of a historian's apprenticeship, such as by having him assist in expanding the abbey's basic book collection into a library suitable for historical study.²¹⁴ Optimistic assertions notwithstanding, expanding Malmesbury's monastic library cannot have been William's 'self-prescribed task',²¹⁵ but one that almost certainly was assigned to him by his superior. We should be careful not to misconstrue the oft-quoted—but rarely contextualized— passage from the *Gesta regum* in which William states to have spent no small amount of money collecting works by foreign historians ('domesticis sumptibus nonnullos exterarum gentium historicos conflassem') and accumulating chronicles from far and wide ('cronica longe lateque corrogavi').²¹⁶ The traditional translation of 'domesticis sumptibus'—that provided in the *Gesta regum*'s standard edition/translation—is '[with] my own money', leading some to conclude that these history books were acquired by William at his own initiative and with personal funds. This is extremely implausible. As a boy, even one from a wealthy family supportive of his education, William is unlikely to have had a substantial collection of books that his parents could have donated to the monastery upon his oblation, let alone one bursting with rare and non-curricular texts. Once a monk, he would no longer have had private capital with which to purchase books, and instead had to rely on his institutional superiors to supply whatever was needed. It seems clear, therefore, that 'sumptus domestici' refers not to any form of personal capital, but rather to domestic funds—literally: 'expenses of the house'—whose use and distribution were subject to the abbot's authorization. Even William's subsequent appointment as Malmesbury's cantor/precentor—an office that typically involved responsibility for a community's liturgical books and, from about the later eleventh century, was habitually combined with the role of librarian/*armarius*—would not have changed that. As discussed elsewhere in this book (3.1), monastic cantors, too, were ultimately allocated their resources and revenues by the heads of their communities.

---

²¹² See Rodney M. Thomson, *William of Malmesbury*, rev. ed. (Woodbridge: Boydell, 2003), pp. 199–201.

²¹³ The exact dates and duration of Godfrey's abbacy are difficult to determine due to the incomplete, and at times conflicting, sources; cf. *The Heads of Religious Houses: England and Wales*, Vol. 1: *940–1216*, ed. by David Knowles et al., 2nd ed. (Cambridge: Cambridge University Press, 2001), p. 55; Thomson, *William*, p. 200.

²¹⁴ The earliest datable books from Malmesbury's monastic library are discussed in Thomson, *William*, pp. 97–115. Also cf. Niskanen, 'William', *passim*.

²¹⁵ Winkler and Dolmans, 'William', p. 7. ²¹⁶ *GRA*, ed./tr. Mynors et al., I, 150–1.

It may not be coincidence, therefore, that William's most prolific phase as a writer of history (c.1125–35) fell squarely within the period when the monastic community was governed by Bishop Roger of Salisbury (1102–39; acting abbot c.1118–39).[217] The titular nature of Roger's abbacy and his frequent absence from Malmesbury may have given William some exceptional liberties in his historiographical pursuits, such as by permitting him to take up a residence at Glastonbury Abbey to produce the foundation history known as *De antiquitate Glastoniensis ecclesiae* and the *Life* of Glastonbury's venerated former abbot, Dunstan.[218] Still, as Rodney Thomson reminds us, 'this historical activity must have necessitated some relaxation of the Benedictine rule',[219] and the sheer size of William's oeuvre suggests that 'he must have been released from a good deal of regular discipline in order to make it possible'.[220] Extraordinary dispensations like these could only have been granted to William by Malmesbury's monastic superior, be that Abbot/Bishop Roger himself or whoever administered the abbey's everyday business in his absence. Thomson's suggestion that William's aim in sending out presentation copies of his *Gesta regum* to powerful magnates like Empress Matilda in the mid-1120s might have been to lobby for the election of a new abbot to replace the externally appointed Roger less than a decade into his tenure is intriguing in this context,[221] and it is tempting to imagine that his ulterior motive was to regain a 'proper' abbatial patron to fill the void left by his late mentor, Godfrey, perhaps indicating that Malmesbury's famous monk-historian had been wanting under the bishop's regime. For all the freedom of movement, lack of supervision, and creative licence William might have enjoyed under Roger, having a 'hands-off' superior also meant having less access to resources and—perhaps most importantly—lacking a patron to lend his name and abbatial title to the finished works and endow them with his official *auctoritas*. Perhaps this last point helps explain why William turned to Glastonbury's abbot as a surrogate in the hope of availing himself of his support and resources whilst living and working under his roof—a hope that, as revealed by the dedication of *De antiquitate*,[222] was not unfounded, and one which, as discussed above (2.4), was entirely in keeping with the support lent to 'resident historians' like Garnier

---

[217] *Heads 1*, ed. Knowles et al., p. 55.
[218] *Saints' Lives*, ed./tr. Winterbottom and Thomson, p. xv; Thomson, *William*, p. 18; Gransden, *Writing*, I, 183–4.
[219] Rodney M. Thomson, 'Malmesbury, William of', in *Oxford Dictionary of National Biography* (2004), n.p., https://doi.org/10.1093/ref:odnb/29461. As Thomson points out, '[t]here was not merely the time and labour of writing. William had to conduct research, to read and transcribe books and documents at religious houses up and down the country'; also cf. Thomson, *William*, p. 17, concluding that William in his 'wide-ranging search for literary materials [...] travelled virtually the length and breadth of the land', and that 'the evidence is such that we have to envisage at least one grand tour, entailing a long absence, perhaps a year or more, from his house, and prolonged stays at certain other monasteries, exploring, noting, summarizing and copying'.
[220] Thomson, *William*, p. 7.   [221] Thomson, *William*, p. 37.
[222] *De antiquitate*, ed./tr. Scott, pp. 40–1.

de Pont-Saint-Maxence and Goscelin of Saint-Bertin by their hosts. Be that as it may, it must be clear that though William did not credit his historiographical productivity to the support of his own superiors in the way contemporary historians such as Orderic and Symeon—both of whom, incidentally, have also been identified as 'cantor-historians'—did,[223] he depended on abbatial patronage just the same.

This was true for William's early activity under Godfrey and Eadwulf (1106–18) as much as it was for his productive years under Roger and his eventual successors, John (1140) and Peter Moraunt (1141–58/9). Some of these abbots lent their support in palpable ways by providing William with the time—and, importantly, resources—to undertake research trips, copy and/or commission history books from far and near, and build a library without which he would have been unable to produce the works that brought him such fame amongst medieval and modern readers. Others, meanwhile, were 'invisible' patrons who operated in the background. The fact that in the scholarly literature their involvement is eclipsed regularly by the towering presence of William 'the historian' offers a powerful reminder of how easy yet misleading it is to project modern preoccupations with the role of the author and his/her individual agency onto institutional environments such as medieval monasteries that demand a more nuanced understanding of the relationship between these authors and their abbatial patrons. As argued below (3.1 and 3.2), examples such as that of William and his abbots compel us to adjust our definition of abbatial patronage by incorporating not just the authorization to write in the first place, but equally the provision of books, documents, and other resources for historical study and composition.

Whilst William did not acknowledge his abbatial patrons at all, others disclosed theirs in ambivalent ways that prevent straightforward identifications and require contextual analysis. A case in point is the *Historia Iherosolimitana* produced by Robert 'the Monk'. In the prologue, Robert reports to have written at the orders of 'a certain abbot named B.' ('quidam [...] abbas, nomine B.'), who was 'distinguished by his knowledge of literature and upright behaviour' ('litterarum scientia et morum probitate preditus'), and who has been identified with Bernard, abbot (1084–1100) of Marmoutier near Tours.[224] This identification is uncompelling. In the *Historia*'s prologue, aptly titled an 'apologetic sermon' ('sermo apologeticus'), Robert issues a plea to 'all those who will read this history, or hear it read to them

---

[223] Rozier, 'Symeon', *passim*; Rozier, 'Orderic', *passim*.

[224] *The* Historia Iherosolimitana *of Robert the Monk*, ed. by Damien Kempf and Marcus Bull (Woodbridge: Boydell, 2013), p. 3, with discussion on ibid., pp. xxv–xxxiv [hereafter *HI*]; translation adapted from *Robert the Monk's History of the First Crusade-Historia Iherosolimitana*, tr. by Carol Sweetenham (Aldershot: Ashgate, 2005), p. 75, who expands 'B.' to 'Bernard' (of Marmoutier). Cf. Marcus Bull, 'Robert the Monk and his Source(s)', in *Writing the Early Crusades: Text, Transmission and Memory*, ed. by Marcus Bull and Damien Kempf (Woodbridge: Boydell, 2014), pp. 127–39 (p. 131); Simon T. Parsons, 'The Use of *Chanson de Geste* Motifs in the Latin Texts of the First Crusade, c.1095–1145' (unpublished PhD dissertation, Royal Holloway, University of London, 2015), pp. 72–4.

and think about it as they listen' ('[u]niversos qui hanc istoriam legerint, sive legere audierint et auditam intellexerint'), informing them that he was compelled to write by obedience ('scribere conpulsus sum per obedientiam'), and that 'if anyone desires to know the place where this history was composed, let him know that it was the cloister of a certain *cella* of Saint-Rémi founded in the bishopric of Reims' ('[s]i quis affectat scire locum quo hec istoria composita fuerit, sciat esse claustrum cuiusdam celle sancti Remigii constitute in episcopatu Remensi').[225] What are we to make of Robert's claim that he wrote history out of obedience? Obedience to whom? As a monk, the only individual to whom Robert could have been obliged by a vow of obedience was his community's abbot, and the examples of Guibert and others studied in this chapter shows that this was taken extremely seriously.[226] But who was this abbot, and which monastic community is meant here?

Robert's monastic career is now widely held to have begun not at Reims, but at Marmoutier, meaning that he supposedly only became associated with Saint-Rémi when he was appointed as its abbot in late 1095/early 1096 in succession of the late Henry I (1076–95).[227] By contrast, the nineteenth-century editors of the *Recueil des historiens des croisades* believed that Robert had initially made his profession at Saint-Rémi and *only then* transferred to Marmoutier before returning to Reims to take up his abbacy.[228] The evidence produced in support of this version of events includes a letter by Pope Gregory VII dated 1077 that has one 'Robertus' amongst Saint-Rémi's monks, and which specifies further that this Robert, along with another monk called Lambert, had been excommunicated by the archbishop of Reims, Manasses I (1069–80).[229] Robert's primary monastic affiliation is of importance because it helps us establish the likely identity of his abbatial patron, the enigmatic 'abbas, nomine B.'. Most scholars now agree that Robert produced the *Historia* in the first decade of the twelfth century, long after his abbacy at Saint-Rémi had been curtailed by his excommunication by Archbishop Manasses II of Reims (1096–1106) and his removal from office in 1097.[230] Though Robert

---

[225] *HI*, ed. Kempf and Bull, p. 3; *Historia*, tr. Sweetenham, p. 75.

[226] *RB*, ed./tr. Venarde, pp. 38–41. Given the close textual and semantic proximity between 'abbas B.' and 'obedientia' in the *Historia*'s preface, it seems highly unlikely, if not outright impossible, that Robert could have intended to use the latter in anything but its literal sense—that is, as a reference to the monastic hierarchy within which he had grown up and spent virtually the entirety of his life.

[227] *HI*, ed. Kempf and Bull, pp. xxi–xxii, who consider it 'unlikely that he [Robert] had had any previous association with Reims [prior to his abbacy]'.

[228] *Recueil des historiens des croisades: Historiens occidentaux*, 5 vols. (Paris: Imprimerie impériale, 1844–95), III, xlii.

[229] *Das Register Gregors VII.*, ed. by Erich Caspar, 2 vols. [= *MGH Epp. sel.* II] (Berlin: Weidmann, 1920–3), I, 326–9 (pp. 327–8) (= no. IV, 20); translated in *The Register of Pope Gregory VII, 1073–1085: An English Translation*, tr. by Herbert E. J. Cowdrey (Oxford: Clarendon, 2002), pp. 230–2 (p. 231); the identification of the 'Robertus' in Gregory VII's letter with Robert the Monk is rejected by *HI*, ed. Kempf and Bull, p. xxii n. 52.

[230] Note, though, that the text's most recent editors suggest a date of completion as late as *c*.1110; *HI*, ed. Kempf and Bull, pp. xxxiv–xli; also cf. James Naus, 'The *Historia Iherosolimitana* of Robert the Monk and the Coronation of Louis VI', in *Writing the Early Crusades: Text, Transmission and Memory*,

challenged the archbishop's ruling and rallied some support that allowed him to force the deposition of his appointed successor, Burchard (1097/8–1100), he would never be reinstated—he even was banned from setting foot in the monastery—but had to withdraw, tail between his legs, to Saint-Rémi's dependent priory of Saint-Oricle at Sénuc, where he is recorded in the office of prior as late as 1122 and called 'the sometime abbot of Saint-Rémi' ('olim Sancti Remigii abbas') in a letter sent by Pope Calixtus II to the then archbishop of Reims.[231] Thus when Robert asserts to have written the *Historia* 'in claustro cuiusdam celle sancti Remigii', this most likely refers to precisely this dependent monastic cell ('cella') of Saint-Oricle.

As Saint-Oricle's prior, Robert would have been answerable to the abbot at the mother house at Reims, rather than to that of Marmoutier. As Pope Urban II proclaimed explicitly shortly after Robert's excommunication in 1097, Bernard of Marmoutier's abbatial authority over him had ceased when he left his community for Saint-Rémi, whence he was 'released entirely from the yoke of domination of his old monastery's abbot' ('se absolute a maioris monasterii abbatis dominationis iugo absolutum fuisse').[232] This unequivocal papal ruling must put Bernard of Marmoutier—and any of his successors—firmly out of the running for the role of the *Historia*'s abbatial patron, regardless of whether or not Robert had professed himself to them previously. Instead, everything points to the abbot(s) of Saint-Rémi who took over from Robert after his deposition. The problem is, however, that at the time Robert wrote the *Historia* at Saint-Oricle, neither Marmoutier nor Saint-Rémi were governed by an abbot whose name begins with 'B'. Bernard of Marmoutier had died in April 1100 and was succeeded by Hilgod (1100–4) and William (1104–24), whereas Burchard of Saint-Rémi had been removed from office that same year by Robert's few remaining political allies and was succeeded by Azenaire (1100–18).[233] Surely, though, Robert's statement that he wrote out of obedience ('obedientia') to his superior refers to the point at which the work was first commissioned, not the point at which it was completed?

---

ed. by Marcus Bull and Damien Kempf (Woodbridge: Boydell, 2014), pp. 105–15. The traditional view that the *Historia* served as inspiration for the so-called *Magdeburger Aufruf* conventionally dated to 1107/8 has been refuted comprehensively.

[231] 'Ad Rodulfum archiepiscopum Remensem', in *Patrologia Latina*, ed. by Jean-Paul Migne, 221 vols. (Paris: Garnier, 1841–55), CLXIII, 1247–8 (p. 1247).

[232] *Annales Ordinis S. Benedicti Occidentalium monachorum Patriarchae*, ed. by Jean Mabillon, 6 vols. (Paris: Robustel, 1703–39), V, 381.

[233] Sharon Farmer, *Communities of Saint Martin: Legend and Ritual in Medieval Tours* (Ithaca, NY: Cornell University Press, 1991), pp. 47–8; Edmond Martène, *Histoire de l'abbaye de Marmoutier*, 2 vols. (Tours: Guilland-Verger, 1874–5), I, 536–7, who dates Bernard's death to 7 April 1100. As others have observed, two of the *Historia*'s manuscripts have the variant 'N.' instead of 'B.', though this is most likely due to the perpetuation of a scribal error and, in any case, would not allow an identification with any of the post-1097 abbots of Saint-Rémi or Marmoutier; cf. Jay Rubenstein, 'The *Deeds* of Bohemond: Reform, Propaganda, and the History of the First Crusade', *Viator* 47 (2016), 113–36 (p. 119 n. 35).

According to the *Historia*'s preface, the commissioning abbot had shown Robert a history of similar subject matter ('unam istoriam secundum hanc materiam') that he deemed unsatisfactory ('ei admodum displicebat'), essentially asking Robert to do a better job than his unnamed predecessor.[234] This substandard source is widely held to have been the anonymous *Gesta Francorum*—or rather, a text from the '*Gesta Francorum* tradition' or, to adopt one scholar's terminology, a 'Jerusalem history'.[235] A version of this *Gesta Francorum*/Jerusalem history was almost certainly circulating in France in the first decade of the twelfth century, yet scholars have been cautious, and with good reason, to pinpoint the exact date it arrived in the Latin West in written form.[236] If the *Historia*'s patron was indeed Robert's successor at Saint-Rémi, Abbot Burchard, then he and Robert must have had access to the narrative—in some form or other—before Burchard's own deposition on 18 November 1100. Whilst this seems rather early given what is known about the *Gesta*'s manuscript tradition,[237] not to mention the considerable speed with which the narrative would have had to reach France after the capture of Jerusalem in July 1099, it is not an entirely impossible scenario, especially if we embrace the aforementioned possibility—convincingly reinforced by Samu Niskanen—that the *Gesta* might have had their primitive origins in a now-lost parent text (a so-called '*Ur-Gesta*' = Rubenstein's Jerusalem history/ Niskanen's α).[238] The existence of such a 'rough-hewn, unpretentious' narrative, an 'awkward collection of texts' written in 'rough-and-ready prose',[239] chimes very well with Robert's assertion that the text his abbatial patron had asked him to replace was unsatisfactory 'partly because the series of beautiful events it contained was thrown together carelessly, and [partly because] the literary composition and expression were haphazard' ('partim quia series tam pulcre materiei inculta iacebat, et litteralium compositio dictionum inculta vacillabat').[240] This

---

[234] *HI*, ed. Kempf and Bull, p. 3; *Historia*, tr. Sweetenham, p. 75.

[235] The terms '*Gesta Francorum* tradition' and 'Jerusalem history' are adopted from Jay Rubenstein, 'What is the *Gesta Francorum*, and Who Was Peter Tudebode', *Revue Mabillon* 16 (2005), 179–204 (p. 189), whose arguments concerning the early textual tradition seem compelling; Rubenstein suggests that '[t]he Jerusalem history itself was probably a work of compilation, a collection of short edifying stories or sermons which were probably originally in the vernacular'; by contrast, Bull, 'Robert', p. 131 believes that Robert used the *Gesta Francorum* 'in a form very close to those in which it now survives'.

[236] The traditional (and still popular) thesis that Robert wrote his *Historia* as part of a literary 'propaganda campaign' orchestrated by Bohemond of Tarento after his return to the West in 1105–7 has been dismantled by Nicholas L. Paul, 'A Warlord's Wisdom: Literacy and Propaganda at the Time of the First Crusade', *Speculum* 85 (2010), 534–66. As Paul could show, Bohemond's efforts are unlikely to have resulted in the strategic production of large textual corpora, but instead relied on the dissemination of information 'mainly in the form of elaborately performed narrative' (ibid., p. 560). Though questioned by some such as Rubenstein, 'Deeds', pp. 115–16, Paul's arguments remain convincing. It is rather telling that the publication of the *Historia*'s new and much-needed critical edition is currently being held back until such time as the dust around these ongoing debates has settled.

[237] *HI*, ed. Kempf and Bull, pp. xlii–xlvii; Parsons, 'Use', p. 72.

[238] Samu Niskanen, 'The Origins of the *Gesta Francorum* and Two Related Texts: Their Textual and Literary Character', *Sacris Erudiri* 51 (2012), 287–316 (pp. 290–6).

[239] Rubenstein, 'Gesta', pp. 184, 188, and 203.   [240] *HI*, ed. Kempf and Bull, p. 3.

statement might indicate that the primitive narrative available to Robert and Burchard was not (yet) a fully-fledged chronicle, perhaps not even a coherent piece of writing, but a motley assortment of texts and documents that had reached Saint-Rémi in the form of various crusader journals, letters, and codicils—and quite possibly orally—that had been assembled hastily with little attempt to reconcile their contents and chronologies.[241] Though the evidence ultimately remains ambivalent, it does, on balance, point most strongly to Burchard of Saint-Rémi as our prime candidate for the identity of 'abbas, nomine B.'.

Accepting this identification casts the *Historia*'s preface in a slightly different light, with Robert using it to express the resentment he felt towards his abbatial patron and successor, who had 'jumped in his grave' and forced him to spend his days cloistered away in a minor dependency, and who, judging from Robert's lament, had made him produce the commissioned text all by himself without any scribal assistants ('[e]go vero, quia notarium non habui alium nisi me, et dictavi et scripsi')—perhaps an indication that as the superior of Saint-Oricle's mother house, Burchard denied Robert copyists in the same way that Abbot Theodemar had done to Paul the Deacon, thereby adding insult to injury.[242] Such enforced acts of abbatial patronage and historiographical commission show us yet another way in which the writing of history was inseparably intertwined with the exercise of institutional authority and lordly *potestas*. The fact that Robert had once held an abbacy himself—the very one that the *Historia*'s patron had taken from him!—makes his a particularly pertinent case study, and it may not be unreasonable to imagine that the ambiguity of the preface's enigmatic reference to 'abbas, nomine B.' was no accident, but rather a deliberate and shrewd manoeuvre to sabotage the memory of an abbatial patron who, in the end, had proven himself more of a rival and usurper than a supporter. Acknowledging Burchard by initial only but not suppressing his name altogether would have constituted a minor form of *damnatio memoriae*, with Robert perhaps trusting that over time readers would struggle and eventually become unable to identify 'B.', a strategy that, as the different identifications proposed in modern scholarship show, proved largely successful.

A major case of *damnatio memoriae* that entirely concealed an abbot's patronage occurs in the work of twelfth-century abbot-historian Suger of Saint-Denis (1122–51). Celebrated for his monastic leadership, architectural campaigns, and sizeable historiographical oeuvre,[243] Suger is often portrayed as an agent of change

---

[241] On the circulation of crusade narratives in letter form and their reception in monastic environments, see Thomas W. Smith, 'First Crusade Letters and Medieval Monastic Scribal Cultures', *Journal of Ecclesiastical History* 71 (2020), 484–501; Simon T. Parsons, 'The Letters of Stephen of Blois Reconsidered', *Crusades* 17 (2018), 1–29; Carol L. Symes, 'Popular Literacies and the First Historians of the First Crusade', *Past and Present* 235 (2017), 37–67.

[242] *HI*, ed. Kempf and Bull, p. 3; *Historia*, tr. Sweetenham, p. 75. Robert describes how the work had flowed from his mind to his pen and thence onto the page ('paruit menti manus, et manui penna, et penne pagina').

[243] Suger's works are edited in *Suger: Œuvres*, ed./tr. by Françoise Gasparri, 2 vols. (Paris: Les Belles Lettres, 1996–2001); on his writings about Saint-Denis, see Andreas Speer, 'Abt Sugers Schriften zur

whose abbacy marked a watershed in the community's history and the way it was committed to written records. As important work by Lindy Grant, Bernard Guenée, and Rolf Große has shown, however, such identifications require adjustment because they tend to ignore the considerable debt Suger's work owed to the influence of his predecessor and mentor, Adam (1094–1122).[244] The fact that '[i]n the collective memory of St-Denis, he [Adam] was bound to fade besides his energetic successor' owes much to Suger's systematic effort to minimize the previous abbot's legacy in his historical writings, and in this Suger found an accomplice in Peter Abelard, whose *Historia calamitatum* paints a less than complimentary picture of Adam's abbatial regime that makes Suger's achievements look even more imposing.[245] Though Suger was in many respects a continuator of Adam's initiatives, he showed great ingenuity, and little reservation, in excising him from the record to claim their collaborative achievements solely as his own.[246] This is true not only for Suger's architectural work that all but eclipses the groundwork laid by his late predecessor,[247] but also for his role in securing the monastery's privileges—if need be with forgeries—and, of main interest here, his historiographical patronage.

fränkischen Königsabtei Saint-Denis', in *Abt Suger von Saint-Denis: Ausgewählte Schriften. Ordinatio, De consecratione, De administratione*, ed. by Andreas Speer et al., 3rd ed. (Darmstadt: Wissenschaftliche Buchgesellschaft, 2008), pp. 13–66, with critical editions in ibid., pp. 174–99 (*Ordinatio*), 200–55 (*De consecratione*), and 256–72 (*De administratione*); these are translated in *Abbot Suger on the Abbey Church of St.-Denis and Its Art Treasures*, tr. by Erwin Panofsky and Gerda Panofsky-Soergel, 2nd ed. (Princeton, NJ: Princeton University Press, 2019).

[244] Bernard Guenée, 'Chancelleries et monastères: La mémoire de la France au Moyen Âge', in *Les Lieux de mémoire*, ed. by Pierre Nora, 3 vols. (Paris: Gallimard, 1984–92), II, 5–30 (pp. 21–7); translated as 'Chanceries and Monasteries', tr. by Deke Dusinberre, in *Rethinking France: Les Lieux de mémoire*, ed. by Pierre Nora and tr. by David P. Jordan, 4 vols. (Chicago, IL: University of Chicago Press, 1999–2010), IV, 1–26 (pp. 16–22). On Adam, see Rolf Große, 'L'abbé Adam, prédécesseur de Suger', in *Suger en question: Regards croisés sur Saint-Denis*, ed. by Rolf Große (Munich: Oldenbourg, 2004), pp. 31–43; Lindy Grant, *Abbot Suger of St-Denis: Church and State in Early Twelfth-Century France* (London: Longman, 1998), pp. 182–5.

[245] Grant, *Suger*, p. 183; also cf. Speer, 'Schriften', pp. 17–18 and 62; on Suger and Abelard, see Louis Grodecki, 'Abélard et Suger', in *Pierre Abélard et Pierre le Vénérable: Les courants philosophiques, littéraires et artistiques en occident au milieu du XIIe siècle*, ed. by René Louis et al. (Paris: Éditions du CNRS, 1975), pp. 279–86; repr. in *Le Moyen Âge retrouvé: De l'an mil à l'an 1200*, ed. by Louis Grodecki (Paris: Flammarion, 1986), pp. 217–22.

[246] See Rolf Große, *Saint-Denis zwischen Adel und König: Die Zeit vor Suger (1053–1122)* (Stuttgart: Thorbecke, 2002), p. 12: '... daß Suger zwar das Werk Abt Adams fortführte, dessen Verdienste aber dem Vergessen anheimzugeben verstand'. It has also been noted that Suger 'enjoyed the confidence of his abbot [Adam]' and, as a result, 'was coming to move in high circles, [...] rapidly gaining administrative experience', which makes his ungenerous treatment of Adam look almost cynical in nature; see *Suger: The Deeds of Louis the Fat*, tr. by Richard C. Cusimano and John Moorhead (Washington, DC: Catholic University of America Press, 1992), p. 3.

[247] Grant, *Suger*, pp. 183–4; Françoise Gasparri, 'L'administration de Suger, Abbé de Saint-Denis, d'après les Gesta Sugerii', in *Aux sources de la gestion publique*, ed. by Elisabeth Magnou-Nortier, 3 vols. (Lille: Presses universitaires de Lille, 1993–7), III, 111–28; Giles Constable, 'Suger's Monastic Administration', in *Abbot Suger and Saint-Denis: A Symposium*, ed. by Paula L. Gerson (New York, NY: The Metropolitan Museum of Art, 1986), pp. 17–32; repr. in *Monks, Hermits and Crusaders in Medieval Europe*, ed. by Giles Constable (Aldershot: Ashgate, 1988), no. X (pp. 1–51); Erik Inglis, 'Remembering and Forgetting Suger at Saint-Denis, 1151–1534: An Abbot's Reputation between Memory and History', *Gesta* 54 (2015), 219–43.

A prime example of this studied by van Houts is a historical compendium (Paris, Bibliothèque Mazarine, MS 2013) assembled c.1117–25/6 that was begun under Adam's patronage and, following his death in 1122, continued by Suger.[248] Intriguingly, several texts contained in MS Mazarine 2013 appear to have been copied from autographs in the libraries of their authors' monasteries, which were centres of historiographical production in their own right,[249] and the anonymous compiler's ability to visit these libraries or borrow their holdings depended on the authority and authorization of his abbatial patrons. This was a collaborative, cross-generational project sponsored by two successive abbots that provided the monks of Saint-Denis with a corpus of recent histories complementing—and serving as a framework for—Suger's historiographical work.[250] Likewise, Suger's ability to continue MS Mazarine 2013 and other projects he had inherited from Adam was facilitated by his previous appointment as Adam's right-hand man, a continuity that contextualizes Suger's work without minimizing it.[251] His historical vision comprised not just written texts, but also buildings and spaces charged with historical meaning within which these texts were situated, brought to live, and experienced by the community.[252] Following in Adam's footsteps, Suger was more than an instigator of historiographical composition—he was the architect of his community's memory.

2.6 Architects of Memory

In this book we have already met several abbots who were intellectual and spatial architects of memory. Besides Adam and Suger of Saint-Denis, there was also, for instance, Leonas of San Clemente a Casauria, patron of the illustrated *Chronicon Casauriense,* who commissioned the construction of a historiated sculpture for his community's abbey church. By creating these communal *lieux de mémoire,*

---

[248] Elisabeth M. C. van Houts, 'Suger, Orderic Vitalis, and the Vexin: Some Observations on Bibliothèque Mazarine MS 2013', in *Political Ritual and Practice in Capetian France: Studies in Honour of Elizabeth A. R. Brown,* ed. by Cecilia Gaposchkin and Jay Rubenstein (Turnhout: Brepols, 2021), pp. 55–76 (pp. 71–2); I am thankful to Elisabeth van Houts for kindly sharing this article with me prior to publication. On Adam's death, see Große, *Saint-Denis,* pp. 228–9.
[249] Van Houts, 'Suger', pp. 68–9.
[250] Speer, 'Schriften', pp. 18–19 describes Suger's domestic histories as a link ('Verbindungsglied') between the abbey and its socio-political environment that had Suger withdraw (if only temporarily) from his secular diplomatic relationships and act primarily in the capacity of a monk and abbot whose attention was focused entirely on the monastic community of Saint-Denis ('Der Staatsmann Suger tritt ganz hinter dem Mönch und Abt zurück, der [...] all sein Trachten und Tun völlig in den Dienst des Klosters des Heiligen Dionysius stellt').
[251] Van Houts, 'Suger', pp. 65–6; Julian Führer, 'Documentation et écriture de l'histoire chez l'abbé Suger', in *L'Écriture de l'histoire au Moyen Âge: Contraintes génériques, contraintes documentaires,* ed. by Étienne Anheim et al. (Paris: Garnier, 2015), pp. 149–60.
[252] Laurent Avezou, 'Du Moyen Âge à la fin des Lumières', in *Lex lieux de l'histoire,* ed. by Christian Amalvi (Paris: Armand Colin, 2005), pp. 13–63 (pp. 34–5).

monastic superiors engaged in 'memoryscaping'—a term that, as noted elsewhere, provides 'a useful conceptual portmanteau' for studying landscapes, natural as well as manmade, that contribute to the creation of memory narratives.[253] An instructive case of just such a 'memoryscaper' is that of Eigil, abbot (818–22) of Fulda.[254] Eigil had joined Fulda's community as a child and spent two decades under the rule of his kinsman, Sturmius (744–79).[255] By the time of his election, he was an old man who had witnessed the monastery's changing fortunes under three heads of house. Though there had been some literary activity under Abbots Ratger and Baugulf (779–802), the writing of history—specifically domestic history—at Fulda had not (yet) developed into a major enterprise as it did under the patronage of, for example, the early abbots of Saint-Wandrille and Wearmouth-Jarrow. This is not to say there had been no chronographical efforts prior to Eigil's abbacy. There were, it is true, the *Annales Fuldenses antiquissimi*, the *Annales necrologici*, and the recension of the *Chronicon Laurissense breve*,[256] none of which, however, provides more than glosses on the history of the community and the succession of its abbots, leading one scholar to conclude that they were 'probably intended for private use only'.[257] Whatever we might make of this suggestion—at least in the case of the *Annales necrologici*, it seems certain that they would have had an application in the communal settings of the monastic liturgy and *memoria*—it is safe to say that these texts did not inspire processes of

---

[253] Quote from Sarah De Nardi et al., 'Introduction', in *The Routledge Handbook of Memory and Place*, ed. by Sarah De Nardi et al. (New York, NY: Routledge, 2019), pp. 1–7 (p. 4); Hamzah Muzaini and Brenda S. A. Yeoh, *Contested Memoryscapes: The Politics of Second World War Commemoration in Singapore* (New York, NY: Routledge, 2016), pp. 9–10.

[254] On what follows, cf. Pohl, '*Locus memoriae*'. On the conflicts that led to Ratger's deposition and Eigil's role in them, see Patzold, 'Konflikte', pp. 137–9; Raaijmakers, *Fulda*, pp. 99–131; most recently Jebe, 'Reform', *passim*.

[255] *Vita*, ed. Becht-Jördens, p. 5; on Eigil's kinship with Sturmius, cf. *Vita*, ed. Engelbert, pp. 6–7 and 131.

[256] 'Annales Fuldensis antiquissimi', in *Annales Fuldenses sive Annales regni Francorum orientalis*, ed. by Friedrich Kurze and Georg H. Pertz [= *MGH SS rer. Germ.* VII] (Hanover: Hahn, 1891), pp. 136–8. The earliest manuscript witnesses are Munich, Bayerische Staatsbibliothek, MS Clm. 14641, fols. 38r–40r, and Vienna, Österreichische Nationalbibliothek, MS Cod. 460, fols. 10v–13r, both of which were begun *c*.780. See also Richard Corradini, 'Zeiträume–Schrifträume: Überlegungen zur Komputistik und Marginalchronographie am Beispiel der "Annales Fuldenses antiquissimi"', in *Vom Nutzen des Schreibens: Soziales Gedächtnis, Herrschaft und Besitz im Mittelalter*, ed. by Walter Pohl and Paul Herold (Vienna: Verlag der österreichischen Akademie der Wissenschaften, 2002), pp. 113–66. The *Annales necrologici* have been edited in *Die Klostergemeinschaft von Fulda im früheren Mittelalter*, ed. by Karl Schmid et al., 3 vols. (Munich: Fink, 1978), I, 271–364; also cf. Otto G. Oexle, 'Die Überlieferung der fuldischen Totenannalen', in *Die Klostergemeinschaft von Fulda im früheren Mittelalter*, ed. by Karl Schmid et al., 3 vols. (Munich: Fink, 1978), II.2, 447–504; principally Eckhard Freise, 'Die Anfänge der Geschichtsschreibung im Kloster Fulda' (unpublished PhD dissertation, University of Münster, 1979).

[257] Raaijmakers, *Fulda*, p. 117, with reference to the *Chronicon*'s recension; also Janneke Raaijmakers, 'Memory and Identity: The *Annales necrologici* of Fulda', in *Texts and Identities in the Early Middle Ages*, ed. by Richard Corradini et al. (Vienna: Verlag der österreichischen Akademie der Wissenschaften, 2006), pp. 303–21 (p. 320), where it is argued that the *Annales necrologici* 'cannot have been more than a list of names on a piece of parchment'.

community-building and the formation of a historical consciousness to the same degree as monastic foundation histories and *gesta abbatum*.[258]

Collective memory relies on narratives, and after three generations the monastic community founded in the 740s had reached a crucial juncture that is known in Memory Studies as the threshold for the transfer of narratives in a group's social or communicative memory—with an average 'shelf-life' of c.80–100 years—to the more durable media of cultural memory.[259] Transfers between these two memory formats do not happen automatically or by accident, but through processes of codification and 'cultural formation'.[260] In his four years as abbot, Eigil initiated and oversaw several such processes. One was a collaborative writing campaign that produced three closely related works of historiography: the *Vita Sturmi* written c.820 by Eigil himself; the *Vita Baugulphi* authored by Brun Candidus around the same time or shortly afterwards; and the *Vita Ratgarii* written after Ratger's resignation.[261] Their narratives together offered the community the first official history of its foundation and the deeds of its earliest abbots—a *gesta abbatum/historia fundationis*—nearly a century before the *Catalogus abbatum Fuldensium*.[262] This dual focus is shared by the *Gesta abbatum Fontanellensium* as well as the *Vita Ceolfridi* and the *Historia abbatum* from Wearmouth-Jarrow, though it seems unlikely that Eigil had first-hand knowledge of these texts.[263]

---

[258] Contrary to the overly optimistic interpretation of the *Annales antiquissimi*'s community-building potential by Raaijmakers, *Fulda*, pp. 56–7. Also cf. Hans-Werner Goetz, 'Zum Geschichtsbewußtsein in der alamannisch-schweizerischen Klosterchronistik des hohen Mittelalters (11.–13. Jahrhundert)', *Deutsches Archiv für Erforschung des Mittelalters* 44 (1988), 455–88 (pp. 461–4).

[259] See principally Assmann, 'Communicative Memory'. Aleida Assmann, 'Memory: Individual and Collective', in *The Oxford Handbook of Contextual Political Analysis*, ed. by Robert E. Goodin and Charles Tilly (Oxford: Oxford University Press, 2006), pp. 210–24 (p. 215) reminds us that '[t]o move from individual and social memory to [...] cultural memory is to cross a threshold of time'; also cf. Aleida Assmann, 'Four Formats of Memory: From Individual to Collective Constructions of the Past', in *Cultural Memory and Historical Consciousness in the German-Speaking World since 1500*, ed. by Christian Emden and David Midgley (Oxford: Peter Lang, 2004), pp. 19–38; on this threshold in historical writing, see Pohl, *Dudo*, pp. 6–17; van Houts, *Memory*, pp. 6–7.

[260] Assmann, 'Communicative Memory', p. 111.

[261] *Vita*, ed. Engelbert. The *Vita Baugulphi* and *Vita Ratgarii* do not survive. Walter Berschin, 'Biographie im karolingischen Fulda', in *Kloster Fulda in der Welt der Karolinger und Ottonen*, ed. by Gangolf Schrimpf (Frankfurt a. M.: Knecht, 1993), pp. 315–24 (pp. 316–17) dates the composition of the *Vita Ratgarii* to 'after 817'. The dates of composition of the *Vita Sturmi* and *Vita Baugulphi* have caused much scholarly debate, on which cf. the recent discussion in Pohl, '*Locus memoriae*'.

[262] Fulda, Hochschul- und Landesbibliothek, MS B1, fols. 4r–5r; edited in *Klostergemeinschaft*, ed. Schmid et al. I, 212–13. Also cf. Mechthild Sandmann, 'Die Äbte von Fulda im Gedenken ihrer Mönchsgemeinschaft', *Frühmittelalterliche Studien* 17 (1983), 393–444. The *Vita Sturmi*'s dual function as a *historia fundationis* was acknowledged as late as the fifteenth century, when it was given the title 'Vita Sturmi primi abbatis et fundatoris Fuldensis coenobii' by the compilers of the *Vitae sanctorum* (Würzburg, Universitätsbibliothek, MS p. th. q. 13).

[263] *Abbots of Wearmouth and Jarrow*, ed./tr. by Christopher Grocock and Ian N. Wood (Oxford: Oxford University Press, 2013), pp. xxv–xxxii. As we will recall, the *Gesta abbatum* of Saint-Wandrille were completed under the patronage of its Abbot Ansegis, who was elected the year after Eigil's death, making it improbable that the unfinished work-in-progress reached Fulda in time to inspire the *Vitae* of its earliest abbots, and rather more likely that the two projects drew inspiration from a similar, and perhaps the same, source. Berschin, 'Bibliographie', pp. 317–18 points to the *Vita abbatum Iurensium*, the *Vita abbatum Acaunensium*, and the *Vitae sanctorum patrum Pladonis, Tatonis et Tasonis* from

A more plausible source of inspiration is the biography of Roman pontiffs known as the *Liber pontificalis*. Though the earliest record of its presence at Fulda is a library inventory from the turn of the sixteenth century, there is some evidence that the *Liber pontificalis* was, if not owned by, then almost certainly known to Fulda's monks considerably earlier.[264] Access to it would have been possible via the libraries of associated institutions like Würzburg Cathedral, which according to a book list from *c*.800 regularly lent books 'to Fulda' ('ad Fultu') and had a copy at the time.[265] Knowledge of the *Liber pontificalis* at such an early date—whether via Würzburg or another associated library—would chime very well with Paul Lehmann's observation of a growing historical interest at Fulda that placed great emphasis on works of classical and, more specifically, Roman history.[266]

As shown elsewhere, this 'Roman connection' was crucial—and indeed central—to Eigil's memoryscaping.[267] We can see textual traces of this in the *Vita Sturmi*, in which Eigil gives a detailed, if highly selective, account of Sturmius's travels in Italy. Just a few years after the community's foundation

San Vincenzo al Volturno as potential sources of inspiration. On these works, see also Ian N. Wood, 'Roman Barbarians in the Burgundian Province', in *Transformations of Romanness: Early Medieval Regions and Identities*, ed. by Walter Pohl et al. (Berlin: De Gruyter, 2018), pp. 275–88.

[264] Basel, Universitätsbibliothek, MS F III 42 fol. 10v; edited in *Mittelalterliche Bücherverzeichnisse des Klosters Fulda und andere Beiträge zur Geschichte der Bibliothek des Klosters Fulda im Mittelalter*, ed. by Schrimpf, Gangolf et al. (Frankfurt a. M.: Knecht, 1992), p. 143 (= no. 473). Previous knowledge and use of the *Liber pontificalis* at Fulda is evidenced by, for example, an eleventh-century epitome in Leiden, Universiteitsbibliotheek, MS Scaliger 49; Rosamond McKitterick, 'Rome and the Popes in the Construction of Institutional History and Identity in the Early Middle Ages: The Case of Leiden, Universiteitsbibliotheek, Scaliger MS 49', in *Rome and Religion in the Medieval World: Studies in Honour of Thomas F. X. Noble*, ed. by Valerie L. Garver and Own M. Phelan (Farnham: Ashgate, 2014), pp. 207–34. As observed by Berschin, 'Biographie', p. 317, it is difficult to imagine that Fulda's tenth-century *Catalogus abbatum* could have been conceptualized without an existing model like the *Liber pontificalis*. Berschin does not, however, consider the possibility that this model may have been none other than the series of abbatial *vitae* written by Eigil and/or under his patronage.

[265] Oxford, Bodleian Library, MS Laud. Misc. 126, fol. 260r; edited in Bernhard Bischoff and Josef Hofmann, *Libri Sancti Kyliani: die Würzburger Schreibschule und die Dombibliothek im VIII. und IX. Jahrhundert* (Würzburg: Schöningh, 1952), pp. 142–9 (p. 145); Michael Lapidge, 'Surviving Booklists from Anglo-Saxon England', in *Learning and Literature in Anglo-Saxon England: Studies Presented to Peter Clemoes on the Occasion of His Sixty-Fifth Birthday*, ed. by Michael Lapidge and Helmut Gneuss (Cambridge: Cambridge University Press, 1985), pp. 33–89 (p. 41); see also *Medieval Manuscripts from Würzburg in the Bodleian Library*, ed. by Daniela Mairhofer (Chicago, IL: University of Chicago Press, 2014), pp. 401–13; Rosamond McKitterick, 'Anglo-Saxon Links with Rome and the Franks in the Light of the Würzburg Book-List', in *Manuscripts in the Anglo-Saxon Kingdoms: Cultures and Connections*, ed. by Claire Breay et al. (Dublin: Four Courts Press, 2021), pp. 86–97 (pp. 90–1).

[266] See Paul Lehmann, 'Fulda und die antike Literatur', in *Aus Fuldas Geistesleben: Festschrift zum 150 jährigen Jubiläum der Landesbibliothek Fulda*, ed. by Joseph Theele (Fulda: Fuldaer Actiendruckerei, 1928), pp. 9–23 (p. 15); Paul Lehmann, 'The Benedictine Order and the Transmission of the Literature of Ancient Rome in the Middle Ages', *Downside Review* 71 (1953), 407–2; also cf. Bernhard Bischoff, 'Das benediktinische Mönchtum und die Überlieferung der klassischen Literatur', *Studien und Mitteilungen zur Geschichte des Benediktinerordens und seiner Zweige* 92 (1981), 165–90; Bernhard Bischoff, *Manuscripts and Libraries in the Age of Charlemagne* (Cambridge: Cambridge University Press, 1994), pp. 134–60. Other institutions known to have had copies of the *Liber pontificalis* include Lorsch, St Gall, and Reichenau; see McKitterick, *Invention*, pp. 172–3, with a distribution map.

[267] See the discussion in Pohl, '*Locus memoriae*'.

and Sturmius's appointment as abbot, Boniface had sent him on an extended journey south of the Alps. Sturmius's primary destination was Benedict's abbey of Montecassino, where he would sojourn for a while to learn how to govern a monastery in accordance with the *Rule*.[268] There can be no doubt that Eigil knew of this formative visit to Montecassino, a record of which survives in the famous petition of 812 known as the *Supplex libellus* that Eigil had co-authored with some fellow monks to oust his abbatial predecessor, Ratger.[269] And yet, he makes no mention of it in the *Vita Sturmi*, which focuses entirely on Sturmius's time in Rome.[270] Whilst this shift of focus may have had to do with a desire to foreground the memory of the exemption privilege Sturmius had received from Pope Zachary (741-52) to help emancipate Fulda's monastic community from its diocesan bishops, this is unlikely to have been Eigil's only reason for glossing over Montecassino in his biography of Fulda's revered founding abbot.[271] Whatever the motivation(s), the effect was that Sturmius's memory at Fulda was re-shaped in the image of St Benedict not as founder and abbot of Montecassino, but as *abbas Romensis*—a tradition that from the seventh century had become increasingly widespread in England and the so-called 'insular province' in Francia,[272] and one which at Fulda maintained its currency all the way to the fifteenth century, when a local compilation of saints' lives featuring the *Vita Sturmi* received an illustrated frontispiece that depicts Boniface and Pope Gregory I (590–604) side by side against the backdrop of Rome's stylized cityscape (Würzburg, Universitätsbibliothek, MS p. th. q. 13, fol. 1v).[273]

Eigil applied this *abbas Romensis* tradition first to Sturmius and then, by extension, to his successors, and even to Boniface. To appreciate the extent of this *imitatio Romana*, Eigil's historiographical activity needs to be contextualized with his patronage in another key area of cultural formation: architecture. This

---

[268] *Vita*, ed. Engelbert, pp. 9 and 17; also cf. Thomas Franke, 'Studien zur Geschichte der Fuldaer Äbte im 11. und frühen 12. Jahrhundert', *Archiv für Diplomatik* 33 (1987), 55–238 (p. 62 n. 34); Bärbel Witten, *Die Vita der Heiligen Lioba: Eine angelsächsische Äbtissin im Karolingerreich* (Hamburg: Kovač, 2012), pp. 212–16.

[269] 'Supplex libellus monachorum Fuldensium Carolo imperatori porrectus (812 et 817)', ed. by Josef Semmler, in *Initia consuetudinis Benedictinae. Consuetudines saeculi octavi et noni*, ed. by Kassius Hallinger, 2nd ed. (Siegburg: Schmitt, 1989), pp. 319–27 (p. 324).

[270] *Vita*, ed. Engelbert, p. 146.

[271] See Franke, 'Studien', pp. 65–6; Hartmut Hoffmann, 'Die älteren Abtslisten von Montecassino', *Quellen und Forschungen aus italienischen Archiven und Bibliotheken* 47 (1967), 224–354 (pp. 338–46); Konrad Lübeck, 'Die Exemtion des Klosters Fulda bis zur Mitte des 11. Jahrhunderts', *Studien und Mitteilungen zur Geschichte des Benediktinerordens und seiner Zweige* 55 (1937), 132–53.

[272] See principally Joachim Wollasch, '"Benedictus abbas Romensis": Das römische Element in der frühen benediktinischen Tradition', in *Tradition als historische Kraft: Interdisziplinäre Forschungen zur Geschichte des früheren Mittelalters*, ed. by Norbert Kamp and Joachim Wollasch (Berlin: De Gruyter, 1982), pp. 119–37; also cf. Pius Engelbert, 'Regeltext und Romverehrung: Zur Frage der Verbreitung der *Regula Benedicti* im Frühmittelalter', *Römische Quartalschrift für christliche Altertumskunde und Kirchengeschichte* 81 (1986), 39–60; Jesse D. Billett, *The Divine Office in Anglo-Saxon England, 597–c.1000* (Woodbridge: Boydell, 2014), pp. 82–4; Klaus Zelzer, *Ambrosius, Benedikt, Gregor: Philologisch-literarisch-historische Studien* (Vienna: LIT, 2015), pp. 189–90.

[273] See Pohl, '*Locus memoriae*', with a photographic reproduction of this frontispiece.

included the re-modelling of Ratger's monumental abbey church, which likewise had been inspired by Roman tradition.[274] Ratger's specific source of inspiration had been the fourth-century *Basilica sancti Petri*—known today as Old St Peter's Basilica—built by Constantine over the apostle's tomb, the measurements of which Ratger requested personally from Rome to serve as a template for his master builders. Though a conversion error left Fulda's transept about twelve meters short of its Roman equivalent, the building for many centuries remained the most faithful imitation of Old St Peter north of the Alps.[275] As Ratger's successor, Eigil re-oriented the church's interior and turned it into a performative space by staging the cult of Boniface along a 'memory trail' that, in a way not dissimilar from our modern museums, guided the monks and their visitors on an itinerary of carefully curated *aides-mémoires*.[276] Chief amongst them was Boniface's tomb, which Eigil had relocated into the western apse, fitted with a submerged walkway to allow pilgrim traffic even during Mass, and surrounded with historiated wall paintings that showed selected scenes from Boniface's life—including the community's foundation—and were designed by none other than Brun, the author of the *Vita Baugulphi*.[277] In addition, Eigil commissioned a programme of altar *tituli* from Rabanus with metric verses that complemented these foundational narratives and facilitated their aural reception.[278]

---

[274] See Werner Jacobsen, 'Die Abteikirche in Fulda von Sturmius bis Eigil–kunstpolitische Positionen und deren Veränderungen', in *Kloster Fulda in der Welt der Karolinger und Ottonen*, ed. by Gangolf Schrimpf (Frankfurt a. M.: Knecht, 1993), pp. 105–27; Heinrich Hahn, 'Die drei Vorgängerbauten des Fuldaer Domes', *Fuldaer Geschichtsblätter* 61 (1985), 180–202.

[275] See Jacobsen, 'Abteikirche', p. 121; Michael Imhof, 'Bischofssitze, Kirchen, Klöster und Pfalzen im Umkreis Karls des Großen', in *Karl der Große: Leben und Wirkung, Kunst und Architektur*, ed. by Michael Imhof and Christoph Winterer, 2nd ed. (Petersberg: Imhof, 2013), pp. 118–236 (pp. 155–6). Ratger's builders failed to notice that the measurements received from Rome had already been converted (1 Roman foot ~ 29.60 cm vs. 1 Carolingian foot ~ 32.24 cm) and thus converted them again; see Richard Krautheimer, 'The Carolingian Revival of Early Christian Architecture', *Art Bulletin* 24 (1942), 1–38 (p. 11 n. 83); Friedrich Oswald, 'Fulda, Dom', in *Vorromanische Kirchenbauten: Katalog der Denkmäler bis zum Ausgang der Ottonen*, ed. by Friedrich Oswald et al. (Munich: Prestel, 1966/71, repr. 1990), pp. 84–7. Other abbey churches that imitate Old St Peter include Durham, Winchester, and Santa Maria de Ripoll; see Charles B. McClendon, *The Origins of Medieval Architecture: Building in Europe, A.D. 600–900* (New Haven, CT: Yale University Press, 2005), pp. 158–61; Kenneth J. Conant, *Carolingian and Romanesque Architecture, 800–1200*, 4th ed. (New Haven, CT: Yale University Press, 1978), pp. 43–86; Malcolm Thurlby, 'The Roles of the Patron and the Master Mason in the First Design of the Romanesque Cathedral of Durham', in *Anglo-Norman Durham, 1093–1193*, ed. by David Rollason et al. (Woodbridge: Boydell, 1994), pp. 161–84 (pp. 163–5); Jonathan Turnock, 'Landscapes of Patronage, Power and Salvation: A Contextual Study of Architectural Stone Sculpture in Northern England, c.1070–c.1155', 2 vols. (unpublished PhD dissertation, Durham University, 2018), I, 56.

[276] A similar trail designed as a *via sacra* for the cult of St Peter existed at Old St Peters in the eighth century; Joanna Story, 'The Carolingians and the Oratory of Saint Peter the Shepherd', in *Old Saint Peter's, Rome*, ed. by Rosamond McKitterick et al. (Cambridge: Cambridge University Press, 2013), pp. 257–73.

[277] On these paintings, see *Vita*, ed. Becht-Jördens, p. 60; Sturmius had commissioned similar paintings for the 'arca' above Boniface's original tomb; *Vita*, ed. Engelbert, p. 156; Dominicus Heller, *Die ältesten Geschichtsschreiber des Klosters Fulda* (Fulda: Parzeller, 1952), p. 26.

[278] Gereon Becht-Jördens, 'Sturmi oder Bonifatius? Ein Konflikt im Zeitalter der anianischen Reform um Identität und monastisches Selbstverständnis im Spiegel der Altartituli des Hrabanus

Last but not least, he installed several vaulted crypts whose occupants combined into nothing short of a 'who's who' for the history of late antique and early medieval monasticism, again with a notable concentration on Roman saints.[279]

Whilst Eigil's 'make-over' of Ratger's abbey church created a communal monument to the memory of Boniface, his next building campaign—and the *pièce de resistance* of his monastic memoryscape: the sepulchral church of St Michael—was dedicated specifically to Sturmius's legacy.[280] Constructed in 820 and situated in the monastery's graveyard,[281] its architecture has been noted for its *imitatio Romana* that includes the classicizing capitals on both levels of the famous 'anastasis rotunda'.[282] As with Eigil's modifications to the abbey church, however, the most significant architectural features are found underground. In the crypt, the only part of the building to survive in its original form, a single stone pillar from Fulda's first church built by Sturmius on the site occupied by its Carolingian successor was re-used as the central support structure for the circular vault that carried—and still carries—the entire building above ground (Fig. 2.4).[283] With its squat shaft and simple Ionic capital, it marks a stark contrast to the tall columns with elaborate Corinthian capitals found on the upper floors and throughout Ratger's basilica. This was no spoliation or pragmatic re-cycling, but a powerful symbolic statement expressed through architecture that has a narrative equivalent in the *Vita Sturmi*'s portrayal of Sturmius as the community's founding figure: just as Eigil's church of St Michael rests on the strong foundation of the 'Sturmius-pillar', the community's history and historical consciousness rest on the shoulders of its venerated

---

Maurus für die Salvatorbasilika zu Fulda', in *Hrabanus Maurus in Fulda: Mit einer Hrabanus Maurus-Bibliographie (1979–2009)*, ed. by Marc-Aeilko Aris and Susana Bullido del Barrio (Frankfurt a. M.: Knecht, 2010), pp. 123–87.

[279] See *Vita*, ed. Becht-Jördens, pp. 53–5; also cf. Gereon Becht-Jördens, 'Text, Bild und Architektur als Träger einer ekklesiologischen Konzeption von Klostergeschichte: Die karolingische Vita Aegil des Brun Candidus von Fulda (ca. 840)', in *Hagiographie und Kunst: Der Heiligenkult in Schrift, Bild und Architektur*, ed. by Gottfried Kerscher (Berlin: Reimer, 1993), pp. 75–106 (pp. 90–3).

[280] Pohl, '*Locus memoriae*'.

[281] Imhof, 'Bischofssitze', pp. 152–61; Johannes Burkhardt, 'Fulda, Michaelsberg', in *Die benediktinischen Mönchs- und Nonnenkloster in Hessen*, ed. by Friedhelm Jürgensmeier et al. [= *Germania Benedictina* VII] (St. Ottilien: EOS, 2004), pp. 456–64.

[282] See Imhof, 'Bischofssitze', pp. 153 and 158–60, with photographic reproductions. The building's round shape may have been modelled on the Holy Sepulchre in Jerusalem, and by *c*.1093—if not earlier—it also featured a physical replica of Christ's tomb; Otfried Ellger, *Die Michaelskirche zu Fulda als Zeugnis der Totensorge: Zur Konzeption einer Friedhofs- und Grabkirche im karolingischen Kloster Fulda* (Fulda: Parzeller, 1989), pp. 20–30; Gereon Becht-Jördens, 'Die Vita Aegil des Brun Candidus als Quelle zu Fragen der Geschichte Fuldas im Zeitalter der anianischen Reform', *Hessisches Jahrbuch für Landesgeschichte* 42 (1992), 19–48 (p. 36); Carsten Fleischhauer, 'Die Vita Eigilis des Brun Candidus und die Michaelskirche in Fulda', *Fuldaer Geschichtsblätter* 68 (1992), 85–103 (pp. 96–7 and 103).

[283] An identical pillar dated *c*.750 survives amongst the exhibits of Fulda's Dommuseum, a photographic reproduction of which is provided by Imhof, 'Bischofssitze', p. 156. Contrary to traditional interpretations, archaeological research shows Sturmius's abbey church to have been a basilica with three aisles, rather than a single-aisled structure as previously thought, Jacobsen, 'Abteikirche', pp. 106–7.

Fig. 2.4 The 'Sturmius-pillar' in the crypt of St Michael's Church, Fulda. Michaelskirche–Bistum Fulda.

first abbot.[284] With Sturmius's body safely interred in the basilica alongside Boniface's, the pillar from his original foundation thus acted as a memory medium that ensured his presence in Eigil's new church—not entirely unlike the holograms allowing famous rock and pop legends to continue to fill stadiums long after their deaths.

Just how much symbolic and commemorative capital Sturmius's presence carried is shown by Eigil's intention to turn the vaulted chambers that circle the Sturmius-pillar into an official mausoleum for Fulda's future abbots, starting with himself.[285] According to the *Vita Aegil*, he designated one of these chambers as his final resting place and even dug out the grave with his own hands in the hope that his abbatial successors would follow suit and be buried alongside him.[286] This remained wishful thinking. Only one more abbot, Hatto I (842–56), was laid to

---

[284] As explained elsewhere, the term 'Sturmius pillar' does not contradict the ecclesiological interpretation of the pillar as resembling Christ, but is actually perfectly compatible given the abbot's role as Christ's appointed representative in the monastery; see Pohl, '*Locus memoriae*'. On this ecclesiological interpretation, see Becht-Jördens, 'Text', pp. 89–90.

[285] Raaijmakers, *Fulda*, pp. 170–3 describes this planned mausoleum as 'a monument for the abbots to strengthen the awareness of a genealogy, and continuity with the past' (ibid., p. 171); also cf. Ellger, *Michaelskirche*, pp. 104–16.

[286] *Vita*, ed. Becht-Jördens, pp. 74–5.

Fig. 2.5 Eigil of Fulda's (empty) grave in the crypt of St Michael's Church, Fulda. Michaelskirche–Bistum Fulda.

rest in the crypt in the sarcophagus right next to Eigil's, and today both graves are empty and the whereabouts of their former occupants unknown (Fig. 2.5). Had Eigil's plan for an abbatial mausoleum come to fruition, the crypt in the church of St Michael would have formed the architectural counterpart of—and a performative space/stage for—the historical narrative of the *gesta abbatum/historia fundationis* produced at his patronage. Calling to mind Jocelyn Wogan-Browne's description of the nuns' cemetery at Barking Abbey as 'a locus of memory and continuity and an ever-present theatre of events',[287] the sepulchral church of St Michael built in Fulda's monastic graveyard as a monument to its founding abbot provided the community with just such a *locus memoriae* that promoted a sense of historical tradition and continuity after a period of discord and upheaval under Eigil's predecessor(s).[288]

---

[287] Jocelyn Wogan-Browne, 'Dead to the World? Death and the Maiden Revisited in Medieval Women's Convent Culture', in *Guidance for Women in Twelfth-Century Convents*, ed./tr. by Vera Morton and Jocelyn Wogan-Browne (Cambridge: Brewer, 2003), pp. 157–80 (p. 179).
[288] Patzold, 'Konflikte', pp. 105–39; Jebe, 'Reform', pp. 57–62; Raaijmakers, *Fulda*, pp. 99–131.

The church of St Michael was not the only 'theatre of events', to adopt Wogan-Browne's expression, in Fulda's monastic memoryscape.[289] As discussed above, there was also the abbey church with its memory trail of tombs and altars, though here the primary emphasis was on Boniface, rather than on Sturmius and his abbatial successors. Another communal space that provided a stage for historical narratives was the monastery's refectory. Unlike the sepulchral church and its crypt, usage of which would have been sporadic and exclusive to the monastic community, the refectory was used multiple times a day by the monks and, occasionally, their visitors. According to Brun, Eigil capitalized on this regularity by setting the *Vita Sturmi* as mealtime reading for Fulda's monks ('fratribus ad mensam recitare praecepit') so they could reflect on the monastery's origins and the life of its founding abbot ('de vita abbatis et origine monasterii').[290] Rehearsed in this context, the work acquired a currency—and authority—that assured it a privileged place in what Aleida Assmann calls a community's 'cultural working memory' or 'memory canon',[291] placing it alongside foundational texts such as the *Rule of St Benedict*, a copy of which (Würzburg, Universitätsbibliothek, MS p. th. q. 22) was made by Brun—quite possibly at Eigil's orders—for table reading in the monks' dining hall.[292] The refectory maintained this important function as a *lieu de mémoire* and venue of historical edification in the daily life and routine of Fulda's religious community throughout the Middle Ages and even beyond. We can still see visual traces of this on the walls of the late baroque refectory painted by *Historienmaler* Johann Andreas Herrlein (†1796) with scenes from the community's history, the earliest of which correspond to those narrated

---

[289] Memory Studies use the term 'arena' to describe similar concepts; Muzaini and Yeoh, *Memoryscapes*, p. 10 thus use it with reference to 'the complex landscape upon which memories and memory practices move, come into contact, are contested by, and contest other forms of remembrance'; see also Kendall R. Phillips and G. Mitchell Reyes, 'Introduction: Surveying Global Memoryscapes: The Shifting Terrain of Public Memory Studies', in *Global Memoryscapes: Contesting Remembrance in a Transnational Age*, ed. by Kendall R. Phillips et al. (Tuscaloosa, AL: University of Alabama Press, 2011), pp. 1–26.

[290] *Vita*, ed. Becht-Jördens, p. 18; also cf. *Vita*, ed. Engelbert, p. 16; Otto G. Oexle, 'Memorialüberlieferung und Gebetsgedächtnis in Fulda vom 8. bis zum 11. Jahrhundert', in *Die Klostergemeinschaft von Fulda im früheren Mittelalter*, ed. by Karl Schmid et al., 3 vols. (Munich: Fink, 1978), I, 136–77 (pp. 146–7).

[291] Aleida Assmann, 'Canon and Archive', in *Cultural Memory Studies: An International and Interdisciplinary Handbook*, ed. by Astrid Erll et al. (Berlin: De Gruyter, 2008), pp. 97–107; Assmann reminds us that '[t]he term "canon" belongs to the history of religion', and a group's memory canon 'is not built up anew by every generation; on the contrary, it outlives the generations who have to encounter and reinterpret it anew according to their time. This constant interaction with the small selection of artifacts keeps them in active circulation and maintains for this small segment of the past a continuous presence' (ibid., p. 100). At Fulda, the *Vita Sturmi* constituted precisely such an artefact designed for regular interaction that lent a continuous presence to the abbot's memory in the community's daily routine.

[292] This is shown by Christine E. Ineichen-Eder, 'Künstlerische und literarische Tätigkeit des Candidus-Brun von Fulda', *Fuldaer Geschichtsblätter* 56 (1980), 201–17 (p. 204), who concludes that the manuscript was used 'für die Tischlesung'; also cf. Bernhard Bischoff, 'Die ältesten Handschriften der Regula S. Benedicti in Bayern', *Studien und Mitteilungen zur Geschichte des Benediktinerordens und seiner Zweige* 92 (1982), 7–16 (pp. 9–10).

in the *Vita Sturmi*.²⁹³ Whether similar paintings also adorned the walls of the medieval refectory is not known, but it would chime well with Eigil's instruction that Fulda's *gesta abbatum/historia fundationis* be consumed by the monks with both their ears and eyes ('auribus et oculis') whilst taking their meals.²⁹⁴

It was not just the abbots of Fulda who considered historical narratives suitable for mealtime reading. As argued above (2.3), when Abbot Simon of Marchiennes requested the *Chronicon Marchianense* from the reluctant monk-historian Andreas towards the very end of the twelfth century, he may well have had a similar application in mind. Even before the turn of the millennium, refectories had become increasingly common venues for the aural delivery and reception of texts other than monastic rules, and by the later eleventh century these regular communal gatherings 'constituted the most extensive programme of public reading within monastic communities outside the liturgy of the mass and Office'.²⁹⁵ Besides Fulda and Marchiennes, we can see evidence of this in, for example, a late thirteenth-/early fourteenth-century compendium of *vitae/gesta* from Campsey. Containing Old French/Anglo-Norman translations of works by Garnier de Pont-Saint-Maxence, Clemence of Barking, and Matthew Paris, the manuscript (London, British Library, MS Additional 70513) has two ownership inscriptions, one of which simply attributes it to the convent ('Cest livere est a covent de Campisse'; fol. 1v), whereas the other specifies further that the codex and the texts contained therein were 'to be read during meals' ('de lire a mengier'; fol. 265v).²⁹⁶ As shown by Sara Gorman, the later medieval nuns and abbesses of Campsey used these narratives as their institutional historiography, and reading them during mealtimes fostered a strong sense of community and historical belonging.²⁹⁷ The same was true at Barking, where a twelfth-century collection of foundation narratives and *gesta abbatissarum* commissioned by Ælfgyva and her abbatial

---

²⁹³ See Werner Kathrein, 'Der Historienmaler Johann Andreas Herrlein–oder: die Gründung des Bistums Fulda in der Historienmalerei des Johann Andreas Herrlein im Refektorium des ehemaligen Benediktinerkonvents in Fulda', *Alte und neue Kunst* 41 (2002), 138–42. On the depicted episodes, cf. Raaijmakers, *Fulda*, pp. 19–40. I enjoyed the privilege of taking several meals a day in this refectory during my appointment as Gangolf-Schrimpf Visiting Fellow.

²⁹⁴ *Vita*, ed. Becht-Jördens, p. 18.

²⁹⁵ Teresa Webber, 'Monastic Space and the Use of Books in the Anglo-Norman World', *Anglo-Norman Studies* 36 (2014), 221–40 (p. 237); also Teresa Webber, 'Reading in the Refectory at Reading Abbey', *Reading Medieval Studies* 42 (2016), 63–88; Teresa Webber, 'Reading in the Refectory: Monastic Practice in England, c.1000–c.1300', an extended version of Webber's Annual John Coffin Memorial Palaeography Lecture 2010 (rev. 2013), available on the author's academia.edu page, https://www.academia.edu/9489001/Reading_in_the_Refectory_Monastic_Practice_in_England_c_1000_c_1300. https://www.ies.sas.ac.uk/sites/default/files/files/Publications/Webber_Teresa_ReadingintheRefectory_Feb2012_RevisedEdition2013_new.pdf.

²⁹⁶ See Delbert Russell, 'The Campsey Collection of Old French Saints' Lives', *Scriptorium* 57 (2003), 51–83; Mary C. Erler, 'Private Reading in the Fifteenth- and Sixteenth-Century English Nunnery', in *The Culture of Medieval English Monasticism*, ed. by James G. Clark, new ed. (Woodbridge: Boydell, 2007), pp. 134–46 (p. 137).

²⁹⁷ Sara Gorman, 'Anglo-Norman Hagiography as Institutional Historiography: Saints' Lives in Late Medieval Campsey Ash Priory', *Journal of Medieval Religious Cultures* 37 (2011), 110–28.

successors (Cardiff, Public Library, MS 1.381) has been shown to have had a primary locus in the nuns' refectory.[298]

A particularly colourful example of a *gesta abbatum* made for communal consumption in the refectory is the *Catalogus abbatum* compiled by Andreas Lang, abbot-historian of Michelsberg. Produced in 1487 by Andreas's chaplain/*amanuensis*, Nonnosus,[299] the authorial manuscript (Bamberg, Staatsbibliothek, MS RB Msc. 48) is a bulky tome unsuitable for much other than private study and reference. Contributing to this sense of unwieldiness are copies of hundreds of charters spanning the period 973–1483,[300] and the *mise-en-page* exhibits signs of redaction and work-in-progress that may suggest the book remained in the author's personal possession to serve as his 'desk copy'.[301] Why the text and decoration remained unfinished is difficult to ascertain, but comparison with another manuscript produced just a few years later provides a plausible explanation. In 1494, less than a decade after its composition, Bamberg's *Catalogus abbatum* was reduced to a quarter of its original length, stripped ruthlessly of all extraneous contents (including the charters), and copied into a much slimmer and more user-friendly codex (Bamberg, Staatsbibliothek, MS RB Msc. 49) by Reinher, a local monk-scribe working under Andreas's supervision.[302] The purpose of this truncation and re-codification is revealed by the title the new book was given: *Fasciculus abbatum*—a reference to the sheaves ('fasciculi') of grain/wheat that were the main ingredient of the monks' daily bread.[303] As the prologue explains, the work's plain style of composition ('stilus humilis') and lack of verbosity ('non

---

[298] See Bussell and Brown, 'Lives', pp. 13–14. On the manuscript's use(s), see Diane Watt, *Women, Writing and Religion in England and Beyond, 650–1100* (London: Bloomsbury Academic, 2019), pp. 135–9; Diane Watt, 'A Manuscript for Nuns: Cardiff, Central Library, MS 1.381', *Postcards from the Archives: Women's Literary Culture before the Conquest* (2018), https://blogs.surrey.ac.uk/early-medieval-women/2018/02/05/a-manuscript-for-nuns-cardiff-central-library-ms-1-381/.

[299] Petersohn, 'Fragmente', pp. 595–7; Machilek, 'Geschichtsschreibung', p. 314. Nonnosus subsequently became the community's prior and authored a 'twin-*vita*' of Emperor Henry II (1014–24) and Empress Kunigunde (1014–24).

[300] Caspar A. Schweitzer, 'Das Urkundenbuch des Abtes Andreas im Kloster Michelsberg bei Bamberg in vollständigen Auszügen', *Bericht über das Wirken des Historischen Vereines zu Bamberg* 16 (1853), i–x and 1–175; Caspar A. Schweitzer, 'Das Urkundenbuch des Abtes Andreas im Kloster Michelsberg bei Bamberg in vollständigen Auszügen (II. Abtheilung)', *Bericht über das Wirken des Historischen Vereines zu Bamberg* 17 (1854), 1–147.

[301] There are various unfinished sections and blank spaces for content to be added later—for example, fols. 61r–67v, 75v–76r, and 98r–99v.

[302] The original in MS Bamberg RB Msc. 48 fills 523 pages (fols. 72r–333r) measuring 39.5 × 27.7 cm with 50–60 lines/page; by contrast, the abbreviated version in MS Bamberg RB Msc. 49 only has 107 pages (fols. 1r–54r) measuring 35.5 × 27.7 cm with 60–70 lines/page. Cf. *Katalog der Handschriften der königlichen Bibliothek zu Bamberg*, ed. by Friedrich Leitschuh et al., 4 vols. (Bamberg: Buchner, 1895–1966), I.3, 21–6; Karin Dengler-Schreiber, *Scriptorium und Bibliothek des Klosters Michelsberg in Bamberg* (Graz: Akademische Druck- und Verlagsanstalt, 1979), pp. 147–8; Karl-Georg Pfändtner, 'Andreas Lang: Chronica abbatum monasterii S. Michaelis (fasciculus abbatum) et pontificum Babenbergensis ecclesiae (= B.14)', in *Im Schutz des Engels: 1000 Jahre Kloster Michaelsberg Bamberg, 1015–2015*, ed. by Norbert Jung and Holger Kempkens (Petersberg: Imhof, 2015), pp. 429–30.

[303] This metaphor chimes well with a stipulation found in the sixth-century monastic rule of Ferreolus of Uzès, according to which monks unable to work in the fields to produce food should

verborum pompa') are meant to resemble the monks' simple diet, making it the perfect choice of reading during the community's daily mealtime gatherings.[304]

Rather than offering exhaustive detail like the *Catalogus*, the *Fasciculus* gives succinct summaries of the abbots' main achievements that could be remembered easily and read out episodically in the monks' refectory. Embellishing these 'bite-sized' biographies of Bamberg's abbots are no fewer than forty-one miniature portraits whose significance in the context of communal commemoration and abbatial self-fashioning are discussed later in this study (3.3), including one for its author (Fig. 2.6). The *Fasciculus*'s effective use of colour and navigation aids like running titles and 'thumbnails' in the page margins to facilitate episodic reading and recital marks a notable contrast to the plain and pragmatic layout of the *Catalogus*, and its prologue explicitly encourages the use of multiple senses by instructing the audience to read and hear ('legere et audire') about these abbots and their deeds with pen ('stilo'), ears ('auribus'), and eyes ('oculis')—instructions strikingly similar to those issued nearly seven hundred years earlier by Eigil for the *Vita Sturmi*.[305] In both cases, the audience gathered in the monastic refectory was expected to experience and 'consume' history in a multi-sensory setting that relied on the combined mnemonic powers of hearing, seeing, and even touching.[306]

---

prepare the pages of books for writing, thereby (so the implication) equally contributing to the community's nourishment; Latin text edited by Vincent Desprez, 'La Regula Ferrioli: Texte critique', *Revue Mabillon* 60 (1982), 117–48 (p. 139) [hereafter *RF*]; *Ferreolus: Mönchsregel*, ed./tr. by Ivo Auf der Maur and Georg Holzherr (St. Ottilien: Eos, 2011). More explicit is the famous parable by Peter the Venerable, abbot of Cluny (1122–56), which compares the production of books in the monastery to the monks' labour in the fields, with the scribe's hand and quill resembling the plough, the pages the Earth's soil, and the finished book God's abundant harvest ('[P]ro aratro convertatur manus ad pennam, pro exarandis agris divinis litteris paginae exarentur, seratur in cartula verbi dei seminarium, quod maturatis segetibus, hoc est libris perfectis, multiplicatis frugibus esurientes lectores repleat, et sic panis caelestis laetalem animae famem depellat'); *The Letters of Peter the Venerable*, ed. by Giles Constable, 2 vols. (Cambridge, MA: Harvard University Press, 1967), I, 27–41 (p. 38) (= no. 20). Reciting the proverb from Matthew 4:4—'Man shall not live on bread alone'—the fifteenth-century constitutions of Żagań stipulate that 'just as the servant gives the brothers the physical bread by putting it in front of them, the librarian gives them the spiritual [bread] by providing [them with] books' ('[E]rgo sicut servitor fratribus ministret cibum corporalem ipsum apponendo, sic librarius spiritualem libros concedendo'); see Karl H. Rother, 'Ein Ausleihregister der Augustiner Chorherren zu Sagan: Ein Beitrag zur Geschichte der Bibliothek', *Zentralblatt für Bibliothekswesen* 43 (1926), 1–22 (pp. 1–2).

[304] MS Bamberg RB Msc. 49, fol. 1r, ll. 49–53. Recalling that as a monk he only ate plain food ('nec unquam repastinatum in mensa apposui'), Andreas states his intention to 'serve up' the *Fasciculus* to the monks as if it were beggar's bread ('vobis tanquam mendicatum panem [...] huiusmodi in mensa apposuit'), trusting that the work's unrefined style will be more palatable to them than the original *Catalogus abbatum*. The inspiration for this allegory may have been the *Supplementum chronicarum* written by Andreas's contemporary and fellow chronicler, Giacomo Filippo Foresti (†1520), a copy of which was present in the monastery's library; *MBKDS*, III.3, 386 and 393 (= nos. 96 and 101); cf. Achim Krümmel, *Das 'Supplementum chronicarum' des Augustinermönches Jacobus Philippus Foresti von Bergamo: Eine der ältesten Bilderchroniken und ihre Wirkungsgeschichte* (Herzberg: Bautz, 1992), pp. 242–3.

[305] MS Bamberg RB. Msc. 49, fol. 1r, ll. 36–9; here, too, Andreas seems to have borrowed from the preface of Foresti's illustrated *Supplementum chronicarum*.

[306] On the power of touch in medieval manuscript culture, cf. Kathryn M. Rudy, 'Touching the Book Again: The Passional of Abbess Kunigunde of Bohemia', in *Codex und Material*, ed. by Patrizia Carmassi and Gia Toussaint (Wiesbaden: Harrassowitz, 2018), pp. 247–57.

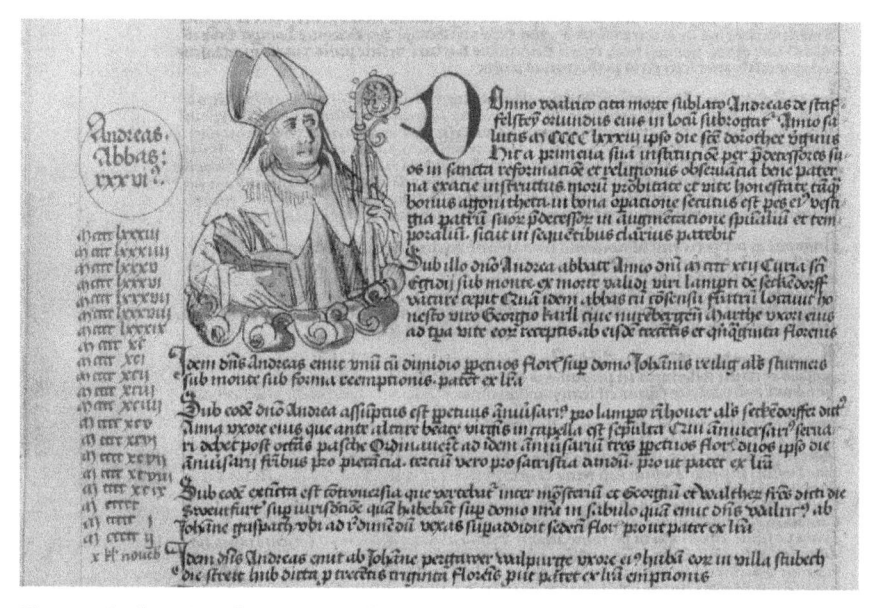

Fig. 2.6 Andreas Lang's portrait in the *Fasciculus abbatum*. Bamberg, Staatsbibliothek, MS RB. Msc. 49, fol. 54v.

It was not just illustrated manuscripts that facilitated this multi-sensory experience. As we saw above, a room's interior design could further amplify the mnemonic potential of the historical narratives recited within its walls. An instructive example of this is the monastic refectory of Sponheim re-designed by prolific abbot-historian, Johannes Trithemius. In 1502, Trithemius ordered for the walls of the community's summer refectory to be painted with portraits of his predecessors, from Bernhelm (1124/5–38) to Johann Kolenhausen. To accompany these images, Trithemius composed a series of *tituli* providing each abbot's biographical details before summarizing his most memorable deeds.[307] Most of the twenty-four incumbents are said to have governed the community well ('bene rexit'; 'bene praefuit') and done much good ('multa bona fecit'; 'optime fecit'), though some also face criticism.[308] Many of these 'mini-*gesta*' have verbatim parallels in, and

---

[307] Thirteen *tituli* were transcribed in the seventeenth century before the entire sequence was destroyed by extensive water damage; they are printed in *Die Inschriften des Landkreises Bad Kreuznach*, ed. by Eberhard J. Nikitsch [= *Die deutschen Inschriften* XXXIV] (Wiesbaden: Reicher, 1993), no. 223†, www.inschriften.net; also cf. Johannes Mötsch and Wolfgang Seibrich, 'Sponheim', in *Die Männer- und Frauenklöster der Benediktiner in Rheinland-Pfalz und Saarland*, ed. by Friedhelm Jürgensmeier and Regina E. Schwerdtfeger [= *Germania Benedictina* IX] (St. Ottilien: EOS, 1999), pp. 801–27 (pp. 821–2).

[308] Abbot Peter (c.1265) thus stands accused of having alienated churches and permitted the community's monks to accumulate personal property, a controversial decision that caused much envy and was soon reversed by his successor, Johann (1296–1306); *Inschriften*, ed. Nikitsch: 'Petrus [...] qui ecclesiam in Genzingen alienavit [...], primus pecculium indulsit'; 'Iohannes [...] homo bonus, qui peculium monachis denuo interdixit'.

were almost certainly copied from, another historical narrative written by Trithemius just a few years earlier, the *Chronicon Sponheimense*.[309] Recited from the pages of the *Chronicon*'s autograph (Würzburg, Universitätsbibliothek, MS ch. f. 126) and/or read directly off the refectory's walls during communal mealtimes, these texts and their corresponding images offered an opportunity for Sponheim's monks to reflect collectively on the achievements (and failures) of their superiors before committing them to memory with the assistance of visual *aides-mémoires*. An almost identical and contemporary text-image ensemble that may have been inspired by Trithemius's work at Sponheim existed at Hirsau. Here, too, the source of the *tituli* that accompanied the paintings on the walls of the summer refectory refurbished in 1517–21 was an existing text produced by Trithemius at the commission of Hirsau's abbots: the *Annales Hirsaugienses*.[310] Judging from the *tituli*'s transcriptions in John Parsimonius's sixteenth-century account book (Wolfenbüttel, Herzog August Bibliothek, MS. Cod. Guelf. 143.1 Extrav.), this programme of illustration was even more ambitious than that at Sponheim with key scenes from the abbey's foundation ('de fundationibus') and the life of St Benedict ('historica de Benedicto patre') alongside portraits of its abbots, patrons, and famous monks ('abbatibus, praeceptoribus et illustrioribus monachis coenobii'),[311] all of whom were afforded a privileged place in the community's historiographical and architectural memory.

It is fitting to end this discussion with one of the best-known illustrated histories made in the Middle Ages, the *Bayeux Tapestry*.[312] At nearly 70m in length, the work's purpose and location have been the subject of much speculation and debate, and the same is true for the identity—or perhaps identities—of its

---

[309] *Opera historica, quotquot hactenus reperiri potuerunt omnia*, ed. by Marquard Freher, 2 vols. (Frankfurt a. M.: Marne & Aubry, 1601; repr. Minerva, 1966), II, 236–435; also cf. *Inschriften*, ed. Nikitsch: 'Die [...] Inschriften wurden wohl von Trithemius selbst konzipiert, da sie zum Teil wörtlich auf den entsprechenden Stellen seiner Sponheimischen Klosterchronik basieren'.

[310] See Karl Wolff, 'Johannes Trithemius und die älteste Geschichte des Klosters Hirsau', *Württembergische Jahrbücher für Statistik und Landeskunde* [no vol. no.] (1863), 229–81 (pp. 268–70); Renate Neumüllers-Klauser, 'Quellen zur Bau- und Kunstgeschichte von Hirsau', in *Hirsau St. Peter und Paul 1091–1991*, ed. by Klaus Schreiner, 2 vols. (Stuttgart: Theiss, 1991), I, 475–99 (pp. 491–2); Christoph Schmitt, '*Trithemii effigies... ex archetype depicta*: Trithemiusbilder des 16. Jahrhunderts', in *Johannes Trithemius (1462-1516): Abt und Büchersammler, Humanist und Geschichtsschreiber*, ed. by Klaus Arnold and Franz Fuchs (Würzburg: Königshausen & Neumann, 2019), pp. 221–46 (pp. 223–38).

[311] Printed in *Die Inschriften des Landkreises Calw*, ed. by Renate Neumüllers-Klauser [= *Die deutschen Inschriften* XXX] (Wiesbaden: Reicher, 1992), pp. xxiii–xxiv (p. xxiii), www.inschriften.net. The original paintings/*tituli* do not survive. Cf. Arno Mentzel-Reuters, 'Serielle Chronographie und historische Unschärfe: Das historiographische Spätwerk des Johannes Trithemius', in *Herbipolis: Studien zu Stadt und Hochstift Würzburg in Spätmittelalter und Früher Neuzeit*, ed. by Markus Frankl and Martina Hartmann (Würzburg: Königshausen & Neumann, 2015), pp. 373–426 (p. 420). On Parsimonius, see Waldemar Kramer, *Johannes Parsimonius: Leben und Wirken des zweiten evangelischen Abtes von Hirsau (1525-1588)* (Frankfurt a. M.: Kramer, 1980).

[312] The scholarly literature on the *Bayeux Tapestry* is too vast to be referenced here. Facsimiles with discussions include *The Bayeux Tapestry*, ed. by David M. Wilson (London: Thames and Hudson, 2004); *The Bayeux Tapestry*, ed./tr. by Lucien Musset and Richard Rex (Woodbridge: Boydell, 2005); a digital facsimile is now available online courtesy of Bayeux Museum, https://www.bayeuxmuseum.com/en/the-bayeux-tapestry/discover-the-bayeux-tapestry/explore-online/.

patron(s). Traditionally, the *Tapestry*'s patronage has been ascribed to Odo, bishop of Bayeux (1049–97) and William the Conqueror's half-brother, leading some to suggest that it was intended for display inside Bayeux's cathedral church.[313] A more recent interpretation locates the *Tapestry*'s origins at St Augustine's Abbey, Canterbury during the tenure, and likely at the commission, of its first Norman abbot, Scolland (1070–87).[314] Even a compromise between the two has been proposed in the form of a joint patronage model that identifies Odo as the work's instigator and Scolland as its designer.[315] Whatever the nature of Scolland's role, it is generally accepted that he was involved in the *Tapestry*'s production in a capacity that can be referred to as a form of patronage. A former monk, treasurer, and scribe of Mont-Saint-Michel, he owed his post-Conquest appointment to King William, which would explain why as abbot he then invested the monastery's human and material resources into the making of an artefact celebrating the Conqueror and his deeds.[316] What is more, his first-hand experience in the production and decoration of manuscripts at Mont-Saint-Michel—a centre of book production, illumination, and historical writing in Normandy with close connections to England even before the Norman Conquest—would offer a compelling explanation for the iconographic similarities that have been observed between the *Tapestry* and contemporary products of the Montoise scriptorium.[317] Whether or not Scolland had a hand in the actual composition and artistic realization of the *Tapestry*'s narrative, as abbot he would have had to authorize the project and agree the allocation of considerable human and material

---

[313] On the *Bayeux Tapestry*'s physical measurements, cf. Derek Renn, 'How Big Is It–And Was It?', in *The Bayeux Tapestry: New Approaches*, ed. by Michael J. Lewis et al. (Oxford: Oxbow, 2011), pp. 52–8. The reconstruction of the embroidery's supposed installation in the eleventh-century nave of Bayeux Cathedral by Christopher Norton, 'Viewing the Bayeux Tapestry, Now and Then', *Journal of the British Archaeological Association* 172 (2019), 52–89 (pp. 53–61) is presented with greater confidence than the evidence permits, and his assertion that '[t]here is no need to look any further for its intended location' (ibid., p. 78) remains disputable. Norton has since gone further by arguing that the work was commissioned and then donated to Bayeux by William the Conqueror himself; Christopher Norton, 'The Helmet and the Crown: The Bayeux Tapestry, Bishop Odo and William the Conqueror', *Anglo-Norman Studies* 43 (2021), 123–50.

[314] See Elizabeth C. Pastan, 'Imagined Patronage', in Elizabeth C. Pastan and Stephen D. White, *The Bayeux Tapestry and Its Contexts: A Reassessment* (Woodbridge: Boydell 2014), pp. 59–81; Elizabeth C. Pastan and Stephen D. White, 'Problematizing Patronage: Odo of Bayeux and the Bayeux Tapestry', in *The Bayeux Tapestry: New Interpretations*, ed. by Martin K. Foys et al. (Woodbridge: Boydell, 2009), pp. 1–24.

[315] See most recently the discussion by Véronique Gazeau, 'Réformateur ou stratège? L'évêque Odon, patron des moines de Saint-Vigor et commanditaire de la tapisserie de Bayeux', in *Évêques et communautés religieuses dans la France médiévale*, ed. by Noëlle Deflou-Leca and Anne Massoni (Paris: Éditions de la Sorbonne, 2022), pp. 319–42; previously Howard B. Clarke, 'The Identity of the Designer of the Bayeux Tapestry', *Anglo-Norman Studies* 35 (2012), 120–39; Richard Gameson, 'The Origin, Art, and Message of the Bayeux Tapestry', in *The Study of the Bayeux Tapestry*, ed. by Richard Gameson (Woodbridge: Boydell, 1997), pp. 157–211.

[316] On Scolland's career, see Stephen D. White, 'Locating Harold's Oath and Tracing His Itinerary', in Elizabeth C. Pastan and Stephen D. White, *The Bayeux Tapestry and Its Contexts: A Reassessment* (Woodbridge: Boydell, 2014), pp. 105–25 (pp. 121–5).

[317] Clarke, 'Identity', pp. 130–1, with references to the relevant literature.

resources.³¹⁸ Such abbatial patronage and investment lends some credence to the suggestion that the *Tapestry* might have been hung in Canterbury's abbey church, one of the building campaigns initiated by Scolland and completed under his successors that attracted praise from Goscelin of Saint-Bertin and others.³¹⁹ If this was indeed where the work had its locus, it would have formed part of a memoryscape not unlike that at ninth-century Fulda. Elizabeth Pastan's suggestion that 'its most competent beholders would have been the monks [of St Augustine's] themselves' finds further support in the presence of several of the *Tapestry*'s *dramatis personae* in the community's martyrology and other records from the abbey's archives.³²⁰ If, as Pastan goes on to suggest, the *Tapestry* was designed to inspire historical contemplation and prompt Canterbury's monks to reflect on the history of their community and its benefactors, it would have served a function similar to that of the other text-image ensembles studied here.³²¹

2.7 Conclusions

Given the range of evidence analysed here, there can be no doubt that the modern notion of a historian as essentially a *homo scribens* conducting historical studies in pursuit of a personal inclination or sense of vocation is hopelessly insufficient to capture the collaborative and intrinsically hierarchical nature of writing history in medieval monastic communities.³²² In institutional environments that relied on the core principles of authority and obedience, and the basic operational structures of which depended fundamentally on the individual's complete and unquestioned subordination to the superior on the one hand, and the superior's ultimate and unchallenged responsibility for the community and all its members on the other, historical writing was no egalitarian exercise, much less a free-for-all. The

---

[318] Clarke, 'Identity', pp. 136–7 is no doubt correct to point out that Scolland 'must have been willing to give his blessing to such a major enterprise', even if his conclusion that the abbot personally 'determined the main storyline' is difficult to substantiate.

[319] See Elizabeth C. Pastan, '*Quid faciat...Scollandus*? The Abbey Church of St Augustine's c.1073–1100', in Elizabeth C. Pastan and Stephen D. White, *The Bayeux Tapestry and Its Contexts: A Reassessment* (Woodbridge: Boydell, 2014), pp. 260–87 (pp. 280–7), with specific reference to 'Historia, miracula et translatio sancti Augustini', in *Acta Sanctorum, Maii VI* (Antwerp: Societé des Bollandistes, 1688), pp. 377–443 (p. 413); also cf. the account in *The Life of Edward the Confessor Who Rests at Westminster Attributed to a Monk of Saint-Bertin*, ed./tr. by Frank Barlow, 2nd ed. (Oxford: Oxford University Press, 1992), pp. 133–49.

[320] Pastan, '*Quid faciat*', p. 261. See also Susan E. Kelly, 'Some Forgeries in the Archive of St. Augustine's Abbey, Canterbury', in *Fälschungen im Mittelalter*, ed. By Jasper Detlev, 5 vols. (Hanover: Hahn, 1988), IV, 347–69.

[321] Michael Crafton, 'Review of Elizabeth C. Pastan and Stephen D. White, *The Bayeux Tapestry and Its Contexts: A Reassessment*', *Speculum* 91 (2016), 550–1 (p. 550) refers to the *Tapestry* as a 'ruminative, memorializing text', one that was well suited to monastic modes of reading and viewing.

[322] The evidence and conclusions presented here cement Cleaver's pertinent observation that the traditional 'focus on the individual as the author of a history risks missing contributions made by others, particularly in monastic communities'; Cleaver, *History Books*, p. 34.

official decision as to which histories were (and were not) written in medieval monasteries rested, first and foremost, with their abbots and abbesses, who alone could grant their monks and nuns the dispensation to write and authorize the allocation of the time and resources required. Their agreement—better still, their sponsorship and support—was a *conditio sine qua non* for historiographical activity to take place and be sustained in a monastic context. Without their consent, let alone against their orders, the only alternative was to write in secret and alienate communal resources at the significant risk of incurring serious and at times severe punishment. As I hope to have shown, abbatial patronage, whilst frequent and widespread across the medieval Latin West, does not map easily onto other forms and contexts of patronage, especially those that were of a transactional nature and allowed for greater autonomy and negotiating powers than were available to the average monastic author when responding to an order from their superior, therefore requiring us to re-think and re-calibrate our common understanding of author-patron relationships when they involve medieval abbots and abbesses.

Perhaps the most important conclusions to be drawn from this discussion concern the ways in which abbatial patronage manifested itself in practice, rather than in theory or according to the prescriptions of monastic rules, customaries, and other normative texts, and the ends to which it was applied, and sometimes enforced, in the day-to-day context of the communal religious life. Whether they commissioned domestic or external writers—judging from the evidence, the former generally seems to have been the preferred *modus operandi*, even if it did not always form an available option—abbots and abbesses have emerged clearly as powerful and resourceful intellectual architects whose historiographical patronage was often part of more comprehensive efforts aimed at the codification, preservation, and re-imagination of communal memories and identities that involved, in the first instance, the institutions over which they presided, but similarly their wider socio-political, dynastic, and family networks. These efforts regularly comprised not only the commissioning of written texts, but also the construction of buildings and spaces within which these texts could be situated and experienced collectively—identified here as memoryscapes—as well as other material and immaterial memory media. To be 'lived' and 'inhabited', history did not just have to be written, but had to be embodied, performed, and activated in communal settings like the monastic refectory that, as my discussion has revealed, served as an important *locus historiae* and a performative stage for foundation histories, *gesta abbatum/abbatissarum*, and other historical narratives commissioned by monastic superiors. Just as the historian's craft involves much more than just putting one's pen to parchment, abbatial patronage is a panorama that only reveals itself when viewed through a wide lens.

3
Abbatial Book Provision and Library Building

3.1 Introduction

As the previous chapters have shown, abbots and abbesses regularly used their authority to champion the writing of history inside (and sometimes outside) their communities, be that by putting pen to parchment personally or by enabling others to do so at their commission. This required not just careful and efficient management of time, assets, and personnel, but also the provision of resources that were instrumental—and indispensable—to the writing of history: books. Without books, Orderic cautions his audience, the deeds of the past are given over to oblivion ('res gestae oblivioni traditae sunt'), and the memories of previous generations are washed away forever like hail or snow in a torrent ('quasi grando vel nix in undis cum rapido flumine irremeabiliter fluente defluunt').[1] As we will recall, Orderic composed the *Historia ecclesiastica* over nearly thirty years under the trans-generational patronage of Saint-Évoult's abbots, and it seems safe to assume, therefore, that it was they who provided him with his substantial and wide-ranging research library, only a fraction of which appears to have been available domestically at the outset of the ambitious writing project.[2]

That book provision was an integral aspect of the abbot's role in monastic historiographical production and recognized as such beyond Saint-Évoult is suggested by an idiom commonly attributed to Geoffrey of Breteuil/Saint-Victor (†c.1194) and recited frequently in subsequent centuries, according to which a cloister without a library is like a castle without an armoury ('Claustrum sine

---

[1] *HE*, ed./tr. Chibnall, III, 282–4, with further discussion in Benjamin Pohl, 'One Single Letter Remained in Excess of All His Sins...: Orderic Vitalis and Cultural Memory', in *Orderic Vitalis: Life, Works and Interpretations*, ed. by Charles C. Rozier et al. (Woodbridge: Boydell, 2016), pp. 333–51 (pp. 340–1). Orderic may well have drawn inspiration for this metaphor from the Charentonne, a river that originated near his monastery of Saint-Évoult in the Forest of Ouche; Hingst, *World*, pp. 1–4.

[2] See *HE*, ed./tr. Chibnall, I, 48–77, who identifies 'over a hundred [literary] sources' cited or mentioned by Orderic (ibid., p. 48). On Saint-Évoult's library, see Geneviève Nortier, *Les bibliothèques médiévales des abbayes bénédictines de Normandie*, 2nd ed. (Paris: Lethielleux, 1971), pp. 98–123; also cf. Jenny Weston and Charles C. Rozier, 'Descriptive Catalogue of Manuscripts Featuring the Hand of Orderic Vitalis', in *Orderic Vitalis: Life, Works and Interpretations*, ed. by Charles C. Rozier et al. (Woodbridge: Boydell, 2016), pp. 385–98.

armario, quasi castrum sine armamentario').[3] More important than the idiom's origins is the context in which Geoffrey uses it. Unlike Orderic, he addresses not a general readership, but a specific individual named Peter Mangot, a monk who with the support of powerful sponsors had obtained his abbot's permission to leave the community and establish a new monastery under his own leadership. In a letter commending Peter on his success and reminding him of the debt he owed to his advocates, himself included,[4] Geoffrey advises the monastic superior-to-be to make sure that the community placed under his governance will be impregnable like a castle, and to assemble within its walls an army of Christ ('Christi militia') ready to fight day and night ('die noctuque') with the arms of righteousness ('armis iustitiae') deposited in its *bibliotheca*.[5] It is Peter who must serve as the procurer and administrator ('procurator et minister') of his monastery's army and provide the weapons for its warriors ('ministrare arma pugnantibus') in the same way that the lord of a castle must provide for his soldiers. Geoffrey knew something of monastic governance and procurement due to his own appointment as prior of Sainte-Barbe-en-Auge, and this experience very likely informed his friendly but firm advice to Peter. As far as he was concerned, there could be no doubt that the provision of books fell, first and foremost, to the head of house. But just how widely held an expectation was this, and to what extent is it corroborated by the evidence of abbatial book provision across the medieval Latin West?

Unlike other monastic personnel whose *ex officio* involvement in the care of books has been investigated at some length, the subject of abbatial book provision has never been studied systematically. By scrutinizing the various means by which abbots and abbesses supplied their communities with books as resources for historical writing, I will showcase them as powerful library builders both in their

---

[3] Hubert Silvestre, 'À propos du dicton "Claustrum sine armario, quasi castrum sine armamentario"', *Medieval Studies* 26 (1964), 351–3. Casting doubt on the identification of Geoffrey as the idiom's inventor is an early twelfth-century compilation from Schäftlarn, which explains that a monastery's bookstore is called *armarium* because monks fight their adversaries with books instead of weapons ('arma'); Munich, Bayerische Staatsbibliothek, MS Clm. 17142, fol. 92v; Martin Steinmann, *Handschriften in Mittelalter: Eine Quellensammlung* (Basel: Schwabe, 2013), p. 227 (= no. 337). In a similar vein, Abbot Peter of Celle (1150–62) refers to books as shields for defence; 'De afflictione et lectione', in *La spiritualité de Pierre de Celle (1115–1183)*, ed. by Jean Leclercq (Paris: Vrin, 1946), pp. 231–9 (pp. 233–4); translated in *Peter of Celle: Selected Works*, tr. by Hugh Feiss (Kalamazoo, MI: Cistercian Publications, 1987), pp. 133–4.

[4] Evreux, Bibliothèque municipale, MS Lat. 46, fol. 104v; edited in 'Gaufridi apud sanctam Barbaram in Neustria canonicorum regularium subprioris epistolae', in *Patrologia Latina*, ed. by Jean-Paul Migne, 221 vols. (Paris: Garnier, 1841–55), CCV, 828–88 (pp. 844–5) (= no. xviii): '[H]abetis quod tam ardenter quaesistis, a nobis plane, a rege per nos, a capitulo Cisterciensis per litteras regis, caeterosque coadiutores, quod voluistis impetrastis'. Geoffrey's recollection that Peter's desire had seemed difficult to achieve at times ('difficillima quidem primo videbantur') may indicate some initial resistance on the abbot's part.

[5] 'Epistolae', ed. Migne, p. 845. In a previous letter (ibid., p. 842 (= no. xvi)), the abbot of Baugercy (Beaugerais?) had asked Geoffrey to write to Peter and admonish him to procure a 'bibliotheca' for his monastery as quickly as possible ('Salutat domnus Petrus Mangot [...], et inter caetera de bibliotheca emenda submoneatis'). As others have observed, Geoffrey uses 'bibliotheca' to refer to *both* a library in the physical sense and the Bible; ibid., p. 845 n. 9; Silvestre, 'Claustrum', p. 352 n. 4.

Latin West via Palladius and Jerome.[24] In the *RA*, the subject of books is confined to three sentences, one of which states that those in charge of the pantry, the brothers' clothing, and the books ('qui cellario, sive qui vestibus, sive qui codicibus praeponuntur') should always fulfil their duty without protest.[25] The next two sentences clarify that books may only be requested and handed out once a day at a certain hour ('[c]odices certa hora singulis diebus petantur'), and that whoever makes a request outside that specific time should be turned away unless they are in urgent need.[26] According to the *RP*, once a week the abbot should appoint a member of the community to tour the monastery after the morning prayer and establish which items are to be assigned to the monks for their weekly tasks, which he may then request from the abbot and distribute with his permission.[27] Those who wish to read a book should be given one ('codicem si ad legendum petierint, accipient') on the proviso that it be restored to its location ('suo restituent loco') at the end of the week. Books must not be left unfastened,[28] and in the evening they should be returned to a recess ('fenestra') or wall cabinet ('riscus parietis') to be counted by the abbot's second-in-command ('sub manu secundi') before being locked away overnight.[29] Apart from these arrangements, no specific mention is made of books or their provision in the *RP* and *RA*. In sum, therefore, the evidence that can be gathered from these monastic rules is limited but not insignificant. Each of the four texts reviewed above acknowledges—and expects—the presence of books within the monastery, and they all concur that books and the materials required for their production should not be freely accessible but distributed by the abbot or his deputy, usually involving a formal request and/or record. The provision of books is presented as an intrinsic part of the abbot's managerial responsibility to supply the tools for the workers in his 'divine workshop' or, to evoke Geoffrey's letter to Peter Mangot, the weapons for his monastic army.[30]

A more detailed (if not exactly uniform) picture emerges from the sizeable corpus of monastic customaries, many of which tend to associate the care of books with the *armarius*. From the eleventh century, the position of *armarius*—named after the Latin term for a book chest or cupboard—was commonly combined with

---

[24] *Pachomiana Latina: Règle et épitres de S. Pachome, épitre de S. Théodore et 'Liber' de S. Orsiesius, texte latin de S. Jérôme*, ed. by Amand Boon (Louvain: Bureaux de la Revue, 1932), pp. 3–74, with Jerome's preface; translated as *Pachomian Koinonia*, tr. by Armand Veilleux, 3 vols. (Kalamazoo, MI: Cistercian Publications, 1980-2), II, 139–95.

[25] *La règle de saint Augustin*, ed. by Luc Verheijen, 2 vols. (Paris: Études augustiniennes, 1967), I, 417-37 (p. 432).

[26] *RA*, ed. Verheijen, I, 432-3. [27] *Pachomiana*, ed. Boon, p. 19; tr. Veilleux, II, 149.

[28] *Pachomiana*, ed. Boon, p. 41; tr. Veilleux, II, 162.

[29] Besides books, this safe storage should contain a pair of tweezers for removing thorns from one's feet, the use of which, and thus access to the cabinet, is strictly limited to the monastery's *secundus* and the housemasters; *Pachomiana*, ed. Boon, pp. 37 and 40; tr. Veilleux, II, 160-1.

[30] On the monastery as a divine workshop, see *RB*, ed./tr. Venarde, pp. 36–7; *RM*, ed./tr. de Vogüé, II, 376-7 and 380-1; tr. Eberle, pp. 118-19.

that of the cantor/precentor, a development that is reflected in the customaries.[31] Their language can be deceptive, however, leading some to overestimate and overplay the autonomy of the 'cantor-*armarius*'. It is surely a stretch, for example, to argue that by assuming the responsibilities traditionally held by the *armarius*, the cantor's control over the library and scriptorium was 'absolute',[32] to the exclusion even of the abbot. Teresa Webber's work on priors and sacristans cautions against such generalizations by showing that their official responsibility for certain kinds of books such as those used by the officiants during Mass has to be distinguished from the cantor's sphere of influence.[33] What is more, Richard Sharpe's review of monastic account books shows that the official revenues allocated to cantors for the provision and maintenance of books barely stretched beyond a community's most essential codices, those needed for the liturgy, but rarely (if ever) to books intended for other purposes such as historical study.[34] When it came to the latter, and indeed generally, monastic cantors and librarians depended fundamentally on the authorization and financial support of their superiors.[35] These realities need to be borne in mind when relying on customaries as evidence of monastic book provision practices, and revisiting them in this light quickly relativizes the notion of the cantor's supposed monopoly and autonomy.

An instructive case in point is the *Liber ordinis* of Saint-Victor that, in an oft-quoted passage, assigns the *armarius* the custody of all the church's books.[36] What is rarely acknowledged, however, is that the *Liber ordinis* obliges the *armarius* to report to the abbot and consult him on all but the most routine book provisions: whilst he may regularly give out certain books to the monks in exchange for a deposit as long as he creates an inventory for the abbot to review on occasion, he is strictly forbidden from distributing the monastery's oldest and most valuable volumes without the abbot's permission ('[m]aiores autem et preciosiores libros sine licentia abbatis praestare non debebit').[37] Even more explicit is a decree issued by Abbot Pierre le Duc (1381–1400) in 1392 that prohibits Saint-Victor's cantor-*armarius* from giving any book to a person outside the monastery without the abbot's licence ('nullum librum accomodare debet extranero sine licentia abbatis'), and even those he distributes internally he must record for the abbot's reference

---

[31] See the examples in Fassler, 'Cantor', pp. 48–51; Webber, 'Libraries', pp. 119–20 n. 51–8.

[32] Fassler, 'Cantor', p. 50, seemingly taking at face value the customaries of Cluny; previously Knowles, *Order*, p. 428.

[33] Webber, 'Cantor', pp. 178–81.

[34] Richard Sharpe, 'The Medieval Librarian', in *The Cambridge History of Libraries in Britain and Ireland*, Vol. 1: *To 1640*, ed. by Teresa Webber and Elizabeth Leedham-Green (Cambridge: Cambridge University Press, 2006), pp. 218–41 (p. 220), concluding that 'there is no religious house where the precentor had regular funds sufficient to build up a library of books for study'.

[35] See Sharpe, 'Librarian', pp. 236–7; Webber, 'Cantor', pp. 182–3.

[36] *Liber ordinis Sancti Victoris Parisiensis*, ed. by Lucas Jocqué and Ludo Milis (Turnhout: Brepols, 1984), p. 78: 'Armarius omnes ecclesiae libros in custodia sua habet'.

[37] *Liber ordinis*, ed. Jocqué and Milis, p. 79.

and approval.³⁸ Likewise, the stipulation that the *armarius* should assume official responsibility for the production of books inside and outside the monastery ('[o]mnes scripturae, quae in ecclesia sive intus sive foris fiunt, ad eius officium pertinent') by providing scribes with parchment, materials, and remuneration ('ut ipse scriptoribus pargamena et cetera, quae ad scribendum necessaria sunt, provideat, et eos qui pro precio scribunt, ipse conducat') includes the important caveat that scribes from within the community must be assigned by the abbot first and then—and only then!—be issued with tools and materials by the *armarius* ('[q]uicumque de fratribus intra claustrum scriptores sunt, et quibus officium scribendi ab abbate iniunctum est, omnibus his armarius providere debet').³⁹ Those who were not appointed thus ('[c]eteros autem fratres, qui scribere sciunt, et tamen officium scribendi eis iniunctum non est') may not be assigned any scribal work without the abbot's permission ('sine licentia abbatis ad scribendum ponere armarius non debet'). Should the *armarius* require their services, he must indicate this to the abbot first ('prius abbati indicare debet') and seek his licence to commission what needs to be done ('per eius licentiam et praeceptum facere, quod faciendum est'). The *armarius* may only commission what the abbot authorizes, and nothing else ('[n]ullus autem praeter id, quod sibi iniunctum est, sine licentia abbatis scribere praesumat').⁴⁰ If scribes are required to leave the community or miss the canonical hours to complete the work assigned to them, this needs to be agreed by the abbot ('sine licentia abbatis nec extra conventum exire, nec horis regularibus deesse potest ille, qui scribit'), who by virtue of his superior authority will determine when the scribes do their work and when they re-join the community ('abbas determinabit eis quibus horis eos scripturae vacare, aut quibus ad conventum redire velit').⁴¹

As discussed above (2.2), provisos restricting the freedom of action of monastic scribes and librarians by subjecting them directly to the abbot's authority were also introduced by other customaries such as the *Liber tramitis* and the *Constitutiones Hirsaugienses*. At Hirsau, the position of cantor-*armarius* ('[p]recentor, qui et armarius') was deemed so important as to be reserved for those raised ('nutritus') within the monastery, and whoever held it was answerable directly and exclusively to the abbot ('nec de hoc habet alium aliquem magistrum nisi solum domnum abbatem').⁴² A similar hierarchical dynamic is also set out in the *Consuetudines Cluniacenses* written by Bernard of Cluny in the final quarter of the eleventh century, a text frequently cited as evidence for the cantor's absolute

---

³⁸ The cantor-*armarius* is admonished to observe these rules under threat of excommunication ('sub pena excommunicationis') because failure to do so in the past had led to the loss of books ('que quidem quia a longis temporibus non fuerunt bene observata, multos libros perdidimus et plures perdemus'); quoted after Delisle, *Cabinet*, II, 226.
³⁹ *Liber ordinis*, ed. Jocqué and Milis, p. 79.   ⁴⁰ *Liber ordinis*, ed. Jocqué and Milis, p. 80.
⁴¹ *Liber ordinis*, ed. Jocqué and Milis, pp. 80–1.
⁴² 'Constitutiones', ed. Migne, p. 1072; *Constitutiones*, ed. Engelbert and Elvert, I, 60.

control because it calls him 'master and provider of all scribes' ('omnium scriptorum magister, atque provisor').⁴³ There is, however, a critical caveat: besides books for Mass and the Divine Office, the cantor-*armarius* must not commission anything from the monastery's scribes without permission from the abbot or prior ('nisi abbatis, aut prioris licentia'). This dependence on the approval of the abbot—or, in his absence, the prior—is evident throughout the *Consuetudines* and epitomized in their opening reference to the *armarius* as the abbot's deputy ('vicarius').⁴⁴ Echoing the *RB* and *RM*, the *Caeremoniae Bursfeldenses* produced in the fifteenth century give the *armarius* custody of all books except those for the Divine Office ('omnes monasterii libros ad Divinum officium non spectantes in custodia sua habeat') on the important condition that the abbot must have an inventory of these books so he can hold the *armarius* to account for their provision ('[a]bbas quoque omnes libros, qui sub sua servantur custodia, similiter brevi annotatos habeat, ut de omnibus rationem exigere aut dare sciat cum fuerit opus').⁴⁵

This brief but insightful review of five of the Latin West's most important and influential customaries leaves little doubt that the view of medieval monastic book provision prevalent in current scholarship requires adjustment, especially as regards the role of the cantor-*armarius*. Whether we look to the customaries of monastic 'powerhouses' such as Farfa, Cluny, Hirsau, Saint-Victor, and Bursfelde—all five of them centres of historical writing—or to the monastic rules revisited above, the picture they paint is one of dependent agents operating under the overarching authority of their institutional superior(s).⁴⁶ Within this hierarchical chain of command, the allocation of resources and responsibilities to officeholders such as cantors and librarians is evidence not of independent or absolute, but of *delegated* and *dependent* authority. This is true of both male and female religious communities.⁴⁷ The cantor/chantress-*armarius* partakes in the abbot/abbess's authority as his/her designated *vicarius*, and for this he/she is answerable to the superior. This has major ramifications for our principal understanding of the abbot's role in the provision of books, even if it tells us little about

---

⁴³ 'Ordo Cluniacensis', in *Vetus disciplina monastica*, ed. by Marquard Hergott (Paris: Osmont, 1726; repr. Siegburg: Schmitt, 1999), pp. 136–364 (p. 161). A new critical edition is being prepared by Susan Boynton and Isabelle Cochelin. On Cluny's customaries, see principally Isabelle Cochelin, 'Discipline and the Problem of Cluny's Customaries', in *A Companion to the Abbey of Cluny in the Middle Ages*, ed. by Scott G. Bruce and Steven Vanderputten (Leiden: Brill, 2021), pp. 204–22, with a helpful summary table (ibid., pp. 205–6). Also cf. Susan Boynton, 'Shaping Cluniac Devotion', in *A Companion to the Abbey of Cluny in the Middle Ages*, ed. by Scott G. Bruce and Steven Vanderputten (Leiden: Brill, 2021), pp. 125–45, who suggests that Bernard may have cantor-*armarius* himself (ibid., p. 131).

⁴⁴ 'Ordo', ed. Hergott, p. 161.

⁴⁵ *Caeremoniae*, ed. Albert, p. 257; also cf. Eifler, *Bibliothek*, I, 211–15.

⁴⁶ A similar picture is created by other customaries that, for reasons of space, are not treated in detail here; see, for example, the various texts from England analysed by Webber, 'Cantor'.

⁴⁷ Lehfeldt, 'Authority', pp. 107–9.

actual practice.⁴⁸ For this, we shall turn our attention to sources whose testimony, though never objective, is closer to lived realities than are the normative stipulations of rules and customaries. The following discussions explore some of these sources in greater detail.

3.2 Book Production and Procurement

In a manuscript culture, one of the most direct and efficient ways for abbots and abbesses to provide domestic historians with books was by expanding their institutional libraries. This could be achieved on a temporary basis via *ad hoc* book loans or exchanges, or permanently through manufacture, purchase, and bequest. Rather than depending exclusively on any one mode of production and procurement, monastic superiors could rely on a range of internal and external supply channels in their book acquisition strategies, allowing them to source not just single volumes but entire collections, the largest of which comprised hundreds or even thousands of items. At the very top of the scale, we can see individuals being credited with—and actively claiming credit for—single-handedly providing more or less the entirety of their communities' book collections. Bede in his *Historia abbatum* records one of the earliest examples of such a 'super provider' by reporting that the founding abbot of Wearmouth-Jarrow, Benedict Biscop, provided his monks with a great many books ('magna [...] copia voluminum') that he had purchased or been gifted on his travels ('vel placito pretio emptos vel amicorum dono largitus retulit').⁴⁹ Upheld by Bede as a devoted purchaser ('religiosus emptor') and tireless provider ('provisor impiger') of books, Benedict on his deathbed is said to have obliged his abbatial successor(s) to preserve the integrity of the rich and well-stocked library he had brought from Rome by preventing its spoliation and dispersal at all costs ('[b]ibliothecam quam de Roma nobilissimam copiosissimamque advexerat [...] sollicite servari integram ne per incuriam fedari aut passim dissipari praecepit').⁵⁰ This dying wish, whilst benefiting multiple generations of library users, Bede included, was not entirely without self-interest: elsewhere in the *Historia abbatum*, Bede recalls that the books given to the monks of Wearmouth-Jarrow by Benedict's companion and abbot of St Martin's in Rome, John the Archchanter ('archicantator'), continued to be preserved together in the library to serve their donor's memory in eternal

---

⁴⁸ Making the point forcefully, Sharpe concludes that 'there is almost nothing to be got from custumals that sheds light on [...] the management of libraries as collections of books'; Sharpe, 'Librarian', p. 224.
⁴⁹ *Abbots*, ed./tr. Grocock and Wood, pp. 30–45 (pp. 30–1).
⁵⁰ *Abbots*, ed./tr. Grocock and Wood, pp. 48–9; also cf. Michael Lapidge, *The Anglo-Saxon Library* (Oxford: Oxford University Press, 2006), p. 35; Rosalind Love, 'The Library of the Venerable Bede', in *The Cambridge History of the Book in Britain*, Vol. 1: *c.400–1100*, ed. by Richard Gameson (Cambridge: Cambridge University Press, 2011), pp. 606–32 (pp. 609–10).

gratitude ('memoriae gratia servantur').[51] If a singular and comparatively minor book donation such as John's could secure him a permanent place in the community's *memoria*, then a major and continuous provision like Benedict's—the scale of which seems to have been without parallel amongst his successors—must have carried substantial commemorative currency, a subject that will be explored further later in this book (3.3).

Unrivalled though Abbot Benedict's book provision was at Wearmouth-Jarrow, it does have parallels elsewhere. The *Liber confraternitatis* of Pfäfers (St Gall, Stiftsarchiv, Cod. Fab. 1) commemorates its long tradition of abbatial book provision by listing the volumes given by Alavicus (973/4–92), Hartmann (*c*.1012–26), Odalrichus (*c*.1067–80), Hesso (*c*.1080–*c*.1100), and Henry (1151–83), who together supplied just shy of three hundred titles including several works of history.[52] At St Godehard's Abbey in Hildesheim, Abbot Frederick (1133/6–51), furnished the embryonic community with a most abundant treasure ('amplissimum thesaurum') that contained books both handsome and useful ('libros tam venustos et utiles quam pretiosos') made from the best parchment ('validissimo pergameno compositos').[53] Almost four centuries later, Johannes Legatius in his *Chronicon coenobii sancti Godehardi*—written at the order of Abbot Henning Kalberg (1493–1535)—recalled that the books provided to the monks of Hildesheim by their first abbot had been so numerous that detailing them all would be tedious ('longum esset memorare').[54] This was no mere *topos*. Those singled out for special mention include the lives of saints, bishops, abbots, priests, and monks ('vitas confessorum multorum, pontificum, abbatum, sacerdotum ac monachorum'), and the remarkable fact that Frederick's original twelfth-century library above the sacristy continued to exist and be used well into the sixteenth century suggests that Legatius still had access to these and Frederick's many other volumes *in situ*.[55] A library of similar proportions was established by Waltram, the first abbot (1138–46) of Fischingen. Waltram came

---

[51] *Abbots*, ed./tr. Grocock and Wood, pp. 34–7; also cf. Peter H. Blair, *The World of Bede* (Cambridge: Cambridge University Press, 1990), pp. 171–2. John had been sent to England by Pope Agatho (687–1) at Benedict's request; *HEGA*, ed./tr. Colgrave and Mynors, pp. 388–9.

[52] 'Thesaurus Fabariensis', in *Libri confraternitatum sancti Galli, Augiensis, Fabariensis*, ed. by Paul Piper [= *MGH Necr.* Suppl.] (Berlin: Weidmann, 1884), pp. 395–8 (pp. 397–8), listing works by Sallust, various saints' lives, a chronicle of kings ('cronica regum'), and a history of Troy ('Troiana historia'), probably that attributed to Dares Phrygius.

[53] *Catalogi bibliothecarum antiqui*, ed. by Gustav Becker (Bonn: Cohen, 1885), pp. 198–9 (p. 198) (= no. 85).

[54] *Scriptores rerum Brunsvicensium*, ed. by Gottfried W. von Leibniz, 3 vols. (Hanover: Förster, 1707–11), II, 404–26 (p. 407) (= no. XXXIII).

[55] Eva Schlotheuber and Wolfgang Beckermann, 'Die Bibliothek des Godehardiklosters in Hildesheim', in *Wandmalerei in Niedersachsen, Bremen und im Groningerland: Fenster in die Vergangenheit*, ed. by Rolf-Jürgen Grote et al., 2 vols. (Munich: Deutscher Kunstverlag, 2001), I, 108–16; Eva Schlotheuber and John T. McQuillen, 'Books and Libraries within Monasteries', in *The Cambridge History of Medieval Monasticism in the Latin West*, ed. by Alison I. Beach and Isabelle Cochelin, 2 vols. (Cambridge: Cambridge University Press, 2020), II, 975–97 (p. 988).

to Fischingen from Petershausen, where the late abbot Dietrich (1086–1116) had left a very well-stocked library ('bibliothecam nobiliter aucmentatam reliquit') that, judging from two contemporary inventories (Heidelberg, Universitätsbibliothek, MS Cod. Sal. IX 42a, fol. 73r, from Petershausen; and Thurgau, Gemeindearchiv, KKG 16, B 6.2.01/1, fol. 1r (*olim* B.VIII 1c/C.XV 13, no. 13), from Fischingen) supplied the exemplars for many of the books Waltram provided for his new community.[56] When the first abbot of Muri, Reginbolt (1032–55), assembled a communal library from scratch, he, too, could draw on exemplars from his previous monastery at Einsiedeln.[57]

Upon his appointment as abbot of Rastede (1142–57), Siward, the former bishop of Uppsala (1123–33), gave the monks just shy of thirty books, several of which, including an enigmatic 'chronica', may have been copied—or physically removed—from Uppsala's episcopal library.[58] The fact that Siward had been driven from his see by unbelievers ('per insolentiam paganorum expulsus') and come to Rastede after a stint in Ireland could indicate that some of the books he brought with him came from Uppsala and/or had been acquired *en route*.[59] Such imports and transfers of institutional library books were not unheard of, nor did they have to result from eviction or exile. At Bury St Edmunds, Abbot Baldwin (1065–97) imported a dozen books from his previous home of Saint-Denis.[60] Though Baldwin's initial book accession strategy relied mostly on external supply, particularly via imports from French/Continental libraries, there is evidence of an increase in domestic production at Bury during the later years of his abbacy, and by the end of the twelfth century most volumes in the monastery's library seem to

---

[56] *MBKDS*, I, 39–40 and 217–18 (= nos. 12 and 46); also cf. the narrative account in *Monastic Experience in Twelfth-Century Germany: The Chronicle of Petershausen in Translation*, tr. by Alison I. Beach et al. (Manchester: Manchester University Press, 2020), pp. 126–7, composed by an anonymous monk who might have been Petershausen's later abbot, Gebhard (1164–70/73); Beach, *Trauma*, p. 48.

[57] *MBKDS*, I, 209–10 (= no. 40); also cf. *Acta Murensia: Die Akten des Klosters Muri mit der Genealogie der frühen Habsburger*, ed. by Charlotte Bretscher-Gisiger and Christian Sieber (Basel: Schwabe, 2012), pp. 12–13 et al.

[58] Oldenburg, Staatsarchiv, Bestd. 23,1, No. 3, pp. 51–3; 'Historia monasterii Rastedensis', ed. by Georg Waitz, in *Gesta episcoporum, abbatum, ducum aliorumque principum saec. XIII* [= *MGH SS* XXV] (Hanover: Hahn, 1880), pp. 495–511 (p. 503).

[59] 'Historia', ed. Waitz, p. 502; Tönnes Kleberg, *Medeltida Uppsalabibliotek*, 2 vols. (Uppsala: Almqvist, 1968–72), I, 24–42; Erik Niblaeus, 'German Influence on Religious Practice in Scandinavia, c.1050–1150' (unpublished PhD dissertation, King's College, London, 2010), pp. 50–4, considers it 'likely that the list of donations [...] is a reasonably accurate reflection of Siward's possessions at the time of his arrival at Rastede' (ibid., p. 51); Peter A. Jorgensen, 'Review of Tönnes Kleberg, *Medeltida Uppsalabibliotek II: Bidrag till deras historia till 1389*', *Speculum* 50 (1975), 132–4, believes that 'the sources of information are insufficient to allow one to state which of the volumes [given to Rastede by Siward], if any, were ever in Siward's possession in Uppsala' (ibid., p. 132 n. 1).

[60] Teresa Webber, 'The Provision of Books for Bury St Edmunds Abbey in the 11th and 12th Centuries', in *Bury St Edmunds: Medieval Art, Architecture, Archaeology and Economy*, ed. by Antonia Gransden (Leeds: British Archaeological Association, 1998), pp. 186–93 (pp. 188–9); Teresa Webber, 'Books and Their Use across the Conquest', in *Bury St Edmunds and the Norman Conquest*, ed. by Tom Licence (Woodbridge: Boydell, 2014), pp. 160–89 (pp. 181–9); on Baldwin, see Antonia Gransden, 'Baldwin, Abbot of Bury St Edmunds, 1065–1097', *Anglo-Norman Studies* 4 (1981), 65–76 and 178–95.

have been produced in-house.⁶¹ Baldwin's abbacy not only marked a major milestone in the history of the monastery's library and scriptorium, but it also promoted a new historical consciousness that manifested itself in historiographical compositions such as the annals found in the Bury Psalter (Vatican, Biblioteca Apostolica Vaticana, MS Reg. lat. 12).⁶²

Whilst some abbots like Baldwin used a 'mixed economy' of book provision that combined external procurement and internal production, others relied primarily, or even exclusively, on domestic means of supply and even lent a hand themselves by acting as scribes and copyists. Having reformed the monastery of Hirsau along Cluniac customs and restored its scriptorium, Abbot William (1069/71-91) made use of the scribal workforce available in-house to lay the foundations for a great new library endowed by himself and his successors, Bruno (1105-20), Volmar (1120-56), and Manegold (1156-65).⁶³ As a result of their collective efforts, these four abbots between them provided almost all ('ferme omnes') the books listed on Hirsau's later twelfth-century library inventory, a treasure which the anonymous scribe deemed to be beyond compare ('[t]hesaurus procul dubio incomparabilis').⁶⁴ The thirteenth-century *gesta abbatum* preserved in the *Codex Hirsaugiensis* report that William's predecessor, Frederick (1065-9), regularly put his own pen to parchment to help expand the undeveloped library, and despite his otherwise tainted legacy—he was deposed in 1069—he continued to be remembered fondly for his generous book provision.⁶⁵ The same source relates that Manegold, who before his election had served first as the cantor's assistant ('adiutor cantoris') and then as prior, arranged the production of over sixty books ('plus quam sexaginta libros fecit conscribi').⁶⁶ As with the examples of Petershausen/Fischingen and Einsiedeln/Muri discussed above, the library built at Hirsau by Abbot William and his successors also acted as a source for the libraries of future monastic foundations. When in 1085 a monk of Hirsau named Azelinus was appointed the first abbot of Blaubeuren, he was given licence by William to take a stock of books with him so he, too, could start building a suitable library at the new foundation. Over the course of his abbacy (1085-1101), Azelinus channelled considerable energy and resources into the development of Blaubeuren's domestic library, and upon his death he left the monks with nearly two hundred

---

⁶¹ Webber, 'Provision', pp. 189-90; Webber, 'Books', pp. 162-3.

⁶² See Webber, 'Books', pp. 170-80.

⁶³ As Alison Beach observes, the 'high degree of control' which William and his abbatial successors exercised over Hirsau's scriptorium led to an 'extraordinary accuracy of transmission' not just within the community, but also through the wider dissemination of exemplars produced there, including, not least, the two hundred or so copies of William's influential *Constitutiones Hirsaugienses*; Beach, *Trauma*, p. 25.

⁶⁴ *Catalogi*, ed. Becker, pp. 219-20 (p. 219) (= no. 100).

⁶⁵ *Codex Hirsaugiensis*, ed. by Eugen Schneider (Stuttgart: Kohlhammer, 1887), p. 3; also 'Historia Hirsaugiensis monasterii', in *Supplementa tomorum I-XII, pars II: Supplementum tomi XIII*, ed. by Georg Waitz [= *MGH SS* XIV] (Hanover: Hahn, 1883), pp. 254-65 (p. 256).

⁶⁶ *Codex*, ed. Schneider, p. 10.

volumes that were recorded in his memory on an inventory (Stuttgart, Landesarchiv Baden-Württemberg–Hauptstaatsarchiv, A 478 Bü 16 (*olim* Rep. Blaubeuren B. 16), fol. 15r–v), a collection that, even if not quite on a par with that cultivated at Hirsau, was certainly a serious contender within the wider region.[67]

The case from Hirsau shows that abbatial book provision was a cross-generational commitment that involved not only a community's founding abbot/abbess, but subsequent incumbents, too, some of whom rivalled or even surpassed the efforts of their venerated predecessors. An early example of this is recorded in the *Historia Croylandensis*, a notorious text compiled in the late fourteenth or fifteenth century but purporting to be the work of Crowlands's eleventh-/twelfth-century abbot, Ingulf (1085–1108). Long dismissed as a forgery, the *Historia*'s detailed account of the abbey's history from its foundation to the very end of the Middle Ages has been partially rehabilitated by research stressing the veracity of the early sources upon which its author(s)—commonly referred to as 'Pseudo-Ingulf'—can be shown to have drawn.[68] The *Historia* reports that Crowlands's library had been humble until the turn of the millennium, when its third abbot, Ægelric II, added forty 'major volumes' (presumably patristic works) and more than a hundred 'minor volumes' to the existing collection, including many works of history ('dedit iste abbas Egelricus communi bibliothecae claustralium monachorum magna volumina diversorum doctorum originalia numero quadraginta, minora vero volumina de diversis tractatibus et historiis quae numerum centenarium excedebant').[69] In a later chapter, we learn that by the time of Ingulf's appointment in 1085, the library had been expanded further through the combined efforts of Ægelric's successors and comprised in excess of seven hundred volumes, all of which were consumed by the great fire that destroyed the library in 1091 and forced Ingulf's successor, Geoffrey d'Orleans (1109–24), to rebuild it virtually from scratch ('[t]ota quoque bibliotheca nostra periit quae amplius quam ccc volumina originalia continebat, praeter minora volumina quae amplius erant quam cccc').[70] The remarkable fact that the *Historia*'s late medieval compiler(s) could enumerate, and in some cases itemize, these lost books hundreds of years after their destruction is vivid testimony to their continuing commemorative currency and suggests that Ægelric and his

---

[67] Edited in *Catalogi*, ed. Becker, pp. 174–7 (= no. 74); see also Theodor Gottlieb, *Über mittelalterliche Bibliotheken* (Leipzig: Harrassowitz, 1890), p. 370 (= no. 785); Ludwig F. Hesse, 'Die Klosterbibliothek in Blaubeuren', *Serapeum* 18 (1857), 59–62 (p. 60).

[68] See David Roffe, 'The *Historia Croylandensis*: A Plea for Reassessment', *English Historical Review* 110 (1995), 93–108; for a more recent reassessment with a summary of the *état présent*, see Lindy Brady, 'Crowland Abbey as Anglo-Saxon Sanctuary in the Pseudo-Ingulf Chronicle', *Traditio* 73 (2018), 19–42 (pp. 19–22).

[69] *The Chronicle of Croyland Abbey by Ingulph*, ed. by Walter de Gray Birch (Wisbech: Leach & Son, 1883), p. 91.

[70] Missing from Birch's edition, this episode of the *Historia Croylandensis* is edited in *Rerum Anglicarum scriptores veteres*, ed. by William Fulman and Thomas Gale, 3 vols. (Oxford: Sheldon, 1684–91), I, 98.

successors had arranged for their titles to be recorded in writing to ensure that their memory—and that of their abbatial providers—would outlast their physical presence.[71]

One such inventory that sustained the communal *memoria* was drawn up at Benediktbeuern to commemorate the library books provided by Gothelm, the second abbot (1032–62) after the monastery's re-foundation in 1031. The badly rubbed original document (Munich, Bayerisches Hauptstaatsarchiv, Kloster Benediktbeuern, Amtsbücher und Akten 1, fol. 4r–v) lists Gothelm's books separate from those provided by his predecessor, Ellinger (1031), and both lists were subsequently copied in Gottschalk's 'house history' of Benediktbeuern known as the *Breviarium* (Munich, Bayerische Staatsbibliothek, MS Clm. 18571, fol. 153v). Gothelm's books include, amongst others, works by Boethius and Caelius Sedulius, Prosper's continuation of Eusebius-Jerome's *Chronicon*, and a 'liber ystoriarum', whereas Ellinger's provision of mostly liturgical codices was humbler in scope and was probably copied from exemplars at Tegernsee, where Ellinger had been abbot from 1017 until his deposition in 1026, and then again, following his contested reinstatement, from 1031 to 1041, when he was made to resign for a second time.[72] Though Ellinger's abbatial legacy at Tegernsee—like Frederick's at Hirsau—was marred by memories of conflict and discord, his library building continued to attract high praise from chroniclers.[73] And just like Frederick, Ellinger also lent a hand in the production of books. Specimens of his handwriting include not only his authorial compositions in the so-called 'Tegernsee Miscellany' (Austin, TX, Harry Ransom Center, MS 29), but also, for example, Tegernsee's copy of Isidore's *Etymologies* (Munich, Bayerische Staatsbibliothek, MS Clm. 18192).[74] Ellinger's scribal work was of such distinction that after his second (and definitive) resignation in 1041, he continued to work as a copyist and, in this capacity, made a regular contribution to the book provision of six consecutive abbots of Tegernsee, Altmann (1041), Udalrich I (1041/2), Herrand (1042–6), Egbert (1046–8), and Siegfried (1048–68), thus continuing to help expand the library he himself had built over several decades despite his

---

[71] Even as late as the seventeenth century, William Dugdale could cite some of these written records in *Monasticon Anglicanum: A History of the Abbies and other Monasteries, Hospitals, Frieries, and Cathedral and Collegiate Churches, with their Dependencies, in England and Wales*, ed. by William Dugdale et al., 6 vols., new ed. (London: Longman, 1846–56), II, 99.

[72] *MBKDS*, III.1, 73–4 (= no. 22); 'Chronicon Benedictoburanum', ed. by Wilhelm Wattenbach, in *Chronica et annales aevi Salici*, ed. by Georg H. Pertz [= *MGH SS* IX] (Hanover: Hahn, 1851), pp. 210–38 (pp. 219 and 222); see also Gottlieb, *Bibliotheken*, p. 369 (= no. 780).

[73] Christine E. Eder, 'Die Schule des Klosters Tegernsee im frühen Mittelalter im Spiegel der Tegernseer Handschriften', *Studien und Mitteilungen zur Geschichte des Benediktiner-Ordens und seiner Zweige* 83 (1972), 6–155 (pp. 52–3).

[74] Eder, 'Schule', pp. 75–81; see also Bernhard Schmeidler, *Abt Ellinger von Tegernsee, 1017–1026 und 1031–1041: Untersuchungen zu seinen Briefen und Gedichten im Clm 19412 und zu den von ihm geschriebenen Handschriften* (Munich: Beck, 1938), pp. 132–64.

increasingly hostile relationship with the community.[75] The single most transformative and memorable act of abbatial book provision at Tegernsee was recorded in the fifteenth century, however, when its abbot, Conrad (1461–92), purchased just over four hundred volumes ('circa ccccv volumina') in addition to those he had produced in-house or secured as donations from benefactors ('praeter volumina a fratribus scripta et a devotis personis ad fraternitatem oblata'), thereby more than doubling the holdings of the library he had inherited from his predecessors.[76]

One of the earliest cases of such serial abbatial provision is recorded in the *Gesta abbatum Fontanellensium*, which offer detailed information about the books given by several of Saint-Wandrille's early medieval abbots, beginning with Wando (*c*.716–19 and *c*.747–54). The anonymous ninth-century author reports that so many volumes still present in the library at the time of writing were owed to Wando that recounting them all would seem onerous ('[c]odicum etiam copiam non minimam, quod dinumerari oneri esse videtur'), words that would be easy to dismiss as a rhetorical device, were it not for the fact that the *Gesta abbatum*—just like the fifteenth-century chronicle from St Godehard discussed above—singles out twenty-two books *pars pro toto* in the abbot's memory ('ob memoriam illius'), including works of history.[77] A similar-sized sample of twenty-one books is associated with Gervold (787–806), and an even larger one for Ansegis (823–33), whose name is attached to thirty-two titles.[78] A confidant of Charlemagne and Louis the Pious, Ansegis had managed several monasteries before Saint-Wandrille, including Saint-Germer-de-Fly, home of twelfth-century abbot-historian Guibert of Nogent, where he had provided fifty-two volumes for the monks' library.[79] Considering that relatively few medieval monastic libraries could boast books in quantities larger than double digits—a better descriptor for them might be 'book collections'[80]—the numbers provided by Ansegis and his

---

[75] Schmeidler, *Ellinger*, pp. 49–94.

[76] Quoted from Tegernsee's monastic chronicle (Munich, Bayerische Staatsbibliothek, MS Clm. 1072, fols. 13v–45v), edited in Roland Götz, 'Kloster Tegernsee im 15. Jahrhundert', in *Die benediktinische Klosterreform im 15. Jahrhundert*, ed. by Franz X. Bischof and Martin Thurner (Berlin: De Gruyter, 2013), pp. 93–142 (p. 139).

[77] *Chronique*, ed./tr. Pradié, pp. 107–10; *Catalogi*, ed. Becker, pp. 1–2; the works of history provided by Wando include the third-century *Historia Apollonii regis Tyri* and Jordanes's *De origine actibusque Getarum*; cf. Nortier, *Bibliothèques*, p. 173.

[78] *Chronique*, ed./tr. Pradié, pp. 141–2 and 162–3; *Catalogi*, ed. Becker, pp. 3–4 and 13–14; Pascal Pradié, 'L'histoire sainte de Fontenelle: Une lecture des *Gesta abbatum*', *Tabularia* (2004), https://doi.org/10.4000/tabularia.1348; Takuro Tsuda, 'Was hat Ansegis gesammelt? Über die zeitgenössische Wahrnehmung der "Kapitularien" in der Karolingerzeit', *Concilium medii aevi* 16 (2013), 209–31. By contrast, Gervold's predecessor, Wido (753/4–87), only seems to have provided two books during his abbacy; see Gottlieb, *Bibliotheken*, p. 399 (= no. 1034).

[79] *Chronique*, ed./tr. Pradié, pp. 172–3; *Catalogi*, ed. Becker, pp. 14–16.

[80] Richard Gameson, 'The Medieval Library (to *c*.1450)', in *The Cambridge History of Libraries in Britain and Ireland*, Vol. 1: *To 1640*, ed. by Teresa Webber and Elizabeth Leedham-Green (Cambridge: Cambridge University Press, 2006), pp. 13–50 (pp. 13–14). See also Richard Sharpe, *Libraries and Books in Medieval England: The Role of Libraries in a Changing Book Economy (The Lyell Lectures for 2018–19)*, ed. by James Willoughby (Oxford: Bodleian Library, 2023), pp. 18–19 and 36–9 (= Tables 3, 5, and 6).

predecessors at Saint-Wandrille are remarkable, and it is no surprise to see subsequent generations attaching considerable importance and commemorative value to these provisions. The library thus assembled by Saint-Wandrille's abbots in the late eighth and early ninth century made the monastery stand out as a centre for historical study in Neustria, but it probably also contributed to its being targeted repeatedly by Scandinavian raiders, even forcing the monks to abandon the site temporarily and seek refuge in Flanders with their most treasured volumes until it was safe for them—and for the books—to return home.[81]

Despite these kinds of risks, the early abbots of Saint-Wandrille were not the only monastic superiors of their day to accumulate considerable assets in their communities' libraries. In his *Cronick des gotzhuses Rychenowe* (Freiburg i. Br., Universitätsbibliothek, MS 15), a vernacular history of Reichenau Abbey composed during the final quarter of the fifteenth century for the monastery's then abbot, Martin of Weißenburg (1492–1508), Gallus Öhem reports to have consulted an old *rotulus* ('alten rodel') detailing the books provided by Reichenau's earliest abbots, from the founding abbot Pirminius (724–7) to Ruadhelm (838–42).[82] When first establishing the famous island monastery on Lake Constance *c.*724, Pirminius is said to have brought with him as many of his books as he could carry ('mit seinen büchern, so vil er by im haben möcht') to provide a basic library for its monks—though if he did indeed provide fifty volumes as specified by Öhem ('dero fünfftzig waren'), this library really would have been anything but basic by contemporary standards—that was expanded further as the community swiftly grew in size ('mit mercklichem zůnemen der brüder und bücher').[83] Due to Pirminius's pioneering efforts, his successor, Etto (727–34), could afford to part with three-quarters of the library's contents to provide for new foundations elsewhere ('Der lieb abbt Etto [...] tailt sine brüder und bücher in viertail, behielt im ainen tail der brüder und bücher, die dry tail schickt er den dry vorbenempten fürsten und satzt und bestimpt jettlichem tail ainen abbt und zwölff brüder').[84] Whilst unable to say which or exactly how many books were given away with the permission of Reichenau's second abbot ('[w]as aber oder wie vil bücher die brüder mit inen hinweg trügen, ist uns onwissend'), Öhem does claim comprehensive knowledge—presumably based on the aforesaid *rotulus*—of what remained on-site and what was added by Etto himself ('wie vil aber und welche hie bliben, es sye von denen die Pirminius braucht oder hernach

---

[81] Cf. Nortier, *Bibliothèques*, pp. 174–5; Katherine Cross, *Heirs of the Vikings: History and Identity in Normandy and England, c.950–c.1015* (York: York Medieval Press, 2018), p. 123. Once the community had returned to its original site, the writing of history experienced another prolific spell during the eleventh century; Elisabeth M. C. van Houts, 'Historiography and Hagiography at Saint-Wandrille: The "Inventio et miracula Sancti Vulfanni"', *Anglo-Norman Studies* 12 (1990), 233–51; Lucile Tran-Duc, 'Une entreprise hagiographique au XIe siècle dans l'abbaye de Fontenelle: Le renouveau du culte de saint Vulfran', *Tabularia* (2008), https://doi.org/10.4000/tabularia.690.

[82] *MBKDS*, I, 234–8 (= no. 48); Öhem's monastic chronicle is edited in *Das Wappenbuch des Gallus Öhem: Neu herausgegeben nach der Handschrift 15 der Universitätsbibliothek Freiburg*, ed. by Harald Drös (Sigmaringen: Thorbecke, 1994), pp. 30–61.

[83] Quoted after *MBKDS*, I, 234.   [84] *MBKDS*, I, 235.

in kurtzem die brüder die alhie bliebend, brachten, syen erkant und wissend'), even if he does not share these insights with his readers for brevity's sake ('die zu erzeilen alle laus ich vallen von kurtzi wegen'). Identical explanations (or excuses) are given for the numerous books ('ettliche bücher'; 'vil bücher'; 'menges būch') provided by Waldo (786–806) ('was bücher das gewesen syen [...] geschwig ich jetzt von kurtze wegen'), Haito (806–22) ('ich geschwigen der bücher'), Erlebald (822–38), and Ruadhelm, the last two of whom are said to have had an extraordinary fondness for books ('besonder liebe zü büchern').[85] According to Öhem, Erlebald engaged both domestic and external scribes to enable the steady provision of books for his monastery ('die bücher, so er hier in der ow und in dem closter sant Dyonisy haut laussen schriben und überkomen'), and Ruadhelm copied many volumes himself ('ettliche selbs geschriben') just as Frederick of Hirsau and Ellinger of Tegernsee would several centuries later.

As with their predecessors, Öhem again declines to give specific information about the books provided by Erlebald and Ruadhelm in his *Cronick*. And yet, we can still get a sense of their respective numbers and contents thanks to a pair of library inventories compiled at Reichenau during the first half of the ninth century, both of which are, if not the *Cronick*'s direct sources, then almost certainly part of a shared textual tradition that also included the now-lost *rotulus*. Recording the results of over one and a half decades of sustained abbatial investment into the abbey's library, Erlebald's inventory is the longer of the two and runs to nearly forty titles, including several multi-volume works, whereas Ruadhelm's inventory lists just shy of a dozen volumes.[86] Accompanying—and transmitted alongside—these lists are two further catalogues produced by the same individual, Reginbert (†846), long-serving head scribe of Reichenau's monastic scriptorium and likely also its librarian/*armarius*. The longer and earlier is a full(?) inventory of the domestic library compiled *c*.821/2, possibly on the occasion of Erlebald's election, whereas the second, produced towards the end of Reginbert's life, contains the books which he copied ('scripsi') and/or had written ('scribere feci') for that same library under the command ('sub dominatu') and with the permission ('permissu') of four successive heads of house: Waldo, Haito, Erlebald, and Ruadhelm.[87] Judging by the 821/2 inventory, Erlebald's predecessors had managed to assemble several hundred volumes in the monastery's *armarium*, most of which likely post-dated Etto's call to give away three of every four volumes he had inherited from Pirminius. In less than a

---

[85] *MBKDS*, I, 237–8.
[86] *MBKDS*, I, 252–7 (= nos. 50–2); also cf. *Catalogi*, ed. Becker, pp. 16–18 (= no. 8). On Erlebald's abbacy, see Wiech, *Amt*, pp. 150–1.
[87] *MBKDS*, I, 240–52 and 257–62 (= nos. 49 and 53); on Reginbert's scribal activity, see Karl Preisendanz, 'Reginbert von der Reichenau: Aus Bibliothek und Skriptorium des Inselklosters', *Neue Heidelberger Jahrbücher* (1952/3), 1–49; Felix Heinzer, 'Ego Reginbertus scriptor'-Reichenauer Büchersorge als Spiegel karolingischer Reformprogrammatik', in *Klosterreform und mittelalterliche Buchkultur im deutschen Südwesten* (Leiden: Brill, 2008), pp. 17–31.

century, his successors turned this slimmed-down collection into one of the richest libraries in Carolingian Europe that could rival the eminent monastic centres of Fulda, Lorsch, and St Gall, on which more below (4.2),[88] with copies of important historical 'bestsellers' such as Eusebius-Jerome's *Chronicon*, Rufinus's Latin translation of Eusebius's *Historia ecclesiastica* alongside his continuation, Flavius Josephus's *Antiquitates Iudaicae/Historiae antiquitatum* and his *De bello Iudaico* (in excepts), the *Liber Pontificalis* ('Gesta pontificum Romanorum'),[89] Darius Phrygius's *De origine Troianorum* and *De excidio Troiae*, Gregory of Tours's *Historia Francorum*, Einhard's *Vita Karoli*,[90] Orosius's *Historiae adversus paganos*, Bede's *Historia ecclesiastica gentis Anglorum*, and over a dozen examples of saints' lives and *vitae patrum*, many of them multi-volume collections. When Erlebald and Ruadhelm expanded this library further during the 820s–40s, Reginbert continued to act as their 'go-to assistant' just as he had done under Waldo and Haito.

Similar dynamics can be observed at St Gall. Here, it was the rule of the tenth abbot, Grimald (841–72), that heralded something of a 'golden age' for the library, second only to the time of Gozbert (816–37), who provided over four hundred volumes.[91] An inventory drawn up after Grimald's death (St Gall, Stiftsbibliothek, MS Cod. Sang. 267, pp. 25–32) contains more than sixty books, most of which Grimald accomplished ('patravit') with the help of his deputy and eventual successor, Harmut ('cum adiutorio Hartmoti praepositi sui').[92] They include Flavius Josephus's *Antiquitates Iudaicae* and *De bello Iudaico*, Pompeius Trogus's *Historiae Philippicae* (in excerpts), the *Gesta Alexandri Magni*, Eusebius-Jerome's *Chronicon*, and some saints' lives. As will be discussed below (4.4), Grimald maintained a separate library for himself that encompassed over thirty titles and was assimilated into the communal library upon his death, thereby supplying further works of history to the monks. Having succeeded Grimald, Hartmut (872–83) continued the work he had begun as the late abbot's assistant by providing books in substantial numbers that are listed on a separate inventory, and just like Grimald he bequeathed his abbatial library to the monks when

---

[88] Johanna Jebe, 'Bücherverzeichnisse als Quellen der Wissensorganisation: Ordnungspraktiken und Wissensordnungen in den karolingerzeitlichen Klöstern Lorsch und St. Gallen', in *Die Bibliothek–The Library–La Bibliothèque: Denkräume und Wissensordnungen*, ed. by Andreas Speer and Lars Reuke (Berlin: De Gruyter, 2020), pp. 1–28.

[89] *MBKDS*, I, 247; McKitterick, *Rome*, p. 172.

[90] Matthias M. Tischler, *Einharts Vita Karoli: Studien zur Entstehung, Überlieferung und Rezeption*, 2 vols. (Hanover: Hahn, 2001), I, 155–6 and 428–30.

[91] *MBKDS*, I, 66–82 (= no. 16); Gozbert's successors, Bernwig (837–40/1) and Engelbert I (840/1), added little during their short tenures. The precise dating of this mid-ninth-century library catalogue remains difficult; also cf. Julius Petzholdt, *Handbuch deutscher Bibliotheken* (Halle: Schmidt, 1853), p. 133.

[92] *MBKDS*, I, 83–4 (= no. 17).

resigning in 883.⁹³ Committed to writing soon after the abbots' deaths/resignations, the inventories from St Gall initially seem to have served pragmatic purposes in the context of the monastery's estate management and library organization, though they subsequently acquired significant commemorative meaning. That these uses were not mutually exclusive is shown by Ratpert's *Casus sancti Galli*, where the same two book lists (probably copied from shared exemplars) are inserted verbatim, and in full, into the historical narrative as evidence for the chronicler's critical appraisal of the two abbots' government and administration,⁹⁴ an assessment which, in turn, would provide an important benchmark for the monks' commemoration of their abbots during subsequent centuries.⁹⁵

A broader look across the map suggests that monastic historians of the Middle Ages regularly relied on the testimony of book lists and library inventories when committing their abbots' achievements to writing, even if they did not always replicate them word-for-word in their narratives in the way Ratpert did. Indeed, accounts of abbatial book provision found with some frequency in monastic chronicles and *gesta abbatum* are often so detailed that it is difficult to imagine how they could have been produced without recourse to written records. The *gesta abbatum* from Saint-Wandrille and the various chronicles from Hirsau, Reichenau, Hildesheim, Petershausen, and Tegernsee are good cases in point, and they have parallels elsewhere. The anonymous continuator of the *Gesta abbatum Sithiensium*—a work originally composed in the 960s by monk-historian Folcuin and then continued by Saint-Bertin's future abbot, Simon (1127–36), at the orders of his predecessor, Lambert (1095–1123)—celebrates Abbot Godescalc (1163–76) for having ordered numerous books for the community's library, many of which were still found on the shelves at the time of writing ('sicut in librariis nostris apparet').⁹⁶ The house historian of Saint-Riquier and subsequent abbot-historian (1105–43) of Oudenburg, Hariulf, dedicated an entire chapter of his *Chronicon Centulense* to the thirty-six volumes assembled ('contulit') by Abbot Gerwin (1045–74) to inspire imitation amongst his successors ('ut futuri horum incitentur exemplis').⁹⁷ And at Saint Trond, the *Gesta abbatum*

---

⁹³ MS Cod. Sang. 267, pp. 28–30; *MBKDS*, I, 85–6 and 86–7 (= nos. 18 and 19); cf. Hannes Steiner, 'Buchproduktion und Bibliothekszuwachs im Kloster St. Gallen unter den Äbten Grimald und Hartmut', in *Ludwig der Deutsche und seine Zeit*, ed. by Winfried Hartmann (Darmstadt: Wissenschaftliche Buchgesellschaft, 2004), pp. 161–83.
⁹⁴ St Gall, Stiftsbibliothek, MS Cod. Sang. 614, pp. 116–17 and 124–7; edited in *Klostergeschichten*, ed./tr. Steiner, pp. 202–15 and 220–9. Hannes Steiner rejects the traditional notion that the two inventories in MS Cod. Sang. 614 were copied directly from MS Cod. Sang. 267 in favour of a common ancestor which likely consisted of multiple, formerly separate lists (ibid., 91–2).
⁹⁵ The eleventh-century continuator of the *Casus sancti Galli*, a monk called Ekkehard (IV), includes no such lists of books provided by the community's subsequent abbots.
⁹⁶ 'Gesta abbatum Sithiensium: Continuatio', ed. by Oswald Holder-Egger, in *Supplementa tomorum I-XII, pars I* [= *MGH SS* XIII] (Hanover: Hahn, 1881), pp. 663–73 (p. 669).
⁹⁷ *Chronique de l'abbaye de Saint-Riquier (Vᵉ siècle-1104)*, ed. by Ferdinand Lot (Paris: Picard, 1894), pp. 261–6 (p. 262). On Hariulf's writing, see Thomas Ledru, 'Hariulf de Saint-Riquier: Un moine historien de la fin du XIᵉ siècle', *Faire de l'histoire au Moyen Âge* 36 (2017), 19–41.

Trudonensium written by Abbot Rudolf (1108–21 and 1123–38) and continued by various redactors between the mid-twelfth and late sixteenth centuries speak of multiple abbots who played an important part in the provision of books for the monks' library.[98] Some contributed books since before their abbacies, including Rudolf, who had previously served as the abbey's prior and installed the earliest book cupboard in the cloister ('armarium in claustro primus ipse fecit'), as well as Wiric (1155–80), who before his election had been both prior and *armarius*.[99] Others, by contrast, did not get involved in library building until after their election, such as William of Brussels (1516–32) and George Sarens (1532–58), the first of whom augmented the library with many books and new furniture for study, whilst the latter went to great lengths to rebuild and restore it to its former splendour after it burned down in 1538.[100]

There were some abbots whose provision of books was deemed so exemplary that chroniclers resorted to elaborate metaphors and drew extravagant comparisons to convey its scale to their audiences. A good example of this is offered by Sigebert of Gembloux, whose *Gesta abbatum Gemblacensium*—a serial biography of Gembloux's abbots later continued by his disciple Godescalc—heap much praise on Abbot Olbert (1018–48) for having built a library that was unparalleled amongst his contemporaries and therefore compelled the historian to look to the distant past in search of suitable parallels. Like a second Philadelphus ('quasi alter quidam Philadelphus'—that is, Ptolemy II 'the Great' (283–246 BC), founder of the Great Library of Alexandria), Olbert is said to have supplied Gembloux's monks with an abundance of books ('sumministravit eis etiam copiam librorum'), many of which he even copied ('transscripsit') personally with the intention of building a comprehensively stocked library ('ad construendam [...] bibliothecam plenariam').[101] Sigebert's choice of words suggest that Olbert had 'built' ('construere') not only the books itself, but also—as Philadelphus had done at Alexandria—a facility to store and organize them. The *Gesta* credit Olbert with

---

[98] *Gesta abbatum Trudonensium*, ed. by Paul Tombeur, 2 vols. (Turnhout: Brepols, 2013); translated as *Kroniek van de abdij van Sint-Truiden*, tr. by Emil Lavigne, 2 vols. (Assen: Van Gorcum, 1986–8); for the continuations, see 'Gesta abbatum Trudonensium', ed. by Rudolf Köpke, in *Annales et chronica aevi Salici: Vitae aevi Carolini et Saxonici*, ed. by Georg H. Pertz [= *MGH SS* X] (Hanover: Hahn, 1852), pp. 227–448. A handlist of Saint Trond's abbots is included in *Chronique de l'abbaye de Saint-Trond*, ed. by Camille de Borman, 2 vols. (Liège: Grandmont-Donders, 1877), I, xiii–xv.

[99] *Gesta*, ed. Tombeur, I, 15; *Kroniek*, tr. Lavigne, I, 100; ibid., II, 27–9.

[100] *Chronique*, ed. de Borman, II, 364 and 389; *Kroniek*, tr. Lavigne, II, 246 and 268–9.

[101] Leipzig, Universitätsbibliothek, MS Rep. II. 69, fols. 13v–56v (fol. 37r); edited as 'Gesta abbatum Gemblacensium', ed. by Georg H. Pertz, in *Chronica et gesta aevi Salici* [= *MGH SS* VIII] (Hanover: Hahn, 1848), pp. 523–42 (p. 540); also cf. Johan P. Gumbert, 'Egberts geschenken aan Egmond', in *In het spoor van Egbert: Aartsbisschop Egbert van Trier, de bibliotheek en geschiedschrijving van het klooster Egmond*, ed. by Georgius N. M. Vis (Hilversum: Verloren, 1997), pp. 25–43 (p. 29 n. 18); on the manuscript (likely Sigebert's autograph), see Michel de Waha, 'Le manuscrit CIV. Rep II 69 de l'Universitätsbibliothek Leipzig, la *Vita Wichberti* (BHL 8882) et les *Gesta Abbatum Gemblacensium* de Sigebert de Gembloux', in *Sigebert de Gembloux*, ed. by Jean-Paul Straus (Turnhout: Brepols, 2015), pp. 117–56.

over one a hundred and fifty volumes,[102] so expanding the monastery's *armarium* into a fully-fledged book room must have seemed an appropriate (and perhaps necessary) investment, one that helped cement Olbert's abbatial legacy with an architectural monument not dissimilar from the wings of our modern libraries sponsored by and named after their major benefactors.

A helpful case for comparison comes from Montecassino. Begun by Leo Marsicanus in c.1099 and then continued by various local authors into the second half of the twelfth century, the *Chronica monasterii sancti Benedicti Casinensis* reports that Abbot Desiderius (1058–87), who subsequently became Pope Victor III (1086–7), excelled in both his monastic building campaigns and his provision of books ('Non solum autem in edificiis, verum etiam in libris describendis operam Desiderius dare permaximam studuit').[103] Desiderius ordered over seventy volumes for the monastery's library from the domestic scriptorium ('in hoc loco describi precepit'), the titles of which are listed meticulously in the *Chronica* for the memory of posterity. This was more than three times the number provided by Theobald (1022–35/37), whose contribution of just over twenty volumes had earned him the title of the library's most generous abbatial patron to date along with a prominent place in the community's *memoria*.[104] Just like at Gembloux, the unprecedented scale of Desiderius's library building at Montecassino forced commentators to abandon their usual frames of reference in search of precedents, though rather than turning to historical characters, they forayed into the realms of pagan mythology. A short laudatory poem (*Carmen acrostichum*) by Alfanus, a former monk of Montecassino who had since become archbishop of Salerno (1058–85), thus compares Desiderius to Boreas, God of the north wind. According to Alfanus, the titles of the books ('tituli librorum') his contemporary Desiderius obtained from near and far ('ex regione varia') to fill the shelves of the abbey's library were as numerous as the leaves ('foliis') with which Boreas covers the barren hillsides at the end of summer—a play on the word *folium* referring to both the leaves on a tree and the pages/leaves bound in a book.[105]

---

[102] 'Gesta', ed. Pertz, p. 540.

[103] *Chronik*, ed. Hoffmann, p. 444; on historical writing at Montecassino, see Laurent Feller, 'L'écriture de l'histoire du Mont-Cassin au XIIe siècle: Chroniques et documentation pragmatique', in *I Longobardi a Venezia: Scritti per Stefano Gasparri*, ed. by Irene Barbiera et al. (Turnhout: Brepols, 2020), pp. 365–81; principally Walter Pohl, *Werkstätte der Erinnerung: Montecassino und die Gestaltung der langobardischen Vergangenheit* (Vienna: Oldenbourg, 2001); on the provision of books, see Francis L. Newton, *The Scriptorium and Library at Monte Cassino, 1058–1105* (Cambridge: Cambridge University Press, 1999), pp. 21–6 and 253–327.

[104] *Chronik*, ed. Hoffmann, pp. 265–6; also cf. *Catalogi*, ed. Becker, pp. 132–3 (= no. 47); Gottlieb, *Bibliotheken*, p. 416 (= no. 1194); Newton, *Scriptorium*, p. 253.

[105] 'Boreas solet ardua quotquot foliis iuga spargere, tot tot titulos tulit hic variorum varia ex regione librorum'; *I Carmi di Alfano I, arcivescovo di Salerno*, ed. by Anselmo Lentini and Faustino Avagliano (Montecassino: Abbazia di Montecassino, 1974), pp. 217–19 (p. 219) (= no. 54); Ernst Dümmler, 'Lateinische Gedichte des neunten bis elften Jahrhunderts', *Neues Archiv der Gesellschaft für ältere deutsche Geschichtskunde* 10 (1884), 333–57 (pp. 356–7); also cf. Newton, *Scriptorium*, pp. 13 n. 63 and 291–307.

The original manuscript (Vatican, Biblioteca Apostolica Vaticana, MS Vat. lat. 1202), juxtaposes the poem's text (fol. 1v) with a full-page miniature showing Desiderius surrounded by the books he provided (fol. 2r), many of them with bejewelled covers, which he offers personally to the community's founder and patron saint, St Benedict: 'Along with the buildings, O Father, accept the[se] many wonderful books' ('Cum domibus miros / plures pater accipe libros') (Fig. 3.1).[106] The message is clear: abbatial book provision and building work are two sides of the same coin, and as such they deserve equal commemoration.[107]

If Alfanus and the authors of the *Chronica monasterii sancti Benedicti Casinensis* intended their praise for Theobald and Desiderius to set an example and spurn on successive abbots to follow in their footsteps, this strategy seems to have paid off. Appointed in 1087, Oderisius I (1087–1105) continued Desiderius's efforts by providing further books for the abbey's library, though his contribution never quite rivalled those of his celebrated predecessors.[108] A fair number of the volumes provided by Montecassino's abbots survive, some of them *in situ*, and they include a notable range of historical narratives such as Widukind's *Rerum gestarum Saxonicarum* (Montecassino, Archivio dell'Abbazia/Biblioteca Statale del Monumento Nazionale, MS 298), Gregory of Tours's *History of the Franks* (MS 275), Anastasius's *Historia tripertita* (MS 6), Justinus's epitome of Pompeius Trogus's *Historiae Philippicae* (Florence, Biblioteca Medicea Laurenziana, MS Plut. 66.21), Tacitus's *Annales* and *Historiae* in one volume (ibid., MS Plut. 68.2), and an illustrated copy of Orosius's *Historiae adversus paganos* (Vatican, Biblioteca Apostolica Vaticana, MS Vat. lat. 3340); works of history provided by these abbots but now assumed lost include Paul the Deacon's *Historia Langobardorum*, Jordanes's *De origine actibusque Getarum*, Flavius Josephus's *De bello Iudaico*, and the *Historia Langobardorum Beneventanorum degentium* by Montecassino's monk-historian, Erchempert.[109] For Alfanus and his successors, the memory of their provision appears to have been of equal—if not greater—significance than the books' production and procurement. To them, these history books were not just objects of use, but also, as we will see now, commemorative currency.

---

[106] Translation adapted from Newton, *Scriptorium*, p. 10 n. 33–4. The adjective 'miros' ('wonderful'; acc. pl.) evidently refers to the many books ('libros plures'), not to the buildings ('domibus'; abl. pl.).

[107] The same conclusion is reached by Francis Newton with regard to the *Chronica monasterii sancti Benedicti Casinensis* when observing that there was 'a clear link in the minds of the chroniclers between these two sides of an abbot's activities: building and book production'; Newton, *Scriptorium*, p. 5; see also ibid., p. 253, concluding that '[t]he Chronicle's authors see this activity [domestic book production] as closely associated with the building of buildings and the acquisition of church furnishings'.

[108] See the discussion in Newton, *Scriptorium*, pp. 26–8.

[109] From the list provided by Newton, *Scriptorium*, pp. 256–7 and 277–8; on the illustrated Orosius, see David J. A. Ross, 'Illustrated Manuscripts of Orosius', *Scriptorium* 9 (1955), 35–56 (pp. 36–46).

Fig. 3.1 Desiderius of Montecassino and his books. Vatican, Biblioteca Apostolica Vaticana, MS Vat. lat. 1202, fol. 2r.

3.3 Books as Commemorative Currency

As discussed previously (2.2), monastic superiors were not just regular authors and subjects of historical narratives, but also frequently their patrons. Such patronage was an expression of leadership and duty towards the community and its history, but it could also be driven by pragmatism, opportunism, and self-interest. That one did not have to exclude the other is shown by *gesta abbatum/abbatissarum*, especially those whose accounts of a community's history—viewed through the deeds of its successive leaders—culminate in the achievements of the sponsoring abbot/abbess, thereby creating a sense of institutional continuity at the same time as promoting the memory of the patron's accomplishments, be they the acquisition of lands and privileges, architectural constructions, or the provision of books for the monastery's library.[110] Rather than leaving it to chance or authorial judgement to decide which attainments would be accentuated in their *gesta*, monastic superiors could influence the selection process by feeding their biographers the right kind of evidence from the start. One way of doing just that was by producing inventories. The advantage of inventories was that they could be copied easily and archived securely even if their contents were lost, alienated, or destroyed. The fact that much of our knowledge of medieval monastic book collections rests on a pan-European corpus of book lists and library inventories—typically more than it does on the comparatively low numbers of extant books—speaks volumes.[111] As the following examples demonstrate, moreover, these documents could develop a significant life of their own.

At San Silvestro di Nonantola, Abbot Rodulf I (1002–35) ordered an inventory to record his provision of thirty-nine library volumes,[112] and a similar record was

---

[110] Cf. the cases discussed in Benjamin Pohl, 'What Sort of Man Should the Abbot Be? Three Voices from the Norman Abbey of Mont-Saint-Michel', in *Abbots and Abbesses as a Human Resource in the Ninth- to Twelfth-Century West*, ed. by Steven Vanderputten (Zurich: LIT, 2018), pp. 101–24; Hans-Werner Goetz, 'Das Bild des Abtes in alamannischen Klosterchroniken des hohen Mittelalters', in *Ecclesia et regnum: Beiträge zur Geschichte von Kirche, Recht und Staat im Mittelalter*, ed. by Dieter Berg and Hans-Werner Goetz (Bochum: Winkler, 1989), pp. 139–53.

[111] Major collections of medieval library inventories include the aforementioned *MBKDS*; *Catalogi*, ed. Becker; Gottlieb, *Bibliotheken*; Delisle, *Cabinet*; as well as *Mittelalterliche Bibliothekskataloge Österreichs*, ed. by Theodor Gottlieb et al., 5 vols. (Vienna: Österreichische Akademie der Wissenschaften, 1915–71) [= *MBKÖ*]; *Bibliothèques médiévales de France: Répertoire des catalogues, inventaires, listes diverses de manuscrits médiévaux (VIIIe–XVIIIe siècles)* [= *BMF*], http://www.libraria.fr/BMF/; *Bibliotheca Belgica manuscripta*, ed. by Antonius Sanderus, 2 vols. (Lille: Insulis, 1641–43) [= *BBM*]; *Corpus of British Medieval Library Catalogues* [= *CBMLC*], ed. by Richard Sharpe et al., 16 vols. (London: British Library, 1990–); *Medieval Libraries of Great Britain* [= *MLGB3*], http://mlgb3.bodleian.ox.ac.uk/. Also cf. Neil R. Ker, *Medieval Libraries of Great Britain: A List of Surviving Books*, 2nd ed. (London: Royal Historical Society, 1987).

[112] Gottlieb, *Bibliotheken*, p. 416 (= no. 1198); Giuseppe Gullotta, *Gli antichi cataloghi e i codici della abbazia di Nonantola* (Vatican City: Biblioteca Apostolica Vaticana, 1955), p. 5. According to this inventory, Rodulf had provided these books via his assistant, a monk named Peter ('per Petrum monachum'). Some of them survive with colophons that mirror the inventory's wording ('adquisito [...] tempore domni Rodulfi abbatis primi per Petrum monachum'; see, for example, Rome, Biblioteca Nazionale Centrale di Roma, MSS Sess. 44 (1473) and 45 (1364)); Mariapia Branchi, *Lo scriptorium e la biblioteca di Nonantola* (Modena: Edizioni Artestampa, 2011), pp. 210–13 (= plates 147–50).

commissioned by Abbot Jerome (1079-1100) of Pomposa halfway through his tenure (c.1093) to commemorate the donation of fifty-eight books.[113] Jerome's inventory soon became known and copied beyond Pomposa: one contemporary, who self-identifies as 'Henricus clericus', furnished his friend, a certain 'Stephanus', with a copy alongside a letter that praises Jerome for building a book collection that, in Henry's opinion, put to shame even the libraries of the Eternal City herself ('[n]ulla autem ecclesia, nec urbs, neque provincia, tandem nec ipsa Roma orbis caput, certet laudibus Pomposiae copia sanctorum fortunatae librorum').[114] Rather than taking his word for it, though, Henry encourages Stephen to peruse the titles of these books himself in the enclosed inventory ('Sed ne tibi parum sufficere videatur quod de libris memoravi, libet etiam titulum uniuscuiusque libri scribere').[115] He signs off by asserting his hope that the good abbot may continue his exemplary work to the end ('argumentosus vero abbas in sancto opere, ut qui bene coeperit, usque in finem perseveret'), and that, as a result, the books in the monastery's library may be copious, useful to posterity, and—importantly—recorded in inventories to preserve their memory for the future ('ut libri posteris profuturi scribantur, et pro futuris temporibus ad memoriam retinendum itidem subnotentur').[116] Whoever 'Henry the cleric' was, he no doubt would have been pleased to see the fulfilment of this wish not just at Pomposa, but also, for example, at Schaffhausen, where a close contemporary of his drew up just such an inventory (Schaffhausen, Ministerialbibliothek, MS 17, fol. 306v) to record the books produced and/or acquired with the support ('adminiculo'), permission ('permissu'), and at the order ('iussu') of Abbot Siegfried (1083-96).[117] And at Oberaltaich, Abbot Poppo (1260-82) commissioned an inventory (Munich, Bayerische Staatsbibliothek, MS Clm. 9540, fol. 271r) of the books he had provided during his first eight years in post.[118] Equally self-serving was the library stocktake ('inquisitio librorum') conducted at Admont in 1370 by Albert II of Lauterbeck (1361-84), the primary purpose of which appears to have been to list Albert's provision of forty volumes.[119] Similar lists were ordered by the abbots of Reichenbach, Prüfening, and Wessobrunn,[120] as well as at St Augustine's Abbey, Canterbury, where the majority of the four hundred or so volumes itemized by a fifteenth-century inventory are marked as having been provided

---

[113] Modena, Biblioteca Estense Universitaria, MS Lat. 390 (a.H.4.6; *olim* VI.F.5), fols. 70r-76r; see also below (4.1).

[114] 'Epistola Henrici clerici ad Stephanum', in *Diarium italicum: Sive monumentorum veterum, bibliothecarum, musaeorum, etc.*, ed. by Bernard de Montfaucon (Paris: Anisson, 1702), pp. 81-96 (p. 82); translation adapted from *The Antiquities of Italy: Being the Travels of the Learned and Reverend Bernard de Montfaucon, from Paris Through Italy, in the Years 1698 and 1699*, tr. by John Henley (London: Darby, 1715), pp. 62-5 (p. 63). Henry's admission that he had learned about these books and their provision directly from Jerome himself ('ex ipsius ore cognovi'; 'Epistola', ed. de Montfaucon, p. 81) may suggest that he was, if not a monk of Pomposa, then perhaps a secular cleric attached to the monastic community.

[115] 'Epistola', ed. de Montfaucon, p. 82. [116] 'Epistola', ed. de Montfaucon, p. 96.
[117] *MBKDS*, I, 293-6 (= no. 63). [118] Edited in *MBKDS*, IV.1, 84-5 (= no. 18).
[119] *Catalogi*, ed. Becker, p. 292 (= nos. 203 and 209).
[120] *MBKDS*, III.1, 190-1 (= no. 66); ibid., IV.1, 439-41 and 487 (= nos. 43 and 52).

by successive generations of abbots, with Thomas Findon (1283–1309) leading the charge with a hefty one hundred and twenty recorded titles.[121]

In creating these records, monastic superiors not only responded to the expectations of their communities, but they also competed with each other and the memory of those who had gone before them. This could lead to significant 'peer-pressure', especially within (and between) institutions like St Augustine's, Canterbury that looked back at a long and proud tradition of abbatial book provision. The more generous previous heads of house had been in their library provisions, and the more fondly they were remembered for it, the greater the pressure for subsequent incumbents to position themselves competitively within this memory tradition by striving to rival or even surpass their predecessors' contributions. Even the most generous contribution would be forgotten over time—or worse, risk being misattributed to a different individual, who would reap the commemorative reward instead—unless a written record was created and preserved for the attention of posterity. At St Eutychius near Nursia, Abbot Jerome (1159–70) thus ordered an inventory of all titles (fifty-eight) in the library at the time of his appointment before appending a separate section for the half a dozen books he had added ('adiunguntur libri quos dominus Hyeronimus abbas conficere studuit').[122] As the rubric of this section makes clear, it was drawn up with the specific aim of preserving the memory of these particular volumes ('nos posteris memorandum significare curamus'), lest they fall victim to oblivion due to negligence, ignorance, or stupidity ('[q]uum quidquid boni negligentia vel oblivione stulta tenebris ignorantiae poenitus relinquitur'). Whilst this might strike us as a disproportionate effort for the memory of a mere six volumes, especially for a monastery that, following its reform in the eleventh century, had assembled a reputable library served by a domestic scriptorium, Jerome increased the existing collection by about 10 per cent—a crucial reminder that for much of the medieval period, even reasonably wealthy and influential communities rarely had the means to establish and sustain libraries with hundreds of titles, meaning that the addition of just a handful of volumes could be considered worthy of memory.

Personal inventories such as Jerome's were also produced by Abbots Geoffrey I of Vendôme (1093–1132) and Ramwold of St Emmeram (975–1001).[123] Like Jerome's list, Ramwold's primarily served the memory of his own book provision, and only in the second instance did it function as a full library catalogue. Having

---

[121] See David Knowles, *The Religious Orders in England*, 2 vols. (Cambridge: Cambridge University Press, 1948–55), II, 340; *St Augustine's Abbey, Canterbury*, ed. by Bruce C. Barker-Benfield, 3 vols. [= *CBMLC* XIII] (London: British Library, 2008), III, 1863–70 (= appendix 6).

[122] *Catalogi*, ed. Becker, pp. 218–19 (= no. 99). On the Abbey of St Eutychius, see Pietro Pirri, *L'abbazia di Sant'Eutizio in val Castoriana presso Norcia e le chiese dipendenti* (Rome: Herder, 1960).

[123] Geoffrey's inventory is Vendôme, Bibliothèque municipale/Médiathèque Parc Ronsard, MS 26, fol. 240r; printed in Gottlieb, *Bibliotheken*, p. 148 (= no. 411). He has been identified as the probable patron of the *Annales Vindocinenses*; Lecouteux, 'Geoffroy'; Lecouteux, 'L'archétype', pp. 247–51.

commissioned a summary account of the library's holdings ('adbreviatio librorum') soon after his abbatial appointment in 975 (Pommersfelden, Gräflich Schönbornsche Schloßbibliothek, Cod. 340 (*olim* 2821), fols. 72v–74r),[124] Ramwold ordered a second, more personalized inventory in 993. Produced nearly two decades into his abbacy, this second list written onto the final page of an evangeliary (Munich, Bayerische Staatsbibliothek, MS Clm. 14222, fol. 199r) comprises nearly a hundred volumes that were provided and committed to memory under Ramwold's abbatial leadership ('sub regimine Ramuoldi abbatis').[125] This inventory acquires additional commemorative currency not only because it survives in a liturgical codex that, judging from its annotations, was used regularly (possibly on a daily basis) during the last decade of Ramwold's tenure, but because there is concrete evidence of its use in subsequent periods.[126] Originally filling about half a page, the inventory was expanded on multiple occasions, and by various scribes, beginning with three shorter lists specifying which members of the community had custody of certain books and/or other items from the abbot's bequest over time.[127] These lists together testify to the sustained memory of Ramwold's books, and they reveal a genuine concern for their preservation and safekeeping after his death. That such concerns were not unfounded is revealed by a fourth list recording the confiscation of several of these treasured volumes by Bishop Gebhard (I) of Regensburg ('Gebahardus episcopus abstulit'), a loss so traumatic that even centuries later an anonymous annotator would call upon God to take vengeance ('Deo vindictam!').[128]

It was not just theft that—in the absence of written records—could jeopardize the memory of abbatial book provisions. Other major risks were damage caused by negligence or inappropriate storage, loss through unreliable borrowers (discussed below; 3.5), sale or pledge by subsequent incumbents to raise funds by liquidating the community's valuable possessions, and, the worst case, accidental—and, rather less common, deliberate—destruction. When Berthold, abbot of Weingarten (1200–32) and patron of the *Berthold Sacramentary* (New York, Pierpont Morgan Library, MS M. 710), became aware that many of

---

[124] *MBKDS*, IV.1, 143–6 (= no. 25); *Catalogi*, ed. Becker, pp. 127–9 (= no. 42).

[125] *MBKDS*, IV.1, 146–9 (= no. 26).

[126] See *MBKDS*, IV.1, 147, concluding that the manuscript was used regularly ('offenbar regelmäßig in Gebrauch') during the later tenth and eleventh centuries based on its numerous annotations and redactions.

[127] MS Clm. 14222, fol. 199r, ll. 26–31, fol. 198v, and fol. 17r, ll. 1–9; on these lists and their relative chronology, see Georg Swarzenski, *Die Regensburger Buchmalerei des X. und XI. Jahrhunderts* (Leipzig: Hiersemann, 1901), pp. 25–6; Swarzenski tentatively dates the second list before Ramwold's inventory of 993, though the palaeography suggests otherwise; it seems plausible that the three monks charged with the safekeeping of these books and liturgical items (Hertin, Baldwin, and Walther) were the community's successive *armarii*/cantors or sacristans; also cf. *MBKDS*, IV.1, 147 n. 2.

[128] MS Clm. 14222, fol. 17r, ll. 10–21; Swarzenski, *Buchmalerei*, p. 25 identifies this 'Gebahardus episcopus' with Gebhard I (995–1023), rather than with Gebhard II (1023–36) or Gebhard III (1036–60).

the old books in his abbey's library had been treated so carelessly that they were damaged beyond repair, he ordered for replacements to be made from scratch ('de novo conscribi fecit'), the titles and *incipits* of which he had recorded meticulously on an inventory (Stuttgart, Württembergische Landesbibliothek, MS HB I 240, fol. 43r-v) so they could be inspected easily in the future ('et ut facilius, si cui aliquo eorum uti placuerit, inspectis eorum titulis, quem maluerit valeat reperire') and would not fall into similar disrepair.[129] Practical applications and safety concerns apart, Berthold's inventory served an important and highly personal commemorative function: at its opening, there is a miniature of Berthold in his abbatial attire lifting a large initial 'L', his cheeks puffed up as if to stress the collective weight—physical and ideological—of the various books ('libri') he provided for Weingarten's library after decades of neglect and dilapidation (Fig. 3.2a).

The placement of this inventory and its miniature within the host manuscript underscores their importance for the monastic community's historical consciousness and, more specifically, for Berthold's *memoria*. Bookending it are an abbatial decree issued by Berthold in 1217 at the consecration of the new abbey church (the previous one had burned down two years earlier) stipulating that Saturday's Mass should be celebrated in honour of the Virgin Mary to seek her protection for the building (fols. 38v-42v) and Berthold's abbatial *gesta* (fols. 44r-52v) that feature another portrait of him in an initial (Fig. 3.2b).[130] The final leaves (fols. 156v-158v) contain the *gesta abbatum* of the monastery's post-reform abbots, from Beringer (c.1070-80) to Conrad I of Wagenbach (1242-65), known as the *Catalogus abbatum Weingartensium* but rubricated here as 'De abbatibus nostris'.[131] The *Gesta Bertholdi*, the charter of 1217, and Berthold's book list together form a semantic unit, a dossier that records Berthold's abbatial

---

[129] Herrad Spilling, 'Abt Bertholds Bücherverzeichnis: Anhaltspunkt zur Datierung seines Sakramentars?', in *Das Berthold-Sakramentar: Vollständige Faksimile-Ausgabe im Originalformat von Ms M. 710 der Pierpont Morgan Library in New York*, ed. by Felix Heinzer and Hans U. Rudolf (Graz: Akademische Druck- und Verlagsanstalt, 1999), pp. 187-92 and 270-1; also cf. the entry (including a full transcription of the book list) in *Württembergisches Urkundenbuch Online*, 12 vols., III, 488-9 (= N28), http://www.wubonline.de/?wub=912; *Die Handschriften der ehemaligen Hofbibliothek Stuttgart*, Vol. 1.2: *Codices ascetici (HB I 151-249)*, ed. by Virgil E. Fiala and Hermann Hauke (Wiesbaden: Harrassowitz, 1970), pp. 162-8.

[130] An edition/translation of the *Gesta Bertholdi abbatis Weingartensis* is provided by Hans U. Rudolf, 'Quellentexte zum Wirken Abt Bertholds von Weingarten (1200-1232)', in *Das Berthold-Sakramentar: Vollständige Faksimile-Ausgabe im Originalformat von Ms M. 710 der Pierpont Morgan Library in New York*, ed. by Felix Heinzer and Hans U. Rudolf (Graz: Akademische Druck- und Verlagsanstalt, 1999), pp. 257-71 (pp. 261-8); on the context of their composition, see Hans U. Rudolf, 'Das Benediktinerkloster Weingarten um 1200 und seine Entwicklung unter Abt Berthold (1200-1232)', in *Das Hainricus-Missale: Vollständige Faksimile-Ausgabe der Handschrift MS M.711 (bisher auch "Hainricus-Sakramentar") aus The Morgan Library and Museum New York*, ed. by Hans U. Rudolf (Graz: Akademische Druck- und Verlagsanstalt, 2010), pp. 13-32.

[131] 'Catalogus abbatum Weingartensium', ed. by Oswald Holder-Egger, in *Supplementa tomorum I-XII, pars III* [= *MGH SS* XV] (Hanover: Hahn, 1861), pp. 1312-14. An illustrated copy with portraits of all twelve abbots survives in Weingarten's thirteenth-century *Codex traditionum* (Stuttgart, Landesarchiv Baden-Württemberg-Hauptstaatsarchiv Stuttgart, MS B 515 2a, fols. 3r-v). See also Goetz, 'Geschichtsbewußtsein', pp. 474-6; Goetz, 'Bild', pp. 145-8.

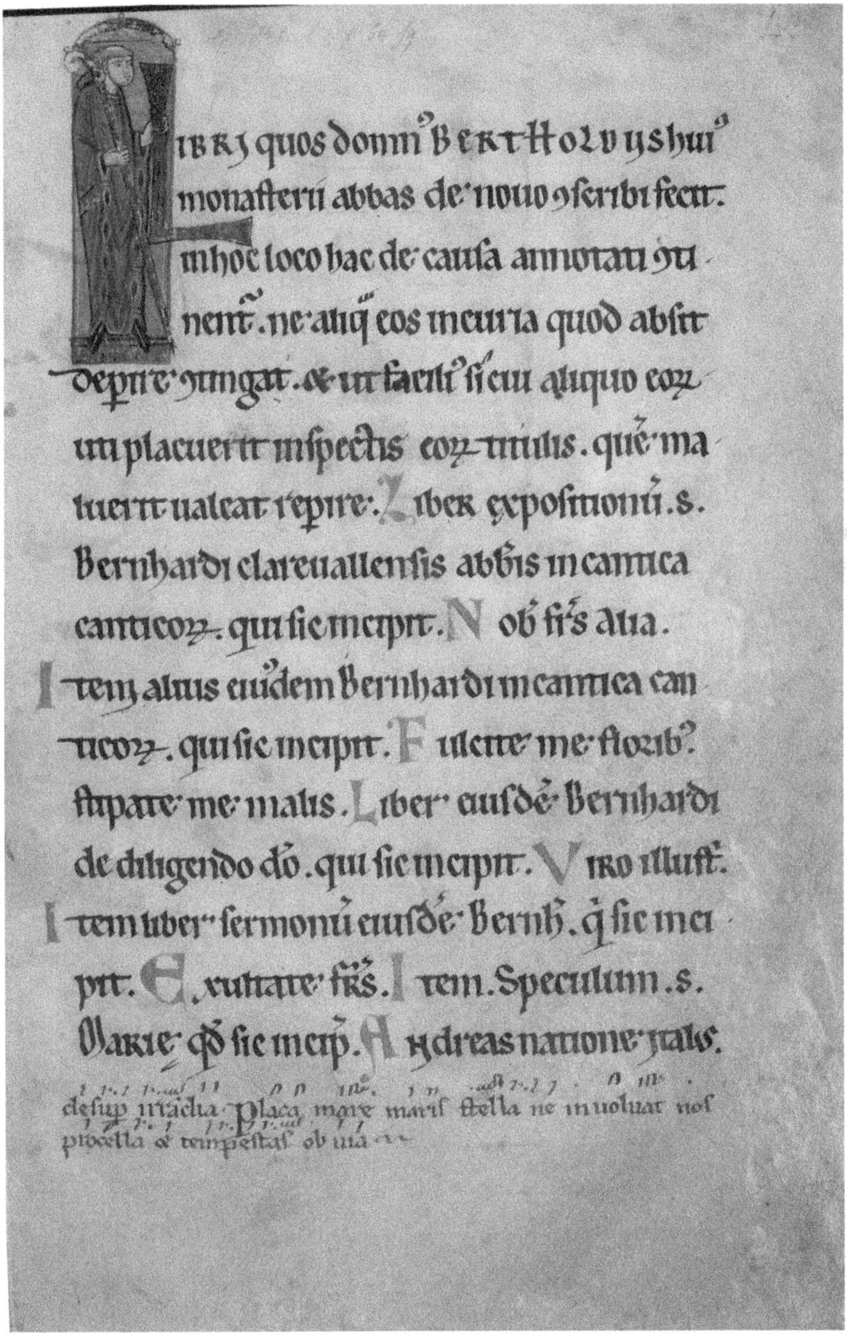

Libri quos domnus Bertholdus huius monasterii abbas de nouo conscribi fecit. in hoc loco hac de causa annotati sunt. ne aliqui eos incuria quod absit deperire sinngat. & ut facilius cui aliquo eorum placuerit inspectis eorum titulis. que maluerit ualeat reperire. Liber expositionum sancti Bernhardi clareuallensis abbis in cantica canticorum. qui sic incipit. Nob sís alia. Item alius eiusdem Bernhardi in cantica canticorum. qui sic incipit. Fulcite me floribus. stipate me malis. Liber eiusdem Bernhardi de diligendo deo. qui sic incipit. Viro illustri. Item liber sermonum eiusdem Bernh. qui sic incipit. Exultate fratres. Item. Speculum. s. Marie qd sic incip. Andreas natione italus.

desup iniacula placa mare maris stella ne inuoluat nos procella & tempestas ob uia

Fig. 3.2a Berthold of Weingarten's book list. Stuttgart, Württembergische Landesbibliothek, MS HB I 240, fol. 43r.

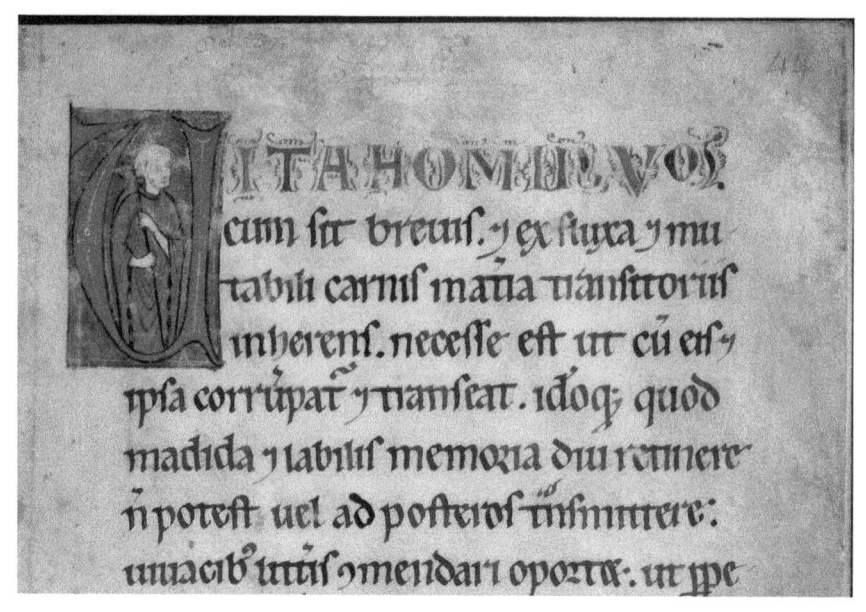

Fig. 3.2b Berthold of Weingarten's *gesta*. Stuttgart, Württembergische Landesbibliothek, MS HB I 240, fol. 44r.

achievements and is complemented by—and contextualized within—the serial narrative of the *gesta abbatum*. The physical juxtaposition of these texts within the manuscript shows that to Berthold and his monks, the provision of books constituted a major building block within Weingarten's historical and historiographical tradition.

Another instructive case of a decimated library that spurred successive abbots into action to safeguard the memory of their own provision comes from Saint-Pierre-le-Vif de Sens, where Abbot Arnaud (1096–1124) rebuilt the institutional book collection virtually from scratch after most of it had perished in a fire under his predecessor, Hermuin (1085–96). To stop his legacy from going up in smoke like Hermuin's, Arnaud effectively 'triple-locked' the memory of his provision: he first had an inventory drawn up the year before his death of all the books he had ordered to be produced and decorated for the monks' library ('iussit apicibus annotari omnia nomina librorum que ipse conscribi fecerat at bene ornaverat [...] ad restaurationem et ad usum ipsius ecclesie').[132] Conscious of his own age and sensing death's fast approach ('considerans debilitatem etatis

---

[132] Auxerre, Bibliothèque municipale, MS 212, fol. 91r–v; *Chronique de Saint-Pierre-le-Vif de Sens, dite de Clarius* (*Chronicon Sancti Petri Vivi Senonensis*), ed./tr. by Robert-Henri Bautier et al. (Paris: CNRS, 1979), pp. 188–95; *Catalogi*, ed. Becker, pp. 194–6 (= no. 81); Gottlieb, *Bibliotheken*, pp. 145–6 (= no. 403). On the abbatial succession at Saint-Pierre-le-Vif de Sens, see *Chronique de l'abbaye de Saint-Pierre-le-Vif de Sens: rédigée vers la fin du XIIIe siècle par Geoffroy de Courlon*, ed./tr. by Gustave Julliot (Sens: Duchemin, 1876), pp. 16–19.

sueque previdens vicinitatem mortis'), Arnaud then added a second safety mechanism by having this inventory ratified by notaries ('per manus notariorum') before depositing it in the monastery's archives ('in archivis ecclesie'). As a third and final layer of security, he had the entire list copied into the *Chronicon sancti Petri Vivi*, a house history commissioned and part-authored by himself (Auxerre, Bibliothèque municipale, MS 212).[133] Rather than letting the integrated document speak for itself, the *Chronicon* reports that Arnaud personally supervised the process from start to finish, from the preparation of membranes to the sourcing of exemplars and the allocation of copyists.[134] The only other achievement to receive similar praise in the *Chronicon* is Arnaud's building activity, which was seen—yet again—as going hand-in-hand with his provision of library books.[135]

The lengths to which Arnaud went to 'futureproof' the memory of his book provision are remarkable but not without parallel. At Garsten, Abbot Otto (1317-33) sought and received external ratification of his domestic provision through a diploma issued by Bishop Albert II of Passau (1320-42).[136] And when Andreas Lang ordered the periodic stocktake of the library he helped cultivate at Michelsberg, he had the records ratified by external notaries (Friedrich Ber from Forchheim and Valentin Cristan from Mainz) before depositing notarized (by Wolfgang Hoheneker) and ratified (by Johannes Balkmacher, dean of St. Jakob's Church) copies in the domestic archives.[137] This level of care may well have been unprecedented, though it is not impossible that Andreas drew inspiration from his celebrated twelfth-century predecessors, Wolfram I (1112-23) and Herman (1123-47), both of whom had been ardent library builders whose book provisions were recorded in writing by their second-in-command and Bamberg's long-serving *armarius*, Burchard (†1149).[138] In fact, we can be sure that Andreas knew these inventories because he copied them in his authorial compositions, the *Catalogus abbatum* and *Fasciculus abbatum*, and it is due to these copies that

---

[133] On Arnaud's scribal work and his contribution to MS Auxerre 212, see *Chronique*, ed./tr. Bautier et al., pp. xiii-xix and xxiii-xxxi.

[134] MS Auxerre 212, fols. 91r-v: 'In his etiam in tantum erat intentus, ut propriis manibus, aliis expers laboribus, ferret libros ac revolveret, membranas etiam secundum modum voluminum incisas numero fratribus ad parandum daret, ipseque postea scriptoribus ad scribendum reportaret'.

[135] As observed by Gabrielle Spiegel, Arnaud's achievements closely resembled those of his abbatial peer and contemporary, Suger of Saint-Denis; Gabrielle M. Spiegel, 'Review of *Chronique de Saint-Pierre-le-Vif de Sens, dite de Clarius (Chronicon Sancti Petri Vivi Senonensis)*', *Speculum* 57 (1982), 114-16 (p. 115).

[136] Gottlieb, *Bibliotheken*, p. 374 (= no. 815) with reference to Albert's original charter.

[137] These notarized inventories are copied in Bamberg, Staatsarchiv, Rep. 29 no. 9 and 187 no. 3030; *MBKDS*, III.3, 370-82, 388-93, and 393-5 (= nos. 93-5, 97-100, and 101-3). For further discussion, see below (4.3).

[138] *MBKDS*, III.3, 355-65 (= no. 90). Burchard's inventory also includes the books provided by Priors Frutolf, Thiemo, and Ellenhard; a generation later, another monk of Bamberg named Ruotger drew up a similar inventory of the books produced and acquired by Abbot Wolfram II (1172-1201); Harry Bresslau, 'Bamberger Studien I', *Neues Archiv der Gesellschaft für ältere deutsche Geschichtskunde* 21 (1896), 141-234 (pp. 163-70).

we have knowledge of them today as the originals are lost. In a sense, therefore, Michelsberg's abbot-historian must be credited for preserving the memory not only of his own book provision, but also of the books given by his distant predecessors that otherwise would likely have been consigned to oblivion.

Examples such as these illustrate the vital importance of book lists and library inventories as monastic memory media. In several cases, we would have little or no knowledge of an abbot's book provision were it not for the survival of these documents in the original, in contemporary copies, or in the pages of chronicles and *gesta abbatum*. Monastic superiors were mindful of the risks faced by the libraries they built with such dedication and expense, hence their creation of records that would help sustain the memory of their involvement even if the books themselves were lost or destroyed. This is not to say that these records acted as surrogates for the objects they listed, nor indeed that the books carried no commemorative currency in their own right. Where they do survive, books can provide vital insights into this commemorative culture by showing us alternative ways in which abbots and abbesses sought to 'make their mark' by inserting clues for the attention of present and future users.

We do not have to venture far into the books to find these clues, as they often feature on their opening and/or closing pages. An ownership mark on the last page of a copy of the *Capitularia Caroli magni et Ludovici pii*—better known as the 'False Capitularies' of Benedictus Levita—from the monastic library of Mont-Saint-Michel informs the reader that it was made at the command of Abbot Robert of Torigni ('Iste liber est sancti Michaelis de periculo maris, quem domnus Robertus abbas fecit fieri'; Avranches, Bibliothèque patrimoniale, MS 145, fol. 110v).[139] Himself a consummate historian, Robert strategically expanded the library assembled by his predecessors with hand-selected and carefully sourced books that, as we shall see below (3.4), benefitted the education of the monks at same time as serving his historiographical projects. Similar ownership marks survive in books from St Albans to commemorate the provision of Robert's contemporary and fellow bibliophile, Abbot Simon (1167–83).[140] Simon's generosity as a book provider is corroborated by the *Gesta abbatum*, according to which he gave only the best books ('libros optimos') and had a hand in their meticulous

---

[139] Pohl, '*Abbas*', p. 84, with a photographic reproduction. For further examples, see J. G. Alexander, *Norman Illumination at Mont St Michel, 966–1100* (Oxford: Oxford University Press, 1970), pp. 37–8; Richard Gameson, 'Les colophons des manuscrits du Mont-Saint-Michel', in *Images de la foi: La bible et les Pères de l'Eglise*, ed. by Jean-Luc Leservoisier (Paris: Fédération française pour la coopération des bibliothèques, 2002), pp. 31–5.

[140] For example, Cambridge, St John's College, MS G.15 (183), fol. 1r: 'Hunc libellum fecit dominus Symon abbas de sancto Albano'; see also *Manuscripts from St Albans Abbey: 1066–1235*, ed. by Rodney M. Thomson, 2 vols. (Woodbridge, Boydell: 1982–5), I, 85 (= no. 9); Richard W. Hunt, 'The Library of the Abbey of St Albans', in *Medieval Scribes, Manuscripts and Libraries: Essays Presented to N. R. Ker*, ed. by Malcolm B. Parkes and Andrew G. Watson (London: Scolar, 1978), pp. 251–77 (p. 252).

preparation ('ad unguem irreprehensibiliter praeparare').[141] Similar to the monastic chroniclers of St Godehard and Saint-Wandrille studied above (3.2), the abbatial biographer of St Albans reports that Simon's books were far too numerous to be enumerated in full, instead encouraging his readers to inspect them with their own eyes in the special painted cupboard ('specialis almarium pictum') which Simon had installed in the abbey church for that very purpose.[142] Commemoration apart, the ownership marks naming Simon might well have been intended to help prevent misshelving and ensure that the books he had given would always be returned to this special 'showcase'.

More easily quantifiable—but no less memorable—levels of provision are recorded for other abbots of St Albans, though none of them is known to have built himself a book shrine like Simon's.[143] It can be no coincidence, therefore, that the miniaturist tasked with illustrating the *Gesta abbatum* in the late fourteenth or early fifteenth century (London, British Library, MS Cotton Claudius E IV) chose to depict them with one or more books, at the same time as accompanying (some) of their portraits with rubrics that explicitly mention the provision of books.[144] The images of Simon (see Fig. 4.4) and his successor Warin (Fig. 3.3) are especially striking thanks to their inclusion of a book chest filled to the rim and a pile of books scattered around Warin's feet in addition to the two volumes in his hand—an iconography reminiscent of Desiderius of Montecassino's abbatial portrait analysed above.

The illustrated *Gesta abbatum* are not the only visual source to commemorate the abbatial provision of books at St Albans. A century earlier, Abbot Thomas de la Mare (1349-96) had commissioned the *Liber benefactorum* (London, British Library, MS Cotton Nero D VII), a detailed survey of the abbey's benefactors kept on the high altar ('super magnum altare') as a communal *aide-mémoire* that features more than two hundred portraits—'a larger number of painted

---

[141] *Gesta abbatum monasterii sancti Albani, a Thoma Walsingham, regnante Ricardo secundo, compilata*, ed. by Henry T. Riley, 3 vols. (Cambridge: Cambridge University Press, 1866-9), I, 184; translation in *The Deeds of the Abbots of St Albans–Gesta abbatum monasterii sancti Albani*, tr. by David Preest and James G. Clark (Woodbridge: Boydell, 2019), p. 290.

[142] *Gesta*, ed. Riley, I, 184 and 192; tr. Preest and Clark, pp. 290 and 300; Hunt, 'Library', p. 258.

[143] *Gesta*, ed. Riley, I, 58, 70, 94, 179, and 482; II, 89, 207, 306, and 363; III, 384, 389, 393, and 403; tr. Preest and Clark, pp. 133, 151, 180, 279, 537-8, 601, 686, 732, 750, 786, 788, 896, 900, 903, and 912.

[144] MS BL Cotton Claudius E IV, fols. 105r (Paul of Caen, 1077-93; 'Nota de libris datis per abbatem Paulum'), 107r (Richard d'Aubigny, 1097-1119; no rubric), 113v (Robert de Gorham, 1151-66; no rubric), 124r (Simon; 'De probitate Simonis et libris datis ecclesiae per eundem'), 125v (Warin, 1183-95; no rubric), 135r (William of Trumpington, 1214-35; 'De libris monasterii Sancti Albani...'), and 157v (Roger de Norton, 1263-91; no rubric). These images must be distinguished from those on fols. 98v (Eadric and Wulsic), 99r (Wulnoth), 100v (Ælfric), 101r (Ealdred), 103v (Frithric), 129v (John de Cella), and 135r (William of Trumpington), whose inclusion of books serves primarily to emphasize the abbot's erudition and learning. In Warin's case, the accompanying text describes how he provided his nephew, Warin the Younger, with 'many books'; *Gesta*, ed. Riley, I, 196; tr. Preest and Clark, pp. 306-7.

Fig. 3.3 Warin of St Albans and his books. London, British Library, MS Cotton Claudius E IV, fol. 125v.

miniatures than almost any other contemporary English codex'.[145] To plan and execute this important book, Abbot Thomas assembled an 'all-star line-up' that consisted of domestic historian Thomas Walsingham, resident monk-scribe William de Wyllum, and, for the many illustrations, renowned lay artist Alan Strayler.[146] Rather than using 'stock imagery', Strayler designed each miniature from scratch, and his portraits are distinguished by a strong sense of liveliness and individuality. As in the *Gesta abbatum*, Strayler's images show their subjects 'proudly clutching the prized objects that they donated',[147] and though many of them had died centuries ago, there can be no doubt that these objects were selected carefully by the books' planners as visual representations of their most memorable accomplishments. Thirty-one of the portraits in the *Liber benefactorum* are of

---

[145] James G. Clark, 'Monastic Confraternity in Medieval England: The Evidence from the St Albans Abbey *Liber Benefactorum*', in *Religious and Laity in Western Europe, 1000–1400: Interaction, Negotiation, and Power*, ed. by Emilia Jamroziak and Janet Burton (Turnhout: Brepols, 2006), pp. 315–31 (pp. 315–16).

[146] Martha Driver and Michael Orr, 'Decorating and Illustrating the Page', in *The Production of Books in England, 1350–1500*, ed. by Alexandra Gillespie and Daniel Wakelin (Cambridge: Cambridge University Press, 2011), pp. 104–28 (p. 115).

[147] Eleanor Jackson, 'The St Albans Benefactors' Book: Precious Gifts and Colourful Characters', *British Library Medieval Manuscripts Blog*, https://blogs.bl.uk/digitisedmanuscripts/2020/05/the-st-albans-benefactors-book.html.

abbots, eleven of whom are described as major book providers.[148] This time, it is Paul who leads the charge with a whole pile of volumes at his feet (Fig. 3.4), followed by Roger de Norton (three books), Richard d'Aubigny, and John of Wheathampstead (one book each).[149]

The *Liber benefactorum* and *Gesta abbatum* offer testimony to the commemorative currency of abbatial book provision at St Albans. With one taking pride of place on the altar and the other stored away safely in the library for the monk's reference and consultation, their vivid images served as powerful memory media that preserved the institutional legacy of these abbots for centuries, even if the books provided by them had been lost or destroyed. That this was not exclusive to St Albans—nor indeed to England—is shown by the contemporary *Fasciculus abbatum* from Bamberg, where no fewer than twenty-five of forty-one abbots

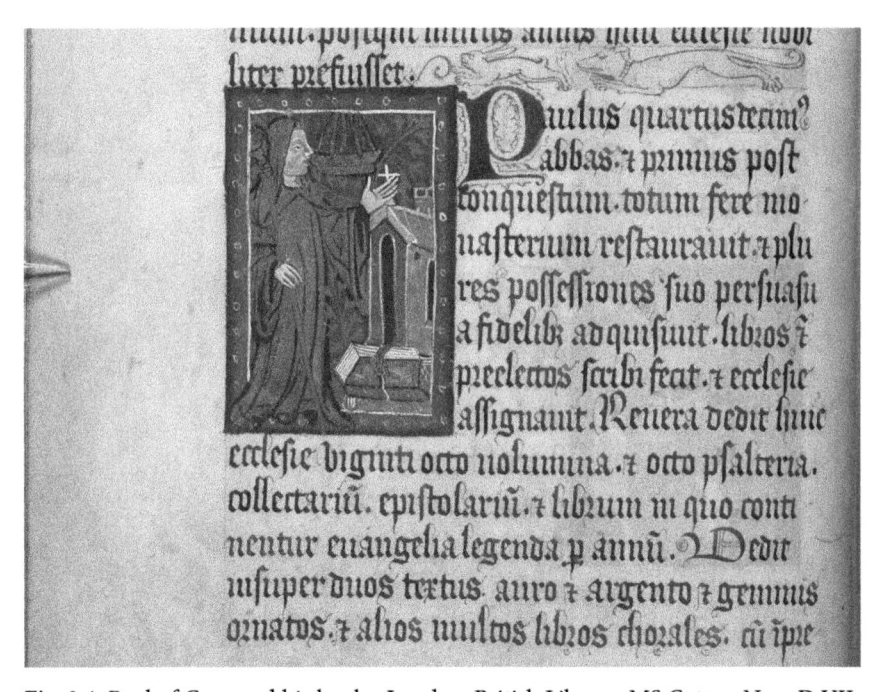

Fig. 3.4 Paul of Caen and his books. London, British Library, MS Cotton Nero D VII, fol. 13v.

---

[148] MS BL Cotton Nero D VII, fols. 13v–14r (Paul), 14r–v (Richard), 14v–15r (Geoffrey), 15v–16r (Robert), 16r–v (Simon), 18v–19r (Roger), 20v–21r (Michael), 21r–24r (Thomas), 27r–35r (John de la Moote), 37r–43r (John of Wheathampstead), and 43v–44r (William Albon). Nine more were added at a later point to continue the abbatial succession to Thomas Ramryge (1492–1520).

[149] The accompanying text relates that Paul provided a large number of books to the community ('plures libros ad usus conventus conscribi fecit, quorum numerum quia longum foret hic explicare').

whose deeds are preserved for posterity—including the author, Andreas Lang (see Fig. 2.6)—have portraits that depict them with books.[150]

The memory of abbatial book provisions relied not just on texts and images, but also on performative practices and carefully choreographed rituals. Amongst the extant books from the monastic library of Saint-Mesmin de Micy are several whose colophons ascribe them to the initiative of Abbot Peter (c.840–59),[151] one of which describes how Peter seized the finished volume and personally placed it on the altar of St Stephen during the liturgy as a means of inscribing its provision in the community's collective memory.[152] This record of Peter's performative book provision offers rare textual testimony to a practice known primarily from visual sources like the dedication scenes on the frontispieces of monastic books.[153] Given their proliferation and shared stylistic repertoire, these images are often treated as iconographic commonplaces with little basis in historical reality, rather than as evidence of actual practice informed by specific precedents. Speaking against this view are cases like that of Robert de Lindsey, abbot (1214–22) of Peterborough, who provided his monks with three lavishly illuminated books, the most famous of which—and the one of primary interest here—is the *Peterborough Psalter* (Cambridge, Fitzwilliam Museum, MS 12).[154] At the opening of the poor man's prayer in Psalm 101 ('Domine exaudi...'; fol. 139v) there is a miniature of

---

[150] MS Bamberg RB Msc. 49, fols. 3r (Henry, 1020–46), 3v (Adelhelm, 1046–71; Ruotpert, 1071–2), 5r (Uto I, 1072–82; Thiemo, 1086–94; Gumpold, 1094–1112), 9r (Herman, 1123–47), 13r (Helmeric, 1147–60), 14v (Wolfram II, 1172–1201), 18r (Herold, 1212–21), 19r (Uto II, 1237), 21r (Udalric II, 1267–95), 23r (Volcold, 1305–11), and 27v (Walter, 1334–50); by a different miniaturist: fols. 41v (Conrad, acting abbot for John I), 42r (Hartung II, 1450–3), 47r (Eberhard III, 1463–75), 52r (Udalric III, 1475–83), and 54v (Andreas, 1483–1502); and, by yet another illustrator, fols. 58r (Wolfgang I, 1502–5; John III, 1505–22), 58v (John IV, 1522–31), 59v (Martin, 1531–9), 60r (George I, 1539–49), and 61r ([Wolfgang II, 1549–64]). The illustrations found throughout the *Fasciculus abbatum* have been identified as the work of eight different artists; Pfändtner, 'Chronica', p. 430.

[151] For example, Leiden, Universiteitsbibliotheek, MS Voss. Lat. Q. 110, fol. 2r; Paris, Bibliothèque nationale de France, MS Lat. 1820, fol. 1r; Paris, Bibliothèque nationale de France, MS Lat. 1862, fols. 40v–41r and 82v. On these books, cf. Thomas Head, *Hagiography and the Cult of Saints: The Diocese of Orléans, 800–1200* (Cambridge: Cambridge University Press, 1990), pp. 207–9; *Colophons de manuscrits occidentaux des origines au XVIe siècle*, 6 vols. (Fribourg: Éditions Universitaires, 1965–82), V, 44 (= no. 15195); John W. Clark, *The Care of Books: An Essay on the Development of Libraries and Their Fittings, from the Earliest Times to the End of the Eighteenth Century* (Cambridge: Cambridge University Press, 1901), pp. 77–8.

[152] Vatican, Biblioteca Apostolica Vaticana, MS Reg. lat. 95, fol. 229r: 'Hic est liber sancti Maximini Miciacensis monasterii, quem Petrus abbas scribere iussit et proprio labore providit atque distinxit et die caenae Domini super sacrum altare sancti Stephani Deo et sancto Maximino habendum obtulit'.

[153] Joachim Prochno, *Das Schreiber- und Dedikationsbild in der deutschen Buchmalerei*, Vol. I: *Bis zum Ende des 11. Jahrhunderts* (Leipzig: Teubner, 1929); Corine Schleif, 'Gifts and Givers that Keep on Giving: Pictured Presentations in Early Medieval Manuscripts', in *Romance and Rhetoric: Essays in Honour of Dhira B. Mahoney*, ed. by Georgiana Donavin and Anita Obermeier (Turnhout: Brepols, 2010), pp. 51–74; Henry Mayr-Harting, *Ottonian Book Illumination: An Historical Study*, 2 vols., 2nd ed. (London: Harvey Miller, 1999).

[154] Robert also provided the *Lindsey Psalter* (London, Society of Antiquaries, MS 59) and a glossed psalter (Cambridge, St John's College, MS D.6), both of which have inscriptions identifying him as their donor; cf. *Peterborough Abbey*, ed. by Karsten Friis-Jensen and James Willoughby [= CBMLC VIII] (London: British Library, 2001), p. 23.

Fig. 3.5 Robert de Lindsey presenting the *Peterborough Psalter*. Cambridge, Fitzwilliam Museum, MS 12, fol. 139v.

an abbot—almost certainly Robert—solemnly approaching an altar alongside a monk who carries a book (Fig. 3.5). To appreciate fully the significance of this miniature and its iconography, we need to situate it within the manuscript's overall programme of illumination and the culture of abbatial book provision at Peterborough generally.

Robert's miniature is the only image in the entire *Peterborough Psalter* that has no point of reference in the narrative by which it is accompanied, whereas the others all show scenes and figures from the main text.[155] This would seem to make it an 'inhabited' initial, rather than a 'historiated' one, the only one of its kind in Robert's manuscripts.[156] It is unlikely that the miniature's purpose is purely ornamental, however, and perhaps a more fruitful approach is to think of

---

[155] MS Fitzwilliam 12, fols. 12v (Christ in Majesty with personifications of Mercy and Truth; Psalm 1), 78r (David and Goliath; Psalm 52), 116r (David slaying a lion; Psalm 80), and 159r (Christ in Majesty; Psalm 109). I do not include in this count the patterned/foliated initials and *litterae notabiliores* on ibid., fols. 13v, 14r, 41v, 60v, 75v, 77r, 138v, 169v, 177v, 182v, 201r, 218r, 223r, and 224r.

[156] It is not impossible that the manuscript now kept at St John's College once featured a similar kind of image which has since been lost, given that the page originally separating the kalendar (fols. 1r–6v) and Prologue to the Psalms (fols. 7r–17v) from the Psalter proper (fols. 18r–159v) has been cut out, leaving behind only a stub (fol. 17a).

it—and others like it—as historiated in a slightly different sense, one in which the reference point is not a scene from the text, but an episode from the history of the book itself. Doing so reveals the elusive scene as the visual equivalent of the ritual described in the ninth-century colophon from Micy: bowing before the altar with one hand stretched out and the other resting on his abbatial staff, Robert implores the saint to accept the book provided by him and carried by his monk-assistant, probably the *Peterborough Psalter* itself.[157] As far as we know, Robert gave little more than a handful of books for Peterborough's library, a gift that pales in comparison with the fifty-five tomes provided by his predecessor, Benedict (1177–93).[158] The books' quality mattered just as much as their quantity, however, enough in any case to warrant Robert's commemoration in the form of a fine miniature that, whilst lacking a clear textual reference point, suggests some degree of strategic consideration with regard to its placement. Inserted about halfway through the volume on a quire's innermost sheet, the image occupies a point at which the codex falls open naturally so that one of the first impressions to catch the reader's eye and be ingrained in his/her memory is the likeness of the commissioning abbot.[159]

Not all images of abbatial book provision involve altars, though, and some depict the superior 'face-to-face' with the monastery's patron saint. A miniature in the *Hitda Codex* (Darmstadt, Universitäts- und Landesbibliothek, MS 1640, fol. 6r) commissioned by Hitda, abbess of Meschede (*c*.978–*c*.1042), has her present the book to the community via its patron saint, St Walburga (Fig. 3.6).[160] As

---

[157] The monk's identity and the reason for his presence (other than to serve as 'book bearer') are unclear, but it is not unthinkable that he played some part or other in the book's production by acting as its copyist, binder, or illuminator.

[158] *CBMLC*, VIII, 22–32 and 34–46 (= BP4–10 and 12–19), with inventories from Robert to Nicholas Elmstow (1391–6); Benedict's books are listed ibid., pp. 15–22 (= BP3). Also cf. Sharpe, 'Medieval Librarian', pp. 236–7. Edward Edwards, *Memoirs of Libraries: Including a Handbook of Library Economy*, 3 vols. (London: Trübner & Co., 1859), I, 116–18 attributes 'nearly eighty works' to Benedict (ibid., p. 116); the historical narratives Benedict provided for his monks include copies of Roger of Howden's *Gesta regis Henrici secundi* (London, British Library, MS Cotton Julius A XI), the *Gesta Alexandri magni*, and the life and deeds of Thomas Becket; *CBMLC*, VIII, pp. 20–1 (= BP3, nos. 40, 42, and 47–8). Simon Gunton, *The History of the Church of Peterburgh* (London: Chiswell, 1686), p. 29 credits Robert with half a dozen volumes, and Robert of Swaffham (fl. 1250–71) mentions no books in his otherwise detailed and complimentary account of his abbacy; see *Historiae Anglicanae scriptores varii*, ed. by Joseph Sparke, 2 vols. (London: Bowyer, 1723), II, 107–14; *CBMLC*, VIII, p. 24 (= BP4).

[159] The *Peterborough Psalter* comprises a total of two hundred and thirty-six folia, but many of the earlier quires consist of fewer sheets than the ones found later in the codex; cf. the helpful collation diagrams on https://www.fitzmuseum.cam.ac.uk/illuminated/manuscript/discover/the-peterborough-psalter/section/make.

[160] *Der Darmstädter Hitda-Codex: Bilder und und Zierseiten aus der Handschrift 1640 der Hessischen Universitäts- und Landesbibliothek*, ed. by Peter Bloch and Erich Zimmermann (Frankfurt: Propyläen, 1968); Christoph Winterer, *Das Evangeliar der Äbtissin Hitda: Eine ottonische Prachthandschrift aus Köln: Miniaturen, Bilder und Zierseiten aus der Handschrift 1640 der Universitäts- und Landesbibliothek Darmstadt* (Darmstadt: Wissenschaftliche Buchgesellschaft, 2016). Hitda's identity remains contested amongst scholars; Dieter Riemer, 'Neue Überlegungen zu Hitda', in *Äbtissin Hitda und der Hitda-Codex (Universitäts- und Landesbibliothek Darmstadt, Hs. 1640): Forschungen zu einem Hauptwerk der ottonischen Kölner Buchmalerei*, ed. by Klaus G. Beuckers

Fig. 3.6 Hitda of Meschede presenting the *Hitda Codex*. Darmstadt, Universitäts- und Landesbibliothek, MS 1640, fol. 6r.

observed by Henry Mayr-Harting, '[n]o image could more effectively have emphasised the power of the abbess over her church', and '[b]y giving the book

(Darmstadt: Wissenschaftliche Buchgesellschaft, 2013), pp. 33–56, tentatively identifies her as the mother of Archbishop Gero of Cologne, commissioner of the *Gero Codex* (Darmstadt, Universitäts- und Landesbibliothek, MS 1948).

to St Walburga, Hitda shows that she is the authoritative channel of access to the patroness'.¹⁶¹ Even the miniature itself, he argues, 'represents a form of gift exchange',¹⁶² one that reflects a mutual acknowledgement between benefactor (abbess) and beneficiary (community) that the provision of a gift—in this case a book—created an obligation on the part of the recipient(s) to repay the donor in kind or in services, the latter of which included commemoration.¹⁶³ The miniature of Hitda providing the book to Walburga and her convent established a visual memorandum of this agreement that perpetuated her legacy—and her *auctoritas*—beyond the grave, and its iconography would have resonated strongly with everyone who picked up the volume and laid eyes on the prominently placed illumination.¹⁶⁴

A striking example of abbatial *auctoritas* visualized on the pages of a monastic book is the illustrated frontispiece of the *Kunigunde Passional* (Prague, National Library of the Czech Republic, MS XIV A 17, fol. 1v) made at the female community of St George in Prague at the command of its abbess, Kunigunde (1302–21). The miniature depicts the princely abbess seated on a pedestal, staff in hand, receiving the book from two tonsured men with rubrics identifying them as, respectively, Colda, the book's 'lector' and 'egregius dictator', and Beneš, its 'scriptor' (Fig. 3.7).¹⁶⁵ A scroll inscribed with Leonine verses running from Colda to Kunigunde further identifies her as the book's commissioning authority ('Suscipe dictata | de regum semine nata, // ad laudem Christi | que me dictare fecisti').¹⁶⁶ With the abbess and her two 'manuscript men' taking centre-stage, the women to their left ('priorissa cum conventu') have received little attention. Two reach out in anticipation, and the fact that their hands—unlike Colda's—are empty suggests that they are about to receive something *from* Kunigunde, rather than offering something *to* her. The most likely object of this expected exchange is that carried by no fewer than half the women: a book. The miniature's iconographic trajectory—from Colda/Beneš to Kunigunde to the

---

¹⁶¹ Mayr-Harting, *Illumination*, II, 100–1.   ¹⁶² Mayr-Harting, *Illumination*, II, 101.

¹⁶³ Cf. Arnoud-Jan Bijsterveld, 'The Medieval Gift as Agent of Social Bonding and Political Power: A Comparative Approach', in *Medieval Transformations: Texts, Power, and Gifts in Context*, ed. by Esther Cohen and Mayke de Jong (Leiden: Brill, 2001), pp. 123–56; Lars Kjær, *The Medieval Gift and the Classical Tradition: Ideals and the Performance of Generosity in Medieval England, 1100–1300* (Cambridge: Cambridge University Press, 2019).

¹⁶⁴ Cf. the discussion by Schleif, 'Gifts', pp. 68–9. Medieval readers seeking additional clarification would find it in the miniature's accompanying *titulus*, which explicitly dedicates the precious codex to the nuns who acted as the primary agents of Hitda's memory ('Hunc librum sancte Walburge Hitda abatissa *pro se* suisque [my emphasis]').

¹⁶⁵ The occasional identification of Beneš as the book's illustrator fails to convince; cf. the discussion by Pamela Sheingorn, 'Review of Gia Toussant, *Das Passional der Kunigunde von Böhmen: Bildrhetorik und Spiritualität*', *Studies in Iconography* 27 (2006), 213–19 (pp. 214–15).

¹⁶⁶ See Allison McCann, 'Women's Books? Gendered Piety and Patronage in Late Medieval Bohemian Illuminated Codices' (unpublished PhD dissertation, University of Pittsburgh, 2019), pp. 71–8, questioning some of the conclusions concerning Kunigunde's agency presented in previous scholarship.

Fig. 3.7 Kunigunde of Prague, her nuns, and her two scribes, Colda and Beneš. Prague, National Library of the Czech Republic, MS XIV A 17, fol. 1v.

community—describes the very sequence in which the *Kunigunde Passional* changed hands to reach the community's library, and it is plausible that the books carried by the nuns had taken the same route. Kunigunde provided books for her nuns from as early as 1303, the year after her appointment,[167] many of

---

[167] The earliest one is Prague, National Library of the Czech Republic, MS XII E 14c (dated 1303), followed by ibid., MSS XIV D 13 (1306), XII D 10 (1310), XIV E 10 (1312), XII D 11 (1318), and XII D 13 (undated); McCann, 'Women's Books?', p. 74 n. 97; Rudy, 'Touching', p. 250, concludes that the *Kunigunde Passional* was part of a 'project to expand the conventual library'. A handlist of Kunigunde's

which have colophons that mention her agency in their acquisition ('comparuit et contulit') or production ('fecit scribi et contulit').[168] By the time the *Kunigunde Passional* was produced in 1312, the community had received at least three, more likely four, codices thus inscribed from her, the exact number of volumes carried by the women on the frontispiece. Kathryn Rudy's forensic examination of the manuscript has revealed traces of physical interaction from page turning to the ritualized touching and kissing of its images as commemorative acts of devotion.[169] As she argues compellingly, the codex 'served as a ritual object that shaped [the] nuns' memories of their most celebrated abbess',[170] a crucial aspect of which—and one emphasized by the frontispiece—was the provision of books.

Abbatial book provision was a collaborative enterprise, but not a democratic one. Scribes, illuminators, and other personnel could expect to be recognized and remembered for their involvement, but not without authorization and mediation of their superiors. Nowhere is this expressed more vividly than in the four-part sequence of dedication images of the *Hornbach Sacramentary* (Solothurn, Sankt-Ursen-Kathedrale, MS U1), 'the longest and largest linear visualisation of a book being given and received' to survive in a monastic manuscript.[171] The opening scene (fol. 7v) shows the commissioning abbot, Adalbert (*c*.972–93), accepting the volume from its scribe, Eburnant, who according to the accompanying verses had followed Adalbert's orders obediently and may therefore request a reward via him.[172] How this was envisaged to operate is shown in the next scenes: Adalbert first hands the book to St Pirmin, the community's founder (fol. 8v), who then passes it on to St Peter (fol. 9v) for its eventual presentation to Christ Himself (fol. 10v).[173] Unlike Eburnant, who quickly disappears from the sequence,

---

books is provided by Jennifer S. Vlček Schurr, 'The Passional of Abbess Cunegund: Protagonists, Production and a Question of Identity' (unpublished MPhil dissertation, University of Glasgow, 2009), pp. 103–4 (= Appendix IV), which distinguishes carefully between books the abbess commissioned for the community (those listed above) and books she had made for her personal use, the latter of which include Prague, National Library of the Czech Republic, MSS VII G 17/d, XII D 8a, XII D 8b, XII D 9, and XII D 12.

[168] MSS Prague XIII E 14c, XIV D 13, XII D 10, XIV E 10, and XII D 11; quoted after Vlček Schurr, 'Passional', p. 17.

[169] Rudy, 'Touching', pp. 250–6. On such 'hands-on' devotional and reading practices, see more generally Kathryn M. Rudy, *Touching Parchment: How Medieval Users Rubbed, Handled, and Kissed Their Manuscripts, Vol. I: Officials and Their Books* (Cambridge: Open Book Publishers, 2023).

[170] Rudy, 'Touching', p. 249.

[171] Schleif, 'Gifts', p. 60; see also Thomas Labusiak, 'Benediktinische Buchmalerei: Die Macht der Bilder', in *Macht des Wortes: Benediktinisches Mönchtum im Spiegel Europas*, ed. by Gerfried Sitar et al., 2 vols. (Regensburg: Schnell & Steiner, 2009), I, 303–15 (p. 311); *Ornamenta Ecclesiae: Kunst und Künstler der Romanik*, ed. by Anton Legner, 3 vols. (Cologne: Schnütgen-Museum, 1985), I, 139–42 (= B2).

[172] MS Solothurn U1, fol. 8r, ll. 7–16: 'Eburnant vilis | tibi tota mente fidelis // Semper ubique tui | promptissimus assecla voti // Scriptor domne tibi | praesens quem porrigo libri // Quo tu cum sanctum | celebres Christicola cultum // Tecum scriptori | pia praemia posce mereri'; cf. Peter Bloch, *Das Hornbacher Sakramentar und seine Stellung innerhalb der frühen Reichenauer Buchmalerei* (Basel: Birkhäuser, 1956), p. 23.

[173] Bloch, *Sakramentar*, pp. 52–67 distinguishes between acts of delivery (*Übergabe*) and presentation (*Darbringung*), and he emphasizes the historicity of the scenes depicted.

Adalbert remains present throughout, with Pirmin and Peter presenting themselves as his ambassadors.[174] As with the *Hitda Codex* discussed above, it is the abbot who by virtue of his/her authority facilitates exclusive and authoritative access to these saints and the services they provide on behalf of the scribe(s).

A similar relationship between an abbot and his scribal workforce can be seen in the books provided by Frowin, fifth abbot (1143/47–78) of Engelberg,[175] whose arrival from St Blasien transformed the abbey's basic collection of mainly liturgical codices into a full-scale library suitable for study. Whilst his predecessors had relied primarily on external supply channels, Frowin utilized domestic means of production to expand and diversify the existing book collection.[176] Despite some losses, the scale of Frowin's abbatial book provision may still be gauged from the survival of more than thirty codices with colophons that name him as their provider by using terminology similar to that employed by the artist/versifier of the *Hornbach Sacramentary*.[177] A detailed analysis of these colophons is offered elsewhere,[178] but what is of interest here is that they style Frowin as their primary agent and the main beneficiary of their commemorative currency. The colophon in Engelberg's copy of Augustine's treatise on the Sermon on the Mount (Engelberg, Stiftsbibliothek, MS Cod. 88, fol. [i]v) asks the rhetorical question as

---

[174] MS Solothurn U1, fol. 10r, ll. 9–16: 'Haec tibi commendans | meus ut mihi credidit abbas // Vilia divini tibi | mittit xenia libri // Quem tibi sacravit | ac tota mente paravit // Caeli cui cardo | pateat pro munere servo'; ibid., fol. 11r, ll. 9–16: 'Do tibi quod praefert | meus abbas munus Adalbert // Cui pro terrenis | de vitae praemia donis // Perpetis ut libri | mereatur margine scribi // Gaudeat hinc scriptor | pariter scriptoris et actor'; Bloch, *Sakramentar*, pp. 26–7. On representations of intercession in medieval art, see Sean Gilsdorf, 'Deēsis Deconstructed: Imagining Intercession in the Medieval West', *Viator* 42 (2012), 131–74.

[175] The successors of Engelberg's first abbot, Aldhelm (1120–31), were remembered less than favourably. The domestic annals do not mention their names and instead present Frowin as 'secundus abbas', a *damnatio memoriae* that was revised in the fifteenth century; 'Annales Engelbergenses, a.1147–1546', in *Annales aevi Suevici* [= *MGH SS* XVII], ed. by Georg H. Pertz (Hanover: Hahn, 1861), pp. 278–82 (p. 279); Placidus Tanner, 'Die ältesten Jahrbücher Engelbergs', *Der Geschichtsfreund* 8 (1852), 101–17 (p. 109).

[176] See Martin Steinmann, 'Die Bücher des Abtes Frowin–ein Skriptorium in Engelberg?', *Scriptorium* 54 (2000), 9–13; *Scriptoria medii aevi Helvetica*, ed. by Albert Bruckner, 14 vols. (Geneva: Roto-Sadag, 1935–79), VIII, 14–18. The surviving contents of Frowin's library have been digitized with funding by the Stavros Niarchos Foundation (2011–12), https://www.e-codices.unifr.ch/en/list/subproject/frowins_library.

[177] Martin Steinmann, 'Abt Frowin von Engelberg (1143–1178) und seine Handschriften', *Der Geschichtsfreund* 146 (1993), 7–36 (pp. 16–17); Ephrem Omlin, 'Abt Frowin als Gründer der Engelberger Schreiberschule', in *Der selige Frowin von Engelberg: Ein Reformabt des 12. Jahrhunderts, 1143–1178* (Engelberg: Stiftsdruckerei, 1943), pp. 26–35 and 47–53 (pp. 47–50). The colophon in a copy of Bede's *Gospel Homilies* informs the reader that '[h]e who governed here was the *auctor* of this book' ('Qui fuit hic rector, | fuit huius codicis auctor'; Engelberg, Stiftsbibliothek, MS Cod. 47, fol. 1r), a term sometimes used interchangeably with *actor* by medieval Latin writers that can be translated as 'maker' or 'provider'; cf. Müller, 'Auctor', pp. 18–20; Chenu, 'Auctor', pp. 82–3. The same terminology is used by the colophon in Engelberg, Stiftsbibliothek, MS Cod. 23, fol. 123v ('Abbas Frowinus | fuit auctor codicis huius'); Similar colophons also feature in books provided by Frowin's successors, Berchtold (1178–97), Henry I (1197–1223), Walter I (1250–67), Ulrich I (1296–8), Rudolph I (1298–1317), and William (1331–47), albeit in considerably smaller numbers.

[178] Benjamin Pohl, *Publishing in a Medieval Monastery: The View from Twelfth-Century Engelberg* (Cambridge: Cambridge University Press, 2023).

to why Frowin should receive any less credit for producing the book than its scribe, given that the latter merely obeyed him with his hand ('Cur aut unde minus | habet a mercede Fro[w]inus? // Cum scriptor scripsi, | manus autem paruit ipsi')? The same verses adorn the frontispiece of a large Bible—the third instalment of a three-volume set copied at Frowin's request—by a scribe called Richene (Engelberg, Stiftsbibliothek, MS Cod. 5, fol. 1r), which reasons further that as long as the abbot leads well and the scribe obeys him, they shall both be rewarded in the heavenly citadel ('Dum bene praecedit | hic, dum catus alter obedit, // merces amborum | florebit in arce polorum').[179] The scribe claims no autonomy as his hand is but an extension of Frowin's, and its movements are directed by the abbot's superior authority. The accompanying miniature shows Richene and Frowin seated next to each other—at notably different heights—under a gallery of painted arches (Fig. 3.8). Perched in front of an open book ready to write, Richene eagerly awaits the abbot's instructions.[180] As with the miniatures from Hornbach and Prague, Richene does not claim his reward independently of Frowin, but via his mediation. The corresponding miniature on the frontispiece of the Bible-set's first volume (Engelberg, Stiftsbibliothek, MS Cod. 4, fol. 1v) therefore shows Frowin—not Richene—presenting the finished manuscript(s) to the patron saint. With the abbot assuming centre-stage, Richene and whoever else might have been involved in the process are relegated to the background.

This is not to say that there were no prospects for scribes and other collaborators to share their superior's limelight. The commemorative currency and prestige of the provision of books by abbots and abbesses sometimes had scribes competing to take part in their production. At Michelsberg, the two monk-scribes Reinher and Nonnosus whom we met above (1.2) went to remarkable lengths in their rivalry to be remembered as the 'go-to scribe' of their abbot and domestic historian, Andreas. When composing an account of Andreas's deeds shortly after his death in 1502, Reinher drew up a detailed inventory of the many books he had procured (MS Bamberg RB. Msc. 49, fol. 57r; Fig. 3.9a).[181] Nonnosus expanded Reinher's inventory by adding, on the reverse of the same page (fol. 57v), a list of Andreas's authorial compositions (Fig. 3.9b), in which Andreas is said never to have put his own pen to parchment ('nullum per se scripserit librum') but tasked Nonnosus to codify his entire oeuvre ('omnia conscribi fecit per capellanum suum fratrem Nonnosum'). As we saw (1.2), however, some of Andreas's authorial

---

[179] On Richene, see Steinmann, 'Frowin', pp. 14–16; Steinmann, 'Bücher', p. 11.

[180] Cf. Reto Bonifazi, 'Die beiden Miniaturen der Frowin-Bibel auf Einzelblättern', in *Die Bilderwelt des Klosters Engelberg: Das Skriptorium unter den Äbten Frowin (1143–1178), Bechtold (1178–1197) and Heinrich (1197–1223)*, ed. by Christoph Eggenberger (Luzern: Diopter, 1999), pp. 27–30 (p. 27). Steinmann, 'Frowin', p. 14 suggests that the miniature's iconography might be adapted from of a scene involving Bede (in the role of the scribe) and Salomon (in the place of the abbot) in a twelfth-century manuscript from Prüfening (Munich, Bayerische Staatsbibliothek, MS Clm. 14,398), though whether the stylistic similarities are strong enough to indicate a direct line of influence remains debatable.

[181] *MBKDS*, III.3, 387–8 (= no. 96.III); Bresslau, 'Studien I', pp. 189–92.

Fig. 3.8 Frowin of Engelberg and his scribe, Richene. Engelberg, Stiftsbibliothek, MS Cod. 5, fol. 1r.

compositions—including the *Fasciculus*—were in fact copied by Reinher. Judging from the palaeographical evidence, Nonnosus's omission did not remain unchallenged, forcing him to set the record straight and share credit with Reinher. Distinguishable by their lighter ink and written with a narrower/sharper nib

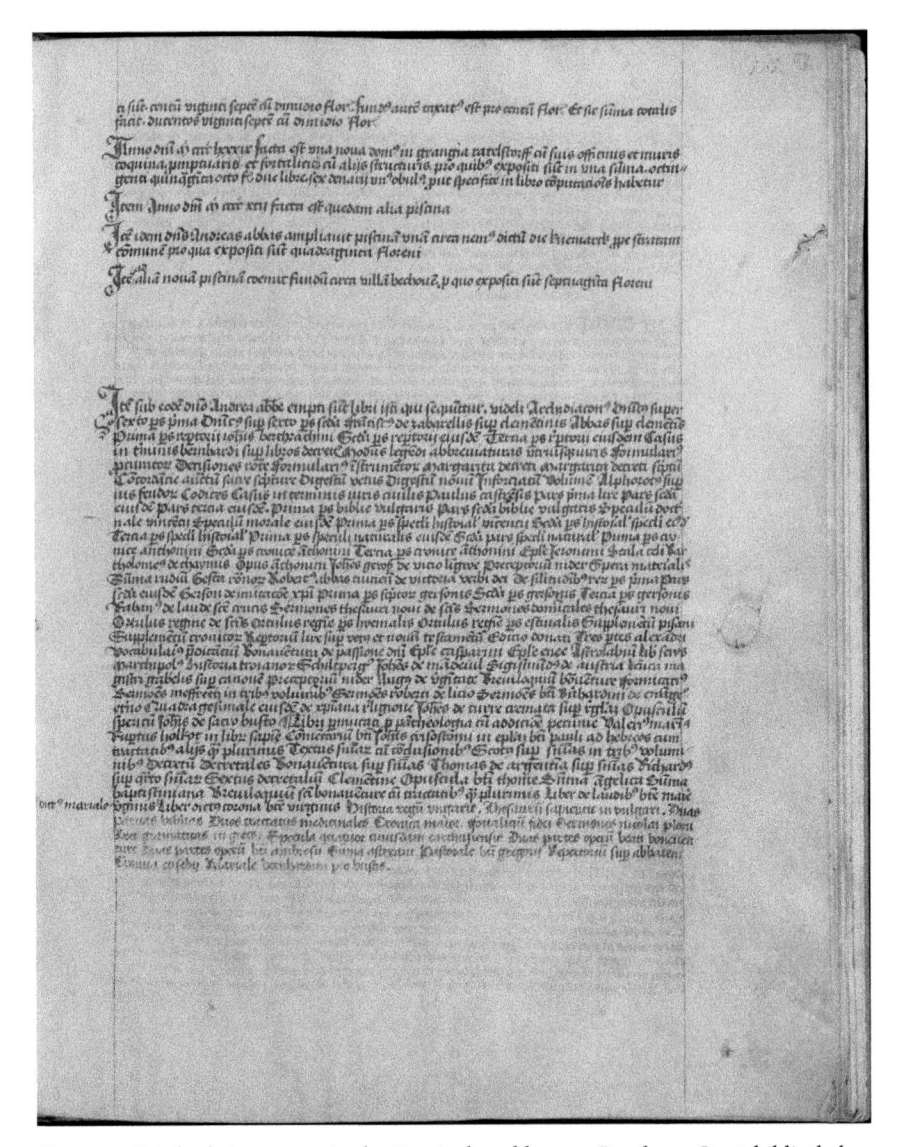

Fig. 3.9a Reinher's inventory in the *Fasciculus abbatum*. Bamberg, Staatsbibliothek, MS RB. Msc. 49, fol. 57r.

than the preceding text, the last three and a half lines are an addition in Nonnosus's own hand that acknowledges Reinher as the copyist of at least a few volumes ('illa scribi fecit per fratrem Reinherum'),[182] though the fact that Reinher's name is written over an erasure suggests that Nonnusus had previously

---

[182] MS Bamberg RB. Msc. 49, fol. 57v, ll. 40–3.

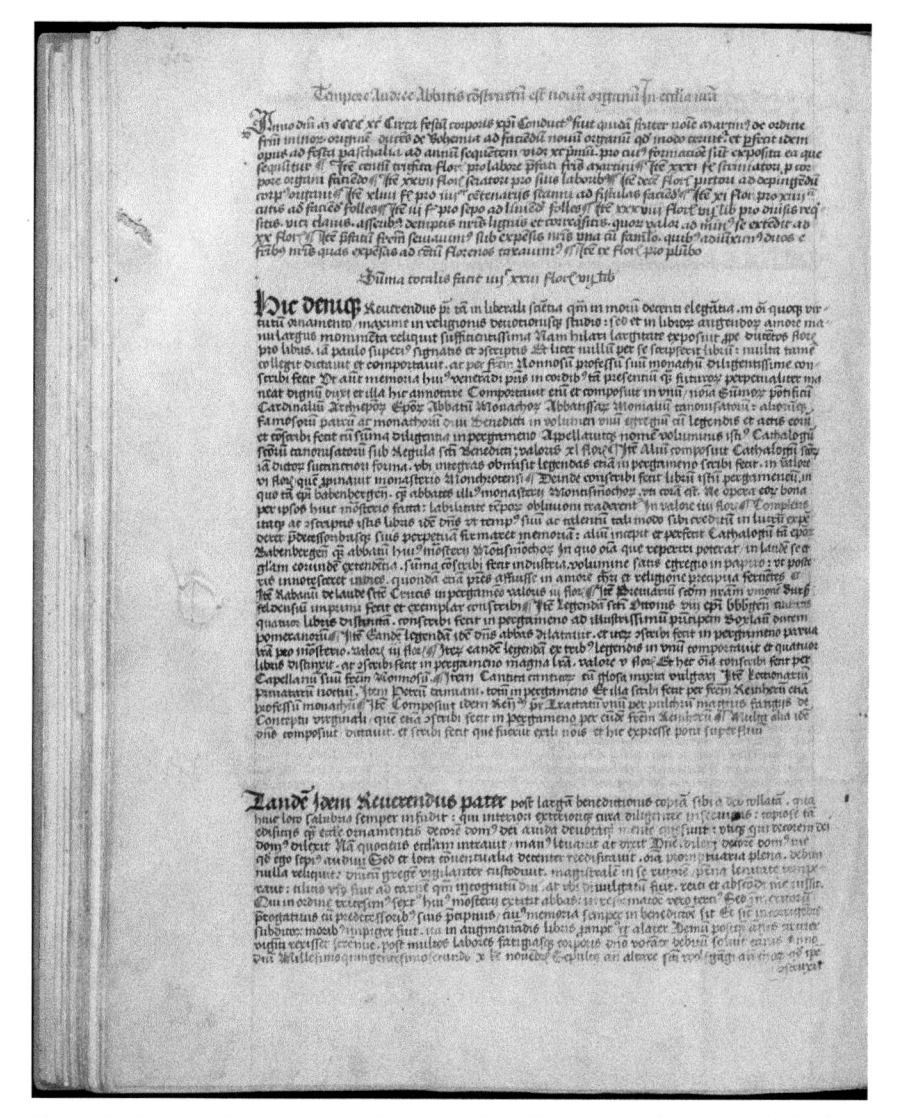

Fig. 3.9b Nonnosus's inventory in the *Fasciculus abbatum*. Bamberg, Staatsbibliothek, MS RB. Msc. 49, fol. 57v.

claimed credit for these volumes himself before relinquishing, quite possibly under duress, his claim in his rival's favour. Both men were determined to have their scribal agency acknowledged and recorded for posterity. Having their names inscribed into the community's collective memory alongside Andreas's, the two scribes claimed their respective share in the reward that the late abbot could expect in return for the books he had provided.

Another scribe who showed great resolve and resourcefulness in his efforts to be remembered alongside his abbot was Swicher of Prüfening. Possibly the most accomplished and industrious copyist in Prüfening's prolific twelfth-century scriptorium who 'was drawn to heroic scribal endeavours',[183] Swicher played an instrumental role in the book provision of three successive heads of house: Erbo (1121–61), Godefrid (1162/3), and Eberhard (1162/3–68).[184] The frontispiece of the *Prüfening Isidore* (Munich, Bayerische Staatsbibliothek, MS Clm. 13031) shows Swicher on his deathbed and two angels with a pair of scales about to weigh his soul, a motif known as *psychostasia*.[185] Tipping the scales in Swicher's favour is a hefty codex—presumably the *Prüfening Isidore*—that outweighs his sins and grants the 'wretched scribe' ('scriptor miser') entry into paradise.[186] The contrast with the contemporary miniatures from Engelberg discussed above is notable: Richene only ever features alongside his abbot Frowin, though as we saw the reverse is not true. In the *Prüfening Isidore*, by contrast, there seems to be no sign of Swicher's abbatial patron; or is there? Tempting though it would be to view Erbo's absence from the miniature as evidence of Swicher's scribal autonomy, a look at his other work reveals a different story.

In 1158, Swicher was tasked by his abbot Erbo to make a copy of the *Glossarium Salomonis* (Munich, Bayerische Staatsbibliothek, MS Clm. 13002) for the monastery's library.[187] About halfway through the book, Swicher briefly strayed from his exemplar to insert a short poem:

May he possess the light of heaven who wrote ('scripsit'), without reward, so large a volume in the hope of Divine mercy, in return for which a reward may be given to him there [in heaven], for here [on Earth] he lacked the reward he deserved. And may the [book's] supervisor ('monitor') and initiator ('cupitor') also rejoice in heaven, one of whom frequently admonished the tardy scribe, whilst the other urged him on continuously.[188]

---

[183] Quote from Elizabeth Sears, 'The Afterlife of Scribes: Swicher's Prayer in the Prüfening Isidore', in *Pen in Hand: Medieval Scribal Portraits, Colophons and Tools*, ed. by Michael Gullick (Walkern: Red Gull, 2006), pp. 75–96 (p. 76).

[184] The books provided by Abbot Godefrid are listed in a contemporary inventory (Munich, Bayerische Staatsbibliothek, MS Clm. 14361, fol. 135v) alongside his obit.

[185] *Die romanischen Handschriften der Bayerischen Staatsbibliothek*, Vol. 1: *Die Bistümer Regensburg, Passau und Salzburg*, ed. by Elisabeth Klemm (Wiesbaden: Reichert, 1980), pp. 64–5 (= no. 89); Sears, 'Afterlife', pp. 75–7 and 84–5. For further examples of *psychostasia*, cf. Michael Gullick, 'How Fast Did Scribes Write? Evidence from Romanesque Manuscripts', in *Making the Medieval Book: Techniques of Production*, ed. by Linda L. Brownrigg (Los Altos Hills, CA: Anderson Lovelace, 1995), pp. 39–58; Pohl, 'Orderic', pp. 339–40.

[186] MS Munich Clm. 13031, fol. 1r: 'Scriptoris miseri | dignare Deus misereri. // Noli culparum | pondus pensare mearum. // Parva licet bona sint | super exaltata malis sint. // Nox luci cedat | vite mors iste recedat'.

[187] *Handschriften*, ed. Klemm, pp. 60–4 (= no. 87).

[188] MS Munich Clm. 13002, fol. 110v: 'Possideat lumen | celi tam grande volumen // qui scripsit gratis | divine spe pietatis. // Pro quo debet ei | merces illic redibereri, // nam qua dignus erat | istic mercede crebat. // Gaudeat et monitor | in celis atque cupitor, // scribam crebro monens | tardantem sepius urgens'; translation adapted from Sears, 'Afterlife', p. 96.

The identities of the two individuals who commissioned the book's production and monitored Swicher's work remain undisclosed, but they are revealed elsewhere in the manuscript. In the preface, Swicher relinquishes his own agency in favour of two others: one—the *monitor*—is Wolfger, a local monk placed in charge of the abbey's library ('qui armarię suę curam gerebat') and perhaps its archives.[189] It is to Wolfger's pen that we owe several important sources for the history of the monastery and its library, including various abbatial charters, a *liber traditionum* (Munich, Bayerisches Hauptstaatsarchiv, Kloster Prüfening, KL 2), and two library inventories, one from the 1140s and the other from 1165.[190] Wolfger's second inventory is prefixed to the *Glossarium*'s opening quire (fols. 5v–6v) with a frontispiece that shows the library's principal providers, Erbo and Eberhard, alongside Christ, the monastery's patron saint, and its episcopal founder, Otto of Bamberg. Both abbots have their names highlighted in red and together are credited with the provision of almost a hundred and forty books, most of which were copied domestically during Erbo's tenure.[191] It is no surprise, therefore, that the second individual identified in Swicher's preface—the *cupitor*—is none other than Erbo. Just like the Engelberg scribe who described his own hand as a mechanical instrument for carrying out his abbot's command, Swicher rejects any claim of independence by referring to himself and Wolfger as labouring under Erbo's gentle yoke ('sub pii patris levi iugo'). His assertion that he made the *Glossarium* without reward ('gratis') is no attempt to liberate himself from this yoke, nor an example of scribal emancipation, but an acknowledgement that monastic scribes—unlike professionals—were not entitled to remuneration for conducting their work in compliance with their superiors' authority. These were no commercial transactions but acts of obedience.

In the mid-thirteenth century, the *Glossarium* was copied by Conrad, a monk of Scheyern who adapted Swicher's verses to refer to himself and his abbot, Henry (1226–59).[192] Conrad was a proficient scribe whose services were requested regularly by Henry and his predecessor, also named Conrad (1206–25), who

---

[189] MS Munich Clm. 13002, fol. 8r. On Wolfger, see Franz J. Worstbrock, 'Wolfger von Prüfening', in *Die deutsche Literatur des Mittelalters–Verfasserlexikon*, ed. by Burghart Wachinger et al., 2nd rev. ed., 14 vols. (Berlin: De Gruyter, 1977–2008), X, 1352–60; Heinrich Fichtenau, 'Wolfger von Prüfening', *Mitteilungen des Instituts für österreichische Geschichtsforschung* 51 (1937), 313–57.

[190] Both inventories are edited in *MBKDS*, IV.1, 416–27 (= nos. 40 and 41). On the *liber traditionum*, cf. Andrea Schwarz, *Die Traditionen des Klosters Prüfening* (Munich: Beck, 1991).

[191] Hans-Georg Schmitz, *Kloster Prüfening im 12. Jahrhundert* (Munich: Wölfle, 1975), p. 71; Elisabeth Klemm, 'Die Klostergemeinschaft von Prüfening im Spiegel ihres Schatzverzeichnisses', in *Cechy jsou plné kostelu/Boemia plena est ecclesiis*, ed. by Milada Studničková (Prague: Nakladatelství Lidové Noviny, 2010), pp. 37–44. On the monastic library under Erbo and Eberhard, see Stephan Kellner, 'Die Prüfeninger Klosterbibliothek–Geschichte und Spuren', in *Die Regensburger Bibliothekslandschaft am Ende des Alten Reiches*, ed. by Manfred Knedlik and Bernhard Lübbers (Regensburg: Universitätsverlag, 2011), pp. 129–40; Manfred Knedlik, 'Die Bibliothek des Benediktinerklosters Prüfening', in *Mönche, Künstler und Fürsten: 900 Jahre Gründung Kloster Prüfening*, ed. by Maria Baumann (Regensburg: Schnell & Steiner, 2009), pp. 89–104.

[192] Munich, Bayerische Staatsbibliothek, MS Clm. 17403, fol. 7v: 'In hoc sane opere predictum fratrem C[huonradum], qui se sub pii patris levi iugo pro sui officii debito devotior impendebat, sua

had authored various works of history before resigning in 1225, including domestic annals, the *Chronicon Schirense*, and the *Series abbatum Schirensium*.[193] About half a dozen of Conrad's books survive, and he himself has left us an inventory in the *Glossarium*'s opening quire.[194] Conrad—who refers to himself in the third person throughout—recalls having worked by himself ('solus laboravit') without access to communal funds ('nichil sibi sumptuum de publico daretur'), forcing him to gather what was needed by his own means ('ipse que necessaria errant ita undecumque contulit') without support ('solus comparavit sine omni emolumento et auxilio')—statements that seem paradoxical considering that he worked exclusively by abbatial mandate.[195] To resolve this, we need to take a closer look at another important aspect of abbatial book provision: resourcing and collaboration.

3.4 Resourcing and Collaboration

A key area of monastic life and administration that offers tangible evidence of the superior's principal involvement in the provision of books is the allocation of official funds and revenues. The fact that monastic officers like cantors, sacristans, and priors were in regular receipt of revenues designated for the production and/or acquisition of books is well established based on documentation surviving from across the medieval Latin West, often in the shape of abbatial charters and account books, but also in narrative form. At Evesham, for example, the prior and cantor were both allocated annual revenues from the abbey's demesne to help maintain the domestic library, with the former receiving the annual tithes of Bengeworth to pay for the parchment and the sustenance of external copyists ('ad parcamenum et exhibitionem'), and the latter being granted five *solidi* annually from lands held in Hampton, Stokes, and Alcester to provide the ink for domestic scribes, pigment

---

omnibus nota et grata sollicitudo commendabat'; edited in 'De codicibus a Chounrado Schirensi exaratis', ed. by Philipp Jaffé, in *Annales aevi Suevici*, ed. by Georg H. Pertz [= *MGH SS* XVII] (Hanover: Hahn, 1861), pp. 623–4; also cf. Joseph von Hefner, 'Über den Mönch Konrad von Scheyern mit dem Beinamen philosophus', *Oberbayerisches Archiv für vaterländische Geschichte* 2 (1840), 150–80 (pp. 158–9); that Prüfening's copy of the *Glossarium Salomonis* provided the exemplar for the Scheyern codex was suspected by Carl T. Gemeiner, *Kurze Beschreibung der Handschriften in der Stadtbibliothek der K[aiserlichen] freien Reichsstadt Regensburg* (Ingolstadt: n/a, 1791), p. 12, and confirmed by Albert Boeckler, 'Zur Conrad von Scheyern-Frage', *Jahrbuch für Kunstwissenschaft* (1923), 83–102 (p. 97).

[193] Though occasionally identified as the same person, these two Conrads are distinguished categorically by Boeckler, 'Scheyern-Frage', pp. 101–2; also cf. Franz J. Worstbrock 'Konrad von Scheyern', in *Die deutsche Literatur des Mittelalters* = *Verfasserlexikon*, ed. by Burghart Wachinger et al., 2nd rev. ed., 14 vols. (Berlin: De Gruyter, 1977–2008), V, 252–4.

[194] MS Munich Clm. 17403, fol. 7v; von Hefner, 'Konrad', p. 159; Schlotheuber and McQuillen, 'Books', pp. 993–5, with identifications of six surviving manuscripts and multiple fragments from Conrad's 1241 catalogue.

[195] MS Munich Clm. 17403, fol. 7v.

for illumination, and whatever was needed for the books' binding ('de hiis debet invenire precentor incaustum omnibus scriptoribus monasterii et colores ad illuminandum et necessaria ad ligandum libros').[196] The source that informs us about these allocations is the *Chronicon* (or *Historia*) *abbatiae de Evesham*, composed by Thomas of Marlborough during his successive tenure as Evesham's sacristan (1217), prior (1218–29), and eventually abbot (1229–36). More specifically, they are recorded in an abbatial charter inserted into the chronicle's narrative that was issued by Thomas's predecessor, Randulf (1214–29), and confirmed by Pope Innocent III, and in which Thomas, a dean of ten years, 'doubtless had a hand'.[197] As the charter explains, some of the revenues given to Evesham's officers were secured by Randulf himself, whereas others had been obtained by previous abbots including Reginald (1130–49), Roger (1159–60), and Adam (1161–89), who likewise had obtained confirmations from Popes Innocent II (1130–43) and Alexander III (1159–81).[198] Not only are these officers themselves appointed by the abbot from within the community ('ab abbate de proprio conventu creentur'), but they must render an account of their spending to him four times a year in the presence of the prior and six monks appointed by the abbot and convent ('officiales omnes qui redditus percipiunt quater in anno coram abbate [...] priore et sex claustralibus, tribus ab abbate et tribus a conventu vocatis, de administratione sua compotum reddant').[199] Any reported over- or underspend may be redistributed at the abbot's discretion in conference with the chapter, and should a revenue stream be diminished or dry up altogether, the abbot and chapter must find a suitable alternative. Whilst communal conferral offered a mutual control mechanism for the allocation of official revenues, at least in theory, it did not change the fact that in practice all revenues generated from the monastic demesne were ultimately subject to the superior's authorization.

At Westminster, a charter by Abbot Gervase (1138–57) earmarks revenues generated from the monastery's demesne for duties pertaining to the cantor's office ('pro ceteris negotiis que ad cantoris nostri pertinent officium'), including the repair of library books ('pro reparandis libris armarii').[200] The allocated funds comprise eight shillings annually from the tithes of Roding in Essex held by the priest Aluric ('viii solidos de decima de Roinges, quam tenet Aluricus presbiter'), which are to be distributed in two instalments, one at the feast of the Annunciation, and the other at Saint Peter in Chains ('ad Annuntiationem sancte

---

[196] *Thomas of Marlborough: History of the Abbey of Evesham*, ed./tr. by Jane Sayers and Leslie Watkiss (Oxford: Oxford University Press, 2003), pp. 392–4.

[197] *History*, ed./tr. Sayers and Watkiss, p. xxi; on Thomas's appointments and the *Historia*'s date of composition, see ibid., pp. xx–xxv.

[198] *History*, ed./tr. Sayers and Watkiss, pp. 386–7.

[199] *History*, ed./tr. Sayers and Watkiss, pp. 388–9.

[200] *Westminster Abbey Charters, 1066–c.1214*, ed. by Emma Mason (London: London Record Society, 1988), p. 125 (= no. 251).

Marie iiii solidos et ad festivitatem sancti Petri ad vincula iiii solidos'), and they both will go to the cantor ('volumus et precipimus ut cantor ecclesie beati Petri Westmonasterii, quisquis ille fuerit, predictos habeat solidos'). As Gervase makes clear, however, this is not an entitlement, but an abbatial bequest ('nostra donatio').[201] A similar arrangement is recorded in the *Consuetudines* from Żagań, stipulating that the librarian manages the book collection at the abbot's behest ('ad iussum abbatis'), and for this he receives an annual recompense of one groschen directly from the abbot ('habet ipse singulis annis unam marcam grossorum in camera abbatis sublevare').[202] At Dargun, the head of house held one manse of land from the lord of Rostock, Henry Borwin III, for the acquisition, repair, and renewal of the community's books ('ad libros comparandos, reficiendos seu quolibet modo alio instaurandos'), the returns from which he could use and/or distribute however he saw fit.[203] Whilst there does not appear to have been an expectation to consult Dargun's community about these revenues, it seems likely that the prior, in turn, would have had to report to the mother house and Cistercian General Chapter. The principle remained the same, whereby the head of the community and beneficiary/administrator of the grant(s) provided the resources for the library either directly, via his officers, or a combination of both, as was the case at St Albans.

According to the *Gesta abbatum*, St Albans's first post-Conquest abbot and a known book lover ('scripturarum amator'), Paul of Caen (1077-93), persuaded a fellow Norman called Robert to donate several tithes at Hatfield and Redbourn to the monastery.[204] Upon receipt of Robert's donation, Paul permanently allocated the tithes to the provision of books for St Albans's church ('ad volumina ecclesiae facienda'), for which he personally selected scribes from far afield ('ab electis et procul quaesitis scriptoribus scribi'). To show his gratitude, Paul gave some of the first books made with these funds to Robert for his chapel ('ad capellam suam in curia de Hathfeld'), but the remainder—and all those made thereafter—he gave to the monks.[205] To 'top up' the revenues secured from Robert, the abbot further decreed that the sustenance for hired scribes should be provided jointly by the cellarer and monks from their alms ('constituit quaedam diaria dari scriptoribus de eleemosyna fratrum et cellarii [...] ad edendum'), thus ensuring that food was always made available to them without interrupting their work ('ne scriptores impedirentur'). Conscious of the financial burden this placed on the abbey's

---

[201] *Charters*, ed. Mason, p. 125.   [202] Rother, 'Ausleihregister', p. 1.
[203] Quoted after Steinmann, *Handschriften*, pp. 355-6 (= no. 432).
[204] *Gesta*, ed. Riley, I, 57-8; tr. Preest and Clark, p. 132.
[205] The chronicler reports that Paul continued to use these resources for the monks' benefit by ordering the production of carefully selected books from exemplars provided by Lanfranc, the Norman archbishop of Canterbury and former abbot of Saint-Étienne de Caen ('continuo in ipso, quod construxit, scriptorio libros praeelectos scribi fecit, Lanfranco exemplaria ministrante'); *Gesta*, ed. Riley, II, 58; tr. Preest and Clark, p. 133.

almoner, he increased the latter's revenues accordingly.[206] Though the books thus supplied for St Albans were financed by the community's almoner, cellarer, abbot, and monks, the only person who is commemorated explicitly for their provision—and praised exuberantly for it in the *Gesta abbatum*—is the abbot. Paul is credited with providing no fewer than sixty-nine volumes without even counting the ordinals, customaries, missals, books of tropes, books of collects, and various other books kept in the communal bookcases,[207] and his use of hired scribes no doubt played a major part in this herculean effort.

Indeed, professional scribes were no rarity in medieval monasteries, and their sustenance and accommodation could incur significant costs for the community and its superior. Paul's direct successors, Richard d'Aubigny and Geoffrey de Gorham, both channelled tithes allocated to the almoner for feeding the poor to the monastic scriptorium ('domui scriptoris') in exchange for rations of food. The almoner was to collect these rations from the monks' lest the scribes had to stop their work to buy food ('ne scriptores in escis emendis impedirentur').[208] The procedure appears to have borne fruit, allowing Richard to provide the monks with many precious books ('volumina pretiosa'), whilst Geoffrey provided two missals written and illuminated in gold ('unum missale, auro redimitum; et aliud in duabus voluminibus, totum auro incomparabiliter illuminatum, et aperte et legibiliter scriptum'), a precious illuminated psalter ('unum psalterium pretiosum, totum similiter auro illuminatum'), and various other books.[209] Robert de Gorham is credited with having contributed more books than could easily be related ('[f]ecit etiam scribi libros plurimos, quos longum esset enarrare'), and his successor, Simon, stationed a team of professional scribes in his abbatial chamber on a permanent basis.[210] As the *Gesta* make clear, Simon went to great lengths in securing revenues to enlarge the abbey's library and scriptorium, so much so that all subsequent abbots would be obliged to employ at least one specialized copyist at all times.[211]

Other abbots and abbesses who permanently employed professional scribes include Guido of Nonantola (1286–1309), who according to Franciscan chronicler Salimbene di Adam instructed his monks always to have two hired scribes in their

---

[206] *Gesta*, ed. Riley, II, 58; tr. Preest and Clark, p. 132. Similar re-allocations are documented at other monasteries; see the cases discussed in Webber, 'Cantor', pp. 182–3.

[207] *Gesta*, ed. Riley, I, 58: 'Dedit igitur huic ecclesiae viginti octo volumina notabilia, et octo psalteria, collectarium, epistolarium, et librum in quo continentur evangelia legenda per annum; duos textus, auro et argento, et gemmis, ornatos; sine ordinalibus, consuetudinariis, missalibus, tropariis, collectariis, et aliis libris, qui in armariolis habentu'; tr. Preest and Clark, p. 133.

[208] *Gesta*, ed. Riley, I, 76; tr. Preest and Clark, p. 163.

[209] *Gesta*, ed. Riley, I, 70 and 94; tr. Preest and Clark, pp. 151 and 180.

[210] *Gesta*, ed. Riley, I, 192; tr. Preest and Clark, p. 300.

[211] The abbatial provision of books and support of scribes at St Albans is recorded throughout the *Gesta abbatum*, most notably in the chapters dedicated to William of Trumpington (1214–35), Roger de Norton (1263–91), Richard of Wallingford (1327–34), Michael of Mentmore (1335–49), and Thomas de la Mare (1349–96).

midst and pay them from the abbey's funds ('rogavit fratres quod simper in illo monasterio cum monasterii expensis duos scriptores haberent propter copiam librorum, que ibi est').[212] When Margaret, abbess of Frauental, paid seven thaler and fourteen pfennig for a book commissioned from a certain sister named Elisabeth in 1342, nearly half the money went to a hired scribe ('precium scriptoris') who seems to have been a regular.[213] A particularly well-documented case comes from Abingdon, where Abbot Faritius (1100–17) overhauled his predecessors' book production and provision policies. The abbatial chronicle history known as *De abbatibus Abbendonie* includes a list of the books provided by Faritius.[214] Writing at the commission of either Faritius himself or one of his successors, the chronicler explains that these volumes were produced not by the members of the monastic community proper, but by copyists from outside the cloister ('scriptores preter claustrales').[215] This is not to suggest that Faritius made no use of his domestic workforce. In fact, the *Historia ecclesie Abbendonensis* reports that he allocated resources to the monastery's obedientiaries specifically so as to upscale in-house book production, such as by reassigning the tithe of Dumbleton (worth 30 *solidi* annually) and 'earmarking' it for buying parchment ('[a]d pergamenum emendum').[216] The text does not specify which of the officers should receive this grant and administer the revenues generated from it on the abbot's behalf, but a clue may be derived from the more detailed, if somewhat formulaic, account of *De obedientiariis abbatiae Abbedonensis*, which states that parchment, ink, and everything else required when producing books for the community ('parcamenam, incaustum, et omnia quae ad preparationem librorum conventus sunt necessaria') should be purchased by the cantor from the revenues assigned to him ('redditibus cantori assignatis') by his abbot.[217] The important

---

[212] *Salimbene de Adam: Cronica*, ed. by Giuseppe Scalia, 2 vols. (Turnhout: Brepols, 1998–9), II, 938.
[213] Erlangen, Universitätsbibliothek, MS 136, fol. 1r; quoted after Steinmann, *Handschriften*, p. 509 (= no. 584).
[214] *De abbatibus Abbendonie*, ed. by Joseph Stevenson, in *Chronicon monasterii de Abingdon*, 2 vols. (London: Longman, 1858), II, 267–95 (= Appendix II) [hereafter *De abbatibus*]; *CBMLC*, IV, 4–7 (= B2). The sole surviving copy of the text (London, British Library, MS Cotton Vitellius A XIII, fols. 83r–87v) was produced during the thirteenth century. On the date of composition, cf. *Historia Ecclesie Abbendonensis-The History of the Church of Abingdon*, ed./tr. by John G. Hudson, 2 vols. (Oxford: Oxford University Press, 2002–7), I, lvi–lvii, arguing that the work was most likely begun under Ingulf (1130–59) and then continued at the command of Hugh (c.1190–1220).
[215] *De abbatibus*, ed. Stevenson, p. 289. Considering Faritius's instrumental role in Abingdon's material and spiritual enrichment as described at length in the *Historia ecclesie Abbendonensis* composed under the patronage of Abbot Walkelin (1158–64), it seems unlikely that the books listed in *De abbatibus* were the only ones he gave to the monks during the seventeen years of his abbacy; see *Historia*, ed./tr. Hudson, I, 332–9; also cf. Antonia Gransden, *Historical Writing in England*, 2 vols. (London: Routledge, 1974–82), I, 271–85. Indeed, it has been suggested that at least some of the books itemized in *De abbatibus* might have been the Faritius's personal books and were incorporated into the communal library upon his death; *CBMLC*, IV, 7.
[216] *Historia*, ed./tr. Hudson, II, 216–17.
[217] *De obedientiariis abbatiae Abbedonensis*, ed. by Joseph Stevenson, in *Chronicon monasterii de Abingdon*, 2 vols. (London: Longman, 1858), II, 296–334 (= Appendix III) [hereafter *De obedientiariis*]. The stipulations recorded in *De obedientiariis* may have been informed by existing practices and customs. Cf. Webber, 'Cantor', pp. 173–7, for a discussion of similar examples from other Anglo-Norman communities.

decision as to whether internal or external scribes are used lies not solely with the cantor, but also, and primarily, with the abbot ('dispositione abbatis et cantoris').[218]

The abbot's overarching authority is re-emphasized by the next stipulation in *De obedientiariis*, according to which the cantor should use the funds allocated to him to reimburse external scribes for their labour ('mercedem laboris') whilst the abbot uses his resources to provide for their physical well-being ('victum corporis') by supplying food and accommodation for them for as long as they remain inside his monastery.[219] This chimes well with the *Rule of St Benedict*'s insistence that guests should be served their meals not in the monks' refectory, but in the abbot's kitchen ('coquina abbatis et hospitum') and at his table ('mensa abbatis').[220] As the abbot's guests—paid guests, of course, but guests nonetheless—external scribes would dine in his company and enjoy food procured with his funds. It is no coincidence, therefore, that the tithes Faritius allocated for the purchase of parchment also provided salt for the abbot's table ('sal ad mensam abbatis'), thereby allowing for the sustenance of external scribes on a regular basis.[221] Faritius's reputation as a provider of books was so great that the abbey's cartulary-chronicle (London, British Library, MS Cotton Claudius C IX, fols. 105r–202r; also known as the *Liber terrarum*) features a miniature that shows him with two insignia: his abbatial staff and, taking centre-stage, a large book (Fig. 3.10).[222] The miniature's physical condition is deserving of comment. Faritius's face, his staff, and—most notably—the book are smudged almost beyond recognition. The specificity of this 'wear and tear' suggests that it was caused not by accidental damage, but by deliberate touching or rubbing, an intimate and performative engagement with manuscripts known primarily from devotional books.[223] It is typically the faces, hands/feet, and the objects associated most strongly with the venerated figures that tend to suffer the most from such physical interaction, suggesting that the cartulary-chronicle's readers mainly remembered and celebrated their former abbot for his book provision.

---

[218] *De obedientiariis*, ed. Stevenson, pp. 370–1.   [219] *De obedientiariis*, ed. Stevenson, p. 371.

[220] *RB*, ed./tr. Venarde, pp. 174–5 and 182–3; cf. Knowles, *Order*, pp. 404–6. A similar stipulation is found in *RM*, according to which all 'visiting outsiders' should be seated at the abbot's own table; *RM*, ed./tr. de Vogüé, II, 346–7; tr. Eberle, p. 250 ('extranei supervenientes').

[221] *De obedientiariis*, ed. Stevenson, p. 393. The long held-view that parchment was less a primary resource than a by-product of medieval monastic husbandry has recently been questioned by Bruce Holsinger, *On Parchment: Animals, Archives, and the Making of Culture from Herodotus to the Digital Age* (New Haven, CT: Yale University Press, 2022), pp. 21–2 and 288–306.

[222] On this cartulary-chronicle and its historical context, see John Hudson, 'The Abbey of Abingdon, its Chronicle and the Norman Conquest', *Anglo-Norman Studies* 19 (1997), 181–202. Faritius's portrait is the only figurative illustration found in the entire manuscript.

[223] Kathryn M. Rudy, 'Kissing Images, Unfurling Rolls, Measuring Wounds, Sewing Badges and Carrying Talismans: Considering Some Harley Manuscripts through the Physical Rituals they Reveal', *Electronic British Library Journal* 5 (2011), 1–56; Kathryn M. Rudy, 'Dirty Books: Quantifying Patterns of Use in Medieval Manuscripts Using a Densitometer', *Journal of Historians of Netherlandish Art* 2 (2010), 1–44.

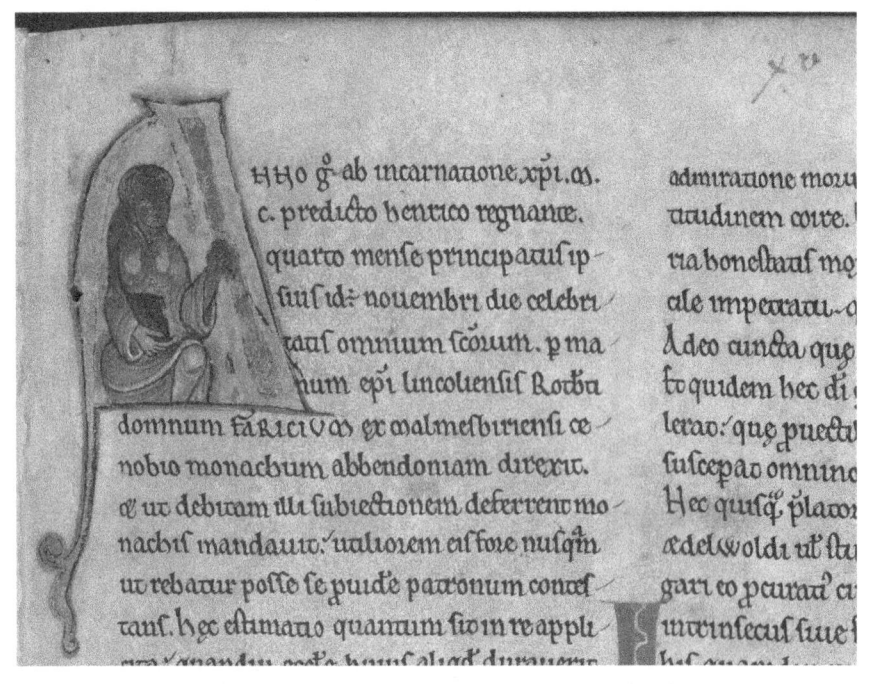

Fig. 3.10 Faritius of Abingdon holding a book. London, British Library, MS Cotton Claudius C IX, fol. 144r.

There is further evidence of abbots raising and allocating funds specifically in support of their book provision. A charter issued in 1146 by Macharius, abbot (1140–61/2) of Fleury, and confirmed by King Louis VII that survives, in abridged form, on the penultimate page of a compendium with writings by Cicero, Quintilian, and others (Paris, Bibliothèque nationale de France, MS Lat. 7696, fol. 157v) introduces a special tax to be levied annually at the feast of St Benedict ('in brumali *tempore* festivitate *beati patris* sancti Benedicti taxam conferre'), the proceeds of which should go to the monastery's cantor and/or *armarius* (likely a single person) and be spent wisely ('diligenter expendet/*expendere debet*') on the repair of the community's damaged books and the making of new ones.[224] Whilst the request for this new levy came from Hatto, Fleury's cantor-*armarius* ('rogatione etiam *cantoris vel armarii* Attonis'), it required Macharius to authorize it after inspecting the library and witnessing the books' sorry state first-hand ('videns bibliothece nostre codices vetustate nimia cariosos et tereredine [*sic!*] ac

---

[224] *Floriacensis vetus bibliotheca*, ed. by Jean Du Bois, 2 vols. (Paris: Cardon, 1605), I, 409–12; Ernst G. Vogel, 'Die Bibliothek der Benedictinerabtei Saint Benoit oder Fleury an der Loire', *Serapeum* 5 (1844), 17–29 and 46–8 (pp. 23–5); Delisle, *Cabinet*, II, 365–6; excerpts in *Catalogi*, ed. Becker, p. 198 (= no. 84); all contain grave errors of transcription, though, which is why the text here is cited directly from the manuscript, with Du Bois's additions (the manuscript source of which is unknown) rendered in italics. Also cf. Giacone, 'Masters', pp. 47–8.

tinea rodente corruptos'). To 'future-proof' this new taxation, the charter urges those charged with the duty to pass it down to their successors (*'[v]olumus etiam, ut eosdem annuos tales reddant eorum successores, quales in propria solvent, qui nunc possident'*). Macharius even lists the taxpayers and their respective dues so he and his successors can collect what is owed more easily in the future ('Quod si eguo [*sic!*] vel abbas qui mihi successerit aliquam obediencia vel internarum vel externarum in manu sua tenere voluerit'). The list names no fewer than forty individuals who together owe two hundred and thirteen *solidi*, to which Macharius adds another ten (or, in Du Bois's transcription, twenty) by committing himself and his successors to an annual payment ('[e]go igitur et qui mihi succedet abbas decem/*viginti* solidos annis singulis dabo').[225] To stop future abbots from reneging on this duty ('*ne aliquis successorum nostrorum hunc statutum infringere aut adnihilare praesumat*'), Macharius confirms it with his own seal and the seal of the chapter ('*sigilli nostri et sigilli capituli impressione roborare et confirmare decrevimus*'). He finishes by ruling that none of the dependent priors summoned to the mother house each year for the feast of St Benedict is allowed to leave until he surrenders what he owes to Fleury's cantor/*armarius* ('*ut nulli priorum ad praedictum festum venientem exeundi licentia concedatur, donec debitum cantori et armario persolvat*'). Even by the standards of wealthy monastery like Fleury with a large institutional library, two hundred and twenty-three solidi would have gone a long way to providing the monks with whatever books they needed on an annual basis,[226] at the same time as securing Macharius a prominent place in the community's collective memory and the commemoration of its abbots.[227]

Macharius of Fleury was not the only abbot to 'crowd-fund' his book provision. A similar arrangement is mentioned in a charter issued in 1145 by Udo, abbot (1130–50) of Chartres.[228] Confidently styling himself as the abbey's foremost book provider, Udo reports that prior to his abbacy the library had been impoverished

---

[225] Intriguingly, the annual amounts differ between the list preserved in MS BnF Lat. 7696, fol. 157v and that printed by Du Bois, with the latter adding up to two hundred and sixty-one *solidi* plus twenty by the abbot. This discrepancy of *c*.20 per cent might indicate that the levy was adjusted periodically in keeping with what was needed or to reflect changes in the local economy.

[226] On Fleury's library, see Marco Mostert, *The Library of Fleury: A Provisional List of Manuscripts* (Hilversum: Verloren, 1989); Marco Mostert, 'La bibliothèque de Fleury-sur-Loire', in *Religion et culture autour de l'an Mil: Royaume capétien et Lotharingie*, ed. by Dominique Iogna-Prat and Jean-Charles Picard (Paris: Picard, 1990), pp. 119–23.

[227] It has been suggested that Macharius's library tax had a precedent in a charter issued by his predecessor, Simon, on 11 July 1103, albeit without a reference to the document in question; *Inventaire des manuscrits de la Bibliothèque d'Orléans: Fonds de Fleury*, ed. by Charles Cuissard (Paris: Herluison, 1885), p. xvi. I have been unable to locate this charter.

[228] *Cartulaire de l'abbaye de Saint-Père de Chartres*, ed. by Benjamin Guérard, 2 vols. (Paris: Crapelet, 1840–50), II, 393–4 (= no. CLXXVIII); on Abbot Udo and his administration, see Robert F. Berkhofer III, *Day of Reckoning: Power and Accountability in Medieval France* (Philadelphia, PA: University of Pennsylvania Press, 2004), p. 149; Robert F. Berkhofer III, 'Abbatial Authority over Lay Agents', in *The Experience of Power in Medieval Europe: 950–1350*, ed. by Robert F. Berkhofer III et al. (Aldershot: Ashgate, 2005), pp. 43–57 (p. 54).

('ecclesie nostre armarium, usque ad meum tempus pauperrimum') and most of its books damaged to the point of being too fragile to use, with the librarian lacking the funds to repair or replace them ('paupertatis enim extreme que armarium deprimebat testes erant manifestissimi corrosi tineis et pene deleti vetustate libelli, sparsim per armarium huc illucque projecti, qui a fratre qui armario preerat, pre paupertate nimia, non poterant renovari nec etiam, quod minus est, religari').[229] To put an end to this, Udo introduces a new revenue for the library ('redditum determinatum armario assignavi'), to be held by its librarian annually ('redditum videlicet talem, qualem frater qui armarium tenuerit singulis annis habeat') and financed with payments collected from the monastery's other obedientiaries at All Saints ('redditum reddent ei annuatim, in festivitate omnium sanctorum, administratores obedientiarum nostrarum'). To ensure that none of them refuse their payment, Udo, like Macharius, inserts a debtors' list into his charter that begins with the abbot himself (contributing ten *solidi*) and the monastery's domestic officers (two *solidi* each) before moving on to the debtors at its various dependencies. The total amount owed is notably close to that collected at Fleury—indeed, if we follow Du Bois's count, it is identical. Udo's charter closes by threatening those foregoing their annual library payments with eternal damnation unless they do penance and pay what they owe ('sciat in tremendi iudicii die se esse dampnandum, nisi inobedientiam suam per penitentiam et congruam satisfactionem correxerit').[230] These taxes are an expression of the abbot's authority, and failure to surrender them constitutes disobedience towards God, the saints, the abbot, and his community ('Deo et sanctis eius et nobis omnibus iobediens erit').

Just over a decade later, Abbot Robert of Vendôme (1144–60) issued a privilege introducing a similar levy that survives in multiple copies.[231] Like Macharius's charter, Robert's was aimed specifically—and explicitly—at posterity. Mindful of the fickleness of human minds, Robert reminds Vendôme's cellarer and chamberlain that it was custom ('fuit consuetudo') for them to share the costs of binding the community's books, but because an argument had arisen between them as to how much each should contribute ('sed quia inter eos contentio oriebatur, quantum quisque prebere deberet'), none had been produced ('nec novi fiebant') in some time, much to Robert's disapproval, nor had the old ones been repaired ('nec [...] veteres corrigebantur'). To break this deadlock, Robert decrees with his abbatial authority ('auctoritate Dei et sua [...] precepit') that all dependencies (barring two) should pay an annual sum in support of library of the

---

[229] *Cartulaire*, ed. Guérard, II, 393.   [230] *Cartulaire*, ed. Guérard, II, 394.
[231] Edited as 'Decretum domni Roberti abbatis Vindocinensis pro bibliotheca' in *Cartulaire de l'abbaye cardinale de la Trinité de Vendôme*, ed. by Charles Métais, 5 vols. (Paris: Picard, 1893–7), II, 399–401 (= no. DXLIX).

mother house ('ut omnes priores obediencarium ad ius Vindocinensis ecclesie pertiencium, excepta cella Andegavensi et Credonensi, annuum censum armario prebeant').[232] As with Fleury and Chartres, the list of Vendôme's debtors runs into the high thirties, but this time the type of payment varies. Most pay their dues in money, with a sum total of one hundred and fifty *solidi*, whereas some pay theirs in kind by surrendering a dry measure of grain ('sextarium frumenti') and/or wheat ('sextarium siliginis'). This was not a unique arrangement. At some point between the mid-1160s and late 1170s, Pope Alexander III wrote to the abbot of Corbie—either John (1158-72) or Hugh (1172-85)—to praise his initiative in introducing a system whereby the production and repair of the community's books was financed through a levy of ten *solidi* from each major dependency and five from the smaller ones ('a singulis prepositis maioribus x et a minoribus v solidi custodi librorum annis singulis persolvantur'), to which were added, at the abbot's discretion, three measures of grain and oats from a tithe held by the canons of Clairfai ('tres quoque modios frumenti et avene, medie distinctos, ad mensuram Encrensem, quos a canonicis de Claro Faio recepistis annuatim') and the revenues from the lands of Branlères by one Walter de Malle ('et redditus terre de Branlers, quam ex dono Galteri de Malli habere noscimini'), both of which were to go to the keeper of books ('custodi librorum nichilominus deputastis').[233]

What is remarkable about these taxations from Fleury, Chartres, Vendôme, and Corbie—all centres of historiographical production—is that within a few decades, four abbots used their authority to raise major funds for their abbeys' libraries. These were not one-off cash injections, but sustainable, long-term investments. And whilst the immediate beneficiaries of these levies were the communities' cantor-*armarii*, they owed these benefits and the licence to use them entirely and exclusively to the lordship of their abbots. Though cantor-*armarii* figure regularly amongst the witnesses and producers of these abbatial charters,[234] it is always the abbot who decrees these provisions by virtue of his *auctoritas* and lordly *potestas*.

The death of a monastic superior and the search for an appointable successor could lead to disruptions and delays in a community's book provision. The *Gesta abbatum* of Saint-Wandrille report that when Ansegis, whom we met above (3.2), died rather unexpectedly in 823, the production of some luxury codices he had commissioned ground to a halt—presumably either because the ensuing interregnum meant that these considerable human and material resources could not be authorized until a new head of house was found, or because Ansegis's eventual

---

[232] *Cartulaire*, ed. Métais, II, 400.
[233] Edited in Delisle, *Cabinet*, II, 124. The papal confirmation survives in multiple copies (Paris, Bibliothèque nationale de France, MSS Lat. 17767, 17768, and 17770).
[234] For example, *Floriacensis bibliotheca*, ed. Du Bois, I, 411: '[S]ignatum [...] Hactonis [sic!] cantoris et armarii'; *Cartulaire*, ed. Métais, II, 401: 'Scriptum per manum Guillemi Sanctonensis tunc temporis armari'.

successors did not consider this a good use of the community's funds.²³⁵ By the same token, though, the appointment of a superior who was supportive of the monastery's library and willing to invest funds and manpower—and, if needed, even the labour of his/her own hands—to its sustenance and expansion could go some way towards compensating the absence, temporary unavailability, and even death of domestic scribes. A good example of this can be found in an illustrated twelfth-century codex from Scheyern produced for Abbot Conrad and known as the *Scheyerer Matutinalbuch* (Munich, Bayerische Staatsbibliothek, MS Clm. 17401). As we saw above (3.3), Conrad was one of the principal patrons of Scheyern's monastic library, and one of the *Matutinalbuch*'s miniatures shows him and his 'go-to copyist'—the other Conrad—opposite each other with verses stipulating that the abbot finished the volume himself.²³⁶ Whatever the reason behind the scribe's inability to complete the task, it was overcome by the initiative of an abbot ready to lend a hand himself. A similar miniature features in a manuscript from Liessies, which shows an abbot personally assisting in the making of a book by holding an ink pot for the scribe/author, St John the Evangelist.²³⁷

Monastic superiors lending a hand in the provision of books for their communities are crucial reminders of the expectation—articulated clearly in the *RB*—that abbatial leadership should manifest itself by both word and example ('verbo et exemplo'). That said, it should be clear by now that abbatial book provision, whilst governed by an unnegotiable sense of hierarchy and authority, relied fundamentally on collaboration and teamwork, to the extent that the abbot or abbess could become almost invisible in the process. A good example of this comes from Saint-Amand. Founded in the early seventh century, the abbey became a regional centre of book production during the Carolingian period, and though its fortunes took a turn for the worse subsequently, Saint-Amand's abbots maintained a library and a scriptorium that continued to operate into the central and later Middle Ages.²³⁸ An inventory from the first half of the twelfth century, most likely the second quarter, lists over three hundred volumes (Paris, Bibliothèque nationale de France, MS Lat. 1850, fols. 199v–202v).²³⁹ Written on either side and between the columns

---

²³⁵ *Chronique*, ed./tr. Pradié, p. 162: 'Quattuor evangelia in membrano purpureo ex auro scriberi iussit Romana littera, ex quibus Mathaei, Iohannis et Lucae complevit, sed interveniente morte eiusdem reliquum inperfectum remansit'.

²³⁶ MS Munich Clm. 17401, fol. 19r: 'Hunc vice scriptoris | ob spem coelestis amoris // Perfeci librum | Divinis laudibus aptum'; also cf. Boeckler, 'Scheyern-Frage', pp. 90–2.

²³⁷ See the photographic reproduction in *Ornamenta*, ed. Legner, I, 233–4 (= B31).

²³⁸ See Rosamond McKitterick, *History and Memory in the Carolingian World* (Cambridge: Cambridge University Press, 2004), pp. 140–1 and 155–7; André Boutémy, 'Le scriptorium et la bibliothèque de Saint-Amand d'après les manuscrits et les anciens catalogues', *Scriptorium* 1 (1946), 6–16; Françoise Simeray, 'Le scriptorium de l'abbaye de Saint-Amand au milieu du XIIe siècle', *Valentiana* 4 (1989), 6–10.

²³⁹ Delisle, *Cabinet*, II, 448–58 (= no. IX). Parts of this inventory appear to have been adopted from an earlier book list in the first volume of St Augustine's *Enarrationes in Psalmos* (Valenciennes,

are the names of the individuals responsible for their provision, provided they were known to the scribe ('quę scire potuimus').

Most individuals on the inventory held an office within the community, though a few appear to have been lay brothers or *conversi* who had entered the monastery as adults and donated the book(s) along with their other possessions.[240] Arranged here in order of the number of volumes provided, from the highest to the lowest, they are:

Name/title	MS BnF Lat. 1850, fol(s).	Role at Saint-Amand[241]	Vols.
Hucbaldus monachus	199v^b, 199v^c, 200r^a, 200r^b, 200r^c, 200v^a, 201r^b, 201r^c	School master (†930) (Cantor?)	19
Gualterus	199v^b, 199v^c, 200r^a, 200v^a	?	9
Magister Gillebertus	199v^a	School master (†1095)	6
Gillebertus[242]	200r^a, 200r^b, 200r^c, 200v^c	Monk (*c*.1153)	6
Hellinus noster prior, postea abbas s. Teoderici	199v^a, 200r^a, 200r^b, 201r^a	Prior (*c*.1133–5); abbot of Mont d'Hor (*c*.1135–45)	5
Floricus prior	199v^a, 200r^a	Prior (*saec*. XI^{ex}/XII^{in}?)	4
Fulco	201r^b	Monk (*c*.1113 × 53)	4
Fulquinus prior	200r^a, 201r^a, 201r^b	Prior (*c*.1123–?)	3
Gualterus noster prior, postea abbas s. Martini	199v^a, 200r^b	Prior (pre-1136); abbot of Tournai (1136–60)	3
Gunterus prior	199v^b, 200r^a	Prior (*c*.1107–?)	3
Amulricus prior	199v^a, 200r^b	Prior (*c*.1149–?)	3
Alardus	199v^a	Monk (*c*.1123)	3
Guntardus	199v^a, 199v^b	Monk (?)	2
Robertus sacerdos	199v^b, 201r^a	Priest (?)	2
Hugo primus abbas	199v^b	Abbot (1085–1107)	1
Bovo secundus abbas	200r^a	Abbot (1107–21)	1
Gualterus primus olim noster abbas	199v^b	Abbot (1121–3)	1
Lotharius	200r^b	Monk (†828)	1

As we can see from this table, the major providers of Saint-Amand's monastic library included three abbots and six priors, two of whom later became abbots themselves when Hellin was appointed at Saint-Thierry du Mont d'Hor and

---

Bibliothèque municipale/Médiathèque Simone Veil, MS 39 (*olim* 33), fol. 2r); what is more, ninety-four of the listed titles were recorded at a later point (fols. 201v–202v: 'Sequitur annotatio librorum qui libris superius annotatis additi sunt ad bibliothecam sancti Amandi'); Delisle, *Cabinet*, I, 308.

[240] For example, Lotharius (fol. 200r^b), Guntardus (fols. 199v^a and 199v^b), Fulco (fol. 201r^b), Alardus (fol. 199v^a), and Gillebertus (fols. 200r^a, 200r^b, 200r^c, and 200v^c); they may be identical with the witnesses in a series of monastic charters issued *c*.1123, *c*.1113 × 53, and *c*.1153; cf. Delisle, *Cabinet*, I, 308.

[241] On these identifications, cf. Delisle, *Cabinet*, I, 308–16.

[242] As pointed out by Delisle, *Cabinet*, I, 309, this 'Gillebertus' cannot be identical with the 'Magister Gillebertus' who gave six volumes but died in 1095.

Walter was placed in charge of Saint-Martin de Tournai.²⁴³ Two entries, both ranking amongst the top three, can be identified with individuals who held the offices of school master and, possibly, cantor. Except for Lotharius (†828) and Hucbald (†930), the abbey's well-known Carolingian hagiographer, poet, and musician,²⁴⁴ all datable entries belong to the first half of the twelfth century. The only eleventh-century entry is Master Gilbert (†1095), a monk of Saint-Amand and sometime canon of Saint-André du Câteau ('noster monachus, prius sancti Andreę canonicus') known for his Bible commentaries and glosses.²⁴⁵ At a glance, it would thus seem that at Saint-Amand the heads of house were less prolific book providers than the priors and other monastic officeholders, with Abbots Hugh I (1085–1107), Bovo II 'the Younger' (1107–21), and Walter I (1121–3) all ranking near the bottom of the table with a single book to their name.²⁴⁶

This impression is misleading, however. Upon closer examination, Gualterus, *proxime accessit* with nine volumes, six of which survive, reveals himself as none other than Abbot Walter I ('Gualterus primus olim noster abbas'). Léopold Delisle in 1886 identified this Walter with the compiler of Saint-Amand's earliest cartulary (written *c*.1117) before Henri Platelle made the connection between this cartulary scribe and the monk who would succeed Bovo II as abbot in 1121.²⁴⁷ Walter continued working on the cartulary throughout his abbacy, bringing it to a (preliminary) point of conclusion in 1123, the year of his death.²⁴⁸ This identification of the cartularist with Abbot Walter I has since been reinforced further, but so far there has been no attempt—to my knowledge—to 'join the dots' by combining these conclusions with Delisle's arguments about the identity of the

---

²⁴³ It has been suggested that Floricus (fols. 199vᵃ and 200rᵃ) might have left Saint-Amand to become abbot, too, and that in this capacity he later added his name to the *rouleau funéraire* for Abbot Hugh I of Saint-Amand (1085–1107); André Boutémy, 'Les enluminures de l'abbaye de Saint-Amand', *Revue Belge d'archéologie et d'histoire de l'art* 12 (1942), 135–41 (pp. 137–8).

²⁴⁴ Rosamond McKitterick has shown that most of Hucbald's personal books, which formed a separate collection from the communal library until his death—were not produced in house, but acquired from elsewhere; Rosamond McKitterick, 'Carolingian Book Production: Some Problems', *The Library* 12 (1990), 1–33 (p. 29).

²⁴⁵ Christopher de Hamel, *Glossed Books of the Bible and the Origins of the Paris Book Trade* (Woodbridge: D. S. Brewer, 1984), pp. 1–13; repr. as 'The Circulation of Glossed Books of the Bible', in *The History of the Book in the West: A Library of Critical Essays*, ed. by Jane Roberts et al., 5 vols. (Farnham: Ashgate, 2010), I, 93–121 (pp. 95–9 and 106 n. 16–17); occasional confusion amongst modern scholars notwithstanding, this Master Gilbert is not identical with Gilbert of Poitiers (†1154).

²⁴⁶ The books they provided are Valenciennes, Bibliothèque municipale/Médiathèque Simone Veil, MSS 498 and 546 (*olim* 458 and 500) (Walter; Hugh); Paris, Bibliothèque nationale de France, MS Lat. 1918 (Bovo).

²⁴⁷ See Delisle, *Cabinet*, I, 309–10; Henri Platelle, 'Le premier cartulaire de l'abbaye de Saint-Amand', *Le Moyen Âge* 62 (1956), 301–29 (pp. 307–8 and 312).

²⁴⁸ By that point, the cartulary comprised just shy of fifty documents, all of which Walter had copied from originals kept in the monastery's archives. Some of them record the restoration of monastic property alienated by Walter's predecessors, Bovo I and Bovo II; see Platelle, 'Cartulaire', p. 325 (= no. 46). No further acts were added to the cartulary until halfway through the abbacy of Absalon (1123–45).

enigmatic 'Gualterus' recorded in the inventory.[249] The codicological evidence permits us to cement this identification beyond reasonable doubt and establish a *terminus ante quem* for at least one of Walter I's volumes: amongst the inventory's extant items is a composite codex in an early twelfth-century binding hosting two works by St Augustine (Paris, Bibliothèque nationale de France, MS Lat. 2012).[250] Inside this binding is an episcopal charter issued in 1107 by Baldric of Noyon/Tournai that was re-used by the twelfth-century binder to create the volume's flyleaves (fols. ii/135).[251] Together with his archdeacon, Lambert, Bishop Baldric concedes a dozen churches to Saint-Amand's abbot, a grant that must have been of great value and strategic importance in the context of the community's well-documented campaign for monastic exemption in the later eleventh and early twelfth centuries, which begs the question as to when and why the charter was discarded and recycled.[252]

Marked by extensive corrections and revisions, often written over substantial erasures, the episcopal charter re-used by the bookbinder is not in fact the ratified or 'official' version of the act, but a preliminary version drawn-up by the recipient that, for reasons unknown, was never authenticated.[253] The ratified version survives independently in the twelfth-century cartulary, as well as in the thirteenth-century continuation known as the *Liber privilegiorum*.[254] As Laurent Morelle has shown, the recycling of charters (and their drafts) at Saint-Amand was a strictly regulated process that involved *ad hoc* appraisals of the monastery's archives by authorized personnel to determine the 'lifespan' of its holdings.[255] In the context of our charter, the most plausible occasion for such an appraisal resulting in the disposal of the draft version was the making of Walter's cartulary. As the work's compiler, Walter—who in the process had been appointed abbot— certainly had the authority to approve the draft's removal from the monastic

---

[249] Laurent Morelle, 'The Metamorphosis of Three Monastic Charter Collections in the Eleventh Century (Saint-Amand, Saint-Riquier, Montier-en-Der)', in *Charters and the Use of the Written Word in Medieval Society*, ed. by Karl Heidecker (Turnhout: Brepols, 2000), pp. 171–204 (p. 176 n. 17).

[250] MS BnF Lat. 1850, fol. 200r^a: 'Augustinus super Iohannem in duobus voluminibus; in secundo habetur liber ipsius de sermone Domini in monte'; Delisle, *Cabinet*, I, 310; ibid., II, 451. In the inventory, the two works share a large coloured initial, a visual marker used with notable consistency by the scribe to demarcate physical volumes, which strongly suggests that they had already been combined into a single volume at that point.

[251] On this charter, cf. Suzanne Solente, 'Une charte-partie de 1107 dans un manuscrit de Saint-Amand', *Bibliothèque de l'école des chartes* 94 (1933), 213–17.

[252] These efforts are studied by Henri Platelle, *Le temporel de l'abbaye de Saint-Amand des origines à 1340* (Paris: Librairie d'Argences, 1962); Henri Platelle, 'L'évolution du temporel de l'abbaye de Saint-Amand des origines à 1340', *Revue du Nord* 177 (1963), 108–10; more recently Vanderputten, *Reform*, pp. 180–4.

[253] Most of these corrections and erasures concern the charter's second half; cf. the edition by Solente, 'Charte-partie', pp. 215–16.

[254] Lille, Archives départementales du Nord, 12 H 1, no. 38; edited in Platelle, 'Cartulaire', pp. 323–4 (= no. 31). Further copies are Paris, Bibliothèque nationale de France, MSS Moreau 42, fols. 225r-v and Nouv. acq. lat. 1219, pp. 64–5; cf. Morelle, 'Metamorphosis', p. 184 n. 46.

[255] Morelle, 'Metamorphosis', pp. 183–6; Bertrand, *Documenting*, pp. 81–107.

archives, and it is probably no coincidence that it should resurface soon afterwards inside the binding of another book provided by Walter and credited to him alongside eight others in the library inventory. With a total of ten books to his name—including two works of history in the shape of the *Historiae Alexandri Magni* and Cassiodorus's *Historia tripartita*—the abbot was amongst the community's foremost book providers.[256] Achieved within just three years, his contribution to the monks' library was second only to that of Hucbald two centuries earlier.

Unlike the cartulary, an abbatial 'pet project' that Walter seems to have completed largely by himself, the provision of the books attributed to him by the library inventory was very much a team effort. For the codex bound in the discarded charter, he joined forces with his second-in-command, Prior Gunther, who is given shared credit for the book's provision by the inventory's annotator.[257] Another product of such joint provision was the monastery's four-volume set of Boethius's *De consolatione philosophiae*, one volume of which was provided by Abbot Hellin ('abbas Hellinus unum'), and another by Prior Fulcuin ('prior Fulquinus unum').[258] Hellin was abbot of Saint-Thierry du Mont d'Hor (1135–45) at the time, but had given at least two books during his previous tenure as Saint-Amand's prior (c.1133–5). Following his departure, he continued for some years to support his former home with books; in fact, the frequency of his bequests seems to have increased post-1135, as the inventory credits another three books to 'Hellinus abbas sancti Theoderici'.[259] This increase suggests that as abbot, Hellin had both the *auctoritas* and the resources to provide his old community with books in ways which had been unavailable to him as prior, when he had had to report to, and receive his funds from, Abbot Absalon. Unlike Walter and Gunther's joint venture, Hellin and Fulcuin cannot have made their respective

---

[256] The *Historiae Alexandri Magni* has been lost, but the *Historia tripartita* survives in Valenciennes, Bibliothèque municipale/Médiathèque Simone Veil, MS 498 (*olim* 458); Walter's other extant books include Valenciennes, Bibliothèque municipale/Médiathèque Simone Veil, MSS 60, 65, 66, and 156 (*olim* 53, 58, 59, and 148); Paris, Bibliothèque nationale de France, MS Lat. 1847.

[257] We do not know precisely when and how long Gunther was prior of Saint-Amand, as his presence in this capacity is attested only in 1107. The next prior mentioned in the inventory, Fulcuin, is not attested until 1123, the first year of Absalon's abbacy, which may suggest that Gunther had assumed the office under Bovo II and continued to serve until the end of Walter's abbacy; Delisle, *Cabinet*, I, 310–12; Henri Platelle, *La justice seigneuriale de l'abbaye de Saint Amand: son organisation judiciaire, sa procédure et sa compétence du XIe au XVIe siècle* (Louvain: Publications universitaires de Louvain, 1965), pp. 109–10.

[258] MS BnF Lat. 1850, fol. 201r^a. Hellin's name is written over an erasure, but the scraped-out letters cannot be reconstructed sufficiently. Similarly, it remains unknown whether the set's sole surviving volume (Valenciennes, Bibliothèque municipale/Médiathèque Simone Veil, MS 298 (*olim* 288)) is Fulcuin's book or the one given by Hellin; the providers of the other two volumes are not identified on the inventory; Delisle, *Cabinet*, II, 453 n. 3.

[259] Besides the Boethius volume (see above), these books contain extracts from St Gregory's explanations on the minor and major prophets and selected commentaries on the Song of Songs by Gregory and Ambrose, respectively (Valenciennes, Bibliothèque municipale/Médiathèque Simone Veil, MS 50 (*olim* 43)).

contributions to the multi-volume set of Boethius at the same time, considering that Fulcuin's priorate ended before Hellin began his abbacy at Saint-Thierry; in fact, it was Hellin who succeeded Fulcuin as Saint-Amand's prior c.1133. This means that the set took between a minimum of three and a maximum of twenty-two years to be completed.[260] Even more time was taken over the completion of Saint-Amand's two-volume set of Martianus Capella's *De nuptiis Philologiae et Mercurii*, one part of which the community received from Hucbald ('Hucbaldus unum') during the early tenth century, and the other from Fulcuin ('Prior Fulquinus alterum'), about two centuries later.[261]

At Saint-Amand and elsewhere, abbatial book provision was a collaborative enterprise that involved multiple individuals working simultaneously and/or over periods of time. This did not make it a democratic exercise, however, as even the most well-staffed and resourced workshop ultimately depended on the authority and leadership of the monastic superior. The fact that the superior's involvement is not always made explicit in the sources and can be concealed—accidentally or on purpose—by the role of others upon whom scholarship has lavished greater attention must not lead us to conclude that the abbot or abbess was absent from the process. Sometimes, such as in Walter's case, it can thus take a second or third look at the evidence to reveal the true extent of their influence.

3.5 'Interlibrary Loans'

As a final aspect of abbatial book provision, we turn to yet another way in which medieval monastic superiors used their authority and resources to source books for their communities' libraries, the historians they patronized, and—as discussed more fully below (4.3)—even themselves. With an ability to draw on extensive personal and institutional connections, abbots and abbesses had privileged and sometimes exclusive access to book exchange networks that connected their monasteries with private and institutional libraries. We already saw evidence of this earlier in this book, such as when Albinus of Canterbury exercised his abbatial authority to provide his protégé, Bede, with copies of rare books and documents from as far afield as Rome, which were copied *in situ* and delivered to Wearmouth-Jarrow by Albinus's scribe, Nothelm (1.2); or when Gerbert of Bobbio approached his peer Eberhard at Tours with a 'wish list' of books he desired to have copied from the latter's institutional library, quickly reassuring Eberhard that

---

[260] The *terminus post quem* for Fulcuin's contribution is 1123, when he is first attested as Saint-Amand's prior, and the *terminus ante quem* c.1133, when he handed over the office to Hellin. Hellin's volume, meanwhile, could date from any point during his abbacy at Saint-Thierry.

[261] Neither volume is known to survive; Delisle, *Cabinet*, I, 309; ibid., II, 454 (= no. 179).

he would furnish the necessary writing materials and scribal wages upfront, presumably from his monastery's coffers (2.3); and, of course, when Laurence, the Benedictine abbot of Westminster, commissioned his northern Cistercian counterpart at Rievaulx, Ælred, to compose a new *Life* of Edward the Confessor and even gave him something of a head start by sending copies of two existing Edward-*Vitae* from exemplars in Westminster's abbey library (2.4). We may also wish to recall Æthelweard's letter to Matilda, abbess of Essen and the commissioning authority behind his *Chronicon*, in which Æthelweard addresses his kinswoman as an abundant fount of historical knowledge thanks to her dynastic pedigree and abbatial *potestas*, clearly implying that she had provided him with oral and, conceivably, written sources of information to support the project (2.4); indeed, the integral role of women—especially those with royal or aristocratic connections—as consumers, owners, and distributors of books across medieval and early modern Europe has been established beyond question, and the same was true of women in positions of monastic leadership.[262]

In the early eighth century, Abbess Eadburga of Minster-in-Thanet/Wimbourne received a letter from Boniface thanking her for the gifts of sacred books ('sanctorum librorum munera') that she had sent across the Channel at Boniface's request to support him on his missionary work in Francia.[263] We do not know whether these books were permanent gifts or long-term loans, but in a follow-up letter Boniface implores Eadburga to show him even greater kindness than before by sending a lavish copy of the Epistles of St Peter written in gold ('cum auro conscribas') that he wishes to have in his possession at all times ('maxime semper in presentia cupiam habere').[264] Mindful of the considerable effort and expense involved in such an extravagant commission, Boniface reassures Eadburga that he will send whatever is needed—not least the gold—via his trusted envoy, Eoban ('ad scribendum hoc, quod rogo, per Eoban presbiterum destino').[265] Eadburga was not the only abbess targeted by requests to send books from England to the Continent and *vice versa*. According to the *Vita Bertilae abbatissae Calensis*, Bertila, founding abbess (*c.*658/60–705) of Chelles, was known so widely for her generosity ('munificentia larga') that even 'pious kings from the parts of Saxony across the sea' ('reges fideles ab transmarinis

---

[262] See Tyler, *England*; Sarah W. Watson and S. C. Kaplan, 'Books of Duchesses: Mapping Women Book Owners in Late Medieval Francophone Europe, 1350–1550: Initial Findings', *Journal of the Early Book Society* 23 (2020), 27–60; Brigitte Büttner, 'Women and the Circulation of Books', *Journal of the Early Book Society* 4 (2001), 9–31; Patricia D. Stirnemann, 'Women and Books in France: 1170–1220', in *Representations of the Feminine in the Middle Ages*, ed. by Bonnie Wheeler (Dallas: Academia, 1993), pp. 247–52.

[263] *Die Briefe des heiligen Bonifatius und Lullus*, ed. by Michael Tangl [= *MGH Epp. sel.* I] (Berlin: Weidmann, 1916), p. 54 (= no. 30).

[264] *Briefe*, ed. Tangl, p. 60 (= no. 35).

[265] *Briefe*, ed. Tangl, p. 60, who also identifies the gold as amongst the items Boniface promises to provide to Eadburga to fulfil his request.

partibus Saxoniae') would ask for her books.[266] Bertila did not deny their requests ('petitionem [...] non denegavit'), but sent many volumes to England ('voluminibus multis librorum') using only the most illustrious emissaries ('electas personas et devotissimos homines illuc direxit').[267] Further evidence of book travel from England to the European mainland occurs in the *Vita* of St Getrude, the cofoundress and first abbess (*c*.647/50–59) of Nivelles. Like her contemporary Bertila, Getrude presided over a large book collection assembled from libraries in Rome and 'beyond the sea' ('sancta volumina de urbe Roma et de transmarinis regionibus gignaros'), the latter of which most likely refers to the English Channel.[268] And though we do not know from which particular repositories Getrude sourced these books, it is not implausible that she availed herself of the institutional libraries of her English abbatial peers.

It was not just female monastic superiors who provided and made available books from their collections across geographical as well as territorial boundaries, but also their male counterparts. When around the middle of the ninth century abbot-historian Lupus of Ferrières (*c*.840–62) decided to expand his library of classical and patristic works by 'search[ing] the empire for the manuscripts he needed', he knew that the best places to look were the libraries curated by his abbatial peers, especially those across the sea in England.[269] In a letter to Altsig, abbot of York(?), Lupus enquires about works by Jerome, Bede, and Quintilian, which he urges his correspondent ('obnixe flagito') to send to Ferrières's reinstated dependency of St Jodocus ('ad cellam sancti Iudoci, quae tandem aliquando nobis reddita est') by envoys ('per certissimos nuntios mihi [...] dirigatis') so they can be handed over to their mutual acquaintance, Lantram ('tradendos Lantramno, qui bene vobis notus est'), copied, and returned promptly ('ibique exscribendos vobisque quam potuerit fieri celeries remittendos').[270] So urgent was Lupus's

---

[266] 'Vita Bertilae abbatissae Calensis', ed. by Wilhelm Levison, in *Passiones vitaeque sanctorum aevi Merovingici (IV)*, ed. by Bruno Krusch and Wilhelm Levison [*MGH SS rer. Merov.* VI] (Hanover: Hahn, 1913), pp. 95–109 (p. 106).

[267] 'Vita', ed. Levison, pp. 106–7; the *Vita*'s anonymous author adds that he/she had no doubt about the veracity of these reports ('Quod ita adimpletum esse a Dei laudem ac domnae Bertilae confidimus'; ibid.); McKitterick, 'Scriptoria', pp. 1 and 29; Nicole Suhl, 'Die "Vita Bertilae Abbatissae Calensis"–eine Quelle für mögliche Unterschiede in der Religiosität von "Volk" und "Ehre" im frühen Mittelalter?', *Medium Aevum Quotidianum* 36 (1997), 39–58 (pp. 43–9).

[268] 'Vita S. Geretrudis', in *Fredegarii et aliorum Chronica. Vitae sanctorum*, ed. by Bruno Krusch [= *MGH SS rer. Merov.* II] (Hanover: Hahn, 1888), pp. 447–74 (p. 457); McKitterick, 'Scriptoria', p. 1 n. 3 likewise identifies these 'volumina de transmarinis regionibus' with books from England; on Getrude and her *Vita*, see Paul Fouracre and Richard A. Gerberding, *Late Merovingian France: History and Hagiography 640–720* (Manchester: Manchester University Press, 1996), pp. 301–29; *Sainted Women*, ed./tr. McNamara et al., pp. 220–34.

[269] Quote from Brian P. McGuire, *Friendship and Community: The Monastic Experience, 350–1250*, new ed. (Ithaca, NY: Cornell University Press, 2010), p. 131; also cf. Michael Gorman, 'Bede's *VIII Quaestiones* and Carolingian Biblical Scholarship', *Revue bénédictine* 109 (1999), 32–74 (p. 32); Philippe Depreux, 'Büchersuche und Büchertausch im Zeitalter der karolingischen Renaissance am Beispiel des Briefwechsels des Lupus von Ferrières', *Archiv für Kulturgeschichte* 76 (1994), 267–84.

[270] *Servati Lupi epistolae*, ed. by Peter K. Marshall (Leipzig: Teubner, 1984), p. 68 (= no. 62); translated in *The Letters of Lupus of Ferrières*, tr. by Graydon W. Regenos (The Hague: Nijhof,

request that in his letter he begs Altsig to send whichever of the desired books he can currently spare, even if he cannot provide them all right away ('[q]uod si omnes non potueritis, at aliquos ne gravemini destinare'). In return, Altsig is promised the eternal reward of God's charity ('recepturi a Deo praemium impletae caritatis') and whatever compensation he may wish from Lupus ('a nobis autem quamcumque possibilem dumtaxat iusseritis vicem tanti laboris').[271] Some twenty years earlier, not long before he became abbot of Ferrières, Lupus had 'tapped up' Einhard, abbot of Seligenstadt, with a similar request.[272] In 847, he told Marcward, abbot of Prüm (829–53), that Einhard's successor, Ratlegius, had agreed to have parts of a book copied for Lupus ('partem quondam cuiusdam libri faciet mihi describi'), which upon completion he would send to him via one of Marcward's couriers ('eamque vestro mihi reddendam nuntio se traditurum promittit').[273] Just a few years earlier, Lupus had asked Marcward to dispatch one of Prüm's monks to Fulda ('queso praeterea ut ad sanctum Bonifatium sollertem aliquem monachum dirigatis') to borrow, with the abbot's permission, a two-volume exemplar of Suetonius's *Lives of the Caesars* ('ex vestra parte Hattonem abbatem deposcat, ut vobis Sueton(ium) Tr(anquillum) *De vita Caesarum* [...] ad exscribendum dirigat'), which he expected to receive from Marcward himself or via a trusted messenger ('mihique eum aut ipsi [...] afferatis aut [...] per certissimum nuntium mittendum curetis').[274]

Sent from one abbot to another, Lupus's letters to Altsig and Marcward give first-hand insights into abbatial book borrowing networks. They demonstrate the efficiency of such reciprocal arrangements if money and resources were not an issue and reliable couriers available to assist with the logistics, provide safe carriage for the books, and deliver the agreed payments and deposits. At the same time, they highlight the basic conditions that had to be met for these arrangements to work. These included, on the part of the lending institution, the expendability of the requested book(s) and the principal agreement of the superior, as well as, on the part of the borrower, the capacity and commitment to process and copy these books promptly to ensure a timely return. If these factors were brought into alignment, abbatial book networks could extend across significant distances, connecting monasteries and their domestic historians across

---

1966), pp. 105–6 (= no. 87). A new critical edition of Lupus's letters to replace Marshall's is being prepared by Michael Allen for Corpus Christianorum, Continuatio Mediaevalis. The reinstatement of St Jodocus as a dependent cell of Ferrières occurred in the early to mid-840s following the receipt of a ducal confirmation charter; see Adelheid Krah, *Die Entstehung der 'potestas regia' im Westfrankenreich während der ersten Regierungsjahre Kaiser Karls II. (840–77)* (Berlin: Akademie Verlag, 2001), pp. 234–5.

[271] *Epistolae*, ed. Marshall, p. 68.
[272] *Epistolae*, ed. Marshall, pp. 1–3 (= no. 1); tr. Regenos, pp. 1–4 (= no. 1).
[273] *Epistolae*, ed. Marshall, pp. 66–7 (= no. 60); tr. Regenos, pp. 78–9 (= no. 65). For further examples of Lupus's book borrowing, see Andrea Reed-Leal, 'Book-Borrowing in the Early Middle Ages: A Case Study of Servatus Lupus (c.805–862)', *Library and Information History* 36 (2020), 194–209.
[274] *Epistolae*, ed. Marshall, pp. 88–90 (= no. 91); tr. Regenos, pp. 51–2 (= no. 35).

Europe (and sometimes beyond) and fuelling a 'medieval knowledge economy' rooted deeply in the production, collection, and exchange of history books between religious communities.[275]

Lupus was not the only abbot to avail himself regularly of other monastic book collections to compile the sources for his personal writing projects or to facilitate historical study and composition amongst the members of his community. In the final quarter of the tenth century, Abbot Gozbert (983–1001) of Tegernsee sent a letter to Ramwold, the bibliophile abbot of St Emmeram whom we met above (3.3), in which he announces the return of a book (presumably enclosed) that Ramwold had lent him for copying because it did not exist in Tegernsee's library ('quia in nostra non habetur bibliotheca').[276] Gozbert recalls that the book's prompt return had been stipulated by its owner as a condition for the loan ('ut nobis praestari praecipiatis'), and having made good on his promise, he felt entitled to request another volume from St Emmeram's abbot. In a follow-up letter, he asks to borrow the *Historia tripartita*, presumably that by Cassiodorus. As Gozbert explains, copies of two parts of the *Historia* were available to him at Tegernsee ('*Tripertitae Historiae* duas partes conscriptas habemus'), but the third part was missing ('tertia pars ideo deest') and had proven impossible to source elsewhere ('quia exemplar alias adquirere non possumus'). Having exhausted all other avenues, Gozbert's last chance to complete the set lay with the exemplar kept at St Emmeram, provided its abbot would kindly agree to lend it to him ('nisi ob gratiam vestri nobis mittere dignemini') in recognition of his track record of returning borrowed volumes in good time.[277] As we will see below, giving—and, on the lender's part, actively seeking—such reassurances before agreeing a book loan was not uncommon, and much hinged on the reliability and authority of the parties involved.

Unless they cultivated a reputation for being untrustworthy or notoriously unpunctual with their returns, abbots stood a better chance than most to succeed in their book borrowing efforts, with some lending volumes from multiple libraries at a time. A recent study of the Norman abbey of Fécamp under the

---

[275] See Jan L. van Zanden and Eltjo Buringh, 'Book Production as a Mirror of the Emerging Medieval Knowledge Economy, 500–1500', in Jan L. van Zanden, *The Long Road to the Industrial Revolution: The European Economy in a Global Perspective, 1000–1800* (Leiden: Brill, 2009), pp. 69–91; Teresa M. Miguel, 'Exchanging Books in Western Europe: A Brief History of International Interlibrary Loan', *International Journal of Legal Information* 35 (2007), 499–513; Sharpe, *Libraries*, p. 2.

[276] Munich, Bayerische Staatsbibliothek, MS Clm. 19412, fols. 15v–16r; printed in *Codex diplomatico-historico-epistolaris*, ed. by Bernhard Pez and Philibert Hueber, 3 vols. (Augsburg: Fratrum Veithiorum, 1729), I, 121 (= no. 1). The borrowed volume is described as 'liber plenariae collationis', that is, a plenarium.

[277] MS Munich Clm. 19412, fols. 36v–37r; printed in *Codex*, ed. Pez and Hueber, I, 127 (= no. 13). Gozbert's eleventh- and twelfth-century successors also engaged frequently in the exchange of books, including his direct successor, Abbot Godehard (1001–2), who in 1101 wrote a letter (MS Munich Clm. 19412, fol. 41r), requesting two books from the monastic library of Oberaltaich, and especially Abbot Conrad I (1126–55), whose activity as a regular book lender/borrower is evidenced in multiple letters (Munich, Bayerische Staatsbibliothek, MS Clm. 19411, fols. 106r-v, 109r-v, and 121r-v).

leadership of Abbot John (1028–78) suggests that when John composed his *Confessio theologica* and various other works, he made first-hand use of several external book collections in addition to Fécamp's substantial domestic library, most notably perhaps the great monastic library of Ravenna, where John had completed his novitiate before traversing the Alps and coming to Normandy via Saint-Bénigne de Dijon in the company of William of Volpiano.[278] John's relationship with Ravenna and its library was one he cultivated throughout his abbacy, liaising with several of Ravenna's superiors to maintain access to their books.[279] Whilst the true extent of John's use of books sourced from Ravenna and elsewhere remains to be established,[280] the efficacy of this *modus operandi* is made evident by comparable cases from Normandy and beyond. A century later, Robert of Torigni used his influence as the newly appointed abbot of Mont-Saint-Michel to source books for his *Chronica*.[281] The flyleaves of his authorial working copy (MS Avranches 159, fols. 1v–3r) show that Robert went further than many by compiling—or ordering a pair of scribes to compile for him—two lists of books kept at Le Bec about 180 km as the crow flies from Mont-Saint-Michel, where Robert had been monk and prior (c.1149–54) before his abbatial election.[282] The *Chronica*'s most recent editor believes these lists to have originated at Le Bec and considers it 'all but certain' that Robert made them whilst he was prior there,[283] but the codicological and palaeographical evidence strongly suggests that they were produced during Robert's abbacy at Mont-Saint-Michel, possibly as late as the 1160s–80s, when he was putting the finishing touches to his *Chronica* and needed quick and easy access to his former monastery's famously well-stocked library, not entirely unlike modern historians using interlibrary loans to double-check the footnotes of their books ahead of publication.[284]

---

[278] Lauren Mancia, *Emotional Monasticism: Affective Piety in the Eleventh-Century Monastery of John of Fécamp* (Manchester: Manchester University Press, 2018), pp. 51–65; also cf. Benjamin Pohl and Steven Vanderputten, 'Fécamp, Cluny, and the Invention of Tradition in the Later Eleventh Century', *Journal of Medieval Monastic Studies* 5 (2016), 1–41. Ravenna was home to multiple monastic and institutional libraries from the early Middle Ages onwards, making it a popular destination amongst writers well before John's age; Judith Herrin, *Ravenna: Capital of Empire, Crucible of Europe* (New Haven, CT: Yale University Press, 2020), pp. 280–4.

[279] Mancia, *Monasticism*, p. 55.

[280] There is, as of yet, no detailed study of the manuscript evidence; cf. Benjamin Pohl, 'Review of Lauren Mancia, *Emotional Monasticism: Affective Piety in the Eleventh-Century Monastery of John of Fécamp*', *Early Medieval Europe* 30 (2022), 1–3; on Fécamp's monastic library, see *La bibliothèque et les archives de l'abbaye de la Sainte-Trinité de Fécamp: Splendeur et dispersion des manuscrits et des chartes d'une prestigieuse abbaye bénédictine normande*, Vol. 1: *La bibliothèque et les archives au Moyen Âge*, ed. by Stéphane Lecouteux et al. (Fécamp: Amis du Vieux Fécamp et du Pays de Caux, 2021).

[281] *RT*, ed./tr. Bisson, I, 2–393.

[282] On Robert's career, see *RT*, ed./tr. Bisson, I, xxvi–xlvii; Pohl, 'Robert and Le Bec'.

[283] *RT*, ed./tr. Bisson, I, xxvii and lxxxiv.

[284] Pohl, '*Abbas*', p. 51; Patricia D. Stirnemann, 'Les bibliothèques princières et privées aux XIIe et XIIIe siècles', in *Histoire des Bibliothèques françaises*, Vol. 1: *Les bibliothèques médiévales, du VIe siècle à 1530*, ed. by André Vernet (Paris: Éditions du Cercle de la Librairie, 1989), pp. 173–91 (pp. 174–6); Richard H. Rouse and Mary A. Rouse, '"Potens in opere et sermone": Philip, Bishop of Bayeux, and His

The first of the two lists contains the titles of one hundred and fourteen volumes donated to Le Bec's monks by Philip de Harcourt, bishop of Bayeux (1142–63), upon his death,[285] a major gift that is recorded also in the *Chronica*, where the number of books is given as one hundred and forty;[286] note, moreover, that when the list was made twenty-seven books were still *en route* ('Summa voluminum cxiii [*sic!*], exceptis xxvii voluminibus quos dedit episcopus, sed nondum habuerunt').[287] The second list contains one hundred and sixty-five titles from Le Bec's monastic library ('Beccensis almarii'), including a copy of Peter Lombard's *Libri quattuor sententiarum*, which gives a *terminus post quem* of 1158.[288] Laura Cleaver draws attention to the fact that the level of information exhibited by these lists is 'unusually detailed' in that they provide the complete contents of each physical volume, rather than simply the first work copied in it.[289] The two lists together record about three times as many work titles ('tituli') than they do physical volumes, which, as Cleaver observes, implies that they were 'not the result of a campaign to organise the library [of Le Bec]',[290] but a bespoke commission by an individual with an interest that justified, and indeed demanded, detailed enumeration of the *all* the texts found in these volumes. Rather than a finding aid for locating and organizing the physical volumes on their shelves, they are more likely to have been intended as handlists for requesting specific loans or copies of the books kept at Le Bec by someone who was not, or no longer, a member of the monastic community. The most plausible context for their production—and perhaps the only compelling explanation as to why both lists should be bound into Robert's personal copy of his *magnum opus*—is that Le Bec's erstwhile prior and abbot-historian of Mont-Saint-Michel commissioned them as a handy overview of the titles he could access quickly and conveniently despite his change of institutional affiliation by combining old connections with his new abbatial authority.[291] The 'richesse exceptionnelle' of Le Bec's library with more than three hundred volumes containing a staggering seven to eight hundred

---

Books', in *Authentic Witnesses: Approaches to Medieval Texts and Manuscripts*, ed. by Richard H. Rouse and Mary A. Rouse (Notre Dame, IN: University of Notre Dame Press, 1991), pp. 323–59 (p. 323); Cleaver, 'Library', pp. 173–6.

[285] Edited in Cleaver, 'Library', pp. 190–205.

[286] *RT*, ed./tr. Bisson, I, 224–5; on Philip's books, see Stirnemann, 'Bibliophiles'; Rouse and Rouse, 'Philip'.

[287] MS Avranches 159, fol. 1v; Cleaver, 'Library', p. 195.

[288] Nortier, *Bibliothèques*, p. 63. The list's handwriting points firmly to the second half of the twelfth century, with a likely date range of c.1163–1200; Stirnemann, 'Bibliothèques', p. 176; Cleaver, 'Library', p. 176; Pohl, '*Abbas*', pp. 51–2.

[289] Cleaver, 'Library', p. 179.   [290] Cleaver, 'Library', p. 179.

[291] Even whilst at Le Bec, Robert had access to a wide range of materials which he sourced both locally and from further afield to support his writing projects; Benjamin Pohl, 'The "Bec Liber Vitae": Robert of Torigni's Sources for Writing the History of the Clare Family at Le Bec, c.1128–54', *Revue bénédictine* 126 (2016), 324–72; Pohl, 'When did Robert'; David Bates, 'Robert of Torigni and the *Historia Anglorum*', in *The English and Their Legacy, 900–1200: Essays in Honour of Ann Williams*, ed. by David Roffe (Woodbridge: Boydell, 2012), pp. 175–84.

works in total was unrivalled within the monastic landscape of twelfth-century Normandy,[292] and it explains why Robert was keen to maintain access to it after his departure. We do not know whether Robert travelled to Le Bec in person to consult, copy, or borrow books he identified as useful for his writing projects or appointed monks of Mont-Saint-Michel to do the work for him, but this last was certainly not unusual practice amongst monastic superiors at the time.

In fact, we do not have to leave Le Bec to find an example of an abbot sending his monks on research trips in search of books that would benefit his own writing projects. When in the final quarter of the eleventh century Abbot Anselm (1078–93) tried to gain access to certain books unavailable in-house, he thus engaged a monk of Le Bec named Maurice who had joined the community in the early 1060s but had been relocated to the monastic cathedral chapter of Christ Church, Canterbury after the archiepiscopal appointment of Lanfranc, Le Bec's former prior (1045–63) and abbot of Saint-Étienne de Caen (1066–70), in c.1070 × 73. Anselm had taught Maurice as a *puer*, and judging from their extant personal correspondence he was heartbroken when Lanfranc requested—or demanded—the relocation to Canterbury.[293] In the years that followed, Anselm exchanged many letters with Maurice, regularly imploring the archbishop to release him,[294] but not until 1078 did Lanfranc agree, reluctantly, to send Maurice home to Le Bec.[295] In the interim, Anselm made the most of his protégé's sojourn across the Channel by sending him frequent requests to copy or send books from Canterbury's famously well-stocked library.[296] The books he requested included the *Regularis concordia*, Bede's *De temporibus*, Hippocrates's *Aphorisms* with Galen's gloss, and a *Libellus de pulsibus*, always insisting that Maurice's transcriptions be accurate and the exemplars corrected if required.[297] Anselm was aware, of course, that Maurice would be unable to copy—let alone send—any volumes without Lanfranc's approval, so he wrote to the archbishop requesting his permission and promising the books' prompt return ('michi cito

---

[292] Stéphane Lecouteux, 'À la recherche des livres du Bec (première partie)', in *Sur les pas de Lanfranc, du Bec à Caen: Recueil d'études en hommage à Véronique Gazeau*, ed. by Pierre Bauduin et al. (Caen: Presses universitaires de Caen, 2018), pp. 267–77. Also cf. Sharpe, *Libraries*, pp. 18–19 and 36–7 (= Tables 3 and 5) on the size of some contemporary Anglo-Norman monastic libraries.

[293] See *Letters*, ed./tr. Niskanen, pp. 74–7, 82–5, 104–7, 106–9, 146–9, 158–61, 184–7, and 190–3 (= nos. i.24, i.28, i.34, i.35, i.51, i.55, i.63, and i.65); for the wider context, see Pohl, '*Anonymus*', pp. 170–2.

[294] *Letters*, ed./tr. Niskanen, pp. 76–7.

[295] As far as we know, however, Maurice did not return to Le Bec straight away, but spent the following years at its dependent priory of Conflans Sainte-Honorine; see Pohl, '*Anonymus*', pp. 173–4.

[296] The volume *The Cathedral Priory of Christ Church, Canterbury* for the Corpus of British Medieval Library Catalogues [= *CBMLC*] is still in preparation by James Willoughby; in the meantime, see principally Montague R. James, *The Ancient Libraries of Canterbury and Dover* (Cambridge: Cambridge University Press, 1903); Teresa Webber, 'Les manuscrits de Christ Church (Cantorbéry) et de Salisbury à la fin du XIe siècle', in *Manuscrits et enluminures dans le monde normand: Xe–XVe siècles*, ed. by Pierre Bouet and Monique Dosdat (Caen: Presses universitaires, 1999), pp. 95–105; Teresa Webber, 'Script and Manuscript Production at Christ Church, Canterbury, after the Norman Conquest', in *Canterbury and the Norman Conquest: Churches, Saints and Scholars, 1066–1109*, ed. by Richard Eales and Richard Sharpe (London: Hambledon, 1995), pp. 145–58.

[297] *Letters*, ed./tr. Niskanen, pp. 146–7; Pohl, '*Anonymus*', p. 172.

eosdem libros remissuro debeant accommodare').[298] In one instance, Anselm justifies his request by explaining that Canterbury's uncorrupted copy of *De temporibus* is required to correct a flawed copy kept at Le Bec.[299] What renders Maurice's appointment as Anselm's interlibrary-loan assistant of particular interest here is that he was himself a capable writer of history. In fact, he has recently been identified with the so-called *Anonymus Beccensis*, a monk of Le Bec who wrote a 'miniature chronicle' in the guise of a commentary on Luke 2:1.[300] In writing this history, Maurice benefited from first-hand access to two of the largest monastic libraries in the Anglo-Norman world, Le Bec and Christ Church, Canterbury.[301] The fact that he also enjoyed the special favour and friendship—and the book provision—of the superiors in charge of these two institutions, Anselm and Lanfranc, played no small part in Maurice's productivity as a monastic historian.

Cases like those of Lupus, Gozbert, Robert, and Anselm are instructive individually and in conjunction. Taken together, they designate a range of ways and means by which monastic superiors secured access to books for both themselves and others within their communities, particularly—but not exclusively—those writing at their abbatial commission. They provide a sense of the geographical distances covered by these arrangements and the speed with which abbots could supply books to one another (and to third parties) when time was of the essence. Whilst cooperation amongst peers could not be taken for granted, there seems to have been a general consensus, and indeed an expectation, that requests would normally be approved—and books made mutually accessible—if the costs and logistics were covered. Evidence of this expectation survives in a letter written by Anselm in 1073 × 74, when he was prior of Le Bec (1063–78), in which he reassures his correspondent—'Abbot O.', plausibly identified by the letter's recent editor as Odilo, abbot of La Croix-Saint-Leufroy (before 1070–9 × 1113)—that '[w]e would gladly comply with your request and send you the book [...], which your holiness asked for by messenger, if only we had it here' ('[l]ibrum [...] quem per nuntium vestrum petivit sanctitas vestra, certe si modo eum apud nos haberemus, libenter secundum iussionem vestram vobis mitteremus').[302] The 'we' here is Prior Anselm speaking as deputy on behalf of his institutional superior, Abbot Herluin (1034–78), whom he would succeed in this position in

---

[298] *Letters*, ed./tr. Niskanen, pp. 106–7.   [299] *Letters*, ed./tr. Niskanen, pp. 106–7.

[300] This identification of Maurice with the 'Anonymus Beccensis' is established in Pohl, '*Anonymus*'; on his other works, see *Three Treatises from Bec on the Nature of Monastic Life*, ed./tr. by Giles Constable and Bernard S. Smith (Toronto: University of Toronto Press, 2008); also cf. van Houts, 'Le Bec', pp. 133–6.

[301] That he did so is evident from the citations identified throughout the work; Pohl, '*Anonymus*', pp. 161–9 and 182–4.

[302] *Letters*, ed./tr. Niskanen, pp. 384–7 (pp. 384–5) (= no. i.312); the book in question was a copy of St Gregory's *Moralia in Iob*. On Odilo, see Gazeau, *Normannia*, II, 86–7.

1078.³⁰³ The reason why they (read: Herluin) could not send the book to Odilo, Anselm adds remorsefully, is that it had been requested by and lent to someone else, another abbot no less: William I 'Bona Anima', abbot (1070–9) of the Conqueror's foundation of Saint-Étienne de Caen, who, at the time of writing, was having two copies produced in-house, one for his own community and the other for Lanfranc, William's abbatial predecessor at Caen and Anselm's predecessor as prior of Le Bec, who in 1070 had been appointed archbishop of Canterbury ('Domnus enim abbas Cadumensis habet illum et ibi scribitur ad exemplum eius, alter ad opus domni archiepiscopi Lanfranci').³⁰⁴ 'I write our excuses to you', Anselm signs off with further words of reassurance, 'lest you think that we did not wish to present you with the book [...], and that you may know our wish that as soon as we get the book back, we will gladly lend it to the messenger of your paternal loftiness according to your wish' ('Quapropter ne putetis quia nos nolimus vobis eum praestare [...], scripsi vobis excusationem nostram, et ut sciatic nostrum voluntatem quia cum citius nos librum eundem recipiemus, libenter eum secundum voluntatem vestram nuntio vestrae paternitatis accommodabimus').³⁰⁵

A similar reassurance was issued by Anselm in 1071 or 1077, this time to Ralph, prior of Caen and later Rochester, who subsequently became abbot (1107–24) of Battle.³⁰⁶ Judging from Anselm's words, a strongly worded letter had reached Ralph and his abbot William at Caen demanding the urgent and immediate return of some overdue books borrowed from Le Bec, an accusation that had caused consternation. Anselm shows himself profoundly embarrassed and deeply displeased ('profundius puderet vel altius poeniteret'), asserting that he never uttered anything of the sort nor sent any letters to that effect, and he then assures his peer and their respective superiors that 'Dom Abbot [Herluin] consenting, me wishing, no brother resisting, we will unreservedly send you whichever books [...] on your demand, for our mutual benefit' ('Domno igitur abbate concedente, me volente, nullo fratrum resistente, nostro pariter et vestro compensato commodo libenter vobis quoscunque libros [...] mittemus quando exigetis').³⁰⁷ Extending the proverbial olive branch to appease the affronted parties and avoid a diplomatic incident, Anselm informs Abbot William (via Ralph) that 'we forsake our [books] that you have with you for as long as you need them' ('quos vero de

---

³⁰³ Gazeau, *Normannia*, II, 7–13, covering both abbacies.
³⁰⁴ *Letters*, ed./tr. Niskanen, pp. 384–7; Gazeau, *Normannia*, II, 38–43. On the production of Lanfranc's copy by the scribes of Saint-Étienne, see two further letters sent by Anselm in 1073 and/or 1074; *Letters*, ed./tr. Niskanen, pp. 59–65 and 380–3 (= nos. i.19 and i.130).
³⁰⁵ This was not the only book Lanfranc had requested from Herluin/Le Bec since his departure, as Anselm reports in another of his letters; *Letters*, ed./tr. Niskanen, pp. 380–1.
³⁰⁶ *Letters*, ed./tr. Niskanen, pp. 32–7 (= i.10); on Ralph's identification as the letter's likely recipient, see ibid., pp. 36–7 n. 1.
³⁰⁷ *Letters*, ed./tr. Niskanen, pp. 34–5.

nostris vos habetis dimittemus, quamdiu indigetis')—a concession that he, as Ralph's equivalent, could never have made without Herluin's abbatial authorization.

Whilst this (near-)incident between Le Bec and Saint-Étienne de Caen may well have been the result of a genuine misunderstanding or miscommunication, with Anselm perhaps standing wrongly accused of sending return notices on behalf of his abbot, there is in fact evidence that some superiors were more territorial and protective of their books than others, turning down requests from their peers due to bad experience—with loaned books being returned late, in poor condition, or not at all—or because the requested item was considered too valuable or indispensable. Intriguingly, it was none other than abbot-historian Lupus of Ferrières who, as discussed above, readily availed himself of the libraries of his peers, but who on at least one occasion was reluctant when asked to lend out books from his library. In a letter to Hincmar, archbishop of Reims, written c.845 × 62, Lupus produces excuses why he cannot comply with Hincmar's request to send him Ferrières's copy of Bede's excerpts from St Augustine and the Pauline Epistles: not only is the book too big to be carried on one's person or be concealed in a bag ('propterea quod tantus est liber, ut nec sinu celari nec pera possit satis commode contineri'), but because of its size and beauty it will attract thieves *en route* ('formidanda esset obvia improborum rapacitas, quam profecto pulchritude ipsius codicis accendisset'), making it too dangerous for Lupus to send it lest it be lost ('ita forsitan et mihi et vobis perisset').[308] Whether these reservations were genuine or a mere pretence is impossible to know, but generally speaking such concerns were neither unfounded nor without parallel.

In a letter written c.1042/3 that survives in a contemporary copy (Paris, Bibliothèque nationale de France, MS Lat. 2858, fol. 68v), a monk of Santa Maria del Ripoll called Pontius reproaches the recipient, a certain monk called John whose monastic affiliation remains unclear, to finish copying the quires sent to him and return them as quickly as possible ('quaterniones quos vobis transmisi quantocius transcribatis et remittatis'). Pontius complains that he himself is being held responsible for John's delay (perhaps suggesting that he held the role of *armarius*) and facing harsh accusations by another monk called Salomon ('quia Salomon valde indignatus est contra fratrem suum pro his et ipse improperat mihi amarissimis verbis').[309] This Salomon was not just anybody, but the secretary and

---

[308] *Epistolae*, ed. Marshall, pp. 77–8 (= no. 76); on the work of Bede requested by Hincmar, see *Bede the Venerable: Excerpts from the Works of Saint Augustine and the Letters of the Blessed Apostle Paul*, tr. by David Hurst (Kalamazoo, MI: Cistercian Publications, 1999). A well-documented case of book theft concerning the personal bible of Abbot Majolus of Cluny is discussed by Scott G. Bruce, 'Clandestine Codices in the Captivity Narratives of Abbot Maiolus of Cluny', in *Teaching and Learning in Medieval Europe: Essays in Honour of Gernot R. Wieland*, ed. by Greti Dinkova-Bruun and Tristan Major (Turnhout: Brepols, 2017), pp. 149–61 (pp. 157–8).

[309] MS BnF Lat. 2858, fol. 68v, ll. 12–16; *Vie de Gauzlin, abbé de Fleury–Vita Gauzlini, abbatis Floriacensis monasterii*, ed./tr. by Robert-Henri Bautier and Gillette Labory (Paris: Éditions du CNRS, 1969), p. 184 (= 'Poncius monachus: Epistola ad Johannem monachum'); also cf. *Diplomatari i escrits*

amanuensis of Oliba, Ripoll's abbot (1008–46) and bishop of Vic (1018–46).[310] It seems plausible that in prompting the librarian(?) Pontius—who, in turn, chased John—Salomon was acting at the abbot's orders, and that his very bitter words ('verba amarissima') were really Oliba's conveyed on his behalf and expressing *his* frustration that a book *he* had authorized to be loaned was not returned promptly. In fact, it was not one but two volumes that Oliba had permitted to be borrowed, the other being a psalter that Pontius urged John either to copy immediately or send back ('Set et psalterium quod misi, si videtur ut transcribatis, transcribite; si non, semper remittite'), even offering to send a messenger ('nuntium vobis transmitterem') who would fetch the book(s) if needed—an offer that probably was less of a courtesy than an attempt at avoiding further delays by applying pressure on the borrowers.[311] According to the *Liber tramitis*, at eleventh-century Farfa the abbots—but nobody else!—could facilitate the timely return of borrowed volumes by authorizing their monks to miss the morning Mass and forego their midday rest in order to copy them ('[s]i domnus abbas aliquem librum de alio monasterio adquisierit et praefinito debet tempore reddere [...] psalmos familiares et missam vel meridianum frater ille propter hanc scripturam dimittat').[312] The fact that the imminent due date of books on loan from other monasteries is one of only a handful of reasons that justify such discretional abbatial exemptions underscores how serious a matter this was, and also how reputationally damaging delayed returns were to the borrowing institution and, by extension, its abbot or abbess.

In the face of such risks and inconveniences, it is no surprise to see institutional superiors introducing 'safety measures' in the form of confirmations of receipt, pledges, and deposits for loaned library books. Thus when in 1452 Abbot Jacob of Kastl borrowed some books from St Emmeram, he personally confirmed their receipt in a letter to its abbot, Hartung.[313] As abbot of Cluny, Peter the Venerable (1122–56) wrote to the prior of the Grande Chartreuse, admonishing him to send the deposit for the volumes he had borrowed from Cluny's library ('Mittite per praesentium latorem vel quemlibet alium fidum tamen vadimonia librorum

---

literaris de l'abat i bisbe Oliba, ed. by Eduard Junyent i Subirà (Barcelona: Institut d'Estudis Catalans, 1992), pp. 387–8 (= no. 1), who identifies both Pontius and John as monks of Ripoll and dates the document to before 1011, which seems unlikely, however.

[310] *Vita*, ed./tr. Bautier and Labory, p. 170; *Hispania Vetus: Musical-Liturgical Manuscripts from Visigothic Origins to the Franco-Roman Transition (9th–12th Centuries)*, ed. by Susana Zapke (Bilbao: Fundación BBVA, 2007), pp. 326–7. On Oliba, see Paul Freedman, 'Oliba', in *La catedral de Sant Pere de Vic*, ed. by Marta Crispi Cantón et al. (Barcelona: Publicacions de l'Abadia de Montserrat, 2019), pp. 107–14; Stefano M. Cingolani, 'L'Abat Oliba, el poder i la paraula', *Acta historica et archaeologica mediaevalia* 31 (2014), 115–62; Matthias M. Tischler, 'From Rome to Ripoll, Rioja, and Beyond: The Iberian Transmission of the Latin *Tiburtine Sibyl* and Oliba of Ripoll and Vic's Europe-Wide Network of Knowledge Transfer and Learning', *Early Medieval Europe* 30 (2022), 558–76.

[311] MS BnF Lat. 2858, fol. 68v, ll. 16–20; *Vita*, ed./tr. Bautier and Labory, p. 184; *Diplomatari*, ed. Junyent i Subirà, p. 387.

[312] *Liber tramitis*, ed. Dinter, p. 227.

[313] Hartung's confirmation of receipt survives in Munich, Bayerische Staatsbibliothek, MS Clm. 14958, fol. 339v.

quos misi'),³¹⁴ no doubt implying that this part of the agreement was yet to be honoured by the recipient. About a century earlier, prolific monk-poet Fromund of Tegernsee—the teacher and advisor of abbot-historian Ellinger—wrote a letter to a certain 'P.', whose identity and institutional affiliation are unknown. 'P.' had asked to borrow a copy of Boethius's work, presumably *De consolatione philosophiae*, which Fromund copied and glossed *manu propria*.³¹⁵ Fromund informs his correspondent that he will be happy to accommodate the request but unfortunately cannot do so straight away because one of these two manuscripts is his personal copy and therefore indispensable ('quorum alterum mecum retinui'), whereas the other is being held in Augsburg—whether at the cathedral or the local abbey of SS Ulrich and Afra is not specified—along with another volume containing works by Juvenal and Persius as a deposit for copies of Boethius's *De institutione arithmetica* and the pseudo-Ciceronian *Invective against Sallust* borrowed from their collection—in other words, two Tegernsee books being pledged in exchange for two books from Augsburg. Fromund signs off by reassuring 'P.' that as soon as he returns the borrowed volumes to Augsburg to redeem the deposited Tegernsee codices, he will send over the latter ('Quos libros mihi prestitos cum remitto nostrosque recipio, iussu vestro voluntarie satisfacio').³¹⁶

In late 1149, Abbot Wibald of Corvey (1146–58)—whom we will meet again below (4.2)—received a letter from Rainald of Dassel, informing him that the works of Cicero he wanted to borrow from Hildesheim's cathedral library had not been sent yet because it was against the canons' customs to do so without a good pledge ('non est consuetudinis apud nos ut sine bonis monimentis aliqui [libros] alicui concedantur').³¹⁷ Reinald reassures Wibald that the desired volumes will be sent immediately upon receipt of an adequate deposit, which he identifies as Corvey's library copies of Gellius's *Attic Nights* and Origen's commentary on the Song of Songs ('Mittite igitur nobis Angellium noctium Atticarum et Originem super cantica canticorum. Nostros autem [...], si qui vobis placent, vobis mittemus').³¹⁸ Agreeing to pledge the latter ('Misimus tibi pro monimentis librorum vestrorum Originem in cantica canticorum'), Wibald in his response regretfully informs Rainald that Gellius's text is unavailable, which is why he is sending him Frontinus's *Strategemata* instead ('et pro Aggellio noctium atticarum, quem ad presens habere nequaquam potuimus, librum, quem grece

---

³¹⁴ *Letters*, ed. Constable, I, 334 (= no. 132).
³¹⁵ *Die Tegernseer Briefsammlung (Froumund)*, ed. by Karl Strecker [= *MGH Epp. sel.* III] (Berlin: Weidmann, 1925), p. 18 (= no. 17), where the identification of 'P.' with Abbot Peringer of Tegernsee is rejected.
³¹⁶ *Briefsammlung*, ed. Strecker, p. 18.
³¹⁷ Rainald's letter has been edited in *Das Briefbuch Abt Wibalds von Stablo und Corvey*, ed. by Martina Hartmann, 3 vols. [= *MGH Briefe d. dt. Kaiserzeit* IX.1-3] (Hanover: Hahn, 2012), II, 401–2 (= no. 189).
³¹⁸ *Briefbuch*, ed. Hartmann, II, 402.

Stratagemmaton vocant, quod militare est').³¹⁹ As Martina Hartmann observes, however, Wibald almost certainly had a copy of the *Attic Nights* in his abbatial library at the time of writing.³²⁰ Perhaps his choice to send the *Strategemata* as a substitute should be seen as an indication that Wibald was unwilling—rather than unable—to part with Gellius's work, if only because it was deemed too valuable.

Whatever the rationale, Wibald's exchange of books with Rainald and their negotiation of appropriate pledges are part of a wider principle operating across medieval Europe that is epitomized by the verses of a mid-fifteenth-century poem in a manuscript from Bursfelde (Marburg, Universitätsbibliothek, MS 75, fol. 383r): 'He/she who wants to receive and be trusted with a book is told this by our order: he/she should first put another [book] in its place that is of equal or greater value' ('Qui sibi concedi | vult librum vel bene credi, / noster hoc ordo sonat: | alium mox ipse reponat, / qui valeat tantum | vel certe plus aliquantum').³²¹ Writing in a similar vein many centuries earlier during his tenure at Reichenau, Abbot Walafrid of Strabo (842–9) concluded one of his poems with a heartfelt reminder that nobody was to lend a book to anyone outside the monastery unless they had sworn an oath or provided a deposit that could only be redeemed once the borrowed book(s) had been returned to the community.³²² Though they were usually introduced with good intentions and the safety of the lent/borrowed books in mind, provisos such as these were not always popular with prospective borrowers. Sometimes requests were rejected out of hand, which could lead to complaints and, if the abbots persisted in their reluctance, interventions from superordinate authorities.

In 1212, the Council of Paris summoned by the freshly appointed English cardinal, Robert of Courçon (1212–19), sought to put an end to the clergy's reported reluctance, and at times downright refusal, to lend books from their institutional libraries. In its statutes, the council prohibited religious individuals and communities—specifically monasteries and their members ('viri regulares')—to take any oaths that prevented them from loaning their books to the needy ('interdicimus inter alia viris religiosis, ne emittant iuramentum de non commodando libros suos indigentibus'). Instead they decreed, after careful consideration

---

³¹⁹ *Briefbuch*, ed. Hartmann, II, 402–4 (p. 404) (= no. 190).

³²⁰ *Briefbuch*, ed. Hartmann, II, 402 n. 8. On Wibald's abbatial residence, which included both a library and study, see below (4.2).

³²¹ Edited in Wilhelm Wattenbach, *Das Schriftwesen im Mittelalter* (Leipzig: Hirzel, 1896), pp. 588–9 (p. 589). About two centuries earlier, the Cambro-Norman historian and poet Gerald of Wales had composed a set of verses as an inscription for his personal book cupboard ('Versus armariolo librorum Giraldi'), stipulating that nobody must remove any of the volumes without leaving a deposit ('sine pignore nemo tollat'); the poem is edited from London, Lambeth Palace Library, MS 236, fol. 164v in *Giraldi Cambrensis Opera*, ed. by John S. Brewer et al., 8 vols. (London: Longman, 1861–91), I, 369 (= no. xxiv).

³²² Edited with translation in Walter Berschin, 'Vier karolingische Exlibris', in *Mittellateinische Studien*, ed. by Walter Berschin, 3 vols. (Heidelberg: Mattes, 2005–17), I, 169–78 (pp. 170–1).

('consideratione diligenti'), that only certain books—presumably service books, liturgical codices, and other kinds of books required for the daily domestic routine—may be withheld from external borrowers and retained for the monks' use ('in domo ad opus fratrum retineantur'); all others should, as a matter of principle and a principal work of compassion ('cum commodare inter praecipua misericordiae opera computetur'), be made available readily to those in need ('alii [...] indigentibus commodentur') on the condition that lending them out would cause no damage or loss to the monastery ('cum indemnitate domus'). History books presumably fell into the latter category. Ascertaining whether a book could be loaned without risk to the community was the abbot's responsibility and subject to his discretion and judgement ('secundum providentiam abbatis').[323]

Acting in a rather different spirit than the Council of Paris, the Dominican General Chapter of Barcelona held in 1323 decreed categorically that none of the books from the libraries of the religious houses over which it had jurisdiction was to be loaned, pawned, sold, or otherwise alienated by anyone, not even their superiors or their deputies ('volumus et ordinamus quod libri in catenis vel armario communi usui deputati per priores vel eorum vicarios sive per conventum impignorari, vendi, commodari vel quomodolibet alienari non possint'), and that whoever did so should be made to pay for the replacement volume(s) from their personal funds ('Si qui vero contrarium fecerint, cogantur per priores provinciales de bonis sibi appropriates valorem libri seu librorum pro communi armario deputare').[324] Not even the chaining of some of these books had prevented them from being removed or sold off, requiring the Chapter to step in and curtail the superiors' freedom of action. The selling and trading of books by monastic superior was not uncommon, sometimes as a way of fundraising that provided much-needed cash injections. Though less common than requests for loans or copies, there are some well-documented cases of abbots and abbesses parting permanently with their books, typically for a hefty sum of money or something of considerable value offered to them in exchange.

A good example of this, specifically in relation to the writing of history, can be found in the monastic cartulary of Ebersberg produced under abbot-historian Williram (1048–85). The partial autograph (Munich, Bayerisches Hauptstaatsarchiv, Kloster Ebersberg, KL 2) contains several historical narratives written by Williram or at his abbatial request, most notably the *Catalogus*

---

[323] 'Statutorum concilii Parisiensis pars secunda: Ad viros regulares', in *Sacrorum conciliorum nova et amplissima collectio*, ed. by Giovanni D. Mansi, 31 vols. (Venice: Zatta, 1758-98), XXII, 825-33 (p. 832) ('Ne religiosi iuramentum faciant de non commodando libros').

[324] *Acta capitulorum generalium ordinis Praedicatorum*, ed. by Franz A. Frühwirth and Benedikt M. Reichert, 9 vols. (Rome: In domo generalitia, 1898-1904), II, 146. On the Dominicans and their involvement in the medieval book trade, see now the contributions by Richard and Mary Rouse, Laura Albiero, and Alison Stones in *The Medieval Dominicans: Books, Buildings, Music, and Liturgy*, ed. by Eleanor J. Giraud and Christian T. Leitmeir (Turnhout: Brepols, 2021).

abbatum Ebersbergensium and the *Chronicon Ebersbergense*.³²⁵ One of the charters copied in Ebersberg's cartulary records a trade between Williram and the bishop of Trient, Henry (1068–80), who gives three fruitful vineyards ('vineas feraces') along the River Talfer—in what is now the world-renowned wine-producing region of South Tyrol—in exchange for certain rights and possessions. One vineyard is traded for a church, whereas the other two are surrendered in exchange for the books the bishop desired from the abbot's bookcase ('pro commutatione librorum, quos idem episcopus concupiverat de scriniis abbatis').³²⁶ Henry had just come into the possession of these vineyards the previous year, and their value, especially when taking into account the territories given alongside them, shows how prized an asset the abbot's library was. The *Liber actorum* of Arnsburg (Lich, Fürst zu Solms-Hohensolms-Lich'sches Archiv, Liber actorum Arnsburg, fols. 135v–136v) records that in 1439 Abbot John sold no fewer than sixty-four books from the monastery's collection to his peer, the abbot of Maulbronn, even though the community's financial situation at the time appears to have been reasonably stable and would not have necessitated such a 'fire sale'.³²⁷

An alternative to the sale or trade of books was provided by semi-permanent loans.³²⁸ A good example of this comes from Reichenau, where Abbot Eberhard (1343–79) temporarily issued a book from the monks' library to Walter, knight and deacon of Basel Cathedral, to be kept for life ('pro tempore vite sue').³²⁹ In return, Walter agreed that upon his death his own copy of Bartholomaeus Anglicus's *De proprietatibus rerum* would be given to the abbot and his chapter in perpetuity ('ad dictum monasterium verissime transmittendum prelibatis dominis abbati et capitulo seudicto monasterio librum suum De proprietatibus rerum [...] causa mortis legaverit'). The agreement was recoded in a charter, ratified publicly ('publice recognoverit'), and Walter swore, likely at the abbot's insistence, that he would not try to renege on it at any point in the future ('promisitque [...] Waltherus bona fide se dictum legatum ratum habere

---

³²⁵ On Abbot Williram and his historiographical activity, see Hans U. Ziegler, 'Das historische Gesamtwerk des Abtes Williram von Ebersberg (1048–1085)', in *Kloster Ebersberg: Prägekraft christlich-abendländischer Kultur im Herzen Altbayerns*, ed. by Bernhard Schäfer (Ebersberg: Garnies, 2002), pp. 161–84; Michael Rupp, 'Williram von Ebersberg', in *Althochdeutsche und altsächsische Literatur*, ed. by Rolf Bergmann (Berlin: De Gruyter, 2013), pp. 518–28; on the cartulary, cf. Hans U. Ziegler, 'Das Ebersberger Urkundenbuch–Ein Großprojekt historischer Forschung im Landkreis Ebersberg', *Land um den Ebersberger Forst* 4 (2001), 8–37.
³²⁶ MS Munich HStA KL 2, fol. 30r (= no. 28); 'Das Cartular des Klosters Ebersberg', ed. by Friedrich H. Hundt, *Abhandlungen der Historischen Klasse der Königlich-Bayerischen Akademie der Wissenschaften* 14 (1879), 115–96 (p. 160) (= no. 28).
³²⁷ Fritz Hermann, 'Verkauf von Handschriften aus Arnsburg nach Maulbronn im Jahr 1439', *Zentralblatt für Bibliothekswesen* 37 (1920), 80–4, who excludes financial difficulties from the abbot's motivations for the sale ('Eine besondere Notlage des Klosters [...] scheint für die Zeit des Verkaufs nicht in Frage zu kommen'; ibid., p. 80).
³²⁸ Reed-Leal, 'Book-Borrowing', pp. 197–8.
³²⁹ *Die Reichenauer Handschriften: Neudruck mit bibliographischen Nachträgen*, ed. by Alfred Holder and Karl Preisendanz, 3 vols. (Wiesbaden: Harrassowitz, 1970–3), III.2, p. 14; quoted after Steinmann, *Handschriften*, pp. 539–40 (= no. 604).

perpetuo atque firmum nec contra ipsum facere vel venire'). At the same time, however, there is evidence of abbots attempting, with varying degrees of success, to buy back books sold or alienated by themselves or their predecessors. The *Catalogus abbatum* from Augsburg (Augsburg, Archiv des Bistums Augsburg, MS 78) reports with great admiration that Abbot Conrad I (1334–55) bought back a copy of the *Mater verborum* (known as *Glosa Salomonis*; the author mistakenly attributes the work to Salomon III, bishop of Constance) that had been sold off by his precursor, Marquard (1315–34). Marquard had shown no interest in the book and sold or pawned it to the local Dominican convent ('venditus vel in vadem traditus fuit fratribus ordinis Praedicatorum huius civitatis') because it was 'written in very ancient script' ('liber scriptus est in antiquissima litera').[330] Unwilling to accept that such a treasure should be alienated from the community for petty cash, Conrad is said to have striven tirelessly to return the book to his monastery's library ('omni tamen studio idem pater laboravit, ut idem librum redimeret in vita et regimine suo') and eventually succeeded in 1344 by retrieving it from the Dominicans for an unspecified sum ('redeptus est ab eo a predictis fratribus pro certa peccunia') that the chronicler could no longer determine ('Numerum peccuniarum non inveni').[331] An attempt to recuperate not just a single book, but fifteen pawned volumes from the monastic library of Loccum that had been used as collateral during a recent economic crisis is documented for 1445, when Mette, abbess of Wöltingerode, and Beate, abbess of Derneburg, together issued a letter of intent (Hanover, Niedersächsisches Landesarchiv, Cal. Or. 100 Loccum, Urkunde 842) addressed to Loccum's abbot, John, in which they commit themselves to returning the books that he had pawned ('vorpendet') to them in return for eighty Dutch guilders.[332] According to the same letter, the original transaction had been agreed by the abbot of Volkolderode (or Volkenroda) during a visitation on the condition that should the books be damaged or lost during their sojourn at Wöltingerode and Derneburg the abbesses would refund their full value to Loccum's abbot, presumably by forfeiting the money he owed them; if John were to renege on the agreement by repossessing these books without surrendering the pledged sum in its entirety, he would forfeit lands of equivalent value until the full eighty guilders were received safely by the abbesses.[333]

The *Gesta abbatum* of St Albans report a story in which one of the abbey's early monks called Egwin is sent to Denmark by his abbot, Wulnoth (*c*.930).[334] Landing in Odense, Egwin spends a year with a local convent of Benedictine monks to

---

[330] The *Catalogus* has been edited as 'Fr. Wilhelmi Wittwer Catalogus abbatum monasterii ss. Udalrici et Afrae Augustensis', ed. by Anton Streichele, *Archiv für die Geschichte des Bisthums Augsburg* 3 (1860), 15–437 (p. 177).
[331] 'Catalogus', ed. Streichele, p. 177.
[332] The abbesses' letter is edited in *Calenberger Urkundenbuch*, ed. by Wilhelm von Hodenberg and Joachim Studtmann, 10 vols. (Hanover: Jänecke, 1855–1990), III, 487–8 (= no. 842).
[333] *Urkundenbuch*, ed. von Hodenberg, III, 488.
[334] *Gesta*, ed. Riley, I, 12–18; tr. Preest and Clark, pp. 62–5.

discover that they have possession of St Albans's relics, which were stolen from his home monastery. Hiding them in a chest, Egwin devises a cunning ruse to return these relics to their rightful owners by entrusting the locked container to a fellow Englishman who is about to embark on a crossing to London. He tells the sailor that the casket contains books Wulnoth had loaned to him over a year ago, and which are long overdue. Unaware of its true contents, the sailor returns the chest to the abbot, with Egwin following separately with the keys. Fictional though this episode may be, its credibility relied fundamentally on the notion that an abbot would lend books to a travelling monk, an idea that evidently was considered plausible by the *Gesta*'s author(s) and, quite possibly, informed by historical precedent.

3.6 Conclusions

Bringing together a range of evidence from across the medieval Latin West, the discussions presented here urge us to revisit and revise our understanding of the roles abbots and abbesses played in the provision of books for (their) monastic libraries. Despite the reservations and occasional pessimism of scholarship cautioning 'not to overestimate the importance of abbatial contributions to monastic libraries',[335] the men and women in charge of monastic communities across Europe were demonstrably amongst the foremost book providers and library builders throughout the Middle Ages. Whilst there are, unsurprisingly, considerable differences in both quantity and quality between their individual contributions—differences that have to do with personal choices as much as they do with specific local and institutional circumstances—as a collective abbots and abbesses rank second to none in the provision of monastic books, many of which are still extant today and/or attested in library inventories. These books constituted vital resources for the writing of history by the members of medieval monastic communities, but they were equally instrumental in the commemoration of their abbatial providers. Equipped with inscriptions and illustrations that stimulated the memory of present and future audiences who would read, view, and touch their pages in worshipful fashion, the commemorative currency of books provided by abbots and abbesses by far exceeded, and indeed justified, the considerable effort and expense of their production and procurement.

Part of the reason why so little of this has been acknowledged is that the kinds of sources cited most regularly in studies of monastic book provision tend to be conspicuously silent about the abbot's role in the provision of books. As we saw, this is true especially of monastic rules and customaries, the normative (and

---

[335] Heale, *Abbots*, p. 86.

aspirational) regulations of which provide relatively limited insights into the realities of everyday life but have frequently been—and still sometimes are—taken at face value. At the same time, the relative prominence of other individuals mentioned regularly in these texts means that scholarship has tended to lavish a disproportionate amount of attention on them, thereby obscuring, unintentionally, the underlying institutional structures and hierarchies within which they operated. These structures typically remain implicit in normative texts, presumably because they were so fundamental to the monastic enterprise that they did not require explicit mention or repetition in the context of book provision. This specifically concerns monastic officers such as the cantor-*armarius*, whom scholars have credited with far greater autonomy and authority than the evidence permits, but also other personnel involved in the production and provision of monastic books down to the level of scribes and copyists, whose individual agency is often overplayed unduly to the exclusion of their institutional superiors' overarching authority. Recognising their reliance on the abbot's approval and support does not mean negating their important contributions, though it does allow us to situate them more accurately in relation to the source from which they, like everyone in a monastic community, ultimately derived their agency and resources. These conclusions echo and corroborate the discussion of authority and obedience as core operational principles in the collaborative yet hierarchical structures that enabled and sustained monastic historiographical activity (2.2). Abbatial *auctoritas* was a decisive factor and facilitator not only in the composition of new historical narratives, but also in the provision of the written sources upon which monastic historians relied to exercise their craft.

4
'In studio abbatis'

4.1 Introduction

The previous chapters have shown us abbots and abbesses investing human and material resources into building environments that enabled and facilitated historiographical activity. One aspect of this not discussed so far was the construction and maintenance of physical workplaces suitable for historical writing and study, some of which were designed for communal use, whereas others were exclusive to the monastic superiors and their personal assistants.[1] That one did not have to exclude the other is shown by examples of abbots and abbesses writing alongside their monks and nuns in the cloister or scriptorium. Orderic famously celebrates his community's former abbot, Thierry de Mathonville (1050–7), as a distinguished scribe ('scriptor egregius') who personally supervised the monks in Saint-Évroult's scriptorium and wrote many books in their presence.[2] The *Liber de restauratione monasterii sancti Martini Tornacensis* recalls that Abbot Rodulf of Tournai (1095–1105) sometimes would not set foot outside the cloister for an entire month ('integro mense de claustro non exiret') whilst completely devoting himself to writing books ('scribendis libris totum studium daret'), and whoever entered the cloister would find him amidst a dozen apprentice scribes seated on exquisitely crafted writing desks ('ut si claustrum ingredereris, videres plerumque duodecim monachos iuvenes in cathedris sedentes et super tabulas diligenter et artificiose compositas cum silentio scribentes).[3] The same *modus operandi* was adopted by Abbot Frederick of Hirsau (1065–9), who according to the abbey's foundation history insisted on being given a workstation amongst the other scribes

---

[1] The literature on medieval writing spaces is limited and rarely focuses on specific individuals; a general overview is provided by Ewan Clayton, 'Workplaces for Writing', in *Pen in Hand: Medieval Scribal Portraits, Colophons and Tools*, ed. by Michael Gullick (Walkern: Red Gull Press, 2006), pp. 1–18.

[2] *HE*, ed./tr. Chibnall, II, 48–50; Pohl, 'Orderic', pp. 337–9; on Thierry, see Gazeau, *Normannia*, II, 273–5.

[3] 'Herimanni liber de restauratione monasterii S. Martini Tornacensis', in *Supplementa tomorum I–XII*, Vol. 2: *Supplementum tomi XIII*, ed. by Georg Waitz [= *MGH SS* XIV] (Hanover: Hahn, 1883), pp. 274–317 (pp. 312–13); translation in *The Restoration of the Monastery of Saint Martin of Tournai*, tr. by Lynn H. Nelson (Washington, DC: Catholic University of America Press, 1996), pp. 113–14. The chronicler and subsequent abbot of Tournai, Herman (1127–36), reports that Rodulf's books were deemed second to none, and whoever wished to correct their own books would request them as exemplars ('vix in aliqua vicinarum ecclesiarum similis inveniretur bibliotheca, omnesque pro corrigendis libris suis de nostra ecclesia peterent exemplaria').

('scriptorium inter alios scriptores habere perhibeatur') to write books for the community's library,[4] as well as by Abbess Caesaria II (c.525–60) of Arles, who is said to have been the mistress ('magistra') of her community's scriptorium and personally taught the nuns how to write the most handsome books.[5] The question is whether cases such as these were related by monastic chroniclers because they conformed to their expectations and were seen as exemplary, or because they were considered exceptional and contrary to general practice, in which case we need to ask where else abbots and abbesses wrote and studied if not in communal spaces.

Unlike the private studies of modern writers, some of which are deemed so iconic as to be preserved *in situ* after their owners' deaths and become popular tourist attractions, personal writing and study spaces of the Middle Ages usually escape our knowledge due to a lack of physical evidence. Little tends to survive of their furnishings and interior design, and in the absence of concrete traces our imagination is easily drawn to the formulaic iconography of scribal portraits such as that of Eadwine (Cambridge, Trinity College, MS R.17.1, fol. 283v) or depictions of the Four Evangelists writing their respective Gospels.[6] Images of abbots in their studies are especially rare, and those that do exist are often posthumous, sometimes by centuries. The nineteenth-century portrait of Robert of Torigni by Édouard de Bergevin that shows the twelfth-century historian 'au milieu de ses manuscrits' in the cosy comfort of his abbatial study at Mont-Saint-Michel offers an instructive case in point (Fig. 4.1).[7] Gaining insight into the workplaces of medieval abbot-historians is essential for our understanding of their working methods and how they went about their craft. It also nuances our broader perception of the logistics and practicalities of writing history in medieval monastic communities. The following discussion thus provides a systematic investigation of abbatial workplaces and the study materials stored therein, the first of its kind, using examples from across medieval Latin Europe. It argues that private studies and libraries were much more common and widespread amongst monastic superiors than so far acknowledged, and from considerably earlier on. To set the scene for this, however, it is instructive to begin by considering a particularly detailed example from the very end of the Middle Ages.

31 December 1514 had been a long day at the Abbey of St James in Würzburg. Whilst the monks used the last daylight hours to prepare the Feast of the Circumcision, their abbot-historian, Johannes Trithemius, was sat at his desk

---

[4] 'Historia', ed. Waitz, p. 256.

[5] *Caesarius Arlatensis opera omnia*, Vol. 2: *Opera varia*, ed. by Germain Morin (Maredsous: Maretioli, 1942), p. 320; Jo A. McNamara, 'Caesaria II, Abbess of Saint Jean of Arles (ca. 550)', in *Sainted Women of the Dark Ages*, ed. by Jo A. McNamara et al. (Durham, NC: Duke University Press, 1992), pp. 112–18.

[6] For discussion, see Michael Gullick, 'Self Referential Artist and Scribe Portraits in Romanesque Manuscripts', in *Pen in Hand: Medieval Scribal Portraits, Colophons and Tools*, ed. by Michael Gullick (Walkern: Red Gull Press, 2006), pp. 97–114.

[7] On this portrait, see Pohl, 'Robert and Le Bec', pp. 96–7; Pohl, 'Memory', pp. 128–31.

Fig. 4.1 Nineteenth-century portrait of Robert of Torigni in his private study. Édouard de Bergevin, 1889.

putting the finishing touches to a project that had taken him fifty-four months ('[m]ensibus quinquaginta quatuor') to complete.[8] The fruit of his labour was a handsome autograph codex (MS Munich Clm. 704) containing the second instalment of the *Annales Hirsaugienses* commissioned by Abbot Blasius of Hirsau twenty years earlier. The first volume's presentation copy (MS Munich Clm. 703) had been sent to Hirsau three years before with a dedication letter addressed to Blasius's successor, John,[9] and the second tome was made to match the

---

[8] *Annales*, II, 5. The liturgical programme for the Circumcision commenced at sunset and continued with an extended Night Office of twelve readings; Susan Boynton, 'The Bible and the Liturgy', in *The Practice of the Bible in the Middle Ages: Production, Reception, and Performance in Western Christianity*, ed. by Susan Boynton and Diane J. Reilly (New York, NY: Columbia University Press, 2011), pp. 10–33 (pp. 15–17 = Table 2.1).

[9] The dedication letter is dated 5 February 1511 (MS Munich Clm. 703, fol. 1v, ll. 50–1: 'scripsi quinta die mensis Februarii. Anno Christianorum millesimo D. XI.'), whereas the text itself concludes with an explicit dated 10 January of that year (ibid., fol. 304v, ll. 44–5: 'decima die mensis Ianuarii. Anno Christianorum millesimo quingentesimo undecimo'). The dedicatory letter has been printed in *Annales*, I, A^{1}r–A^{2}r.

appearance of its sibling. Despatched virtually as soon as the ink was dry, it reached Hirsau a few days later with another letter to John enclosed.[10] With both volumes off his desk and *en route* to their patron, Trithemius wearily put down his pen after nearly five years of writing ('fatigatus quintum in annum calamum deposui').[11]

What is remarkable about this episode is not how long it took Trithemius to complete the assignment; in fact, for the single-handed writing of two holograph codices with over six hundred folia, four and a half years was anything but slow work given what we know about the writing speed of medieval scribes.[12] The main reason why the *Annales*—or rather their accompanying dedication letters—are of interest is because they provide insights into the working conditions Trithemius experienced during his abbatial appointments. As abbot of Sponheim, he reportedly had found little time to immerse himself in his historiographical projects due to an endless list of mind-numbing administrative chores ('vanis caducisque mundi curis et sollicitudinibus quasi continuę nimium occupatus'), a complaint that brings to mind the abbots' protests at the 1480 Bursfelde General Chapter in response to Gunther of Nordhausen's sermon.[13] According to the 1511 epistle, these duties had been so incessant ('tantis me laboribus rei familiaris, mundique curis absque intermissione oppressit'; 'plena laboribus abbatia') that the only way for Trithemius to accomplish any writing had been to sacrifice his sleep and work during the small hours ('ut mihi raro, ac solum per intervalla nocturnis, quas ipse mihi de somno plerumque suffurabar, horis codicem liceret contingere').[14] Unless

---

[10] *Annales*, II, 5–8; again, the date of the dedication letter (MS Munich Clm. 704, fol. 3v, ll. 10–11: 'ultima die mensis Decembris. Anno Domini M. D. XIII') differs from that in the text itself (ibid., fol. 312v, ll. 8–9 and 14–15: '[A]nno Dominice nativitatis prenotato millesimo quingentesimo tercio decimo; etatis mee quinquagesimo primo; ultima die mensis Decembris [...] M. D. XIIII. Anno Iohannis abbatis huius monasterii nostri Hirsaugiensis undecimo').

[11] MS Munich Clm. 704, fol. 312v.

[12] See Michael Gullick, 'How Fast Did Scribes Write? Evidence from Romanesque Manuscripts', in *Making the Medieval Book: Techniques of Production*, ed. by Linda L. Brownrigg (London: Red Gull Press, 1995), pp. 39–58; Eef A. Overgaauw, 'Fast or Slow, Professional or Monastic: The Writing Speed of Some Late-Medieval Scribes', *Scriptorium* 49 (1995), 211–27; Johann P. Gumbert, 'The Speed of Scribes', in *Scribi e colofoni: Le sottoscrizioni di copisti dalle origini all'avvento della stampa*, ed. by Emma Condello and Giuseppe de Gregorio (Spoleto: Centro italiano di studi sull'alto medioevo, 1995), pp. 57–69. Cases of scribal work taking place at impressive speed include Columba's *Book of Durrow* (Dublin, Trinity College, MS 57 (A.4.5)), which according to its colophon (fol. 247v) was produced in just twelve days ('per XII dierum spatium'), as well as Munich, Bayerische Staatsbibliothek, MS Clm. 14437, fol. 109r, which judging by its colophon was made within seven days and corrected on the eighth ('[s]cribus est autem diebus septem et in octavo correctus'); Steinmann, *Handschriften*, p. 112 (= no. 126). These cases are exceptions, rather than the norm. Indeed, the scribal colophon in the first instalment of a monumental three-volume Bible produced at St Isidore in León under Abbot Menendo in 1162 anticipates the reader's great surprise upon hearing that the work was completed in just seven months ('[q]uodque maxime mireris, in sex mensum spacio scriptus septimoque colorum pulcritudine iste fuit liber compositus'); León, Biblioteca de la Real Colegiata de San Isidoro, MS Cod. I 3., fol. 1r; Steinmann, *Handschriften*, p. 302 (= no. 361). The colophon in a 'commonplace book' from the later thirteenth century (Oxford, Bodleian Library, MS Digby 86, fol. 205v) states that it took the scribe one and a quarter years to write it ('scripsi librum in anno et iii mensibus').

[13] *Annales*, I, A¹r.   [14] *Annales*, I, A¹r–v.

he was roaming the deserted cloister at night-time, the implication is that Trithemius wrote history in the same place where he ought to have slept: in his abbatial quarters.

Tinged with melodrama though it may be, the letter's account is supported by Duraclusius, a monk of Würzburg who sojourned at Sponheim for a year during Trithemius's abbacy and studied under his tutelage. When years later Duraclusius wrote, largely from memory, an account of Trithemius's *gesta* with a list of his writings, he recalled how his host had been struggling to set aside time for quiet study amidst his many abbatial occupations ('in medio curarum et continua rei familiaris occupatione').[15] Duraclusius reports that Trithemius had regularly been labouring after dark ('lucubravit', which we may translate idiomatically as 'burning the midnight oil'), reading and writing day and night ('legens aut scribens die ac nocte') and withdrawing himself whenever possible ('quotiens sibi otium licuit subfurari').[16] As if to prove a point, Duraclusius called his work *Vita et lucubrationes Iohannis Trithemii* ('The Life and Nightly Labours of Johannes Trithemius'), and Trithemius used the same expression in his *Annales*.[17] Johannes Centurianus, a priest who had joined the monastic community as a lay brother to improve his education, wrote to Trithemius in 1507 recalling that the prolific abbot-historian had often been working when everyone else was sleeping, always reading or writing in the privacy of his quarters.[18] The concurring testimony of Trithemius's autobiography and two eye-witnesses suggests that this image of the reclusive abbot-historian working long hours in his study is accurate, even if it was embellished for dramatic effect.

Trithemius was not the only medieval abbot to forego his sleep regularly in favour of scribal activity. Marianus Scotus, the founder and first abbot (though

---

[15] Trithemius also produced catalogues of his own works; Klaus Arnold, 'Ein Würzburger Schriftenverzeichnis des Johannes Trithemius aus dem Jahr 1514', in *Herbipolis: Studien zu Stadt und Hochstift Würzburg in Spätmittelalter und Früher Neuzeit*, ed. by Markus Frankl, Martina Hartmann, and Dorothea Klein (Würzburg: Königshausen, 2015), pp. 357–72.

[16] *Johannes Duraclusius: Vita et lucubrationes Iohannis Trithemii*, in *Johannes Trithemius: Opera historica*, ed. by Marquard Freher, 2 vols. (Frankfurt a. M.: Marne and Aubry, 1601; repr. Minerva, 1966), I, 5–7. The medieval Latin term *lucubratio* usually describes work conducted at night; *Glossarium mediae et infimae Latinitatis*, ed. by Charles Dufresne du Cange, 10 vols. (Niort: Favre, 1883–7), V, 148; *Mittellateinisches Glossar*, ed. by Edwin Habel and Friedrich Gröbel, 2nd ed. (Paderborn: Schöningh, 1989), p. 227.

[17] *Vita*, ed. Freher, p. 5; MS Munich Clm. 704, fol. 312v: 'Hec sunt lucubrationum mearum capita tituli et nomina'.

[18] [Johannes Centurianus:] 'Letter to Johannes Trithemius, 18 April 1507', in *Johannes Trithemius: Opera historica*, ed. by Marquard Freher, 2 vols. (Frankfurt a. M.: Marne and Aubry, 1601; repr. Minerva, 1966), II, 527–9 (p. 528): 'Caeteris dormientibus tu in sancto scripturarum studio vigilabas, semper aut legens, aut scribens aliquid pro communi utilitate multorum'. Trithemius gives a similar account in a letter sent to Sponheim the previous year; [Johannes Trithemius:] 'Letter to the prior and community of Sponheim, 31 October 1506 (= Epistola II)', in *Johannes Trithemius: Opera historica*, ed. by Marquard Freher, 2 vols. (Frankfurt a. M.: Marne and Aubry, 1601; repr. Minerva, 1966), II, 507–12 (p. 508).

uncertainty remains as to whether he ever officially carried this title) of St Peter's Abbey in Regensburg, not to be confused with the Mainz-based chronicler of the same name, seems to have had a habit of writing at night. In his *Vita*, we learn that when one night the sacristan forgot to provide Marianus with his writing lamp ('contigit negligente custode eiusdem ecclesiae lumina sibi non praeberi'), three of his fingers lit up so he could complete the work with God's support ('divina misericordia tres digitos manus suae sinistrae, ad instar trium lampadarum, splendescere faciebat, ut inceptum opus in tali lumine coelesti incessanter perageret').[19] Less miraculous is the account by the anonymous continuator of Cosmas of Prague's *Chronica Bohemorum*, who reports that when Diethard was made abbot of Sázava (1097–1133) and found only Slavonic books in its library, he spent both day and night copying the missing (Latin?) volumes with great effort ('[i]dem abbas libros [...] nocte et die immenso labore conscripsit'), and those he did not write himself he bought or had made by hired scribes ('quosdam emit, quosadam scriptores scribere conduxit et omnimodis acquisivit').[20] According to abbot-historian Menko (1242–73) of Bloemhof in Wittewierum, his predecessor, Emo (1214–37), who was also a writer of history, composed most of his *Chronicon abbatum in Werum* at night, a habit Emo apparently had picked up from his brother, Addo, during their student days in Oxford and Paris ('propter consuetudinem observatam Parisius et Oxonie tempore studii, quando, fratre suo domno Addone priorem partem noctis vigilante ac scribende').[21] John of Salerno reports that Abbot Odo of Cluny (927–42) made a habit of shunning the company of his community at night to find quiet time for writing by going on extended walks. A prolific writer of sermons, commentaries, and a biography of Gerald of Aurillac, Odo is said to have embarked on his nightly excursions to the nearby tomb of St Martin by himself carrying only a pair of wax tablets ('non college fultus latere, non bacilli corroboratus munimine, sed duas tabellas manu baiulans, scribendi

---

[19] 'Vita [Mariani] auctore Scoto monacho Ratispon', in *Acta Sanctorum Februarii II* [= *AASS* V] (Paris: Palmé, 1864), pp. 365–73 (p. 367); Helmut Flachenecker, *Schottenklöster: Irische Benediktinerkonvente im hochmittelalterlichen Deutschland* (Paderborn: Schöningh, 1995), pp. 95–8, observes that Marianus was not identified as abbot in contemporary sources.

[20] 'Über Diethard, Abt des Klosters Sazawa', in *Die Chronik der Böhmen des Cosmas von Prag*, ed. by Berthold Bretholz [= *MGH SS rer. Germ. N. S.* II] (Berlin: Weidmann, 1923), pp. 255–6 (p. 255) (= Appendix II); the most recent edition and translation of the *Chronica*'s continuation is *Cosmas of Prague: The Chronicle of the Czechs–Cosmae Pragensis Chronica Bohemorum*, ed./tr. by János M. Bak et al. (Budapest: Central European University Press, 2020), pp. 429–53 (= Appendix). Also cf. David Kalhous, *Anatomy of a Duchy: The Political and Ecclesiastical Structures of Early Přemyslid Bohemia* (Leiden: Brill, 2000), pp. 223–5.

[21] 'Emonis et Wenkonis Werumensium Chronica', ed. by Ludwig Weiland, in *Chronica aevi Suevici* [= *MGH SS* XXIII] (Hanover: Hahn, 1874), pp. 454–572 (p. 531); the most recent edition is *Kroniek van het klooster Bloemhof te Wittewierum*, ed./tr. by Hubertus P. H. Jansen and Antheun Janse (Hilversum: Verloren, 1991), pp. 290–1 and 320–1; the *Chronicon* specifies that Emo regularly stayed awake to copy texts after Matins (3 a.m. to sunrise), whilst Addo did so before Matins; also cf. *Kronijken van Emo en Menko, Abten van het klooster te Wittewierum, met het vervolg van een ongenoemde*, ed. by Hendrikus O. Feith and Gozewijn A. Stratingh (Utrecht: Kemink, 1866), pp. vi–vii.

officio aptissimas').[22] An anonymous medieval Latin poem on how to be a good monk composed in the thirteenth or fourteenth century even explicitly recommends spending the night over the pages of books whilst enduring hunger and thirst in the day, and what was good enough for the monk certainly was considered good enough for the abbot.[23]

This *modus operandi* came at a cost, however. In the case of Trithemius, it earned him the criticism of his monks, many of whom saw the abbot's nightly studies and solitary writing retreats as vanity projects that drained the community's resources unduly. Not only did they complain that their abbot spent too much time in the privacy of his lodgings and was rarely seen around the monastery, sometimes leaving for weeks on end to visit libraries whilst neglecting his managerial duties, but they also felt increasingly alienated by the visitors flocking to Sponheim from near and far to marvel at his famous book collection.[24] What Herman of Tournai considered exemplary behaviour for an abbot, the monks of Sponheim viewed as gross misconduct and neglect. Trithemius later admitted to having taken great pleasure in showing his library to guests, many of whom had never been to Sponheim and stayed for months to read the books and have learned conversations with the bookish abbot-historian.[25] Whilst Trithemius himself was eager to indulge such requests, the community protested that his hospitality put strains on its finances and supplies, not least because he exempted his guests from all expenses and offered them food and accommodation for the duration of their stay.[26] He was accused of abusing the authority of his abbatial office to bankroll his bibliophilia by tapping into communal funds (*mensa fratrum*) to purchase ever more books for himself without so much as consulting the monks.

Similar criticism was levelled at Abbot Jerome of Pomposa (1079–1100) for gratuitously wasting the monastery's funds to buy books, with some suspecting that he was planning on 'buying' himself an episcopal seat and then make off with the books at the first opportunity ('[a]lii eum frustra in nugis bona monasterii dissipare, alii autem illum hoc ob id agere, ut aliquando cum totis libris fugiens aliquem acquireret episcopatum sibi, instanter asserebant').[27] Jerome appears to have considered the books he acquired with his abbey's resources his personal

---

[22] 'Vita sancti Odonis', ed. by Jacques-Paul Migne, in *Patrologia Latina CXXXIII* (Paris: Garnier Fratres, 1853), pp. 43–86 (p. 49); *St. Odo of Cluny: Being the Life of St. Odo of Cluny by John of Salerno and the Life of St. Gerald of Aurillac by St. Odo*, tr. by Gerard Sitwell (London: Sheen & Ward, 1958), p. 16; Edmund M. McCaffray, 'The Culture of Literate Power at Cluny, 910–1156 CE' (unpublished PhD dissertation, Arizona State University, 2015), pp. 190–317.

[23] Munich, Bayerische Staatsbibliothek, MS Clm. 6911, fol. 107v: 'Est aliquid vigiles cartis impendere noctes, continuare dies, pallere fameque sitique'; Steinmann, *Handschriften*, pp. 468–9 (p. 468) (= no. 543).

[24] Arnold, *Trithemius*, pp. 228–52; Brann, *Trithemius*, pp. 20–7.

[25] [Johannes Trithemius:] 'Chronicon Sponheimense', in *Johannes Trithemius: Opera historica*, ed. by Marquard Freher, 2 vols. (Frankfurt a. M.: Marne and Aubry, 1601; repr. Minerva, 1966), II, 236–435 (p. 396).

[26] *Chronicon*, ed. Freher, pp. 396–7.

[27] Modena, Biblioteca Estense Universitaria, MS Lat. 390 (a.H.4.6; *olim* VI.F.5), fols. 70r–v; *Handschriften*, pp. 228–31 (pp. 228–9) (= no. 281).

property that he could use as he pleased and even take with him should he opt to abandon the community. Whether or not the monks were right to suspect their abbot of harbouring such plans—as far as we know, Jerome never obtained a bishopric despite his influential contacts with Countess Matilda of Tuscany and other magnates[28]—they were certainly correct about the remarkable extent and frequency of Jerome's book acquisitions. According to a library inventory from 1093 (Modena, Biblioteca Estense Universitaria, MS Lat. 390 (a.H.4.6; *olim* VI. F.5), fols. 70r–76r), Pomposa's monks owed virtually all their books—fifty-eight volumes—to Jerome, including the earliest complete copy of Seneca's *Tragedies* attested in the Latin West.[29] Jerome's monks, like Trithemius's, were decidedly unappreciative of the means by which he had acquired this collection, however, and whilst there is no trace of Jerome's reaction to their accusations, we do know how Trithemius responded to his critics at Sponheim. According to Duraclusius's *Vita*, the abbot sought to appease his allegators by reassuring them that though he had spent in excess of 2,000 *fl.* on books, the money had never been taken from their coffers ('non de monasterii substantia'), which apparently were always empty to begin with ('quae semper valde fuit exilis'), but had been donated by external patrons and benefactors.[30] Duraclusius's recollection that he had witnessed these explanations being given frequently ('saepius') and from Trithemius's own mouth ('ab eius ore') suggests that the monks remained sceptical and demanded regular spending reviews from their abbot. But was it the amassing of books and study resources in itself to which they objected, the spiralling costs associated with their acquisition, or the fact that their abbot treated them as his personal property, rather than communal goods?

Hints can be found in Trithemius's *De laude scriptorium*, a dialogue between the author and those who reproach book lovers for having too many volumes ('qui amatores librorum de multitudine velut nimietate reprehendunt').[31] We do not know the extent to which the text's wording was informed by Trithemius's arguments with his monks, but they may well have enquired why he chose to bury himself under more books than he could ever

---

[28] Countess Matilda wrote a letter in Abbot Jerome's support in 1106 to help settle a dispute between him and his diocesan bishop, Dodo of Modena; edited in *Die Urkunden und Briefe der Markgräfin Mathilde von Tuszien*, ed. by Elke Goez and Werner Goez (Hanover: Hahn, 1998), pp. 266–9 (= no. 97); also available online with an English translation, https://epistolae.ctl.columbia.edu/letter/1275.html.

[29] Gottlieb, *Bibliotheken*, pp. 223–4 (= no. 625); Tyler, *England*, p. 183; Peter L. Schmidt, 'Rezeption und Überlieferung der Tragödien Senecas bis zum Ausgang des Mittelalters', in *Traditio Latinitatis: Studien zur Rezeption und Überlieferung der lateinischen Literatur*, ed. by Peter L. Schmidt and Joachim Fugmann (Stuttgart: Steiner, 2000), pp. 207–46 (p. 241).

[30] *Vita*, ed. Freher, p. 6. Arnold, 'Leben', p. 24 suspects that these reassurances may be disingenuous, and that Trithemius did in fact use communal funds to expand his library.

[31] *Scribes*, ed./tr. Arnold and Berendt, pp. 88–9; Arnold, 'Leben', pp. 27–8. The chapter bears the title 'Whether it is commendable to have many books in monasteries' ('An sit commendabile in cenobiis multos habere codices'), and it shows notable echoes of Seneca's *On the Tranquility of the Mind*; *Seneca: Philosophische Schriften: Latein–Deutsch*, ed./tr. by Manfred Rosenbach, 5 vols., 2nd ed. (Darmstadt: Wissenschaftliche Buchgesellschaft, 2010), II, 138–40.

hope to read ('[q]uid vos tanta librorum multitudine obruitis, cum eos legere omnes non possistis quos habetis?'). The abbot's response was simple: it cannot be wrong to amass books since the venerated Fathers—Trithemius names Origen, Augustine, and Jerome—wrote and collected more volumes than could be counted, and what is good for one cannot be bad for another ('[n]am si illis bonum fuit, nec istis malum erit'). Having many good books in a monastery must therefore be good ('[b]onum est [...] et multos et bonos in coenobio habere codices'), even if nobody could read them all ('etiam si omnes legere non sufficiant').[32] If these were indeed Trithemius's words, they must have fallen on deaf ears. Centurianus reports that the relationship between the monks and their abbot had been damaged beyond repair, leaving Trithemius with no choice but to resign from office in 1506.[33] To add insult to injury, his successor began selling off his books to recoup at least some of the money he had spent on them.[34]

The move to Würzburg appears to have improved matters for Trithemius, at least initially, providing him with a sense of optimism that stands in contrast to the frustration and bitter resentment with which he looked back on his Sponheim years. In an acrimonious letter addressed to the monks of Sponheim and sent within weeks of his arrival at Würzburg, Trithemius recapitulates that nobody had been less appreciative of his writings than them ('nemini umquam lucubrationes nostrae minus placuerunt quam filiis nostris'), and that his studies had always greatly displeased them ('sacra vobis semper displicuere studia nostra').[35] Elsewhere Trithemius refers to them as 'know-nothings' ('ignorati') so ignorant that they required a ploughman ('arator') and not a preacher ('orator'), a keeper of pigs ('curator porcorum') rather than minds ('curator animorum').[36] Abandoning this pigsty, Trithemius reports to have felt the relief of spewing out ('evomere') a disease.[37] At the same time, this transfer brought some new challenges. Fairly modest in size and status, Würzburg placed relatively few managerial demands on its superiors, but by the same token it carried little prestige and resources, two things that—as we saw—mattered a great deal to Trithemius and were instrumental to his historiographical pursuits. On the one hand, the new appointment offered more time for writing, which is why in a letter to Tholey's abbot Trithemius could cheerfully refer to his new home as 'a haven of great calm and tranquillity' ('portus magne quietis et tranquillitatis [...] am[o]enus et

---

[32] *Scribes*, ed./tr. Arnold and Berendt, pp. 90–1.   [33] 'Letter 18 April 1507', ed. Freher, p. 528.
[34] *Vita*, ed. Freher, p. 6; Eifler, *Bibliothek*, I, 183.
[35] [Johannes Trithemius:], 'Letter to the prior and community of Sponheim, 31 October 1506 (= Epistola II)', in *Johannes Trithemius: Opera historica*, ed. by Marquard Freher, 2 vols. (Frankfurt a. M.: Marne and Aubry, 1601; repr. Minerva, 1966), II, 507–12 (pp. 508–9).
[36] [Johannes Trithemius:] 'De lectione et studio divinarum scripturarum (= Homilia IV)', in *Opera pia et spiritualia*, ed. by Johannes Busaeus (Mainz: Johannes Albinus, 1604), pp. 422–7 (p. 426).
[37] 'Letter 31 Oct. 1506', ed. Freher, p. 511.

quietissimus').[38] On the other hand, he was soon reminded of just how difficult it was to write history with little more than a basic book collection.

When first arriving at Sponheim in 1482, Trithemius had found only a few dozen volumes in the abbey's *armarium*.[39] After his election as abbot, he made it his priority to remedy this 'poverty of books' ('paucitas librorum') by assembling a library of over 2,000 volumes that was deemed second to none in Germany ('hodie in tota Germania nulla bibliotheca nostra similis esse dicatur').[40] Trithemius later referred to these books as his own ('libri mei'), and when forced to leave them behind upon his resignation he protested that he could not live without them ('sine quibus [...] vivere non potui').[41] Arriving at Würzburg in 1506 with no more than a handful of volumes, he had no choice but to rebuild his beloved library from scratch, and though he never quite managed to replicate the extensive collection amassed at Sponheim, his renewed efforts were recorded—not without a sense of admiration—in an inventory of his abbatial estate made shortly after his death in 1517, crediting him with the acquisition of nearly four hundred volumes

---

[38] The letter (dated 16 November 1507) has been edited by Johann C. Lager, 'Ein Brief des Abtes Trithemius an Gerhard von Hassel, Abt von Tholey (1489-1517)', *Trierisches Archiv* 17/18 (1911), 189-91 (p. 190).

[39] *Chronicon*, ed. Freher, II, 395, which speaks of 'vix XLVIII volumina, imputatis omnibus, tempore ordinationis suae in hoc monasterio reperta sunt, parvae aestimationis, et minoris utilitatis ad veram eruditionem'. In one of his homilies, written c.1486, he recalls merely fourteen volumes; [Johannes Trithemius:], 'De labore monachorum manuali (= Homilia VII)', in *Opera pia et spiritualia*, ed. by Johannes Busaeus (Mainz: Johannes Albinus, 1604), pp. 434-8 (p. 436); Arnold, *Trithemius*, pp. 56-62.

[40] *Chronicon*, ed. Freher, II, 396. For a contemporary witness, see Susann El Kholi, 'Ein Besuch bei Johannes Trithemius: Der Brief des Matthäus Herbenus an Jodokus Beissel vom 14. August 1495', *Archiv für mittelrheinische Kirchengeschichte* 56 (2004), 143-57. The comparison with the library of Saint-Victor occurs in a letter from Trithemius to Cornelius Aurelius composed in 1499 and edited in Philip C. Molhuysen, 'Cornelius Aurelius', *Nederlands archief voor kerkgeschiedenis* 2 (1902), 1-35 (pp. 28-30 = no. III). In 1502, Trithemius counted 1,646 volumes in Sponheim's library (ibid., p. 416), though in his autobiography (*Nepachius*, written 1505) this number increased further to 'circiter duo milia volumina tam scripta, quam impressa'; [Johannes Trithemius:] 'Nepachius', in *Corpus historicum Medii Aevi*, ed. by Johann G. von Eckhart, 2 vols. (Leipzig: Gleditsch, 1723), II 1825-44 (p. 1828). Similar numbers appear in two of Trithemius's letters, dated 13 August 1505 and 31 October 1506, respectively; [Johannes Trithemius:] 'Letter to Johannes Nutius, 13 October 1505 (= Epistola XXXII)'; 'Letter to Prior Johannes Bracht of St Matthew's in Trier, 31 October 1506 (= Epistola III)', in *Johannes Trithemius: Opera historica*, ed. by Marquard Freher, 2 vols. (Frankfurt a. M.: Marne and Aubry, 1601; repr. Minerva, 1966), II, 469-70 and 512-14. On Trithemius's expansion of Sponheim's library, cf. Paul Lehmann, 'Nachrichten von der Sponheimer Bibliothek des Abtes Johannes Trithemius', in *Festgabe zum 7. September 1910: Hermann Grauert zur Vollendung des 60. Lebensjahres gewidmet von seinen Schülern*, ed. by Max Jansen (Freiburg i. Br.: Herder, 1910), pp. 205-20; Michael Embach, 'Johannes Trithemius OSB (1462-1516) und die Bibliothek von Kloster Sponheim–mit einem Blick auf die Vita Juttas von Sponheim (1092-1136)', in *Zur Erforschung mittelalterlicher Bibliotheken: Chancen-Entwicklungen-Perspektiven*, ed. by Andrea Rapp (Frankfurt a. M.: Klostermann, 2009), pp. 101-36, including a list of the extant manuscripts made and acquired during Trithemius's abbacy (ibid., pp. 131-3).

[41] [Johannes Trithemius:] 'Letter to Jakob Kimolanus, 16 August 1507', in *Johannes Trithemius: Opera historica*, ed. by Marquard Freher, 2 vols. (Frankfurt a. M.: Marne and Aubry, 1601; repr. Minerva, 1966), II, 556-7 (p. 556); also 'Letter 31 October 1506', ed. Freher, p. 513; cf. Embach, 'Trithemius', p. 124; Arnold, 'Leben', pp. 25 and 30.

in little over a decade.⁴² As shown below (4.3), Trithemius kept most of these books close at hand in his abbatial lodgings, the self-same lodgings that, as we saw in the dedication letters of the *Annales*, served as his personal workplace.

Despite the optimism expressed in Trithemius's letters, there is evidence to suggest that the working conditions at Würzburg were not always quite as idyllic as he would have his correspondents believe.⁴³ The letter that accompanied the *Annales*'s second volume in 1514 gives the impression that by then Trithemius had regressed into his old habit of carving out precious writing time in ways that affected both his wellbeing and his presence within the community. Setting aside time for writing without interruption ('sine intermissione'), he withdrew himself from the company of Würzburg's monks.⁴⁴ Taking his meals at the writing desk and reading long into the night, he pushed himself to the point of exhaustion and self-loathing ('usque ad taedium et abominationem'). Exerting himself more and more ('desudavi adeo constanter atque tenaciter'), the *Annales* grew into an all-consuming obsession that occupied him both day and night ('die ac nocte'), awake and asleep ('vigilans et dormiens'; 'noctem dormiens interruptam'), taking over his mind and body ('aut mente aut corpore Hirsuagianis occupatus fui annalibus').⁴⁵ It is tempting to link these statements to a contemporary entry in Würzburg's account book ('Registrum receptorum et expositorum'; Würzburg, Universitätsbibliothek, MS ch. f. 340). Written in Trithemius's hand, the entry in question (fol. 12v) records expenses filed by the prior whilst the abbot himself visited the thermal baths near Hirsau ('me [Trithemius] absente in termis et Hirsaugia') in early 1515. Even if delivery of the *Annales* to their abbatial patron was the primary motivation for travelling to Hirsau on this occasion, might this little 'spa visit' have been intended as a recovery break for the weary abbot-historian before he embarked on his next two writing projects, the *Lives* of Bishop Maximus of Mainz and Rabanus Maurus?⁴⁶

Whilst the last point must remain conjecture, we can use this case study to draw out the parameters for our broader investigation of abbatial workplaces. As abbot of Sponheim and Würzburg, Trithemius routinely—and perhaps

---

⁴² Ivo Fischer, 'Der Nachlaß des Abtes Johannes Trithemius von St. Jakob in Würzburg', *Archiv des historischen Vereins für Unterfranken und Aschaffenburg* 67 (1928), 41–82; with revised numbers in Klaus Arnold, 'Das Nachlaßverzeichnis des Johannes Trithemius, Abt des Klosters St. Jakob in Würzburg, aus dem Jahr 1517', in *Johannes Trithemius (1462-1516): Abt und Büchersammler, Humanist und Geschichtsschreiber*, ed. by Klaus Arnold and Franz Fuchs (Würzburg: Königshausen & Neumann, 2019), pp. 279–339. When the community was dissolved in 1803, it had *c.*8,000 volumes; Otto Handwerker, 'Dreihundert Jahre Würzburger Universitätsbibliothek, 1619-1919', in *Aus der Vergangenheit der Universität Würzburg*, ed. by Max Buchner (Berlin: Springer, 1932), pp. 102–33 (p. 111).

⁴³ The statements in these letters have often been taken too literally in scholarship; see, for example, Brann, *Trithemius*, pp. 81–5.

⁴⁴ *Annales*, ed. Freher, II, 5.   ⁴⁵ *Annales*, ed. Freher, II, 5.

⁴⁶ On these texts and Trithemius's, see Arnold, *Trithemius*, pp. 157–61; also cf. ibid., p. 223 on the context of the visit to Hirsau in January 1515 and the abbot's physical ailments.

exclusively—wrote and studied outside the community's shared spaces in the privacy of his own quarters. This was a choice, not a necessity, considering that a writing workshop/scriptorium had been built under Abbot Bernhelm (1124–51) and continued to operate, with some ebb and flow, until the end of the Middle Ages.[47] Contemporary accounts by Trithemius and others suggest that his abbatial lodgings were equipped with facilities for writing, reading, and book storage, and that they were quiet enough to allow focused work at day and night without disturbance. And there seems to have been a distinction, formal or informal, between the abbot's books and those belonging to the community, which might reflect, to some degree, the separation between *mensa fratrum* and *mensa abbatis*. How common (or not) was this, though, and is there evidence that monastic superiors elsewhere had similar facilities at their disposal?

4.2 Abbatial Workplaces

The fact that Trithemius had access to abbatial lodgings at Sponheim and Würzburg (4.1) conforms to wider trends that, over the course of the centuries, had made it customary for medieval superiors—male and female—to reside away from their communities in a private area of the monastic complex. An abbatial residence could be in the cloister, usually in the western range, in a detached building, and even on an independent estate.[48] In the case of Sponheim, we are relatively well informed about the location of the private lodgings that doubled as Trithemius's abbatial workplace. In 1478, his predecessor, Johann Kolenhausen (1469/70–83), had taken up residence in the community's old guest house from the early fourteenth century.[49] Located above the south gate, these lodgings were noisy, so the gate was bricked up and a new one built on the eastern end of the

---

[47] Embach, 'Trithemius', pp. 104–13. The longevity of Sponheim's scriptorium is unusual. As Rodney Thomson reminds us, we cannot assume that monastic scriptoria were ubiquitous or permanent facilities that once established would operate continuously, and '[t]he general rule seems to be that they lasted long enough to provide the basic stock for the library of the community. One or two generations of scribes might be sufficient to achieve this'; Rodney M. Thomson, 'Scribes and Scriptoria', in *The European Book in the Twelfth Century*, ed. by Erik Kwakkel and Rodney M. Thomson (Cambridge: Cambridge University Press, 2018), p. 79.

[48] Matthias Untermann, *Handbuch der mittelalterlichen Architektur* (Darmstadt: Wissenschaftliche Buchgesellschaft, 2009), pp. 135–7 and 138–9; Werner Jacobsen, 'Die Klosterresidenz im frühen und hohen Mittelalter', in *Wohn- und Wirtschaftsbauten frühmittelalterlicher Klöster*, ed. by Hans R. Sennhauser (Zurich: Hochschulverlag, 1996), pp. 59–68. For England, see Heale, *Abbots*, pp. 155–67; Michael Thompson, *Cloister, Abbot and Precinct in Medieval Monasteries* (Stroud: Tempus, 2001), pp. 65–78, including two useful appendices that show the situation of the abbot's residence in medieval English monasteries (ibid., pp. 133–5) and locations of rural abbatial houses (ibid., 137–8), respectively; Harold Brakspear, 'The Abbot's House at Battle', *Archaeologia* 83 (1933), 139–66. On abbesses' lodgings, see Diana K. Coldicott, *Hampshire Nunneries* (Chichester: Phillimore, 1989); Lehfeldt, 'Authority', p. 116.

[49] The opposite development can be observed at Cerne Abbey, where the fifteenth-century Abbot John Vanne (1458–70) converted the abbatial quarters into a large guest house, at the same time as

abbey.⁵⁰ When he succeeded Kolenhausen in 1483, Trithemius found the abbot's lodgings agreeably quiet, but small and sparsely furnished.⁵¹ Making do for just over a decade, he built a new abbatial residence ('domus abbatia') in 1494 that had a heated parlour ('stuba'), a chapel ('capella'), and two private chambers ('duae camerae pro abbate').⁵² Whereas the old lodgings had been spartan and good for little more than resting, the new house's interior was highly ornate with wall paintings and inscriptions in Latin, Greek, and Hebrew.⁵³ In stark contrast to Kolenhausen's apartment, where nothing could be locked away and there was no deskspace for writing, Trithemius's house had lockable doors, desks ('mensae'), and chests ('cistae') for storing books and other personal items.⁵⁴ Nothing survives of these furnishings, but written descriptions indicate a study chamber similar to those of some of the Humanist scholars who were Trithemius's personal acquaintances and visitors.⁵⁵ It has even been suggested that one such illustrious visitor, Nuremberg-born engraver and printmaker Albrecht Dürer (†1528), might have modelled two of his world-famous master prints on the interior of Trithemius's abbatial residence at Würzburg.⁵⁶

Whilst some abbatial residences were moderately furnished and pragmatic in design, others were more elaborate, and some were so ostentatious as to rival, unapologetically, the great episcopal and princely palaces of their day. For example, an anonymous continuation of the *Gesta abbatum Trudonensium* spanning the years 1138–83 reports that Abbot Wiric of Saint Trond (1155–80) built

building a new residence for himself and his successors; *An Inventory of the Historical Monuments in Dorset*, Vol. I: *West* (London: Her Majesty's Stationery Office: 1952), pp. 74–85. Also cf. the case of Kirkstall Abbey in Leeds discussed by Thompson, *Cloister*, p. 86.

⁵⁰ Wilhelm Schneegans, *Abt Johannes Trithemius und Kloster Sponheim* (Kreuznach: Schmithals, 1882), pp. 87–8.

⁵¹ *Chronicon*, ed. Freher, II, 405: 'Eo namque die, quo Trithemius abbatiam intravit, praeter libam unam, byretum et stratum cum necessariis suis, nihil fuit in domo abbatiali repertum'.

⁵² *Chronicon*, ed. Freher, II, 405.

⁵³ See Renate Neumüllers-Klauser, 'Quellen zur Bau- und Kunstgeschichte von Hirsau', in *Hirsau St. Peter und Paul 1091-1991*, ed. by Klaus Schreiner, 2 vols. (Stuttgart: Theiss, 1991), I, 475–99 (p. 492).

⁵⁴ *Chronicon*, ed. Freher, II, 405.

⁵⁵ Michael Embach, 'Anhänger und Nachfolger des Abtes Johannes Trithemius (1462–1516)', in *Johannes Trithemius (1462-1516): Abt und Büchersammler, Humanist und Geschichtsschreiber*, ed. by Klaus Arnold and Franz Fuchs (Würzburg: Königshausen and Neumann, 2019), pp. 201–20; Arnold, 'Nachlaßverzeichnis', pp. 332–5; Arnold, *Trithemius*, pp. 201–2. Trithemius gives the names and occupations of many of his acquaintances in his authorial works; for example, *Chronicon*, ed. Freher, II, 395–6.

⁵⁶ The depiction of St Jerome behind a writing desk, pen in hand, surrounded by books and other study resources in Dürer's *St Jerome in His Study* (1514) incorporates elements from Dürer's own study in his Nuremberg house and Trithemius's workspace at Würzburg; see Franz F. Leitschuh, 'Trithemius und Dürer' [= *Quellen und Studien zur Geschichte des Kunst- und Geisteslebens in Franken I*], *Archiv des historischen Vereins von Unterfranken und Aschaffenburg* 44 (1902), 185–95, who sees Trithemius as the direct inspiration for Dürer's *Jerome* and *Melancholia I*: 'Die Gestalt des Trithemius [...] war es aber ohne Zweifel, die Dürer zu seinen Kupferstichen die Melancholie und Hieronymus anregte' (ibid., p. 193). Dürer's study later provided the model for the abbot's chamber ('Abtsstube') in Thomas Mann's novel *Doktor Faustus* (1947); Johannes Elema, 'Thomas Mann, Dürer und Doktor Faustus', *Euphorion* 59 (1965), pp. 97–117; repr. in *Thomas Mann*, ed. by Helmut Koopmann (Darmstadt: Wissenschaftliche Buchgesellschaft, 1975), pp. 320–50 (pp. 321–2).

himself a monastic palace so magnificent that it outshone all other palaces in the land.[57] And when former Frankish Queen Radegund retired from the world in 558 in her own monastic foundation of Holy Cross at Poitiers, she continued her career as 'quasi-abbess'—having appointed her foster daughter Agnes in her place—by occupying several private rooms inside the monastery that were suitably luxurious and exclusive to receive high-status guests and political relations on a regular basis.[58] The terms used by medieval writers to define abbatial residences range from 'domus abbatis' ('abbot's house') and 'aula abbatis' ('abbot's hall/ palace') to 'mansio abbatis' ('abbot's lodgings'), 'camera abbatis' ('abbot's chamber'), 'stuba abbatis' ('abbot's parlour'), and other cognate terms designating reserved spaces within larger buildings as well as entire architectural units.[59] Traditionally associated with the later Middle Ages, such abbatial spaces—both male and female—are recorded regularly from about the middle of the twelfth century.[60] Their establishment is usually linked with two socio-political and

---

[57] 'Gesta abbatum Trudonensium, continuatio secunda', ed. by Rudolf Köpke, in *Annales et cronica aevi Salici: Vitae aevi Carolini et Saxonici* [= *MGH SS* X], ed. by Georg H. Pertz (Hanover: Hahn, 1852), pp. 333–61 (p. 353): 'Tantum ei decoris contulit studium industrii artificis, ut omnibus in terra nostra, licet operosa varietate splendissimis, emineat palatiis'; Tombeur's more recent edition of the *Gesta abbatum Trudonensium* does not include this second continuation.

[58] Melville, *Monasticism*, pp. 16–17. Abbesses' lodgings were used regularly to entertain guests and offer hospitality to important visitors; Lehfeldt, 'Authority', p. 116. On Radegund's life and career, see now Erin T. Dailey, *Radegund: The Trials and Triumphs of a Merovingian Queen* (Oxford: Oxford University Press, 2023).

[59] Examples of 'domus/aula(e) abbatis' include St Gall (ninth century), Ramsey (c.1114–33), Mossaic (twelfth century), Gloucester (1301), Fleury (1316), and Lièges (c.1372–93); *Cartularium monasterii de Rameseia*, ed. by William H. Hart and Ponsonby A. Lyons, 3 vols. (London: Longman, 1884–93), I, 130; *Historia et Cartularium monasterii sancti Petri Gloucestriae*, ed. by William H. Hart, 2 vols. (Cambridge: Cambridge University Press: 1863–5), I, lxxxvii; *Glossarium*, ed. du Cange, IV, 314. The specific and exclusive purpose of these and similar abbots' houses speaks against the assertion made by Thompson, *Cloister*, p. 78, according to whom '[s]trictly speaking there is no such thing as a type of dwelling that is specially that of an abbot'. Nearly as frequent are references to 'camera(e) abbatis' such as at thirteenth-century Peterborough; twelfth-century Ramsey and St Albans; and eleventh-century Westminster and Evesham; *Cartularium*. Hart and Lyons, II, 197–8; Joseph A. Robinson, *The Abbot's House at Westminster* (Cambridge: Cambridge University Press, 1911), pp. 1–8 and 73–4; Richard D. Gem and William T. Ball, 'The Romanesque Rebuilding of Westminster Abbey', *Anglo-Norman Studies* 3 (1981), 33–60 and 203–7 (p. 59); Christopher N. Brooke, 'Adrian IV and John of Salisbury', in *Adrian IV: The English Pope (1154–1159)*, ed. by Brenda Bolton and Anne Duggan (London: Routledge, 2003), pp. 3–13 (p. 6). Examples of 'stuba(e) abbatis' include fourteenth-century Benediktbeuern and St Emmeram (1474), and the Cistercian Abbey of Heilsbronn; Otto Meyer, 'Überlieferung und Verbreitung des Dekrets des Bischofs Burchard von Worms', *Zeitschrift der Savigny-Stiftung für Rechtsgeschichte, Kanonistische Abteilung* 24 (1935), 141–83 (p. 165); Georg Muck, *Geschichte von Kloster Heilsbronn: Von der Urzeit bis zur Neuzeit*, 3 vols. (Nördlingen: Beck, 1879–80), II, 460; Caspar A. Schweitzer, 'Das Copialbuch der Cistercienzer-Abtei Langheim in vollständigen Auszügen der Urkunden von 1142–1500: Schluss, 1452–1504', *Bericht über das Wirken des Historischen Vereines zu Bamberg* 26 (1863), 1–47 (p. 26). Further Cistercian examples are Cleeve, Croxden, Eberbach, Kaisheim, Kappel, Meaux, Melk, Rein, Salem, Stams, and Zwettl.

[60] See Julie Kerr, *Monastic Hospitality: The Benedictines in England, c.1070–c.1250* (Woodbridge: Boydell, 2007), pp. 50–93; Heale, *Abbots*, p. 155 concludes that '[b]y the end of the twelfth century [...], the heads of the greater Benedictine abbeys had taken residence apart from their community', and 'by the later Middle Ages even the superior of a modest dependent priory could expect to have his own private quarters'. Examples of spaces inhabited by abbesses are given by Power, *Nunneries*, pp. 59–60 n. 2, who likewise concludes that 'the superior [of a female community] nearly always had a separate room, or suite of rooms [...], especially if she were the head of one of the great abbeys' (ibid.).

economic developments: on the one hand, the involvement of abbots in secular hierarchies of lordship, specifically the *servitium regis*, which resulted in a growing number and frequency of visitors who needed catering, entertainment, and accommodation in a separate space lest they disturb the monks; on the other hand, the emancipation of a form of abbatial lordship in its own right with an increasingly formalized separation between the resources and revenues for the abbot, the 'abbot's table' or *mensa abbatis*, and those for the community, the 'monks' table' or *mensa fratrum* (also known as *mensa monachorum/conventualis/communis*).[61] Though there are robust reasons for these common associations, their chronology is not always as clear and straightforward as traditionally assumed, and several developments typically linked with the separation of abbatial spaces had their origins before the twelfth century. It is now widely acknowledged, for example, that the integration of monasteries into secular spheres of influence and the resulting need—and socio-political pressure—to accommodate visitors demanded structural adjustments from at least the Carolingian period, which is when the earliest concrete traces of abbatial residences begin to appear in the written, visual, and archaeological sources.[62]

One of the most prominent examples of this is the *Plan of St Gall* (St Gall, Stiftsbibliothek, MS Cod. Sang. 1092), an idealized schematic drawing of a Carolingian monastery and its facilities produced at the time of Abbot Gozbert (816–37) that depicts a two-story palace ('aula') for the abbot. Accessible from the abbey church via a private corridor, this palace features—according to its Latin *tituli*—a heated 'mansio abbatis', two porticoes, a reception room, the abbot's bedroom with a chamber ('camera') above, a sun room ('solarium'), a kitchen with pantry, a bathroom and latrine, and rooms for servants.[63] These lodgings are separate from the abbey's main guest house, and the fact that they feature eight beds might indicate that the abbot could accommodate selected visitors inside his

---

[61] The precise chronology and pervasiveness of this separation have caused much scholarly debate; important contributions include, in chronological order, Émile Lesne, *L'origine des menses dans le temporel des eglises et des monasteres de France au IXe siecle* (Lille: Giard, 1910); Eric John, 'The Division of the Mensa in Early English Monasteries', *Journal of Ecclesiastical History* 6 (1955), 143–55; Margaret Howell, 'Abbatial Vacancies and the Divided *Mensa* in Medieval England', *Journal of Ecclesiastical History* 33 (1982), 173–92; Steffen Patzold, '*Mensa fratrum* und *consensus fratrum*: Überlegungen zu zwei parallelen Entwicklungen im fränkischen Mönchtum des 9. Jahrhunderts', in *Kloster und Wirtschaftswelt im Mittelalter*, ed. by Claudia Dobrinski, Brunhilde Gedderth, and Katrin Wipfler (Munich: Fink, 2007), pp. 25–38.

[62] Untermann, *Handbuch*, p. 135; Patzold, '*Mensa*', pp. 26–8.

[63] Walter Berschin, 'Der St. Galler Klosterplan als Literaturdenkmal', in *Studien zum St. Galler Klosterplan*, ed. by Johannes Duft, Peter Ochsenbein, and Karl Schmuki, 2 vols. (St Gall: Fehr/Historischer Verein des Kantons St, Gallen, 1962–2002), II, 107–50 (p. 119 = no. 10); Andrea zur Nieden, *Der Alltag der Mönche: Studien zum Klosterplan von St. Gallen* (Hamburg: Diplomatica, 2008), pp. 175–8; Alfons Zettler, 'Spaces for Servants and *provendarii* in Early Medieval Monasteries: The Example of the Virtual Monastery on the Plan of Saint Gall', *Bulletin du centre d'études médiévales d'Auxerre* 8 (2015), 1–17 (p. 8), http://journals.openedition.org/cem/13624.

own palace.⁶⁴ Indeed, the presence of a separate pantry for the abbot's kitchen has been cited as evidence that the separation between the *mensa abbatis* and the *mensa fratrum* was already underway at St Gall—and in the Frankish world more widely—by the middle of the ninth century.⁶⁵ Though we must be cautious with such assertions given that the *Plan* reflects aspirations more than realities, we do know that an abbatial residence existed at St Gall from at least the time of Abbot Grimald (841–72).⁶⁶ According to Ratpert's history of the monastery's origins and its changing fortunes composed c.880–900 and known as the *Casus sancti Galli*, Grimald had appointed his deputy ('proabbas'), Hartmut, to build him a residence ('domicilium') that, as Grimald insisted, had to be very useful ('utilissime') as well as very handsome ('pulcherrime'), with everything needed ('cum omnibus necessariis') to go about his abbatial business.⁶⁷ To what extent this bespoke residence resembled that on the *Plan* is impossible to know, but it is not implausible that it followed a similar design.

Grimald of St Gall was not the only early medieval abbot to reside in a building designed according to his particular demands and specifications. About a generation earlier, a similar building project had been launched by Abbot Eigil of Fulda, whom we already met above (2.6),⁶⁸ and by the end of the millennium abbatial residences existed at Lorsch, Reichenau, Corbie, and elsewhere.⁶⁹ As we move forward in time, the evidence for abbots' residences in the written and archaeological documentation increases exponentially, both quantitatively and qualitatively. Prominent examples from the high Middle Ages are Evesham, where a 'camera abbatis' existed since the abbacy of Robert (after 1104–before 1130),⁷⁰ Bardney, Battle, Bosau, Chester, Cluny, Corvey, Glastonbury, Gloucester, Peterborough, Pomposa, Ramsey, St Albans, Trier, Waltham (Holy Cross), Werden, and Westminster, to name but a few well-attested cases.⁷¹ Amongst the

---

⁶⁴ Jacobsen, 'Klosterresidenz', p. 60; also cf. Lynda L. Coon, *Dark Age Bodies: Gender and Monastic Practice in the Early Medieval West* (Philadelphia, PA: University of Pennsylvania Press, 2011), p. 185, referring to the abbot's palace of St Gall as a 'hybrid space'.
⁶⁵ Untermann, *Handbuch*, p. 135; Dieter Hägermann, 'Der Abt als Grundherr: Kloster und Wirtschaft im frühen Mittelalter', in *Herrschaft und Kirche: Beiträge zur Entstehung und Wirkungsweise episkopaler und monastischer Organisationsformen*, ed. by Friedrich Prinz (Stuttgart: Hiersemann, 1988), pp. 345–85 (pp. 375–82); Patzold, '*Mensa*', pp. 28 and 38. The need for a separate kitchen for the abbot and his guests is stated in *RB*, ed./tr. Venarde, pp. 172–5.
⁶⁶ Cf. the discussion in Thompson, *Cloister*, pp. 65–6.
⁶⁷ *Klostergeschichten*, ed./tr. Steiner, pp. 194–5; also cf. zur Nieden, *Alltag*, pp. 202–3; Alfons Zettler, 'Überlegungen zu den karolingerzeitlichen Herrscherbesuchen in den Bodenseeklöstern', in *Pfalz–Kloster–Klosterpfalz: Historische und archäologische Fragen*, ed. by Hans R. Sennhauser (Zurich: Hochschulverlag, 2009), pp. 105–20 (pp. 108–10), with some important corrections to previous scholarship.
⁶⁸ *Vita*, ed. Becht-Jördens, p. 20.
⁶⁹ Zur Nieden, *Alltag*, p. 178 and the references provided there; also cf. Jacobsen, 'Klosterresidenz', pp. 60–1.
⁷⁰ *History*, ed./tr. Sayers and Watkiss, pp. 570–1; Anthony Emery, *Greater Medieval Houses of England and Wales, 1300–1500*, 3 vols. (Cambridge: Cambridge University Press, 1996–2006), III, 72 n. 10.
⁷¹ For further examples, see Untermann, *Handbuch*, p. 137; Brakspear, 'House', pp. 140–3.

Norman/Romanesque survivals of St Augustine's Abbey, Bristol (founded c.1140 by Robert FitzHarding) are a vaulted chapter house, a double-arched gate house, and, to the south-west of the cloister, a single archway that has been identified as part of the abbatial lodgings constructed under Bristol's first abbot, Richard of Warwick (1148–76/7), who had come to England from St Victor in Paris.[72] By the later medieval and early modern periods, abbatial residences had become so ubiquitous as to constitute a standard feature of monastic architecture across the Latin West.[73] The abbess's chamber at Amesbury recorded at the time of the community's dissolution under Henry VIII is said to have measured a generous 24 × 14 ft (~7.3 × 4.3 m), and there is a possibility, albeit one impossible to validate due to the buildings' subsequent destruction, that this chamber dated from *before* Amesbury's conversion into a priory under King Henry II in 1177.[74] At the very top of the scale is a list of expenses incurred by John of Wheathampstead, abbot of St Albans (London, British Library, MS Arundel 34; discussed in more detail below; 4.3) that records the construction of a 'noble chamber' ('camera nobilis') measuring a colossal ninety-five feet (~29 m) in length ('in longitudine iiii^{xx} xv pedes') for John and his successor to inhabit ahead of royal visits ('pro inhospitatione abbatis in adventu domini regis') at the princely cost of three hundred pounds taken from the communal funds ('ex parte conventus').[75] Whether the monks considered this investment into their abbot's suitably representative accommodation good value for money remains unknown.

The increasing largesse of abbatial residences fuelled the medieval imagination, and abbots' chambers—and especially abbesses' chambers—are popular tropes in works of literature and romance. Thus when Malory's Lancelot enters a nunnery at Pentecost, he is shown to the abbess's chamber to be stripped of his armour ('they ladde hym unto the abbas chambir and unarmed hym') only to find his cousins, Bors and Lionel, resting on the abbess's bed; the chamber is described as large enough comfortably to accommodate these three knights, the abbess, Sir Galahad, and twelve nuns eager to participate in the heavily gendered spectacle

---

[72] Nigel Baker et al., *Bristol: A Worshipful Town and Famous City: An Archaeological Assessment from Prehistory to 1900* (Oxford: Oxbow, 2018), p. 111; Roland W. Paul, 'The Plan of the Church and Monastery of St. Augustine, Bristol', *Archaeologia* 63 (1912), 213–50 (pp. 237 and 246–7). Except for the gate house, Bristol's twelfth-century abbatial lodgings were replaced with sixteenth-century buildings (cf. the ground plan in ibid., plate XXXIV).

[73] For England and Wales, the cases discussed in Emery, *Houses* give a good sense of how regular these buildings were in the later Middle Ages; also cf. Heale, *Abbots*, pp. 155–67.

[74] 'Houses of Benedictine Nuns: Abbey, Later Priory, of Amesbury', in *A History of the County of Wiltshire*, Vol. 3, ed. by Ralph B. Pugh and Elizabeth Crittall (London: Institute of Historical Research, 1956), pp. 242–59, http://www.british-history.ac.uk/vch/wilts/vol3/pp242-259.

[75] London, British Library, MS Arundel 34, fol. 68r; printed in *Gesta*, ed. Riley, II, 258 (= 'Appendix A'); Riley's transcription of the chamber's length ('xcv' instead of 'iiii^{xx} xv') is mistaken, however; also cf. *English Benedictine Libraries: The Shorter Catalogues*, ed. by Richard Sharpe et al. [= *CBMLC* IV] (London: British Library, 1996), pp. 563–4 (= B88).

('there com in twelve nunnes that brought with hem Galahad').[76] Whilst the sexual hints in Malory's *Morte Darthur* are mostly implicit, they are less subtle elsewhere. In Boccaccio's *Decameron*, we meet one Madonna Usimbalda, a Lombard abbess known for her strictness who falls in her own trap when attempting to convict a nun called Isabetta of illicit sexual relations.[77] Having caught Isabetta and her lover in the act, the other nuns fetch Usimbalda from her abbatial chamber so she can inspect the scene of the crime with her own eyes. Unbeknownst to them, however, Usimbalda has also smuggled a secret lover—a priest, no less—into her abbatial chamber. Rising from her sleep and fearing the exposure of her sin, Usimbalda rushes to the door and in the darkness inadvertently grabs the priest's trousers instead of her veil. Having summoned the community in the chapter house to pronounce judgement over Isabetta, the abbess, still wearing the priest's breeches on her head, is found guilty of the same crime and afterwards 'returns to lie with her priest'.[78] Both Malory and Boccaccio present the abbess's chamber as a private space wherein sexual and other deviant actions can take place away from the eyes of the community. This trope of the sexually insatiable abbess is also found in the Old French fabliau *L'abbesse qui fu grosse*, where the abbess's chamber doubles as a secret maternity ward, as well as in the Middle High German *Der turnei von dem zers*, where a detached penis runs riot in a nunnery with the abbess desperately trying to claim it for herself.[79]

Needless to say, the historical reality usually reveals itself rather less scandalous than the authors of literary texts would have us believe, though there are records of if not outright scandals then at least dubious practices conducted inside the privacy of abbatial chambers. When Archbishop Eudes Rigaud (1248–75) of Rouen undertook a survey of the monastic communities—male and female—within Normandy's metropolitan province, he reported numerous examples of such devious behaviour in his extant register (Paris, Bibliothèque nationale de France, MS Lat. 1245). At Villarceaux, a dependent priory of Saint-Cyr, the episcopal visitation on 9 July 1249 revealed not only that many of its twenty-three nuns, including the cellaress and the subprioress, had regular sexual relations with men, which repeatedly resulted in pregnancy, but also that the prioress was drunk virtually every night ('priorissa ebria est fere qualibet nocte') and, in her

---

[76] *Sir Thomas Malory: Le Morte Darthur*, ed. by Peter J. C. Field, 2 vols. (Cambridge: D. S. Brewer, 2013), I, 665–7, from London, British Library, MS Add. 59678, fols. 349r–v.

[77] *Giovanni Boccaccio: Decameron*, ed. by Vittore Branca, 9th ed. (Milan: Mondadori, 2008), pp. 752–5; translated as *Giovanni Boccaccio: Decameron*, tr. by Mark Musa and Peter Bondanella (New York, NY: Norton, 1983), pp. 563–6; my own translation is adapted from https://www.brown.edu/Departments/Italian_Studies/dweb/.

[78] *Decameron*, ed. Branca, p. 755; tr. Musa and Bondanella, p. 566.

[79] Katherine A. Brown, 'Boccaccio Reading Old French: Decameron IX. 2 and La Nonete', *Modern Language Notes* 125 (2010), 54–71; 'Der turnei von dem zers/Das Nonnenturnier', in *Novellistik des Mittelalters: Märendichtung*, ed./tr. by Klaus Grubmüller (Frankfurt a. M.: Deutscher Klassiker Verlag, 1996), pp. 944–77.

hangover, did not get up for Matins ('[p]riorissa nec surgit ad matutinas').[80] When Eudes returned to check up on Villarceaux's wayward superior on 12 September 1253, and then again in November 1254, July 1257, November 1258, June 1261, and May 1264, he found to his dismay that she still regularly overslept for Matins ('nec surgit ad matutinas sepe'), presumably as a result of inebriation.[81] Only upon Eudes's next visit in January 1265 does the register report some improvement, but all was undone again by 1268, when the archbishop made his final trips to Villarceaux.[82] Eudes's *Registrum* contains no shortage of examples of misbehaving monastic superiors, and whilst his reports might well have been tinged by prejudice and reform agendas, particularly towards female religious, it would be a mistake to dismiss them as entirely fictitious.[83]

Eudes and his visitations apart, some of the most intriguing cases of abbatial misconduct recorded in non-literary sources concern the two English nunneries of Romsey and Barking. At Romsey, Abbess Gundela (or Joyce) Rowse (1502–23) stood accused by her diocesan bishop of summoning the nuns and sacristan to her private quarters on most nights after Compline to make them indulge in heavy drinking, an accusation that resulted in a new regulation according to which the doors of the abbess's chamber had to be bolted shut every evening and remain locked until morning.[84] An almost identical accusation that likewise resulted in 'house arrest' had been made two centuries earlier against the then abbesses of Romsey and Barking by their episcopal visitor, John Peckham, archbishop of Canterbury (1279–92), who further chastized a thirteenth-century abbess of Wherwell for recurrently ordering overindulgent suppers to be prepared in her abbatial quarters whilst enforcing austerity on her nuns by rationing food and drink in the communal refectory.[85] And at Nun Monkton, those invited into the abbess's private chamber and leaving in a state of inebriation reportedly included members of the local clergy.[86] Romsey belonged to what David Bell calls the

---

[80] Edited in *Regestrum visitationum archiepiscopi Rothomagensis: Journal des visites pastorales d'Eude Rigaud, archevêque de Rouen, MCCXLVIII–MCCLXIX*, ed. by Théodose Bonnin (Rouen: Le Brument, 1852), pp. 43–4; translated as *The Register of Eudes of Rouen*, tr. by Sydney M. Brown and Jeremiah F. O'Sullivan (New York, NY: Columbia University Press, 1964), pp. 48–50. On Eudes and his reforms, see Adam J. Davis, *The Holy Bureaucrat: Eudes Rigaud and Religious Reform in Thirteenth-Century Normandy* (Ithaca, NY: Cornell University Press, 2006).

[81] *Regestrum*, ed. Bonnin, pp. 166–7, 194, 281–2, 323, 402, and 490; tr. Brown and O'Sullivan, pp. 182, 209, 317, 368–9, 458, and 558–9.

[82] *Regestrum*, ed. Bonnin, pp. 534, 572, and 602; tr. Brown and O'Sullivan, pp. 608–9, 658, and 692–3.

[83] Eva Schlotheuber, 'Der Erzbischof Eudes Rigaud, die Nonnen und das Ringen um die Klosterreform im 13. Jahrhundert', in *Institution und Charisma: Festschrift für Gert Melville*, ed. by Franz J. Felten at al. (Cologne: Böhlau, 2009), pp. 99–110.

[84] See *Female Monastic Life in Early Tudor England: With an Edition of Richard Fox's Translation of the Benedictine Rule for Women 1517*, ed. by Barry Collett (London: Routledge, 2002), p. 36; also cf. Charles Spence, *The Abbey Church of Romsey in Hampshire*, 5th ed. (Romsey: Jordan, 1886) p. 80; Mackenzie Walcott, 'Romsey Abbey', *Gentleman's Magazine and Historical Review* 14 (1863), 198–200 (p. 199).

[85] Power, *Nunneries*, pp. 60–2, with the relevant references.

[86] See Valerie G. Spear, *Leadership in Medieval English Nunneries* (Woodbridge: Boydell, 2005), pp. 129–30.

'second tier' of medieval English nunneries with an annual income between £250–499, placing it alongside houses like Dartford, Elstow, and Godstow. Barking was wealthier still, being counted amongst Bell's 'top five' nunneries in England with an income of more than £500 per annum.[87] It is no surprise, therefore, that the later medieval abbesses of both these houses resided in relatively large lodgings and had considerable resources at their disposal. Barking's abbesses had their own quarters with a private kitchen from at least the fourteenth century, probably located in a building separate from the abbey complex.[88] This included a private chamber that under Abbess Katherine de Sutton (1358–76) became the performance space for a curious ritual: a bell dedicated to the community's seventh-century founder, St Erkenwald, was rung ceremoniously before being taken into the abbess's chamber, where it was filled to the rim with wine and passed around until it was drunk dry.[89] Examples like these should not be taken to suggest that the lodgings of abbesses were (ab)used regularly as venues of debauchery, or at least no more regularly than those of their male peers. What they do show, however, is that these spaces offered a kind of privacy that was exceptional and exclusive in the communal setting of a medieval monastery, one which could lead to suspicion, prejudice, and sometimes vivid imagination.

It is this sense of privacy that also explains why abbatial residences were used with some frequency for writing and study, especially during the later Middle Ages. When Gunther of Nordhausen claimed to have written in his cell ('cella mea'), for example, he was in fact referring to a spacious apartment next to the monks' dormitory that was available to Erfurt's abbots in addition to an abbatial manor located off-site.[90] At Kappel, the infirmary built in c.1210 was turned into a spacious residence for Abbot Ulrich Trinkler (1492–1508),[91] and when Heinrich Bullinger arrived as the monks' new teacher in 1523, he found Tinkler's successor, Wolfgang Joner (1520–7 × 31), residing in an apartment so grand and well appointed that he felt compelled to describe it in detail. Though the building was old and constructed in archaic fashion ('vetusta et veterum more constructa'), Bullinger deemed it palatial ('amplia est et regia').[92] The abbot's lodgings filled the

---

[87] Bell, *Nuns*, pp. 10–11.

[88] See Anne M. Dutton, 'Women's Use of Religious Literature in Medieval England' (unpublished PhD dissertation, University of York, 1995), p. 228.

[89] Anne B. Yardley, 'Liturgy as the Site of Creative Engagement: Contributions of the Nuns of Barking', in *Barking Abbey and Medieval Literary Culture: Authorship and Authority in a Female Community*, ed. by Jennifer N. Brown and Donna A. Bussell (Woodbridge: Boydell, 2012), pp. 267–82 (p. 272).

[90] Frank, *Peterskloster*, pp. 135 and 387; Eifler, *Bibliothek*, I, 86.

[91] Hans R. Sennhauser, 'Das Kloster Kappel im Mittelalter: Bemerkungen zur Klosterkirche und zur Klosteranlage', in *Zisterzienserbauten in der Schweiz: Neue Forschungsergebnisse zur Archäologie und Kunstgeschichte*, ed. by Karl Grunder and Hans R. Sennhauser, 2 vols. (Zurich: Verlag der Fachvereine, 1990), II, 85–126 (pp. 109–12).

[92] Bullinger's notes are printed by Sennhauser, 'Kappel', pp. 120–6. Also cf. Hans U. Bächtold, 'Heinrich Bullinger als Historiker der Schweizer Geschichte', in *Heinrich Bullinger und seine Zeit: Eine Vorlesungsreihe*, ed. by Emidio Campi (Zurich: Theologischer Verlag, 2004), pp. 251–73.

top floor ('[mansionem] supremam, quae ex omnibus et saluberrima est et expolitissima, abbas inhabitat') with a hall befitting a king ('aula vere regia'), a heated parlour ('hypocaustum haud exgiuum'),[93] a bedroom ('cubiculum'), a large chamber ('cubiculum amplissimum') furnished with chests ('arcis') and bookshelves ('armariis'), most likely a private library, and the abbot's study ('domini museon') that had its own fireplace, a bed on which to read and rest, and large windows overlooking the monastery's quiet and peaceful graveyard with a gushing font situated against the idyllic vista of the nearby fields, hills, and woodlands—a true *locus amoenus* ideally suited for study and writing at any time of day or night.[94]

Abbatial studies and libraries were no rarity during the later medieval and early modern periods, even if few attracted as much praise as Joner's.[95] How does this compare to the situation in earlier centuries, though, especially in monasteries where historical writing is known to have taken place? A particularly insightful example comes from Corvey, where Abbot Wibald (1146–58) upon his appointment gave orders for the construction of a new abbatial residence, with building works commencing in the spring of 1148.[96] Wibald was a well-connected man. Educated at Liège by Rupert of Deutz, he became abbot of Stavelot (where he had been a teacher) and Malmedy in 1130, Montecassino in 1137, and Corvey in 1146, at the same time as acting as counsellor of Emperor Lothar III (1125–37) and King Conrad III (1138–52) and tutor to the latter's son, Henry Berengar— appointments which required him to spend considerable time at court and introduced him to a certain kind of lifestyle and habitus.[97] Judging by the evidence

---

[93] According to Bullinger, this parlour could, on occasion, provide accommodation for the abbot's guests, but only the most noble ('et hoc solent excipi hospites, non usquequaque ignobiles'); Sennhauser, 'Kappel', p. 125.

[94] See Sennhauser, 'Kappel', pp. 124–5: 'Ea ad septentrionem hypocaustum et cubiculum habet, domini museon, et vere museon admoenissimum, nam vincit in primis prospectus ita iocundus, ut nihil plane desiderati possit, quum ante fenestras cimiterium cristallo sit viridius, in quo fons vivacissimae acquae per cannas ferreas in lintrem spaciosissimum non sine leni prorrumpit murmure; adiacent prata, campi, montes, sylvae, omnia illa in ipso sunt obtutot, et ultro se apperienti fenestras, suavianda parebent'. Bullinger's words evoke the image of the Mouseion, one of the two ancient libraries of Alexandria.

[95] Cf. Maria Rottler, '"Catalogus bibliothecae abbatialis S. Emmerami"–ein Katalog der St. Emmeramer Abtsbibliothek aus der Zeit Frobenius Forsters', in *Netzwerke gelehrter Mönche: St. Emmeram im Zeitalter der Aufklärung*, ed. by Bernhard Löffler and Maria Rottler (Munich: Beck, 2015), pp. 297–304; James G. Clark, 'An Abbot and His Books in Late Medieval and Pre-Reformation England', in *The Prelate in England and Europe, 1300–1560*, ed. by Martin Heale (York: York Medieval Press, 2014), pp. 101–26; *Handbuch deutscher historischer Buchbestände in Europa*, Vol. 3: *Tschechische Republik*, ed. by Vincenc Streit et al. (Hildesheim: Olms-Weidmann, 1998), pp. 42–3; Nigel F. Palmer, *Zisterzienser und ihre Bücher: Die mittelalterliche Bibliotheksgeschichte von Kloster Eberbach im Rheingau* (Regensburg, Schnell & Steiner, 1998), pp. 293–4.

[96] Hilde Claussen, 'Zum Abtshaus des Wibald von Stablo im Kloster Corvey', in *Wohn- und Wirtschaftsbauten frühmittelalterlicher Klöster*, ed. by Hans R. Sennhauser (Zurich: Hochschulverlag, 1996), pp. 27–31; Hans-Georg Stephan, 'Zur Siedlungs- und Baugeschichte von Corvey-vornehmlich im frühen und hohen Mittelalter', *Archaeologia historica* 20 (1995), 447–67.

[97] See Franz-Josef Jakobi, *Wibald von Stablo und Corvey (1098–1158): Benediktinischer Abt in der frühen Stauferzeit* (Münster, Aschendorff, 1979); Nicolas Schroeder, 'Wibald en questions: Historiographie et nouvelles perspectives', in *Wibald en questions: Un grand abbé lotharingien du*

in Wibald's letter book (Liège, Archives de l'État, Abbaye impériale de Stavelot, MS I 341), the construction of the abbot's house ('domus') to the north-west of Corvey's abbey church took rather longer than anticipated, necessitating that Wibald take up temporary accommodation in a local church.[98] In a letter written in the winter of 1148, the abbey's provost, Adalbert, apologizes profusely for the inconvenience, and he reassures Wibald—who was clearly disgruntled by this point—that these lodgings will be sufficiently spacious and private ('valde commodum et secretum') to serve as an interim solution.[99]

Wibald must have insisted that having a private space to himself was important and non-negotiable. In a letter dated 1149, he recalls that the rooms inhabited by his predecessors ('habitacula Corbeiensis abbatis') had been narrow and derelict ('angusta et ruinosa'), deliberately contrasting them with the spaciousness of the new and solid ('nova et fortia') structure that had his name inscribed above the front door along with his abbatial ordinal number ('cum numero, quotus sim in cathalogo abbatum Corbeiensium') in accordance with the *catalogus abbatum* spanning the years 822–1146 that he himself had helped produce (Münster, Landesarchiv Nordrhein-Westfalen/Staatsarchiv, MS I 133, pp. 1–6).[100] Wibald's residence had not only rooms for sleeping, dining, and entertaining, but also a private study that is mentioned in a communication between him and the archbishop of Bremen, Hartwig (1148–68), who had visited the monastery in 1150 and been accommodated in the abbot's house along with his entourage.[101] Wibald thanks Hartwig for the kind words about his lodgings—specifically his study ('studium')—and adds that if the archbishop were to visit again and stay for a little longer ('longiorem inibi habitationem facere'), he would gladly accommodate his wish to study the books ('volumina') and documents ('scedulae') in his abbatial library ('armarii nostri').[102] Nothing survives of Wibald's study, but the

---

XIIe siècle. D'or et de parchemin, ed. by Albert Lemeunier and Nicolas Schroeder (Stavelot: Abbaye de Stavelot, 2010), pp. 5–11. A detailed itinerary of Wibald's movements in the years 1117–59 is provided in *Briefbuch*, ed. Hartmann, pp. xiii–xx.

[98] Claussen, 'Abtshaus', p. 28.

[99] *Monumenta Corbeiensia*, ed. by Philipp Jaffé [= *Bibliotheca rerum Germanicarum* I] (Berlin: Weidmann, 1864), pp. 174–5 (= no. 99) (p. 174); more recently *Briefbuch*, ed. Hartmann, I, 133–5 (= no. 76) (p. 134). The building was finally completed in 1149; on its location, see Stephan, 'Baugeschichte', p. 449.

[100] *Monumenta*, ed. Jaffé, pp. 276–88 (= no. 167) (p. 287); *Briefbuch*, ed. Hartmann, I, 290–306 (= no. 142) (pp. 304–5); Wilhelm Hemmen, 'Der Brief des Magisters Manegold an Abt Wibald von Corvey (1149)', in *Von der Domschule zum Gymnasium in Paderborn*, ed. by Klemens Honselmann (Paderborn: Bonifatius, 1962), pp. 79–105. On Wibald's role in the making of the *liber vitae*, see Hermann-Josef Schmalor, 'Die Bibliothek der ehemaligen Reichsabtei Corvey', *Westfälische Zeitschrift* 147 (1997), 251–70 (pp. 257–8); Karl H. Krüger, 'Die Corveyer Gründungsberichte des 12. Jahrhunderts im *Liber vitae*', in *Der Liber Vitae der Abtei Corvey*, ed. by Karl Schmid and Joachim Wollasch, 2 vols. (Wiesbaden: Reichert, 1983–9), II, 8–28; *Der Liber Vitae der Abtei Corvey*, ed. by Karl Schmid and Joachim Wollasch, 2 vols. (Wiesbaden: Reichert, 1983–9).

[101] Claussen, 'Abtshaus', pp. 29–30.

[102] *Monumenta*, ed. Jaffé, pp. 384–5 (= no. 259) (p. 384); *Briefbuch*, ed. Hartmann, II, 501–4 (= no. 235) (p. 502). As Hilde Claussen argues compellingly, the context here strongly suggests that this 'armarium' was not the communal library, but a separate facility located in Wibald's residence; Claussen, 'Abtshaus', p. 30 n. 29. Exactly when Corvey's abbots first acquired their own library and

breadth of knowledge and textual quotations in his hundreds of letters suggests a reference library of medieval and classical works that facilitated historiographical projects like the *catalogus abbatum* of Waulsort (the location of Wibald's monastic profession), *De constructione ecclesiae Corbeinensis*, and the *Chronographus Corbeiensis* (Münster, Landesarchiv Nordrhein-Westfalen/Staatsarchiv, MS I 243), a continuation of the *Annales Corbeienses* spanning the years 1145-8.[103] Perhaps the best-known volume from Wibald's library is a compendium of works by Cicero copied at his abbatial command (Berlin, Staatsbibliothek–Preußischer Kulturbesitz, MS lat. fol. 252).[104] Not only did Wibald personally gather the exemplars for this compendium by drawing on his large network of contacts to borrow the desired books from libraries near Corvey and further afield,[105] but he also commissioned a bespoke frontispiece that shows him prostrate before the monastery's patrons saints, Vitus, Stephen, and Justin (Fig. 4.2).[106] Underneath we can see Cicero and a student next to an abandoned writing desk of a type likely to have featured in Wibald's abbatial study at Corvey.[107]

Wibald was not the only medieval abbot with a private study that served as a location for producing and storing books. Other examples include the *studium*

study is difficult to know, but these facilities seem to have existed, in some form or other, from at least the time of Abbot Erkenbert (1107-28), and perhaps earlier; Joseph Prinz, *Die Corveyer Annalen: Textbearbeitung und Kommentar* (Münster: Aschendorff, 1982), p. 25.

[103] *Annalium Corbeiensium continuatio saeculi XII et Historia Corbeiensis Monasterii annorum MCXLV–MCXLVII cum additamentis (Cronographus Corbeiensis)–Fortsetzung der Corveyer Annalen des 12. Jahrhunderts und die Geschichte des Klosters Corvey der Jahre 1145–1147 mit Zusätzen (Der Corveyer Chronograph)*, ed. by Irene Schmale-Ott (Münster: Aschendorff, 1989), pp. 60–86 and 88–96. The *catalogus abbatum* was likely made c.1152; *Monumenta*, ed. Jaffé, p. 498 (= nos. 370–1); *Briefbuch*, ed. Hartmann, II, 728–30 (= nos. 347–8).

[104] *Die illuminierten lateinischen Handschriften deutscher Provenienz der Staatsbibliothek Preußischer Kulturbesitz Berlin, 8.–12. Jahrhundert*, ed. by Andreas Fingernagel, 2 vols. (Wiesbaden: Harrassowitz, 1991), I, 7–8 (= no. 5); *Glanz alter Buchkunst: Mittelalterliche Handschriften der Staatsbibliothek Preußischer Kulturbesitz, Berlin*, ed. by Tilo Brandis and Peter J. Becker (Wiesbaden: Reichert, 1988), pp. 72–3 (= no. 30); Birger Munk Olsen, *L'étude des auteurs classiques latins aux XIe et XIIe siècles*, 4 vols. (Paris: IRHT, 1982–2009), I.1, 148–50. I must thank Harald Wolter-von dem Knesebeck for drawing my attention to this manuscript.

[105] One of Wibald's lenders, the provost of Hildesheim (1148–59) and later archbishop of Cologne (1159–67), Rainald of Dassel, teasingly(?) admonished him for betraying his Christian convictions by hunting high and low for the writings of the famous heathen orator; *Monumenta*, ed. Jaffé, pp. 326–7 (= no. 207) (p. 326); *Briefbuch*, ed. Hartmann, II, 401–2 (= no. 189) (p. 401); Julien Maquet, 'Wibald, un "Cicéron chrétien"? Les connaissances juridiques et la pratique judiciaire d'un grand abbé d'Empire (†1158)', in *Wibald en questions: Un grand abbé lotharingien du XIIe siècle. D'or et de parchemin*, ed. by Albert Lemeunier and Nicolas Schroeder (Stavelot: Abbaye de Stavelot, 2010), pp. 33–42. It is not impossible that Rainald's seemingly flippant remark might have reflected a genuine concern for Wibald's reading habits. In return for lending him the desired Ciceronian works, Rainald requested to borrow Corvey's copies of Aulus Gellius and Origen.

[106] The *titulus* identifying the figure as 'Adelbertus abbas Corbeye' is a thirteenth-century addition, and there is little doubt that in its original form the miniature was in fact meant to depict Wibald; *Handschriften*, ed. Fingernagel, I, 8; *Glanz*, ed. Brandis and Becker, p. 72.

[107] An interesting parallel survives in Munich, Bayerische Staatsbibliothek, MS Clm. 19472, fol. 1r, an eleventh-century manuscript from Tegernsee containing works by Cicero and Sallust. Though commonly attributed to Cicero, it is not impossible that the writing desk depicted in the Corvey codex was meant to depict that of Wibald, especially considering his personal involvement in the manuscript's production.

Fig. 4.2 Wibald of Corvey's(?) writing desk. Berlin, Staatsbibliothek zu Berlin–Preußischer Kulturbesitz, MS lat. fol. 252, fol. 1v.

abbatis at the Cistercian abbey of Stična, a major centre of monastic book production in medieval Slovenia with a library that by the end of the twelfth century contained copies of historical narratives such as Otto of Freising's *Gesta Friderici* and William of Saint-Thierry's *Vita prima Bernardi*.[108] There is also the intriguing case of Abbot Bernard of Rein (1265–80), whose *gesta* were appended to the community's necrology (Rein, Stiftsarchiv, MS D) in the mid-1390s by its abbot-historian, Angelus Manse (1399–1425), author of the *Series abbatum Runensium*.[109] Angelus reports that Bernard had built himself a new residence next to the infirmary with a private chamber ('camera abbatis') and an *armarium*, though this probably refers to a book chest/shelf, rather than to a separate room.[110] By contrast, when a new monastic library was built at Heilsbronn, the existing *armarium*—this time certainly a designated book room—became the abbot's private study and library.[111] The abbatial lodgings at Admont built for Bernard (1265–81/2) featured a library and scriptorium, and the abbots of St Matthew's, Trier (formerly dedicated to St Eucharius) had similar facilities from at least the thirteenth century.[112] Located in the western range of the cloister and fitted with heating and running water, the *curia abbatis* at Trier had two floors with a study on the upper level.[113] It later became known as the *vetus abbatia* when a new residence was built at the order of Abbot Johannes Rode (1421–39), who installed a library room in the cloister's eastern range and converted the

---

[108] See Nataša Golob, *Twelfth-Century Cistercian Manuscripts: The Sitticum Collection* (Ljubljana: Slovenska knjiga, 1996), pp. 22–39.

[109] 'Necrologium Runense', in *MGH Necr.* II, ed. by Sigismund Herzberg-Fränkel (Berlin: Weidmann, 1904), pp. 341–56, though the *gesta* still await their critical edition. On the manuscript, see Norbert Müller, 'Stiftsarchiv: Geistige Bewahrungsstätte', in *Erlesenes und Erbauliches: Kulturschaffen der Reiner Mönche*, ed. by Norbert Müller (Rein: Zisterzienserstift, 2003), pp. 103–33 (pp. 123–5); Johannes Gießauf, 'Totenmemoria im Südostalpenraum und seiner südlichen Nachbarschaft: Eine begrenzte Bestandsaufnahme bis 1300', in *Schriftkultur zwischen Donau und Adria bis zum 13. Jahrhundert*, ed. by Reinhard Härtel et al. (Klagenfurt: Wieser, 2008), pp. 151–202 (pp. 168–9). Heinrich R. von Zeissberg, 'Fragmente eines Nekrologs des Klosters Reun in Steiermark', *Archiv für österreichische Geschichte* 58 (1879), 217–29 (pp. 221–3) believed the *gesta* to have been written shortly after Bernhard's death and then copied by Angelus. On the *Series abbatum*, see *Handschriftenverzeichnis der Stiftsbibliothek zu Rein*, ed. by Anton Weis and Walter Steinmetz (Rein: self-published, 1999–2014), pp. 365–6.

[110] Rein, Stiftsarchiv, MS D, fol. 50v. I would like to express my thanks to Dr David Zettl, archivist at the Zisterzienserstift Rein, for kindly providing me with photographs of this manuscript during the COVID-19 pandemic. Rein's communal *armarium* was a niche in the eastern wall of the cloister that reached its capacity by c.1270, leading Bernard to provide additional library space on the floor above next to the dormitory; see the reconstruction in Leopold Grill, 'Reportage über den einstigen romanischen Kreuzgang in Rein', *Marienbote des Stiftes Rein* 9 (1950), 17–20 (p. 18); also cf. Walter Steinmetz, '*Armarium Runense*: Kleiner Führer durch die Reiner Stiftsbibliothek', in *Stift Rein: Geschichte–Kultur–Glaube*, ed. by Elisabeth Brenner and Reiner Kreises (Kumberg: Sublilium Schaffer, 2018), pp. 171–8 (pp. 171–2).

[111] Ladislaus Buzas, *Deutsche Bibliotheksgeschichte des Mittelalters* [= *Elemente des Buch- und Bibliothekswesens* III] (Wiesbaden: Reichert, 1975), p. 64.

[112] Petrus Becker, *Die Benediktinerabtei St. Eucharius-St. Matthias vor Trier* [= *Germania Sacra* NF XXXIV; *Das Erzbistum Trier* VIII] (Berlin: De Gruyter, 1996), pp. 51–9.

[113] Cf. Becker, *Benediktinerabtei*, p. 54, who suspects that the abbot might have hired Cistercian architects for the construction of the water conduit.

thirteenth-century abbatial chapel ('sacellum abbatis') into a repository for the monastery's archives ('archivum').[114]

Conversions of abbatial chambers and chapels into libraries and archives—and *vice versa*—were facilitated by the fact that these spaces often came equipped with adequate storage for books and documents.[115] The presence of books, especially (but not exclusively) liturgical codices, in abbatial chapels is confirmed by inscriptions and inventories from as early as the eleventh century, though the practice likely reaches back further.[116] The boundaries between liturgical, residential, and working spaces are not always easy to establish, and sometimes a 'hybrid' function must be assumed. The abbesses of Lacock had their own quarters from at least the fourteenth century, located above the cloister's western range in close proximity to the tomb of Lacock's foundress and first abbess, Ela (1240–57), and accessible via a spiral staircase leading up from the ground level.[117] Below the abbatial lodgings and accessible at ground level was (and still is) a vaulted chamber whose medieval wall plaster shows images of the Crucifixion and portraits of SS Christopher and Andrew. Though traditionally viewed as a 'male space' for the abbey's resident priest and (mis)labelled 'the Chaplain's Room', this painted chamber has recently been identified as a space for the abbess herself, and thus a 'female-only space'.[118] The wall paintings were almost certainly commissioned by Ela herself—either in

---

[114] Becker, *Benediktinerabtei*, p. 58.

[115] Clark, 'Abbot', pp. 110–12; also cf. Edgar Lehmann, *Die Bibliotheksräume der deutschen Klöster im Mittelalter* (Berlin: Akademie, 1957), who distinguishes, rather too categorically, between so-called Romanesque 'treasury libraries' ('Schatzkammerbibliotheken') and 'study libraries' ('Studienbibliotheken'); the rigidity of Lehmann's approach has been criticised in subsequent scholarship, for example, by Buzas, *Bibliotheksgeschichte*, p. 152.

[116] For example, a late fourteenth-/early fifteenth-century consuetudinary from St Mary's Abbey, York (Cambridge, St John's College, MS D.27, fol. 275v: 'ad capellam domini abbatis'); *Catalogue of Dated and Datable Manuscripts c.737–1600 in Cambridge Libraries*, ed. by Pamela R. Robinson, 2 vols. (Cambridge: Cambridge University Press, 1988), I, 86–7 (= no. 299); by the late fifteenth century, York's abbots lived in a two-storey house; Heale, *Abbots*, p. 161; likewise, a late eleventh-century book list from the Abbey of Weihenstephan (Munich, Bayerische Staatsbibliothek, MS Clm. 21521, fol. 159v) allocates three liturgical volumes 'ad capellam abbatis'; *MBKDS*, IV.2, 649–50 (p. 649) (= no. 87); Schlotheuber and McQuillen, 'Books', pp. 976–7; and a book list made at Reading Abbey in 1192 records several books 'in capella abbatis', presumably referring to the chapel of the community's then abbot, Hugh (1186–99), at the same time as including a designated section for the books kept in the chapel of the previous incumbent, Joseph (1173–86) ('Libri de capella abbatis Ioseph'); *CBMLC*, IV, 419–47 (pp. 443 and 446–7) (= B71); also cf. Webber, 'Space', p. 224. Books were also stored in infirmary chapels, as is shown by a thirteenth-century Missal from St Albans (Oxford, Bodleian Library, MS Laud. Misc. 279, fol. 4v: 'ex permissione domini Willelmi abbatis ad capellam infirmarum'); *Illuminated Manuscripts in the Bodleian Library Oxford*, ed. by Otto Pächt and J. J. G. Alexander, 3 vols. (Oxford: Oxford University Press, 1966–73), III, 49 (= no. 534).

[117] Ela's remains were translated twice, first in the sixteenth, and then again in the late nineteenth century. She was a powerful and well-connected lord in her own right, being both the countess of Salisbury (and sole heiress to Earl William FitzPatrick of Salisbury) and the wife of William Longespée, Henry II's illegitimate son, making Ela the king's daughter-in-law. Her grant of c.1236 giving Lacock Manor to the future abbesses and nuns in perpetuity has been translated in Jennifer C. Ward, *Women of the English Nobility and Gentry, 1066–1500* (Manchester: Manchester University Press, 1995), pp. 201–2 (= no. 146).

[118] Ellie Pridgeon and Susan Sharp, 'Patronage and Function: The Medieval Wall Paintings at Lacock Abbey in Wiltshire', *Journal of Medieval Monastic Studies* 5 (2016), 113–37 (p. 119).

the early years of her tenure or after her retirement in 1257, when she continued to live on-site until her death in 1261—and likely finished under her successor, Beatrice of Kent (1257–80). Though the room's precise function remains contested, its residential nature with a large fireplace and window suggests that it served as a living and, potentially, working space for Ela and her successors until the larger lodgings on the floor above were constructed a century or so later.[119]

In a reversal of the developments seen in some contemporary (male) communities, it seems that at Lacock the abbatial chamber was converted into a private chapel following the construction of the fourteenth-century residence. And yet, the wall paintings predate this expansion by a century, which would speak against an exclusively devotional function. Pridgeon and Sharp's suggestion that Ela might have intended the wall paintings in her chamber 'as a commemorative, familial, and personal mark on the institution she once governed', and that she 'envisaged the images assuming a mnemonic function to record her deeds', is pertinent here.[120] Even if the chamber would have been closed to most visitors, it almost certainly would have remained accessible to the women of the monastic community proper to serve as a communal memory space, though given Ela's pedigree and political connections, we should not exclude the possibility that the room was used on occasion to entertain high-status guests of both genders. The cellareress's accounts for 1346/7 record that Robert Wyvil, bishop of Salisbury (1330–75), was entertained by the abbess, presumably in her private quarters, and served an extravagant feast of expensive fish, shellfish, meat, and poultry.[121] The wall paintings apart, little is known about the interior of Lacock's abbatial quarters, and whilst we cannot know for sure whether the abbess's chamber provided a space for private study and literary composition, it certainly remains a possibility.

What we do know, though, is that the construction and decoration of the abbess's quarters at Lacock coincided closely with the production of several historical narratives integral to the community's sense of the past. Under the rule of Beatrice, the nuns began the compilation of the *Lacock Annals* (London, British Library, MS Cotton Vitellius A VIII, fols. 113r–132v, a historical compendium badly damaged in the Ashburnham House fire in 1731), which were supplemented later by a more comprehensive house chronicle relating the history of the community's foundation and the deeds of its first abbess known as the *Book of Lacock* (fragment in MS Cotton Vitellius A VIII, fols. 128r–130v, with a fuller transcript in London, British Library, MS Harley 5019).[122] In the late thirteenth

---

[119] Pridgeon and Sharp, 'Patronage', pp. 116–20; Charles H. Talbot, 'Lacock Abbey: Notes on the Architectural History of the Building', *Journal of the British Archaeological Association* 11 (1905), 176–210 (p. 192).
[120] Pridgeon and Sharp, 'Patronage', pp. 129–30.   [121] Spear, *Leadership*, p. 99.
[122] In their present form, the *Lacock Annals* are bound in one volume with a later twelfth-century copy of Robert of Torigni's redaction of William of Jumièges's *Gesta Normannorum ducum* from Reading Abbey (MS Cotton Vitellius A viii, fols. 5r–100v); *GND*, ed./tr. van Houts, 2 vols. (Oxford:

and early fourteenth centuries, the nuns made two cartularies at the order of their abbesses, the first of which (London, British Library, MS Add. 88973) combines acts in Latin and French, whereas the second (London, British Library, MS Add. 88974) is entirely in Latin.[123] Where these volumes were kept is difficult to establish, but by the mid-fourteenth century the communal collection was large enough to warrant a separate book room besides the shelved wall-niche in the cloister still visible today. If Lacock's abbesses had a designated storage space for the books they commissioned from the nuns, then this was most likely the chamber (and later chapel) constructed by Ela.

Other monastic superiors who immersed themselves, physically and mentally, in historical subject matter within the privacy of their abbatial quarters include the abbots of Cleeve, a community of English Cistercians founded in 1198 and dissolved under Henry VIII. Here, Abbot David Juyner (1435–87) built himself a new residence above the refectory that comprised of a lobby/antechamber, a private chamber, and two rooms in the loft space above.[124] There was also a painted chamber accessible via the antechamber, the function of which remains unclear, though the presence of a large window and fireplace may suggest a space at once private enough for study and sufficiently representative to be 'public-facing'. Opposite the fireplace survives a mural with an episode from the *Gesta Romanorum*, a text whose historical dimension would not have been lost on those admitted into the abbot's lodgings.[125] As with Ela, we cannot know whether Juyner and his successors kept a private library in their painted chamber, but given the room's configuration and probable usage, we should at least consider the possibility that it provided a suitable environment for collecting and storing books.

Oxford University Press, 1992–5), I, cxii–cxiii. On the *Book of Lacock*, see William L. Bowles and John G. Nichols, *Annals and Antiquities of Lacock Abbey* (London: Nichols & Son, 1835), p. 374 and i–v (= Appendix I).

[123] See James Freeman, 'The Lacock Cartularies' (2014), https://blogs.bl.uk/digitisedmanuscripts/2014/08/the-lacock-abbey-cartularies.html. Besides these cartularies, the *Book of Lacock*, and the *Lacock Annals*, extant books from Lacock's thirteenth- and fourteenth-century collections include a copy of William Brito's *Expositiones vocabulorum Bibliae* (sold at Christie's in 2011 for £46,850; now at Lacock Abbey), an anthology of Anglo-Norman poetry commencing with *Le Tretiz* by Walter of Bibbesworth (sold for £205,250; current location unknown), and an illuminated Psalter (Oxford, Bodleian Library, MS Laud. Lat. 114; likely produced in-house) with a miniature of a nun (or abbess?) clutching a small booklet (fol. 148r); on the two auctioned manuscripts, see https://www.christies.com/en/lot/lot-5495253; https://www.christies.com/en/lot/lot-5495254.

[124] See Emery, *Houses*, III, 512–13, with a floor plan. On Juyner's abbacy, see *Heads*, ed. Knowles et al., III, 279.

[125] *Gesta Romanorum*, ed. by Herman Oesterley (Berlin: Weidmann, 1872), p. 597 (= 191, germ. 53); on the mural, see Caroline Babington et al., *Our Painted Past: Wall Paintings of English Heritage* (London: English Heritage, 1999), pp. 46–7; Miriam Gill, 'The Role of Images in Monastic Education: The Evidence from Wall Painting in Late Medieval England', in *Medieval Monastic Education*, ed. by George Ferzoco and Carolyn Muessig (London: Leicester University Press, 2000), pp. 117–35 (pp. 120–2).

4.3 Private Collections

Narrative and archaeological sources apart, some of the best evidence of abbatial studies is provided by the books stored therein. Though many of these books do not survive and are known only (if at all) from book lists and inventories, those that have come down to us sometimes have inscriptions allocating them to the private lodgings of an abbot or abbesses. The expense list from St Albans introduced above (4.2) itemizes not only the building of John of Wheathampstead's new abbatial chamber, but also a library attached to it ('librariae ibidem, prope cameram prius dictam').[126] The costs of this library are excluded from the tally, suggesting that it, unlike the chamber itself, was paid not *ex parte conventus*, but from a different source. The most plausible explanation is that the money came from the abbot's coffers, the *mensa abbatis*, and that the books were for his personal use and 'cultural consumption'.[127] John certainly was an avid consumer, and just like Trithemius he had the walls of his study inscribed with learned proverbs reiterating his investment—financially and ideologically—in books.[128] John was not the first abbot of St Albans to maintain a private library. An earlier list (Cambridge, University Library, MS Ee. 4.20) from 1382 made by William, chaplain of Thomas de la Mare, already mentions an abbot's library and study ('librarium sive studium') with storage for books,[129] and a similar facility also existed at the abbot's summer house at Redbourne.[130] Thomas's predecessor, Michael of Mentmore, is recorded in the *Gesta abbatum* to have assigned various books to his study ('suo studio assignavit') in addition to those he provided for the communal library.[131] That this was no invention on the chronicler's part is shown by nearly a dozen volumes with inscriptions assigning them to this *studium abbatis*, at least some of which were acquired by Michael's predecessor, Richard of Wallingford, indicating that he, too, might have had a library in his study.[132]

---

[126] MS Arundel 34, fol. 68v; *Gesta*, ed. Riley, II, 258; London, British Library, MS Cotton Otho B. IV, fols. 12v–16r, for 1452–65; *CBMLC*, IV, 563–71 and 572–81 (= B88 and B89).

[127] Clark, 'Abbot', p. 117; also cf. Haye, *Mittelalter*, p. 35.

[128] One inscription reads: 'When studying, may you see to it that virtue and honesty be the ultimate motive of your endeavours, here and elsewhere' ('Cum studeas, videas, | ut sit virtus et honestas // hic et ubique tibi | finalis causa studendi'); Kenelm H. Digby, *Mores Catholici*, 3 vols. (London: Dolman, 1831–42), III, 300; also cf. the account by John Leland: *De rebus Britannicis collectaneorum*, ed. by Thomas Hearne, 6 vols., 3rd ed. (1770–4), VI, 135; Henry Chauncy, *The Historical Antiquities of Hertfordshire [...] Also the Characters of the Abbots of St Albans* (London: Griffin, 1700), pp. 276–7.

[129] *A Catalogue of the Manuscripts Preserved in the Library of the University of Cambridge*, ed. by Charles Hardwick and Henry Luard, 6 vols. (Cambridge: Cambridge University Press, 1856–67), II, 126–30 (= no. 1037) (p. 127).

[130] *Gesta*, ed. Riley, III, 399; tr. Preest and Clark, pp. 786–7; Hunt, 'Library', pp. 260–2; Clark, 'Abbot', p. 109. The abbot's house at Redbourne was built on the site of the former communal latrine ('in loco vero ubi fuit prius latrina communis').

[131] *Gesta*, ed. Riley, III, 363; tr. Preest and Clark, p. 750; Hunt, 'Library', p. 261.

[132] These are Cambridge, Corpus Christi College, MS 77 ('de studio dompni abbatis sancti Albani'); Cambridge, Trinity College, MS B.14.36 ('de studio abbatis'); Cambridge, University Library, MS Gg. 4.11 ('studio abbatis specialiter deputatus'); Dublin, Trinity College, MS 444 ('de studio abbatis'); London,

The abbatial library of St Albans is no isolated case. A homiliary from Westminster Abbey (Cambridge, University Library, MS Ee. 4.23) has an inscription stating that it was found in the cupboard of Abbot Richard (1246–58) ('inventus fuit in armariolo R. de Crok. abbas'), with similar inscriptions surviving in books from Bury St Edmunds, Peterborough, and Canterbury Cathedral Priory.[133] At Cerne Abbey, the gatehouse built by/for Abbot Thomas Sam (1497–1509) (known as the 'Abbot's Porch') is purported to have had a study chamber with space for a library, though no inscriptions survive to corroborate this.[134] The later medieval abbesses of Barking kept their books separate from those of the community and passed them down from one incumbent to the next. A customary commissioned by Sibyl de Felton for her personal use (Oxford, University College, MS 169) has an inscription designating it to be inherited by her successors alongside other books with similar inscriptions.[135] One of the earliest cases of an abbess having a personal book collection is Cuthswith of Inkberrow (c.693–709), whose copy of Jerome's *Commentary on Ecclesiastes* (Würzburg, Universitätsbibliothek, MS p. th. q. 2) has a declaration of ownership on its opening page (fol. 1r: 'Cuthsuuithae boec thaerae abbatissan').[136] Whether

British Library, MS Royal 8 G I ('de studio abbatis'); London, British Library, MS Royal 9 C X ('de studio abbatis'); London, British Library, MS Royal 10 D III ('de studio abbatis'); Mount Stuart, Marquess of Bute ('de studio domini abbatis'); Oxford, Bodleian Library, MS Bodley 292 ('de studio abbatis'); Oxford, Bodleian Library, MS Laud Misc. 264 ('de studio abbatis'); San Marino, CA, Huntington Library, MS 27187 ('de studio abbatis'). Cf. Clark, 'Abbot', 108–9; James G. Clark, *A Monastic Renaissance at St Albans: Thomas Walsingham and His Circle c.1350–1440* (Oxford: Clarendon, 2004), pp. 86–7; James G. Clark, 'The Regular Clergy', in *A Companion to the Early Printed Book in Britain: 1476–1558*, ed. by Vicent J. Gillespie (Woodbridge: Boydell, 2014), pp. 176–206 (p. 185); Michelle Still, *The Abbot and the Rule: Religious Life at St Albans, 1290–1349* (Aldershot: Ashgate, 2002), pp. 169–80.

[133] From Bury, Cambridge, Jesus College, MS 18 ('pro studio abbatis'); from Peterborough, Cambridge, Corpus Christi College, MS 92 ('liber abbatis et conventus de Burgo sancti Petri'); from Canterbury, Canterbury, Cathedral Archives, DCC/ChAnt/Z/141, an early sixteenth-century book list written by the local monk William Ingram; a copy survives in Canterbury, Cathedral Archives, DCC/LitMS/C/11, fols. 95r–104v; cf. Clark, 'Abbot', p. 109; Heale, *Abbots*, p. 162.

[134] Thompson, *Cloister*, p. 88. An information board installed by the Heritage Lottery Fund and The Countryside Agency states that '[a]bove the entrance itself were the living quarters for the abbot', and that '[t]hese rooms are where the abbot would have lived, studied and received visitors, with space enough for a library; perhaps holding the Book of Cerne [Cambridge, University Library, MS Ll. 1.10], but certainly the manuscripts which became scattered in 1539 following the Dissolution'. The architectural remains allow for such an interpretation, especially with regard to the large niche on the eastern wall of the first-floor parlour, which might well have been used for storing books; a floor plan has been printed in *Inventory*, n.p. I am grateful to the present-day owners and inhabitants of Cerne Abbey, Michael and Barbara Fulford-Dobson, for kindly inviting me to investigate the interior of the Abbot's Porch first-hand. On Cerne's architectural history, see Emery, *Houses*, III, 509–10.

[135] See Dutton, 'Use', pp. 235–55; Bugyis, *Care*, pp. 49–50; Katie A.-M. Bugyis, 'Women Priests at Barking Abbey in the Late Middle Ages', in *Women Intellectuals and Leaders in the Middle Ages*, ed. by Kathryn Kerby-Fulton et al. (Cambridge: Cambridge University Press, 2020), pp. 319–34 (pp. 319–20). Similar inscriptions survive from other female houses; cf. Bell, *Nuns*, pp. 133 (Dartford), 134 (Denney), 137 (Estow), 145 (Kingston St Michael), and 210 (Tarrant Keynston).

[136] *Anglo-Saxon Manuscripts: A Bibliographical Handlist of Manuscripts and Manuscript Fragments Written or Owned in England up to 1100*, ed. by Helmut Gneuss and Michael Lapidge (Toronto: University of Toronto Press, 2014), p. 687 (= no. 944). Patrick Sims-Williams, 'Cuthswith, Seventh-Century Abbess of Inkberrow, Near Worcester, and the Würzburg Manuscript of Jerome on Ecclesiastes', *Anglo-Saxon England* 5 (1976), 1–21; McKitterick, 'Scriptoria', pp. 26–7; Lifshitz, *Women*, p. 30.

the volumes Boniface borrowed from Eadburga, abbess of Minster-in-Thanet/ Wimbourne came from a similar collection is not known, but it is certainly a possibility.[137] It was not just the superiors of large and wealthy monasteries who collected books, as is shown by an illuminated thirteenth-century psalter (London, British Library, MS Harley 5765) with fifteenth-century inscriptions that locate it in the abbatial chamber at St Mary, Pipewell ('De camera abbatis Pippewell').[138] By that point, the monastery was impoverished and in poor repair, so much so that a petition presented to (Anti-)Pope John XXIII complains that its demesne was insufficient to sustain the abbot and his monks any longer.[139] Comparable examples survive from other religious orders, too.[140]

These English examples have parallels elsewhere in Europe. When Kunigunde of Bohemia, daughter of King Ottokar II (1253–78), became abbess (1302–21) of St George in Prague following her divorce from Boleslaus II of Masovia, she used her new office to assemble a large personal book collection that included not only the *Kunigunde Passional* (Prague, National Library of the Czech Republic, MS XIV A 17), but also several other books with inscriptions in Kunigunde's own hand that assign them to her library.[141] An inventory from Zwettl drawn up in 1405 (Zwettl, Stiftsbibliothek, MS 22) allocates many volumes to the abbot's library ('ad bibliothecam domini abbatis'), which is remarkable considering that the monastery was plundered more than once during the later thirteenth and early fourteenth centuries.[142] At Erfurt, an early printed copy of Angelus de Clavasio's *Summa angelica* (Rudolstadt, Historische Bibliothek, 2° Ink 3) is inscribed as one of the books from the old abbatial chamber ('ex libris antiquae cellae abbatiae'),[143] and a fifteenth-century inventory from Tegernsee (Munich, Bayerische Staatsbibliothek, MS Clm. 1925, fol. 13r) locates a manuscript of the same work 'in curia abbatis'.[144] In 1198, the abbot of Marseille had to reassure his community by promising—in a charter—that he and his successors henceforth would place

---

[137] Boniface's letter to Eadburga is printed with translation in Andy Orchard, 'Old Sources, New Resources: Finding the Right Formula for Boniface', *Anglo-Saxon England* 47 (2001), 15–31 (p. 21); see also Lifshitz, *Women*, pp. 4 and 85.

[138] Ker, *Libraries*, p. 152; *A Catalogue of the Harleian Manuscripts in the British Museum*, 4 vols. (London: Eyre and Strahan, 1808–12), III, 294 (= no. 5765).

[139] On this petition, dated 13 December 1412, see *Calendar of Papal Registers Relating to Great Britain and Ireland*, Vol. 6: *1404–1415*, ed. by William H. Bliss and Jessis A. Twemlow (London: Her Majesty's Stationery Office, 1904), p. 393.

[140] At the Dominican convent of St Albert, Leipzig, a fourteenth-century copy of Cicero's *Tusculan Disputations* was marked as the property of the late Abbot Stephen ('Liber abbatis Stephani, obiit anno MCCC 8 octob.'); see *Catalogue d'une bibliothèque exquise, très considérable en toutes sortes de sciences de langues*, ed. by Abraham De Hondt (The Hague: 1722), n.p. On book ownership amongst the Mendicant orders, see Hans-Joachim Schmidt, 'Bücher im Privatbesitz und im Besitz der Konvente: Regelungen der Bettelorden', in *Die Bibliothek-The Library-La Bibliothèque: Denkräume und Wissensordnungen*, ed. by Andreas Speer und Lars Reuke (Berlin: De Gruyter, 2020), pp. 157–71.

[141] See Alfred Thomas, *Anne's Bohemia: Czech Literature and Society, 1310–1420* (Minneapolis, MN: University of Minnesota Press, 1998), pp. 35–40; Rudy, 'Touching', pp. 251 and 326.

[142] *MBKÖ*, I, 516–20 (= no. 75).   [143] Eifler, *Bibliothek*, I, 181 and II, 1042 (= no. 206).

[144] *MBKDS*, IV.2, 751–849 (= no. 109) (p. 765); Schlotheuber and McQuillen, 'Books', p. 984.

books received by donation in the monks' library and not incorporate them into their private collection as his predecessors had done, a custom that had earned them much criticism.[145] A similar regulation was issued in 1324 by the Augustinian General Chapter in Montpellier.[146]

Another hundred and fifty years later, a copy of the *Thebaid* (Wolfenbüttel, Herzog August Bibliothek, MS. Cod. Guelf. 265.4 Extrav.) was presented to Johannes Trithemius by fellow bibliophile Jakob Wipfeling with the explicit instruction—inscribed prominently on its frontispiece—that it was to be placed in the monks' library and *not* amongst the abbot's belongings, perhaps insinuating that Trithemius, too, had a habit of quietly adding donated books to his own library rather than the communal collection.[147] The size and location of Trithemius's abbatial library can be gauged from two pieces of evidence from Würzburg, where Trithemius held the abbacy following his resignation from Sponheim. The first is an inventory of the abbatial estate made for his successor, Matthias Dietrich (1516–35).[148] Meticulously recording almost five hundred items that range from pieces of furniture, paintings, musical and astronomical instruments, and even firearms to individual pieces of cutlery, the inventory is divided into the locations in which these items were discovered ('reperti') after Trithemius's death. The first and largest section contains three hundred and seventy-five books found 'in abbacia', a term that can refer both to a monastery and, more specifically, to an abbot's residence.[149] Scholarship so far has associated these books with Würzburg's communal library, with the possible exception of certain medical and scientific texts.[150] This interpretation is at odds, however, with the fact that all other locations on the inventory can be linked directly with the provision of living and workspaces for the abbot and/or the reception and entertainment of guests: the abbot's chamber ('camera abbatis'), a parlour ('stuba

---

[145] *Cartulaire de l'abbaye de Saint-Victor de Marseille*, ed. by Benjamin E. C. Guérard, 2 vols. (Paris: Lahure, 1857), II, 286–7 (= no. 898).

[146] Edited in *Chartularium universitatis Parisiensis*, ed. by Emile Chatelain and Heinrich Denifle, 4 vols. (Paris: Delalain, 1889–97), II.1, 275–6 (= no. 831).

[147] 'Stacium hunc dono domino Ioanni de Trittenheym abbati Spanheymensis bibliothecę non privatę applicandum. Iacobus v. Sletstat. Manu propria anno Domini MCCCCXCIII' (fol. 1r); Wipfeling had bought the book in 1474 before donating it to Sponheim in 1493; Lehmann, 'Nachrichten', p. 216 dates the manuscript 'saec. XIII', whereas the more recent description in *Die mittelalterlichen Handschriften der Gruppen Extravagantes, Novi und Novissimi*, ed. by Hans Butzmann [= *Kataloge der Herzog August Bibliothek Wolfenbüttel: Die Neue Reihe XV*] (Frankfurt a. M.: Klostermann, 1972), pp. 126–8 (p. 126) has 'XII. Jh., 2. Hälfte'.

[148] Vatican, Biblioteca Apostolica Vaticana, MS Vat. lat. 11051, fols. 17r–29v, edited by Arnold, 'Nachlaßverzeichnis', pp. 289–337, who suggests that no library inventory existed when Andreas succeeded Trithemius in 1516 (ibid., p. 282).

[149] Arnold, 'Nachlaßverzeichnis', pp. 291–332. On the term *abbacia/abbatia*, see *Mediae Latinitatis Lexicon minus*, ed. by Jan F. Niermeyer and Co van de Kieft, rev. ed., 2 vols. (Leiden: Brill, 2002), I, 2–4. A good example of a separate abbatial residence referred to as 'abdye' (the vernacular equivalent of *abbacia*) is found on the plan of St Bavo's, Ghent in Antonius Sanderus's *Flandria illustrata* (1641); reproduced in *Ghent: A City of All Times*, ed. by Marc Boone and Gita Deneckere (Ghent: Stadsmuseum/Mercatorfonds, 2010), pp. 32–3.

[150] Arnold, 'Nachlaßverzeichnis', p. 286; Arnold, *Trithemius*, pp. 212–15; Fischer, 'Nachlaß', p. 45.

abbacie'), an antechamber ('ante stubam abbacie'), a granary ('granarium'), a dining room ('refectorium'), a larder ('promptuarium'), a kitchen ('coquina'), and a guest chamber ('camera hospitum').[151] Following Trithemius's death in 1516, these rooms were inspected one-by-one and had their contents recorded in turn. The fact that the section following from the 'libri in abbacia' is called 'alia sequ[e]ntur que reperi in camera abbatis' suggests that they relate to a single location, and that this location was none other than the abbatial chamber, the primary repository for the abbot's belongings and, as seen above (4.1), Trithemius's preferred writing and study space.[152]

This identification is corroborated by another inventory of the same facilities made after Matthias's death in 1535 for his successor, Erhard (1535–42), which explicitly records three book chests 'in camera abbatis': a large book container ('grosser buchbeheltter') with one hundred and ten volumes, a large container painted with the image of a grape ('ein grosser beheltter an dem ein treubel gemalt') with nineteen volumes, and a third decorated with the image of a scallop ('ein grosser beheltter doran ein jacobsmuschel gemalt') with thirty-two volumes, plus a large chest of drawers ('ein grosser beheltter mit viln schubladen') with numerous letters and unbound booklets ('darin etlich alt brieff und ungebunden buchlin').[153] In addition to these one hundred and sixty-one volumes stored in Matthias's chamber, there were another one hundred and three in his summer house ('im sumer haus vor der aptey').[154] If Matthias could store that many books in his abbatial lodgings, then there is no reason to doubt that his predecessor—a self-confessed bibliophile and prolific historian—could have done so as well. In fact, it is entirely plausible that Matthias simply preserved Trithemius's library *in situ* and adjusted it to his personal needs by adding or removing individual books over the course of his abbacy, though the lack of titles from the 1535 inventory means we cannot be certain. What we do know is that he had inherited, if not necessarily the books themselves, then certainly their storage containers from his predecessor: as noted above, one of the three book chests discovered in his chamber bore the image of a grape ('ein treubel'), the emblem of Trithemius's crest as shown in his portrait in the monastery's refectory.[155] Whether the chest with a scallop (the symbol of the community's patron saint) and the one without decoration had also been part of the furniture when Matthias succeeded Trithemius and moved into his abbatial chamber can no longer be known, but it seems likely.

---

[151] Arnold, 'Nachlaßverzeichnis', pp. 334–7.
[152] The two sections together constitute nearly 90 percent of the items on the inventory.
[153] Printed by Michael Wieland, 'Das Schottenkloster St. Jakob in Würzburg', *Archiv des historischen Vereins für Unterfranken und Aschaffenburg* 16 (1863), 1–183 (pp. 72–5).
[154] Wieland, 'Schottenkloster', p. 72; Arnold, 'Nachlaßverzeichnis', p. 286.
[155] Arnold, *Trithemius*, pp. 20 and 215; on the iconography, cf. ibid., pp. 276–81.

The number of books accumulated by Würzburg's abbots within their private chamber is remarkable but not out of step with the personal libraries assembled by some of their peers. The abbatial library at Hildesheim comprised two hundred volumes or more by the later fifteenth century, several of which survive with inscriptions designating them 'pro camera abbatis'.[156] Similar in size was the library of Raphael de Marcatellis, abbot (1437–1508) of Saint-Bavo in Ghent.[157] Even if the size of Würzburg's abbatial library was therefore not exceptional, its contents certainly were. In fact, the collection left behind by Trithemius constituted what would easily have been one of the most well-stocked and wide-ranging corpora of historical narratives anywhere in later medieval Germany, if not the Latin West. Over eighty volumes—a quarter of the entire collection!—contained works of history, from Roman and Greek authorities like Thucydides, Livy, Julius Caesar, Tacitus, Justinus, Valerius Maximus, and Flavius Josephus, to historians of early and central medieval Europe such as Bede, Gregory of Tours, Einhard, Regino of Prüm, Aimoin of Fleury, Lampert of Hersfeld, Ekkehard of Aura, Liutprand of Cremona, Widukind of Corvey, Otto of Freising, Benzo of Alba, Burchard of Ursperg, Saxo Grammaticus, Sigebert of Gembloux, Geoffrey of Viterbo, William of Jumièges, and Geoffrey of Monmouth, but also more recent and contemporary histories by Antoninus of Florence, Marcus Sabellicus, Robert Gaguin, Guillaume Caoursin, Giacomo Filippo Foresti, Ulrich of Richenthal, Werner Rolevinck, and others.[158] If their order on the 1517 inventory permits any speculation as to their arrangement, these history books would have been grouped together and—in a deviation from the arrangement of most monastic libraries—given pride of place even before volumes of Scripture, patristic commentaries, and books of observance.[159] That this was so may be inferred also from Trithemius's *De laude scriptorum*, in which he urges fellow book lovers to store their collections

---

[156] For example, Hildesheim, Dombibliothek, MSS 313b and 785; Wolfenbüttel, Herzog August Bibliothek, MS Cod. Astron. 13.4; see Helmar Härtel, 'Die Bibliothek des Godehardiklosters in Hildesheim', in *Der Schatz von Sankt Godehard*, ed. by Michael Brandt, 2nd ed. (Hildesheim: Diözesan-Museum, 1988, pp. 28–31 (pp. 30 and 31 n. 15)); Schlotheuber and Beckermann, 'Bibliothek', pp. 113–14.

[157] Albert Derolez, *The Library of Raphael de Marcatellis, Abbot of St. Bavon's, Ghent, 1437–1508* (Ghent: Scientia, 1979); Albert Derolez, 'Early Humanism in Flanders: New Data and Observations on the Library of Abbot Raphael de Mercatellis (†1508)', in *Les humanistes et leur bibliothèque*, ed. by Rudolf de Smet (Leuven: Peeters, 2002), pp. 37–57; Kamiel G. Van Acker, 'De librije van Raphael de Marcatellis, abt van Sint-Baafs en bisshop van Rhosus', *Archief- en Bibliotheekwezen in België* 48 (1977), 143–98; Hanno Wijsman, *Luxury Bound: Illustrated Manuscript Production and Noble and Princely Book Ownership in the Burgundian Netherlands (1400–1550)* (Turnhout: Brepols, 2010), pp. 281–3. Similar-sized abbatial libraries existed at other Flemish monasteries, including Saint-Peter's Ghent; Willem P. Blockmans, 'The Devotion of a Lonely Duchess', in *Margaret of York, Simon Marmion, and 'The Visions of Tondal'*, ed. by Thomas Kren (Malibu, CA: Getty Museum, 1992), pp. 29–46 (p. 41).

[158] Arnold, 'Nachlaßverzeichnis', pp. 291–301 (= nos. 1–88, with a few exceptions).

[159] The pressmarks on the books surviving from Würzburg that can be identified with entries on the 1517 inventory assign these histories the signatures A–D before continuing with theology and other subjects from E onwards; Arnold, 'Nachlaßverzeichnis', pp. 293–6 and 299–301 (= nos. 18, 30, 36, 38, 44, 67–9, 74–5, 77, and 80–2). For a useful comparison, see Schlotheuber and Beckermann, 'Bibliothek', pp. 111–12; on medieval monastic library arrangements, cf. Richard Sharpe, 'Accession, Classification, Location: Shelfmarks in Medieval Libraries', *Scriptorium* 50 (1996), pp. 279–87; Teresa Webber,

in chests ('armarii') that prevent theft ('qui nichil ex ea surripi permittant') and arrange them by subject matter ('secundum materias').[160] Practising what he preached, Trithemius arranged his abbatial book chests in such a way as to prioritize the subject that shaped his life and legacy like no other: history.[161]

A question crucial to our understanding of abbatial books is whether they had their home permanently in the abbot's private quarters or whether at least some of them were 'on loan' temporarily from the communal collection. Monasteries offered various locations for storing books—the cloister, the sacristy, the chapter house, the abbey church, the refectory, the infirmary, the dormitory, and even the monks' cells—and access to some of these locations, and the books stored therein, was reserved for certain office holders such as the cantor, the sacrist, the prior, and the abbot.[162] An inventory from Cluny made shortly after the death of Abbot Ivo I (1256–75) records not only the books which the late abbot had provided for the community ('fecit fieri conventui'), but also the various locations in which these books had been deposited in keeping with Ivo's explicit instructions. Some were placed in the monks' library, others taken to the cloister to be fastened with iron chains ('fecit poni in claustro [...] cum cathenis ferreis'), and others again Ivo retained for himself until he donated them to the monks at the end of his life ('dedit et tradidit conventui').[163] Ivo was not the first abbot of Cluny to collect his own books, and a similar collection had existed under his precursor, Majolus (964–94).[164] The *Catalogus abbatum* from the Abbey of SS Ulrich and Afra in Augsburg

---

'Where Were Books Made and Kept?', in *The Cambridge Companion to Medieval British Manuscripts*, ed. by Orietta Da Rold and Elaine Treharne (Cambridge: Cambridge University Press, 2020), pp. 214–33 (pp. 224–8).

[160] *Scribes*, ed./tr. Arnold and Berendt, pp. 92–5; Arnold, 'Leben', pp. 27–8.

[161] Brann, *Trithemius*, p. 306 remarks that '[i]f sheer pagination be our measure[,] Trithemius should be thought of first and foremost as an historian'.

[162] Gameson, 'Library', pp. 15–21; Teresa Webber, 'The Libraries of Religious Houses', in *The European Book in the Twelfth Century*, ed. by Erik Kwakkel and Rodney M. Thomson (Cambridge: Cambridge University Press, 2018), pp. 103–21 (pp. 104–11); Webber, 'Collections', pp. 124–5. According to the *Chronicon Sponheimense*, the books gathered at Sponheim by Trithemius were so numerous that they could not be stored in a single location ('[t]antus enim hodie [c.1503] est in hoc monasterio numerus librorum, quod locus unus non sufficit ad eorum repositionem'); *Chronicon Sponheimense*, II, 396. Other well-studied examples are Durham and Bury St Edmunds; Piper, 'Libraries'; Webber, 'Books'. Similar practices of keeping books also existed amongst other orders such as the Dominicans; Martina Wehrli-Johnsin, '*Libri in cella*: Beobachtungen zu den Privatbibliotheken observanter Dominikaner aus dem Basler Predigerkloster', in *Die Bibliothek–The Library–La Bibliothèque: Denkräume und Wissensordnungen*, ed. by Andreas Speer und Lars Reuke (Berlin: De Gruyter, 2020), pp. 172–86.

[163] Paris, Bibliothèque nationale de France, MS Lat. 10938, fols. 84v–85r, 93v; printed in Delisle, *Cabinet*, II, 483–5, who mistakenly gives the shelfmark as 'Lat. 18938'. On the use of chains to fasten books in the monastic cloister, cf. Gameson, 'Library', pp. 37–42; Schlotheuber and McQuillen, 'Books', p. 978.

[164] Zur Nieden, *Alltag*, pp. 211 n. 810 and the references provided therein. Cluny's early hagiographical sources repeatedly praise Majolus's learning and erudition; cf. Franz Neiske, 'Charismatischer Abt oder charismatische Gemeinschaft? Die frühen Äbte Clunys', in *Charisma und religiöse Gemeinschaften im Mittelalter*, ed. by Giancarlo Andenna, Mirko Breitenstein, and Gert Melville (Münster: LIT, 2005), pp. 55–72 (p. 62); Dominique Iogna-Prat, *Agni Immaculati: Recherches sur les sources hagiographiques relatives à saint Maieul de Cluny (954–994)* (Paris: Éditions du Cerf, 1988).

(Augsburg, Archiv des Bistums, MS 78) records that Abbot Melchior (1459–74) built an abbatial library ('abbatum bibliothecam seu librariam') accessible from the chapter house rather than the dormitory, as was the case with the communal library, so he and his successors would not disturb the sleeping monks ('ut per eius aditum nulla fieret fratribus inquietatio').[165] We should not assume, however, that the allocation of books to one specific location was always or necessarily a permanent arrangement, nor that they could not move between different locations to reflect changes in usage and demand within the community, except perhaps in the case of chained libraries.

A prime example of such mobility is provided by the notarized library inventories from Michelsberg mentioned above (3.3), which enable us to trace, with unusual accuracy, the fluctuation of books between the communal collection and the library of its abbot-historian, Andreas Lang.[166] Initially conducted in 1483 at the occasion of Andreas's appointment, the inquest was repeated twice over the next five years, first in 1486, and then again in 1488. Each time, the record was updated by distinguishing carefully between the volumes in the sacristy ('in sacristia'), those in the library ('in armario sive bibliotheca'), and those in the abbot's private quarters ('libri abbacie'). Amongst the various types of books stored in these locations, there is one that allows us to follow the movements between them with particular precision: history books. Just like his friend Trithemius, albeit on a smaller scale, Bamberg's abbot-historian kept a selection of historical writings close at hand in the comfort of his private rooms, presumably to assist him with his historiographical projects. When the first inventory was produced in 1483, the history books in his custody included Vincent of Beauvais's *Speculum historiale* (in three volumes), William of Tyre's *Historia Ierosolymitana*, Martin of Troppau's *Chronicon pontificum et imperatorum*, Rolevinck's *Fasciculus temporum*, the *Historia Troianorum*, two *Historiae Alexandri magni*, the *Gesta ducis Ernesti*, and the *Deeds* of Archduke Sigismund of Austria (1427–96) and Landgrave William III of Thuringia (1425–82).[167] That

---

[165] 'Catalogus', ed. Streichele, pp. 235–6.

[166] Bamberg, Staatsarchiv, Rep. 29 no. 9 and 187 no. 3030; *MBKDS*, III.3, 370–82, 388–93, and 393–5 (= nos. 93–5, 97–100, and 101–3).

[167] *MBKDS*, III.3, 381–2. The identification of some of these works is not entirely straightforward. It is not unthinkable, for example, that the 'Historia ducis Gotfredi de terra sancta' was a copy of Caxton's *Godeffroy of Boloyne*, rather than William of Tyre's Latin original; the 'Historia ducis Wilhelmi, alias Schiltberger, cum aliis contentis' was almost certainly a copy of the German twelfth-century epic *Herzog Ernst*; there is, moreover, a noticeable focus on extra-European history, and in addition to William of Tyre/Caxton the inventory also lists a certain 'Historia Iohannis de Monte Villa cum aliis historiis insertis', which we may identify with John Mandeville's travellers' tales. We know that Andreas had been responsible for the acquisition of several of these volumes from a register made by his biographer, Nonnosus; MS Bamberg RB. Msc. 49, fol. 57r; *MBKDS*, III.3, 382–8. Juding from this register, Andreas also acquired copies of the *Historia regum Hungarie*, Eusebius's *Chronicon*, and the *Facta et dicta memorabilia* by Valerius Maximus, though none of these can be identified with the extant volumes in *Katalog*, ed. Leitschuh et al., I.2.2, 117–34, nor with the later inventory of books drawn up in the process of the abbey's dissolution in 1803 (Bamberg, Staatsbibliothek, MS Misc. 182.1–2).

this was a temporary allocation is shown by the second inquest of 1486 ('Inventarius novus comportatus librorum abbacie'). Here, neither the *Historia Troianorum* nor the second volume of the *Speculum historiale* is listed amongst the books in the abbot's chamber, but both are back in the main library, suggesting that they had been returned in the interim. Volumes one and three of the *Speculum* stayed with Andreas, presumably because he still made regular use of them. Meanwhile, Andreas added further works of history to his private collection by relocating Foresti's *Supplementum cronicorum* from the communal library to his private collection and procuring copies of Antoninus of Florence's *Chronicon* and the *Gesta Romanorum* not previously recorded at Bamberg, which were still present in his chamber at the third and final inquest in 1488.[168]

The most plausible explanation for this two-way traffic of books—and specifically history books—between the library of the monks and that of their abbot is that the 'libri abbacie' recorded in the inventories of 1483–8 served as the abbot's working library, a reference collection that could be adjusted to suit his needs at a given point in time. It surely was no accident that this periodic review of Andreas's abbatial library coincided closely with the biggest surge in historiographical activity at Michelsberg since the 'glory days' of Abbots Thiemo (1086–94), Gumpold (1094–1112), and Herman (1123–47), which had generated major historical works such as Frutolf's *Chronicle* subsequently continued by Ekkehard of Aura and other redactors, as well as a continuation of Herman and Berthold of Reichenau's *Kaiserchronik*.[169] Unlike in the twelfth century, in the late fifteenth and early sixteenth centuries the writing of history at Bamberg took place, first and foremost, within the abbot's private quarters. It was here that Andreas wrote the *Catalogus abbatum* and the *Chronica episcoporum Babenbergensium*, the *Vitae sancti Ottonis*, and several other works with easy on-site access to a well-stocked working library.[170] That said, we should not think of him as working in perfect isolation like Trithemius. As seen above (1.2), turning the drafts of his historical narratives into fine copies was not a task Andreas took on himself, but one he delegated to a scribal team led by his *amanuensis* and biographer Nonnosus, who faithfully copied whatever was dictated or supplied to him in notes.[171] Where in the monastery this collaboration took place is difficult to know, but an entry in the *Fasciculus abbatum* gives reason to suspect it happened within the confines of the abbot's lodgings.

---

[168] *MBKDS*, III.3, 385–6, 389, and 393–4.
[169] Machilek, 'Geschichtsschreibung', pp. 307–9; *Chronicles of the Investiture Contest: Frutolf of Michelsberg and His Continuators*, tr. by Thomas J. H. McCarthy (Manchester: Manchester University Press, 2014), pp. 1–84; Harry Bresslau, 'Bamberger Studien II' [= 'Die Chroniken des Frutolf von Bamberg und des Ekkehard von Aura'], *Neues Archiv der Gesellschaft für ältere deutsche Geschichtskunde* 21 (1896), 197–234.
[170] Machilek, 'Geschichtsschreibung', pp. 313–14.   [171] MS Bamberg RB. Msc. 49, fol. 57v.

The *Fasciculus* records that in 1484, the year after the compilation of the first inventory, Andreas installed an underground lead-pipe system ('cannas plumbeas subterraneas') to channel fresh water ('aqua recens') from a nearby spring to his abbatial palace ('versus curiam') and supply the abbot's kitchen, the servants' quarters, and—of interest here—the scribes' parlour ('stuba scriptorum').[172] Pipe-based water conduits existed in many medieval monasteries, most prominently perhaps the one installed at Canterbury Cathedral Priory by Prior Wibert (1151–67).[173] They supplied various facilities around the monastery such as infirmaries, washrooms, toilets, laundries, kitchens, refectories, brew- and bake-houses, fishponds, and, especially during later centuries, the lodgings of abbots and priors.[174] These systems were notoriously expensive to build and maintain, and in the case of Bamberg the expenditure exceeded 200 *fl.*[175] Such a substantial

---

[172] MS Bamberg RB. Msc. 49, fol. 55v: 'Anno Domini M° CCCC° LXXXIIII. Idem dominus Andreas abbas continuari fecit venam fontis in plumbeis cannis quem predecessor suus utpote morte preventus profitere non poterat [...] Item de eodum vase fecit fieri cannas plumbeas subterraneas, que ipsam aquam deducunt versus curiam ubi aqua recens ad manum habetur. Item ad stubam scriptorum. Ad stubam familie. Item ad coquinam'. The term 'stuba'—from Old High German *stuba* > Middle High German *stube*; cf. Old English *stofa* ('stove')—suggests a heated room, presumably via a tile stove given the presence of paper and other flammable materials; *Glossarium*, ed. du Cange, VII, 618; 'Stube, *Sf std.*', in *Etymologisches Wörterbuch der deutschen Sprache*, ed. by Friedrich Kluge, rev. by Elmar Seebold, 25th ed. (Berlin: De Gruyter, 2011), pp. 893–4; Konrad Bedal, 'Stube', in *Lexikon des Mittelalters*, 9 vols. (Munich: Artemis, 1980–98), VIII, 249–51. Rainer Atzbach, 'The "Stube" and Its Heating: Archaeological Evidence for a Smoke-Free Living Room between Alps and North Sea', in *Dwellings, Identities and Homes: European Housing Culture from the Viking Age to the Renaissance*, ed. by Kate Giles and Mette Svart Kristiansen (Hoebjerg: Jutland Archaeological Society, 2014), pp. 195–210.

[173] Canterbury's conduit is depicted in the famous *Eadwine Psalter* (Cambridge, Trinity College Library, MS R.17.1, fols. 284v–285r) and has been studied in detail by Francis Woodman, 'The Waterworks Drawings of the Eadwine Psalter', in *The Eadwine Psalter: Text, Image, and Monastic Culture in Twelfth-Century Canterbury*, ed. by Margaret Gibson et al. (London: MHRA, 1992), pp. 168–77; see also Peter J. Fergusson, 'Canterbury Cathedral Priory's Bath House and Fish Pond', *Anglo-Norman Studies* 37 (2015), 115–30; Klaus Grewe, 'Der Wasserversorgungsplan des Klosters Christchurch in Canterbury (12. Jahrhundert)', in *Die Wasserversorgung in Mittelalter*, ed. by Klaus Grewe (Mainz: Zabern, 1991), pp. 229–36.

[174] Early examples are Großkomburg (late eleventh century), St Emmeram in Regensburg (c.1177–1201), and Hirsau, where Abbot Gebhard (1091–1105) extended the *aquaeductus subterraneus* constructed by his predecessor, William (1069–91); 'Historia', ed. Waitz, p. 257; at St Emmeram, the construction of the conduit was the only achievement commemorated on the tombstone of Abbot Peringer (†1201): 'ANNO · D(OMI)NI · M · CC · I · IIII · ID(IBVS) · IAN(VARII) · O(BIIT) · S(AN)C (T)E · MEM(ORIE) · P(ER[I])NG(ER)V(S) · ABB(A)S · HVI(VS) · LOCI · QVI · FEC(IT) · AQ(VE) · DVCTU(M) · PLU(M)BEVM'; for a photographic reproduction of this tomb stone, see Klaus Grewe, 'Wasserversorgung und -entsorgung im Mittelalter–ein technikgeschichtlicher Überblick', in *Die Wasserversorgung in Mittelalter*, ed. by Klaus Grewe (Mainz: Zabern, 1991), pp. 11–86 (p. 42); for additional examples, see James Bond, 'Monastic Water Management in Great Britain: A Review', in *Monastic Archaeology: Papers on the Study of Medieval Monasteries*, ed. by Graham Keevill et al. (Oxford: Oxbow, 2001), pp. 88–136; Roberta J. Magnusson, *Water Technology in the Middle Ages: Cities, Monasteries, and Waterworks after the Roman Empire* (Baltimore, MD: Johns Hopkins University Press, 2001), pp. 5–7.

[175] MS Bamberg RB. Msc. 49, fol. 55v: '[P]lusquem ducenti floreni'. At St Emmeram, repairing the twelfth-century water pipes had cost Abbot Adalbert II (1324–58) in excess of twenty-six pounds of silver, and three centuries later the same pipes were again in such bad repair that 1,000 *fl.* had to be spent on a replacement; '*Fontes monasterii s. Emmerami Ratisbonensis*: Bau- und kunstgeschichtliche

investment only seems justifiable if the facilities served by the new conduit were in regular use, and whilst this may be taken for granted for the abbot's kitchen and servants' quarters, both of which would have been used daily to cater for the abbot and/or his guests, the *stuba scriptorum* might require additional explanation. Just how long this *stuba scriptorum* had existed in the *curia abbatis* is not recorded, but thanks to the *Fasciculus* we know that Andreas's predecessor but one, Abbot Eberhard (1463–75), had given it a new location when he renovated the servants' quarters.[176] This is all we hear about the scribes' parlour during Eberhard's abbacy, and his successor, Ulrich (1475–83), appears to have purchased his books from external sources, rather than having them made in-house.[177] Though it was Ulrich who had laid the foundations for the abbey's water supply by installing pipework worth over 300 *fl.* in 1482, it was Andreas who completed the project and redistributed the water to those facilities which he considered of particular importance, including the *stuba scriptorum*.[178] This decision soon led to a steep increase in domestic book production with a focus on historical writing, driven no doubt by Andreas's investment as both a prolific author and patron of history.

Casting our view to earlier centuries, we find that abbatial book collections existed in many places, and from much earlier than the case studies discussed so far might suggest. One particularly well-documented example of just such a collection from before the turn of the millennium is that of Adso, abbot of Montier-en-Der (968–92) and Saint-Bénigne in Dijon (987–89). Adso was himself a prolific writer of historical narratives that dealt with both the past and the future. During his abbacy, he composed two *gesta*, one of them dedicated to a previous abbot of Montier-en-Der, and an apocalyptical treatise about the arrival of the Antichrist.[179] When in 992 news reached the monks of Montier-en-Der that their abbot-historian had died on pilgrimage to the Holy Land, they produced an inventory of the books Adso had left behind upon his departure. This inventory—not a 'catalogue', as it has been called—survives on the final page of Montier-en-Der's copy of the *Martyrologium Usuardi* (Paris, Bibliothèque

---

Quellen', in *Quellen und Forschungen zur Geschichte des ehemaligen Reichsstiftes St. Emmeram in Regensburg*, ed. by Max Piendl (Kallmünz: Lassleben, 1961), pp. 1–183 (pp. 78, 113–14, and 135–6); cited in Grewe, 'Wasserversorgung', p. 44.

[176] MS Bamberg RB. Msc. 49, fol. 51r: 'Item stuba scriptorum translata est et annexa stube familie expositi sunt'; the same entry appears in MS Bamberg RB. Msc. 48, fol. 271v, but neither of them mentions the specific location of the *stuba scriptorum* before/after its relocation. The *Fasciculus* further credits Eberhard with the construction of a bookbinding workshop ('stuba ligature librorum') and a new scraping room ('stuba rasure'), the latter of which was probably used to prepare animal skins so they could be made into vellum; MS Bamberg RB. Msc. 49, fol. 51v.

[177] MS Bamberg RB. Msc. 49, fol. 54r; *MBKDS*, III.3, 368–9.

[178] MS Bamberg RB. Msc. 49, fol. 53v: 'Idem dominus abbas Anno Domini M° CCCC° LXXXII renovari fecit fontem de vicina silva cum novis cannis, que usque ad sanctam fidem eo vivente adducta fuit pro cuius labore expositi sunt plusquam trecenti floreni. Qui videlicet fons postea per dominum Andream abbatem perfectum fuit, pro ut modo cernitur'.

[179] On Adso, his career, and his writings, see Manitius, *Geschichte*, II, 432–42; Bernd Schneidmüller, 'Adso von Montier-en-Der und die Frankenkönige', *Trierer Zeitschrift* 40/1 (1977/8), 189–99.

nationale de France, MS Lat. 5547, fol. 104v).[180] A large percentage of the inventory's twenty-three titles are by classical and early Christian authorities such as Cicero, Terence, Maurus Servius Honoratus, Caelius Sedulius, Eutyches (more likely the sixth-century grammarian than the fifth-century heretic by the same name), and Martianus Capella, but they also include more recently produced historical narratives such as the 'Vita sancti Iohannis elemosinarii' and Freculf's *Historiarum libri XII*.[181]

As noted by Franck Collard, it is unlikely that Adso had bequeathed these books to his community before he left for Jerusalem, and more likely that they were discovered when his abbatial lodgings were searched posthumously and an inventory of their contents compiled on behalf of his successor, Abbot Berengar (992–c.1000)—a procedure that reminds us of the succession arrangements at later medieval Würzburg seen above.[182] In fact, the inventory's rubric specifies that the books were found in Adso's book chest *after* his departure ('Hii sunt libri domni abbatis Adsonis, quos in arca eius repperimus, *postquam* ipse Hierosolimam petiit').[183] That they had indeed constituted the late abbot's personal library is evidenced further by a letter from Gerbert, abbot of Bobbio (982/3–99)—better known as Gerbert of Aurillac and, from 999, Pope Sylvester II—to Adalbero, archbishop of Reims (969–89), dated 983, nine years before Adso's death, in which Gerbert asks Adalbero to use his episcopal clout to help him acquire Adso's copy of the historical work by Julius Caesar, presumably his *Gallic Wars*, so he can have it copied by his scribes at Bobbio ('[i]storiam Iulii Cęsaris a domno Azone abbate Dervensi ad rescribendum nobis adquirite').[184] Though it is true that no such manuscript features on the inventory of 992, Collard's suggestion that Gerbert might have failed to return the borrowed book to Adso—which is supported by the fact that a copy of Caesar's work does feature on Gerbert's own book list—seems compelling.[185] If this was so, then the manuscript in question ended up being part of not one, but two abbatial book collections, finding its eventual home not in Adso's personal book chest at Montier-en-Der, but in Gerbert's at Bobbio.

---

[180] Henri Omont, 'Catalogue de la bibliothèque de l'abbé Adson de Montier-en-Der (992)', *Bibliothèque de l'École des chartes* 42 (1881), 157–60; Franck Collard, 'Les livres de l'abbé Adson et l'abbaye de Montier-en-Der', in *Les moines du Der 673–1790*, ed. by Patrick Corbet, Jackie Lusse, and Georges Viard (Langres: Guéniot, 2000), pp. 147–59, with a critique of Omond's use of terminology (ibid., p. 148 n. 8).

[181] Edited, with possible identifications for most of the list's entries, in Omont, 'Catalogue', pp. 159–60. Adso is known to have possessed other classical works, too, including a history of Julius Caesar which is mentioned in his private correspondence; Collard, 'Livres', pp. 150–2 with the relevant references and discussion.

[182] Collard, 'Livres', p. 150. A handlist of Montier-en-Der's abbots is provided in *The Cartulary of Montier-en-Der, 666–1129*, ed. by Constance B. Bouchard (Toronto: University of Toronto Press, 2004), pp. 363–6.

[183] MS Lat. 5547, fol. 104v, ll. 1–3, my emphasis; Omont, 'Catalogue', p. 159.

[184] *Briefsammlung*, ed. Weigle, pp. 30–1 (p. 31) (= no. 8); *Correspondence*, ed. Riché and Callu, I, 16–19 (= no. 8).

[185] Collard, 'Livres', p. 151, with reference to Pierre Riché, *Gerbert d'Aurillac: Le pape de l'an mil* (Paris: Fayard, 1987), p. 257.

Even earlier than Adso's books are three codices from Bobbio—Gerbert/ Sylvester II's sometime home—with inscriptions assigning them to an abbot's book chest.[186] The first, a copy of Jerome's commentary on Isaiah produced c.622, comes from the chest of Abbot Attalanus (615–25/6) (Milan, Biblioteca Ambrosiana, MS S 45 sup., p. 2; 'L[i]b[er] de arca domno Ata[l]ani').[187] The second, written c.580–620 and containing works by Lactantius, Hilarius, and others, belongs to the chest of Vorgust, whose abbacy is otherwise unattested (Turin, Archivio Di Stato, MS IB.II.27, fol. 1v: 'De arca dom[ni] Vorgusti abb [at]i').[188] The third, a copy of St Augustine's *Sermones* and other works contemporary with the previous codex, is from the chest of Bobulenus (c.643–54) (Vatican, Biblioteca Apostolica Vaticana, MS Vat. lat. 5758, p. 1: 'Liber de arca domini Bobuleni').[189] Michal Richter believes these chests to have been installed during the early eighth century and labelled after Bobbio's previous abbots to organize and commemorate, retrospectively, the books each of them had provided for the community.[190] This seems an unnecessarily cumbersome explanation, and a more plausible one is that these chests—just like those at Montier-en-Der and elsewhere—served as repositories for the personal book collections of three seventh-century abbots that were created during their respective tenures and inherited, along with their contents, by subsequent incumbents.[191] Another

---

[186] Bernhard Bischoff, *Latin Palaeography: Antiquity and the Middle Ages*, tr. by Daibhm O. Cróinin and David Ganz (Cambridge: Cambridge University Press, 1990), p. 192. Michael Lapidge proposes that the Latin term 'arca', at least during the early medieval/Anglo-Saxon period, typically designated 'a wooden chest placed on the floor'; Lapidge, *Library*, p. 61.

[187] See the entry in the 'Earlier Latin Manuscripts' database [hereafter *ELM*] at the National University of Ireland, Galway developed on the basis of *Codices Latini Antiquiores*, ed. by Elias A. Lowe, 12 vols. (Oxford: Clarendon, 1934–82), III, no. 365, with photographic reproductions; https://elmss.nuigalway.ie/catalogue/703. The book's date remains contested; Pius Engelbert, 'Zur Frühgeschichte des Bobbieser Skriptoriums', *Revue bénédictine* 78 (1986), 220–60 (pp. 227–30); Michael Richter, *Bobbio in the Early Middle Ages: The Abiding Legacy of Columbanus* (Dublin: Four Courts Press, 2008), pp. 73–5 and 83–6.

[188] *Codici Bobbiesi della Biblioteca Nazionale Universitaria in Torino*, ed. by Carlo Cipolla [= *Collezione Paleografica Bobbiese* I] (Milan: Hoepli, 1907), pp. 90–1; also cf. the entry in *ELM*, https://elmss.nuigalway.ie/catalogue/784.

[189] *Specimina codicum Latinorum Vaticanorum*, ed. by Franz Ehrle and Paul Libaert [= *Tabulae in usum scholarum* III] (Berlin: De Gruyter, 1932), p. xix (= no. 8); James J. John, 'The Ex-Libris in Codices Latini Antiquiores', *Scriptorium* 50 (1996), 239–43 (p. 242); also cf. the entry in *ELM*, https://elmss.nuigalway.ie/catalogue/44.

[190] Richter, *Bobbio*, p. 74, quoting a previous suggestion by Pius Engelbert that 'at the beginning of the eight century a librarian of Bobbio put into order the steadily growing amount of manuscripts and marked them with a kind of guideline note'; Engelbert, 'Frühgeschichte', p. 233 (English translation by Richter).

[191] Richter suspects that the chests had a room of their own, but there is no support for his identification of this room with the monastery's library or scriptorium; Richter, *Bobbio*, p. 74. By the time of Abbot Agilulf (c.883–96), Bobbio had come to resemble a 'monastic town' (ibid., p. 124) with a wide range of buildings and facilities that included a designated house for the abbot, which seems the more obvious location for these book chests. An intriguing parallel is found in the *Rule of the Master* (XVII.1-2 and 10-13) from sixth-century Italy or southern Gaul, according to which a monastery's tools must be stored in one room ('in uno cubiculo'), the custody of which the abbot will assign to a single brother he knows to be responsible. In this room there should be various chests ('arcae'), including one for the abbot's personal belongings ('res abbatis') and one for the monastery's books

possibility is that they were not three separate chests, but a single chest that was handed down from one abbot to the next and re-named in the process.

Considering their material composition—they were probably made from wood—and the unfortunate fate or destruction of the buildings in which they were housed in the process of their dissolution or as a result of medieval as well as modern warfare, it is no surprise that neither Adso's chest nor those from Bobbio survive, and the same is true elsewhere, such as at Montecassino.[192] To my knowledge, no abbatial book chests or *armariola* are known to survive *in situ*, and in the absence of tangible material or archaeological evidence we must turn to written and artistic sources for information about their design. Fortunately, there are depictions, particularly manuscript illuminations, that can furnish us with ideas about the physical appearance of abbatial book chests. They include the so-called *Maius chronicon Fontanellense* (Le Havre, Bibliothèque municipale, MS 332), a compilation of historical works from Saint-Wandrille produced c.1075 that encompasses, amongst others, the *Gesta abbatum Fontanellensium* and *Vita Ansberti* introduced earlier in this book (2.1).[193] Opposite the *Vita*'s prologue is a full-page miniature of Abbot/Bishop Asbert in his insignia set against the backdrop of Saint-Wandrille's monastic architecture (fol. 41v). Below Ansbert's feet are a monk and, in the bottom right-hand corner, a large chest filled with books in ornate bindings (Fig. 4.3). That this was likely meant to depict Ansbert's personal book chest, rather than a communal *armarium*, is suggested by an episode related in the *Vita* (fol. 45r), informing us that when Ansbert first decided to become a monk of Saint-Wandrille after a high-flying career at the court of Chlothar III, the abbey's then abbot and namesake, Wandregisel, recognized the novice's sharpness of mind ('acumen ingenii') and ordered for him to be issued with a large and diverse book collection ('diversorum voluminum copiam ei concite tribui iussit') for his personal use.[194] The *Vita* provides no information as to what happened with these books following Ansbert's own election as abbot in 678, but it is not

---

and documents ('arca cum diversis codicibus, membranis, et cartis monasterii'); *RM*, ed./tr. de Vogüé, I, 175; tr. Eberle, pp. 165–6. Engelbert identifies the 'res abbatis' with vestments, though there is nothing to suggest that these could not have included books belonging to the abbot that were considered distinct from the 'codices monasterii' in the communal book and deed chest; Engelbert, 'Frühgeschichte', p. 232. On the relationship between the *RM* and the *RB*, see Bernd Jaspert, *Die Regula Benedicti- Regula Magistri-Kontroverse* (Hildesheim: Gerstenberg, 1977).

[192] On the destruction(s) of Montecassino, see Kriston R. Rennie, *The Destruction and Recovery of Monte Cassino, 529–1964* (Amsterdam: Amsterdam University Press, 2020). An important but little-known primary source not considered by Rennie is the travel diary by Dom Bede Camm (1864–1942), a monk of Downside Abbey in Stratton-on-the-Fosse, Somerset, which includes detailed drawings and floorplans of Montecassino's monastic buildings prior to their bombing in 1944; see 'History & Community: 20 Exhibits from Downside Abbey', https://historyandcommunity.com/room2D.html.

[193] On the manuscript, see *Chronique*, ed./tr. Pradié, pp. lxxviii–lxxxiv; *La France romane au temps des premiers Capétiens (987–1152)*, ed. by Danielle Gaborit-Chopin et al. (Paris: Musée du Louvre Éditions, 2005), p. 333 (= no. 255).

[194] 'Vita', ed. Krusch and Levison, p. 622; the *Gesta abbatum* make surprisingly little mention of Ansbert and his abbatial deeds, perhaps because the *Vita Ansberti* already existed at the time of its composition and was easily accessible in-house; *Chronique*, ed./tr. Pradié, pp. 2–25.

Fig. 4.3 Ansbert of Saint-Wandrille and his book chest. Le Havre, Bibliothèque municipale Armand Salacrou, MS 332, fol. 41v.

implausible that he kept a personal library during his abbacy (and episcopate) in the way subsequent abbots of Saint-Wandrille are known to have done, and that this abbatial library was stored in chests like that later depicted in the *Maius chronicon*.

Possibly the most striking visual example of an abbatial book chest is found in a late fourteenth-/early fifteenth-century manuscript from St Albans (London, British Library, MS Cotton Claudius E IV), the better part of which

Fig. 4.4 Simon of St Albans and his book chest. London, British Library, MS Cotton Claudius E IV, fol. 124r.

(fols. 97v–321r) is occupied by the *Gesta abbatum* in Thomas Walsingham's recension.[195] The chapter dedicated to Abbot Simon is decorated with a miniature that shows him perched in front of a large book chest (Fig. 4.4). The outside of the chest is fortified with wrought iron(?) brackets along all edges and a big rectangular lock centred on the front panel, its inside bursting with various books and documents, one of which is being studied attentively by the abbot. The *Gesta*'s author celebrates Simon as a man of letters ('vir litteratus'), a book lover ('amator scripturarum').[196] As we will recall (3.3), Simon gave numerous books to his monks and installed a bespoke painted cupboard for them inside the abbey church.[197] This is unlikely to be the plain and unornamented wooden chest depicted by the *Gesta*'s miniaturist, though, and the scene's intimate setting is more suggestive of a private study than a church nave. Further supporting this distinction is the presence of several unbound documents amongst the chest's visible contents, whereas the text refers exclusively to bound volumes. As we will see below (4.4), abbatial lodgings regularly provided storage for charters and archival documents, and the mixed contents of Simon's chest with its discernible

---

[195] On this manuscript and its recension of the *Gesta abbatum*, cf. *Gesta*, tr. Preest and Clark, pp. 36–7; Clark, *Renaissance*, pp. 163–6.

[196] See *Gesta*, ed. Riley, I, 184 and 192; tr. Preest and Clark, pp. 290 and 300, who translate 'amator scripturarum' as 'a great lover of the Scriptures', though to my mind the context does not necessitate such a semantic reduction of the term.

[197] *Gesta*, ed. Riley, I, 184.

reinforcements (iron brackets and a locking mechanism) may indicate that this was not just a repository for books, but also, perhaps, an abbatial deed chest.

This is not to say that abbots' personal book chests had to be entirely functional, plain, and unadorned—in fact, the painted chests of Würzburg's late medieval abbots discussed above are evidence to the contrary, and they are not the only ones. Abbot John V (1065–1117) of Subiaco not only copied various books himself, but he also built—possibly with his own hands—a chest for them that was marvelled at by chroniclers for its remarkable beauty and craftsmanship ('fecit arcile ad recondendum libros sculptum mira pulcritudine').[198] The nature of these books suggests that they—and by extension their beautiful container—were made not just *by* the abbot, but also for *his* use.[199] Ornate book chests were not unique to monastic superiors. As early as the eighth century, Stephen of Ripon reported that Bishop Wilfrid of York (664–78) had ordered gift copies of the Gospels written in pure gold and on purple parchment, a gift that was accompanied by a book chest made from the purest gold and the precious gemstones ('et bibliothecam librorum eorum omnem de auro purissimo et gemmis pretiosissimis fabricatam'), which Wilfrid had custom-built by master jewellers ('conpaginare inclusores gemmarum praecepit').[200] When the Dominican convent of Blackfriars, Scarborough was searched and looted during its dissolution, the inquest stated that '[o]n the site of the palace of the abbot [...], there was found an elegant and ingeniously-constructed box, made of iron', the outside of which was lavishly adorned with gold and some silver-like precious metal, and its interior 'painted with vermillion, as is the support of the lid'.[201] Even the sturdiest and most luxurious chests sometimes failed to protect their contents, however. Much to the disapproval of the author(s) of St Albans's *Gesta abbatum*, several of the books from Simon's

---

[198] *Chronicon Sublacense: AA. 593–1369*, ed. by Raffaello Morghen (Bologna: Zanichelli, 1927), p. 16.

[199] They included St Augustine's *Confessions*, an unspecified work by Isidor (possibly his *Etymologies*), St Jerome's psalter, antiphonaries for both day and night, an unspecified rule (presumably that of St Benedict), a customary, and a book of letters.

[200] 'Vita Wilfridi I. episcopi Eboracensis auctore Stephano', ed. by Wilhelm Levison, in *Passiones vitaeque sanctorum aevi Merovingici (IV)*, ed. by Bruno Krusch and Wilhelm Levison [= *MGH SS rer. Merov.* VI] (Hanover: Hahn, 1913), pp. 163–263 (pp. 212–13).

[201] See Joseph B. Baker, *The History of Scarborough, from the Earliest Date* (London: Longmans, Green & Co., 1882), pp. 133–4, with a drawing of the chest labelled 'Ancient Deed Chest' (ibid., p. 133), which is described in great detail as being 'one foot two inches long, seven and a half inches broad, and seven inches deep, and is composed of hammered iron one-eighth of an inch in thickness, bound with thin bars of the same metal, so as to divide it into compartments. The keyhole in front, which has been richly gilt, is false, and only placed there for ornament. The outward foliated border has also been gilded. The several compartments have been painted with various devices, chiefly landscapes. The handles and bases are painted with vermillion. The lid [...] is almost entirely occupied with the lock, which is of curious workmanship, having five string bolts which, when the lid is pressed down, lock instantaneously, and are opened by a key in the centre of the lid, the keyhole for which is hid by a sliding bar. The embellishment on the front of the lock is curiously chased and filled with a white metal, not unlike to silver'. The chest is said subsequently to have 'passed into the hands of a gentleman at Retford named Hudson'. To my knowledge, its whereabouts today remain unknown, making it impossible to date it with certainty.

book chest had been sold by his fourteenth-century successor, Richard of Wallingford, though at least one of them (London, British Library, MS Royal 13 D IV) had since been retrieved, for a rather hefty ransom, by the subsequent incumbent, Michael of Mentmore.[202] The dynamics governing this cross-generational legacy and inheritance of abbatial libraries in the Middle Ages are the subject of the next part of this study.

4.4 Custodianship, Inheritance, and Bequest

The evidence presented thus far leaves no real doubt that abbatial libraries were a regular phenomenon from the early medieval period onwards. But what happened to these libraries when their owners died, resigned, or had their abbacy curtailed/terminated by other means? Perhaps the most obvious option, and one already seen at Würzburg and Barking, was for the departed/departing superior's books to be preserved *in situ* so they could be passed on to and inherited by the successor. In some cases, this took the shape of formalized legislation and codified custom, such as when a memorandum was drawn up at St Augustine's Abbey, Canterbury (Canterbury, Cathedral Archives and Library, DCC/ChAnt/A/66C) in the later fifteenth century, stipulating that an abbot quitting his office—whether due to resignation, change of institution, or death is not specified—must not only part with his insignia, but also leave behind his books ('libri'), charters ('munimenta'), and other documents ('scripta') so they can be handed over to his successor.[203] A similar if less formalized arrangement existed at St Blasien, whose abbots

---

[202] *Gesta*, ed. Riley, III, 200–1; tr. Preest and Clark, pp. 677–9; see also Jenny Stratford and Teresa Webber, 'Bishops and Kings: Private Book Collections in Medieval England', in *The Cambridge History of Libraries in Britain and Ireland*, Vol. 1: *To 1640*, ed. by Teresa Webber and Elizabeth Leedham-Green (Cambridge: Cambridge University Press, 2006), pp. 178–217 (p. 193). Similar charges were brought against two later twelfth-/early thirteenth-century abbots of Mont-Saint-Michel, Jordan (1191–1212) and Raoul (III) de Villedieu (1229–37), who stood accused of having sold off their monastery's books; Jean Chazelas, 'La vie monastique au Mont Saint-Michel au XIIIe siècle', in *Millénaire monastique du Mont Saint-Michel*, ed. by Jean Laporte et al., 5 vols. (Paris: Lethielleux, 1967–93), I, 127–50 (pp. 140–46). The primary evidence of these accusations survives in Avranches, Bibliothèque patrimoniale, MS 149, fols. 118r–v and 149v–151v. I owe this reference to Fabien Paquet.
[203] Canterbury, Cathedral Archives and Library, DCC/ChAnt/A/66C, ll. 11–13. I am grateful to Dr Alison Ray, then Assistant Archivist at Canterbury Cathedral, now College Archivist and Records Manager at St Peter's College, Oxford, for kindly assisting me in locating this document and supplying me with images. Also cf. Clark, 'Abbot', p. 108. The monastic customary of St Augustine's, Canterbury contains some regulations that might belong in a similar context, stipulating that upon the death of a monk, any books he may have acquired were to be incorporated into the communal library after the cantor had inscribed the deceased's name into each of them; *Customary*, ed. Thompson, I, 362; cf. Malcom B. Parkes, 'The Provision of Books', in *The History of the University of Oxford*, ed. by Jeremy I. Catto et al., 8 vols. (Oxford: Clarendon, 1984–2000), II, 407–83; repr. in *Pages from the Past: Medieval Writing Skills and Manuscript Books*, ed. by Pamela R. Robinson and Rivkah Zim (Aldershot: Ashgate, 2012), pp. 407–83 (= no. XIV) (p. 455).

maintained a cumulative library over several generations.²⁰⁴ A book list from Meaux (London, British Library, MS Cotton Vitellius C VI, fol. 242v) dated 1396 records a small collection of seven books for the abbot's daily use, and their central location inside the abbey church ('in communi almario in ecclesia') might suggest that they were passed down between incumbents. In other cases, the inheritance of books between successive generations of abbots appears to have been the result not of custom or legislation, but primarily of the care and foresight of specific individuals. According to his biographer, Abbot Hugh II (1150-69) of Saint-Amand always carried some of his books with him on his official business, annotating them carefully so that his successors, who stood to inherit them after his death, would have something to occupy them on their journeys, too ('ut habeant, inquit, posteri mei, dum saecularibus implicantur et equitant, ubi figant intentionem, si tamen velint').²⁰⁵ Of course, abbots could also inherit books from individuals other than their predecessors. In his testament, thirteenth-century canon lawyer Henry of Segusio (†1271) designated a range of benefactors for his large book collection. Having stipulated that his 'green decretals' were to go to Archbishop Aiglerius of Naples, Henry added that, if Aiglerius died before him, the book in question should go to his brother, the abbot of Montecassino.²⁰⁶

Such arrangements do not seem to have existed everywhere, though, nor were they always applied rigorously. Rather than surrendering their books to their successors, some abbots held on to them beyond their tenure. A prominent example of this is Benedict Biscop, founder and first abbot of Monkwearmouth-Jarrow who had previously held the abbacy (669-71) of St Augustine's, Canterbury. According to Bede's *Historia abbatum*, Benedict in the second year of his Canterbury abbacy had brought back many books ('libros non paucos') from a journey to Rome, some of which he then used to endow his new foundation in the North.²⁰⁷ More striking still is the case of Seiwold, abbot of Bath. Banished from his native England after the Battle of Hastings, Seiwold found sanctuary in Flanders and was appointed abbot of Saint-Vaast.²⁰⁸ According to an inventory in a copy of Augustine's commentary on the Gospel of John (Arras, Bibliothèque

---

²⁰⁴ Gerhard Stamm, 'Zur Geschichte der Bibliothek', in *Das tausendjährige St. Blasien: 200jähriges Domjubiläum*, ed. by Chistel Römer and Ernst Petrasch, 2 vols. (Karlsruhe: Badenia, 1984), II, 171-200 (pp. 199-200 n. 160).

²⁰⁵ This is recorded in St Amand's twelfth-century book inventory; Paris, Bibliothèque nationale de France, MS Lat. 1850, fol. 202r.

²⁰⁶ Edited in Agostino Paravicini Bagliani, *I testamenti dei cardinali del Duecento* (Rome: Presso la Società alla Biblioteca Vallicelliana, 1980), pp. 134-5 (p. 135).

²⁰⁷ *Abbots*, ed./tr. Grocock and Wood, pp. 30-1. Benedict Biscop's journey to Rome in 671 is also reported, albeit without any mention of books, in *The Chronicle of John of Worcester*, ed./tr. Reginald R. Darlington and Patrick McGurk, 2 vols. (Oxford: Oxford University Press, 1995-8), II, 120-1. Also cf. above (3.2).

²⁰⁸ We cannot be certain about the precise dates of Seiwold's abbacy, though the years sometimes suggested in previous scholarship (for example, 986-1008 and 993-1005) are certainly mistaken; Philip Grierson, 'Les livres d'abbé Seiwold de Bath', *Revue bénédictine* 52 (1940), 96-116 (p. 96 n. 2). He was certainly in post in the early to-mid-1060s and expelled by 1077; he died on 19 April 1084 (ibid., pp. 97-100).

municipale, MS 849 (539), fol. 159r), Seiwold personally carried ('contulit') some thirty-three books to his new home across the English Channel, all of which, as far as we know, had previously been with him at Bath.[209] A rare example of a 'personal library of an English ecclesiastic at the time of the Conquest',[210] Seiwold's inventory shows a notable concentration of history books. Besides the lives and deeds of the desert fathers (Brussels, Koninklijke Bibliotheek van België, MS 9850-52), we can find Alcuin's *Vita* of Richard the Hermit (lost), the *Lives* of SS Cuthbert, Guthlac, Filibert, Dunstan, Waleric, Maurus, Lucian, Maxian, and Julian collected in two volumes (both lost), Fulbert's *Gesta* of Abbot Aichard of Jumièges (Arras, Bibliothèque municipale, MS 1029 (812)), Cassiodorus's *Historia tripartita* (lost), and Bede's *Historia ecclesiastica gentis Anglorum* (possibly New York, NY, Pierpont Morgan Library and Museum, MS M.826).[211] Historical narratives also figure prominently amongst the books in the personal library of Alcuin, abbot of Tours, some of which he had inherited from Ælberht, Archbishop of York, and delivered to Tours upon his appointment in 796.[212] Besides Paulinus of Nola's *Carmina* on St Felix and Avitus of Vienne's historio-exegetical poem *De spiritualis historiae gestis*, Alcuin's abbatial library included copies of Justinus's epitome of the *Histories* by Pompeius Trogus and Pliny the Elder's *Historia naturalis*.

Another early medieval abbot whose custody of books seems to have extended beyond his tenure is Baugulf of Fulda. One of the earliest book lists to survive from Fulda records seventeen volumes under the rubric 'De cella Paugolfi' (Vatican, Biblioteca Apostolica Vaticana, MS Pal. lat. 1877, fol. 35v; hereafter B1). The dominant scholarly interpretation is that these books and six others itemized on a second inventory found in the same codex (B2) were relocated temporarily to Fulda's dependent cell at Wolfsmünster (founded by Baugulf) before being returned to the mother house and (re-)integrated into its communal library after Baugulf's death in 815.[213] According to this interpretation, Baugulf removed

---

[209] Michael Lapidge, 'Surviving Book Lists from Anglo-Saxon England', in *Learning and Literature in Anglo-Saxon England*, ed. by Michael Lapidge and Hemlut Gneuss (Cambridge: Cambridge University Press, 1985), pp. 33-89; repr. and rev. in *Anglo-Saxon Manuscripts: Basic Readings*, ed. by Mary P. Richards (New York, NY: Routledge, 1994), pp. 87-167 (pp. 125-30; = no. VII). I would like to thank Pascal Rideau at the Médiathèque d'Arras and Dominique Stutzmann at the IRHT, Paris for kindly providing me with information on and images of the manuscript containing the book list.

[210] Lapidge, 'Lists', p. 126; Lapidge, *Library*, pp. 136-7. Lapidge also allows for the possibility that Seiwold abducted these books from the communal library of Bath's monks, though on balance this seems less likely.

[211] On these identifications, see Lapidge, 'Lists', pp. 127-30; Grierson, 'Livres', pp. 107-11. Whether or not the codex containing the book list also arrived at Saint-Vaast with Seiwold we do not know, but it certainly belonged to the monks' library during the twelfth century as evidenced by an ownership mark on fol. 159v ('Liber sancti Vedasti Atrebatensis, quique eum furaverit anathema sit') written in a twelfth-century hand. Similar ownership marks are also found in other eleventh- to thirteenth-century books from Saint-Vaast, for example, Arras, Bibliothèque municipale, MSS 294 (849), 573 (462), and 1071 (274).

[212] Printed with commentary in Lapidge, 'Lists', pp. 105-12 (= no. I).

[213] *Bücherverzeichnisse*, ed. Schrimpf et al., pp. 17-21 (= B1-2); Paul Lehmann, 'Quot et quorum libri fuerint in libraria Fuldensi', in *Bok- och bibliotekshistoriska Studier: Tillägnade Isak Collijn på hans 50-årsdagpp*, ed. by Axel Nelson (Uppsala: Almqvist & Wiksells, 1925), pp. 47-57 (pp. 54-5).

these twenty-three volumes from Fulda when resigning from office in 802 and kept them at Wolfsmünster for the rest of his life. Though it is tempting to see a parallel with Seiwold's case, there is another possibility that deserves exploration, namely that the *cella Paugolfi* described not Baugulf's minor foundation at Wolfsmünster, but rather the lodgings he and his abbatial successors inhabited at Fulda—indeed, this is the very sense in which the word 'cella' was used by Gregory the Great when describing the early monastic architecture of St Benedict's foundation of Montecassino.[214] Such a reading gains further support from a third book list contemporary with B1 and B2 and copied alongside them in the Vatican manuscript (B3), according to whose enigmatic rubric an unnamed abbot extracted some seventeen volumes from an unspecified location ('istos libros abstulit abbas inde') at an unknown point in time.[215] Scholars generally agree that this abbot was probably Baugulf and the location the *cella* mentioned in B1, but so far they have struggled to explain where the books were taken from there, when, and why. Identifying this *cella* with the abbot's quarters at Fulda resolves many of these questions, especially if we assume, as some have before,[216] that all three book lists were compiled in the immediate aftermath of Baugulf's resignation, quite possibly at the explicit order of his abbatial successor, Ratger. Their shared purpose, then, would have been to furnish the newly invested abbot with an inventory of his predecessor's library, not dissimilar from the inventories at Würzburg. In keeping with this possibility, B1/B2 would represent the abbatial library Baugulf had accrued at Fulda over the course of his tenure, and B3 a selection of books from this library that were relocated to Wolfsmünster in 802 and therefore no longer present in the abbot's quarters when they were prepared for Ratger after Baugulf's departure. Indeed, this would explain why just about half of the seventeen titles in B3 reappear verbatim in B1/B2, another conundrum that has remained unsolved to date. Whichever interpretation we adopt, the likelihood is that Baugulf took a selection of books with him *after* he resigned from Fulda's abbacy, thus leaving his successor, Ratger, with a diminished library to inherit.

That abbatial book custody and ownership were not uncommon at early medieval Fulda is suggested also by the famous *Cadmug Codex* (Fulda, Hochschul- und Landesbibliothek, MS B3), a 'pocket Gospel book' from Ireland that might have found its way to Fulda in the company of Boniface. The manuscript then seems to have passed into the possession of the East Frankish rulers until it was returned by

---

[214] *Grégoire le Grand: Dialogues*, ed. by Adalbert de Vogüé and tr. by Paul Antin, 3 vols. (Paris: Éditions du Cerf, 1978-80), II, 156-7 and 170-1. On Fulda's residence, cf. Marc-Aeilko Aris et al., 'Fulda, St. Salvator', in *Die benediktinischen Mönchs- und Nonnenkloster in Hessen*, ed. by Friedhelm Jürgensmeier, Franziskus Büll, and Regina E. Schwerdtfeger [= *Germania Benedictina* VII] (St. Ottilien: EOS, 2004), pp. 374-5 (pp. 367-74).

[215] *Bücherverzeichnisse*, ed. Schrimpf et al., pp. 21-3 (= B3).

[216] Wesley M. Stevens, 'Fulda Scribes at Work: Bodleian Library, Manuscript Canonici Miscellaneous 353', *Bibliothek und Wissenschaft* 8 (1972), 287-317 (p. 308).

Arnulf of Carinthia at some point prior to 896.[217] A note in golden letters found on the book's final page (fol. 65v) records that Abbot Huoggi (891–915), procured the codex from King Arnulf ('a rege piissimo Arnolfo impetravit') and honourably restored it to Fulda ('sanctae Fuldensi aeclesiae honorabiliter restituit').[218] As argued by Franz Staab, Huoggi probably received the book in a location other than Fulda, possibly in Regensburg, where he met with the king soon after his abbatial election.[219] The note does not specify whether Huoggi handed over the recuperated codex to the monks immediately upon his return, nor at which point it was incorporated into the monastery's library, and there is a chance that it stayed in his personal custody for the remainder of his abbacy. This would not have been unusual. One of Huoggi's predecessors, Hatto I (842–56), styled himself a 'book custodian' ('custos librorum') in a letter to Pope Leo IV.[220] Just like Hatto, who prior to his election had served as Fulda's *armarius*, Huoggi formerly held the office of monastic librarian ('bibliothecarius'),[221] and both seem to have used this curatorial expertise to continue collecting books during their abbacies. Despite repeated attempts, it remains impossible to identify the *Cadmug Codex*—or any of the so-called *Codices Bonifatiani*, for that matter—amongst the recorded holdings of Fulda's medieval library.[222] Whilst the fragmentary nature of the inventories prohibits definitive conclusions, we can suspect cautiously that the book might have been part of the abbot's library for some time before it was eventually incorporated into the communal book collection, quite possibly at Huoggi's death in 915, with the note on the book's final page denoting a posthumous bequest.

Such a 'deathbed donation' would chime well with the practices we can observe across the wider European map. In fact, posthumous bequests to the monastic community followed by incorporation, wholly or in part, into its institutional

---

[217] *Handschriften*, ed. Hausmann, p. 12; Franz Staab, 'Fulda (B)', in *Die deutschen Königspfalzen: Repertorium der Pfalzen, Königshöfe und übrigen Aufenthaltsorte der Könige im deutschen Reich des Mittelalters*, Vol. I.5: *Hessen*, ed. by Caspar Ehlers, Lutz Fenske, and Thomas Zotz (Göttingen: Vandenhoeck & Ruprecht, 1983), pp. 511–612 (p. 532) (= no. 9).

[218] Printed in full in Staab, 'Fulda', p. 532. The entire note was later copied, by a late fifteenth- or early sixteenth-century hand, onto the book's rear pastedown (n.p.).

[219] Staab, 'Fulda', p. 532; Rudolf Schieffer, 'Fulda, Abtei der Könige und Kaiser', in *Kloster Fulda in der Welt der Karolinger und Ottonen*, ed. by Gangolf Schrimpf (Frankfurt a. M.: Knecht, 1993), pp. 39–55 (p. 46).

[220] 'Appendix ad Hrabanum: Epistolarum Fuldensium fragmenta', in *Epistolae Karolini aevi III* [= *MGH Epp.* V] (Berlin: Weidmann, 1899), pp. 517–33 (pp. 530–1) (= no. 31); Edmund E. Stengel and Oskar Semmelmann, 'Fuldensia IV: Untersuchungen zur Frühgeschichte des Fuldaer Klosterarchivs', *Archiv für Diplomatik* 4 (1958), 120–82 (p. 174); Mechthild Sandmann, 'Wirkungsbereiche fuldischer Mönche', in *Die Klostergemeinschaft von Fulda im früheren Mittelalter*, ed. by Karl Schmid et al., 3 vols. (Munich: Fink, 1978), II.2, 692–791 (pp. 766–7). It has been proposed that Abbot Hatto's self-identification as 'custos librorum' might refer not to his abbacy, but retrospectively to the office he had held under his predecessor, Rabanus Maurus; *Bücherverzeichnisse*, ed. Schrimpf et al., p. 96. This seems unconvincing, however.

[221] Huoggi carried the titles of 'bibliothecarius' and 'primiscrinius', which at Fulda were usually held by a single person, in charters from at least 874; *Codex diplomaticus Fuldensis*, ed. by Ernst F. J. Dronke (Kassel: Fischer, 1850), pp. 275–6 (= no. 611); cf. Sandmann, 'Wirkungsbereiche', p. 767; Stengel and Semmelmann, 'Fuldensia IV', pp. 142 and 169–74.

[222] *Bücherverzeichnisse*, ed. Schrimpf et al., pp. 12–13 and 94.

library was one of the most common arrangements—if not *the* most common besides inheritance by the next incumbent—for abbatial libraries at the end of the current owner's tenure or life. Contemporary to Hatto and Huoggi of Fulda are the cases of Abbots Grimald and Hartmut of St Gall whom we met briefly above (4.2). An ardent patron of domestic book production, Grimald greatly enlarged the abbey's library during his long abbacy, and he also built a sizeable book collection for himself.[223] According to an inventory produced early in Hartmut's abbacy, possibly in the context of his succession, this abbatial library contained some thirty-four volumes at the moment of Grimald's death, and they all were incorporated into the monks' library (St Gall, Stiftsbibliothek, MS Cod. Sang. 267, pp. 30–2).[224] Judging from the titles, Grimald collected various works of history in his abbatial library. These included a copy of 'De sex aetatibus mundi' (presumably Bede's *Chronica maiora/De temporum ratione*) bound in one volume with Julius Caesar's *Cosmographia* ('chronica Iulii Caesaris'), the Trojan histories by Darius Phrygius and (Pseudo-)Dictys of Crete, and a composite codex which contained, amongst other historical works, Einhard's *Vita Karoli* (presumably Vatican, Biblioteca Apostolica Vaticana, MS Reg. lat. 339).[225] Succeeding Grimald in 872, Hartmut followed in his footsteps by further enlarging the monastic library and building from scratch his own abbatial library that rivalled Grimald's in both size and scope. Thus when Ratpert composed his *Casus sancti Galli*, he could list not only the books Hartmut had provided for the community, but also, under a separate rubric, those he had collected for his personal use ('proprii causa videlicet usus').[226] Hartmut acquired computistical works such as Bede's *De temporibus* and *De natura rerum* bound into one volume with other related treatises on the reckoning of time ('unus grandis et alia argumenta computandi in volumine i'), as well as a large *mappa mundi*.[227] Following Hartmut's resignation in 883, his abbatial library, like Grimald's before him, was assimilated fully and permanently into the abbey's communal library ('similiter post finem dierum suorum sancti Galli servitio perpetualiter contradidit').[228]

These kinds of bequests were not limited to the early Middle Ages. At the end of the twelfth century, the monks of Arnstein inherited the books collected by their

---

[223] Steiner, 'Buchproduktion'; McKitterick, *Carolingians*, pp. 182–5.

[224] MS St Gall 267, pp. 30–2; *MBKDS*, I, 87–9 (= no. 20): 'Istos autem libros domnus Grimoldus de suo dedit ad sanctum Gallum'. It is not always evident by which means these books had been obtained in the first place, and it is perfectly possible that Grimald had owed some of them to his long service as arch-chaplain and chancellor of King Louis the German (843–76).

[225] *MBKDS*, I, 89; Tischler, *Studien*, I, 102–51, with a detailed discussion of the Vatican manuscript on ibid., pp. 109–40 (= Va 7).

[226] MS SB St Gall 614, pp. 126–7; *MBKDS*, I, 86–7 (= no. 19). The books made for the community are listed in MS SB St Gall 614, pp. 124–6 and MS SB St Gall 267, pp. 28–30; *MBKDS*, I, 85–6 (= no. 18).

[227] *MBKDS*, I, 87: 'Inter hos etiam unam mappam mundi subtili opere patravit, quam inter hos quoque libros connumeravit'.

[228] *MBKDS*, I, 86–7; also cf. Buzas, *Bibliotheksgeschichte*, p. 28; on Hartmut's resignation, see Wiech, *Amt*, pp. 159–61.

late abbot, Richolfus (1180–96), which are recorded in a contemporary inventory (London, British Library, MS Harley 3045, fol. 47v). John, abbot (1274–91) of Glastonbury, left two dozen books for his monks, which he had acquired with zeal and diligence ('suo studio et diligentia adquisivit') over the course of his abbacy. According to Adam de Damerham's *Historia de rebus gestis Glastoniensibus* (Cambridge, Trinity College, MS R. 5.33, fols. 68r–v), the late abbot's books were carried into the chapter house in the presence of the entire community ('libri deportati fuerunt in capitulo, presente conventu') before their incorporation into the communal library, a ritual that served practical as well as commemorative purposes.[229] Nearly a century later, Balduin, abbot (1316–48) of Beaumont, on his deathbed gave his library of twenty-one volumes to the canons of Belleval, who diligently recorded its contents in an inventory (Charleville-Mézières, Bibliothèque municipal/Médiathèque Voyelles, MS 25, fol. B).[230] Besides a state-of-the-art collection of medieval canon law, Balduin's abbatial library also included a single-volume history of the Roman emperors ('liber hystoriarum imperatorum Romanorum, volumen unum').[231] Around the same time, two large abbatial libraries with a combined value of more than two hundred and fifty silver pounds were bequeathed to the monks of Bury St Edmunds by their abbots, William of Bernham (1335–61) and John of Brinkley (1361–79), which prior to their donation had been stored in the *studium abbatum* recorded in a fifteenth-century dossier of the abbey's charters and administrative documents (Cambridge, Jesus College, MS 18).[232] William's contemporary and abbot of St Emmeram, Albert von Schmidmüln (1324–58), upon his death bequeathed his abbatial library of more than forty volumes to his monks, all of which he had acquired by his own (financial) means ('libros propriis nostris sumptibus comparatos'), and which he had itemized carefully in a charter dated 20 December 1357 that is sealed with both Albert's own seal and the monks' communal seal (Munich, Bayerisches Hauptstaatsarchiv, Kloster St. Emmeram, Regensburg, Urkunden 526). Serving as the abbot's last will and testament, the charter sets out detailed stipulations for the future safekeeping of these volumes with specific conditions for their lending/borrowing that are reminiscent of those discussed earlier (3.5).[233] Another century later, Richard Guthrie likewise left all his books to the monks of Arbroath, whom he had governed as abbot for just over half a decade (1449–55), and in

---

[229] *CBMLC*, IV, 216–18 (= B40) (p. 216); Julia Crick, 'The Marshalling of Antiquity: Glastonbury's Historical Dossier', in *The Archaeology and History of Glastonbury Abbey*, ed. by Lesley Abrams and James P. Carley (Woodbridge: Boydell, 1991), pp. 217–43 (p. 222).

[230] Edited in *Bibliothèques de l'ordre de Prémontré dans la France d'Ancien Régime*, ed. by Anne Bondéelle-Souchier, 2 vols. (Paris: CNRS Éditions, 2000–6), II, 91–2; *CGM*, V, 555 (= no. 25): 'Hii sunt libri quos domnus bone memorie abbas Balduynus emit fierique fecit atque demum conventui dedit'.

[231] *Bibliothèques*, ed. Bondéelle-Souchier, II, 92; *CGM*, V, 555.

[232] *CBMLC*, IV, 90–4 (= B15) (p. 91); Stratford and Webber, 'Bishops', p. 190.

[233] Edited in *MBKDS*, IV.1, 161–4 (pp. 163–4) (= no. 31).

1499 the monks of Kamp inherited the entire library assembled by their recently abdicated abbot, Henry, a bequest that is reported in some detail in the *Chronicon monasterii Campensis*.[234]

As noted at several points throughout this study, there is evidence that abbatial lodgings and the storage facilities found therein were home not just to collections of books, but also to charters and other kinds of administrative and archival documents that constituted integral sources for the history of a monastic community, and which would have been essential to consult when seeking to commit its history to writing. As we will recall, Abbot Wibald of Corvey invited the archbishop of Bremen to stay in his abbatial house again specifically so they could inspect the documents ('scedulae') in his private study and library.[235] It makes perfect sense, therefore, that abbatial residences often served not just as repositories (*Aufbewahrungsorte*), but also, and with some regularity, as the very places of issue (*Ausstellungsorte*) for these documents. The abbots of Saint-Bertin/Saint-Omer used their lodgings in this capacity from as early as 1107, when Lambert (1095–1125) issued a charter (Bruges, Rijksarchief, S. Bertijns Poperinge 3) in his own chamber ('in camera abbatis') to resolve a quarrel with his namesake, Lambert of Reninghelst, in the presence of several witnesses.[236] A confirmation charter of Hugh of Cyfeiliog, Earl of Chester, was issued and witnessed in the abbatial chamber at Chester ('in camera abbatis Cestr[ie] apud Cestram') in the presence of Abbot Robert I (1157–75), the earl and his personal chaplain William ('Willelmo capellano comitis'), and many others ('et multis aliis').[237]

---

[234] Edited in *MBKDS*, V.1, 18–23 (= no. 5); also cf. Hermann Keussen, 'Die Bibliothek des Abtes von Camp, Heinrich von der Heyden aus Calcar', in *Fontes adhuc inediti rerum Rhenanarum: Niederrheinische Chroniken*, ed. by Gottfried Eckertz, 2 vols. (Cologne: Heberle, 1870), II, 437–44. According to the *Chronicon*, Henry's resignation—and the resulting bequest of his abbatial library—occurred by his own free will ('sponte') (ibid., p. 437). On Guthrie's bequest, see David N. Bell, 'The Libraries of Religious Houses in the Late Middle Ages', in *The Cambridge History of Libraries in Britain and Ireland*, Vol. 1: *To 1640*, ed. by Teresa Webber and Elizabeth Leedham-Green (Cambridge: Cambridge University Press, 2006), pp. 126–51 (p. 128).

[235] As demonstrated by Martina Hartmann, Wibald's use of the term 'scedula(e)' must be understood as a reference to archival documents; Martina Hartmann, *Studien zu den Briefen Abt Wibalds von Stablo und Corvey sowie zur Briefliteratur in der frühen Stauferzeit* (Hanover: Hahn, 2011), pp. 102–3 ('Der von Wibald gebrauchte Plural *scedulae* dürfte dann im weiteren Sinne auch das Archiv des jeweiligen Klosters [...] bezeichnet haben [...] Der Erzbischof [Hartwig] wollte also demnach nicht nur die Bücher der Corveyer Bibliothek studieren, sondern auch die Sammlung der Briefe und Urkunden').

[236] Bruges, Rijksarchief, S. Bertijns Poperinge 3, ll. 19–21: 'Hec conventio facta est anno M° C° VII° in camera abbatis sub his testibus quorum nomina subscripta sunt. Elembertus de Kelmes, Alardus de Menteka, Wido de Crumbeke, Heremarus garetir et Robertus filius eius, Meingerus filius Bovonis, Almarus et Scinelinus, Winredus et Hagebarnus clericus, Ascelinus et Fulbertus. Postremo huius conventionis totum capitulum est testis'. Copies of Lambert's charter of 1107 survive in two twelfth-century cartularies (Boulogne-sur-Mer, Bibliothèque municipale des Annonciades, MS 146, fols. 95r–v; Boulogne-sur-Mer, Bibliothèque municipale des Annonciades, MS 146A, fols. 47v–48r). The text has been edited in *Cartularium: Recueil des chartes du prieuré de Saint-Bertin à Poperinghe, et de ses dépendances à Bas-Warneton et à Couckelaere déposées aux archives de l'Etat à Gand* (Bruges: Vandecasteele-Webrouck, 1870), pp. 5–6 (= no. 3).

[237] Manchester, University Library–John Rylands Library, Rylands Charter 1436. Hugh's charter is an original with a fragmentary seal on tag; see *The Charters of the Anglo-Norman Earls of Chester, c.1071–1237*, ed. by Geoffrey Barraclough (Gloucester: Sutton, 1988), pp. 144–5 (= no. 131).

Just as abbots kept their book collections safe in personal book chests inscribed with their names or painted with their crests—examples of both of which we saw above (4.3)—they also furnished their lodgings with appropriate storage for the safekeeping of charters and documents. Such 'deed chests' are attested at a wide range of monastic houses, male and female. Holding some of their communities' (and their superiors') most valued documents, they were often secured with multiple locks, the keys to which were entrusted to officiaries including the sacristan, the prior(ess), and, above all, the abbot/abbess. When the archives of the Bursfelde Congregation were relocated from Bursfelde to Erfurt in 1460, they were transported and stored in a single chest ('archa cum privilegiis nostre unionis') secured with three locks, the keys to which (and thus access to the documents) were given, after some deliberation, to the two ruling abbots of Erfurt and Bursfelde (one key each) and to the Congregation's acting co-presidents (one between them).[238] Similar examples include the nunneries of Syon, Nunnaminster, Ankerwyke, and Broadholme.[239] An inventory from Chesthunt produced at the time of the community's dissolution in 1536 records that the last abbess had not one, but two such chests in her chamber ('Item ij Chestes in my Ladys Chamber'), one of which was filled with charters ('wherof one of them ys full of Evydence [deeds?] prysed at xij d').[240] The contents of the abbess's second chest are not specified, but it is not unthinkable that it also included documents or perhaps a collection of books similar to those owned by other late medieval and early modern abbesses in England and elsewhere.[241]

The autobiographical account of the election of Agnès de Thieuville, abbess-historian of La Trinité de Caen, written in or shortly after 1482 and introduced above (1.4) reports that the newly invested abbess was handed not only the keys to the monastery ('clefz dicelui monastere'), a symbolic act, but also a bunch of keys ('ung paquet de clefz') that gave her access to the abbatial residence ('maison abbatialle') and some lockable chests ('coffres') stored therein, and which had been kept in the prioress's custody during the interregnum ('dequoy laditte prieure

---

[238] Volk, *Generalkapitels-Rezesse*, pp. 14 and 28; Eifler, *Bibliothek*, I, 96.   [239] Bell, *Nuns*, p. 47.
[240] Quoted in Bell, *Nuns*, p. 129.
[241] Books with inscriptions designating them as part of an abbess's personal collection survive from, for example, the English Benedictines at Brussels, as well as from Poznań, where a separate library for the abbesses continued to exist until the eighteenth century; Caroline Bowden, 'Building Libraries in Exile: The English Convents and their Book Collections in the Seventeenth Century', *British Catholic History* 32 (2015), 343–82 (p. 315); Grażyna Jurkowlaniec and Magdalena Herman, 'Introduction: People Between Multiplied Things and Modified Images', in *The Reception of the Printed Image in the Fifteenth and Sixteenth Centuries: Multiplied and Modified*, ed. by Grażyna Jurkowlaniec and Magdalena Herman (New York, NY: Routledge, 2020), pp. 1–23 (pp. 10–11). Abbess Adelgundis Pettenkofer (1730–56) of St Walburg near Eichstätt had her own *ex libris* found in nearly six hundred volumes. Adelgundis's library was inherited, and her *ex libris* continued to be used by her successors, who together added another one hundred and seventy-two volumes to the book collection; Mechtildis Denz, 'Die Bibliothek der Abtei St. Walburg im Laufe der Jahrhunderte', in *Die Bibliothek der Abtei St. Walburg zu Eichstätt*, ed. by Andreas Friedel (Wiesbaden: Harrassowitz, 2000), pp. xv–xiv (p. xix). Such inscriptions are much rarer with regard to the medieval centuries.

estoit gardaine et conservateure').[242] At the same time, Agnès took possession—as her predecessors had done—of the documents and letters confirming the community's liberties and possessions ('libertes et franchises biens meubles et imeubles'), and it is reasonable to assume that these documents (likely deeds and exemption charters) were kept in her abbatial chests.[243] Caen's abbesses had personal possession of their monastery's most vital archival documents right until the dawn of the French Revolution, when the last abbess, Marie VI de Pontécoulant (1787–92), deposited their original charters and most treasured deeds ('les chartes originales et les titres les plus précieux') in wooden(?) trunks ('malles'), which she then buried in the vault of the abbey church ('qu'elle fit enterrer sur la voûte de son église').[244] The documents remained in their secret hiding place after Marie's death sixteen years later, though over time rainwater ingress rotted away the trunks and corroded the tin cylinders containing the foundation charters and other historical documents ('la rouille attaqua les tubes de fer-blanc qui renfermoient les chartes de fondation et de rôles historiques'), causing them to mould and disintegrate into shreds ('lambeaux'). Unfortunate though Marie's choice turned out, this was not the first time that the abbey church's loft (*grenier*) served as a repository for archival documents. The *Éloges* written by Jacqueline Bouette de Blémur, a former prioress of La Trinité, reports that Abbess Laurence de Budos (1598–1650), whom Jacqueline had served as secretary, found an old chest there filled with the abbey's most important deeds ('un vieux coffre, remply des plus importans papier de la maison'); eager to learn what they contained, the abbess took possession of the principal charters and carried them away in her habit ('elle voulut connoistre par la lecture dequoy ils traitoient [...], elle se charge des pincipaux, et les emporte dans sa robe').[245] Laurence kept hold of these charters for the remainder of her abbacy, enabling Jacqueline to boast that there was no house whose deeds were in better shape than Laurence had left hers when death snatched her from the nuns ('il ny'a point de maison, où les papier soient en meilleur ordre, qu'elle laisse le siens lors que la mort nous la ravit'). When earlier in the same century the monastic community of Hinton finally surrendered to Henry VIII's Lord Privy Seal, Thomas Cromwell, after some initial resistance by its last ever prior, Edmund Horde (1529–39), the appointed steward, Sir Walter Hungerford, complained to the king that his contemporary and Justice of the Peace for Somerset, Thomas Arundel, had broken

---

[242] MS BL Harley 3661, fols. 26r and 33v, where it is stated that this handover of keys was performed 'par la tradition'.

[243] MS BL Harley 3661, fol. 34r. Again, I would like to thank Laura Gathagan for her kind assistance with this case.

[244] Gervais de la Rue, *Essais historiques sur la ville de Caen et son arrondissement*, 2 vols. (Caen: Mancel, 1820), II, 28.

[245] Jacqueline Bouette de Blémur, *Éloges de plusieurs personnes illustres en piété de l'ordre de Saint-Benoît*, 6 vols. (Paris: Billaine, 1679), II, 116.

into the monastic superior's cell and disturbed the important documents and charters kept therein.[246]

An instructive yet little-known example of an abbatial deed chest is recorded in the composite chronicle of Gloucester Abbey (*Historia monasterii sancti Petri Gloucestriae*), which reports that abbot-historian Walter Frocester (1382–1412)— the chronicle's (partial) author—possessed a chest ('capsa'/'capsula') inscribed with his name ('intitulata') that contained records of the many important rights and privileges he had secured during his abbacy, and which was kept separate from the archives.[247] According to the *Historia*, the documents in Walter's private chest included various privileges ('multa et diversa privilegia [...] in capsula praedicta inde confecta') that he had obtained from England's bishops, the archbishops of Canterbury, and even the Roman popes ('a Romanis pontificibus, quam a Cantuariensi archiepiscopo Willelmo Corteney, quam ab episcopis Angliae impetravit').[248] The abbey's former chamberlain ('camerarius'), Walter was well versed in administrative matters and record-keeping, and he applied this expertise both by reorganizing the existing registers of deeds shortly after his appointment in 1482 and, between 1493–7, by directing the making of two new registers and the copying of *Magna Carta*.[249] As abbot, Walter was so invested in recording the history of his community that a short poem about the monastery's foundation ('[V]ersus de prima fundatione huius loci, videlicet Gloucestrensis monasterii') inserted amongst the *Historia*'s prefatory chapters credits him above everyone else with educating Gloucester's monks about their past.[250]

In the light of these activities, it made sense for Walter to keep certain archival documents close at hand in his abbatial lodgings, and it is plausible that his predecessors had done the same. Looking back from the early fifteenth century, the *Historia* draws attention to the initiative of several of Gloucester's earlier abbots in the procurement and codification of privileges ever since the days of the community's first post-Conquest abbot, Serlo (1072–1104), a former canon of Avranches and monk of Mont-Saint-Michel. Both Serlo and his successor, Peter (1104–13), receive praise in the *Historia* for their respective agency in expanding

---

[246] Margaret Connolly, *Sixteenth-Century Readers, Fifteenth-Century Books: Continuities of Reading in the English Reformation* (Cambridge: Cambridge University Press, 2019), p. 159.

[247] '[E]t et alia diversa quae prolonga erant narranda ut in capsa inde confecta, et Walteri Froucestre intitulata, et in archivis ecclesiae condita plenius continentur'; Gloucester, Cathedral Library, MS 34, fol. 23v, ll. 18–21; also London, British Library, MS Cotton Domitian A VIII, fol. 143v, ll. 27–9. The *Historia*'s Latin text has been printed, with some mistakes, in *Historia*, ed. Hart, I, 3–125 (p. 56).

[248] MS Gloucester 34, fol. 24r, ll. 2–6; MS Domitian A VIII, fol. 144r, ll. 4–7; *Historia*, ed. Hart, I, 56.

[249] Gloucester, Cathedral Library, Frocester Register 1397 (*olim* Reg. A); David Walker, 'The Organisation of Material in Medieval Cartularies', in *The Study of Medieval Records: Essays in Honour of Kathleen Major*, ed. by Donald A. Bullough and Robin L. Storey (Oxford: Clarendon, 1971), pp. 132–50 (pp. 133 and 146); Nigel E. Saul, 'Feature of the Month: March 2015–Magna Carta and the Politics of the Reign of Richard II', *The Magna Carta Project*, https://magnacartaresearch.org/read/feature_of_the_month/Mar_2015_2.

[250] MS Gloucester 34, fols. 1v–2r; MS Domitian A VIII, fol. 127r; *Historia*, ed. Hart, I, 5–6: 'Walterus studuit Froucestre, et haec memoranda / in scriptis posuit claustralibus enucleanda'.

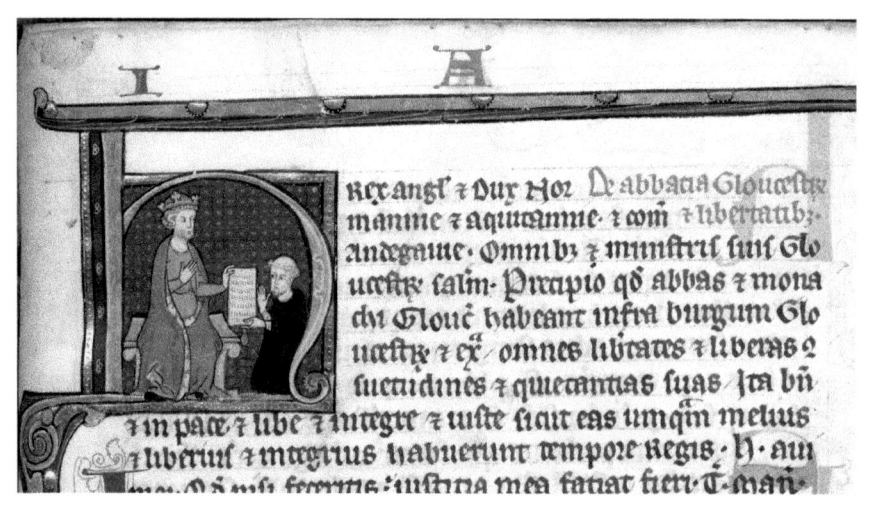

Fig. 4.5 Hamelin of Gloucester(?) receiving a charter from King Henry II. Kew, National Archives, C 150/1, stamped fol. 18.

the monastery's demesne, and their late thirteenth-/early fourteenth-century successor, John de Gamages (1284–1306), is remembered, amongst other achievements, for his provision of a new monastic cartulary.[251] On the opening page of this cartulary (Kew, National Archives, C 150/1, stamped fol. 18) is a historiated initial of Gloucester's abbot—most likely Hamelin (1148–79), given that the adjacent text is a mandate by King Henry II safeguarding the abbey's liberties within the city of Gloucester—receiving a sealed charter from his royal patron (Fig. 4.5).[252]

Just like elsewhere, at Gloucester the production of charters and the writing of history frequently went hand in hand, and here, too, the abbots themselves were either at the very forefront of these activities or pulling strings behind the scenes. Indeed, Gloucester was a prolific centre of monastic historiographical production, even if many of the narratives originating there during the period *c*.1100–1400 have not survived in manuscript form.[253] Walter's involvement in commissioning and part-composing the *Historia* has already been mentioned, and he was not the only abbot to initiate and patronize historical writings at Gloucester. Other historical narratives produced by the community include a now-lost chronicle

---

[251] MS Gloucester 34, fols. 3v–5r and 16r; MS Domitian A VIII, fols. 128v–129v and 138v; *Historia*, ed. Hart, I, 10–14 and 40.

[252] Kew, National Archives, C 150/1, fol. 18r/1r, ll. 1–7; the text of Henry II's mandate is printed in *Historia*, ed. Hart, I, 154 (= no. V); ibid., II, 349 (= no. CCCXLVI); *The Letters and Charters of Henry II, King of England 1154–1189*, ed. by Nicholas Vincent, 7 vols. (Oxford: Oxford University Press, 2020–2), II, 378 (= no. 1161), who dates the mandate '1155 × May 1172, ?1155 × August 1158'.

[253] Paul A. Hayward, 'Chronicles of Gloucester Abbey', in *The Encyclopedia of the Medieval Chronicle*, ed. by R. Graeme Dunphy, 2 vols. (Leiden: Brill, 2020), I, 341–2 (p. 341).

(or possibly multiple chronicles) used by the compilers of the *Tewkesbury Annals* and *Winchcombe Chronicle*, Gervase of Canterbury, and John of Worcester, whose *magnum opus*—the *Chronicon ex chronicis*—was then continued at Gloucester under Abbot Gilbert (1139–48) and/or his successor, Hamelin.[254] Whether Gloucester's early chronicle(s) were 'cartulary-chronicles' like the *Historia* is difficult to know given the absence of manuscript witnesses, but it is not implausible given the regular diplomatic involvement of the abbots under whose rule, and at whose initiative, they were produced. Even Gloucester's last abbot, William Malvern (1514–39; also known as William Parker), played a part in the writing of history by composing a historical poem—in the vernacular— about the abbey's distant foundation and its changing fortunes that runs to some one hundred and fifty-four lines and was inscribed in the nave of the abbey church.[255]

Another insightful example of an abbot whose private space was a site of both documentary and historiographical production comes from the island monastery of Mont-Saint-Michel in Normandy, where abbot-historian Robert of Torigni hosted King Henry II of England in late September/early October 1158. In his *Chronica*, Robert reports that after several invitations, the king with whom he shared a close political and personal connection—Robert would subsequently act as godfather to Henry II's daughter, Eleanor, personally receiving her from the baptismal font at Domfront in 1161/2—came to Mont-Saint-Michel after the feast of St Michael and granted him and his successors control over the churches of Pontorson, thus confirming a previous grant (now lost) by Henry II's maternal grandfather, King Henry I.[256] The royal confirmation was issued not just anywhere, but in Robert's new abbatial chamber ('in nova camera abbatis') in the presence of several high-ranking officials that included Ranulf, the abbey's prior and Robert's second-in-command, Master Gervase of Chichester, clerk to Henry II and Thomas Becket, and Adam, Robert's personal scribe ('scriba Roberti abbatis') (Fig. 1.2c).[257] There are several points of interest here: first of all, the document issued and witnessed in Robert's chamber formed part of an ongoing dispute ('controversia') between the abbot of Mont-Saint-Michel and the bishop of Avranches about the jurisdiction over Pontorson's churches that would not be resolved until 1160, and which over the years generated a substantial documentary

---

[254] Hayward, 'Chronicles', p. 342; *Heads*, ed. Knowles et al., pp. 52–3.

[255] A sixteenth-century transcript survives in Cambridge, Gonville and Caius College, MS 391/611; printed in *Chronicle*, ed. Hearne, II, 578–85 (= Appendix II); Luxford, *Art*, p. 11.

[256] The king's visit to Mont-Saint-Michel is described in detail in *RT*, ed./tr. Bisson, I, 210–11; on the relationship between Robert and King Henry II, see Elisabeth M. C. van Houts, 'Le roi et son historien: Henri II Plantagenêt et Robert de Torigni, abbé du Mont-Saint-Michel', *Cahiers de civilisation médiévale* 37 (1994), 115–18. Robert was the godfather of Henry II's daughter, Eleanor, the later queen of Castile, and he dedicated substantial sections of the *Chronica* to relating the king's celebrated deeds, even naming him explicitly in the prologue.

[257] *RT*, ed./tr. Bisson, I, 210–11.

trail in the form of charters, confirmations, and letters issued by the Anglo-Norman/Angevin kings, Rouen's archbishops, and even the popes.[258] Such disputes were no rarity between the episcopate and the heads of larger monasteries,[259] and to obtain Henry II's confirmation Robert would have had to produce evidence from the monastic archives cultivated and reorganized by his predecessors, Bernard (1131–49) and Geoffrey (1149–50).[260] The chronological coverage of the acts copied into the lavishly illuminated cartulary (Avranches, Bibliothèque patrimoniale, MS 210) that Robert inherited from these abbots upon his appointment in 1154, and which was continued thereafter in a rather more 'pragmatic' format under his own direction,[261] originally extended only as far as 1149, and none of these acts pertained to the specific matter at hand in the autumn of 1158.[262] This changed when a copy of the decisive archiepiscopal settlement of 1160 was added to this cartulary during a subsequent redaction, very likely at Robert's behest, though for the time being the abbot-historian had to

---

[258] As mentioned above, King Henry I's original grant is not known to survive; a notification of Henry II's confirmation (undated) sent to Archbishop Hugh of Rouen has survived as a photographed original (Saint-Lô, Archives départementales de la Manche, 15 Fi 13; original destroyed in 1944; photographic reproduction in Pohl, 'Pragmatic Literacy', p. 16 = fig. 1), whilst the later confirmations by Pope Adrian IV (23 July 1158) and Archbishop Hugh of Rouen (Saint-Lô, Archives départementales de la Manche, 1 H 13; dated 1160) both survive in the original; *Letters*, ed. Vincent, III, 493–4 (= no. 1862); see also Richard Allen, 'Unknown Copies of the Lost Charters of Le Mont Saint-Michel (11th–13th Centuries): The Henry Chanteux Collection at the Archives Départementales du Calvados', *Revue Mabillon* 29 (2018), 45–82 (pp. 65–6; nos. 43 and 44); *Chronique*, ed. Delisle, II, 265–7 (= nos. v–vii). Robert subsequently was granted control of Pontorson Castle in 1162, which Henry II had ordered to be reconstructed the same year in which he confirmed Pontorson's churches to Mont-Saint-Michel; *RT*, ed./tr. Bisson, I, 232–3.

[259] See the examples discussed in Benjamin Pohl, 'Processions, Power and Public Display: Ecclesiastical Rivalry and Ritual in Ducal Normandy', *Journal of Medieval Monastic Studies* 6 (2017), 1–49; Grégory Combalbert, 'Règlement des conflits, gestion du risqué et clercs paroissiaux: l'affermage des dîmes (Normandie, XIIe–XIIIe siècles)', in *La dime, l'Église et la société féodale*, ed. by Michel Lauwers (Turnhout: Brepols, 2012), pp. 335–68.

[260] Stéphane Lecouteux, 'Écrire l'histoire des abbés du Mont Saint-Michel, 2: Robert de Torigni, ses outils, ses sources et sa méthode de travail', *Tabularia* (2018), 1–68 (p. 27), https://doi.org/10.4000/tabularia.2973; Katherine S. B. Keats-Rohan, 'Bibliothèque Municipale d'Avranches, 210: Cartulary of Mont-Saint-Michel', *Anglo-Norman Studies* 21 (1999), 95–112 (p. 101); Thomas N. Bisson, 'The "Annuary" of Robert of Torigni', *Anglo-Norman Studies* 33 (2011), 61–74 (pp. 65–6).

[261] Pohl, 'Literacy'.

[262] This 'primitive version' of the cartulary comprises Avranches, Bibliothèque patrimoniale, MS 210, fols. 5r–112r; edited in *The Cartulary of the Abbey of Mont-Saint-Michel*, ed. by Katherine S. B. Keats-Rohan (Donington: Shaun Tyas, 2006), pp. 63–186. Keats-Rohan dismissed the continuations made under Robert (fols. 112v–117v) and his successors (fols. 118r–137v) as 'an undesirable distraction' (ibid., p. 4), an editorial decision that has been criticized by Coraline Coutant in *Bibliothèque de l'école des chartes* 165 (2007), 535–6 (p. 535). The post-1149 sections of the cartulary have been edited in Coraline Coutant, 'Le cartulaire de l'abbaye du Mont-Saint-Michel et ses additions (XIIe–XIVe siècles): Étude et édition critique', 2 vols. (Thèse diplôme d'archiviste-paléographe, École nationale des chartes, 2009), II, 224–53. I am grateful to Coraline Daydé (née Coutant) for sharing a copy of her thesis with me. Thomas Bisson's identification of fols. 112v–117v (the so-called 'Annuary') with Robert's own handwriting is not sustained by the palaeographical evidence; Bisson, 'Annuary', p. 66, repeated in *RT*, ed./tr. Bisson, II, xxx–xxxii. It is now widely accepted that the cartulary and its miniatures originated under Bernard and/or Geoffrey, though the exact chronology of its composition remains uncertain; Cleaver, *History Books*, pp. 122–3 still argues that these illuminations were likely produced at Mont-Saint-Michel during Robert's abbacy.

return *ad fontes* and mine the relevant originals first-hand ahead of the much-anticipated royal visit.²⁶³

Moreover, there is evidence to suggest that these originals were stored *in situ* in Robert's abbatial chamber, and not just temporarily, but possibly as a more permanent fixture. Information on the location and organizational structure of Mont-Saint-Michel's monastic archives before the fifteenth century is scarce, but what little can be gleaned from the documentary and archaeological sources indicates that they were first given a (semi-)permanent physical home around the middle of the twelfth century, that is, under Robert's abbacy.²⁶⁴ There is no trace of a designated archival space amongst the eleventh-century monastery's remains, nor in the imposing thirteenth-century abbatial palace to the east/south-east of the church with 'admin offices' for the community's proctor. It was the abbot's *residence* that appears to have served as the monastery's primary archival facility (*chartrier*) until at least the thirteenth century, and perhaps as late as the early fifteenth century, when Abbot Pierre Le Roy (1386–1410) ordered a systematic inventory and re-organization of the archives, then kept in a two-storey archival tower adjacent to the Merveille's cloister, and supervised the compilation of two cartularies known as the *Guanandrier* and *Livre blanc*, respectively.²⁶⁵ Preceding these cartularies and likely reflecting the holdings of the Merveille's archive is a fourteenth-century inventory (Avranches, Bibliothèque patrimoniale, MS 211, fols. 113v–137r) listing the privileges kept in the *armarium* of Mont-Saint-Michel ('in armariolo montis') followed by those stored in its dependent priories in Normandy, England ('Anglia'), and the Channel Islands.²⁶⁶ Predating

---

²⁶³ MS Avranches 210, fol. 118v; Coutant, 'Cartulaire', II, 258 (= no. 54).
²⁶⁴ For a concise overview with a list of extant documents, see Marie Bisson, 'Où sont les archives du Mont Saint-Michel?', in *Sur les pas de Lanfranc, du Bec à Caen: Recueil d'études en hommage à Véronique Gazeau*, ed. by Pierre Bauduin et al. (Caen: Annales de Normandie, 2018), pp. 451–63; there is some evidence that an early (re-)organization of the abbey's archives might have taken place under Abbot Bernard, possibly in the context of making the cartulary in MS Avranches 210, but there is nothing to suggest that he or his successor, Geoffrey, arranged a physical space for these documents; Lecouteux, 'Écrire l'histoire 2', p. 27, citing a passage from Robert of Torigni's *De abbatibus* that credits Bernard with this organisational undertaking; for this passage, see the recent edition of *De abbatibus* by Pierre Bouet et al., 'Écrire l'histoire des abbés du Mont Saint-Michel, 3: Édition critique et traduction', *Tabularia* (2019), pp. 1–31 (p. 8), https://doi.org/10.4000/tabularia.3773.
²⁶⁵ See now Benjamin Pohl, 'L'atelier de l'abbé-historian du Mont Saint-Michel: Où Robert de Torigni a-t-il écrit?', in *1023–2023: Le Mont Saint-Michel en Normandie et en Europe*, ed. by Fabien Paquet et al., forthcoming; previously Paul E. Gout, *Le Mont-Saint-Michel: Histoire de l'abbaye et de la ville. Étude archéologique et architecturale des monuments*, 2 vols. (Paris: Armand Colin, 1910; repr. 1979), II, 503–10, 514–15 (= plate XXIII), and 579–80 (= plate XXVI); Mathilde Gardeux, 'Espace d'assistance, espace de pouvoir: les dispositifs d'accueil et d'hébergements dans quelques monastères bénédictins en Normandie aux XIIe et XIIIe siècles', *Bulletin du centre d'études médiévales d'Auxerre* 8 (2015), 1–33 (pp. 25–6); Chazelas, 'Vie', pp. 136–7; on Pierre Le Roy's re-organization of the archives, see Bisson, 'Archives', pp. 454–5, citing the narrative account by Thomas Le Roy; for a map, see Maylis Baylé et al., *Le Mont-Saint-Michel: Histoire et imaginaire* (Paris: Éditions du patrimoine, 1998), p. 247 (= Annexes, plan niveau 4, no. 4.16); also cf. Marc Déceneux, 'Notes sur le logis abbatial du Mont-Saint-Michel a la fin du XIVe siècle', *Les Amis du Mont Saint-Michel* 95 (1990), 41–58.
²⁶⁶ The inventory begins with the words 'In armariolo privilegi[orum?]. In subsequentibus signantur litterae efficaces contente in armariolis cartarii, et primo de armariolo in quo privilegia apostolica

this inventory by nearly two centuries were building campaigns authorized by Robert between the mid-1150s and mid-1180s, one of which—completed by c.1164—included the construction of a range of new facilities to the west/southwest of the Romanesque abbey church.[267] These included a guest house or *hôtellerie* with a hall overlooking the bay, an infirmary, and—amongst the first to be finished as a matter of priority—the very *camera abbatis* in which Henry II issued his charter in 1158 (see above). These facilities superseded, both physically and functionally, the rooms that had occupied this location since the eleventh century, and which despite their smaller size had served simultaneously as the abbot's parlour, reception room, and court room.[268] It seems improbable for a space that changed its use and occupants regularly to have housed the community's most treasured and safeguarded privileges, if only for risk of damage or theft. Robert's new abbatial apartment, by contrast, would have been a perfectly safe and suitable home for the monastic archives, given that it formed part of a suite of rooms providing accommodation and workspace for the abbot with easy access to, yet separate from, the *hôtellerie* with a capacity to accommodate large numbers of pilgrims and visitors.[269] And though these abbatial spaces were in many respects private, they also on occasion served as public spaces in which to entertain selected guests, conduct official business, and perform—and possibly store records of—legal acts such as that conducted in 1158.

It has long been suspected that the abbatial lodgings built by Robert might have housed his personal library alongside a writing or study chamber,[270] and even if ultimately this must remain conjecture, it does chime rather well with the possibility of the monastic archives having also found their locus within these same walls—especially considering Robert's involvement in the continuation of the cartulary in MS Avranches 210, fols. 112v–117v, as well as the established fact that he had first-hand access to these archives and used them regularly when writing his *Chronica* and other works of history. Indeed, one might well argue—as

---

continentur'; the first part of the list (fols. 113v–114v) relates to Mont-Saint-Michel proper and carries the rubric *in armariolo montis*, followed by the various priories; these lists have been edited by Coutant, 'Cartulaire', II, 150–217; also cf. Keats-Rohan, *Cartulary*, pp. 40–1.

[267] Gout, *Mont-Saint-Michel*, II, 448–59.

[268] Gout, *Mont-Saint-Michel*, II, 433: 'L'abbé recevait là les visiteurs, les pèlerins, et à certains jours rendait la justice'. It has recently been proposed that a building located west of Robert's new *hôtellerie* and abbatial lodgings, which previous scholarship had identified as a chapel, might have been a kind of palace built *c*.1000 to house the Norman dukes and other high-status visitors that in the eleventh century was turned into a guest house, but this must remain conjecture; George Gandy, 'Who Built What at Mont Saint-Michel during the 10th Century?', *Annales de Normandie* 65 (2015), 153–82 (pp. 172–80).

[269] Gout, *Mont-Saint-Michel*, II, 456. Mont-Saint-Michel's abbots slept alongside their monks in the dormitory well into the twelfth century; ibid., II, 431 and 432–3 (= plate XVII). Robert's chamber and antechamber are located by Pierre André Lablaude on an architectural plan reproduced in Baylé et al., *Mont-Saint-Michel*, p. 247. I am grateful to François Saint-James for kindly granting me exclusive access to Robert's abbatial apartment in June 2023.

[270] Most prominently Jean Huynes, *Histoire générale de l'abbaye du Mont Saint-Michel au péril de la mer*, 2 vols. (Rouen: Le Brument, 1872–3), I, 176; more recently *RT*, ed./tr. Bisson, I, xxxvi.

the recent editors of Robert's writings have—that it would have been altogether impracticable for Robert to chronicle the history of the monastery and its abbots with such proficiency and precision had he not kept certain books— and, importantly, records—close at hand in his personal workspace.[271] As discussed in more detail elsewhere, Robert rarely put pen to parchment himself, and certainly with regard to his own authorial compositions he primarily relied on assistant scribes and *amanuenses*. How many such assistants he employed and whether these were domestically trained monks or hired professionals (or both) we do not know, but the presence of Adam *scriba Roberti abbatis* amongst the people gathered in his *camera abbatis* to witness the grant of 1158 makes it possible, and plausible, that Robert's working method resembled that of the contemporary abbots of St Albans, who according to their *Gesta abbatum* always had at least one—and in the case of Abbot Simon as many as three—personal scribe(s) present in their abbatial chamber.[272] At Clairvaux, the *amanuensis* of Abbot Bernard (1115–28), a former monk of Montiéramey named Nicholas, could even boast a private 'writing cubicle' ('scriptoriolum').[273] Examples like these substantiate Christopher Brooke's observation that by the thirteenth century, if not indeed earlier, the *camera abbatis* was established as an official institution,[274] and they further emphasize the importance of archival documents for the production of historical works, especially in monasteries that developed into centres of historiographical activity under the leadership of abbots who actively promoted and/or were themselves writers of history.

4.5 Conclusions

The evidence set out here cannot claim to be exhaustive, but it allows us to draw useful conclusions regarding the existence, pervasiveness, and design of abbatial workplaces—specifically spaces for writing and study—in the medieval Latin West. Contrary to previous scholarship, which has viewed the establishment of designated abbatial workspaces and resources as a later medieval phenomenon, it has been demonstrated that these facilities were in fact much more common and existed from significantly earlier than has so far been acknowledged. The

---

[271] *RT*, ed./tr. Bisson, I, xxxii; Lecouteux, 'Écrire', pp. 6, 22–3, and 26–8; Pohl, 'L'atelier', forthcoming.
[272] *Gesta*, ed. Riley, I, 192; tr. Preest and Clark, p. 300; incidentally, one of Simon's scribes also seems to have been called Adam, and like his contemporary namesake at Mont-Saint-Michel this Adam appears as a witness in one of his abbot's charters preserved in St Albans's late medieval (post-1393) cartulary (London, British Library, MS Cotton Julius D III, fol. 76r) (cf. ibid., p. 300 n. 50, albeit with the wrong folio reference).
[273] Quoted from Steinmann, *Handschriften*, pp. 290–1 (p. 290) (= no. 347).
[274] Brooke, 'Adrian IV', p. 6 n. 15.

provision of private study rooms and resources for the men and women in charge of medieval monastic communities was not restricted to the great abbatial palaces and estates dotted across Europe on the eve of the Reformation, but a historical development that had its roots many centuries earlier. Abbots and abbesses collected their own books from as early as the seventh century, if not earlier, and they kept them safe in personal book chests, which were sometimes inscribed with their names. When they passed away or resigned from office, their books (and their receptacles) were usually passed on to their successors or incorporated into the monasteries' communal libraries, though in some cases individuals managed to hold on to their collections beyond their abbatial tenure.

As many European monasteries increased in size and wealth, these arrangements became increasingly formalized from about the Carolingian period, which is when we begin to find ever more concrete evidence of abbatial living and working facilities that were separated physically from their communities and capable of accommodating sizeable corpora of books, charters, and other archival documents. These developments continued across the turn of the millennium, and in the eleventh and twelfth centuries there is consistent evidence of private studies and libraries amongst abbots and abbesses of not only the wealthiest and most well-endowed monasteries, but also the many small- and medium-sized houses. By the late Middle Ages, these kinds of facilities had become all but ubiquitous. Those that survived the age of dissolutions and reformations more or less intact would sometimes find heirs amongst the educated secular elites of early modern Europe for whom owning a private study and library was part of their literate self-fashioning and aristocratic *bella figura*, though few of them showed much of an interest in preserving the kinds of books that previously adorned their chests and shelves.

An observation made several times throughout this discussion concerns the prominence of certain types of books in abbatial libraries. Besides liturgical codices, monastic rules and customaries, account books, and other kinds of books and documents traditionally associated with the abbatial office and the routine pastoral and administrative responsibilities of abbots and abbesses, the 'genre' found most frequently in the possession of medieval monastic superiors is that of historical narratives. These regularly included records of a community's own history such as monastic annals, house chronicles, foundation histories (*historiae fundationum*), the deeds of previous abbots (*gesta abbatum*), and the *lives* of patron saints, but equally historical works whose scope extended far beyond the cloister walls such as episcopal, imperial, and universal histories, dynastic chronicles and genealogies, travel histories and crusade chronicles, and, with some frequency, the secular works of Roman and Greek historians. Perhaps unsurprisingly, the greatest concentration of such historical narratives can be witnessed in the possession of medieval abbots and abbesses who were themselves writers and patrons of history. For them, the cultivation of study and writing facilities with direct access to books and other relevant materials within the privacy and comfort of their own quarters served more than just practical purposes: as private working libraries and reference collections, they enabled these abbot-historians to carve out precious writing time amongst their administrative responsibilities and busy schedules, even if that meant some of them virtually became abbots by day and historiographers by night.

Conclusion

> The Greeks call craftsmen or artisans τέκτωνες, that is, builders. But the master builders (*architecti*) are those who lay the foundations, which is why the apostle Paul says of himself: 'As a wise architect (*sapiens architectus*), I have laid the foundation'.
>
> Isidore of Seville, *Etymologiae* XIX.viii.1.[1]

This notion of the *sapiens architectus* coined in St Paul's First Epistle to the Corinthians and popularized amongst medieval writers by Isidore of Seville provides a fitting analogy for the abbot's role in the writing of history. As this book has shown, the involvement of abbots and abbesses in monastic historiographical production in the period *c*.500–1500 was a fundamental and all-encompassing one, the extent and significance of which cannot be captured fully by focusing exclusively on authorial personae. Writing history was—and is—a communal and collaborative enterprise, and nowhere more so than within monastic communities steeped in historical tradition. Most monasteries in the medieval Latin West committed their history to writing at some point of their existence, some more than once. This community-building and identity-affirming activity was not the task of 'professional historians'—a concept alien to the Middle Ages that would not emerge until the nineteenth century—but of individuals and groups whose primary occupations, offices, and vocations were different, and who required special dispensation and institutional support to engage with it.[2] Writing history was not the regular manual and spiritual labour of medieval monks and nuns, nor was it work for which time and resources were set aside routinely in an abbey's day-to-day life and administration. Each act of historiographical production thus constituted an extraordinary event, one for which

---

[1] Adapted from *Etymologies*, tr. Barney et al., p. 377, with Isidore quoting 1 Corinthians 3:10 ('Secundum gratiam Dei, quae data est mihi, ut sapiens architectus fundamentum posui: alius autem superaedificat'). On the *sapiens architectus* trope, see Günther Binding, *Der früh- und hochmittelalterliche Bauherr als sapiens architectus*, 2nd ed. (Darmstadt: Wissenschaftliche Buchgesellschaft, 2017), pp. 245–82; Günther Binding, 'Bauwissen im Früh- und Hochmittelalter', in *Wissensgeschichte der Architektur*, Vol. 3: *Vom Mittelalter bis zur frühen Neuzeit*, ed. by Jürgen Renn et al., new ed. (Berlin: Max-Planck-Gesellschaft, 2014), pp. 11–94 (pp. 17–18); Nikolaus Pevsner, 'The Term "Architect" in the Middle Ages', *Speculum* 17 (1942), 549–62 (pp. 550–2).

[2] An intriguing case for the exceptional existence of professional historians in medieval Ireland has recently been made by Katharine Simms, 'The Professional Historians of Medieval Ireland', in *Medieval Historical Writing: Britain and Ireland, 500–1500*, ed. by Jennifer Jahner et al. (Cambridge: Cambridge University Press, 2019), pp. 279–98.

singular provision had to be made, workers and materials assigned, time carved out, and—crucially—licence granted. This authorization and allocation of human and material resources was the prerogative of the monastic superior and a *conditio sine qua non* for the writing of history in medieval monasteries. As *sapientes architecti*, the abbots and abbesses studied in this book exercised their authority to lay the foundations on which their communities' historiographical traditions were built by themselves and others.

Medieval monasteries were hierarchical institutions, and this book has helped us understand the structural and operational dynamics that governed their historiographical production by having showcased the role of those at the very top of this hierarchy. The exercise of abbatial authority in support of historical writing either directly or in delegated form was shown to have involved different modes, the most essential of which—and the subjects of the first three chapters—were authorship, patronage, and the provision of books and libraries. These modes were not mutually exclusive, and our understanding of any one of them is contingent upon their consideration and contextualisation as a collective. Only the first mode, that of abbatial authorship, has been the subject of previous scholarship, and much of our knowledge so far has relied on the evidence gathered in Kersken's survey. By contrast, the role of abbots and abbesses as patrons and facilitators of historical writing so far has escaped systematic treatment beyond the level of individual case studies, and these important modes of their historiographical involvement—arguably of greater importance than authorial composition—have been studied in detail for the first time here alongside authorship to reveal the full extent of the relationship between abbatial authority and the writing of history in the Middle Ages.

As demonstrated in Chapter 1, authorial composition was a significant facet of abbatial historiographical activity. As a group—albeit a heterogeneous one—monastic superiors were amongst the most prolific authors of historical narratives across the medieval Latin West with a concentration in the German(-speaking) and Frankish/French lands of the twelfth and fifteenth centuries. By far the most common histories written by abbots and abbesses were domestic narratives about the communities over which they themselves presided; in fact, this is the *only* form of history that monastic superiors authored continuously across the entire period, whereas others such as dynastic, national, or universal chronicles were produced more sporadically and subject to considerable ebb and flow. Latin prose was the preferred format, but vernacular and poetic histories were also composed, more frequently so by abbesses than by their male counterparts. Many wrote during their tenure, and some also before and/or after their abbacies. The former in particular found that carving out time and resources could be a delicate balancing act, with superiors who chose to devote too much to their historiographical pursuits running the risk of alienating their communities and, in the worst case, facing resignation/expulsion from office. Sometimes the solution was delegation. The more menial and time-consuming tasks could be assigned to workforces of domestic and/or professional scribes or to personal *amanuenses*, examples of which we saw in both written and visual sources, including author portraits. Some, however, preferred to commit their authorial compositions to the page *manu propria* whenever possible. Abbatial authors were set apart less by *what* they wrote than by their ability to imbue their works with a unique sense of authority that combined internal/institutional *auctoritas* with external/lordly *potestas*. This sense of power and authority is strongest—or at least most discernible—in histories that served as vehicles of abbatial self-fashioning, with their authors strategically aligning themselves with or distancing themselves from the memory of their predecessors. Some placed themselves so centrally and prominently as to marginalize or even exclude their predecessors altogether, whilst others 'weaponized' the histories they wrote against communal or indeed personal enemies.

The conclusions about abbatial authorship summarized above build on and develop Kersken's work, lending further depth and insight to his quantitative and qualitative findings as well as exploring many new topics and avenues of enquiry. One of the most significant amongst these, and one that breaks new ground, is the authorship of historical works by female monastic superiors—or abbess-historians. Contrary to some scholars' rather pessimistic assessments of historiographical production in communities of medieval religious women with little regard for the endeavours of their female leaders, the evidence presented in Chapter 1 paints a picture of abbesses as regular and instrumental authors of historical narratives, even if not with the same levels of frequency as their male equivalents. The reason why these abbess-historians are less common—or at least less visible to us—may have to do with a frequent renunciation of their authorial self in favour of their communities and communal authorship models, something we observe less regularly amongst abbot-historians. Indeed, abbesses appear to have been more willing than their male colleagues to 'take one for the team' by removing themselves and their authorial personas from the histories they wrote, meaning that their authorship can be easily obscured and often remains undetected. The analyses offered in this book leave no doubt that abbesses frequently acted as guardians of their communities' memory and champions of both domestic and external historiographical activity. Their primary *modus operandi* was not that of authorial composition, however, but that of patronage and facilitation as a way of empowering others within their communities to write history, which is why we saw their presence increase exponentially in subsequent chapters.

Chapter 2 showed us the critical mass of historiography produced on the commission and patronage of abbots and abbesses, comprising many of the best-known works of monastic historical writing to survive from the Middle Ages. These histories and the manuscripts in which they are transmitted sometimes acknowledge their abbatial sponsors explicitly in their prefaces, dedicatory letters, and illuminations, whereas others contain more subtle marks that need to be uncovered. Abbatial patronage could be obscured or even deliberately concealed, requiring considerable detective work to reveal the true *architectus*. The fact that some monastic authors chose not to disclose their abbatial patrons does not allow us to conclude that they wrote of their own volition or on their own authority. Some deliberately (ab)used the (temporary) absence of abbatial control during a vacancy/interregnum or as a result of incapacitation to exercise more authorial freedom and creative agency than normally possible, but acting on their own they lacked internal resources and the support of a patron whose *auctoritas/ potestas* could open important doors for historians by granting them access to external networks, including other libraries. Abbatial patronage differed from other forms of medieval patronage through the absence—in a domestic environment—of a commercial relationship based on remuneration or other material rewards. It was governed not by the transactional laws of supply and demand, but by the fundamental and unnegotiable monastic principles of authority and obedience. This was different, of course, when they commissioned external authors and scribes. Internally as well as externally, monastic superiors were accountable for whatever was written in their communities, not just the histories they explicitly commissioned, but also those they patronized *ex officio* by granting historians the resources and licence to write.

Taking this abbatial accountability to its logical conclusion, some superiors personally exercised 'quality control' by checking, correcting, or supervising the works they sponsored through to publication, even occasionally 'strong-arming' reluctant authors into writing the histories they wanted. Writing (history) without the superior's licence was subject to serious and sometimes severe repercussions, from admonitions and castigations to the destruction of works/drafts, the withholding of food and sustenance, physical isolation, and corporal punishment. In short, a supportive abbot could make all the difference, but so could an unsupportive one. As much as abbots and abbesses could enable and empower historiographers within and without their communities by 'ringfencing' time and resources, they could equally deploy their authority to inhibit and immobilize them by serving as 'gatekeepers' to resources such as books and writing materials, as well as by denying them the time to write or withholding copyists and scribal assistants. Abbatial patronage sometimes extended into trans-/cross-generational arrangements, especially for histories that took a long time to complete, and whose authors depended on the *continuous* support of their monastic superiors, with changes in leadership risking the stalling or termination—or, conversely, the 'turbocharging'—of inherited historiographical projects and commissions.

The third mode of abbatial historiographical facilitation showcased here, and the subject of Chapter 3, was that of book provision and library building. Books were indispensable resources for monastic historians, and without ready access to them few (if any) of the histories studied in this book could have been produced.

Abbots and abbesses were amongst the most prolific providers of monastic books, from individual items to entire libraries comprising hundreds or thousands of volumes. Unlike studies of monastic book provision that focus primarily on the evidence of normative sources, the analysis presented here has taken into consideration a broad range of documentary, narrative, visual, and material sources that were studied alongside, and contextualized with, monastic rules and customaries. Abbatial book provision helped sustain historiographical production in the short and long term, and the libraries built by monastic superiors enabled not just individual authors and protégés, but future generations of domestic historians, too. These books also carried major commemorative currency for the providers themselves. Like patronage, book provision and library building sometimes turned into cross-/trans-generational enterprises that set expectations and created significant peer-pressure, with some superiors competing with their contemporaries and predecessors to be remembered as the most generous providers of books for their abbeys' chroniclers. To 'futureproof' the memory of their provision and safeguard their legacy against loss, theft, or alienation/appropriation by ruthless successors, many abbots and abbesses commissioned detailed inventories that they had ratified, notarized, and copied into the pages of their communities' cartularies, domestic chronicles, and *gesta abbatum/abbatissarum*, the most elaborate of which are illustrated with portraits showing the commissioning superiors with the books they provided. Some went further by installing customized (and sometimes highly ornate) repositories for these books in their monastery's communal spaces to serve as physical monuments and permanent mementos of their library building, whereas others inscribed their provision into the community's memory by staging elaborate performative rituals.

Monastic book provision was a collaborative enterprise, but not a democratic one. It relied on authority that was delegated and devolved downwards from the abbot/abbess according to the monastery's internal hierarchy. Whilst this necessarily—and deliberately—placed considerable emphasis on the superior, sometimes to the exclusion and marginalization of others involved, it also created opportunities for certain collaborators to 'share the limelight' with their abbatial providers, to the point that monks and nuns would rival each other over the privilege of being remembered as their superiors' 'go-to assistants'. We have seen abbots and abbesses channelling resources into the provision of books both *ad hoc* and on a more permanent basis, such as by ringfencing funds or earmarking specific revenues, taxes, and other forms of income for the creation and maintenance of their monasteries' libraries—a kind of 'crowdfunding' that relied fundamentally on their lordly *potestas* and ability to attract external benefactors. Combining external procurement with domestic production, many of the superiors studied in this book operated a 'mixed economy' in their book accession strategies. In addition, the significance of interlibrary loans as an instrumental means of equipping monastic historians with the resources necessary for their craft cannot be overstated, with abbots and abbesses drawing on their wide-ranging networks to provide chroniclers with unparalleled access to books not available domestically—indeed, it is difficult to imagine a better-connected library network in medieval Europe than that created by confederations of monasteries. Access to an(other) abbey's book collection was subject to the superior's approval, and whilst many were rather protective—and some downright territorial—about granting access to their collections, the overall expectation witnessed in this study appears to have been that access requests would normally be granted between abbatial peers as long as the credentials were established, assurances made, costs met, and logistics arranged. Such peer-to-peer access offered a 'fast track' for monastic historians requiring borrowing rights and/or admission to external libraries, showing us yet another way in which abbatial authority could open doors for the writing of history.

Another door open to abbot- and abbess-historians but closed to others—this time in a literal sense—was that of private spaces conducive to historical writing and study, which formed the subject of Chapter 4. Knowledge of the physical workplaces available to medieval monastic superiors is essential to understanding their historiographical involvement and contribution, yet little attention has been paid to them in scholarship. Some abbots and abbesses made use of communal spaces by studying and writing amongst and alongside their monks and nuns, whereas many—indeed a majority—had access to separate facilities, access to which was exclusive to themselves, their assistants, and those admitted at their discretion. Usually part of abbatial residences, these workplaces existed from much earlier than previously assumed, and though very little of their interior and furnishings tends to survive, let alone *in situ*, we have seen evidence allowing us to reconstruct at least some of their former contents in the shape of inventories, account books, and books for study with inscriptions assigning them to the *studium abbatis*. Many monastic superiors maintained personal/official libraries alongside those they curated for their communities, the contents of which they usually passed on to their successors or donated to the monks/nuns for incorporation into the communal library upon their deaths or resignations. Some, however, managed to hold on to their book collections beyond their abbatial tenures, allowing them to transfer books between different locations and institutions. The abbatial studies and libraries investigated in this book offered a kind of privacy unavailable to other members of medieval monasteries, allowing abbot- and abbess-historians to write in the quiet and comfort of their quarters and keep their study and research materials close at hand, including books, archival documents, and sometimes even scribal workforces who helped them codify their authorial compositions.

Drawing together these findings from across the book's individual chapters, the picture that emerges is one of abbatial authority as a continuous conceptual factor and cultural force in the writing of history during the period c.500–1500. This is not to suggest that the very concept of abbatial authority and the remit of the abbatial office remained unchanged or unchallenged between the early Middle Ages and the age of Gunther of Nordhausen, Sophia of Stolberg, and Johannes Trithemius that set us on the path of our investigation in the book's Introduction. The appointment of so-called 'lay abbots' (*Laienäbte*) in the ninth and tenth centuries affected the relationship between the superior and his/her community in different ways than the monastic reform movements of the eleventh and twelfth centuries, and the same is true of the increasing separation of the *mensa abbatis* and *mensa conventualis*. I also do not wish to imply that the exercise of abbatial authority within the community was unrelated to or unaffected by social, political, and economic change in the world outside the cloister. There can be no question that when Eugippius of Lucullanum authored his *Vita Severini* in the sixth century, the conditions in which he wrote differed from those that marked the historiographical authorship of Heilwig of Chelles in the ninth, Robert of Torigni in the twelfth, and Ursula of Frauen-Chiemsee in the late fifteenth / early sixteenth centuries. The *Gesta abbatum* patronized by the early abbots of Saint-Wandrille were no doubt a product of different circumstances than Æthelweard's chronicle commissioned by Matilda of Essen, the *Chronicon Casauriense* written at the order of Abbot Leonas, or the *Grand cartulaire* compiled for Abbess Petronilla of Fontevraud. The extent to which the abbots and abbesses studied in this book exercised their authority to champion historiographical production within and without their communities was subject to a range of factors, internal and external, from economic constraints (size and wealth of the community, availability of resources and personnel, etc.) and political constellations (influence of external agents, wars and conquests, etc.) to environmental conditions (natural disasters, pandemics, etc.) and cultural transformations (literacy, technology, etc.). My intention is not to gloss over these important differences and developments, but to emphasize that the intrinsic relationship between abbatial authority and the writing of history was one that could accommodate and adapt to significant change. Indeed, it is notable that in the face of this change there is such constancy of practice—across both time and place—between the individuals and institutions included in this study. More remarkable still is the steadfastness with which abbatial authority informed, inspired, and influenced historiographical production in each case.

The close connection between abbatial authority and the writing of history in the Middle Ages identified in this study urges us to revisit our understanding of monastic historiography, its processes, and its protagonists in ways that require some fundamental—and perhaps radical—rethinking of what constituted the essence of the medieval historian's craft in a communal and institutional context. Contrary to the expectations expressed in Gunther of Nordhausen's *De historiae* and perpetuated by modern notions of history written in academic and professional environments, the actual 'writing' or authoring was arguably the least important and impactful facet or mode of abbatial historiographical involvement, one that was ultimately secondary—if complementary—to the facilitation of historical writing in ways other than by putting pen to parchment, thereby enabling not just themselves, but others inside as well as outside their communities. This recalibration not only shifts the focus from the authors to the authorizers and enablers—or, in Isidore's words, from the τέκτωνες to the *architecti*—of monastic historical writing, but it also helps showcase individuals and groups who have remained underrepresented and marginalized because of our preoccupation with authorial composition. Besides scribes, bookmakers, and *amanuenses*, these also—and particularly—include abbesses. Though abbesses were less prolific (or at least less visible) as authors of historical writings than their male equivalents, they were instrumental as patrons and facilitators, perhaps suggesting that their historiographical engagement was, if anything, even more community-minded. Recalling Gunther's words quoted in the Introduction of this book, there was no community without history—and, as this study has argued, there was no history without community.

APPENDIX

The Abbots of Flavigny and Their Deeds
(*Series abbatum Flaviniacensium*)

'In the sixth-hundredth and first year after the incarnation of the Lord, in the fifth indiction, with King Chilperic of the Franks reigning in his fourth year, in the time of Emperor Maurice, in the ninth year of Pope Gregory's governing the pontificate of the Roman Church, a church was built in honour of St Praejectus by lord Widerard in the city of Flavigny in the ager of Bornet; and Magoald was ordained abbot. In the first year of King Theoderic, the six hundred sixth after the incarnation of the Lord, and the third of Emperor Phocas, the same lord Theoderic had the lord Widerard's testament concerning the city and monastery of Flavigny confirmed and corroborated with his seal at Semur (dép. Côte-d'Or, cant. Semur-en-Auxois) under the administration of Archbishop Secundinus of the church of Lyon in the second year after the death of the venerable [Pope] Gregory, that is, in the first [year] of the papacy of Sabinian. In the six hundred and fifty-first year of the incarnation of the Lord, that is, in the eleventh year of Clovis, son of Dagobert, Magoald, the first abbot of Flavigny, died after having ruled this place for forty-eight years, and the lord Widerard was ordained abbot on 21 April; he ruled [Flavigny] for twelve years. The Lord Abbot Widerard died on 3 October of the year of the incarnation of the Lord 658;[1] Bishop Geruin succeeded [him] and died on the king's campaign on 6 July. In the year 755, in the eighth indiction, Manasses was ordained abbot by conferral of King Pippin. He transferred the body of St Praejectus from Volvic (dép. Puy-de-Dôme, cant. Châtel-Guyon) to the church of Flavigny. He died in 787, in the fifteenth indiction, and after two years Adalbert was ordained [abbot]; he died in his fourth year, and Zacho succeeded [him], being ordained on 1 May and dying in his fourth year, on 9 May. After him came Alcuin, who in the seventh year relinquished the [abbatial] seat to Apollinaris by conferral of Emperor Charles. How great this was, and what it involved, is enshrined in the official deeds. He [Apollinaris] died during the time of Emperor Louis, in the fourth indiction, 826, and upon his death Vigilius succeeded [as abbot]. He was succeeded by Adrevald in the year 839, who died in his third year. Marianus succeeded [him] in 845, in the eighth indiction, and he relinquished the [abbatial] seat to Vulfald, upon whose death Count Warin ruled as 'quasi-abbot' (*vice abbatis*) by conferral of Emperor Charles;[2] under him [Warin], Sarulf succeeded as deacon, and after him Goszer [succeeded] as abbot. Upon his death, Hugh succeeded [as abbot] in Charles's sixteenth year; and after him followed Eigil, the later archbishop of Sens, who transferred the body of St Regina [to Flavigny]. He was succeeded by Sigard, who in his fifth year relinquished the [abbatial] seat to Wolfhard, brother-in-law of Emperor Louis II, by the latter's conferral. In

---

[1] Up to this point, my translation is based on the beginning of the text as reconstructed by Hlawitschka, 'Textkritisches', p. 262. What follows after has been translated from 'Chronicon', ed. Pertz and rev. Lawo, pp. 502–3, taking into account the corrections in Hlawitschka, 'Textkritisches', pp. 253–4 and 254–6 n. 24.

[2] Warin is referred to elsewhere as *dux* of Flavigny by royal appointment; see Geoffrey Koziol, *The Politics of Memory and Identity in Carolingian Royal Diplomas: The West Frankish Kingdom (840–987)* (Turnhout: Brepols, 2012), p. 181.

the third year after his [Wolfhard's] ordination, in the year 878, in the eleventh indiction, Flavigny's church was consecrated by Pope John and eighteen bishops. In that same year Emperor Louis died, and he was succeeded by Carloman. After this, Bishop Adalgar of Autun sought and obtained control over the abbacy of Flavigny from Charles the Simple in the first year of this king's reign;[3] and on account of this he was summoned to Rome by the pope, but he died *en route* at Tournus (dép. Saône-et-Loire, cant. Tournus) in that same year, that is, in 893; and under him Aquinus was provost [of Flavigny] for a short while. *This same provost Aquinus was implored and elected to be bishop of Autun, but Duke Richard and Ingelbert ordered for the ordination of Walo, brother of Count Manasses, who was—or rather they [both] were—born from Duke Richard's sister.*[4] Having ordained him [Walo], Argrim was removed from the bishopric of Langres by Pope Stephen, but he was re-instated at Lyon by [Pope] Formosus although he did not have the pallium, nor did he have the sustained authority to consecrate a bishop, and the ordination was contested by Bishop Tetbaldus of Langres on the part of the pope.[5] Famosus therefore deposed Argrim irrevocably, and he excommunicated Walo along with his supporters—that is, Richard, Manasses, and the others—for their invasion of the church of Flavigny. Still Walo obtained the bishopric [of Autun], being propped up by secular power, and making himself abbot of Flavigny he kept the lordship in his grasp and installed Otbert as provost under him.[6] As a consequence, the church of Flavigny remained without an abbot for many years, and the bishops of Autun maintained control of the church's lordship as they succeeded each other. Following [the death of] the provost Otbert, [his successor] Girfred was accused of the murder of Adalgar, but being acquitted by the court of bishops, he retained the prelacy.[7] He was succeeded by Raingus, [a man] of great ability and integrity, who died on 15 May. Walo died in the year of the incarnation of the Lord 913, in the fifteenth indiction. In the first

---

[3] The first part of this sentence has been translated from 'Post haec Adalgarius episcopus Eduensis a Karolo Simplice primo anno regni eius subditione [*rather than* sub Odone] abbatiam perquisivit et obtinuit', which Hlawitscka argues to be the correct reading; cf. Hlawitschka, 'Textkritisches', p. 254. If, however, the lost manuscript did indeed read 'sub Odone', this might suggest that Adalgar had actually requested—but not (yet) obtained—the abbacy of Flavigny under Charles the Simple's predecessor, King Odo. This is not impossible, and perhaps not altogether unlikely, given that Adalgar had been Odo's archchancellor, having previously acted as Charles the Bald's notary, envoy, and, from c.875, 'chancellor of the sacred palace' ('sacri palatii cancellarius'); Koziol, *Politics*, p. 188, as well as pp. 81–5, 216–17, 358–9. On Adalgar's diplomatic and administrative appointments, see *Recueil des actes d'Eudes, roi de France (888–898)*, ed. by Robert-Henri Bautier and Georges Tessier (Paris: Imprimerie nationale, 1967), pp. xxix–xxxiii.

[4] Translated from the text provided in Hlawitschka, 'Textkritisches', pp. 253–4.

[5] On this conflict, cf. the discussion in Eduard Hlawitschka, 'Die Todesdaten Teutbalds I. und Teutbalds II. von Langres: Bemerkungen zur Geschichte von Langres in der zweiten Hälfte des 9. Jahunderts', in *Mélanges offerts à Szabolcs de Vajay à l'occasion de son cinquantième anniversaire*, ed. by Pierre Brièrre (Braga: Cruz, 1971), pp. 321–8 (pp. 323–5). Also Koziol, *Politics*, pp. 12–13. On the ambiguity of the expression 'restitutam dignitatem' (translated here as 'sustained authority') with regard to Argrim's contested position as Archbishop of Lyon, see Steven A. Schoenig, *Bonds of Wool: The Pallium and Papal Power in the Middle Ages* (Washington, DC: Catholic University of America Press, 2016), p. 371 n. 32.

[6] This is likely the same Otbert who previously had been archdeacon of Langres and, in this capacity, had received two royal diplomas from Carloman II and Charles the Fat on 8 August and 4 November 882, respectively, both of which have survived as originals (Chaumont, Archives départementales de la Haute-Marne, G 1 nos. 7 and 8). On Otbert's position at Langres, see also Simon MacLean, *Kingship and Politics in the Late Ninth Century: Charles the Fat and the End of the Carolingian Empire* (Cambridge: Cambridge University Press, 2003), pp. 111–14.

[7] Girfred seems to have administered Flavigny on Adalgar's behalf prior to the latter's death and the ensuing murder allegations; he continued this appointment under Adalgar's successor, Walo of Autun, who in an episcopal charter dated 909 still refers to Girfred as 'nostrae ecclesiae [= Flavigny?] abbas et archidiaconus'; cf. Koziol, *Politics*, p. 12 n. 9.

indiction, Hervé succeeded [him] and retained this abbacy [of Flavigny] for himself, and he appointed Gausarius as provost under him. Likewise, when Hervé died he was replaced by Rotmund. This [Rotmund] relinquished the command over the church of Flavigny to Abbot Raino of Mesvres (dép. Saône-et-Loire, cant. Autun-2) in the time of King Rudolph, son of Richard the Justicier. Upon his [Raino's] death, Wichard succeeded [him], and after him came the lord Fulcher in the time of Louis, son of Charles the Simple. He [Fulcher] departed for Jerusalem in the year of the incarnation of the Lord 944, in the second indiction, bringing home to his church part of a nail [from the crucifixion] of the Lord and a piece of His cross, as well as a belt, a handkerchief, and a staff. He also ruled over the church of [Saint-Bénigne de] Dijon. He transferred [the relics of] Saint Paschasia, namely the middle section of her body, to the church [of Flavigny]. He died on 28 April 955 and was succeeded by Milo of Mesvres. Rotmund died in the year 968, in the eleventh indiction, and Gerard succeeded him. Abbot Milo went to Rome and obtained a privilege from Pope Benedict. Bishop Gerard of Autun was succeeded by the lord Walter in the year 978, in the sixth indiction. Following Milo's death, he [Walter] gave the church of Flavigny to Robert, who through utter carelessness completely wrecked the same church. Deposed from the abbacy, he [Robert] was entrusted with the priorate of the cell of Corbigny (dép. Nièvre, cant. Corbigny) because he was a relative of Count Landric of Nevers, and Heldric, a monk of Cluny, was appointed abbot [of Flavigny]. Coming to Corbigny, Robert had himself pronounced abbot, and because of this Corbigny is called an abbey.[8] Heldric died in the year of the incarnation of the Lord 1010, and Amadeus succeeded [him], who recovered the cell of Corbigny [for Flavigny]. He also established the cells of Couches (dép. Saône-et-Loire, cant. Chagny), Semur (dép. Côte-d'Or, cant. Semur-en-Auxois), and Beaulieu (dép. Vaucluse, cant. Cheval-Blanc), and he died in great authority and dignity; Aymo succeeded [him], but he was convicted of simony and surrendered the pastoral care into the hand of Pope Leo IX in the year 1045.[9] He was

[8] Corbigny's abbatial status and its relationship to Flavigny form a very complicated subject, especially considering that there still is no scholarly consensus as to the authenticity of the relevant documentary sources. For example, a royal charter pertaining to be issued by Charlemagne in the mid-770s (that is, as king of the Franks) that grants Flavigny perpetual authority over Corbigny and its monks—a copy of which survives in Flavigny's monastic cartulary—has long been considered an eleventh-century forgery, though Bouchard treats it as if authentic and argues that as far back as Flavigny's foundation, 'Wideradus seems to have intended to establish monks at Corbigny, even though he never did so, because he settled property on Corbigny in his testament'; *Cartulary*, ed. Bouchard, pp. 48–9 (p. 49). The cartulary further includes a memorandum of Charlemagne's act in the form of a charter claiming to have been issued by Abbot Eigil on 22 March 864; ibid., pp. 125–8 (= no. 52). Bouchard believes this charter to be authentic, whereas Winzer and others have provided evidence to suggest that it might in fact be a forgery made at Flavigny during the eleventh century; Winzer, 'Studien', p. 79. Corbigny subsequently formed part of Charles the Bald's gift to Bishop Adalgar of Autun and his successors in 877, copies of which survive in the cartularies of both Flavigny and Autun; *Cartulary*, ed. Bouchard, pp. 69–72 (= no. 23); *Cartulaire de l'église d'Autun*, ed. by Anatole de Charmasse, 2 vols. (Paris: Pédone, 1865–1900; repr. Geneva: Mégariotis, 1978), I, 11–12 (= no. VII), 40–1 (= no. XXV). It seems that the rights over Corbigny were not returned to Flavigny until after Abbot Heldric's election in 990, which had marked the end of Autun's episcopal rule over the abbey and its dependencies; Heldric's successor, Amadeus, later requested and received a confirmation of this restoration act from Bishop Elmuin of Autun in 1034; *Cartulary*, ed. Bouchard, pp. 119–22 (= no. 49). This confirmation—unlike the two acts of 775/6 and 864—is unanimously considered authentic.

[9] Hlawitschka, 'Textkritisches', p. 254 corrects the final part of this sentence to 'in manu Leonis IX curam pastoralem [*rather than* virgam pastoralem] dimisit anno MXLV'. If the reading 'virgam pastoralem' is correct, however, this might suggest that Aymo symbolically surrendered his abbatial staff to Pope Leo IX at the Council of Reims in 1049; also cf. *Regesta Imperii* III 5,2 n. 623, available online: http://www.regesta-imperii.de/id/1049-10-03_2_0_3_5_2_295_623.

succeeded by Odo I, a monk of the abbey of Montiéramey (dép. Aube, cant. Vendeuvre-sur-Barse); after two years, he [Odo I] relinquished the [abbatial] seat to Odo II, who at the time when Elmuin controlled the [episcopal] seat of Autun restored Corbigny, which he had not held previously, to our church; there [at Corbigny], he [Odo II] received a procession by the monks, and when during this procession he accepted with little worry the pastoral staff which the devil's henchman, Robert, had carried, he was unjustly accused of this by our brothers [of Corbigny] who then withdrew from the procession. And on account of the reinforced apostolic orders, according to which an abbot should not hold two monasteries, he [Odo II] was accused by them [the monks of Corbigny] at the synod of Issoudun of leading two churches contrary to the apostolic decrees, so he returned the [abbatial] staff and did not maintain any of the rights requested regarding his cell, that is, the territory of the church of Flavigny. After the death of Bishop Elmuin, when the election of Hagano was made public, the abbot [Odo II] went to the court of King Henry of France and presented his complaint to the ears of the king, and the bishop was coerced by law to swear an oath that immediately after his consecration he would restore his right [over Corbigny] to the church of Flavigny.[10] And given that the voice of Flavigny's abbot is the primary one in the election of the bishop, as everyone can confirm, when the bishop elect went to the chapter of Flavigny he gave his word to the brethren both small and powerful concerning the restoration of the church of Flavigny, that is, the reinstatement of the cell of Corbigny. But charmed by the servility of Corbigny, he did not keep what he promised, still his oath will forever be remembered both privately and publicly. When Odo [II] died, he was replaced by Rainald, the duke's brother and a monk of this place [Flavigny]. This [Rainald] re-enshrined the body of St Praejectus in a coffin made of gold, silver, and gemstones, which he had made with great care and effort, and he invited Abbot Hugh of Cluny to attend this translation. Likewise, he adorned the church entrusted to him with cloaks, capes, and various ornaments; but with the resolve of his mind impeded by illness, he could not carry out what he wished for and died in the youthful blossom of his tender age, not having completed the seventh year of his abbacy. And after this the church [of Flavigny] remained without a governor for almost seven years, except only for Elmuin who ruled for just two months.'

---

[10] On the following events and the likelihood of their actual occurrence, see the discussion in Winzer, 'Studien', p. 88 n. 233. Also cf. André-Joseph Ansart, *Histoire de Sainte Reine d'Alise et de l'abbaye Flavigny* (Paris: Herissant & Barrois, 1783), pp. 195–200.

Abbots of Flavigny*	Dates of abbacy[11]	Calendar/necrology (MS Berlin Phill. 1870, fols. 1r–3v)	Series abbatum, ed. Pertz, pp. 502–3**	Hugh's *Chronicon* (MS Berlin Phill. 1870, fols. 10r–148r)	*Cartulary*, ed. Bouchard***
Magoald	719–32	2v (VIII Kal. Aug.)	(502)**	36v(add.), 37v(add.), 51r(add.)	19–28 (= no. 1), 28–33 (= no. 2), 135–40 (= no. 57), 140–4 (= no. 58)
Widerard	732–44	1v (XI Kal. Mai = ord.), 3r (V Non. Oct.)	(502)**	36v(add.), 37r(add.), 37v(add.), 51r(add.), 51v(add.)	19–28 (= no. 1), 28–33 (= no. 2), 106–8 (= no. 42), 125–8 (= no. 52), 135–40 (= no. 57), 140–4 (= no. 58)
Geruin	744–55	2r (II Non. Iul.)	502 (II Non. Iul.)	51v(add.), 52r(add.), 59v(add.)	33–4 (= no. 3), 38–40 (= no. 6), 40–1 (= no. 7)
Manasses	755–87	3v (Non. Nov.)	502 (a. 787)	52r(add.), 59v(add.), 60v(add.), 60bisr(add.)	34–6 (= no. 4), 43–4 (= no. 9), 44–5 (= no. 10), 45–6 (= no. 11), 48–9 (= no. 13), 125–8 (= no. 52)
Adalbert	789–93/4	-	502 (a. 4°)	59v(add.), 60bisr(add.)	-
Zacho	793/4–96/7	1r (VIII Kal. Mart. = ord.), 2r (VII Id. Mai.)	502 (Kal. Mart. = ord.,[12] VII Id. Mai)	60bisr(add.)	-
Alcuin	796/7–803	-	502 (a. 7° *sedem reliquit*)	-	-
Apollinaris	803–26	1v (IIII Kal. Mai.)[13]	502 (a. 826)	60bisr(add.), 61v(add.), 62r(add.)	36–7 (= no. 5)

[11] Some of the beginnings and/or end dates are obscure and cannot be reconstructed with absolute certainty (or at all) from the extant sources. The dates given largely follow those in the detailed prosopographical catalogue provided by Winzer, 'Studien', pp. 66–100; also cf. *Cartulary*, ed. Bouchard, pp. 145–8. Winzer's dates generally have been given priority where they differ from Bouchard's.

[12] Pertz mistakenly corrects this to '9. Kal. Mart.'; Hugh of Flavigny, 'Chronicon', ed. Pertz and rev. Lawo, p. 502 n. 41.

[13] Winzer, 'Studien', p. 60 did not match Apollinaris's *obit* to this date using the symbolic key 'Θ' inserted by Hugh, but instead concluded that the entry cannot be assigned to any specific date (ibid.: 'keinem Datum zuweisbar').

Continued

Abbots of Flavigny*	Dates of abbacy	Calendar/necrology (MS Berlin Phill. 1870, fols. 1r–3v)	Series abbatum, ed. Pertz, pp. 502–3**	Hugh's Chronicon (MS Berlin Phill. 1870, fols. 10r–148r)	Cartulary, ed. Bouchard***
Vigilius	826/28–?	-	502 (a. 839)	60^{bis}r$^{(add.)}$, 62r$^{(add.)}$, 62^{bis}v$^{(add.)}$	-
Adrevald	834 × 39–40/1	-	502 (a. 839?)	62^{bis}v$^{(add.)}$	-
Marianus	840/1 × 45–?	-	502 (a. 841/2?)	62^{bis}v$^{(add.)}$	-
Vulfald	?–?	3r (VIII. Id. Sept.)	502 (*sedem reliquit*)	62^{bis}v$^{(add.)}$	-
Warin	c.849–?	-	502	62^{bis}v$^{(add.)}$	61–3 (= **no. 19**), 64–5 (= **no. 20**)
Goszer	?–855	-	502 (a. 855/6?)	-	-
Hugh	856–60	-	502 (a. 856)	62^{bis}v$^{(add.)}$	-
Eigil	860–5	2r (III Kal. Iun.)	502	62^{bis}v$^{(add.)}$	65–7 (= **no. 21**), 125–8 (= **no. 52**)
(Geylo)[14]	(866–70)	2r (III Kal. Iul.)	-	62^{bis}v$^{(add.)}$	65–7 (= **no. 21**)
Sigard	870–2 × 75	-	502 (*sedem reliquit*)	62^{bis}v$^{(add.)}$	128–9 (= **no. 53**)
Wolfhard	875–88 × 93	3r (VIII Id. Sept.)	502	-	-
Adalgar^{ep}	877–93	-	502 (a. 877)	62^{bis}v$^{(add.)}$	69–72 (= **no. 23**), 73–5 (= **no. 24**), 75–8 (= **no. 25**)
Walo^{ep}	894[15]–913	-	502–3 (a. 913)	62v$^{(add.)}$, 62^{bis}v$^{(add.)}$, 63v$^{(add.)}$	75–8 (= **no. 25**), 78–80 (= **no. 26**)
Hervé^{ep}	914–35	2r (II Kal. Iul.)	503	63v$^{(add.)}$, 64v$^{(add.)}$	-
Rotmund^{ep}	935–68	-	503 (a. 968)	64v$^{(add.)}$, 72v	106–8 (= **no. 42**)
Fulcher	937/8–55	1v (IIII Kal. Mai.)	503 (a. 955)	62v$^{(add.)}$	-
Adrald	?–?	-	-	-	55–7 (= **no. 16**)

[14] Winzer, 'Studien', pp. 80–2 suspects that Geilo was not in fact abbot of Flavigny, and that his inclusion in the succession of abbots recorded in Hugh's *Chronicon*—but not in the *Series abbatum*—was likely a mistake on the part of the author.

[15] This date for Walo's appointment is suggested by Hlawitschka, 'Todesdaten', p. 323.

Name	Dates				
Milo	955–?	3v (Non. Dec.)	503	62v[(add.)]	55–7 (= no. 16), **59–61 (= no. 18)**
Gerard[ep]	968–77	–	503 (a. 978)	–	67–9 (= no. 22)
Walter[ep]	977–1018	–	503	–	59–61 (= **no. 18**), **80–2 (= no. 27)**, **82–6 (= no. 28)**, 86–8 (= no. 29), 88–90 (= no. 30), 92–3 (= no. 33), 106–8 (= **no. 42**), **109–12 (= no. 43)**, 119–22 (= no. 49), 123–4 (= no. 51)
Robert	?–990	–	503	–	–
Heldric	990–1009/10	3v (XVIII Kal. Ian.)	503 (a. 1010)	73r[(add.)]	82–6 (= no. 28), **86–8 (= no. 29)**, 88–90 (= **no. 30**), 90–1 (= **no. 31**), 91–2 (= **no. 32**), 92–3 (= no. 33), 96–7 (= **no. 36**)
Amadeus	1010–38	1v (XIII Kal. Apr.)	503	73r[(add.)], 91v[(add.)]	**52–5 (= no. 15)**, 55–7 (= no. 16), **80–2 (= no. 27)**, 88–90 (= no. 30), 106–8 (= **no. 42**), **109–12 (= no. 43)**, 119–22 (= no. 49), 123–4 (= **no. 51**)
Aymo	1038–49	3v (VII Kal. Ian.)	503	–	(52–5 (= no. 15))[16]
Odo I	1049–50	2v (VI Kal. Sept.)	503 (*sedem reliquit*)	–	–
Odo II	1050–84	2v (V Id. Aug.)	503 (a. 1051)	–	67–9 (= no. 22)
Rainald	1084/5–90	1r (IIII Id. Feb.)	503	–	122 (= **no. 50**), 133–4 (= **no. 56**)
Elmuin	?–?	–	503	–	–

* *italics* = Abbot/provost/rector ruling Flavigny under and/or on behalf of a bishop of Autun; [ep] = bishop of Autun.
** (brackets) = not edited by Pertz; reconstructed by Hlawitschka.
*** **bold** = directly involving the abbot in question (as issuing authority, solicitor, benefactor, witness, etc.) and issued during his abbacy.

[16] Whilst it is possible that Abbot Aymo might be responsible for the entry 'Aymonis' in the act's list of witnesses, this cannot be established with certainty.

Bibliography

Manuscripts and Archival Sources

Arras, Bibliothèque municipale,
 MS 294 (849).
 MS 364 (453).
 MS 573 (462).
 MS 849 (539).
 MS 1029 (812).
 MS 1071 (274).
Augsburg, Archiv des Bistums, MS 78.
Austin, TX, Harry Ransom Center, MS 29.
Auxerre, Bibliothèque municipale, MS 212.
Avranches, Bibliothèque patrimoniale,
 MS 145.
 MS 149.
 MS 159.
 MS 210.
Bamberg,
 Staatsarchiv,
  Rep. 29 no. 9.
  Rep. 187 no. 3030.
 Staatsbibliothek,
  MS Misc. 182.1-2.
  MS Msc. Hist. 146.
  MS Msc. Hist. 147.
  MS RB Msc. 48.
  MS RB Msc. 49.
Basel, Universitätsbibliothek, MS F III 42.
Berlin, Staatsbibliothek zu Berlin–Preußischer Kulturbesitz,
 MS lat. fol. 252.
 MS Phill. 1870.
Boulogne-sur-Mer, Bibliothèque municipale,
 MS 146.
 MS 146A.
Bruges, Rijksarchief, S. Bertijns Poperinge 3.
Brussels, Koninklijke Bibliotheek van België, MS 9850–52.
Cambridge,
 Corpus Christi College,
  MS 51.
  MS 77.
  MS 92.
  MS 139.

Fitzwilliam Museum, MS 12.
Gonville and Caius College, MS 391/611.
Jesus College, MS 18.
St John's College,
    MS D.6.
    MS D.27.
    MS G.15 (183).
Trinity College,
    MS B.14.36.
    MS R.5.33.
    MS R.17.1.
University Library,
    MS Ee.4.20.
    MS Ee.4.23.
    MS Gg.4.11.
    MS Ll.1.10.
Canterbury, Cathedral Archives and Library,
    DCC/ChAnt/A/66C.
    DCC/ChAnt/Z/141.
    DCC/LitMS/C/11.
Cardiff, Public Library, MS 1.381.
Charleville-Mézières, Bibliothèque municipale–Médiathèque Voyelles, MS 25.
Darmstadt, Universitäts- und Landesbibliothek,
    MS 1640.
    MS 1948.
Dijon, Bibliothèque municipale, MS 448.
Douai, Bibliothèque Marceline Desbordes-Valmore, MS 850.
Dublin, Trinity College,
    MS 57 (A.4.5).
    MS 444.
Engelberg, Stiftsbibliothek,
    MS Cod. 4.
    MS Cod. 5.
    MS Cod. 23.
    MS Cod. 47.
    MS Cod. 88.
Erlangen, Universitätsbibliothek, MS 136.
Evreux, Bibliothèque municipale, MS Lat. 46.
Florence, Biblioteca Medicea Laurenziana,
    MS Plut. 66.21.
    MS Plut. 68.2.
Frankfurt, Universitätsbibliothek, MS Barth. 104.
Freiburg i. Br., Universitätsbibliothek, MS 15.
Fulda, Hochschul- und Landesbibliothek,
    MS B1.
    MS B3.
Gloucester, Cathedral Library,
    Frocester Register 1397 (*olim* Reg. A).
    MS 34.

Hanover, Niedersächsisches Landesarchiv,
    Cal. Or. 100 Loccum, Urkunde 842.
    Dep. 76, C 113.
Heidelberg, Universitätsbibliothek,
    MS Cod. Sal. IX 42a.
    MS Cod. Sal. X.16.
Hildesheim, Dombibliothek,
    MS 313b.
    MS 785.
Kew, National Archives, C 150/1.
Laon, Archives départementales de l'Aisne, H 325.
Le Havre, Bibliothèque municipale Armand Salacrou, MS 332.
Leiden, Universiteitsbibliotheek,
    MS Scaliger 49.
    MS Voss. Lat. Q. 110.
Leipzig, Universitätsbibliothek, MS Rep. II. 69.
León, Biblioteca de la Real Colegiata de San Isidoro, MS Cod. I 3.
Lich, Fürst zu Solms-Hohensolms-Lich'sches Archiv, Liber actorum Arnsburg.
Liège, Archives de l'État, Abbaye impériale de Stavelot, MS I 341.
Lille, Archives départementales du Nord, 12 H 1, no. 38.
London,
    British Library,
        MS Add. 38816.
        MS Add. 40007.
        MS Add. 59678.
        MS Add. 70513.
        MS Add. 88973.
        MS Add. 88974.
        MS Arundel 34.
        MS Cotton Claudius C IX.
        MS Cotton Claudius E III.
        MS Cotton Claudius E IV.
        MS Cotton Domitian A VIII.
        MS Cotton Julius A XI.
        MS Cotton Julius D III.
        MS Cotton Nero D VII.
        MS Cotton Otho B IV.
        MS Cotton Otho C XI.
        MS Cotton Vitellius A XIII.
        MS Cotton Vitellius A VIII.
        MS Cotton Vitellius C VI.
        MS Harley 3045.
        MS Harley 3661.
        MS Harley 5019.
        MS Harley 5765.
        MS Royal 8 G I.
        MS Royal 9 C X.
        MS Royal 10 D III.
        MS Royal 13 D IV.
    Society of Antiquaries, MS 59.

Lucca, Biblioteca Statale, MS 1942.
Manchester, University Library–John Rylands Library, Rylands Charter 1436.
Marburg, Universitätsbibliothek, MS 75.
Melk, Stiftsbibliothek, MS 20.
Milan, Biblioteca Ambrosiana, MS S 45 sup.
Modena, Biblioteca Estense Universitaria, MS Lat. 390 (a.H.4.6; *olim* VI.F.5).
Montecassino, Archivio dell'Abbazia–Biblioteca Statale del Monumento Nazionale,
    MS Casin. 175.
    MS 6.
    MS 275.
    MS 298.
Montpellier, Bibliothèque interuniversitaire–Bibliothèque universitaire historique de médecine,
    MS H 151.
Munich,
    Bayerische Staatsbibliothek,
        MS Clm. 703.
        MS Clm. 704.
        MS Clm. 1072.
        MS Clm. 1925.
        MS Clm. 4623.
        MS Clm. 6911.
        MS Clm. 9540.
        MS Clm. 13002.
        MS Clm. 13031.
        MS Clm. 14222.
        MS Clm. 14355.
        MS Clm. 14361.
        MS Clm. 14398.
        MS Clm. 14437.
        MS Clm. 14641.
        MS Clm. 14958.
        MS Clm. 17142.
        MS Clm. 17401.
        MS Clm. 17403.
        MS Clm. 18192.
        MS Clm. 18571.
        MS Clm. 19411.
        MS Clm. 19412.
        MS Clm. 19472.
        MS Clm. 21521.
    Bayerisches Hauptstaatsarchiv,
        Kloster Benediktbeuern, Amtsbücher und Akten 1.
        Kloster Ebersberg, KL 2.
        Kloster Prüfening, KL 2.
        Kloster St. Emmeram, Regensburg Urkunden 526.
Münster, Landesarchiv Nordrhein-Westfalen–Staatsarchiv,
    MS I 133.
    MS I 243.

New York, NY, Pierpont Morgan Library,
   MS M.710.
   MS M.826.
Oldenburg,
   Landesbibliothek, MS 99i.
   Staatsarchiv, Bestd. 23,1, No. 3.
Oxford,
   Bodleian Library,
      MS Bodley 39.
      MS Bodley 292.
      MS Bodley 309.
      MS Digby 86.
      MS Douce 136.
      MS Laud Lat. 114.
      MS Laud Misc. 126.
      MS Laud Misc. 264.
      MS Laud Misc. 279.
   University College, MS 169.
Paris,
   Bibliothèque nationale de France,
      Coll. Picardie 233.
      Coll. Picardie 268.
      Coll. Picardie 291.
      MS Baluze 42.
      MS fr. 10468.
      MS fr. 13513.
      MS Lat. 529.
      MS Lat. 1245.
      MS Lat. 1820.
      MS Lat. 1847.
      MS Lat. 1850.
      MS Lat. 1862.
      MS Lat. 1918.
      MS Lat. 2012.
      MS Lat. 2502.
      MS Lat. 2858.
      MS Lat. 5411.
      MS Lat. 5547.
      MS Lat. 7696.
      MS Lat. 10912.
      MS Lat. 10938.
      MS Lat. 11757.
      MS Lat. 12681.
      MS Lat. 14651.
      MS Lat. 17545.
      MS Lat. 17767.
      MS Lat. 17768.
      MS Lat. 17770.
      MS Lat. 17775.

MS Moreau 42.
MS Nouv. acq. lat. 1219.
Institut de France–Bibliothèque Mazarine,
MS 753.
MS 2013.
Pommersfelden, Gräflich Schönbornsche Schloßbibliothek, Cod. 340 (*olim* 2821).
Prague, National Library of the Czech Republic,
MS VII G 17/d.
MS XII D 10.
MS XII D 11.
MS XII D 12.
MS XII D 13.
MS XII D 8a.
MS XII D 8b.
MS XII D 9.
MS XII E 14c.
MS XIV A 17.
MS XIV D 13.
MS XIV E 10.
Rein, Stiftsarchiv, MS D.
Rome, Biblioteca Nazionale Centrale di Roma,
MS Sess. 44 (1473).
MS Sess. 45 (1364).
Rudolstadt, Historische Bibliothek, 2° Ink 3.
Saint-Lô, Archives départementales de la Manche,
1 H 13.
15 Fi 13.
San Marino, CA, Huntington Library, MS 27187.
Schaffhausen, Ministerialbibliothek, MS 17.
Solothurn, Sankt-Ursen-Kathedrale, MS U1.
St-Omer, Bibliothèque d'Agglomération, MS 815.
St Gall,
Stiftsarchiv, Cod. Fab. 1.
Stiftsbibliothek,
MS Cod. Sang. 267.
MS Cod. Sang. 614.
MS Cod. Sang. 1092.
Stuttgart, Landesarchiv Baden-Württemberg–Hauptstaatsarchiv,
A 478 Bü 16 (*olim* Rep. Blaubeuren B. 16).
MS B 515 2a.
MS HB I 240.
Thurgau, Gemeindearchiv, KKG 16, B 6.2.01/1 (*olim* B.VIII 1c/C.XV 13, no. 13).
Turin, Archivio Di Stato, MS IB.II.27.
Valenciennes, Bibliothèque municipale–Médiathèque Simone Veil,
MS 39 (*olim* 33).
MS 50 (*olim* 43).
MS 60 (*olim* 53).
MS 65 (*olim* 58).
MS 66 (*olim* 59).

MS 156 (*olim* 148).
MS 298 (*olim* 288).
MS 498 (*olim* 458).
MS 546 (*olim* 500).
Vatican, Biblioteca Apostolica Vaticana,
MS Pal. lat. 929.
MS Pal. lat. 1877.
MS Reg. lat. 12.
MS Reg. lat. 95.
MS Reg. lat. 124.
MS Reg. lat. 339.
MS Vat. lat. 1202.
MS Vat. lat. 3340.
MS Vat. lat. 5758.
MS Vat. lat. 11051.
Vendôme, Bibliothèque municipale-Médiathèque Parc Ronsard, MS 26.
Verdun, Bibliothèque d'étude du Grand Verdun, MS 8.
Vienna, Österreichische Nationabibliothek, MS Cod. 460.
Wiesbaden, Hochschul- und Landesbibliothek RheinMain, MS 1.
Wolfenbüttel, Herzog August Bibliothek,
MS Cod. 164.1 Extrav.
MS Cod. Astron. 13.4.
MS Cod. Guelf. 143.1 Extrav.
MS Cod. Guelf. 265.4 Extrav.
Würzburg, Universitätsbibliothek,
MS ch. f. 126.
MS ch. f. 340.
MS p. th. q. 2.
MS p. th. q. 13.
MS p. th. q. 22.
Zwettl, Stiftsbibliothek, MS 22.

Edited and Printed Sources

'*A Gest of Robyn Hode*', in *Robin Hood and Other Outlaw Tales*, ed. by Stephen Knight and Thomas Ohlgren, 2nd ed. (Kalamazoo, MI: Medieval Institute Publications, 2000), pp. 80–168.

'Ad Rodulfum archiepiscopum Remensem', in *PL*, CLXIII, 1247–8.

'Aelredi Rievallis Abbatis: Operum Pars Prima–Ascetica; Operum Pars Secunda–Historica', in *PL*, CLXXXXV, 209–796.

'Annales Engelbergenses, a.1147–1546', in *Annales aevi Suevici* [= *MGH SS* XVII], ed. by Georg H. Pertz (Hanover: Hahn, 1861), pp. 278–82.

'Annales Fuldensis antiquissimi', in *Annales Fuldenses sive Annales regni Francorum orientalis*, ed. by Friedrich Kurze and Georg H. Pertz [= *MGH SS rer. Germ.* VII] (Hanover: Hahn, 1891), pp. 136–8.

'Annales sancti Benigni Divionensis, a. 564–1285', ed. by Georg Waitz, in *Annales et chronica aevi Salici*, ed. by Georg H. Pertz [= *MGH SS* V] (Hanover: Hahn, 1844), pp. 37–50.

'Appendix ad Hrabanum: Epistolarum Fuldensium fragmenta', in *Epistolae Karolini aevi III* [= MGH Epp. V] (Berlin: Weidmann, 1899), pp. 517-33.

'Catalogus abbatum Weingartensium', ed. by Oswald Holder-Egger, in *Supplementa tomorum I-XII, pars III* [= MGH SS XV] (Hanover: Hahn, 1861), pp. 1312-14.

'Chronica Sancti Benedicti Casinensis', in *Scriptores rerum Langobardicarum et Italicarum saec. VI-IX*, ed. by Georg Waitz [= *MGH SS rer. Lang.* I] (Hanover: Hahn, 1878), 468-88.

'Chronicon Andrense', ed. by Johannes Heller, in *Annales aevi Suevici: Supplementa tomorum XVI et XVII* [= MGH SS XXIV] (Hanover: Hahn, 1879), pp. 684-773.

'Chronicon Benedictoburanum', ed. by Wilhelm Wattenbach, in *Chronica et annales aevi Salici*, ed. by Georg H. Pertz [= *MGH SS IX*] (Hanover: Hahn, 1851), pp. 210-38.

'Chronicon Casauriense, sive historia monasterii Casauriensis', in *Rerum Italicarum scriptores*, ed. by Lodovico A. Muratori, 25 vols. (Milan: Societas Palatina in Regia Curia, 1723-51), II.2, 775-1018.

'Das Cartular des Klosters Ebersberg', ed. by Friedrich H. Hundt, *Abhandlungen der Historischen Klasse der Königlich-Bayerischen Akademie der Wissenschaften* 14 (1879), 115-96.

'De afflictione et lectione', in *La spiritualité de Pierre de Celle (1115-1183)*, ed. by Jean Leclercq (Paris: Vrin, 1946), pp. 231-9.

'De codicibus a Chounrado Schirensi exaratis', ed. by Philipp Jaffé, in *Annales aevi Suevici*, ed. by Georg H. Pertz [= *MGH SS XVII*] (Hanover: Hahn, 1861), pp. 623-4.

'De immutatione ordinus monachorum–Concerning Change in the Order of Monks', in *The Chronography of Robert of Torigni*, ed./tr. by Thomas N. Bisson, 2 vols. (Oxford: Oxford University Press, 2020), II, 250-75.

'De vita s. Radegundis, Liber II.', in *Fredegarii et aliorum Chronica. Vitae sanctorum*, ed. by Bruno Krusch [= *MGH SS rer. Merov.* II] (Hanover: Hahn, 1888), pp. 377-95.

'Decretum domni Roberti abbatis Vindocinensis pro bibliotheca' in *Cartulaire de l'abbaye cardinale de la Trinité de Vendôme*, ed. by Charles Métais, 5 vols. (Paris: Picard, 1893-7), II, 399-401.

'Der turnei von dem zers/Das Nonnenturnier', in *Novellistik des Mittelalters: Märendichtung*, ed./tr. by Klaus Grubmüller (Frankfurt a. M.: Deutscher Klassiker Verlag, 1996), pp. 944-77.

'Die ältesten Jahrbücher Engelbergs', ed. by Placidus Tanner, *Der Geschichtsfreund* 8 (1852), 101-17.

'Écrire l'histoire des abbés du Mont Saint-Michel, 3: Édition critique et traduction', ed. by Pierre Bouet, *Tabularia* (2019), pp. 1-31, https://doi.org/10.4000/tabularia.3773.

'Ein Brief des Abtes Trithemius an Gerhard von Hassel, Abt von Tholey (1489-1517)', ed. by Johann C. Lager, *Trierisches Archiv* 17/18 (1911), 189-91.

'Emonis et Wenkonis Werumensium Chronica', ed. by Ludwig Weiland, in *Chronica aevi Suevici* [= *MGH SS XXIII*] (Hanover: Hahn, 1874), pp. 454-572.

'Epistola Henrici clerici ad Stephanum', in *Diarium italicum: Sive monumentorum veterum, bibliothecarum, musaeorum, etc.*, ed. by Bernard de Montfaucon (Paris: Anisson, 1702), pp. 81-96.

'Expositio regulae ab Hildemaro tradita', ed. by Rupert Mittermüller, in *Vita et regula SS. P. Benedicti una cum expositione regulae*, Vol. 3 (Regensburg: Pustet, 1880), pp. 481-8.

'Fontes monasterii s. Emmerami Ratisbonensis: Bau- und kunstgeschichtliche Quellen', in *Quellen und Forschungen zur Geschichte des ehemaligen Reichsstiftes St. Emmeram in Regensburg*, ed. by Max Piendl (Kallmünz: Lassleben, 1961), pp. 1-183.

'Fr. Wilhelmi Wittwer Catalogus abbatum monasterii ss. Udalrici et Afrae Augustensis', ed. by Anton Streichele, *Archiv für die Geschichte des Bisthums Augsburg* 3 (1860), 15–437.
'Gaufridi apud sanctam Barbaram in Neustria canonicorum regularium subprioris epistolae', in *PL*, CCV, 828–88.
'Gesta abbatum Gemblacensium', ed. by Georg H. Pertz, in *Chronica et gesta aevi Salici* [= *MGH SS* VIII] (Hanover: Hahn, 1848), pp. 523–42.
'Gesta abbatum s[ancti] Bertini continuatio', ed. by Oswald Holder-Egger, in *Supplementa tomorum I–XII, pars I* [= *MGH SS* XIII] (Hanover: Hahn, 1881), pp. 663–73.
'Gesta abbatum Sithiensium: Continuatio', ed. by Oswald Holder-Egger, in *Supplementa tomorum I–XII, pars I* [= MGH SS XIII] (Hanover: Hahn, 1881), pp. 663–73.
'Gesta abbatum Trudonensium, continuatio secunda', ed. by Rudolf Köpke, in *Annales et cronica aevi Salici: Vitae aevi Carolini et Saxonici* [= MGH SS X], ed. by Georg H. Pertz (Hanover: Hahn, 1852), pp. 333–61.
'Gesta abbatum Trudonensium', ed. by Rudolf Köpke, in *Annales et chronica aevi Salici: Vitae aevi Carolini et Saxonici*, ed. by Georg H. Pertz [= *MGH SS* X] (Hanover: Hahn, 1852), pp. 227–448.
'Gesta Ottonis', in *Hrosvit: Opera Omnia*, ed. by Walter Berschin (Munich: Saur, 2001), pp. 271–305.
'Goscelin of St Bertin: Lives of the Abbesses at Barking (Extracts)', tr. by Vera Morton, in *Guidance for Women in Twelfth-Century Convents*, ed./tr. by Vera Morton and Jocelyn Wogan-Browne (Cambridge: Brewer, 2003), pp. 139–56.
'Herimanni liber de restauratione monasterii S. Martini Tornacensis', in *Supplementa tomorum I–XII*, Vol. 2: *Supplementum tomi XIII*, ed. by Georg Waitz [= *MGH SS* XIV] (Hanover: Hahn, 1883), pp. 274–317.
'Historia Hirsaugiensis monasterii', in *Supplementa tomorum I–XII, pars II: Supplementum tomi XIII*, ed. by Georg Waitz [= *MGH SS* XIV] (Hanover: Hahn, 1883), pp. 254–65.
'Historia monasterii Rastedensis', ed. by Georg Waitz, in *Gesta episcoporum, abbatum, ducum aliorumque principum saec. XIII* [= *MGH SS* XXV] (Hanover: Hahn, 1880), pp. 495–511.
'Historia, miracula et translatio sancti Augustini', in *AASS, Maii* VI, 377–443.
'Hrabani Mauri Carmina', in *Poetae Latini aevi Carolini (II)*, ed. by Ernst Dümmler [= *MGH Poetae* III] (Berlin: Weidmann, 1884), pp. 154–258.
'La *Regula Ferrioli*: Text critique', ed. by Vincent Desprez, *Revue Mabillon* 60 (1982), 117–48.
'Liber de quadripartito exercitio cellae', in *PL*, CLIII, 787–884.
'Necrologium Runense', in *MGH Necr.* II, ed. by Sigismund Herzberg-Fränkel (Berlin: Weidmann, 1904), pp. 341–56.
'Ordo Cluniacensis', in *Vetus disciplina monastica*, ed. by Marquard Hergott (Paris: Osmont, 1726; repr. Siegburg: Schmitt, 1999), pp. 136–364.
'Paulus Adalhardo abbati Corbeiensi sanitate vix recuperata epistolas Gregorii papae a se ex parte emendatas mittit', in *Epistolae Karolini aevi II*, ed. by Ernst Dümmler [= *MGH Epp.* IV] (Berlin: Weidmann, 1895), pp. 508–9.
'Primordia coenobii Gandeshemensis', in *Hrosvit: Opera Omnia*, ed. by Walter Berschin (Munich: Saur, 2001), pp. 306–29.
'S[ancti] Wilhelmi Constitutiones Hirsaugienses', in *PL*, CL, 923–1146.
'Simonis gesta abbatum sancti Bertini Sithiensium', ed. by Oswald Holder-Egger, in *Supplementa tomorum I–XII, pars I* [= *MGH SS* XIII] (Hanover: Hahn, 1881), pp. 635–63.

'Statutorum concilii Parisiensis pars secunda: Ad viros regulares', in *Sacrorum conciliorum nova et amplissima collectio*, ed. by Giovanni D. Mansi, 31 vols. (Venice: Zatta, 1758-98).

'The Foundation Narrative', ed./tr. by Nicholas Karn, in *Foundation Documents from St Mary's Abbey, York 1085-1137*, ed. by Richard Sharpe et al. (Woodbridge: Boydell, 2022), pp. 379-407.

'Thesaurus Fabariensis', in *Libri confraternitatum sancti Galli, Augiensis, Fabariensis*, ed. by Paul Piper [= *MGH Necr.* Suppl.] (Berlin: Weidmann, 1884), pp. 395-98.

'Über Diethard, Abt des Klosters Sazawa', in *Die Chronik der Böhmen des Cosmas von Prag*, ed. by Berthold Bretholz [= *MGH SS rer. Germ. N. S.* II] (Berlin: Weidmann, 1923), pp. 255-6.

'Vita [Mariani] auctore Scoto monacho Ratispon', in *AASS Februarii* II, 365-73.

'Vita Ansberti episcopi Rotomagensis', in *Passiones vitaeque sanctorum aevi Merovingici*, Vol. 3, ed. by Bruno Krusch and Wilhelm Levison [= *MGH SS rer. Merov.* V] (Hanover: Hahn, 1910), pp. 613-43.

'Vita Bertilae abbatissae Calensis', ed. by Wilhelm Levison, in *Passiones vitaeque sanctorum aevi Merovingici (IV)*, ed. by Bruno Krusch and Wilhelm Levison [*MGH SS rer. Merov.* VI] (Hanover: Hahn, 1913), pp. 95-109.

'Vita Mathildis reginae antiquior', in *Die Lebensbeschreibungen der Königin Mathilde*, ed. by Bernd Schütte [= *MGH SS rer. Germ.* LXVI] (Hanover: Hahn, 1994), pp. 107-42.

'Vita Mathildis reginae posterior', in *Die Lebensbeschreibungen der Königin Mathilde*, ed. by Bernd Schütte [= *MGH SS rer. Germ.* LXVI] (Hanover: Hahn, 1994), pp. 145-202.

'Vita S. Geretrudis', in *Fredegarii et aliorum Chronica. Vitae sanctorum*, ed. by Bruno Krusch [= *MGH SS rer. Merov.* II] (Hanover: Hahn, 1888), pp. 447-74.

'Vita sancti Godefredi Ambianensis episcopi', in *AASS Novembri* III, 905-44.

'Vita sancti Odonis', ed. by Jacques-Paul Migne, in *PL*, CXXXIII, 43-86.

'Vita Wilfridi I. episcopi Eboracensis auctore Stephano', ed. by Wilhelm Levison, in *Passiones vitaeque sanctorum aevi Merovingici (IV)*, ed. by Bruno Krusch and Wilhelm Levison [= *MGH SS rer. Merov.* VI] (Hanover: Hahn, 1913), pp. 163-263.

[Johannes Centurianus:] 'Letter to Johannes Trithemius, 18 April 1507', in *Johannes Trithemius: Opera historica*, ed. by Marquard Freher, 2 vols. (Frankfurt a. M.: Marne and Aubry, 1601; repr. Minerva, 1966), II, 527-9.

[Johannes Trithemius:] 'Chronicon Sponheimense', in *Johannes Trithemius: Opera historica*, ed. by Marquard Freher, 2 vols. (Frankfurt a. M.: Marne and Aubry, 1601; repr. Minerva, 1966), II, 236-435.

——, 'De lectione et studio divinarum scripturarum (= Homilia IV)', in *Opera pia et spiritualia*, ed. by Johannes Busaeus (Mainz: Johannes Albinus, 1604), pp. 422-7.

——, 'Letter to Jakob Kimolanus, 16 August 1507', in *Johannes Trithemius: Opera historica*, ed. by Marquard Freher, 2 vols. (Frankfurt a. M.: Marne and Aubry, 1601; repr. Minerva, 1966), II, 556-7.

——, 'Letter to Johannes Nutius, 13 October 1505 (= Epistola XXXII)', in *Johannes Trithemius: Opera historica*, ed. by Marquard Freher, 2 vols. (Frankfurt a. M.: Marne and Aubry, 1601; repr. Minerva, 1966), II, 469-70.

——, 'Letter to Prior Johannes Bracht of St Matthew's in Trier, 31 October 1506 (= Epistola III)', in *Johannes Trithemius: Opera historica*, ed. by Marquard Freher, 2 vols. (Frankfurt a. M.: Marne and Aubry, 1601; repr. Minerva, 1966), II, 512-14.

——, 'Letter to the prior and community of Sponheim, 31 October 1506 (= Epistola II)', in *Johannes Trithemius: Opera historica*, ed. by Marquard Freher, 2 vols. (Frankfurt a. M.: Marne and Aubry, 1601; repr. Minerva, 1966), II, 507-12.

——, 'Nepachius', in *Corpus historicum Medii Aevi*, ed. by Johann G. von Eckhart, 2 vols. (Leipzig: Gleditsch, 1723), II 1825–44.
——, 'De labore monachorum manuali (= Homilia VII)', in *Opera pia et spiritualia*, ed. by Johannes Busaeus (Mainz: Johannes Albinus, 1604), pp. 434–8.
——, 'Letter to the prior and community of Sponheim, 31 October 1506 (= Epistola II)', in *Johannes Trithemius: Opera historica*, ed. by Marquard Freher, 2 vols. (Frankfurt a. M.: Marne and Aubry, 1601; repr. Minerva, 1966), II, 507–12.
[Smaragdus:] Commentary on the Rule of St Benedict, tr. by David Barry et al. (Kalamazoo, MI: Cistercian Publications, 2007).
[Trithemii] Opera historica, quotquot hactenus reperiri potuerunt omnia, ed. by Marquard Freher, 2 vols. (Frankfurt a. M.: Marne & Aubry, 1601; repr. Minerva, 1966).
A Monk's Confession: The Memoirs of Guibert of Nogent, tr. by Paul J. Archambault (University Park, PA: Pennsylvania State University Press, 1996).
Abbot Suger on the Abbey Church of St.-Denis and Its Art Treasures, tr. by Erwin Panofsky and Gerda Panofsky-Soergel, 2nd ed. (Princeton, NJ: Princeton University Press, 2019).
Abbots of Wearmouth and Jarrow, ed./tr. by Christopher Grocock and Ian N. Wood (Oxford: Oxford University Press, 2013).
Abt Suger von Saint-Denis: Ausgewählte Schriften. Ordinatio, De consecratione, De administratione, ed. by Andreas Speer et al., 3rd ed. (Darmstadt: Wissenschaftliche Buchgesellschaft, 2008).
Acta capitulorum generalium ordinis Praedicatorum, ed. by Franz A. Frühwirth and Benedikt M. Reichert, 9 vols. (Rome: In domo generalitia, 1898–1904).
Acta Murensia: Die Akten des Klosters Muri mit der Genealogie der frühen Habsburger, ed. by Charlotte Bretscher-Gisiger and Christian Sieber (Basel: Schwabe, 2012).
Actes des évêques de Laon: Des origines à 1151, ed. by Annie Dufour-Malbezin (Paris: Éditions du CNRS, 2001).
Adalberon de Laon: Poème au roi Robert, ed./tr. by Claude Carozzi (Paris: Belles Lettres, 1979).
Adamnan: Das Leben des heiligen Columba von Iona–Vitae S. Columbae, tr. by Theodor Klüppel (Stuttgart: Hiersemann, 2010).
Adgar: Le Gracial–Miracles de la Vierge, tr. by Jean-Louis Benoit and Jerry Root (Turnhout: Brepols, 2021).
Annales Ordinis S. Benedicti Occidentalium monachorum Patriarchae, ed. by Jean Mabillon, 6 vols. (Paris: Robustel, 1703–39).
Annalium Corbeiensium continuatio saeculi XII et Historia Corbeiensis Monasterii annorum MCXLV–MCXLVII cum additamentis (Cronographus Corbeiensis)– Fortsetzung der Corveyer Annalen des 12. Jahrhunderts und die Geschichte des Klosters Corvey der Jahre 1145-1147 mit Zusätzen (Der Corveyer Chronograph), ed. by Irene Schmale-Ott (Münster: Aschendorff, 1989).
Antiquitates Bursfeldenses, ed. by Johann G. Leuckfeld (Leipzig: Freytag, 1713).
Baudri de Bourgueil: Poèmes, ed./tr. by Jean-Yves Tilliette, 2 vols. (Paris: Les Belles Lettres, 1998–2002).
Bede the Venerable: Excerpts from the Works of Saint Augustine and the Letters of the Blessed Apostle Paul, tr. by David Hurst (Kalamazoo, MI: Cistercian Publications, 1999).
Bede's Ecclesiastical History of the English People, ed./tr. by Bertram Colgrave and Roger A. B. Mynors (Oxford: Clarendon, 1969).
Caeremoniae Bursfeldenses, ed. by Marcel Albert (Siegburg: Schmitt, 2002).
Caesarii Heisterbacensis monachi ordinis Cisterciensis Dialogus miraculorum, ed. by Joseph Strange, 3 vols. (Cologne: Heberle, 1851–7).

Caesarius Arlatensis opera omnia, Vol. 2: *Opera varia*, ed. by Germain Morin (Maredsous: Maretioli, 1942).
Caesarius of Heisterbach: The Dialogue on Miracles, tr. by Henry von Essen Scott and Charles C. Swinton Bland, 2 vols. (London: Routledge, 1929).
Calenberger Urkundenbuch, ed. by Wilhelm von Hodenberg and Joachim Studtmann, 10 vols. (Hanover: Jänecke, 1855–1990).
Calendar of Papal Registers Relating to Great Britain and Ireland, Vol. 6: *1404–1415*, ed. by William H. Bliss and Jessis A. Twemlow (London: Her Majesty's Stationery Office, 1904).
Cartulaire de l'abbaye de Saint-Père de Chartres, ed. by Benjamin Guérard, 2 vols. (Paris: Crapelet, 1840–50).
Cartulaire de l'abbaye de Saint-Victor de Marseille, ed. by Benjamin E. C. Guérard, 2 vols. (Paris: Lahure, 1857).
Cartulaire de l'église d'Autun, ed. by Anatole de Charmasse, 2 vols. (Paris: Pédone, 1865–1900; repr. Geneva: Mégariotis, 1978).
Cartularium monasterii de Rameseia, ed. by William H. Hart and Ponsonby A. Lyons, 3 vols. (London: Longman, 1884–93).
Cartularium: Recueil des chartes du prieuré de Saint-Bertin à Poperinghe, et de ses dépendances à Bas-Warneton et à Couckelaere déposées aux archives de l'Etat à Gand (Bruges: Vandecasteele-Webrouck, 1870).
Catalogi bibliothecarum antiqui, ed. by Gustav Becker (Bonn: Cohen, 1885).
Catalogue des actes d'Henri Ier, roi de France, 1031–1060, ed. by Frédéric Soehnée (Paris: Champion, 1907).
Chartularium universitatis Parisiensis, ed. by Emile Chatelain and Heinrich Denifle, 4 vols. (Paris: Delalain, 1889–97).
Chronicles of the Investiture Contest: Frutolf of Michelsberg and His Continuators, tr. by Thomas J. H. McCarthy (Manchester: Manchester University Press, 2014).
Chronicon Hirsaugiense, in *Johannes Trithemius: Opera historica, quotquot hactenus reperiri potuerunt omnia*, ed. by Marquard Freher, 2 vols. (Frankfurt a. M.: Marne & Aubry, 1601; repr. Minerva, 1966), II, 1–235.
Chronicon monasterii de Abingdon, ed. by Joseph Stevenson, 2 vols. (London: Longman, 1858).
Chronicon Sublacense: AA. 593–1369, ed. by Raffaello Morghen (Bologna: Zanichelli, 1927).
Chronique de l'abbaye de Saint-Pierre-le-Vif de Sens: Rédigée vers la fin du XIIIe siècle par Geoffroy de Courlon, ed./tr. by Gustave Julliot (Sens: Duchemin, 1876).
Chronique de l'abbaye de Saint-Riquier (Ve siècle–1104), ed. by Ferdinand Lot (Paris: Picard, 1894).
Chronique de l'abbaye de Saint-Trond, ed. by Camille de Borman, 2 vols. (Liège: Grandmont-Donders, 1877).
Chronique de Robert de Torigni, abbé du Mont-Saint-Michel, ed. by Léopold Delisle, 2 vols. (Rouen: Le Brument, 1872–3).
Chronique de Saint-Pierre-le-Vif de Sens, dite de Clarius (Chronicon Sancti Petri Vivi Senonensis), ed./tr. by Robert-Henri Bautier et al. (Paris: CNRS, 1979).
Chronique des abbés de Fontenelle (Saint-Wandrille), ed./tr. by Pascal Pradié (Paris: Les Belles Lettres, 1999).
Codex diplomatico-historico-epistolaris, ed. by Bernhard Pez and Philibert Hueber, 3 vols. (Augsburg: Fratrum Veithiorum, 1729).
Codex diplomaticus Fuldensis, ed. by Ernst F. J. Dronke (Kassel: Fischer, 1850).
Codex diplomaticus Quedlinburgensis, ed. by Anton U. von Erath (Frankfurt a. M.: Moeller, 1764).

Codex Hirsaugiensis, ed. by Eugen Schneider (Stuttgart: Kohlhammer, 1887).
Colophons de manuscrits occidentaux des origines au XVIe siècle, ed. by Bénédictins de Bouveret, 6 vols. (Fribourg, CH: Éditions Universitaires, 1965-82).
Consuetudines et Regulae: Sources for Monastic Life in the Middle Ages and the Early Modern Period, ed. by Carolyn Marino Malone and Clark Maines (Turnhout: Brepols, 2014).
Cosmas of Prague: The Chronicle of the Czechs–Cosmae Pragensis Chronica Bohemorum, ed./tr. by János M. Bak et al. (Budapest: Central European University Press, 2020).
Customary of the Benedictine Monasteries of Saint Augustine, Canterbury, and Saint Peter, Westminster, ed. by Edward M. Thompson, 2 vols. (London: Henry Bradshaw Society, 1902-4).
Das Briefbuch Abt Wibalds von Stablo und Corvey, ed. by Martina Hartmann, 3 vols. [= *MGH Briefe d. dt. Kaiserzeit* IX.1-3] (Hanover: Hahn, 2012).
Das Register Gregors VII., ed. by Erich Caspar, 2 vols. [= *MGH Epp. sel.* II] (Berlin: Weidmann, 1920-3).
Das Wappenbuch des Gallus Öhem: Neu herausgegeben nach der Handschrift 15 der Universitätsbibliothek Freiburg, ed. by Harald Drös (Sigmaringen: Thorbecke, 1994).
De abtenkroniek van Aduard: Studies, editie en vertaling, ed. by Jaap J. van Moolenbroek et al. (Hilversum: Verloren, 2010).
De Blémur, Jacqueline Bouette, *Éloges de plusieurs personnes illustres en piété de l'ordre de Saint-Benoîst*, 6 vols. (Paris: Billaine, 1679).
De duodecim excidiis observantiae regularis, edited in Barbara Frank, 'Ein Entwurf zu einer Kapitelsansprache des Abtes Johannes Trithemius aus dem Jahr 1496', *Studien und Mitteilungen zur Geschichte des Benediktinerordens und seiner Zweige* 80 (1969), 145-204 (pp. 158-204).
De moribus et actis primorum Normanniae ducum, ed. by Jules Lair (Caen: Le Blanc-Hardel, 1865).
Der Darmstädter Hitda-Codex: Bilder und und Zierseiten aus der Handschrift 1640 der Hessischen Universitäts- und Landesbibliothek, ed. by Peter Bloch and Erich Zimmermann (Frankfurt, a. M.: Propyläen, 1968).
Der Liber Vitae der Abtei Corvey, ed. by Karl Schmid and Joachim Wollasch, 2 vols. (Wiesbaden: Reichert, 1983-9).
Die Annales Quedlinburgenses, ed. by Martina Giese [= *MGH SS rer. Germ.* LXXII] (Hanover: Hahn, 2004).
Die Briefe des heiligen Bonifatius und Lullus, ed. by Michael Tangl [= *MGH Epp. sel.* I] (Berlin: Weidmann, 1916).
Die Briefsammlung Gerberts von Reims, ed. by Fritz Weigle [= *MGH Briefe d. dt. Kaiserzeit* II] (Weimar: Böhlau, 1966).
Die Chronik von Montecassino–Chronica monasterii Casinensis, ed. by Hartmut Hoffmann [= *MGH SS* XXXIV] (Hanover: Hahn, 1980).
Die Corveyer Annalen: Textbearbeitung und Kommentar, ed. by Joseph Prinz (Münster: Aschendorff, 1982).
Die Inschriften des Landkreises Bad Kreuznach, ed. by Eberhard J. Nikitsch [= *Die deutschen Inschriften* XXXIV] (Wiesbaden: Reicher, 1993).
Die Inschriften des Landkreises Calw, ed. by Renate Neumüllers-Klauser [= *Die deutschen Inschriften* XXX] (Wiesbaden: Reicher, 1992).
Die Sachsengeschichte des Widukind von Korvei, ed. by Paul Hirsch and Hans-Eberhard Lohmann, 5th ed. [= *MGH SS rer. Germ.* LX] (Hanover: Hahn, 1935).

Die Tegernseer Briefsammlung (Froumund), ed. by Karl Strecker [= *MGH Epp. sel.* III] (Berlin: Weidmann, 1925).
Die Traditionen des Klosters Prüfening, ed. by Andrea Schwarz (Munich: Beck, 1991).
Die Urkunden und Briefe der Markgräfin Mathilde von Tuszien, ed. by Elke Goez and Werner Goez (Hanover: Hahn, 1998).
Die Vita Sturmi des Eigil von Fulda: Literarkritisch-historische Untersuchung und Edition, ed. by Pius Engelbert (Marburg: Elwert, 1968).
Diplomatari i escrits literaris de l'abat i bisbe Oliba, ed. by Eduard Junyent i Subirà (Barcelona: Institut d'Estudis Catalans, 1992).
Documents Illustrating the Activities of the General and Provincial Chapters of the English Black Monks, 1215-1540, ed. by William A. Pantin, 3 vols. (London: Royal Historical Society, 1931-7).
Dudo of St Quentin: History of the Normans, tr. by Eric Christiansen (Woodbridge: Boydell, 1998).
Eadmeri monachi Cantuariensis vita sancti Anselmi archiepiscopi Cantuariensis–The Life of St Anselm, Archbishop of Canterbury by Eadmer, ed./tr. by Richard W. Southern (Oxford: Clarendon, 1972).
Ekkehard IV: Fortune and Misfortune at Saint Gall, tr. by Emily Albu and Natalia Lozovsky (Cambridge, MA: Harvard University Press, 2021).
——, *St Galler Klostergeschichten* (Casus sancti Galli), ed./tr. by Hans F. Haefele and Ernst Tremp [= MGH SS rer. Germ. LXXXII] (Hanover: Hahn, 2020).
English Benedictine Libraries: The Shorter Catalogues, ed. by Richard Sharpe et al. [= *CBMLC* IV] (London: British Library, 1996).
Epistolae Karolini aevi III, ed. by Ernst Dümmler [= *MGH Epp.* V] (Berlin: Weidmann, 1899).
Eugippius: Vita Sancti Severini–Das Leben des heiligen Severin, ed./tr. by Theodor Nüßlein (Stuttgart: Reclam, 2004).
Female Monastic Life in Early Tudor England: With an Edition of Richard Fox's Translation of the Benedictine Rule for Women 1517, ed. by Barry Collett (London: Routledge, 2002).
Ferreolus, Mönchsregel, tr. by Ivo auf der Mauer and Georg Holzherr (St Ottilien: Eos, 2011).
Floriacensis vetus bibliotheca, ed. by Jean Du Bois, 2 vols. (Paris: Cardon, 1605).
Foundation Documents from St Mary's Abbey, York 1085-1137, ed. by Richard Sharpe et al. (Woodbridge: Boydell, 2022).
Frechulfi Lexoviensis episcopi opera omnia, ed. by Michael I. Allen (Turnhout: Brepols, 2002).
Gallia Christiana in provincias ecclesiasticas distributa, ed. by Denys de Sainte-Marthe et al., 13 vols. (Paris: Ex Typographia regia, 1715-1877).
Gerbert d'Aurillac: Correspondence, ed./tr. by Pierre Riché and Jean P. Callu, 2 vols. (Paris: Les Belles Lettres, 1993).
Gesta abbatum monasterii sancti Albani, a Thoma Walsingham, regnante Ricardo secundo, compilata, ed. by Henry T. Riley, 3 vols. (Cambridge: Cambridge University Press, 1866-9).
Gesta abbatum Trudonensium, ed. by Paul Tombeur, 2 vols. (Turnhout: Brepols, 2013).
Gesta Romanorum, ed. by Herman Oesterley (Berlin: Weidmann, 1872).
Giovanni Boccaccio: Decameron, ed. by Vittore Branca, 9th ed. (Milan: Mondadori, 2008).
——, *Decameron*, tr. by Mark Musa and Peter Bondanella (New York, NY: Norton, 1983).
Giraldi Cambrensis Opera, ed. by John S. Brewer et al., 8 vols. (London: Longman, 1861-91).

Grégoire le Grand: Dialogues, ed. by Adalbert de Vogüé and tr. by Paul Antin, 3 vols. (Paris: Éditions du Cerf, 1978-80).
Gualbert of Marchiennes, 'De patrocinio sancti Rictrudis', in *AASS Maii* III, 139-53.
Guernes de Pont-Sainte-Maxence: A Life of Thomas Becket in Verse–La Vie de saint Thomas Becket, tr. by Ian Short (Toronto: Pontifical Institute of Mediaeval Studies, 2013).
——, *La Vie de Saint Thomas Becket*, ed. by Emmanuel Walberg (Paris: Champion, 1936).
Guibert de Nogent: Autobiographie, ed./tr. by Edmond-René Labande (Paris: Les Belles Lettres, 1981).
——, *Dei gesta per Francos et cinq autres textes*, ed. by Robert B. C. Huygens (Turnhout: Brepols, 1996).
——, *Monodiae-'Einzelgesänge': Bekenntnisse und Memoiren eines Abtes aus Nordfrankreich*, ed./tr. by Reinhold Kaiser and Anne Liebe, 2 vols. (Freiburg i. B.: Herder, 2019).
Guillaume de Volpiano: Un réformateur en son temps (962-1031)–Vita domni Willelmi de Raoul Glaber: Texte, traduction, commentaire, ed./tr. by Veronique Gazeau and Monique Goullet (Caen: Publications du CRAHM, 2008).
Handschriften in Mittelalter: Eine Quellensammlung, ed./tr. by Martin Steinmann (Basel: Schwabe, 2013).
Henry of Huntingdon: Historia Anglorum–The History of the English People, ed./tr. by Diana E. Greenway (Oxford: Oxford University Press, 1996).
Hildegard von Bingen: Liber scivias–Rüdesheimer Codex aus der Benediktinerinnenabtei St. Hildegard (Graz: Akademische Druck- und Verlagsanstalt, 2013).
——, *Scivias–Die Miniaturen vom Rupertsberg*, ed. by Hildegard Schönfeld and Wolfgang Podehl (Bingen: Pennrich, 1979).
Historia Ecclesie Abbendonensis–The History of the Church of Abingdon, ed./tr. by John G. Hudson, 2 vols. (Oxford: Oxford University Press, 2002-7).
Historia et Cartularium monasterii sancti Petri Gloucestriae, ed. by William H. Hart, 2 vols. (Cambridge: Cambridge University Press: 1863-5).
Historiae Anglicanae scriptores varii, ed. by Joseph Sparke, 2 vols. (London: Bowyer, 1723).
Historiae Franco-Merovingicae synopsis seu historia succincta de gestis et successione regum Francorum, ed. by Raphael de Beauchamps (Douai: Bogard, 1633).
Historiae Francorum scriptores coaetanei, ed. by André Duchesne, 5 vols. (Paris: Cramoisy, 1636-49).
Hrosvithae Liber Tertius, tr. by Mary B. Bergman (Covington, KY: Sisters of St. Benedict Press, 1962).
Hrotsvitha Gandeshemensis: Gesta Ottonis Imperatoris. Lotte, drammi e trionfi nel destino di un imperatore, ed./tr. by Maria P. Pillolla (Firenze: Galluzzo, 2003).
Hugh of Flavigny: 'Chronicon', in *Chronica et gesta aevi Salici*, ed. by Georg H. Pertz [= *MGH SS* VIII] (Hanover: Hahn, 1848), pp. 288-502.
I Carmi di Alfano I, arcivescovo di Salerno, ed. by Anselmo Lentini and Faustino Avagliano (Montecassino: Abbazia di Montecassino, 1974).
I testamenti dei cardinali del Duecento, ed. by Agostino Paravicini Bagliani (Rome: Presso la Società alla Biblioteca Vallicelliana, 1980).
Idung of Prüfening: Cistercians and Cluniacs: The Case for Cîteaux. A Dialogue between Two Monks. An Argument on Four Questions, tr. by Jeremiah F. O'Sullivan (Kalamazoo, MI: Cistercian Publications, 1977).
Johannes Duraclusius: Vita et lucubrationes Iohannis Trithemii, in *Johannes Trithemius: Opera historica*, ed. by Marquard Freher, 2 vols. (Frankfurt a. M.: Marne and Aubry, 1601; repr. Minerva, 1966), I, 5-7.

Johannes Trithemius: Annales Hirsaugienses, 2 vols. (St. Gall: Schlegel, 1690).
——, *In Praise of Scribes (De laude scriptorum)*, ed./tr. by Klaus Arnold and Roland Berendt (Lawrence, KS: Coronado, 1974).
John Leland: De rebus Britannicis collectaneorum, ed. by Thomas Hearne, 6 vols., 3rd ed. (London: Benjamin White, 1770-4).
John of Salisbury: Historia pontificalis–Memoirs of the Papal Court, ed./tr. by Marjorie Chibnall (Oxford: Clarendon, 1986).
Kroniek van de abdij van Sint-Truiden, tr. by Emil Lavigne, 2 vols. (Assen: Van Gorcum, 1986-8).
Kroniek van het klooster Bloemhof te Wittewierum, ed./tr. by Hubertus P. H. Jansen and Antheun Janse (Hilversum: Verloren, 1991).
Kronijken van Emo en Menko, Abten van het klooster te Wittewierum, met het vervolg van een ongenoemde, ed. by Hendrikus O. Feith and Gozewijn A. Stratingh (Utrecht: Kemink, 1866).
L'histoire-polyptyque de l'Abbaye de Marchiennes (1116–1121): Étude critique et édition, ed. by Bernard Delmaire (Louvain-la-Neuve: Centre belge d'histoire rurale, 1985).
La règle de saint Augustin, ed. by Luc Verheijen, 2 vols. (Paris: Études augustiniennes, 1967).
La Régle du Maître, ed./tr. by Adalbert de Vogüé, 3 vols. (Paris: Éditions du Cerf, 1964).
La Vie d'Edouard le Confesseur, by a Nun of Barking Abbey, tr. by Jane Bliss (Liverpool: Liverpool University Press, 2014).
Lantbert von Deutz: Vita Heriberti–Miracula Heriberti–Gedichte–Liturgische Texte, ed. by Bernhard Vogel [= *MGH SS rer. Germ.* LXXIII] (Hanover: Hahn, 2001).
Le moine Idung et ses deux ouvrages: 'Argumentum super quatuor questionibus' et 'Dialogus duorum monachorum', ed. by Robert B. C. Huygens (Spoleto: Cento Italiano di studi sull'alto medioevo, 1972; repr. 1980).
Les Deux vies de Robert d'Arbrissel, fondateur de Fontevraud: Légendes, écrits et témoignages–The Two Lives of Robert of Arbrissel, Founder of Fontevraud: Legends, Writings, and Testimonies, ed. by Jacques Dalarun et al. (Turnhout: Brepols, 2006).
Letters of Anselm, Archbishop of Canterbury, Vol. 1: *The Bec Letters*, ed./tr. by Samu Niskanen (Oxford: Clarendon, 2019).
Liber ordinis Sancti Victoris Parisiensis, ed. by Lucas Jocqué and Ludo Milis (Turnhout: Brepols, 1984).
Liber tramitis aevi Odilonis abbatis, ed. by Petrus Dinter (Siegburg: Schmitt, 1980).
Monastic Experience in Twelfth-Century Germany: The Chronicle of Petershausen in Translation, tr. by Alison I. Beach et al. (Manchester: Manchester University Press, 2020).
Monasticon Anglicanum: A History of the Abbies and other Monasteries, Hospitals, Frieries, and Cathedral and Collegiate Churches, with their Dependencies, in England and Wales, ed. by William Dugdale et al., 6 vols., new ed. (London: Longman, 1846-56).
Monumenta Corbeiensia, ed. by Philipp Jaffé [= *Bibliotheca rerum Germanicarum* I] (Berlin: Weidmann, 1864).
Narrative and Legislative Texts from Early Citeaux, ed. by Chrysogonus Waddell (Citeaux: Comentarii cistercienses, 1999).
Nova bibliotheca manuscriptorum librorum sive specimen antiquarum lectionum latinarum et graecarum, ed. by Philippe Labbé, 2 vols. (Paris: Henault, 1657).
Pachomian Koinonia, tr. by Armand Veilleux, 3 vols. (Kalamazoo, MI: Cistercian Publications, 1980-2).
Pachomiana Latina: Règle et épitres de S. Pachome, épitre de S. Théodore et 'Liber' de S. Orsiesius, texte latin de S. Jérôme, ed. by Amand Boon (Louvain: Bureaux de la Revue, 1932).

Peter of Celle: Selected Works, tr. by Hugh Feiss (Kalamazoo, MI: Cistercian Publications, 1987).
Pouillé du diocèse de Verdun, ed. by Nicolas Robinet et al., 4 vols. (Verdun: Charles Laurent, 1888–1910).
Queenship and Sanctity: The Lives of Mathilda and the Epitaph of Adelheid, tr. by Sean Gilsdorf (Washington, DC: Catholic University of America Press, 2004).
Ratpert: St Galler Klostergeschichten (Casus sancti Galli), ed./tr. by Hannes Steiner [= MGH SS rer. Germ. LXXV] (Hanover: Hahn, 2002).
Recueil des actes de Philippe Ier, roi de France, 1059–1108, ed. by Maurice Prou (Paris: Imprimerie Nationale, 1908).
Recueil des historiens des croisades: Historiens occidentaux, 5 vols. (Paris: Imprimerie impériale, 1844–95).
Regestrum visitationum archiepiscopi Rothomagensis: Journal des visites pastorales d'Eude Rigaud, archevêque de Rouen, MCCXLVIII–MCCLXIX, ed. by Théodose Bonnin (Rouen: Le Brument, 1852).
Rerum Anglicarum scriptores veteres, ed. by William Fulman and Thomas Gale, 3 vols. (Oxford: Sheldon, 1684–91).
Robert of Gloucester's Chronicle, ed. by Thomas Hearne, 2 vols. (Oxford: Theater, 1724).
Robert the Monk's History of the First Crusade-Historia Iherosolimitana, tr. by Carol Sweetenham (Aldershot: Ashgate, 2005).
Rodulfus Glaber: Historiarum libri quinque, in *Rodulfus Glaber Opera*, ed./tr. by John France et al. (Oxford: Clarendon, 1989).
——, *Vita domni Willelmi abbatis*, in *Rodulfus Glaber Opera*, ed./tr. by John France et al. (Oxford: Clarendon, 1989), pp. 254–99.
Rouleaux des morts du IXe au XVe siècle, ed. by Léopold Delisle (Paris: Renouard, 1866).
Sainted Women of the Dark Ages, ed./tr. by Jo A. McNamara et al. (Durham, NC: Duke University Press, 1992).
Salimbene de Adam: Cronica, ed. by Giuseppe Scalia, 2 vols. (Turnhout: Brepols, 1998–9).
Scriptores rerum Brunsvicensium, ed. by Gottfried W. von Leibniz, 3 vols. (Hanover: Förster, 1707–11).
Seneca: Philosophische Schriften: Latein–Deutsch, ed./tr. by Manfred Rosenbach, 5 vols., 2nd ed. (Darmstadt: Wissenschaftliche Buchgesellschaft, 2010).
Servati Lupi epistolae, ed. by Peter K. Marshall (Leipzig: Teubner, 1984).
Sir Thomas Malory: Le Morte Darthur, ed. by Peter J. C. Field, 2 vols. (Cambridge: D. S. Brewer, 2013).
Smaragdus: Expositio in regulam s. Benedicti, ed. by Alfred Spannagel and Pius Engelbert (Siegburg: Schmitt, 1974).
St. Odo of Cluny: Being the Life of St. Odo of Cluny by John of Salerno and the Life of St. Gerald of Aurillac by St. Odo, tr. by Gerard Sitwell (London: Sheen & Ward, 1958).
Statuta Capitulorum Generalium ordinis Cisterciensis ab anno 1116 ad annum 1786, ed. by Joseph-Marie Canivez, 8 vols. (Louvain: Bureaux de la Revue, 1933–41).
Suger: Œuvres, ed./tr. by Françoise Gasparri, 2 vols. (Paris: Les Belles Lettres, 1996–2001).
——, *The Deeds of Louis the Fat*, tr. by Richard C. Cusimano and John Moorhead (Washington, DC: Catholic University of America Press, 1992).
Symeon of Durham: Libellus de exordio atque procursu istius, hoc est Dunhelmensis, ecclesie, ed./tr. David W. Rollason (Oxford: Oxford University Press, 2000).
The Antiquities of Italy: Being the Travels of the Learned and Reverend Bernard de Montfaucon, from Paris Through Italy, in the Years 1698 and 1699, tr. by John Henley (London: Darby, 1715).

The Bayeux Tapestry, ed. by David M. Wilson (London: Thames and Hudson, 2004).
——, ed./tr. by Lucien Musset and Richard Rex (Woodbridge: Boydell, 2005).
The Cartulary of Flavigny, 717–1113, ed. by Constance B. Bouchard (Cambridge, MA: Medieval Academy of America, 1991).
The Cartulary of Montier-en-Der, 666–1129, ed. by Constance B. Bouchard (Toronto: University of Toronto Press, 2004).
The Cartulary of the Abbey of Mont-Saint-Michel, ed. by Katherine S. B. Keats-Rohan (Donington: Shaun Tyas, 2006).
The Cartulary-Chronicle of St-Pierre of Bèze, ed. by Constance B. Bouchard (Toronto: University of Toronto Press, 2019).
The Charters of the Anglo-Norman Earls of Chester, c.1071–1237, ed. by Geoffrey Barraclough (Gloucester: Sutton, 1988).
The Chronicle of Æthelweard, ed./tr. by Alistair Campbell (London: Nelson, 1962).
The Chronicle of Arnold of Lübeck, tr. by Graham A. Loud (London: Routledge, 2019).
The Chronicle of Croyland Abbey by Ingulph, ed. by Walter de Gray Birch (Wisbech: Leach and Son, 1883).
The Chronicle of John of Worcester, ed./tr. Reginald R. Darlington and Patrick McGurk, 2 vols. (Oxford: Oxford University Press, 1995–8).
The Chronicle of St. Mary's Abbey, York, from Bodley MS. 39, ed. by Herbert H. E. Craster and Mary E. Thornton (Durham, Andrews & Co., 1934).
The Chronography of Robert of Torigni, ed./tr. by Thomas N. Bisson, 2 vols. (Oxford: Oxford University Press, 2020).
The Deeds of God through the Franks: A Translation of Guibert de Nogent's 'Gesta Dei per Francos', tr. by Robert Levine (Woodbridge: Boydell, 1997).
The Deeds of the Abbots of St Albans–Gesta abbatum monasterii sancti Albani, tr. by David Preest and James G. Clark (Woodbridge: Boydell, 2019).
The Early History of Glastonbury: An Edition, Translation and Study of William of Malmesbury's 'De Antiquitate Glastonie Ecclesie', ed./tr. by John Scott (Woodbridge: Boydell, 1981).
The Ecclesiastical History of Orderic Vitalis, ed./tr. by Marjorie Chibnall, 6 vols. (Oxford: Oxford University Press, 1968–80).
The Etymologies of Isidore of Seville, tr. by Stephen A. Barney et al. (Cambridge: Cambridge University Press, 2006).
The Gesta Normannorum Ducum of William of Jumièges, Orderic Vitalis and Robert of Torigni, ed./tr. by Elisabeth M. C. van Houts, 2 vols. (Oxford: Oxford University Press, 1992–5).
The Historia Ierosolimitana *of Baldric of Bourgueil*, ed. by Steven Biddlecombe (Woodbridge: Boydell & Brewer, 2014).
The Historia Iherosolimitana *of Robert the Monk*, ed. by Damien Kempf and Marcus Bull (Woodbridge: Boydell, 2013).
The Letters and Charters of Henry II, King of England 1154–1189, ed. by Nicholas Vincent, 7 vols. (Oxford: Oxford University Press, 2020–2).
The Letters of Lupus of Ferrières, tr. by Graydon W. Regenos (The Hague: Nijhof, 1966).
The Letters of Peter the Venerable, ed. by Giles Constable, 2 vols. (Cambridge, MA: Harvard University Press, 1967).
The Life of Ailred of Rievaulx, ed. by Frederick M. Powicke (London: Nelson, 1950).
The Life of Edward the Confessor Who Rests at Westminster Attributed to a Monk of Saint-Bertin, ed./tr. by Frank Barlow, 2nd ed. (Oxford: Oxford University Press, 1992).
The Register of Eudes of Rouen, tr. by Sydney M. Brown and Jeremiah F. O'Sullivan (New York, NY: Columbia University Press, 1964).

The Register of Pope Gregory VII, 1073–1085: An English Translation, tr. by Herbert E. J. Cowdrey (Oxford: Clarendon, 2002).
The Restoration of the Monastery of Saint Martin of Tournai, tr. by Lynn H. Nelson (Washington, DC: Catholic University of America Press, 1996).
The Rule of St Benedict, ed./tr. by Bruce L. Venarde (Cambridge, MA: Harvard University Press, 2011).
The Rule of the Master, tr. by Luke Eberle (Kalamazoo, MI: Cistercian Publications, 1977).
The Writings of Medieval Women: An Anthology, ed./tr. by Marcelle Thiébaux, 2nd ed. (New York, NY: Routledge, 2018).
Thomas of Marlborough: History of the Abbey of Evesham, ed./tr. by Jane Sayers and Leslie Watkiss (Oxford: Oxford University Press, 2003).
Three Treatises from Bec on the Nature of Monastic Life, ed./tr. by Giles Constable and Bernard S. Smith (Toronto: University of Toronto Press, 2008).
Urkundenbuch der Klöster der Grafschaft Mansfeld, ed. by Max Krühne (Halle: Hendel, 1888).
Vie de Gauzlin, abbé de Fleury–Vita Gauzlini, abbatis Floriacensis monasterii, ed./tr. by Robert-Henri Bautier and Gillette Labory (Paris: Éditions du CNRS, 1969).
Vita Aegil abbatis Fuldensis a Candido ad modestum edita prosa et versibus: Ein Opus geminum des IX. Jahrhunderts–Einleitung und kritische Edition, ed. by Gereon Becht-Jördens (Marburg: self-published, 1994).
Vitae quatuor primorum abbatum Cavensium Alferii, Leonis, Petri et Constabilis auctore Hugone abbate Venusino, ed. by Leone M. Cerasoli (Bologna: Zanichelli 1941).
Westminster Abbey Charters, 1066–c.1214, ed. by Emma Mason (London: London Record Society, 1988).
Widukind of Corvey: Deeds of the Saxons, tr. by Bernard S. Bachrach and David S. Bachrach (Washington, DC: Catholic University of America Press, 2014).
Willehelmi Abbatis Constitutiones Hirsaugienses, ed. by Pius Engelbert and Candida Elvert, 2 vols. (Siegburg: Schmitt, 2010).
William of Andres: The Chronicle of Andres, tr. by Leah Shopkow (Washington, DC: Catholic University of America Press, 2017).
William of Malmesbury: Gesta pontificum Anglorum–The History of the English Bishops, ed./tr. by Michael Winterbottom and Rodney M. Thomson, 2 vols. (Oxford: Clarendon, 2007).
——, *Gesta regum Anglorum–The History of the English Kings*, ed./tr. by Roger A. B. Mynors et al., 2 vols. (Oxford: Clarendon, 1998–9).
——, *Historia Novella–The Contemporary History*, ed./tr. by Edmund King and Kenneth R. Potter (Oxford: Clarendon, 1998).
——, *Saints' Lives. Lives of SS. Wulfstan, Dunstan, Patrick, Benignus and Indract*, ed./tr. by Michael Winterbottom and Rodney M. Thomson (Oxford: Clarendon, 2002).
Württembergisches Urkundenbuch Online, 12 vols., http://www.wubonline.de.

Secondary Literature

'Houses of Benedictine Nuns: Abbey, Later Priory, of Amesbury', in *A History of the County of Wiltshire*, Vol. 3, ed. by Ralph B. Pugh and Elizabeth Crittall (London: Institute of Historical Research, 1956), pp. 242–59.
A Catalogue of the Harleian Manuscripts in the British Museum, 4 vols. (London: Eyre and Strahan, 1808–12).

Aigner, Petra, 'Poetry and Networking in High Medieval France (ca. 1100): Baudri de Bourgueil and His Scholarly Contacts', in *Networks of Learning: Perspectives on Scholars in Byzantine East and Latin West*, ed. by Sita Steckel et al. (Berlin: De Gruyter, 2015), pp. 33–56.

Aird, William M., 'The Political Context of the Libellus de Exordio', in *Symeon of Durham: Historian of Durham and the North*, ed. by David W. Rollason (Stamford: Tyas, 1999), pp. 32–45.

Airlie, Stuart, *Making and Unmaking the Carolingians, 751–888* (London: Bloomsbury Academic, 2021).

Alexander, J. G., *Norman Illumination at Mont St Michel, 966–1100* (Oxford: Oxford University Press, 1970).

Allen, Michael I., 'Universal History 300–1000: Origins and Western Developments', in *Historiography in the Middle Ages*, ed. by Deborah M. Deliyannis (Leiden: Brill, 2003), pp. 17–42.

Allen, Richard, 'History, Memory and Community in Cistercian Normandy (12th–13th Centuries)', *Downside Review* 139 (2021), 44–64.

——, 'The Abbey of Savigny (Manche) in Britain and Ireland in the 12th Century: Three Overlooked Documents', *Annales de Normandie* 68 (2018), 9–33.

——, 'Unknown Copies of the Lost Charters of Le Mont Saint-Michel (11th–13th Centuries): The Henry Chanteux Collection at the Archives Départementales du Calvados', *Revue Mabillon* 29 (2018), 45–82.

An Inventory of the Historical Monuments in Dorset, Vol. I: *West* (London: Her Majesty's Stationery Office: 1952).

Arbabzadah, Moreed, 'Word Order in Goscelin and Folcard: Implications for the Attribution of the *Vita Ædwardi regis* and Other Works', *Journal of Medieval Latin* 31 (2021), 191–218.

Aris, Marc-Aeilko and Regina Pütz, *Bibliotheca Fuldensis: Ausgewählte Handschriften und Handschriftenfragmente aus der mittelalterlichen Bibliothek des Klosters Fulda* (Fulda: Parzellers Buchverlag, 2010).

Aris, Marc-Aeilko et al., 'Fulda, St. Salvator', in *Die benediktinischen Mönchs- und Nonnenkloster in Hessen*, ed. by Friedhelm Jürgensmeier, Franziskus Büll, and Regina E. Schwerdtfeger [= *GB* VII] (St. Ottilien: EOS, 2004), pp. 374–5.

Aris, Marc-Aeilko, 'Hrabanus Maurus und die Bibliotheca Fuldensis', in *Hrabanus Maurus: Gelehrter, Abt von Fulda und Erzbischof von Mainz*, ed. by Franz J. Felten and Karl Lehmann (Mainz: Bistum Mainz, 2006), pp. 51–70.

Arnold, John H., *What Is Medieval History?* 2nd ed. (Medford, MA: Polity, 2021).

Arnold, Klaus, 'Das Nachlaßverzeichnis des Johannes Trithemius, Abt des Klosters St. Jakob in Würzburg, aus dem Jahr 1517', in *Johannes Trithemius (1462–1516): Abt und Büchersammler, Humanist und Geschichtsschreiber*, ed. by Klaus Arnold and Franz Fuchs (Würzburg: Königshausen & Neumann, 2019), pp. 279–339.

——, 'Ein Würzburger Schriftenverzeichnis des Johannes Trithemius aus dem Jahr 1514', in *Herbipolis: Studien zu Stadt und Hochstift Würzburg in Spätmittelalter und Früher Neuzeit*, ed. by Markus Frankl, Martina Hartmann, and Dorothea Klein (Würzburg: Königshausen, 2015), pp. 357–72.

——, 'Von Trittenheim nach Sponheim und Würzburg: Zu Leben und Werk des Büchersammlers Johannes Trithemius (1462–1516)', in *Johannes Trithemius (1462–1516): Abt und Büchersammler, Humanist und Geschichtsschreiber*, ed. by Klaus Arnold and Franz Fuchs (Würzburg: Königshausen & Neumann, 2019), pp. 19–34.

——, *Johannes Trithemius (1462–1516)*, 2nd ed. (Würzburg: Schöningh, 1991).

Assmann, Aleida, 'Canon and Archive', in *Cultural Memory Studies: An International and Interdisciplinary Handbook*, ed. by Astrid Erll et al. (Berlin: De Gruyter, 2008), pp. 97–107.

——, 'Four Formats of Memory: From Individual to Collective Constructions of the Past', in *Cultural Memory and Historical Consciousness in the German-Speaking World since 1500*, ed. by Christian Emden and David Midgley (Oxford: Peter Lang, 2004), pp. 19–38.

——, 'Memory: Individual and Collective', in *The Oxford Handbook of Contextual Political Analysis*, ed. by Robert E. Goodin and Charles Tilly (Oxford: Oxford University Press, 2006), pp. 210–24.

——, *Zeit und Tradition: Kulturelle Strategien der Dauer* (Cologne: Böhlau, 1999).

Assmann, Jan, 'Communicative and Cultural Memory', in *Cultural Memory Studies: An International and Interdisciplinary Handbook*, ed. by Astrid Erll et al. (Berlin: De Gruyter, 2008), pp. 109–18.

——, 'Introduction: What Is Cultural Memory?', in *Religion and Cultural Memory: Ten Studies*, ed./tr. by Jan Assmann and Rodney Livingstone (Stanford, CA: Stanford University Press, 2006), pp. 1–30.

Atzbach, Rainer, 'The "Stube" and Its Heating: Archaeological Evidence for a Smoke-Free Living Room between Alps and North Sea', in *Dwellings, Identities and Homes: European Housing Culture from the Viking Age to the Renaissance*, ed. by Kate Giles and Mette Svart Kristiansen (Hoebjerg: Jutland Archaeological Society, 2014), pp. 195–210.

Auslander, Diane, 'Clemence and Catherine: The Life of St Catherine in Its Norman and Anglo-Norman Context', in *Barking Abbey and Medieval Literary Culture: Authorship and Authority in a Female Community*, ed. by Jennifer N. Brown and Donna A. Bussell (Woodbridge: Boydell, 2012), pp. 164–82.

Avezou, Laurent, 'Du Moyen Âge à la fin des Lumières', in *Lex lieux de l'histoire*, ed. by Christian Amalvi (Paris: Armand Colin, 2005), pp. 13–63.

Babington, Caroline et al., *Our Painted Past: Wall Paintings of English Heritage* (London: English Heritage, 1999).

Bächtold, Hans U., 'Heinrich Bullinger als Historiker der Schweizer Geschichte', in *Heinrich Bullinger und seine Zeit: Eine Vorlesungsreihe*, ed. by Emidio Campi (Zurich: Theologischer Verlag, 2004), pp. 251–73.

Bailey, Anne E., '*Gesta Pontificum Anglorum*: History of Hagiography?', in *Discovering William of Malmesbury*, ed. by Rodney M. Thomson et al. (Woodbridge: Boydell, 2019), pp. 13–26.

Baker, Joseph B., *The History of Scarborough, from the Earliest Date* (London: Longmans, Green & Co., 1882).

Baker, Nigel et al., *Bristol: A Worshipful Town and Famous City: An Archaeological Assessment from Prehistory to 1900* (Oxford: Oxbow, 2018).

Barthélemy, Dominique, *Les deux ages de la seigneurie banale: Pouvoir et société dans la terre des sires de Coucy (milieu XIe–milieu XIIIe siècle)* (Paris: Publications de la Sorbonne, 1984).

Bates, David, 'Robert of Torigni and the *Historia Anglorum*', in *The English and Their Legacy, 900–1200: Essays in Honour of Ann Williams*, ed. by David Roffe (Woodbridge: Boydell, 2012), pp. 175–84.

Baylé, Maylis et al., *Le Mont-Saint-Michel: Histoire et imaginaire* (Paris: Éditions du patrimoine, 1998).

Beach, Alison I. and Isabelle Cochelin, 'General Introduction', in *CHMMLW*, I, 1–15.

Beach, Alison I., 'Listening for the Voices of Admont's Twelfth-Century Nuns', in *Voices in Dialogue: Reading Women in the Middle Ages*, ed. by Linda Olson and Kathryn Kerby-Fulton (Notre Dame, IN: University of Notre Dame Press, 2005), pp. 187–98.

——, 'Shaping Liturgy, Shaping History: A Cantor-Historian from Twelfth-Century Peterhausen', in *Medieval Cantors and Their Craft: Music, Liturgy and the Shaping of History, 800–1500*, ed. by Margot E. Fassler et al. (Woodbridge: Boydell, 2017), pp. 297–309.

——, 'The Double Monastery as a Historiographical Problem (Fourth to Twelfth Century)', in *CHMMLW*, I, 561–78.

——, *The Trauma of Monastic Reform: Community and Conflict in Twelfth-Century Germany* (Cambridge: Cambridge University Press, 2017).

——, *Women as Scribes: Book Production and Monastic Reform in Twelfth-Century Bavaria* (Cambridge: Cambridge University Press, 2004).

Becher, Matthias, 'Die Chronologie der Äbte von Saint-Wandrille in der ersten Hälfte des 8. Jahrhunderts: Studien zu den Gesta abbatum Fontanellensium', in *Vielfalt der Geschichte: Lernen, Lehren und Erforschen vergangener Zeiten*, ed. by Sabine Happ and Ulrich Nonn (Berlin: WVB, 2004), pp. 25–47.

Becht-Jördens, Gereon, 'Die Vita Aegil des Brun Candidus als Quelle zu Fragen der Geschichte Fuldas im Zeitalter der anianischen Reform', *Hessisches Jahrbuch für Landesgeschichte* 42 (1992), 19–48.

——, 'Sturmi oder Bonifatius? Ein Konflikt im Zeitalter der anianischen Reform um Identität und monastisches Selbstverständnis im Spiegel der Altartituli des Hrabanus Maurus für die Salvatorbasilika zu Fulda', in *Hrabanus Maurus in Fulda: Mit einer Hrabanus Maurus-Bibliographie (1979–2009)*, ed. by Marc-Aeilko Aris and Susana Bullido del Barrio (Frankfurt a. M.: Knecht, 2010), pp. 123–87.

——, 'Text, Bild und Architektur als Träger einer ekklesiologischen Konzeption von Klostergeschichte: Die karolingische Vita Aegil des Brun Candidus von Fulda (ca. 840)', in *Hagiographie und Kunst: Der Heiligenkult in Schrift, Bild und Architektur*, ed. by Gottfried Kerscher (Berlin: Reimer, 1993), pp. 75–106.

——, *Die Vita Aegil abbatis Fuldensis des Brun Candidus: Ein Opus geminum aus dem Zeitalter der anianischen Reform in biblisch-figuralem Hintergrundstil* (Frankfurt a. M.: Knecht, 1992).

Becker, Petrus, *Die Benediktinerabtei St. Eucharius-St. Matthias vor Trier* [= *Germania Sacra* NF XXXIV; *Das Erzbistum Trier* VIII] (Berlin: De Gruyter, 1996).

Bedal, Konrad, 'Stube', in *Lexikon des Mittelalters*, 9 vols. (Munich: Artemis, 1980–98), VIII, 249–51.

Bell, David N., 'The Libraries of Religious Houses in the Late Middle Ages', in *CHLBI* I, 126–51.

——, 'What Nuns Read: The State of the Question', in *The Culture of Medieval English Monasticism*, ed. by James G. Clark (Woodbridge: Boydell & Brewer, 2007), pp. 113–33.

——, *What Nuns Read: Books and Libraries in Medieval English Nunneries* (Kalamazoo, MI: Cistercian Publications, 1995).

Benedict, Kimberley, *Empowering Collaborations: Writing Partnerships between Religious Women and Scribes in the Middle Ages* (New York, NY: Routledge, 2014).

Benz, Stefan, 'Geschichtsschreibung der Frauenklöster Zentraleuropas im 18. Jahrhundert', in *Between Revival and Uncertainty: Monastic and Secular Female Communities in Central Europe in the Long Eighteenth Century*, ed. by Veronika Čapská et al. (Opava: Silesian University, 2012), pp. 214–65.

Bérat, Emma, 'The Authority of Diversity: Communal Patronage in *Le Gracial*', in *Barking Abbey and Medieval Literary Culture: Authorship and Authority in a Female Community*, ed. by Jennifer N. Brown and Donna A. Bussell (Woodbridge: Boydell, 2012), pp. 210–32.

Berkhofer, Robert F. III, 'Abbatial Authority over Lay Agents', in *The Experience of Power in Medieval Europe: 950–1350*, ed. by Robert F. Berkhofer III et al. (Aldershot: Ashgate, 2005), pp. 43–57.

——, 'Rewriting the Past: Monastic Forgeries and Plausible Narratives', in *Rewriting History in the Central Middle Ages, 900–1300*, ed. by Emily A. Winkler and Christopher P. Lewis (Turnhout: Brepols, 2022), pp. 151–67.

——, *Day of Reckoning: Power and Accountability in Medieval France* (Philadelphia, PA: University of Pennsylvania Press, 2004).

——, *Forgeries and Historical Writing in England, France, and Flanders, 900–1200* (Woodbridge: Boydell, 2022).

Berschin, Walter, 'Biographie im karolingischen Fulda', in *Kloster Fulda in der Welt der Karolinger und Ottonen*, ed. by Gangolf Schrimpf (Frankfurt a. M.: Knecht, 1993), pp. 315–24.

——, 'Der St. Galler Klosterplan als Literaturdenkmal', in *Studien zum St. Galler Klosterplan*, ed. by Johannes Duft, Peter Ochsenbein, and Karl Schmuki, 2 vols. (St Gall: Fehr/Historischer Verein des Kantons St, Gallen, 1962–2002).

——, '*Os meum aperui*: Die Autobiographie Ruperts von Deutz (†um 1130)', *Studien und Mitteilungen zur Geschichte des Benediktinerordens und seiner Zweige* 119 (2008), 69–121.

——, 'Vier karolingische Exlibris', in *Mittellateinische Studien*, ed. by Walter Berschin, 3 vols. (Heidelberg: Mattes, 2005–17), I, 169–78.

Bertrand, Paul, *Documenting the Everyday in Medieval Europe: The Social Dimensions of a Writing Revolution, 1250–1350* (Turnhout: Brepols, 2019).

——, *Les écritures ordinaires: Sociologie d'un temps de révolution documentaire (1250–1350)* (Paris: Publications de la Sorbonne, 2015).

Bijsterveld, Arnoud-Jan, 'The Medieval Gift as Agent of Social Bonding and Political Power: A Comparative Approach', in *Medieval Transformations: Texts, Power, and Gifts in Context*, ed. by Esther Cohen and Mayke de Jong (Leiden: Brill, 2001), pp. 123–56.

Billett, Jesse D., *The Divine Office in Anglo-Saxon England, 597–c.1000* (Woodbridge: Boydell, 2014), pp. 82–4.

Binding, Günther, 'Bauwissen im Früh- und Hochmittelalter', in *Wissensgeschichte der Architektur*, Vol. 3: *Vom Mittelalter bis zur frühen Neuzeit*, ed. by Jürgen Renn et al., new ed. (Berlin: Max-Planck-Gesellschaft, 2014), pp. 11–94.

——, *Der früh- und hochmittelalterliche Bauherr als sapiens architectus*, 2nd ed. (Darmstadt: Wissenschaftliche Buchgesellschaft, 2017).

Bischoff, Bernhard and Josef Hofmann, *Libri Sancti Kyliani: Die Würzburger Schreibschule und die Dombibliothek im VIII. und IX. Jahrhundert* (Würzburg: Schöningh, 1952).

Bischoff, Bernhard, 'Das benediktinische Mönchtum und die Überlieferung der klassischen Literatur', *Studien und Mitteilungen zur Geschichte des Benediktinerordens und seiner Zweige* 92 (1981), 165–90.

——, 'Die ältesten Handschriften der Regula S. Benedicti in Bayern', *Studien und Mitteilungen zur Geschichte des Benediktinerordens und seiner Zweige* 92 (1982), 7–16.

——, *Latin Palaeography: Antiquity and the Middle Ages*, tr. by Daibhm O. Cróinin and David Ganz (Cambridge: Cambridge University Press, 1990).

——, *Manuscripts and Libraries in the Age of Charlemagne* (Cambridge: Cambridge University Press, 1994).

Bisson, Marie, 'Où sont les archives du Mont Saint-Michel?', in *Sur les pas de Lanfranc, du Bec à Caen: Recueil d'études en hommaga à Véronique Gazeau*, ed. by Pierre Bauduin et al. (Caen: Annales de Normandie, 2018), pp. 451–63.

Bisson, Thomas N., 'The "Annuary" of Robert of Torigni', *Anglo-Norman Studies* 33 (2011), 61–74.

——, 'The Scripts of Robert of Torigni: Some Notes of Conjectural History', *Tabularia* (2019), https://doi.org/10.4000/tabularia.3938.

Blair, Peter H., *The World of Bede* (Cambridge: Cambridge University Press, 1990).

Bliss, Jane, 'Who Wrote the Nun's Life of Edward?', *Reading Medieval Studies* 38 (2012), 77–98.

Bloch, Peter, *Das Hornbacher Sakramentar und seine Stellung innerhalb der frühen Reichenauer Buchmalerei* (Basel: Birkhäuser, 1956).

Blockmans, Willem P., 'The Devotion of a Lonely Duchess', in *Margaret of York, Simon Marmion, and 'The Visions of Tondal'*, ed. by Thomas Kren (Malibu, CA: Getty Museum, 1992), pp. 29–46.

Blough, Karen, 'Abbatial Effigies and Conventual Identity at St. Servatius, Quedlinburg', in *A Companion to the Abbey of Quedlinburg in the Middle Ages*, ed. by Karen Blough (Leiden: Brill, 2023), pp. 181–222.

Blume, Dieter, 'Abt Berns von der Reichenau "Vita (III) S. Uodalrici": Ein frühes Zeugnis des Reformwillens in der Reichskirche?', in *Scripturus vitam: Lateinische Biographie von der Antike bis zur Gegenwart*, ed. by Dorothea Walz (Heidelberg: Mattes, 2002), pp. 833–40.

——, *Bern von Reichenau (1008–1048): Abt, Gelehrter, Biograph* (Ostfildern: Thorbecke, 2008).

Blumenthal, Uta-Renate, 'Hugh of Die and Lyons, Primate and Papal Legate', in *Scripturus vitam: Lateinische Biographie von der Antike bis in die Gegenwart. Festgabe für Walter Berschin zum 65. Geburtstag*, ed. by Dorothea Walz (Heidelberg: Mattes, 2002), pp. 487–95.

——, *The Early Councils of Pope Paschal II, 1100–1110* (Toronto: Pontifical Institute of Mediaeval Studies, 1978).

Blurton, Heather F., 'Guibert of Nogent and the Subject of History', *Exemplaria* 15 (2003), 111–31.

Bodarwé, Katrinette, Sanctimoniales litteratae: *Schriftlichkeit und Bildung in den ottonischen Frauenkommunitäten Gandersheim, Essen und Quedlinburg* (Münster: Aschendoff, 2004).

Boeckler, Albert, 'Zur Conrad von Scheyern-Frage', *Jahrbuch für Kunstwissenschaft* (1923), 83–102.

Bond, James, 'Monastic Water Management in Great Britain: A Review', in *Monastic Archaeology: Papers on the Study of Medieval Monasteries*, ed. by Graham Keevill et al. (Oxford: Oxbow, 2001).

Bondéelle-Souchier, Anne, ed., *Bibliothèques de l'ordre de Prémontré dans la France d'Ancien Régime*, 2 vols. (Paris: CNRS Éditions, 2000–6).

Bonifazi, Reto, 'Die beiden Miniaturen der Frowin-Bibel auf Einzelblättern', in *Die Bilderwelt des Klosters Engelberg: Das Skriptorium unter den Äbten Frowin (1143–1178), Bechtold (1178–1197) and Heinrich (1197–1223)*, ed. by Christoph Eggenberger (Luzern: Diopter, 1999), pp. 27–30.

Borgolte, Michael, 'Fiktive Gräber in der Historiographie: Hugo von Flavigny und die Sepultur der Bischöfe von Verdun', in *Fälschungen im Mittelalter*, 5 vols. (Hanover: Hahn, 1988), I, 205–40.

Borst, Arno, *Der karolingische Reichskalender und seine Überlieferung bis ins 12. Jahrhundert*, 3 vols. (Hanover: Hahn, 2001).
Bourgin, Georges, *Guibert de Nogent: Histoire de sa vie (1053–1124)* (Paris: Picard, 1907).
Boutémy, André, 'Le scriptorium et la bibliothèque de Saint-Amand d'après les manuscrits et les anciens catalogues', *Scriptorium* 1 (1946), 6–16.
——, 'Les enluminures de l'abbaye de Saint-Amand', *Revue Belge d'archéologie et d'histoire de l'art* 12 (1942), 135–41.
Bouter, Nicole, ed., *Écrire son histoire: Les communautés régulières face à leur passé* (Saint-Étienne: Publications de l'Université de Saint-Étienne, 2005).
Bowden, Caroline, 'Building Libraries in Exile: The English Convents and Their Book Collections in the Seventeenth Century', *British Catholic History* 32 (2015), 343–82.
Bowles, William L. and John G. Nichols, *Annals and Antiquities of Lacock Abbey* (London: Nichols & Son, 1835).
Boynton, Susan, 'Shaping Cluniac Devotion', in *A Companion to the Abbey of Cluny in the Middle Ages*, ed. by Scott G. Bruce and Steven Vanderputten (Leiden: Brill, 2021), pp. 125–45.
——, 'The Bible and the Liturgy', in *The Practice of the Bible in the Middle Ages: Production, Reception, and Performance in Western Christianity*, ed. by Susan Boynton and Diane J. Reilly (New York, NY: Columbia University Press, 2011), pp. 10–33.
Brady, Lindy, 'Crowland Abbey as Anglo-Saxon Sanctuary in the Pseudo-Ingulf Chronicle', *Traditio* 73 (2018), 19–42.
Brakspear, Harold, 'The Abbot's House at Battle', *Archaeologia* 83 (1933), 139–66.
Branchi, Mariapia, *Lo scriptorium e la biblioteca di Nonantola* (Modena: Edizioni Artestampa, 2011).
Brandis, Tilo and Peter J. Becker, eds., *Glanz alter Buchkunst: Mittelalterliche Handschriften der Staatsbibliothek Preußischer Kulturbesitz, Berlin* (Wiesbaden: Reichert, 1988).
Brandt, Gisela, 'Textsorten weiblicher Chronistik: Beobachtungen an den chronikalischen Aufzeichnungen von Agnes Sampach (–1406/07), Elisabeth Kempf (um 1470), Ursula Pfaffinger (1494–1509) und Caritas Pirckheimer (1524–1527)', in *Textsortentypologien und Textallianzen von der Mitte des 15. bis zur Mitte des 16. Jahrhunderts*, ed. by Franz Simmler and Claudia Wich-Reif (Berlin: Weidler, 2004), pp. 217–42.
Brann, Noel L., *The Abbot Trithemius (1462–1516): The Renaissance of Monastic Humanism* (Leiden: Brill, 1981).
Bresslau, Harry, 'Bamberger Studien I', *Neues Archiv der Gesellschaft für ältere deutsche Geschichtskunde* 21 (1896), 141–234.
——, 'Bamberger Studien II' [= 'Die Chroniken des Frutolf von Bamberg und des Ekkehard von Aura'], *Neues Archiv der Gesellschaft für ältere deutsche Geschichtskunde* 21 (1896), 197–234.
Brett, Martin, 'Escures, Ralph d'', in *Oxford Dictionary of National Biography*, https://doi.org/10.1093/ref:odnb/23047.
——, 'John of Worcester and His Contemporaries', in *The Writing of History in the Middle Ages: Essays Presented to Richard William Southern*, ed. by Ralph H. C. Davis and John M. Wallace-Hadrill (Oxford: Clarendon, 1981), pp. 106–26.
Britnell, Richard H., ed., *Pragmatic Literacy, East and West, 1200–1330* (Woodbridge, Boydell, 1997).
Brooke, Christopher N., 'Adrian IV and John of Salisbury', in *Adrian IV: The English Pope (1154–1159)*, ed. by Brenda Bolton and Anne Duggan (London: Routledge, 2003), pp. 3–13.
Brown, Katherine A., 'Boccaccio Reading Old French: Decameron IX. 2 and *La Nonete*', *Modern Language Notes* 125 (2010), 54–71.

Bruce, Scott G., 'Clandestine Codices in the Captivity Narratives of Abbot Maiolus of Cluny', in *Teaching and Learning in Medieval Europe: Essays in Honour of Gernot R. Wieland*, ed. by Greti Dinkova-Bruun and Tristan Major (Turnhout: Brepols, 2017), pp. 149-61.

——, 'Local Sanctity and Civic Typology in Early Medieval Pavia: The Example of the Cult of Abbot Maiolus of Cluny', in *Cities, Texts, and Social Networks 400-1500*, ed. by Caroline J. Goodson et al. (Farnham: Routledge, 2010), pp. 177-92.

Bruckner, Albert, ed., *Scriptoria medii aevi Helvetica*, 14 vols. (Geneva: Roto-Sadag, 1935-79).

Bugyis, Katie A.-M., 'Dating the Translations of Barking's Abbess-Saints by Goscelin of Saint-Bertin and Abbess Ælfgifu', *Journal of Medieval Monastic Studies* 11 (2022), 97-130.

——, 'Women Priests at Barking Abbey in the Late Middle Ages', in *Women Intellectuals and Leaders in the Middle Ages*, ed. by Kathryn Kerby-Fulton et al. (Cambridge: Cambridge University Press, 2020), pp. 319-34.

——, *The Care of Nuns: The Ministries of Benedictine Women in England during the Central Middle Ages* (Oxford: Oxford University Press, 2019).

Bull, Marcus, 'Robert the Monk and his Source(s)', in *Writing the Early Crusades: Text, Transmission and Memory*, ed. by Marcus Bull and Damien Kempf (Woodbridge: Boydell, 2014), pp. 127-39.

Bulst, Neithard, *Untersuchungen zu den Klosterreformen Wilhelms von Dijon (962-1031)* (Bonn: Röhrscheid, 1973).

Buringh, Eltjo, *Medieval Manuscript Production in the Latin West: Explorations with a Global Database* (Leiden: Brill, 2011).

Burkhardt, Johannes, 'Fulda, Michaelsberg', in *Die benediktinischen Mönchs- und Nonnenkloster in Hessen*, ed. by Friedhelm Jürgensmeier et al. [= *GB* VII] (St. Ottilien: EOS, 2004), pp. 456-64.

Bussell, Donna A. and Jennifer N. Brown, 'Barking's Lives, the Abbey and Its Abbesses', in *Barking Abbey and Medieval Literary Culture: Authorship and Authority in a Female Community*, ed. by Jennifer N. Brown and Donna A. Bussell (Woodbridge: Boydell, 2012), pp. 1-30.

Büttner, Brigitte, 'Women and the Circulation of Books', *Journal of the Early Book Society* 4 (2001), 9-31.

Butzmann, Hans, ed., *Die mittelalterlichen Handschriften der Gruppen Extravagantes, Novi und Novissimi* [= Kataloge der Herzog August Bibliothek Wolfenbüttel: Die Neue Reihe XV] (Frankfurt a. M.: Klostermann, 1972).

Buzas, Ladislaus, *Deutsche Bibliotheksgeschichte des Mittelalters* [= Elemente des Buch- und Bibliothekswesens III] (Wiesbaden: Reichert, 1975).

Campopiano, Michele and Henry Bainton, eds., *Universal Chronicles in the High Middle Ages* (Woodbridge: York Medieval Press, 2017).

Chazelas, Jean, 'La vie monastique au Mont Saint-Michel au XIIIe siècle', in *Millénaire monastique du Mont Saint-Michel*, ed. by Jean Laporte et al., 5 vols. (Paris: Lethielleux, 1967-93), I, 127-50.

Chauncy, Henry, *The Historical Antiquities of Hertfordshire [...] Also the Characters of the Abbots of St Albans* (London: Griffin, 1700).

Chaurand, Jacques, 'La conception de l'histoire de Guibert de Nogent (1053-1124)', *Cahiers de civilisation médiévale* 31/2 (1965), 381-95.

Chenu, Marie-Dominique, 'Auctor, actor, autor', *Archivum latinitatis medii aevi* 3 (1927), 81–86; repr. in *Studi di lessicografia filosofica medievale*, ed. by Marie-Dominique Chenu and Giacinta Spinosa (Florence: Olschki, 2001), pp. 51–6.
Chibnall, Marjorie, *The World of Orderic Vitalis: Norman Monks and Norman Knights* (Woodbridge: Boydell, 2001).
Cingolani, Stefano M., 'L'Abat Oliba, el poder i la paraula', *Acta historica et archaeologica mediaevalia* 31 (2014), 115–62.
Cipolla, Carlo, ed., *Codici Bobbiesi della Biblioteca Nazionale Universitaria in Torino* [= *Collezione Paleografica Bobbiese* I] (Milan: Hoepli, 1907).
Clark, James G., 'An Abbot and His Books in Late Medieval and Pre-Reformation England', in *The Prelate in England and Europe, 1300–1560*, ed. by Martin Heale (York: York Medieval Press, 2014), pp. 101–26.
——, 'Monastic Confraternity in Medieval England: The Evidence from the St Albans Abbey *Liber Benefactorum*', in *Religious and Laity in Western Europe, 1000–1400: Interaction, Negotiation, and Power*, ed. by Emilia Jamroziak and Janet Burton (Turnhout: Brepols, 2006), pp. 315–31.
——, 'The Regular Clergy', in *A Companion to the Early Printed Book in Britain: 1476–1558*, ed. by Vicent J. Gillespie (Woodbridge: Boydell, 2014), pp. 176–206.
——, *A Monastic Renaissance at St Albans: Thomas Walsingham and His Circle c.1350–1440* (Oxford: Clarendon, 2004).
——, *The Benedictines in the Middle Ages* (Woodbridge: Boydell, 2011).
Clark, John W., *The Care of Books: An Essay on the Development of Libraries and Their Fittings, from the Earliest Times to the End of the Eighteenth Century* (Cambridge: Cambridge University Press, 1901).
Clarke, Howard B., 'The Identity of the Designer of the Bayeux Tapestry', *Anglo-Norman Studies* 35 (2012), 120–39.
Classen, Albrecht, '…und sie schrieben doch: Frauen als Schriftstellerinnen im deutschen Mittelalter', *Wirkendes Wort* 44 (1994), 7–24.
Claussen, Hilde, 'Zum Abtshaus des Wibald von Stablo im Kloster Corvey', in *Wohn- und Wirtschaftsbauten frühmittelalterlicher Klöster*, ed. by Hans R. Sennhauser (Zurich: Hochschulverlag, 1996), pp. 27–31.
Clayton, Ewan, 'Workplaces for Writing', in *Pen in Hand: Medieval Scribal Portraits, Colophons and Tools*, ed. by Michael Gullick (Walkern: Red Gull Press, 2006), pp. 1–18.
Cleaver, Laura and Andrea Worm, 'Introduction: Making and Reading History Books in the Anglo-Norman World', in *Writing History in the Anglo-Norman World: Manuscripts, Makers and Readers, c.1066–1250*, ed. by Laura Cleaver and Andrea Worm (Woodbridge: York Medieval Press, 2018), pp. 1–6.
Cleaver, Laura, '"A Most Studious Man, a Researcher and Collector of Sacred and Profane Books": Robert of Torigni and the Making of the Mont-Saint-Michel Chronicle (Avranches Bibliothèque Municipale MS 159)', in *Mapping New Territories in Art and Architectural Histories: Essays in Honour of Roger Stalley*, ed. by Niamh NicGhabhann and Danielle O'Donovan (Turnhout: Brepols, 2022), pp. 327–39.
——, 'The Monastic Library at Le Bec', in *A Companion to the Abbey of Le Bec in the Central Middle Ages (11th–13th Centuries)*, ed. by Benjamin Pohl and Laura L. Gathagan (Leiden: Brill, 2017), pp. 171–205.
——, *Illuminated History Books in the Anglo-Norman World, 1066–1272* (Oxford: Oxford University Press, 2018).

Cochelin, Isabelle, 'Customaries as Inspirational Sources', in *Consuetudines et Regulae: Sources for Monastic Life in the Middle Ages and the Early Modern Period*, ed. by Carolyn Marino Malone and Clark Maines (Turnhout: Brepols, 2014), pp. 27–72.

——, 'Discipline and the Problem of Cluny's Customaries', in *A Companion to the Abbey of Cluny in the Middle Ages*, ed. by Scott G. Bruce and Steven Vanderputten (Leiden: Brill, 2021), pp. 204–22.

Coldicott, Diana K., *Hampshire Nunneries* (Chichester: Phillimore, 1989).

Collard, Franck, 'Les livres de l'abbé Adson et l'abbaye de Montier-en-Der', in *Les moines du Der 673–1790*, ed. by Patrick Corbet, Jackie Lusse, and Georges Viard (Langres: Guéniot, 2000), pp. 147–59.

Combalbert, Grégory, 'Règlement des conflits, gestion du risqué et clercs paroissiaux: L'affermage des dîmes (Normandie, XIIe–XIIIe siècles)', in *La dime, l'Église et la société féodale*, ed. by Michel Lauwers (Turnhout: Brepols, 2012), pp. 335–68.

Conant, Kenneth J., *Carolingian and Romanesque Architecture, 800–1200*, 4th ed. (New Haven, CT: Yale University Press, 1978), pp. 43–86.

Connolly, Margaret, *Sixteenth-Century Readers, Fifteenth-Century Books: Continuities of Reading in the English Reformation* (Cambridge: Cambridge University Press, 2019).

Constable, Giles, 'Suger's Monastic Administration', in *Abbot Suger and Saint-Denis: A Symposium*, ed. by Paula L. Gerson (New York, NY: The Metropolitan Museum of Art, 1986), pp. 17–32; repr. in *Monks, Hermits and Crusaders in Medieval Europe*, ed. by Giles Constable (Aldershot: Ashgate, 1988), no. X (pp. 1–51).

——, 'The Authority of Superiors in Religious Communities', in *La notion d'autorité au Moyen Âge: Islam, Byzance, Occident*, ed. by George Makdisi et al. (Paris: Presses universitaires de France, 1982), pp. 189–210; repr. in *Monks, Hermits and Crusaders in Medieval Europe*, ed. by Giles Constable (London: Variorum, 1988), no. III (pp. 189–210).

Conti, Aidan K., 'Scribes as Authors, Transmission as Composition: Towards a Science of Copying', in *Modes of Authorship in the Middle Ages*, ed. by Ingvil B. Budal and Slavia Rankovic (Toronto: Pontifical Institute of Mediaeval Studies, 2012), pp. 267–88.

Coon, Lynda L., *Dark Age Bodies: Gender and Monastic Practice in the Early Medieval West* (Philadelphia, PA: University of Pennsylvania Press, 2011).

Corradini, Richard, 'Zeiträume–Schrifträume: Überlegungen zur Komputistik und Marginalchronographie am Beispiel der "Annales Fuldenses antiquissimi"', in *Vom Nutzen des Schreibens: Soziales Gedächtnis, Herrschaft und Besitz im Mittelalter*, ed. by Walter Pohl and Paul Herold (Vienna: Verlag der österreichischen Akademie der Wissenschaften, 2002), pp. 113–66.

Costambeys, Marios, 'Albinus (d. 732)', in *Oxford Dictionary of National Biography* (Oxford: Oxford University Press, 2004), https://doi.org/10.1093/ref:odnb/285.

Crafton, Michael, 'Review of Elizabeth C. Pastan and Stephen D. White, *The Bayeux Tapestry and Its Contexts: A Reassessment*, *Speculum* 91 (2016), 550–1.

Crick, Julia C., *The Historia regum Britanniae of Geoffrey of Monmouth*, Vol. 3: *A Summary Catalogue of the Manuscripts* (Woodbridge: D. S. Brewer, 1989).

——, 'The Marshalling of Antiquity: Glastonbury's Historical Dossier', in *The Archaeology and History of Glastonbury Abbey*, ed. by Lesley Abrams and James P. Carley (Woodbridge: Boydell, 1991), pp. 217–43.

Cross, Katherine, *Heirs of the Vikings: History and Identity in Normandy and England, c.950–c.1015* (York: York Medieval Press, 2018).

Crusius, Irene, 'Im Dienst der Königsherrschaft: Königinnen, Königswitwen und Prinzessinnen als Stifterinnen und Äbtissinnen von Frauenstiften und -klöstern', in *Nonnen, Kanonissen und Mystikerinnen: Religiöse Frauengemeinschaften in*

Süddeutschland, ed. by Eva Schlotheuber et al. (Göttingen: Vandenhoeck & Ruprecht, 2008), pp. 59–77.

Dailey, Erin T., *Radegund: The Trials and Triumphs of a Merovingian Queen* (Oxford: Oxford University Press, 2023).

Damian-Grint, Peter, 'Adam of Dryburgh', in *The History of Scottish Theology*, ed. by David Fergusson and Mark W. Elliott, 3 vols. (Oxford: Oxford University Press, 2019), I, 39–53.

——, *The New Historians of the Twelfth-Century Renaissance: Inventing Vernacular Authority* (Woodbridge: Boydell, 1999).

Davis, Adam J., *The Holy Bureaucrat: Eudes Rigaud and Religious Reform in Thirteenth-Century Normandy* (Ithaca, NY: Cornell University Press, 2006).

Davis, Henry W. C., 'Waldric, the Chancellor of Henry I', *English Historical Review* 26 (1911) 84–8.

De Cardevacque, Adolphe, *Histoire de l'abbaye d'Auchy-les-Moines* (Arras: Sueur-Charruey, 1875).

De Charmasse, Anatole, 'Flavigny et les évêques d'Autun', *Mémoires de la Société Eduenne* 46 (1929/31), 159–71, 269–91, and 342–53.

De Hamel, Christopher, *Glossed Books of the Bible and the Origins of the Paris Book Trade* (Woodbridge: D. S. Brewer, 1984).

De Hondt, Abraham, ed., *Catalogue d'une bibliothèque exquise, très considérable en toutes sortes de sciences de langues* (The Hague: 1722).

De la Rue, Gervais, *Essais historiques sur la ville de Caen et son arrondissement*, 2 vols. (Caen: Mancel, 1820).

De Nardi, Sarah et al., 'Introduction', in *The Routledge Handbook of Memory and Place*, ed. by Sarah De Nardi et al. (New York, NY: Routledge, 2019), pp. 1–7.

De Vogüé, Adalbert, *Community and Abbot in the Rule of Saint Benedict* (Kalamazoo, MI: Cistercian Publications, 1979).

De Waha, Michel, 'Le manuscrit CIV. Rep II 69 de l'Universitätsbibliothek Leipzig, la *Vita Wichberti* (BHL 8882) et les *Gesta Abbatum Gemblacensium* de Sigebert de Gembloux', in *Sigebert de Gembloux*, ed. by Jean-Paul Straus (Turnhout: Brepols, 2015), pp. 117–56.

Déceneux, Marc, 'Notes sur le logis abbatial du Mont-Saint-Michel a la fin du XIVe siècle', *Les Amis du Mont Saint-Michel* 95 (1990), 41–58.

Deflou-Leca, Noëlle, 'L'élaboration d'un cartulaire au XIIIe siècle: Le cas de Saint-Germain d'Auxerre', *Revue Mabillon* 8 (1997), 183–207.

Defries, David, *From Sithiu to Saint-Bertin: Hagiographic Exegesis and Collective Memory in the Early Medieval Cults of Omer and Bertin* (Turnhout: Brepols, 2019).

Delisle, Léopold, *Le cabinet des manuscrits de la Bibliothèque impériale/nationale*, 3 vols. (Paris: Imprimerie impériale/nationale, 1868–81).

Dengler-Schreiber, Karin, *Scriptorium und Bibliothek des Klosters Michelsberg in Bamberg* (Graz: Akademische Druck- und Verlagsanstalt, 1979).

Denz, Mechtildis, 'Die Bibliothek der Abtei St. Walburg im Laufe der Jahrhunderte', in *Die Bibliothek der Abtei St. Walburg zu Eichstätt*, ed. by Andreas Friedel (Wiesbaden: Harrassowitz, 2000), pp. xv–xiv.

Depreux, Philippe, 'Büchersuche und Büchertausch im Zeitalter der karolingischen Renaissance am Beispiel des Briefwechsels des Lupus von Ferrières', *Archiv für Kulturgeschichte* 76 (1994), 267–84.

Derolez, Albert, 'Early Humanism in Flanders: New Data and Observations on the Library of Abbot Raphael de Mercatellis (†1508)', in *Les humanistes et leur bibliothèque*, ed. by Rudolf de Smet (Leuven: Peeters, 2002), pp. 37–57.

——, *The Library of Raphael de Marcatellis, Abbot of St. Bavon's, Ghent, 1437–1508* (Ghent: Scientia, 1979).

Despy, Georges, 'Review of K. F. Werner, Andreas von Marchiennes und die Geschichtsschreibung von Anchin und Marchiennes in der zweiten Hälfte des 12. Jahrhunderts', *Scriptorium* 9 (1955), 156–8.

Deutinger, Roman, 'From Lake Constance to the Elbe: Rewriting a Reichenau World Chronicle from the Eleventh to the Thirteenth Century', in *Rewriting History in the Central Middle Ages, 900–1300*, ed. by Emily A. Winkler and Christopher P. Lewis (Turnhout: Brepols, 2022), pp. 39–65.

——, 'Lateinische Weltchronistik des Hochmittelalters', in *Handbuch der Chroniken des Mittelalters*, ed. by Gerhard Wolf and Nobert H. Ott (Berlin: De Gruyter, 2016), pp. 77–103.

Die illuminierten lateinischen Handschriften deutscher Provenienz der Staatsbibliothek Preußischer Kulturbesitz Berlin, 8.–12. Jahrhundert, ed. by Andreas Fingernagel, 2 vols. (Wiesbaden: Harrassowitz, 1991).

Diem, Albrecht and Philip Rousseau, 'Monastic Rules (Fourth to Ninth Century)', in *CHMMLW*, I, 162–94.

Diem, Albrecht, 'The Gender of the Religious: Wo/Men and the Invention of Monasticism', in *The Oxford Handbook of Women and Gender in Medieval Europe*, ed. by Judith Bennett and Ruth M. Karras (Oxford: Oxford University Press, 2013), pp. 432–47.

Digby, Kenelm H., *Mores Catholici*, 3 vols. (London: Dolman, 1831–42).

Dolbeau, François, 'Deux nouveaux manuscrits des "Mémoires" de Guibert de Nogent', *Sacris Eruditi* 26 (1983), 155–76.

Dominique Stutzmann and Sébastien Barret, "L'écriture pragmatique: (1) Objet historique et problématique; (2) Italie; (3) Allemagne, Suisse, Autriche; (4) Angleterre; (5) France; (6) Perspectives et nouveaux concepts', *Paléographie médiévale* (2012), https://ephepaleographie.wordpress.com/2012/04/18/.

Dorrer, Erika S., *Angelus Rumpler, Abt von Formbach (1501–1513) als Geschichtsschreiber: Ein Beitrag zur klösterlichen Geschichtsschreibung in Bayern am Ausgang des Mittelalters* (Kallmünz: Lassleben, 1965).

Doyle, A. Ian, 'Publication by Members of the Religious Orders', in *Book Production and Publishing in Britain, 1375–1475*, ed. by Jeremy Griffiths and Derek Pearsall (Cambridge: Cambridge University Press, 2007), pp. 109–23.

Driver, Martha W. and Michael Orr, 'Decorating and Illustrating the Page', in *The Production of Books in England, 1350–1500*, ed. by Alexandra Gillespie and Daniel Wakelin (Cambridge: Cambridge University Press, 2011), pp. 104–28.

Driver, Martha W., 'Medieval Women Writers and What They Read, c.1000–c.1500', in *The Edinburgh History of Reading: Early Readers*, ed. by Mary Hammond (Edinburgh: Edinburgh University Press, 2020), pp. 54–73.

Dronke, Peter, *Women Writers of the Middle Ages: A Critical Study of Texts from Perpetua (†203) to Marguerite Porete († 1310)* (Cambridge: Cambridge University Press, 1984).

Dugdale, William et al., eds., *Monasticon Anglicanum: A History of the Abbies and Other Monasteries, Hospitals, Frieries, and Cathedral and Collegiate Churches, with Their Dependencies, in England and Wales*, 6 vols., new ed. (London: Longman, 1846–56).

Duggan, Joseph J., 'Turoldus, Scribe or Author? Evidence from the Corpus of Chansons de Geste', in *'Moult a sans et vallour': Studies in Medieval French Literature in Honor of William W. Kibler*, ed. by Monica L. Wright et al. (Amsterdam: Rodopi, 2012), pp. 135–44.

Dümmler, Ernst, 'Lateinische Gedichte des neunten bis elften Jahrhunderts', *Neues Archiv der Gesellschaft für ältere deutsche Geschichtskunde* 10 (1884), 333–57.

Écriture et enluminure en Lorraine au Moyen Âge, ed. by Simone Collin-Roset et al. (Nancy: Société Thierry Alix, 1984).

Eder, Christine E., 'Die Schule des Klosters Tegernsee im frühen Mittelalter im Spiegel der Tegernseer Handschriften', *Studien und Mitteilungen zur Geschichte des Benediktiner-Ordens und seiner Zweige* 83 (1972), pp. 6-155.

Edwards, Edward, *Memoirs of Libraries: Including a Handbook of Library Economy*, 3 vols. (London: Trübner & Co., 1859).

Edwards, Jennifer C., *Superior Women: Medieval Female Authority in Poitiers' Abbey of Sainte-Croix* (Oxford: Oxford University Press, 2019).

Ehrle, Franz and Paul Libaert, eds., *Specimina codicum Latinorum Vaticanorum* [= *Tabulae in usum scholarum* III] (Berlin: De Gruyter, 1932).

Eifler, Matthias, *Die Bibliothek des Erfurter Petersklosters im späten Mittelalter: Buchkultur und Literaturrezeption im Kontext der Bursfelder Klosterreform*, 2 vols. (Cologne: Böhlau, 2017).

El Kholi, Susann, 'Ein Besuch bei Johannes Trithemius: Der Brief des Matthäus Herbenus an Jodokus Beissel vom 14. August 1495', *Archiv für mittelrheinische Kirchengeschichte* 56 (2004), 143-57.

Elema, Johannes, 'Thomas Mann, Dürer und Doktor Faustus', *Euphorion* 59 (1965), pp. 97-117; repr. in *Thomas Mann*, ed. by Helmut Koopmann (Darmstadt: Wissenschaftliche Buchgesellschaft, 1975), pp. 320-50.

Ellger, Otfried, *Die Michaelskirche zu Fulda als Zeugnis der Totensorge: Zur Konzeption einer Friedhofs- und Grabkirche im karolingischen Kloster Fulda* (Fulda: Parzeller, 1989).

Elm, Kaspar, 'Monastische Reformen zwischen Humanismus und Reformation', in *900 Jahre Kloster Bursfelde: Reden und Vorträge zum Jubiläum 1993*, ed. by Lothar Perlitt (Göttingen: Vandenhoeck and Rupprecht, 1994), pp. 59-111.

Embach, Michael, 'Anhänger und Nachfolger des Abtes Johannes Trithemius (1462-1516)', in *Johannes Trithemius (1462-1516): Abt und Büchersammler, Humanist und Geschichtsschreiber*, ed. by Klaus Arnold and Franz Fuchs (Würzburg: Königshausen and Neumann, 2019), pp. 201-20.

——, 'Johannes Trithemius OSB (1462-1516) und die Bibliothek von Kloster Sponheim- mit einem Blick auf die Vita Juttas von Sponheim (1092-1136)', in *Zur Erforschung mittelalterlicher Bibliotheken: Chancen-Entwicklungen-Perspektiven*, ed. by Andrea Rapp (Frankfurt a. M.: Klostermann, 2009), pp. 101-36.

——, *Die Kreuzesschrift des Hrabanus Maurus 'De laudibus sanctae crucis'* (Trier: Paulinus, 2007).

Emery, Anthony, *Greater Medieval Houses of England and Wales, 1300-1500*, 3 vols. (Cambridge: Cambridge University Press, 1996-2006).

Engelbert, Pius, 'Die Bursfelder Kongregation: Werden und Untergang einer benediktinischen Reformbewegung', in *925 Jahre Kloster Bursfelde-40 Jahre Geistliches Zentrum Kloster Bursfelde*, ed. by Rüdiger Krause and Thomas Kaufmann (Göttingen: Wallstein, 2020), pp. 83-101.

——, 'Regeltext und Romverehrung: Zur Frage der Verbreitung der *Regula Benedicti* im Frühmittelalter', *Römische Quartalschrift für christliche Altertumskunde und Kirchengeschichte* 81 (1986), 39-60.

——, 'Zur Frühgeschichte des Bobbieser Skriptoriums', *Revue bénédictine* 78 (1986), 220-60.

Erler, Mary C., 'Private Reading in the Fifteenth- and Sixteenth-Century English Nunnery', in *The Culture of Medieval English Monasticism*, ed. by James G. Clark, new ed. (Woodbridge: Boydell, 2007), pp. 134-46.

Farmer, Sharon, *Communities of Saint Martin: Legend and Ritual in Medieval Tours* (Ithaca, NY: Cornell University Press, 1991).

Fassler, Margot E. et al., eds., *Medieval Cantors and Their Craft: Music, Liturgy and the Shaping of History, 800-1500* (Woodbridge: Boydell, 2017).

Fassler, Margot E., 'Hildegard of Bingen and Her Scribes', in *The Cambridge Companion to Hildegard of Bingen*, ed. by Jennifer Bain (Cambridge: Cambridge University Press, 2021), pp. 280–305.

——, 'The Office of the Cantor in Early Western Monastic Rules and Customaries: A Preliminary Investigation', *Early Music History* 5 (1985), 29–51.

——, 'Volmar, Hildegard, and St. Matthias', in *Medieval Music in Practice: Studies in Honor of Richard Crocker*, ed. by Judith A. Pereino (Middleton, WI: American Institute of Musicology, 2013), pp. 85–112.

——, *Cosmos, Liturgy, and the Arts in the Twelfth Century: Hildegard's Illuminated* Scivias (Philadelphia, PA: University of Pennsylvania Press, 2022).

Feller, Laurent, 'L'écriture de l'histoire du Mont-Cassin au XIIe siècle: Chroniques et documentation pragmatique', in: *I Longobardi a Venezia: Scritti per Stefano Gasparri*, ed. by Irene Barbiera et al. (Turnhout: Brepols, 2020), pp. 365–81.

——, 'La foundation de San Clemente a Casauria et sa representation iconographique', *Mélanges de l'École française de Rome: Moyen-Age, Temps modernes* 94 (1982), 711–28.

Felten, Franz J., 'Herrschaft des Abtes', in *Herrschaft und Kirche: Beiträge zur Entstehung und Wirkungsweise episkopaler und monastischer Organisationsformen*, ed. by Friedrich Prinz (Stuttgart: Hiersemann, 1988), pp. 147–296.

Fergusson, Peter J., 'Canterbury Cathedral Priory's Bath House and Fish Pond', *Anglo-Norman Studies* 37 (2015), 115–30.

Fiala, Virgil E. and Hermann Hauke *Die Handschriften der ehemaligen Hofbibliothek Stuttgart*, Vol. 1.2: *Codices ascetici (HB I 151–249)* (Wiesbaden: Harrassowitz, 1970).

Fichtenau, Heinrich, 'Wolfger von Prüfening', *Mitteilungen des Instituts für österreichische Geschichtsforschung* 51 (1937), 313–57.

Fischer, Ivo, 'Der Nachlaß des Abtes Johannes Trithemius von St. Jakob in Würzburg', *Archiv des historischen Vereins für Unterfranken und Aschaffenburg* 67 (1928), 41–82.

Fisher, Matthew N., *Scribal Authorship and the Writing of History in Medieval England* (Columbus, OH: Ohio State University Press, 2012).

Fleischhauer, Carsten, 'Die Vita Eigilis des Brun Candidus und die Michaelskirche in Fulda', *Fuldaer Geschichtsblätter* 68 (1992), 85–103.

Foot, Sarah and Chase F. Robinson, eds., *The Oxford History of Historical Writing*, Vol. 2: *400–1400* (Oxford: Oxford University Press, 2015).

Foot, Sarah, 'Bede's Abbesses', in *Women Intellectuals and Leaders in the Middle Ages*, ed. by Kathryn Kerby-Fulton et al. (Cambridge: Brewer, 2020), pp. 261–76.

Fouracre, Paul and Richard A. Gerberding, *Late Merovingian France: History and Hagiography, 640–720* (Manchester: Manchester University Press, 1996).

Frank, Barbara, 'Ein Entwurf zu einer Kapitelsansprache des Abtes Johannes Trithemius aus dem Jahr 1496', *Studien und Mitteilungen zur Geschichte des Benediktinerordens und seiner Zweige* 80 (1969), 145–204.

——, *Das Erfurter Peterskloster im 15. Jahrhundert* (Göttingen: Vandenhoeck and Ruprecht, 1973).

Franke, Thomas, 'Studien zur Geschichte der Fuldaer Äbte im 11. und frühen 12. Jahrhundert', *Archiv für Diplomatik* 33 (1987), 55–238.

Freedman, Paul, 'Oliba', in *La catedral de Sant Pere de Vic*, ed. by Marta Crispi Cantón et al. (Barcelona: Publicacions de l'Abadia de Monserrat, 2019), pp. 107–14.

Freeman, Elizabeth, 'Aelred as a Historian among Historians', in *A Companion to Aelred of Rievaulx (1110–1167)*, ed. Marsha Dutton (Leiden: Brill, 2017), pp. 113–46.

——, *Narratives of a New Order: Cistercian Historical Writing in England, 1150–1220* (Turnhout: Brepols, 2002).

Freise, Eckhard, 'Kalendarische und annalistische Grundformen der Memoria', in *'Memoria': Der geschichtliche Zeugniswert des liturgischen Gedenkens im Mittelalter*, ed. by Karl Schmid and Joachim Wollasch (Munich: Fink, 1984), pp. 441–577.

Fromentin, Charles-Antoine, *Essai historique sur l'abbaye de Saint-Silvin d'Auchy-les-Moines* (Arras: Bradier, 1876).

Führer, Julian, 'Documentation et écriture de l'histoire chez l'abbé Suger', in *L'Écriture de l'histoire au Moyen Âge: Contraintes génériques, contraintes documentaires*, ed. by Étienne Anheim et al. (Paris: Garnier, 2015), pp. 149–60.

Gaillard, Michèle, 'Les *Vitae* des saintes Salaberge et Anstrude de Laon, deux sources exceptionnelles pour l'étude de la construction hagiographique et du contexte socio-politique' *Revue du Nord* 391/2 (2011), 655–69.

Gameson, Richard, 'Les colophons des manuscrits du Mont-Saint-Michel', in *Images de la foi: La bible et les Pères de l'Eglise*, ed. by Jean-Luc Leservoisier (Paris: Fédération française pour la coopération des bibliothèques, 2002), pp. 31–35.

——, 'The Medieval Library (to *c*.1450)', in *CHLBI* I, 13–50.

——, 'The Origin, Art, and Message of the Bayeux Tapestry', in *The Study of the Bayeux Tapestry*, ed. by Richard Gameson (Woodbridge: Boydell, 1997), pp. 157–211.

Gandy, George, 'Who Built What at Mont Saint-Michel during the 10th Century?', *Annales de Normandie* 65 (2015), 153–82.

Ganz, David, '*Historia*: Some Lexicographical Considerations', in *Medieval Cantors and Their Craft: Music, Liturgy and the Shaping of History, 800–1500*, ed. by Margot E. Fassler et al. (Woodbridge: Boydell, 2017), pp. 8–22.

Garand, Monique-Cécile, 'Le scriptorium de Guibert de Nogent', *Scriptorium* 31 (1977), 3–29.

——, *Guibert de Nogent et ses secretaires* (Turnhout: Brepols, 1995).

Gardeux, Mathilde, 'Espace d'assistance, espace de pouvoir: Les dispositifs d'accueil et d'hébergements dans quelques monastères bénédictins en Normandie aux XIIe et XIIIe siècles', *Bulletin du centre d'études médiévales d'Auxerre* 8 (2015), 1–33.

Gasparri, Françoise, 'L'administration de Suger, Abbé de Saint-Denis, d'après les Gesta Sugerii', in *Aux sources de la gestion publique*, ed. by Elisabeth Magnou-Nortier, 3 vols. (Lille: Presses universitaires de Lille, 1993–97), III, 111–28.

Gathagan, Laura L., 'Family and Kinship', in *The Cambridge Companion to the Age of William the Conqueror*, ed. by Benjamin Pohl (Cambridge: Cambridge University Press, 2022), pp. 143–62.

Gazeau, Véronique, 'Du secretarius au secretaire: Remarques sur un office médiéval méconnu', in *Faire lien: Aristocratie, réseaux et échanges compétitifs*, ed. by Laurent Jégou et al. (Paris: Publications de la Sorbonne, 2015), pp. 63–72.

——, 'Réformateur ou stratège? L'évêque Odon, patron des moines de Saint-Vigor et commanditaire de la tapisserie de Bayeux', in *Évêques et communautés religieuses dans la France médiévale*, ed. by Noëlle Deflou-Leca and Anne Massoni (Paris: Éditions de la Sorbonne, 2022), pp. 319–42.

——, *Normannia monastica (Xe–XIIe siècle)*, 2 vols. (Caen: Publications du CRAHM, 2007).

Geary, Patrick J., *Phantoms of Remembrance: Memory and Oblivion at the End of the First Millennium* (Princeton, NJ: Princeton University Press, 1994).

Gem, Richard D. and William T. Ball, 'The Romanesque Rebuilding of Westminster Abbey', *Anglo-Norman Studies* 3 (1981), 33–60 and 203–7.

Gemeiner, Carl T., *Kurze Beschreibung der Handschriften in der Stadtbibliothek der K[aiserlichen] freien Reichsstadt Regensburg* (Ingolstadt: n/a, 1791).

Gerzaguet, Jean-Pierre, *L'abbaye d'Anchin de sa foundation (1079) au XIVe siècle: Essor, vie et rayonnement d'une grande communauté bénédictine* (Lille: Presses Universitaires, 1997).
——, *L'abbaye de Marchiennes, milieu VII–début XIIIe siècle* (Turnhout: Brepols, 2022).
Ghent: A City of All Times, ed. by Marc Boone and Gita Deneckere (Ghent: Stadsmuseum/ Mercatorfonds, 2010).
Gießauf, Johannes, 'Totenmemoria im Südostalpenraum und seiner südlichen Nachbarschaft: Eine begrenzte Bestandsaufnahme bis 1300', in *Schriftkultur zwischen Donau und Adria bis zum 13. Jahrhundert*, ed. by Reinhard Härtel et al. (Klagenfurt: Wieser, 2008), pp. 151–202.
Gill, Miriam, 'The Role of Images in Monastic Education: The Evidence from Wall Painting in Late Medieval England', in *Medieval Monastic Education*, ed. by George Ferzoco and Carolyn Muessig (London: Leicester University Press, 2000), pp. 117–35.
Gilsdorf, Sean, 'Deësis Deconstructed: Imagining Intercession in the Medieval West', *Viator* 42 (2012), 131–74.
Giraud, Eleanor J. and Christian T. Leitmeir, eds., *The Medieval Dominicans: Books, Buildings, Music, and Liturgy* (Turnhout: Brepols, 2021).
Glossarium mediae et infimae Latinitatis, ed. by Charles Dufresne du Cange, 10 vols. (Niort: Favre, 1883–7).
Gneuss, Helmut and Michael Lapidge, eds., *Anglo-Saxon Manuscripts: A Bibliographical Handlist of Manuscripts and Manuscript Fragments Written or Owned in England up to 1100* (Toronto: University of Toronto Press, 2014).
Goetz, Hans-Werner, 'Das Bild des Abtes in alamannischen Klosterchroniken des hohen Mittelalters', in *Ecclesia et regnum: Beiträge zur Geschichte von Kirche, Recht und Staat im Mittelalter*, ed. by Dieter Berg and Hans-Werner Goetz (Bochum: Winkler, 1989), pp. 139–53.
——, 'Kirchenfest und weltliches Alltagsleben im früheren Mittelalter', *Mediaevistik* 2 (1989), 123–71.
——, 'Zum Geschichtsbewußtsein in der alamannisch-schweizerischen Klosterchronistik des hohen Mittelalters (11.–13. Jahrhundert)', *Deutsches Archiv für Erforschung des Mittelalters* 44 (1988), 455–88.
——, *Geschichtsschreibung und Geschichtsbewußtsein im hohen Mittelalter* (Berlin: De Gruyter, 2008).
Goez, Werner, 'Zur Weltchronik des Bischofs Frechulf von Lisieux', in *Festgabe für Paul Kirn zum 70. Geburtstag*, ed. by Ekkehard Kaufmann (Berlin: Schmidt, 1961), pp. 93–110.
Golding, Brian, *Gilbert of Sempringham and the Gilbertine Order, 1130–1300* (Oxford: Clarendon, 1995).
Golob, Nataša, *Twelfth-Century Cistercian Manuscripts: The Sitticum Collection* (Ljubljana: Slovenska knjiga, 1996).
Górecki, Piotr, 'Rhetoric, Memory, and Use of the Past: Abbot Peter of Henrykow as Historian and Advocate', *Citeaux* 48 (1997), 261–94.
Gorman, Michael, 'Bede's *VIII Quaestiones* and Carolingian Biblical Scholarship', *Revue bénédictine* 109 (1999), 32–74.
Gorman, Sara, 'Anglo-Norman Hagiography as Institutional Historiography: Saints' Lives in Late Medieval Campsey Ash Priory', *Journal of Medieval Religious Cultures* 37 (2011), 110–28.
Gottlieb, Theodor, *Über mittelalterliche Bibliotheken* (Leipzig: Harrassowitz, 1890).

Götz, Roland, 'Kloster Tegernsee im 15. Jahrhundert', in *Die benediktinische Klosterreform im 15. Jahrhundert*, ed. by Franz X. Bischof and Martin Thurner (Berlin: De Gruyter, 2013), pp. 93–142.

Goullet, Monique, 'De Normandie en Angleterre: Enquête sur la poétique de trois rouleaux mortuaires', *Tabularia* (2016), 217–78, http://journals.openedition.org/tabularia/2782.

——, 'Poésie et mémoire des morts: Le rouleau funèbre de Mathilde, abbesse de la Sainte-Trinité de Caen (†1113)', in *'Ad libros': Mélanges offerts à Denise Angers et Joseph-Claude Poulin*, ed. by Jean-François Cottier et al. (Montreal: Presses de l'Université de Montréal, 2010), pp. 163–98.

Gout, Paul E., *Le Mont-Saint-Michel: Histoire de l'abbaye et de la ville. Étude archéologique et architecturale des monuments*, 2 vols. (Paris: Armand Colin, 1910; repr. 1979).

Gowers, Bernard, 'Review of Edward Roberts, Flodoard of Rheims and the Writing of History in the Tenth Century', *The Medieval Review* (2021), https://scholarworks.iu.edu/journals/index.php/tmr/article/view/32206/36018.

Graf, Katrin, 'Les portraits d'auteur de Hildegarde de Bingen: Une étude iconographique', *Scriptorium* 55 (2001), 179–96.

Gransden, Antonia, 'Baldwin, Abbot of Bury St Edmunds, 1065–1097', *Anglo-Norman Studies* 4 (1981), 65–76 and 178–95.

——, 'Prologues in the Historiography of Twelfth-Century England', in *England in the Twelfth Century*, ed. by Daniel Williams (Woodbridge: Boydell, 1990), pp. 55–81; repr. in *Legends, Traditions and History in Medieval England*, ed. by Antonia Gransden (London: Ashgate, 1992), pp. 125–51.

Grant, Lindy, *Abbot Suger of St-Denis: Church and State in Early Twelfth-Century France* (London: Longman, 1998), pp. 182–5.

Greer, Sarah, *Commemorating Power in Early Medieval Saxony: Writing and Rewriting the Past at Gandersheim and Quedlinburg* (Oxford: Oxford University Press, 2021).

Gresser, Georg, *Die Syonden und Konzilien in der Zeit des Reformpapsttums in Deutschland und Italien von Leo IX. bis Calixt II., 1049–1123* (Paderborn: Schöningh, 2006).

Gretsch, Mechthild, 'Historiography and Literary Patronage in Late Anglo-Saxon England: The Evidence of Æthelweard's *Chronicon*', *Anglo-Saxon England* 41 (2013), 205–48.

Grewe, Klaus, 'Der Wasserversorgungsplan des Klosters Christchurch in Canterbury (12. Jahrhundert)', in *Die Wasserversorgung in Mittelalter*, ed. by Klaus Grewe (Mainz: Zabern, 1991), pp. 229–36.

——, 'Wasserversorgung und -entsorgung in Mittelalter–ein technikgeschichtlicher Überblick', in *Die Wasserversorgung in Mittelalter*, ed. by Klaus Grewe (Mainz: Zabern, 1991), pp. 11–86.

Grierson, Philip, 'Les livres d'abbé Seiwold de Bath', *Revue bénédictine* 52 (1940), 96–116.

Grill, Leopold, 'Reportage über den einstigen romanischen Kreuzgang in Rein', *Marienbote des Stiftes Rein* 9 (1950), 17–20.

Grodecki, Louis, 'Abélard et Suger', in *Pierre Abélard et Pierre le Vénérable: Les courants philosophiques, littéraires et artistiques en occident au milieu du XIIe siècle*, ed. by René Louis et al. (Paris: Éditions du CNRS, 1975), pp. 279–86; repr. in *Le Moyen Âge retrouvé: De l'an mil à l'an 1200*, ed. by Louis Grodecki (Paris: Flammarion, 1986), pp. 217–22.

Große, Rolf, 'L'abbé Adam, prédécesseur de Suger', in *Suger en question: Regards croisés sur Saint-Denis*, ed. by Rolf Große (Munich: Oldenbourg, 2004), pp. 31–43.

Grundmann, Herbert, *Geschichtsschreibung im Mittelalter: Gattungen, Epochen, Eigenart*, 3rd ed. (Göttingen: Vandenhoeck & Ruprecht, 1978).

Guenée, Bernard, 'Chancelleries et monastères: La mémoire de la France au Moyen Âge', in *Les Lieux de mémoire*, ed. by Pierre Nora, 3 vols. (Paris: Gallimard, 1984–92), II, 5–30.

——, 'Chanceries and Monasteries', tr. by Deke Dusinberre, in *Rethinking France: Les Lieux de mémoire*, ed. by Pierre Nora and tr. by David P. Jordan, 4 vols. (Chicago, IL: University of Chicago Press, 1999-2010), IV, 1-26.

——, *Histoire et culture historique dans l'Occident medieval* (Paris: Aubier-Montaigne, 1980).

Guiliano, Zachary, *The Homiliary of Paul the Deacon: Religious and Cultural Reform in Carolingian Europe* (Turnhout: Brepols, 2021).

Gullick, Michael, 'A Foundation Book? Three Twelfth-Century Booklets', in *Foundation Documents from St Mary's Abbey, York 1085-1137*, ed. by Richard Sharpe et al. (Woodbridge: Boydell, 2022), pp. 1-10.

——, 'How Fast did Scribes Write? Evidence from Romanesque Manuscripts', in *Making the Medieval Book: Techniques of Production*, ed. by Linda L. Brownrigg (Los Altos Hills, CA: Anderson Lovelace, 1995), pp. 39-58.

——, 'Self Referential Artist and Scribe Portraits in Romanesque Manuscripts', in *Pen in Hand: Medieval Scribal Portraits, Colophons and Tools*, ed. by Michael Gullick (Walkern: Red Gull Press, 2006), pp. 97-114.

Gullotta, Giuseppe, *Gli antichi cataloghi e i codici della abbazia di Nonantola* (Vatican City: Biblioteca Apostolica Vaticana, 1955).

Gumbert, Johan P., 'Egberts geschenken aan Egmond', in *In het spoor van Egbert: Aartsbisschop Egbert van Trier, de bibliotheek en geschiedschrijving van het klooster Egmond*, ed. by Georgius N. M. Vis (Hilversum: Verloren, 1997), pp. 25-43.

——, 'The Speed of Scribes', in *Scribi e colofoni: Le sottoscrizioni di copisti dalle origini all'avvento della stampa*, ed. by Emma Condello and Giuseppe de Gregorio (Spoleto: Centro italiano di studi sull'alto medioevo, 1995), pp. 57-69.

Gunton, Simon, *The History of the Church of Peterburgh* (London: Chiswell, 1686).

Haarländer, Stephanie, 'Welcher Bonifatius soll es sein? Bemerkungen zu den Vitae Bonifatii', in *Bonifatius: Leben und Nachwirken (754-2004)*, ed. by Franz J. Felten et al. (Mainz: Gesellschaft für mittelrheinische Kirchengeschichte, 2007), pp. 353-61.

Hägele, Günter, 'Melker Reform und Buchdruck: Zur Druckerei im Augsburger Benediktinerkloster St. Ulrich und Afra', in *Reformen vor der Reformation: Sankt Ulrich und Afra*, ed. by Gisela Drossbach and Klaus Wolf (Berlin: De Gruyter, 2018), pp. 187-204.

Hägermann, Dieter, 'Der Abt als Grundherr: Kloster und Wirtschaft im frühen Mittelalter', in *Herrschaft und Kirche: Beiträge zur Entstehung und Wirkungsweise episkopaler und monastischer Organisationsformen*, ed. by Friedrich Prinz (Stuttgart: Hiersemann, 1988), pp. 345-85.

Hahn, Heinrich, 'Die drei Vorgängerbauten des Fuldaer Domes', *Fuldaer Geschichtsblätter* 61 (1985), 180-202.

Hamburger, Jeffrey F., *The Birth of the Author: Pictorial Prefaces in Glossed Books of the Twelfth Century* (Toronto: Pontifical Institute of Mediaeval Studies, 2021).

Handwerker, Otto, 'Dreihundert Jahre Würzburger Universitätsbibliothek, 1619-1919', in *Aus der Vergangenheit der Universität Würzburg*, ed. by Max Buchner (Berlin: Springer, 1932), pp. 102-33.

Hardwick, Charles and Henry Luard, eds., *A Catalogue of the Manuscripts Preserved in the Library of the University of Cambridge*, 6 vols. (Cambridge: Cambridge University Press, 1856-67).

Harris, Jennifer A., 'The Bible and the Meaning of History in the Middle Ages', in *The Practice of the Bible in the Middle Ages: Production, Reception, and Performance in Western Christianity*, ed. by Susan Boynton and Diane J. Reilly (New York, NY: Columbia University Press, 2011), pp. 84-104.

Härtel, Helmar, 'Die Bibliothek des Godehardiklosters in Hildesheim', in *Der Schatz von Sankt Godehard*, ed. by Michael Brandt, 2nd ed. (Hildesheim: Diözesan-Museum, 1988), pp. 28–31.
Hartmann, Martina, '*Concubina vel regina*: Zu einigen Ehefrauen und Konkubinen der karolingischen Könige', *Deutsches Archiv für Erforschung des Mittelalters* 63 (2007), 545–68.
——, *Studien zu den Briefen Abt Wibalds von Stablo und Corvey sowie zur Briefliteratur in der frühen Stauferzeit* (Hanover: Hahn, 2011).
Haye, Thomas, *Verlorenes Mittelalter: Ursachen und Muster der Nichtüberlieferung mittellateinischer Literatur* (Leiden: Brill, 2016).
Hayward, Paul A., 'Chronicles of Gloucester Abbey', in *The Encyclopedia of the Medieval Chronicle*, ed. by R. Graeme Dunphy, 2 vols. (Leiden: Brill, 2020), I, 341–2.
——, 'William of Malmesbury as a Cantor-Historian', in *Medieval Cantors and Their Craft: Music, Liturgy and the Shaping of History, 800–1500*, ed. by Margot E. Fassler et al. (Woodbridge: Boydell, 2017), pp. 222–39.
Head, Thomas, *Hagiography and the Cult of Saints: The Diocese of Orléans, 800–1200* (Cambridge: Cambridge University Press, 1990).
Heale, Martin, *The Abbots and Priors of Late Medieval and Renaissance England* (Oxford: Oxford University Press, 2016).
Healy, Patrick, 'Hugh of Flavigny and Canon Law as Polemic in the Investiture Contest', *Zeitschrift der Savigny-Stiftung für Rechtsgeschichte: Kanonistische Abteilung* 91 (2005), 17–58.
——, *The Chronicle of Hugh of Flavigny: Reform and the Investiture Contest in the Late Eleventh Century* (Aldershot: Ashgate, 2006).
Heath, Anne, 'Elevating Saint Germanus of Auxerre: Architecture, Politics, and Liturgy in the Reclaiming of Monastic Identity', *Speculum* 90 (2015), 60–113.
Heath, Christopher, *The Narrative Worlds of Paul the Deacon: Between Empires and Identities in Lombard Italy* (Amsterdam: Amsterdam University Press, 2017).
Heinzer, Felix, 'Buchkultur und Bibliotheksgeschichte Hirsaus', in *Klosterreform und mittelalterliche Buchkultur im deutschen Südwesten*, ed. by Felix Heinzer (Leiden: Brill, 2008), pp. 85–167.
——, 'Ego Reginbertus scriptor'–Reichenauer Büchersorge als Spiegel karolingischer Reformprogrammatik', in *Klosterreform und mittelalterliche Buchkultur im deutschen Südwesten* (Leiden: Brill, 2008), pp. 17–31.
Heller, Dominicus, *Die ältesten Geschichtsschreiber des Klosters Fulda* (Fulda: Parzeller, 1952).
Helvétius, Anne-Marie, 'Pour une biographie de Gisèle, sœur de Charlemagne, abbesse de Chelles', in *Splendor Reginae: Passions, genre et famille. Mélanges en l'honneur de Régine Le Jan*, ed. by Laurent Jégou et al. (Turnhout: Brepols, 2015), pp. 161–7.
Hemmen, Wilhelm, 'Der Brief des Magisters Manegold an Abt Wibald von Corvey (1149)', in *Von der Domschule zum Gymnasium in Paderborn*, ed. by Klemens Honselmann (Paderborn: Bonifatius, 1962), pp. 79–105.
Hen, Yitzhak, 'Gender and the Patronage of Culture in Merovingian Gaul', in *Gender in the Early Medieval World: East and West, 300–900*, ed. by Leslie Brubaker and Julia M. H. Smith (Cambridge: Cambridge University Press, 2004), pp. 217–33.
Henley, Georgia, 'Geoffrey of Monmouth and the Conventions of History Writing in Early 12th-Century England', in *A Companion to Geoffrey of Monmouth*, ed. by Georgia Henley and Joshua B. Smith (Leiden: Brill, 2020), pp. 291–314.
Herbst, Hermann, 'Niedersächsische Geschichtsschreibung unter dem Einfluss der Bursfelder Reform', *Jahrbuch des Braunschweigischen Geschichtsvereins* 5 (1933), 74–94.

Herding, Otto, 'Johannes Trithemius (1462-1516) als Geschichtsschreiber des Klosters Hirsau', in *Beiträge zur südwestdeutschen Historiographie*, ed. by Otto Herding and Dieter Mertens (Stuttgart: Kohlhammer, 2005), pp. 63-9.

Hermann, Fritz, 'Verkauf von Handschriften aus Arnsburg nach Maulbronn im Jahr 1439', *Zentralblatt für Bibliothekswesen* 37 (1920), 80-4.

Herrick, Samantha K., 'Introduction', in *Hagiography and the History of Latin Christendom, 500-1500*, ed. by Samantha K. Herrick (Leiden: Brill, 2019), pp. 1-10.

Herrin, Judith, *Ravenna: Capital of Empire, Crucible of Europe* (New Haven, CT: Yale University Press, 2020).

Hesse, Ludwig F., 'Die Klosterbibliothek in Blaubeuren', *Serapeum* 18 (1857), 59-62.

Hexter, Ralph and David Townsend, eds., *The Oxford Handbook of Medieval Latin Literature* (Oxford: Oxford University Press, 2012).

Hingst, Amanda J., *The Written World: Past and Place in the Work of Orderic Vitalis* (Notre Dame, IN: University of Notre Dame Press, 2009).

Hlawitschka, Eduard, 'Textkritisches zur Series abbatum Flaviniacensium', in *Landschaft und Geschichte: Festschrift für Franz Petri zu seinem 65. Geburtstag*, ed. by Georg Droege et al. (Bonn: Röhrscheid, 1970), pp. 250-65.

Hodgson, Victoria, 'History and Hagiography: The *Vita Sancti Servani* and the Foundation of Culross Abbey', *Downside Review* 139 (2021), 65-81.

Hoffmann, Hartmut, 'Die älteren Abtslisten von Montecassino', *Quellen und Forschungen aus italienischen Archiven und Bibliotheken* 47 (1967), 224-354.

——, 'Studien zur Chronik von Montecassino', *Deutsches Archiv für Erforschung des Mittelalters* 29 (1973), 59-162.

——, 'Zu den *Annales Quedlinburgenses*', *Sachsen und Anhalt* 27 (2015), 139-78.

——, *Untersuchungen zur karolingischen Annalistik* (Bonn: Röhrscheid, 1958).

Holder, Alfred and Karl Preisendanz, eds., *Die Reichenauer Handschriften: Neudruck mit bibliographischen Nachträgen*, 3 vols. (Wiesbaden: Harrassowitz, 1970-3).

Holdsworth, Christopher, 'Dryburgh, Adam of (c.1140-1212?)', *Oxford Dictionary of National Biography* (Oxford: Oxford University Press, 2004), https://doi.org/10.1093/ref:odnb/97.

Holsinger, Bruce, On Parchment: Animals, Archives, and the Making of Culture from Herodotus to the Digital Age (New Haven, CT: Yale University Press, 2022).

Hotchin, Julie, '*Reformatrices* and Their Books: Religious Women and Reading Networks in Fifteenth-Century Germany', in *Communities of Learning: Networks and the Shaping of Intellectual Identity in Europe, 1100-1500*, ed. by Constant J. Mews and John N. Crossley (Turnhout: Brepols, 2011), pp. 251-91.

Houben, Hubert, 'L'autore delle "Vitae quatuor priorum abbatum Cavensium"', *Studi medievali* 26 (1985), 871-9.

Hourlier, Jacques, *Saint Odilon, abbé de Cluny* (Louvain: Bibliothèque de l'Université, 1964).

Howe, John, 'The Hagiography of Saint-Wandrille (Fontenelle) (Province of Haute-Normandie)', in *L'hagiographie du haut Moyen Âge en Gaule du Nord: Manuscrits, textes et centres de production*, ed. by Martin Heinzelmann (Stuttgart: Thorbecke, 2001), pp. 127-92.

Howell, Margaret, 'Abbatial Vacancies and the Divided *Mensa* in Medieval England', *Journal of Ecclesiastical History* 33 (1982), 173-92.

Hucker, Bernd U., 'Die Chronik Arnolds von Lübeck als "Historia regum"', *Deutsches Archiv für Erforschung des Mittelalters* 44 (1988), 98-119.

Hudson, John, 'The Abbey of Abingdon, Its Chronicle and the Norman Conquest', *Anglo-Norman Studies* 19 (1997), 181-202.

Hummer, Hans, 'Die merowingische Herkunft der *Vita Sadalbergae*', *Deutsches Archiv für Erforschung des Mittelalters* 59 (2003), 459-93.

Hunt, Richard W., 'The Library of the Abbey of St Albans', in *Medieval Scribes, Manuscripts and Libraries: Essays Presented to N. R. Ker*, ed. by Malcolm B. Parkes and Andrew G. Watson (London: Scolar, 1978), pp. 251-77.

Hunt, William and Henry Mayr-Harting, 'Nothhelm (Nothelm) (d. 739)', *Oxford Dictionary of National Biography* (Oxford: Oxford University Press, 2004), https://doi.org/10.1093/ref:odnb/20368.

Huygens, Robert B. C., 'Idungus', in *Die deutsche Literatur des Mittelalters-Verfasserlexikon*, ed. by Burghart Wachinger et al., 2nd rev. ed., 14 vols. (Berlin: De Gruyter, 1977-2008), IV, 362-4.

——, *La tradition manuscrite de Guibert de Nogent* (Steenbrugge: In Abbatia S. Petri, 1991).

Huynes, Jean, *Histoire générale de l'abbaye du Mont Saint-Michel au péril de la mer*, 2 vols. (Rouen: Le Brument, 1872-3).

Illuminated Manuscripts in the Bodleian Library Oxford, ed. by Otto Pächt and J. J. G. Alexander, 3 vols. (Oxford: Oxford University Press, 1966-73).

Imhof, Michael, 'Bischofssitze, Kirchen, Klöster und Pfalzen im Umkreis Karls des Großen', in *Karl der Große: Leben und Wirkung, Kunst und Architektur*, ed. by Michael Imhof and Christoph Winterer, 2nd ed. (Petersberg: Imhof, 2013), pp. 118-236.

Ineichen-Eder, Christine E., 'Künstlerische und literarische Tätigkeit des Candidus-Brun von Fulda', *Fuldaer Geschichtsblätter* 56 (1980), 201-17.

Inglis, Erik, 'Remembering and Forgetting Suger at Saint-Denis, 1151-1534: An Abbot's Reputation between Memory and History', *Gesta* 54 (2015), 219-43.

Innes, Matthew J., 'Keeping It in the Family: Women and Aristocratic Memory, 700-1200', in *Medieval Memories: Men, Women and the Past, 700-1300*, ed. by Elisabeth M. C. van Houts (London: Harlow, 2001), pp. 17-35.

Inventaire des manuscrits de la Bibliothèque d'Orléans: Fonds de Fleury, ed. by Charles Cuissard (Paris: Herluison, 1885).

Iogna-Prat, Dominique, *Agni Immaculati: Recherches sur les sources hagiographiques relatives à saint Maieul de Cluny (954-994)* (Paris: Éditions du Cerf, 1988).

Jacobsen, Werner, 'Die Abteikirche in Fulda von Sturmius bis Eigil-kunstpolitische Positionen und deren Veränderungen', in *Kloster Fulda in der Welt der Karolinger und Ottonen*, ed. by Gangolf Schrimpf (Frankfurt a. M.: Knecht, 1993), pp. 105-27.

——, 'Die Klosterresidenz im frühen und hohen Mittelalter', in *Wohn- und Wirtschaftsbauten frühmittelalterlicher Klöster*, ed. by Hans R. Sennhauser (Zurich: Hochschulverlag, 1996), pp. 59-68.

Jahner, Jennifer et al., 'General Introduction', in *Medieval Historical Writing: Britain and Ireland, 500-1500*, ed. by Jennifer Jahner et al. (Cambridge: Cambridge University Press, 2019), pp. 1-15.

Jahner, Jennifer et al., eds., *Medieval Historical Writing: Britain and Ireland, 500-1500* (Cambridge: Cambridge University Press, 2019).

Jakobi, Franz-Josef, *Wibald von Stablo und Corvey (1098-1158): Benediktinischer Abt in der frühen Stauferzeit* (Münster, Aschendorff, 1979).

James, Montague R., *The Ancient Libraries of Canterbury and Dover* (Cambridge: Cambridge University Press, 1903).

Jaspert, Bernd, *Die Regula Benedicti- Regula Magistri-Kontroverse* (Hildesheim: Gerstenberg, 1977).

Jebe, Johanna, 'Bücherverzeichnisse als Quellen der Wissensorganisation: Ordnungspraktiken und Wissensordnungen in den karolingerzeitlichen Klöstern Lorsch und St. Gallen', in *Die Bibliothek–The Library–La Bibliothèque: Denkräume und Wissensordnungen*, ed. by Andreas Speer and Lars Reuke (Berlin: De Gruyter, 2020), pp. 1–28.

——, 'Reform als Bedrohung? Diagnosen aus der Fuldaer Mönchsgemeinschaft im Spiegel des *Supplex libellus* und der *Vita Sturmi*', in *Les communautés menacées au haut Moyen Âge (vie–xie siècles)*, ed. by Geneviève Bührer-Thierry et al. (Turnhout: Brepols, 2021), pp. 57–79.

Jiroušková, Lenka, *Der heilige Wikingerkönig Olav Haraldson und sein hagiographisches Dossier: Text und Kontext der 'Passio Olavi' (mit kritischer Edition)*, 2 vols. (Leiden: Brill, 2014).

Joachimsen, Paul, *Geschichtsauffassung und Geschichtsschreibung in Deutschland unter dem Einfluss des Humanismus* (Stuttgart: Teubner, 1910; repr. 1968).

John, Eric, 'The Division of the Mensa in Early English Monasteries', *Journal of Ecclesiastical History* 6 (1955), 143–55.

John, James J., 'The Ex-Libris in Codices Latini Antiquiores', *Scriptorium* 50 (1996), 239–43.

Johnson, Charles, 'Waldric, the Chancellor of Henry I', *English Historical Review* 51 (1936), 103.

Jorgensen, Peter A., 'Review of Tönnes Kleberg, *Medeltida Uppsalabibliotek II: Bidrag till deras historia till 1389*', *Speculum* 50 (1975), 132–4.

Jurkowlaniec, Grażyna and Magdalena Herman, 'Introduction: People between Multiplied Things and Modified Images', in *The Reception of the Printed Image in the Fifteenth and Sixteenth Centuries: Multiplied and Modified*, ed. by Grażyna Jurkowlaniec and Magdalena Herman (New York, NY: Routledge, 2020), pp. 1–23.

Kalhous, David, *Anatomy of a Duchy: The Political and Ecclesiastical Structures of Early Přemyslid Bohemia* (Leiden: Brill, 2000).

Kantor, Jonathan, 'A Pseudo-Historical Source: The Memoirs of Abbot Guibert of Nogent', *Journal of Medieval History* 2 (1976), 281–304.

Karn, Nicholas, 'Introduction to the Foundation Narrative', in *Foundation Documents from St Mary's Abbey, York 1085–1137*, ed. by Richard Sharpe et al. (Woodbridge: Boydell, 2022), pp. 339–78.

Kathrein, Werner, 'Der Historienmaler Johann Andreas Herrlein–oder: Die Gründung des Bistums Fulda in der Historienmalerei des Johann Andreas Herrlein im Refektorium des ehemaligen Benediktinerkonvents in Fulda', *Alte und neue Kunst* 41 (2002), 138–42.

Kay, Sarah, *Courtly Contradictions: The Emergence of the Literary Object in the Twelfth Century* (Stanford, CA: Stanford University Press, 2001).

Keats-Rohan, Katherine S. B., 'Bibliothèque Municipale d'Avranches, 210: Cartulary of Mont-Saint-Michel', *Anglo-Norman Studies* 21 (1999), 95–112.

Kehl, Petra, *Kult und Nachleben des heiligen Bonifatius im Mittelalter (754–1200)* (Fulda: Parzeller, 1993).

Keller, Hagen et al., eds., *Pragmatische Schriftlichkeit im Mittelalter: Erscheinungsformen und Entwicklungsstufen* (Munich: Fink, 1992).

Kellner, Stephan, 'Die Prüfeninger Klosterbibliothek–Geschichte und Spuren', in *Die Regensburger Bibliothekslandschaft am Ende des Alten Reiches*, ed. by Manfred Knedlik and Bernhard Lübbers (Regensburg: Universitätsverlag, 2011), pp. 129–40.

Kelly, Susan E., 'Some Forgeries in the Archive of St. Augustine's Abbey, Canterbury', in *Fälschungen im Mittelalter*, ed. by Jasper Detlev, 5 vols. (Hanover: Hahn, 1988), IV, 347–69.

Kempshall, Matthew, *Rhetoric and the Writing of History, 400-1500* (Manchester: Manchester University Press, 2011).
Kennedy, Elspeth, 'The Scribe as Editor', in *Mélanges de langue et de littérature du Moyen Age et de la Renaissance offerts à Jean Frappier*, 2 vols. (Paris: Minard, 1970), I, 523-31.
Ker, Neil R., *Medieval Libraries of Great Britain: A List of Surviving Books*, 2nd ed. (London: Royal Historical Society, 1987).
Kerr, Julie, *Monastic Hospitality: The Benedictines in England, c.1070-c.1250* (Woodbridge: Boydell, 2007).
Kersken, Norbert, 'Äbte als Historiker: Klöster als Zentren der Geschichtsschreibung im Mittelalter', in *Chronicon Aulae regiae-Die Königsaaler Chronik: Eine Bestandsaufnahme*, ed. by Stefan Albrecht (Frankfurt a. M.: Peter Lang, 2013), pp. 11-62.
———, 'High and Late Medieval National Historiography', in *Historiography in the Middle Ages*, ed. by Deborah M. Deliyannis (Leiden: Brill, 2003), pp. 181-216.
Kestemont, Mike and Folgert Karsdorp, 'Estimating the Loss of Medieval Literature with an Unseen Species Model from Ecodiversity', *CEUR Workshop Proceedings* 2723 (2020), 44-55.
Kestemont, Mike et al. 'Forgotten Books: The Application of Unseen Species Models to the Survival of Culture', *Science* 375 (2022), 765-9.
Keussen, Hermann, 'Die Bibliothek des Abtes von Camp, Heinrich von der Heyden aus Calcar', in *Fontes adhuc inediti rerum Rhenanarum: Niederrheinische Chroniken*, ed. by Gottfried Eckertz, 2 vols. (Cologne: Heberle, 1870), II, 437-44.
Kirby, David P., 'Bede's Native Sources for the *Historia Ecclesiastica*', *Bulletin of the John Rylands Library* 48 (1965/6), 341-71; repr. in *Anglo-Saxon History: Basic Readings*, ed. by David A. E. Pelteret (New York, NY: Garland, 2000), pp. 55-81.
Kjær, Lars, *The Medieval Gift and the Classical Tradition: Ideals and the Performance of Generosity in Medieval England, 1100-1300* (Cambridge: Cambridge University Press, 2019).
Kleberg, Tönnes, *Medeltida Uppsalabibliotek*, 2 vols. (Uppsala: Almqvist, 1968-72).
Klemm, Elisabeth, 'Die Klostergemeinschaft von Prüfening im Spiegel ihres Schatzverzeichnisses', in *Cechy jsou plné kostelu/Boemia plena est ecclesiis*, ed. by Milada Studničková (Prague: Nakladatelství Lidové Noviny, 2010), pp. 37-44.
———, ed., *Die romanischen Handschriften der Bayerischen Staatsbibliothek*, Vol. 1: *Die Bistümer Regensburg, Passau und Salzburg* (Wiesbaden: Reichert, 1980).
Klueting, Edeltraud, 'Fromme Frauen als Chronistinnen und Historikerinnen', in *Fromme Frauen als gelehrte Frauen: Bildung, Wissenschaft und Kunst im weiblichen Religiosentum des Mittelalters und der Neuzeit*, ed. by Edeltraud Klueting and Harm Klueting (Cologne: Erzbischöfliche Diözesan- und Dombibliothek, 2010), pp. 217-30.
Kluge, Friedrich, ed., *Etymologisches Wörterbuch der deutschen Sprache*, rev. by Elmar Seebold, 25th ed. (Berlin: De Gruyter, 2011).
Knedlik, Manfred, 'Die Bibliothek des Benediktinerklosters Prüfening', in *Mönche, Künstler und Fürsten: 900 Jahre Gründung Kloster Prüfening*, ed. by Maria Baumann (Regensburg: Schnell & Steiner, 2009), pp. 89-104.
Knowles, David and R. Neville Hadcock, *Medieval Religious Houses: England and Wales*, 2nd ed. (London: Longman, 1971).
Knowles, David et al., eds., *The Heads of Religious Houses: England and Wales*, Vol. 1: *940-1216*, 2nd ed. (Cambridge: Cambridge University Press, 2001).
Knowles, David, *The Monastic Order in England: A History of Its Development from the Times of St Dunstan to the Fourth Lateran Council, 940-1216*, 2nd ed. (Cambridge: Cambridge University Press, 1966).

——, *The Religious Orders in England*, 2 vols. (Cambridge: Cambridge University Press, 1948–55).
Kochskämper, Birgit, 'Die germanistische Mediävistik und das Geschlechterverhältnis: Forschungen und Perspektiven', in *Germanistische Mediävistik*, ed. by Volker Honemann and Tomas Tomasek (Münster: LIT, 2000), pp. 309–52.
Kortüm, Hans-Henning, 'Silvester II.', in *Neue Deutsche Biographie*, 28 vols. (Berlin: Duncker & Humblot, 1953–2023), XXIV, 415–16.
Krah, Adelheid, *Die Entstehung der 'potestas regia' im Westfrankenreich während der ersten Regierungsjahre Kaiser Karls II. (840–877)* (Berlin: Akademie Verlag, 2001).
Kramer, Waldemar, *Johannes Parsimonius: Leben und Wirken des zweiten evangelischen Abtes von Hirsau (1525–1588)* (Frankfurt a. M.: Kramer, 1980).
Krautheimer, Richard, 'The Carolingian Revival of Early Christian Architecture', *Art Bulletin* 24 (1942), 1–38.
Krönert, Klaus, 'La production hagiographique en Germanie à l'époque de Louis le Pieux: Productivité littéraire et crises, mais quel rapport?', in *Politische Kultur und Textproduktion unter Ludwig dem Frommen/Culture politique et production littéraire sous Louis le Pieux*, ed. by Martin Gravel and Sören Kaschke (Ostfildern: Thorbecke, 2019), pp. 269–373.
Krumm, Markus, *Herrschaftsumbruch und Historiographie: Zeitgeschichtsschreibung als Krisenbewältigung bei Alexander von Telese und Falco von Benevent* (Berlin: De Gruyter, 2021).
Krümmel, Achim, *Das 'Supplementum chronicarum' des Augustinermönches Jacobus Philippus Foresti von Bergamo: Eine der ältesten Bilderchroniken und ihre Wirkungsgeschichte* (Herzberg: Bautz, 1992).
L'écriture pragmatique: Un concept d'histoire médiévale à l'échelle européenne (2012) [= *Cahiers électroniques d'histoire textuelle du LAMOP* V], https://archive-2013-2016.lamop.fr/spip.php%3Frubrique261.html.
La France romane au temps des premiers Capétiens (987–1152), ed. by Danielle Gaborit-Chopin et al. (Paris: Musée du Louvre Éditions, 2005).
Labusiak, Thomas, 'Benediktinische Buchmalerei: Die Macht der Bilder', in *Macht des Wortes: Benediktinisches Mönchtum im Spiegel Europas*, ed. by Gerfried Sitar et al., 2 vols. (Regensburg: Schnell & Steiner, 2009), I, 303–15.
Lambert, Peter and Björn Weiler, eds., *How the Past Was Used: Historical Cultures, c.750–2000* (Oxford: Oxford University Press, 2018).
Lapidge, Michael, 'Surviving Book Lists from Anglo-Saxon England', in *Learning and Literature in Anglo-Saxon England*, ed. by Michael Lapidge and Hemlut Gneuss (Cambridge: Cambridge University Press, 1985), pp. 33–89; repr. and rev. in *Anglo-Saxon Manuscripts: Basic Readings*, ed. by Mary P. Richards (New York, NY: Routledge, 1994), pp. 87–167.
——, *The Anglo-Saxon Library* (Oxford: Oxford University Press, 2006).
Lapina, Elizabeth, '"Nec signis nec testibus creditur...": The Problem of Eyewitnesses in the Chronicles of the First Crusade', *Viator* 38 (2007), 117–39.
Lawo, Mathias, 'Hugo von Flavigny und die lateinische Dichtkunst', in *Latin Culture in the Eleventh Century*, ed. by Michael W. Herren et al., 2 vols. (Turnhout: Brepols, 2002) II, 34–50.
——, *Studien zu Hugo von Flavigny* (Hanover: Hahn, 2010).
Leader, Anne, *The Badia of Florence: Art and Observance in a Renaissance Monastery* (Bloomington, IN: Indiana University Press, 2012).

Lecouteux, Stéphane et al., eds., *La bibliothèque et les archives de l'abbaye de la Sainte-Trinité de Fécamp: Splendeur et dispersion des manuscrits et des chartes d'une prestigieuse abbaye bénédictine normande*, Vol. 1: *La bibliothèque et les archives au Moyen Âge* (Fécamp: Amis du Vieux Fécamp et du Pays de Caux, 2021).

Lecouteux, Stéphane, 'À la recherche des livres du Bec (première partie)', in *Sur les pas de Lanfranc, du Bec à Caen: Recueil d'études en hommage à Véronique Gazeau*, ed. by Pierre Bauduin et al. (Caen: Presses universitaires de Caen, 2018), pp. 267–77.

——, 'Écrire l'histoire des abbés du Mont Saint-Michel, 2: Robert de Torigni, ses outils, ses sources et sa méthode de travail', *Tabularia* (2018), 1–68, https://doi.org/10.4000/tabularia.2973.

——, 'L'abbé Geoffroy de Vendôme (1093–1132), initiateur des Annales de Vendôme?', *Cahiers de Civilisation Médiévale* 52 (2009), 37–43.

——, 'L'Archétype et le stemma des annales angevines et vendômoises', *Revue d'histoire des textes* 3 (2008), 229–61.

Ledru, Thomas, 'Hariulf de Saint-Riquier: Un moine historien de la fin du XIe siècle', *Faire de l'histoire au Moyen Âge* 36 (2017), 19–41.

Lees, Clare A., 'Gender and the Subjects of History in the Early Middle Ages', in *Medieval Historical Writing: Britain and Ireland, 500–1500*, ed. by Jennifer Jahner et al. (Cambridge: Cambridge University Press, 2019), pp. 299–318.

Legner, Anton, ed., Ornamenta Ecclesiae: *Kunst und Künstler der Romanik*, 3 vols. (Cologne: Schnütgen-Museum, 1985).

Lehfeldt, Elizabeth A., 'Authority and Agency: Women as Heads of Religious Houses', in *Medieval Women Religious, c.800–c.1500: New Perspectives*, ed. by Kimm Curran and Janet Burton (Woodbridge: Boydell, 2023), pp. 105–20.

Lehmann, Edgar, *Die Bibliotheksräume der deutschen Klöster im Mittelalter* (Berlin: Akademie, 1957).

Lehmann, Paul, 'Fulda und die antike Literatur', in *Aus Fuldas Geistesleben: Festschrift zum 150 jährigen Jubiläum der Landesbibliothek Fulda*, ed. by Joseph Theele (Fulda: Fuldaer Actiendruckerei, 1928), pp. 9–23.

——, 'Nachrichten von der Sponheimer Bibliothek des Abtes Johannes Trithemius', in *Festgabe zum 7. September 1910: Hermann Grauert zur Vollendung des 60. Lebensjahres gewidmet von seinen Schülern*, ed. by Max Jansen (Freiburg i. Br.: Herder, 1910), pp. 205–20.

——, 'Quot et quorum libri fuerint in libraria Fuldensi', in *Bok- och bibliotekshistoriska Studier: Tillägnade Isak Collijn på hans 50-årsdagpp*, ed. by Axel Nelson (Uppsala: Almqvist & Wiksells, 1925), pp. 47–57.

——, 'The Benedictine Order and the Transmission of the Literature of Ancient Rome in the Middle Ages', *Downside Review* 71 (1953), 407–2.

Leitschuh, Franz F., 'Trithemius und Dürer' [= *Quellen und Studien zur Geschichte des Kunst- und Geisteslebens in Franken I*], *Archiv des historischen Vereins von Unterfranken und Aschaffenburg* 44 (1902), 185–95.

Leitschuh, Friedrich, ed., *Katalog der Handschriften der königlichen Bibliothek zu Bamberg*, 4 vols. (Bamberg: Buchner, 1895–1966).

Lesne, Émile, *L'origine des menses dans le temporel des eglises et des monasteres de France au IXe siecle* (Lille: Giard, 1910).

Licence, Tom, 'A New Source for the *Vita Ædwardi Regis*', *Journal of Medieval Latin* 29 (2019), 1–19.

——, 'The Date and Authorship of the *Vita Ædwardi Regis*', *Anglo-Saxon England* 44 (2016), 259–85.

Lifshitz, Felice, 'Beyond Positivism and Genre: "Hagiographical" Texts as Historical Narrative', *Viator* 25 (1994), 95–113.

——, 'Is Mother Superior? Towards a History of Feminine *Amtscharisma*', in *Medieval Mothering*, ed. by John C. Parsons and Bonnie Wheeler (New York, NY: Routledge, 1996), pp. 117–38.

——, 'Still Useless after All These Years: The Concept of "Hagiography" in the Twenty-First Century', in *Writing Normandy: Stories of Saints and Rulers*, ed. by Felice Lifshitz (London: Routledge, 2020), pp. 26–46.

——, *Religious Women in Early Carolingian Francia: A Study of Manuscript Transmission and Monastic Culture* (New York, NY: Fordham University Press, 2014).

——, *The Norman Conquest of Pious Neustria: Historiographic Discourse and Saintly Relics, 684–1090* (Toronto: Pontifical Institute of Mediaeval Studies, 1995).

Loud, Graham A., 'Monastic Chronicles in the Twelfth-Century Abruzzi', *Anglo-Norman Studies* 27 (2005), 101–31.

——, 'Review of Kriston R. Rennie, *The Destruction and Recovery of Monte Cassino, 529–1964*', *Catholic Historical Review* 108 (2020), 602–3.

——, 'The Posthumous Reputation of Abbot Peter of Cava', in *Medioevo e Mediterraneo: Incontri, scambi e confronti. Studi per Salvatore Fodale*, ed. by Patrizia Sardina et al. (Palermo: Palermo University Press, 2020), pp. 389–403.

——, *The Social World of the Abbey of Cava, c.1020–1300* (Woodbridge: Boydell, 2021).

Love, Rosalind, 'The Library of the Venerable Bede', in *The Cambridge History of the Book in Britain*, Vol. 1: *c.400–1100*, ed. by Richard Gameson (Cambridge: Cambridge University Press, 2011), pp. 606–32.

Lowe, Elias A., ed., *Codices Latini Antiquiores*, 12 vols. (Oxford: Clarendon, 1934–82).

Lübeck, Konrad, 'Die Exemtion des Klosters Fulda bis zur Mitte des 11. Jahrhunderts', *Studien und Mitteilungen zur Geschichte des Benediktinerordens und seiner Zweige* 55 (1937), 132–53.

Lucile Tran-Duc, 'Une entreprise hagiographique au XIe siècle dans l'abbaye de Fontenelle: Le renouveau du culte de saint Vulfran', *Tabularia* (2008), https://doi.org/10.4000/tabularia.690.

Luxford, Julian M., *The Art and Architecture of English Benedictine Monasteries, 1300–1540* (Woodbridge: Boydell, 2012).

Machilek, Franz, 'Geschichtsschreibung im und über das Kloster Michaelsberg unter besonderer Berücksichtigung der Memoria Bischof Ottos des Heiligen', in *Im Schutz des Engels: 1000 Jahre Kloster Michaelsberg Bamberg, 1015–2015*, ed. by Norbert Jung and Holger Kempkens (Petersberg: Imhof, 2015), pp. 306–25.

Madicott, John R., 'Birth and Setting of the Ballads', *English Historical Review* 93 (1978), 276–99; repr. in *Robin Hood: An Anthology of Scholarship and Criticism*, ed. by Stephen Knight (Woodbridge: Brewer, 1999), pp. 233–55.

Magnusson, Roberta J., *Water Technology in the Middle Ages: Cities, Monasteries, and Waterworks after the Roman Empire* (Baltimore, MD: Johns Hopkins University Press, 2001).

Mairhofer, Daniela, ed., *Medieval Manuscripts from Würzburg in the Bodleian Library* (Chicago, IL: University of Chicago Press, 2014).

Manaresi, Cesare, 'Il "Liber instrumentorum seu Chronicorum monasterii Casauriensis" della Nazionale di Parigi', *Istituto lombardo di scienze e lettere, rendiconti della Classe de lettere* 80 (1946/7), 29–62.

Mancia, Lauren, *Emotional Monasticism: Affective Piety in the Eleventh-Century Monastery of John of Fécamp* (Manchester: Manchester University Press, 2018).

Maniaci, Marilena, 'Quantificare la produzione manoscritta del passato: Ambizioni, rischi, illusioni di una "bibliometria storica globale"', *IASLonline* (2013), http://www.iaslonline.de/index.php?vorgang_id=3567.

Manitius, Max, *Geschichte der lateinischen Literatur des Mittelalters*, 3 vols. (Munich: Beck, 1923-31).

Mannheim, Karl, 'The Problem of Generations', in *Essays on the Sociology of Knowledge*, ed. by Karl Mannheim and Paul Kecskemeti (London: Routledge, 1952; repr. 1972), pp. 276-322.

——, ' Das Problem der Generationen', in *Wissenssoziologie: Auswahl aus dem* Werk, ed. by Karl Mannheim and Kurt H. Wolff (Berlin: Luchterhand, 1964), pp. 509-65.

Maquet, Julien, 'Wibald, un "Cicéron chrétien"? Les connaissances juridiques et la pratique judiciaire d'un grand abbé d'Empire (†1158)', in *Wibald en questions: Un grand abbé lotharingien du XIIe siècle. D'or et de parchemin*, ed. by Albert Lemeunier and Nicolas Schroeder (Stavelot: Abbaye de Stavelot, 2010), pp. 33-42.

Martène, Edmond, *Histoire de l'abbaye de Marmoutier*, 2 vols. (Tours: Guilland-Verger, 1874-5).

Mayr-Harting, Henry, *Ottonian Book Illumination: An Historical Study*, 2 vols., 2nd ed. (London: Harvey Miller, 1999).

McCarthy, Thomas J., *The Continuations of Frutolf of Michelsberg's Chronicle* (Wiesbaden: Harrassowitz, 2018).

McClendon, Charles B., *The Origins of Medieval Architecture: Building in Europe, A.D. 600-900* (New Haven, CT: Yale University Press, 2005).

McCready, William D., 'Leo of Ostia, the Montecassino Chronicle, and the Dialogues of Abbot Desiderius', *Mediaeval Studies* 62 (2000), 125-60.

McGrady, Deborah, 'Challenging the Patronage Paradigm: Late-Medieval Francophone Writers and the Poet-Prince Relationship', in *The Oxford Handbook of Chaucer*, ed. by Suzanne C. Akbari and James Simpson (Oxford: Oxford University Press, 2020), pp. 270-85.

——, 'Introduction: Rethinking the Boundaries of Patronage', *Digital Philology: A Journal of Medieval Cultures* 2 (2013), 145-54.

McGuire, Brian P., *Friendship and Community: The Monastic Experience, 350-1250*, new ed. (Ithaca, NY: Cornell University Press, 2010).

McKitterick, Rosamond, 'Anglo-Saxon Links with Rome and the Franks in the Light of the Würzburg Book-List', in *Manuscripts in the Anglo-Saxon Kingdoms: Cultures and Connections*, ed. by Claire Breay et al. (Dublin: Four Courts Press, 2021), pp. 86-97.

——, 'Carolingian Book Production: Some Problems', *The Library* 12 (1990), 1-33.

——, 'Charles the Bald (823-877) and His Library: The Patronage of Learning', *English Historical Review* 95 (1980), 28-47.

——, 'Frauen und Schriftlichkeit im Frühmittelalter', in *Weibliche Lebensgestaltung im frühen Mittelalter*, ed. by Hans-Werner Goetz (Cologne: Böhlau, 1991), pp. 65-118.

——, 'Nun's Scriptoria in England and Francia in the Eighth Century', *Francia* 19 (1992), 1-35.

——, 'Rome and the Popes in the Construction of Institutional History and Identity in the Early Middle Ages: The Case of Leiden, Universiteitsbibliotheek, Scaliger MS 49', in *Rome and Religion in the Medieval World: Studies in Honour of Thomas F. X. Noble*, ed. by Valerie L. Garver and Own M. Phelan (Farnham: Ashgate, 2014), pp. 207-34.

——, *Charlemagne: The Formation of a European Identity* (Cambridge: Cambridge University Press, 2008).

——, *History and Memory in the Carolingian World* (Cambridge: Cambridge University Press, 2004), pp. 140-1 and 155-7.
——, *Rome and the Invention of the Papacy: The* Liber pontificalis (Cambridge: Cambridge University Press, 2020).
McMonagle, M. Xavier, 'Service of Authority: The Abbot in the Rule of Benedict', *Cistercian Studies* 17 (1982), 316-37.
McNally, Robert E., *The Bible in the Early Middle Ages* (Westminster: Newman, 1959).
McNamara, Jo A., 'Caesaria II, Abbess of Saint Jean of Arles (ca. 550)', in *Sainted Women of the Dark Ages*, ed. by Jo A. McNamara et al. (Durham, NC: Duke University Press, 1992), p. 112-18.
Meeder, Sven, 'Monte Cassino's Network of Knowledge: The Earliest Manuscript Evidence', in *Writing the Early Medieval West: Studies in Honour of Rosamond McKitterick*, ed. by Elina Scree and Charles West (Cambridge: Cambridge University Press, 2018), pp. 131-45.
Mégier, Elisabeth, 'Jesus Christ, a Protagonist of Anglo-Norman History? History and Theology in Orderic Vitalis's *Historia ecclesiastica*', in *Orderic Vitalis: Life, Works and Interpretations*, ed. by Charles C. Rozier et al. (Woodbridge: Boydell, 2016), pp. 260-83.
Melleville, Maximilien, *Histoire de la ville et des sires de Coucy-le-chateau* (Laon: Journal de l'Aisne, 1848).
Melot, Michel, *Histoire de l'abbaye de Fontevraud-Notre-Dame-des-pleurs, 1101-1793* (Paris: CNRS Éditions, 2022).
Melville, Gert, 'The Institutionalization of Religious Orders (Twelfth and Thirteenth Centuries)', in *CHMMLW*, II, 783-802.
——, *The World of Medieval Monasticism: Its History and Forms of Life* (Collegeville, MN: Cistercian Publications, 2016).
Mentzel-Reuters, Arno, 'Serielle Chronographie und historische Unschärfe: Das historiographische Spätwerk des Johannes Trithemius', in *Herbipolis: Studien zu Stadt und Hochstift Würzburg in Spätmittelalter und Früher Neuzeit*, ed. by Markus Frankl and Martina Hartmann (Würzburg: Königshausen & Neumann, 2015), pp. 373-426.
Mereminskiy, Stanislav, 'William of Malmesbury and Durham: The Circulation of Historical Knowledge in Early Twelfth-Century England', in *Discovering William of Malmesbury*, ed. by Rodney M. Thomson et al. (Woodbridge: Boydell, 2019), pp. 107-16.
Meyer zu Ermgassen, Heinrich, *Der Buchschmuck des Codex Eberhardi* (Marburg: Elwert, 2009).
Meyer, Otto, 'Überlieferung und Verbreitung des Dekrets des Bischofs Burchard von Worms', *Zeitschrift der Savigny-Stiftung für Rechtsgeschichte, Kanonistische Abteilung* 24 (1935), 141-83.
Miguel, Teresa M., 'Exchanging Books in Western Europe: A Brief History of International Interlibrary Loan', *International Journal of Legal Information* 35 (2007), 499-513.
Milward, Celia, 'The Medieval Scribe as Editor: The Case of *La Estorie del Evangelie*', *Manuscripta* 41 (1997), 155-70.
Mindermann, Arend, 'Abt Albert von Stade: Ein Chronist des 13. Jahrhunderts', in *Stupor Saxoniae inferioris: Ernst Schubert zum 60. Geburtstag*, ed. by Wiard Hinrichs et al. (Göttingen: Duehrkohp & Radicke, 2001), pp. 51-8.
Mittellateinisches Glossar, ed. by Edwin Habel and Friedrich Gröbel, 2nd ed. (Paderborn: Schöningh, 1989).
Molhuysen, Philip C., 'Cornelius Aurelius', *Nederlands archief voor kerkgeschiedenis* 2 (1902), 1-35.

Monagle, Clare, 'John of Salisbury and the Writing of History', in *A Companion to John of Salisbury*, ed. by Christophe Grellard and Frédérique Lachaud (Leiden: Brill, 2015), pp. 215–34.
Monod, Bernard, 'De la méthode historique chez Guibert de Nogent', *Revue Historique* 84 (1904), 51–70.
Mordek, Hubert, *Bibliotheca capitularium regum Francorum manuscripta: Überlieferung und Traditionszusammenhang der fränkischen Herrschererlasse* (Munich: Harrassowitz, 1995).
Morelle, Laurent, 'The Metamorphosis of Three Monastic Charter Collections in the Eleventh Century (Saint-Amand, Saint-Riquier, Montier-en-Der)', in *Charters and the Use of the Written Word in Medieval Society*, ed. by Karl Heidecker (Turnhout: Brepols, 2000), pp. 171–204.
Morrison, Karl F., 'Widukind's Mirror for a Princess: An Exercise in Self-Knowledge', in *Forschungen zur Reichs-, Papst- und Landesgeschichte: Peter Herde zum 65. Geburtstag von Freunden, Schülern und Kollege dargebracht*, ed. by Karl Borchardt and Enno Bünz, 2 vols. (Stuttgart: Hiersemann, 1998), I, 49–71.
Mortensen, Lars B., 'The Glorious Past: Entertainment, Example or History? Levels of Twelfth-Century Historical Culture', *Culture and History* 13 (1994), 57–71.
Mostert, Marco, 'La bibliothèque de Fleury-sur-Loire', in *Religion et culture autour de l'an Mil: Royaume capétien et Lotharingie*, ed. by Dominique Iogna-Prat and Jean-Charles Picard (Paris: Picard, 1990), pp. 119–23.
——, *The Library of Fleury: A Provisional List of Manuscripts* (Hilversum: Verloren, 1989).
Mötsch, Johannes and Wolfgang Seibrich, 'Sponheim', in *Die Männer- und Frauenklöster der Benediktiner in Rheinland-Pfalz und Saarland*, ed. by Friedhelm Jürgensmeier and Regina E. Schwerdtfeger [= *GB* IX] (St. Ottilien: EOS, 1999), pp. 801–27.
Mötsch, Johannes, 'Frühgeschichte, Fälschungen und Verwaltung des Klosters Sponheim zur Zeit des Trithemius', in *Johannes Trithemius (1462–1516): Abt und Büchersammler, Humanist und Geschichtsschreiber*, ed. by Klaus Arnold and Franz Fuchs (Würzburg: Königshausen & Neumann, 2019), pp. 121–31.
Muck, Georg, *Geschichte von Kloster Heilsbronn: Von der Urzeit bis zur Neuzeit*, 3 vols. (Nördlingen: Beck, 1879–80).
Mula, Stefano, 'Exempla and Historiography: Alberic of Trois-Fontaines's Reading of Caesarius's *Dialogus miraculorum*', in *The Art of Cistercian Persuasion in the Middle Ages and Beyond: Caesarius of Heisterbach's 'Dialogue on Miracles' and Its Reception*, ed. by Victoria Smirnova et al. (Leiden: Brill, 2015), pp. 143–61.
Müller, Jan-Dirk, '*Auctor–Actor–Author*: Einige Anmerkungen zum Verständnis vom Autor in lateinischen Schriften des frühen und hohen Mittelalters', in *Der Autor im Dialog: Beiträge zu Autorität und Autorschaft*, ed. by Felix P. Ingold and Wener Wunderlich (St Gall: UVK, 1995), pp. 17–31.
Müller, Norbert, 'Stiftsarchiv: Geistige Bewahrungsstätte', in *Erlesenes und Erbauliches: Kulturschaffen der Reiner Mönche*, ed. by Norbert Müller (Rein: Zisterzienserstift, 2003), pp. 103–33.
Munk Olsen, Birger, *L'étude des auteurs classiques latins aux XIe et XIIe siècles*, 4 vols. (Paris: IRHT, 1982–2009).
Muzaini, Hamzah and Brenda S. A. Yeoh, *Contested Memoryscapes: The Politics of Second World War Commemoration in Singapore* (New York, NY: Routledge, 2016), pp. 6–11.

Naus, James, 'The *Historia Iherosolimitana* of Robert the Monk and the Coronation of Louis VI', in *Writing the Early Crusades: Text, Transmission and Memory*, ed. by Marcus Bull and Damien Kempf (Woodbridge: Boydell, 2014), pp. 105-15.

Neiske, Franz, 'Charismatischer Abt oder charismatische Gemeinschaft? Die frühen Äbte Clunys', in *Charisma und religiöse Gemeinschaften im Mittelalter*, ed. by Giancarlo Andenna, Mirko Breitenstein, and Gert Melville (Münster: LIT, 2005), pp. 55-72.

Nelson, Janet L., 'Carolingian Royal Funerals', in *Rituals of Power from Late Antiquity to the Early Middle Ages*, ed. by Frans Theuws and Janet L. Nelson (Leiden: Brill, 2000), pp. 131-84.

——, 'Gender and Genre in Women Historians of the Early Middle Ages', in *L'historiographie médiévale en Europe*, ed. by Jean-Philippe Genet (Paris: Éditions du CNRS, 1999), pp. 149-63; repr. in *The Frankish World, 750-900*, ed. by Janet L. Nelson (London: Bloomsbury Academic, 1993), pp. 183-98.

Neumüllers-Klauser, Renate, 'Quellen zur Bau- und Kunstgeschichte von Hirsau', in *Hirsau St. Peter und Paul 1091-1991*, ed. by Klaus Schreiner, 2 vols. (Stuttgart: Theiss, 1991), I, 475-99.

Newton, Francis L., *The Scriptorium and Library at Monte Cassino, 1058-1105* (Cambridge: Cambridge University Press, 1999).

Nierhoff, Anna C., 'Die Hirsauer Ruhmesliste und ihre Rezeption: Zum "Chronicon Hirsaugiense" und zu den "Annales Hirsaugienses" des Johannes Trithemius', in *Johannes Trithemius (1462-1516): Abt und Büchersammler, Humanist und Geschichtsschreiber*, ed. by Klaus Arnold and Franz Fuchs (Würzburg: Königshausen & Neumann, 2019), pp. 59-96.

Niermeyer, Jan F. and Co van de Kieft, eds., *Mediae Latinitatis Lexicon minus*, rev. ed., 2 vols. (Leiden: Brill, 2002).

Niskanen, Samu, 'The Origins of the *Gesta Francorum* and Two Related Texts: Their Textual and Literary Character', *Sacris Erudiri* 51 (2012), 287-316.

——, 'William of Malmesbury as Librarian: The Evidence of his Autographs', in *Discovering William of Malmesbury*, ed. by Rodney M. Thomson et al. (Woodbridge: Boydell, 2019), pp. 117-27.

Nortier, Geneviève, *Les bibliothèques médiévales des abbayes bénédictines de Normandie*, 2nd ed. (Paris: Lethielleux, 1971).

Norton, Christopher, 'The Helmet and the Crown: The Bayeux Tapestry, Bishop Odo and William the Conqueror', *Anglo-Norman Studies* 43 (2021), 123-50.

——, 'Viewing the Bayeux Tapestry, Now and Then', *Journal of the British Archaeological Association* 172 (2019), 52-89.

O'Donnell, Thomas, '"The Ladies Have Made Me Quite Fat': Authors and Patrons at Barking Abbey', in *Barking Abbey and Medieval Literary Culture: Authorship and Authority in a Female Community*, ed. by Jennifer N. Brown and Donna A. Bussell (Woodbridge: Boydell, 2012), pp. 94-114.

O'Mara, Veronica, 'The Late Medieval English Nun and Her Scribal Activity: A Complicated Quest', in *Nuns' Literacies in Medieval Europe: The Hull Dialogue*, ed. by Virginia Blanton et el. (Turnhout: Brepols, 2013), pp. 69-93.

Oexle, Otto G., 'Die Überlieferung der fuldischen Totenannalen', in *Die Klostergemeinschaft von Fulda im früheren Mittelalter*, ed. by Karl Schmid et al., 3 vols. (Munich: Fink, 1978), II.2, 447-504.

——, 'Memorialüberlieferung und Gebetsgedächtnis in Fulda vom 8. bis zum 11. Jahrhundert', in *Die Klostergemeinschaft von Fulda im früheren Mittelalter*, ed. by Karl Schmid et al., 3 vols. (Munich: Fink, 1978), I, 136-77.

Oliva, Marilyn, 'Rendering Accounts: The Pragmatic Literacy of Nuns in Late Medieval England', in *Nuns' Literacies in Medieval Europe: The Hull Dialogue*, ed. by Virginia Blanton et el. (Turnhout: Brepols, 2013), pp. 51-68.

Omlin, Ephrem, 'Abt Frowin als Gründer der Engelberger Schreiberschule', in *Der selige Frowin von Engelberg: Ein Reformabt des 12. Jahrhunderts, 1143-1178* (Engelberg: Stiftsdruckerei, 1943), pp. 26-35 and 47-53.

Omont, Henri, 'Catalogue de la bibliothèque de l'abbé Adson de Montier-en-Der (992)', *Bibliothèque de l'École des chartes* 42 (1881), 157-60.

Orchard, Andy, 'Old Sources, New Resources: Finding the Right Formula for Boniface', *Anglo-Saxon England* 47 (2001), 15-31.

Orofino, Giulia, *I codici decorati dell'Archivio di Montecassino*, 3 vols. (Rome: Istituto poligrafico e zecca dello Stato, 1994-2006).

Oswald, Friedrich, 'Fulda, Dom', in *Vorromanische Kirchenbauten: Katalog der Denkmäler bis zum Ausgang der Ottonen*, ed. by Friedrich Oswald et al. (Munich: Prestel, 1966/71; repr. 1990), pp. 84-7.

Ott, John S., 'Writing Godfrey of Amiens: Guibert of Nogent and Nicholas of Saint-Crépin between Sanctity, Ideology, and Society', *Mediaeval Studies* 67 (2005), 317-65.

Otter, Monika, 'Baudri of Bourgueil, "To Countess Adela", *Journal of Medieval Latin* 11 (2001), 61-141.

Overgaauw, Eef A., 'Fast or Slow, Professional or Monastic: The Writing Speed of Some Late-Medieval Scribes', *Scriptorium* 49 (1995), 211-27.

Pächt, Otto and J. J. G. Alexander, eds., *Illuminated Manuscripts in the Bodleian Library Oxford*, 3 vols. (Oxford: Oxford University Press, 1966-73).

Padberg, Lutz E. V. and Thomas Klein, 'Hrabanus Maurus', in *Reallexikon der Germanischen Altertumskunde*, ed. by Heinrich Beck et al., 35 vols., 2nd ed. (Berlin: De Gryter, 1972-2008), XV, 139-46.

Pagani, Ileana, 'Ionas-Ionatus: A proposito della biografia di Giona di Bobbio', *Studi medievali* 29 (1988), 45-85.

Palmer, Nigel F., *Zisterzienser und ihre Bücher: Die mittelalterliche Bibliotheksgeschichte von Kloster Eberbach im Rheingau* (Regensburg, Schnell & Steiner, 1998).

Pansters, Krijn, 'Medieval Rules and Customaries Reconsidered', in *A Companion to Medieval Rules and Customaries*, ed. by Krijn Pansters (Leiden: Brill, 2020), pp. 1-36.

——, ed., *A Companion to Medieval Rules and Customaries* (Leiden: Brill, 2020).

Parkes, Malcolm B., *Their Hands before Our Eyes: A Closer Look at Scribes* (Aldershot: Ashgate, 1999).

Parkes, Malcom B., 'The Provision of Books', in *The History of the University of Oxford*, ed. by Jeremy I. Catto et al., 8 vols. (Oxford: Clarendon, 1984-2000), II, 407-83; repr. in *Pages from the Past: Medieval Writing Skills and Manuscript Books*, ed. by Pamela R. Robinson and Rivkah Zim (Aldershot: Ashgate, 2012), pp. 407-83.

Parsons, Simon T., 'The Letters of Stephen of Blois Reconsidered', *Crusades* 17 (2018), 1-29.

Passabì, Gabriele, 'Robert of Torigni's *Liber Chronicorum*: The Chronography as a Textual Project in Avranches, Bibliothèque patrimoniale, MS 159', *Tabularia* (2021), https://doi.org/10.4000/tabularia.5475.

Pastan, Elizabeth C. and Stephen D. White, 'Problematizing Patronage: Odo of Bayeux and the Bayeux Tapestry', in *The Bayeux Tapestry: New Interpretations*, ed. by Martin K. Foys et al. (Woodbridge: Boydell, 2009), pp. 1-24.

Pastan, Elizabeth C., 'Imagined Patronage', in Elizabeth C. Pastan and Stephen D. White, *The Bayeux Tapestry and Its Contexts: A Reassessment* (Woodbridge: Boydell 2014), pp. 59-81.

——, 'Quid faciat... Scollandus? The Abbey Church of St Augustine's c.1073–1100', in Elizabeth C. Pastan and Stephen D. White, *The Bayeux Tapestry and Its Contexts: A Reassessment* (Woodbridge: Boydell, 2014), pp. 260–87.

Patze, Hans, 'Klostergründung und Klosterchronik', *Blätter für deutsche Landesgeschichte* 113 (1977), 89–121; repr. in *Ausgewählte Aufsätze von Hans Patze*, ed. by Peter Johanek et al. (Stuttgart: Thorbecke, 2002), pp. 251–84.

Patzold, Steffen, 'Konflikte im Kloster Fulda zur Zeit der Karolinger', *Fuldaer Geschichtsblätter* 76 (2000), 69–162.

——, '*Mensa fratrum* und *consensus fratrum*: Überlegungen zu zwei parallelen Entwicklungen im fränkischen Mönchtum des 9. Jahrhunderts', in *Kloster und Wirtschaftswelt im Mittelalter*, ed. by Claudia Dobrinski, Brunhilde Gedderth, and Katrin Wipfler (Munich: Fink, 2007), pp. 25–38.

——, *Episcopus: Wissen über Bischöfe im Frankenreich des späten 8. bis frühen 10. Jahrhunderts.* (Ostfildern: Thorbecke, 2008), pp. 173–5.

——, *Konflikte im Kloster: Studien zu Auseinandersetzungen in monastischen Gemeinschaften des ottonisch-salischen Reichs* (Husum: Matthiesen, 2000).

Paul, Nicholas L., 'A Warlord's Wisdom: Literacy and Propaganda at the Time of the First Crusade', *Speculum* 85 (2010), 534–66.

Paul, Roland W., 'The Plan of the Church and Monastery of St. Augustine, Bristol', *Archaeologia* 63 (1912), 213–50.

Petersohn, Jürgen, 'Fragmente einer unbekannten Fassung der Ottoviten-Kompilationen des Michelsberger Abtes Andreas Lang', *Deutsches Archiv für Erforschung des Mittelalters* 67 (2011), 593–608.

Pettegree, Andrew, *Brand Luther: 1517, Printing, and the Making of the Reformation* (London: Penguin, 2015).

Petzholdt, Julius, *Handbuch deutscher Bibliotheken* (Halle: Schmidt, 1853).

Pevsner, Nikolaus, 'The Term "Architect" in the Middle Ages', *Speculum* 17 (1942), 549–62.

Pezzini, Domenico, 'Aelred of Rievaulx's *Vita Sancti Edwardi Regis et Confessoris*: Its Genesis and Radiation', *Cîteaux: Commentarii Cistercienses* 60 (2009), 27–77.

Pfändtner, Karl-Georg, 'Andreas Lang: Chronica abbatum monasterii S. Michaelis (fasciculus abbatum) et pontificum Babenbergensis ecclesiae (= B.14)', in *Im Schutz des Engels: 1000 Jahre Kloster Michaelsberg Bamberg, 1015–2015*, ed. by Norbert Jung and Holger Kempkens (Petersberg: Imhof, 2015), pp. 429–30.

——, 'Die Klosterreform von St. Ulrich und Afra in Augsburg im Spiegel der illuminierten Handschriften', in *Reformen vor der Reformation: Sankt Ulrich und Afra*, ed. by Gisela Drossbach and Klaus Wolf (Berlin: De Gruyter, 2018), pp. 239–54.

Phillips, Kendall R. and G. Mitchell Reyes, 'Introduction: Surveying Global Memoryscapes: The Shifting Terrain of Public Memory Studies', in *Global Memoryscapes: Contesting Remembrance in a Transnational Age*, ed. by Kendall R. Phillips et al. (Tuscaloosa, AL: University of Alabama Press, 2011), pp. 1–26.

Pierre Riché, 'Gerbert d'Aurillac et Bobbio', in *Gerberto d'Aurillac da abate di Bobbio a papa dell'anno 1000*, ed. by Flavio G. Nuvolone (Bobbio: Associazione culturale Amici di Archivum bobiense, 2001), pp. 49–64.

Piétri, Luce, 'Les premières abbesses du monastère Saint-Jean d'Arles', in *Paul-Albert Février de l'Antiquité au Moyen Âge*, ed. by Michel Fixot (Aix-en-Provence: Publications de l'Université de Provence, 2003), pp. 73–86.

Pirri, Pietro, *L'abbazia di Sant'Eutizio in val Castoriana presso Norcia e le chiese dipendenti* (Rome: Herder, 1960).

Plassmann, Alheydis, *Origo gentis: Identitäts- und Legitimitätsstiftung in früh- und hochmittelalterlichen Herkunftserzählungen* (Berlin: Akademie Verlag, 2006).
Platelle, Henri, 'Le premier cartulaire de l'abbaye de Saint-Amand', *Le Moyen Âge* 62 (1956), 301–29.
——, 'L'évolution du temporel de l'abbaye de Saint-Amand des origines à 1340', *Revue du Nord* 177 (1963), 108–10.
——, *La justice seigneuriale de l'abbaye de Saint Amand: Son organisation judiciaire, sa procédure et sa compétence du XIe au XVIe siècle* (Louvain: Publications universitaires de Louvain, 1965).
——, *Le temporel de l'abbaye de Saint-Amand des origines à 1340* (Paris: Librairie d'Argences, 1962).
Pohl, Benjamin and Elisabeth M. C. van Houts, 'History and Memory', in *The Cambridge Companion to the Age of William the Conqueror*, ed. by Benjamin Pohl (Cambridge: Cambridge University Press, 2022), pp. 244–71.
Pohl, Benjamin and Laura L. Gathagan, eds., *A Companion to the Abbey of Le Bec in the Central Middle Ages (11th–13th Centuries)* (Leiden: Brill, 2017).
Pohl, Benjamin and Steven Vanderputten, 'Fécamp, Cluny, and the Invention of Tradition in the Later Eleventh Century', *Journal of Medieval Monastic Studies* 5 (2016), 1–41.
Pohl, Benjamin, 'A Reluctant Historian and His Craft: The Scribal Work of Andreas of Marchiennes Reconsidered', *Anglo-Norman Studies* 45 (2023), 141–61.
——, '*Abbas qui et scriptor*? The Handwriting of Robert of Torigni and His Scribal Activity as Abbot of Mont-Saint-Michel (1154–1186)', *Traditio* 69 (2014), 45–86.
——, 'L'atelier de l'abbé-historian du Mont Saint-Michel: Où Robert de Torigni a-t-il écrit?', in *1023–2023: Le Mont Saint-Michel en Normandie et en Europe*, ed. by Fabien Paquet et al., forthcoming.
——, '*Locus memoriae–locus historiae*: Die Fuldaer Michaelskirche im Zentrum der monastischen Geschichts- und Erinnerungslandschaft im frühen und hohen Mittelalter', *Archiv für mittelrheinische Kirchengeschichte* (2023), forthcoming.
——, 'Processions, Power and Public Display: Ecclesiastical Rivalry and Ritual in Ducal Normandy', *Journal of Medieval Monastic Studies* 6 (2017), 1–49.
——, 'Review of Felice Lifshitz, *Religious Women in Early Carolingian Francia*', *Reviews in History* (2015), https://reviews.history.ac.uk/review/1844.
——, 'Review of Lauren Mancia, *Emotional Monasticism: Affective Piety in the Eleventh-Century Monastery of John of Fécamp*', *Early Medieval Europe* 30 (2022), 1–3.
——, 'Review of Thomas N. Bisson, *The Chronography of Robert of Torigni*', *History* 106 (2021), 293–98, https://doi.org/10.1111/1468-229X.13109.
——, 'Robert of Torigni and Le Bec: The Man and the Myth', in *A Companion to the Abbey of Le Bec in the Central Middle Ages (11th–13th Centuries)*, ed. by Benjamin Pohl and Laura L. Gathagan (Leiden: Brill, 2017), pp. 94–124.
——, 'Robert of Torigni's "Pragmatic Literacy": Some Theoretical Considerations', *Tabularia* (2022), 1–29, https://doi.org/10.4000/tabularia.5576.
——, 'The "Bec Liber Vitae": Robert of Torigni's Sources for Writing the History of the Clare Family at Le Bec, *c*.1128–54', *Revue bénédictine* 126 (2016), 324–72.
——, 'The (Un)Making of a History Book: Revisiting the Earliest Manuscripts of Eadmer of Canterbury's *Historia novorum in Anglia*', *The Library* 20 (2019), 340–70.
——, 'The Memory of Robert of Torigni: From the Twelfth Century to the Present Day', in *Maîtriser le temps et façonner l'histoire: Les historiens normands aux époques médiévale et moderne*, ed. by Fabien Paquet (Caen: Presses universitaires de Caen, 2022), pp. 111–34.

——, 'The Problem of Cluniac Exemption', in *A Companion to the Abbey of Cluny in the Middle Ages*, ed. by Scott G. Bruce and Steven Vanderputten (Leiden: Brill, 2021), pp. 288–305.

——, 'What Sort of Man Should the Abbot Be? Three Voices from the Norman Abbey of Mont-Saint-Michel', in *Abbots and Abbesses as a Human Resource in the Ninth- to Twelfth-Century West*, ed. by Steven Vanderputten (Zurich: LIT, 2018), pp. 101–24.

——, 'When Did Robert of Torigni First Receive Henry of Huntingdon's *Historia Anglorum*, and Why Does It Matter?', *Haskins Society Journal* 26 (2015), 143–67.

——, 'Who Wrote Paris, BnF, Latin 2342? The Identity of the *Anonymus Beccensis* Revisited', in *France et Angleterre: Manuscrits médiévaux entre 700 et 1200*, ed. by Charlotte Denoël and Francesco Siri (Turnhout: Brepols, 2020), pp. 153–89.

——, *Dudo of Saint-Quentin's* Historia Normannorum: *Tradition, Innovation and Memory* (York: York Medieval Press, 2015).

——, *Publishing in a Medieval Monastery: The View from Twelfth-Century Engelberg* (Cambridge: Cambridge University Press, 2023).

Pohl, Walter, *Werkstätte der Erinnerung: Montecassino und die Gestaltung der langobardischen Vergangenheit* (Vienna: Oldenbourg, 2001).

Power, Eileen, *Medieval English Nunneries, c.1275 to 1535* (Cambridge: Cambridge University Press, 1922).

Prache, Anne and Dominique Barthélémy, 'Notre-Dame de Nogent-sous-Coucy, une abbaye bénédictine disparue', *Bulletin Monumental* 140 (1982), 7–14.

Pradié, Pascal, 'L'histoire sainte de Fontenelle: Une lecture des *Gesta abbatum*', *Tabularia* (2004), https://doi.org/10.4000/tabularia.1348.

——, 'L'historiographie à Fontenelle au temps d'Eginhard: Une lecture des Gesta Abbatum, l'histoire sainte de Fontenelle', in *Einhard: Leben und Werk*, ed. by Hermann Schefers, 2 vols. (Regensburg: Schnell & Steiner, 1997–2019), II, 62–74.

——, 'Un fragment de manuscrit inédit du IXe siècle découvert à l'abbaye Saint-Wandrille', *Tabularia* 4 (2004), 131–42, https://doi.org/10.4000/tabularia.1381.

Preisendanz, Karl, 'Reginbert von der Reichenau: Aus Bibliothek und Skriptorium des Inselklosters', *Neue Heidelberger Jahrbücher* (1952/3), 1–49.

Pridgeon, Ellie and Susan Sharp, 'Patronage and Function: The Medieval Wall Paintings at Lacock Abbey in Wiltshire', *Journal of Medieval Monastic Studies* 5 (2016), 113–37.

Prochno, Joachim, *Das Schreiber- und Dedikationsbild in der deutschen Buchmalerei*, Vol. I: *Bis zum Ende des 11. Jahrhunderts* (Leipzig: Teubner, 1929).

Raaijmakers, Janneke, 'Imitemur nos, qui alumni eius sumus...: Boniface's Nachleben in Early Medieval Fulda', in *A Companion to Boniface*, ed. by Michel Aaij and Shannon Godlove (Leiden: Brill, 2020), pp. 379–403.

——, 'Memory and Identity: The *Annales necrologici* of Fulda', in *Texts and Identities in the Early Middle Ages*, ed. by Richard Corradini et al. (Vienna: Verlag der österreichischen Akademie der Wissenschaften, 2006), pp. 303–21.

——, *The Making of the Monastic Community of Fulda, c.744–c.900* (Cambridge: Cambridge University Press, 2012).

Radini, Anita et al., 'Medieval Women's Early Involvement in Manuscript Production Suggested by Lapis Lazuli Identification in Dental Calculus', *Science Advances* 5 (2019), 1–8.

Reed-Leal, Andrea, 'Book-Borrowing in the Early Middle Ages: A Case Study of Servatus Lupus (*c.*805–862)', *Library and Information History* 36 (2020), 194–209.

Renn, Derek, 'How Big Is It–And Was It?', in *The Bayeux Tapestry: New Approaches*, ed. by Michael J. Lewis et al. (Oxford: Oxbow, 2011), pp. 52–8.

Rennie, Kriston R., *Law and Practice in the Age of Reform: The Legatine Work of Hugh of Die* (1073–1106) (Turnhout: Brepols, 2010).

——, *The Destruction and Recovery of Monte Cassino, 529–1964* (Amsterdam: Amsterdam University Press, 2020).

Riché, Pierre, *Gerbert d'Aurillac: Le pape de l'an mil* (Paris: Fayard, 1987).

Richter, Michael, *Bobbio in the Early Middle Ages: The Abiding Legacy of Columbanus* (Dublin: Four Courts Press, 2008).

Riemer, Dieter, 'Neue Überlegungen zu Hitda', in *Äbtissin Hitda und der Hitda-Codex (Universitäts- und Landesbibliothek Darmstadt, Hs. 1640): Forschungen zu einem Hauptwerk der ottonischen Kölner Buchmalerei*, ed. by Klaus G. Beuckers (Darmstadt: Wissenschaftliche Buchgesellschaft, 2013), pp. 33–56.

Roach, Daniel, 'Orderic Vitalis and the First Crusade', *Journal of Medieval History* 42 (2016), 177–201.

Robinson, Ian S., *Authority and Resistance in the Investiture Contest: The Polemical Literature of the Late Eleventh Century* (Manchester: Manchester University Press, 1978).

Robinson, Joseph A., *The Abbot's House at Westminster* (Cambridge: Cambridge University Press, 1911).

Robinson, Pamela R., ed., *Catalogue of Dated and Datable Manuscripts c.737–1600 in Cambridge Libraries*, 2 vols. (Cambridge: Cambridge University Press, 1988).

Roffe, David, 'The *Historia Croylandensis*: A Plea for Reassessment', *English Historical Review* 110 (1995), 93–108.

Rollason, David W., 'Symeon of Durham's *Historia de regibus Anglorum et Dacorum* as a Product of Twelfth-Century Historical Workshops', in *The Long Twelfth-Century View of the Anglo-Saxon Past*, ed. by Martin Brett and David A. Woodman (Farnham: Routledge, 2015), pp. 95–112.

——, ed., *Symeon of Durham: Historian of Durham and the North* (Stamford: Tyas, 1999).

Ross, David J. A., 'Illustrated Manuscripts of Orosius', *Scriptorium* 9 (1955), 35–56.

Rother, Karl H., 'Ein Ausleihregister der Augustiner Chorherren zu Sagan: Ein Beitrag zur Geschichte der Bibliothek', *Zentralblatt für Bibliothekswesen* 43 (1926), 1–22.

Rottler, Maria, '"Catalogus bibliothecae abbatialis S. Emmerami"–ein Katalog der St. Emmeramer Abtsbibliothek aus der Zeit Frobenius Forsters', in *Netzwerke gelehrter Mönche: St. Emmeram im Zeitalter der Aufklärung*, ed. by Bernhard Löffler and Maria Rottler (Munich: Beck, 2015), pp. 297–304.

Rouse, Richard H. and Mary A. Rouse, '"Potens in opere et sermone": Philip, Bishop of Bayeux, and His Books', in *Authentic Witnesses: Approaches to Medieval Texts and Manuscripts*, ed. by Richard H. Rouse and Mary A. Rouse (Notre Dame, IN: University of Notre Dame Press, 1991), pp. 323–59.

Rozier, Charles C. et al., eds., *Orderic Vitalis: Life, Works and Interpretations* (Woodbridge: Boydell, 2016).

Rozier, Charles C., 'Orderic Vitalis as Librarian and Cantor of Saint-Evroul', in *Orderic Vitalis: Life, Works and Interpretations*, ed. by Charles C. Rozier et al. (Woodbridge: Boydell, 2016), pp. 61–77.

——, 'Symeon of Durham as Cantor and Historian at Durham Cathedral Priory c.1090–1129', in *Medieval Cantors and Their Craft: Music, Liturgy and the Shaping of History, 800–1500*, ed. by Margot E. Fassler et al. (Woodbridge: Boydell, 2017), pp. 190–206.

——, *Writing History in the Community of St Cuthbert, c.700–1130: From Bede to Symeon of Durham* (Woodbridge: York Medieval Press, 2020).

Rubenstein, Jay, 'The *Deeds* of Bohemond: Reform, Propaganda, and the History of the First Crusade', *Viator* 47 (2016), 113–36.

——, 'What Is the *Gesta Francorum*, and Who Was Peter Tudebode', *Revue Mabillon* 16 (2005), 179–204.

——, *Guibert of Nogent: Portrait of a Medieval Mind* (New York, NY: Routledge, 2002).

Rudolf, Hans U., 'Das Benediktinerkloster Weingarten um 1200 und seine Entwicklung unter Abt Berthold (1200–1232)', in *Das Hainricus-Missale: Vollständige Faksimile-Ausgabe der Handschrift MS M.711 (bisher auch "Hainricus-Sakramentar") aus The Morgan Library and Museum New York*, ed. by Hans U. Rudolf (Graz: Akademische Druck- und Verlagsanstalt, 2010), pp. 13–32.

——, 'Quellentexte zum Wirken Abt Bertholds von Weingarten (1200–1232)', in *Das Berthold-Sakramentar: Vollständige Faksimile-Ausgabe im Originalformat von Ms M. 710 der Pierpont Morgan Library in New York*, ed. by Felix Heinzer and Hans U. Rudolf (Graz: Akademische Druck- und Verlagsanstalt, 1999), pp. 257–71.

Rudy, Kathryn M., 'Dirty Books: Quantifying Patterns of Use in Medieval Manuscripts Using a Densitometer', *Journal of Historians of Netherlandish Art* 2 (2010), 1–44.

——, 'Kissing Images, Unfurling Rolls, Measuring Wounds, Sewing Badges and Carrying Talismans: Considering Some Harley Manuscripts through the Physical Rituals They Reveal', *Electronic British Library Journal* 5 (2011), 1–56.

——, 'Touching the Book Again: The Passional of Abbess Kunigunde of Bohemia', in *Codex und Material*, ed. by Patrizia Carmassi and Gia Toussaint (Wiesbaden: Harrassowitz, 2018), pp. 247–57.

——, *Touching Parchment: How Medieval Users Rubbed, Handled, and Kissed Their Manuscripts, Vol. I: Officials and Their Books* (Cambridge: Open Book Publishers, 2023).

Ruh, Kurt, 'Das "St. Klara Buch"', *Wissenschaft und Weisheit* 46 (1983), 192–206.

Rupp, Michael, 'Williram von Ebersberg', in *Althochdeutsche und altsächsische Literatur*, ed. by Rolf Bergmann (Berlin: De Gruyter, 2013), pp. 518–28.

Russell, Delbert, 'The Campsey Collection of Old French Saints' Lives', *Scriptorium* 57 (2003), 51–83.

Sackur, Ernst, 'Reise nach Nord-Frankreich im Frühjahr 1889', *Neues Archiv der Gesellschaft für ältere deutsche Geschichtskunde* 15 (1890), 437–73.

Salmon, Pierre, *L'abbé dans la tradition monastique: Contribution à l'histoire du caractère perpétuel des supérieurs religieux en Occident* (Paris: Sirey, 1992).

Sandmann, Mechthild, 'Die Äbte von Fulda im Gedenken ihrer Mönchsgemeinschaft', *Frühmittelalterliche Studien* 17 (1983), 393–444.

——, 'Theoderich von Verdun und die religiösen Gemeinschaften seiner Diözese', in *Person und Gemeinschaft im Mittelalter: Festschrift für Karl Schmid zum fünfundsechzigsten Geburtstag*, ed. by Gerd Althoff et al. (Sigmaringen: Thorbecke, 1988), pp. 315–44.

——, 'Wirkungsbereiche fuldischer Mönche', in *Die Klostergemeinschaft von Fulda im früheren Mittelalter*, ed. by Karl Schmid et al., 3 vols. (Munich: Fink, 1978), II.2, 692–791.

Sansterre, Jean-Marie, 'Figures abbatiales et distribution des rôles dans les *Vitae Quatuor Priorum Abbatum Cavensium* (milieu du XIIe siècle)', *Mélanges de l'école française de Rome, Moyen Âge* 111 (1999), 61–104.

Schieffer, Rudolf, 'Fulda, Abtei der Könige und Kaiser', in *Kloster Fulda in der Welt der Karolinger und Ottonen*, ed. by Gangolf Schrimpf (Frankfurt a. M.: Knecht, 1993), pp. 39–55.

——, 'Von der Geschichte der Äbte und der Klöster zur Geschichte des Ordens: Grundlinien benediktinischer Historiographie im Mittelalter', in *Benediktiner als Historiker*, ed. by Andreas Sohn (Bochum: Winkler, 2016), pp. 23–39.

Schleif, Corine, 'Gifts and Givers that Keep on Giving: Pictured Presentations in Early Medieval Manuscripts', in *Romance and Rhetoric: Essays in Honour of Dhira B. Mahoney*, ed. by Georgiana Donavin and Anita Obermeier (Turnhout: Brepols, 2010), pp. 51-74.

Schlotheuber, Eva and John T. McQuillen, 'Books and Libraries within Monasteries', in *CHMMLW*, II, 975-97.

Schlotheuber, Eva and Wolfgang Beckermann, 'Die Bibliothek des Godehardiklosters in Hildesheim', in *Wandmalerei in Niedersachsen, Bremen und im Groningerland: Fenster in die Vergangenheit*, ed. by Rolf-Jürgen Grote et al., 2 vols. (Munich: Deutscher Kunstverlag, 2001), I, 108-16.

Schlotheuber, Eva, 'Der Erzbischof Eudes Rigaud, die Nonnen und das Ringen um die Klosterreform im 13. Jahrhundert', in *Institution und Charisma: Festschrift für Gert Melville*, ed. by Franz J. Felten at al. (Cologne: Böhlau, 2009), pp. 99-110.

Schmale, Franz-Josef, *Funktion und Formen mittelalterlicher Geschichtsschreibung* (Darmstadt: Wissenschaftliche Buchgesellschaft, 1985).

Schmalor, Hermann-Josef, 'Die Bibliothek der ehemaligen Reichsabtei Corvey', *Westfälische Zeitschrift* 147 (1997), 251-70.

Schmeidler, Bernhard, *Abt Ellinger von Tegernsee, 1017-1026 und 1031-1041: Untersuchungen zu seinen Briefen und Gedichten im Clm 19412 und zu den von ihm geschriebenen Handschriften* (Munich: Beck, 1938).

Schmid, Karl et al., eds., *Die Klostergemeinschaft von Fulda im früheren Mittelalter*, 3 vols. (Munich: Fink, 1978).

Schmidt, Hans-Joachim, 'Bücher im Privatbesitz und im Besitz der Konvente: Regelungen der Bettelorden', in *Die Bibliothek–The Library–La Bibliothèque: Denkräume und Wissensordnungen*, ed. by Andreas Speer und Lars Reuke (Berlin: De Gruyter, 2020), pp. 157-71.

Schmidt, Peter L., 'Rezeption und Überlieferung der Tragödien Senecas bis zum Ausgang des Mittelalters', in *Traditio Latinitatis: Studien zur Rezeption und Überlieferung der lateinischen Literatur*, ed. by Peter L. Schmidt and Joachim Fugmann (Stuttgart: Steiner, 2000), pp. 207-46.

Schmitt, Christoph, '*Trithemii effigies... ex archetype depicta*: Trithemiusbilder des 16. Jahrhunderts', in *Johannes Trithemius (1462-1516): Abt und Büchersammler, Humanist und Geschichtsschreiber*, ed. by Klaus Arnold and Franz Fuchs (Würzburg: Königshausen & Neumann, 2019), pp. 221-46.

Schmitz, Hans-Georg, *Kloster Prüfening im 12. Jahrhundert* (Munich: Wölfle, 1975).

Schneegans, Wilhelm, *Abt Johannes Trithemius und Kloster Sponheim* (Kreuznach: Schmithals, 1882).

Schneidmüller, Bernd, 'Adso von Montier-en-Der und die Frankenkönige', *Trierer Zeitschrift* 40/41 (1977/8), 189-99.

Schreiner, Klaus, 'Abt Johannes Trithemius (1462-1516) als Geschichtsschreiber des Klosters Hirsau: Überlieferungsgeschichtliche und quellenkritische Bemerkungen zu den "Annales Hirsaugienses"', *Rheinische Vierteljahrsblätter* 31 (1966/7), 72-138.

——, 'Erneuerung durch Erinnerung: Reformstreben, Geschichtsbewußtsein und Geschichtsschreibung im benediktinischen Mönchtum Südwestdeutschlands an der Wende vom 15. zum 16. Jahrhundert', in *Historiographie am Oberrhein im späten Mittelalter und in der frühen Neuzeit*, ed. by Kurt Andermann (Sigmaringen: Thorbecke, 1988), pp. 35-87.

——, 'Geschichtsschreibung im Interesse der Reform: Die "Hirsauer Jahrbücher" des Johannes Trithemius (1462-1516)', in *Hirsau St. Peter und Paul 1091-1991*, ed. by Klaus Schreiner, 2 vols. (Stuttgart: Theiss, 1991), II, 297-324.

——, 'Verschriftlichung als Faktor monastischer Reform: Funktionen von Schriftlichkeit im Ordenswesen des hohen und späten Mittelalters', in *Pragmatische Schriftlichkeit im Mittelalter: Erscheinungsformen und Entwicklungsstufen*, ed. by Hagen Keller et al. (Munich: Funk, 1992), p. 37–75.

Schrimpf, Gangolf et al., eds., *Mittelalterliche Bücherverzeichnisse des Klosters Fulda und andere Beiträge zur Geschichte der Bibliothek des Klosters Fulda im Mittelalter* (Frankfurt a. M.: Knecht, 1992).

Schroeder, Nicolas, 'Wibald en questions: Historiographie et nouvelles perspectives', in *Wibald en questions: Un grand abbé lotharingien du XIIe siècle. D'or et de parchemin*, ed. by Albert Lemeunier and Nicolas Schroeder (Stavelot: Abbaye de Stavelot, 2010), pp. 5–11.

Schwarzbauer, Fabian, *Geschichtszeit: Über Zeitvorstellungen in den Universalchroniken Frutolfs von Michelsberg, Honorius' Augustodunensis und Ottos von Freising* (Berlin: Akademie Verlag, 2005).

Schweitzer, Caspar A., 'Das Copialbuch der Cisterzienser-Abtei Langheim in vollständigen Auszügen der Urkunden von 1142–1500: Schluss, 1452–1504', *Bericht über das Wirken des Historischen Vereines zu Bamberg* 26 (1863), 1–47.

——, 'Das Urkundenbuch des Abtes Andreas im Kloster Michelsberg bei Bamberg in vollständigen Auszügen', *Bericht über das Wirken des Historischen Vereines zu Bamberg* 16 (1853), i–x and 1–175.

——, 'Das Urkundenbuch des Abtes Andreas im Kloster Michelsberg bei Bamberg in vollständigen Auszügen (II. Abtheilung)', *Bericht über das Wirken des Historischen Vereines zu Bamberg* 17 (1854), 1–147.

Scior, Volker, 'Zwischen *terra nostra* und *terra sancta*: Arnold von Lübeck als Geschichtsschreiber', in *Die Chronik Arnolds von Lübeck: Neue Wege zu ihrem Verständnis*, ed. by Bernd Schütte and Stephan Freund (Frankfurt a. M.: Peter Lang, 2008), pp. 149–74.

Sears, Elizabeth, 'The Afterlife of Scribes: Swicher's Prayer in the Prüfening Isidore', in *Pen in Hand: Medieval Scribal Portraits, Colophons and Tools*, ed. by Michael Gullick (Walkern: Red Gull, 2006), pp. 75–96.

Sennhauser, Hans R., 'Das Kloster Kappel im Mittelalter: Bemerkungen zur Klosterkirche und zur Klosteranlage', in *Zisterzienserbauten in der Schweiz: Neue Forschungsergebnisse zur Archäologie und Kunstgeschichte*, ed. by Karl Grunder and Hans R. Sennhauser, 2 vols. (Zurich: Verlag der Fachvereine, 1990), II, 85–126.

Sharpe, Richard, 'Anselm as Author: Publishing in the Late Eleventh Century', *Journal of Medieval Latin* 19 (2009), 1–87.

——, 'The Foundation of the Abbey: A Material Perspective', in *Foundation Documents from St Mary's Abbey, York 1085–1137*, ed. by Richard Sharpe et al. (Woodbridge: Boydell, 2022), pp. 11–119.

——, 'The Medieval Librarian', in *CHLBI* I, 218–41.

——, *A Handlist of the Latin Writers of Great Britain and Ireland before 1540, with Additions and Corrections* (Turnhout: Brepols, 2001).

——, *Libraries and Books in Medieval England: The Role of Libraries in a Changing Book Economy (The Lyell Lectures for 2018–19)*, ed. by James Willoughby (Oxford: Bodleian Library, 2023).

Shaw, Richard, *How, When and Why Did Bede Write His Ecclesiastical History?* (London: Routledge, 2022).

Sheingorn, Pamela, 'Review of Gia Toussant, *Das Passional der Kunigunde von Böhmen: Bildrhetorik und Spiritualität*', *Studies in Iconography* 27 (2006), 213–19.

Shopkow, Leah, 'Dynastic History', in *Historiography in the Middle Ages*, ed. by Deborah M. Deliyannis (Leiden: Brill, 2003), pp. 217–48.
——, 'The Man from Vermandois: Dudo of Saint-Quentin and his Patrons', in *Religion, Text, and Society in Medieval Spain and Northern Europe: Essays in Honor of J. N. Hillgarth*, ed. by Thomas E. Burman (Toronto: Pontifical Institute for Mediaeval Studies, 2002), pp. 302–18.
Silvas, Anna M., *Jutta and Hildegard: The Biographical Sources* (University Park, PA: Pennsylvania State University Press, 1999).
Silvestre, Hubert, 'À propos du dicton "Claustrum sine armario, quasi castrum sine armamentario"', *Medieval Studies* 26 (1964), 351–3.
Simeray, Françoise, 'Le scriptorium de l'abbaye de Saint-Amand au milieu du XIIe siècle', *Valentiana* 4 (1989), 6–10.
Simms, Katharine, 'The Professional Historians of Medieval Ireland', in *Medieval Historical Writing: Britain and Ireland, 500–1500*, ed. by Jennifer Jahner et al. (Cambridge: Cambridge University Press, 2019), pp. 279–98.
Sims-Williams, Patrick, 'Cuthswith, Seventh-Century Abbess of Inkberrow, near Worcester, and the Würzburg Manuscript of Jerome on Ecclesiastes', *Anglo-Saxon England* 5 (1976), 1–21.
Smith, Julia M. H., 'A Hagiographer at Work: Hucbald and the Library at Saint-Amand', *Revue bénédictine* 106 (1996), 151–71.
Smith, Thomas W., 'First Crusade Letters and Medieval Monastic Scribal Cultures', *Journal of Ecclesiastical History* 71 (2020), 484–501.
Solente, Suzanne, 'Une charte-partie de 1107 dans un manuscrit de Saint-Amand', *Bibliothèque de l'école des chartes* 94 (1933), 213–17.
Sønnesyn, Sigbjørn O., *William of Malmesbury and the Ethics of History* (Woodbridge: Boydell, 2012).
Sot, Michel, *Gesta episcoporum, gesta abbatum* (Turnhout: Brepols, 1981).
Southern, Richard W., *Saint Anselm and His Biographer: A Study of Monastic Life and Thought, 1059–c.1130* (Cambridge: Cambridge University Press, 1963).
——, *St Anselm: A Portrait in a Landscape* (Cambridge: Cambridge University Press, 1990).
Späth, Markus, *Verflechtung von Erinnerung: Bildproduktion und Geschichtsschreibung im Kloster San Clemente a Casauria während des 12. Jahrhunderts* (Berlin: Akademie Verlag, 2007).
Spear, Valerie G., *Leadership in Medieval English Nunneries* (Woodbridge: Boydell, 2005).
Speer, Andreas, 'Abt Sugers Schriften zur fränkischen Königsabtei Saint-Denis', in *Abt Suger von Saint-Denis: Ausgewählte Schriften. Ordinatio, De consecratione, De administratione*, ed. by Andreas Speer et al., 3rd ed. (Darmstadt: Wissenschaftliche Buchgesellschaft, 2008), pp. 13–66.
Spence, Charles, *The Abbey Church of Romsey in Hampshire*, 5th ed. (Romsey: Jordan, 1886).
Spiegel, Gabrielle M., 'Review of *Chronique de Saint-Pierre-le-Vif de Sens, dite de Clarius (Chronicon Sancti Petri Vivi Senonensis)*', *Speculum* 57 (1982), 114–16.
Spilling, Herrad, 'Abt Bertholds Bücherverzeichnis: Anhaltspunkt zur Datierung seines Sakramentars?', in *Das Berthold-Sakramentar: Vollständige Faksimile-Ausgabe im Originalformat von Ms M. 710 der Pierpont Morgan Library in New York*, ed. by Felix Heinzer and Hans U. Rudolf (Graz: Akademische Druck- und Verlagsanstalt, 1999), pp. 187–92 and 270–1.

Staab, Franz, 'Fulda (B)', in *Die deutschen Königspfalzen: Repertorium der Pfalzen, Königshöfe und übrigen Aufenthaltsorte der Könige im deutschen Reich des Mittelalters*, Vol. I.5: *Hessen*, ed. by Caspar Ehlers, Lutz Fenske, and Thomas Zotz (Göttingen: Vandenhoeck & Ruprecht, 1983), pp. 511–612.

Stacy, N. E., 'Henry of Blois and the Lordship of Glastonbury', *English Historical Review* 114 (1999), 1–33.

Stamm, Gerhard, 'Zur Geschichte der Bibliothek', in *Das tausendjährige St. Blasien: 200jähriges Domjubiläum*, ed. by Chistel Römer and Ernst Petrasch, 2 vols. (Karlsruhe: Badenia, 1984), II, 171–200.

Staubach, Nikolaus, 'Auf der Suche nach der verlorenen Zeit: Die historiographischen Fiktionen des Johannes Trithemius im Lichte seines wissenschaftlichen Selbstverständnisses', in *Fälschungen im Mittelalter*, 5 vols. (Hanover: Hahn, 1988), I, 263–316.

Staunton, Michael, *Thomas Becket and his Biographers* (Woodbridge: Boydell, 2006).

Steckel, Sita, *Kulturen des Lehrens im Früh- und Hochmittelalter: Autorität, Wissenskonzepte und Netzwerke von Gelehrten* (Cologne: Böhlau, 2011).

Steiner, Hannes, 'Buchproduktion und Bibliothekszuwachs im Kloster St. Gallen unter den Äbten Grimald und Hartmut', in *Ludwig der Deutsche und seine Zeit*, ed. by Winfried Hartmann (Darmstadt: Wissenschaftliche Buchgesellschaft, 2004), pp. 161–83.

Steinmann, Martin, 'Abt Frowin von Engelberg (1143–1178) und seine Handschriften', *Der Geschichtsfreund* 146 (1993), 7–36.

——, 'Die Bücher des Abtes Frowin–ein Skriptorium in Engelberg?', *Scriptorium* 54 (2000), 9–13.

Steinmetz, Walter, '*Armarium Runense*: Kleiner Führer durch die Reiner Stiftsbibliothek', in *Stift Rein: Geschichte-Kultur-Glaube*, ed. by Elisabeth Brenner and Reiner Kreises (Kumberg: Sublilium Schaffer, 2018), pp. 171–8.

Stengel, Edmund E. and Oskar Semmelmann, 'Fuldensia IV: Untersuchungen zur Frühgeschichte des Fuldaer Klosterarchivs', *Archiv für Diplomatik* 4 (1958), 120–82.

Stephan, Hans-Georg, 'Zur Siedlungs- und Baugeschichte von Corvey-vornehmlich im frühen und hohen Mittelalter', *Archaeologia historica* 20 (1995), 447–67.

Stevens, Wesley M., 'Fulda Scribes at Work: Bodleian Library, Manuscript Canonici Miscellaneous 353', *Bibliothek und Wissenschaft* 8 (1972), 287–317.

Stieldorf, Andrea, 'Frauenbildung in der Vormoderne', in *Doch plötzlich jetzt emanzipiert will die Wissenschaft sie treiben: Frauen an der Universität Bonn (1818–2018)*, ed. by Andrea Stieldorf et al. (Göttingen: Vandenhoeck & Ruprecht, 2018), pp. 11–30.

Still, Michelle, *The Abbot and the Rule: Religious Life at St Albans, 1290–1349* (Aldershot: Ashgate, 2002).

Stirnemann, Patricia D., 'Les bibliothèques princières et privées aux XIIe et XIIIe siècles', in *Histoire des Bibliothèques françaises*, Vol. 1: *Les bibliothèques médiévales, du VIe siècle à 1530*, ed. by André Vernet (Paris: Éditions du Cercle de la Librairie, 1989), pp. 173–91.

——, 'Two Twelfth-Century Bibliophiles and Henry of Huntingdon's *Historia Anglorum*', *Viator* 24 (1993), 121–42.

——, 'Women and Books in France: 1170–1220', in *Representations of the Feminine in the Middle Ages*, ed. by Bonnie Wheeler (Dallas: Academia, 1993), pp. 247–52.

Stock, Brian, *The Implications of Literacy: Written Language and Models of Interpretation in the 11th and 12th Centuries* (Princeton, NJ: Princeton University Press, 1983).

Story, Joanna, 'The Carolingians and the Oratory of Saint Peter the Shepherd', in *Old Saint Peter's, Rome*, ed. by Rosamond McKitterick et al. (Cambridge: Cambridge University Press, 2013), pp. 257–73.

Stratford, Jenny and Teresa Webber, 'Bishops and Kings: Private Book Collections in Medieval England', in *CHLBI* I, 178–217.
Streit, Vincenc et al., eds., *Handbuch deutscher historischer Buchbestände in Europa*, Vol. 3: *Tschechische Republik* (Hildesheim: Olms-Weidmann, 1998).
Suhl, Nicole, 'Die "Vita Bertilae Abbatissae Calensis"-eine Quelle für mögliche Unterschiede in der Religiosität von "Volk" und "Ehre" im frühen Mittelalter?', *Medium Aevum Quotidianum* 36 (1997), 39–58.
Summit, Jennifer, 'Women and Authorship', in *The Cambridge Companion to Medieval Women's Writing*, ed. by Carolyn Dinshaw and David Wallace (Cambridge: Cambridge University Press, 2003), pp. 91–108.
Swan, Mary 'Authorship and Anonymity', in *A Companion to Anglo-Saxon Literature*, ed. by Phillip Pulsiano and Elaine Treharne (Oxford: Wiley, 2001), pp. 71–83.
Swarzenski, Georg, *Die Regensburger Buchmalerei des X. und XI. Jahrhunderts* (Leipzig: Hiersemann, 1901).
Sykes, Katharine, *Inventing Sempringham: Gilbert of Sempringham and the Origins of the Role of the Master* (Zurich: LIT, 2011).
Symes, Carol L., 'Popular Literacies and the First Historians of the First Crusade', *Past and Present* 235 (2017), 37–67.
Tahkokallio, Jaakko, *The Anglo-Norman Historical Canon: Publishing and Manuscript Culture* (Cambridge: Cambridge University Press, 2019).
Talbot, Charles H., 'Lacock Abbey: Notes on the Architectural History of the Building', *Journal of the British Archaeological Association* 11 (1905), 176–210.
Talbot, Daniel, 'Review of Charles C. Rozier, *Writing History in the Community of St Cuthbert, c.700–1130: From Bede to Symeon of Durham*', *History* 106 (2021), 477–8.
Tether, Leah, *Publishing the Grail in Medieval and Renaissance France* (Cambridge: D. S. Brewer, 2017).
Thomas, Alfred, *Anne's Bohemia: Czech Literature and Society, 1310–1420* (Minneapolis, MN: University of Minnesota Press, 1998).
Thompson, James W., *The Medieval Library* (New York, NY: Hafner, 1923).
Thompson, Michael, *Cloister, Abbot and Precinct in Medieval Monasteries* (Stroud: Tempus, 2001).
Thomson, Rodney M., 'Malmesbury, William of', in *Oxford Dictionary of National Biography* (2004), https://doi.org/10.1093/ref:odnb/29461.
——, 'Scribes and Scriptoria', in *The European Book in the Twelfth Century*, ed. by Erik Kwakkel and Rodney M. Thomson (Cambridge: Cambridge University Press, 2018), pp. 68–84.
——, ed., *Manuscripts from St Albans Abbey: 1066–1235*, 2 vols. (Woodbridge, Boydell: 1982–5).
——, *William of Malmesbury*, rev. ed. (Woodbridge: Boydell, 2003), pp. 199–201.
Thurlby, Malcolm, 'The Roles of the Patron and the Master Mason in the First Design of the Romanesque Cathedral of Durham', in *Anglo-Norman Durham, 1093–1193*, ed. by David Rollason et al. (Woodbridge: Boydell, 1994), pp. 161–84.
Tinti, Francesca and D. A. Woodman, eds., *Constructing History across the Norman Conquest: Worcester, c.1050–c.1150* (York: York Medieval Press, 2022).
Tischler, Matthias M., 'From Rome to Ripoll, Rioja, and Beyond: The Iberian Transmission of the Latin *Tiburtine Sibyl* and Oliba of Ripoll and Vic's Europe-Wide Network of Knowledge Transfer and Learning', *Early Medieval Europe* 30 (2022), 558–76.
——, 'Reginbert-Handschriften: Mit einem Neufund in Kloster Einsiedeln', *Scriptorium* 50 (1996), 175–83.

———, *Einharts Vita Karoli: Studien zur Entstehung, Überlieferung und Rezeption*, 2 vols. (Hanover: Hahn, 2001).
Tsuda, Takuro, 'Was hat Ansegis gesammelt? Über die zeitgenössische Wahrnehmung der "Kapitularien" in der Karolingerzeit', *Concilium medii aevi* 16 (2013), 209–31.
Tyler, Elizabeth M., *England in Europe: English Royal Women and Literary Patronage, c.1000–c.1150* (Toronto: University of Toronto Press, 2017).
Ugé, Karine, 'The Legend of Saint Rictrude: Formation and Transformations (Tenth–Twelfth Century), *Anglo-Norman Studies* 23 (2001), 281–97.
———, *Creating the Monastic Past in Medieval Flanders* (York: York Medieval Press, 2005).
Uhlirz, Mathilde, 'Studien zu Gerbert von Aurillac, Teil 2: Die ottonischen Kaiserprivilegien für das Kloster Bobbio. Gerbert als Abt', *Archiv für Urkundenforschung* 13 (1935), 437–74.
Untermann, Matthias, *Handbuch der mittelalterlichen Architektur* (Darmstadt: Wissenschaftliche Buchgesellschaft, 2009).
Van Acker, Kamiel G., 'De librije van Raphael de Marcatellis, abt van Sint-Baafs en bisshop van Rhosus', *Archief- en Bibliotheekwezen in België* 48 (1977), 143–98.
Van Els, Ad, *A Man and His Manuscripts: The Notebooks of Ademar of Chabannes (989–1034)* (Turnhout: Brepols, 2020).
Van Engen, John H., 'Rupert von Deutz und das sogenannte *Chronicon sancti Laurentii Leodiensis*: Zur Geschichte des Investiturstreites in Lüttich', *Deutsches Archiv für Erforschung des Mittelalters* 35 (1979), 33–81.
Van Houts, Elisabeth M. C., 'Historiography and Hagiography at Saint-Wandrille: The "Inventio et miracula Sancti Vulfanni"', *Anglo-Norman Studies* 12 (1990), 233–51.
———, 'Le roi et son historien: Henri II Plantagenêt et Robert de Torigni, abbé du Mont-Saint-Michel', *Cahiers de civilisation médiévale* 37 (1994), 115–18.
———, 'Review of *William of Andres: The Chronicle of Andres*, tr. by Leah Shopkow', *Church History and Religious Culture* 99 (2019), 6–7.
———, 'Suger, Orderic Vitalis, and the Vexin: Some Observations on Bibliothèque Mazarine MS 2013', in *Political Ritual and Practice in Capetian France: Studies in Honour of Elizabeth A. R. Brown*, ed. by Cecilia Gaposchkin and Jay Rubenstein (Turnhout: Brepols, 2021), pp. 55–76.
———, 'The Abbess, the Empress and the "Constitutions of Clarendon"', in *English Legal History and Its Sources: Essays in Honour of Sir John Baker*, ed. by David Ibbetson et al. (Cambridge: Cambridge University Press, 2019), pp. 247–64.
———, 'The Writing of History at Le Bec', in *A Companion to the Abbey of Le Bec in the Central Middle Ages (11th–13th Centuries)*, ed. by Benjamin Pohl and Laura L. Gathagan (Leiden: Brill, 2017), pp. 125–43.
———, 'Women and the Writing of History in the Early Middle Ages: The Case of Abbess Matilda of Essen and Aethelweard', *Early Medieval Europe* 1 (1992), 53–68.
———, *Local and Regional Chronicles* (Turnhout: Brepols, 1995).
———, *Memory and Gender in Medieval Europe, 900–1200* (Basingstoke: Macmillan, 1999).
Van Moolenbroek, Jaap J., 'De abtenkroniek van Aduard: Geleerdheid en devocie in een overgangstijd', in *De abtenkroniek van Aduard: Studies, editie en vertaling*, ed. by Jaap J. van Moolenbroek et al. (Hilversum: Verloren, 2010), pp. 21–52.
Van Zanden, Jan L. and Eltjo Buringh, 'Book Production as a Mirror of the Emerging Medieval Knowledge Economy, 500–1500', in Jan L. van Zanden, *The Long Road to the Industrial Revolution: The European Economy in a Global Perspective, 1000–1800* (Leiden: Brill, 2009), pp. 69–91.
Vanderputten, Steven, "Against the Custom": Hagiographical Rewriting and Female Abbatial Leadership at Mid-Eleventh-Century Remiremont', *Journal of Medieval Monastic Studies* 10 (2021), 41–66.

——, 'Benedictine Local Historiography from the Middle Ages and Its Written Sources: Some Structural Observations', *Revue Mabillon* 76 (2004), 107-29.
——, 'Compilation et réinvention a la fin du douzieme siècle: André de Marchiennes, le *Chronicon Marchianense* et l'histoire primitive d'une abbaye bénédictine (édition et critique des sources)', *Sacris erudiri* 42 (2003), 403-36.
——, 'Fulcard's Pigsty: Cluniac Reformers, Dispute Settlement and the Lower Aristocracy in Early-Twelfth-Century Flanders', *Viator* 38 (2007), 91-115.
——, 'Monastic Literary Practices in Eleventh- and Twelfth-Century Northern France', *Journal of Medieval History* 32 (2006), 101-26.
——, 'Pourquoi les moines du Moyen Âge écrivaient-ils l'histoire? Une approche socio-constructiviste du problème', *Studi medievali* 42 (2001), 705-23.
——, *Dark Age Nunneries: The Ambiguous Identity of Female Monasticism, 800-1050* (Ithaca, NY: Cornell University Press, 2018).
——, *Dismantling the Medieval: Early Modern Perceptions of a Female Convent's Past* (Turnhout: Brepols, 2021).
——, *Medieval Monasticisms: Forms and Experiences of the Monastic Life in the Latin West* (Berlin: De Gruyter, 2020).
——, *Monastic Reform as Process: Realities and Representations in Medieval Flanders, 900-1100* (Ithaca, NY: Cornell University Press, 2013).
Venarde, Bruce L., 'Making History at Fontevraud: Abbess Petronilla de Chemillé and Practical Literacy', in *Nuns' Literacies in Medieval Europe: The Hull Dialogue*, ed. by Virginia Blanton et al. (Turnhout: Brepols, 2013), pp. 19-31.
Virginia Blanton et al., eds., *Nuns' Literacies in Medieval Europe: The Hull Dialogue* (Turnhout: Brepols, 2013).
——, eds., *Nuns' Literacies in Medieval Europe: The Kansas City Dialogue* (Turnhout: Brepols, 2015).
——, eds., *Nuns' Literacies in Medieval Europe: The Antwerp Dialogue* (Turnhout: Brepols, 2017).
Vogel, Bernhard, 'Das hagiographische Werk Lantberts von Deutz über Heribert von Köln', in *Hagiographie im Kontext: Wirkungsweisen und Möglichkeiten historischer Auswertung*, ed. by Dieter R. Bauer and Klaus Herbers (Stuttgart: Steiner, 2000), pp. 117-29.
Vogel, Ernst G., 'Die Bibliothek der Benedictinerabtei Saint Benoit oder Fleury an der Loire', *Serapeum* 5 (1844), 17-29 and 46-8.
Volk, Paulus, *Die Generalkapitel der Bursfelder Benediktiner-Kongregation* (Münster: Aschendorff, 1928).
——, *Die Generalkapitels-Rezesse der Bursfelder Kongregation*, Vol. I: *1458-1530* (Siegburg: Republica, 1955).
Von Hefner, Joseph, 'Über den Mönch Konrad von Scheyern mit dem Beinamen philosophus', *Oberbayerisches Archiv für vaterländische Geschichte* 2 (1840), 150-80.
Von Zeissberg, Heinrich R., 'Fragmente eines Nekrologs des Klosters Reun in Steiermark', *Archiv für österreichische Geschichte* 58 (1879), 217-29.
Walcott, Mackenzie, 'Romsey Abbey', *The Gentleman's Magazine and Historical Review* 14 (1863), 198-200.
Walker, David, 'The Organisation of Material in Medieval Cartularies', in *The Study of Medieval Records: Essays in Honour of Kathleen Major*, ed. by Donald A. Bullough and Robin L. Storey (Oxford: Clarendon, 1971), pp. 132-50.
Ward, Graeme, 'The Sense of an Ending in the Histories of Frechulf of Lisieux', in *Historiography and Identity III: Carolingian Approaches*, ed. by Rutger Kramer et al. (Turnhout: Brepols, 2021), pp. 291-315.

——, *History, Scripture, and Authority in the Carolingian Empire: Frechulf of Lisieux* (Oxford: Oxford University Press, 2022).

Ward, Jennifer C., *Women of the English Nobility and Gentry, 1066–1500* (Manchester: Manchester University Press, 1995).

Watson, Sarah W. and S. C. Kaplan, 'Books of Duchesses: Mapping Women Book Owners in Late Medieval Francophone Europe, 1350–1550: Initial Findings', *Journal of the Early Book Society* 23 (2020), 27–60.

Watt, Diane, 'A Manuscript for Nuns: Cardiff, Central Library, MS 1.381', *Postcards from the Archives: Women's Literary Culture before the Conquest* (2018), https://blogs.surrey.ac.uk/early-medieval-women/2018/02/05/a-manuscript-for-nuns-cardiff-central-library-ms-1-381/.

——, 'Lost Books: Abbess Hildelith and the Literary Culture of Barking Abbey', *Philological Quarterly* 91 (2012), 1–22.

——, *Medieval Women's Writing: Works by and for Women in England, 1100–1500* (Cambridge: Polity, 2007).

——, *Women, Writing and Religion in England and Beyond, 650–1100* (London: Bloomsbury Academic, 2019).

Wattenbach, Wilhelm, *Das Schriftwesen im Mittelalter* (Leipzig: Hirzel, 1896).

Weakland, Rembert, 'Obedience to the Abbot and the Community in the Monastery', *Cistercian Studies* 5 (1970), 309–16.

Webber, Teresa, 'Books and Their Use across the Conquest', in *Bury St Edmunds and the Norman Conquest*, ed. by Tom Licence (Woodbridge: Boydell, 2014), pp. 160–89.

——, 'Cantor, Sacrist or Prior? The Provision of Books in Anglo-Norman England', in *Medieval Cantors and Their Craft: Music, Liturgy and the Shaping of History, 800–1500*, ed. by Margot E. Fassler, Andrew B. Kraebel, and Katie A.-M. Bugyis (Woodbridge: Boydell, 2017), pp. 172–89.

——, 'Les manuscrits de Christ Church (Cantorbéry) et de Salisbury à la fin du XIe siècle', in *Manuscrits et enluminures dans le monde normand: Xe–XVe siècles*, ed. by Pierre Bouet and Monique Dosdat (Caen: Presses universitaires, 1999), pp. 95–105.

——, 'Monastic and Cathedral Book Collections in the Late Eleventh and Twelfth Centuries', in *CHLBI* I, 109–25.

——, 'Monastic Space and the Use of Books in the Anglo-Norman World', *Anglo-Norman Studies* 36 (2014), 221–40.

——, 'Reading in the Refectory at Reading Abbey', *Reading Medieval Studies* 42 (2016), 63–88.

——, 'Script and Manuscript Production at Christ Church, Canterbury, after the Norman Conquest', in *Canterbury and the Norman Conquest: Churches, Saints and Scholars, 1066–1109*, ed. by Richard Eales and Richard Sharpe (London: Hambledon, 1995), pp. 145–58.

——, 'The Libraries of Religious Houses', in *The European Book in the Twelfth Century*, ed. by Erik Kwakkel and Rodney M. Thomson (Cambridge: Cambridge University Press, 2018), pp. 103–21.

——, 'The Provision of Books for Bury St Edmunds Abbey in the 11th and 12th Centuries', in *Bury St Edmunds: Medieval Art, Architecture, Archaeology and Economy*, ed. by Antonia Gransden (Leeds: British Archaeological Association, 1998), pp. 186–93.

——, 'Where Were Books Made and Kept?', in *The Cambridge Companion to Medieval British Manuscripts*, ed. by Orietta Da Rold and Elaine Treharne (Cambridge: Cambridge University Press, 2020), pp. 214–33.

Wehrli-Johnsin, Martina, '*Libri in cella*: Beobachtungen zu den Privatbibliotheken observanter Dominikaner aus dem Basler Predigerkloster', in *Die Bibliothek–The Library–La Bibliothèque: Denkräume und Wissensordnungen*, ed. by Andreas Speer und Lars Reuke (Berlin: De Gruyter, 2020), pp. 172–86.

Wei, Ian P., *Thinking about Animals in Thirteenth-Century Paris: Theologians on the Boundary between Humans and Animals* (Cambridge: Cambridge University Press, 2020).

Weiler, Björn, 'Historical Writing in Europe, c.1100–1300', in *The Chronicles of Medieval Wales and the March: New Contexts, Studies, and Texts*, ed. by Ben Guy et al. (Turnhout: Brepols, 2020), pp. 33–67.

Weis, Anton and Walter Steinmetz, eds., *Handschriftenverzeichnis der Stiftsbibliothek zu Rein* (Rein: self-published, 1999–2014).

Werner, Karl F., 'Andreas von Marchiennes und die Geschichtsschreibung von Anchin und Marchiennes in der zweiten Hälfte des 12. Jahrhunderts', *Deutsches Archiv für Erforschung des Mittelalters* 9 (1952), 402–63.

West, Charles, *Reframing the Feudal Revolution: Political and Social Transformation between Marne and Moselle, c.800–c.1100* (Cambridge: Cambridge University Press, 2013).

Westgard, Joshua A., 'New Manuscripts of Bede's Letter to Albinus', *Revue bénédictine* 120 (2010), 208–15.

Weston, Jenny and Charles C. Rozier, 'Descriptive Catalogue of Manuscripts Featuring the Hand of Orderic Vitalis', in *Orderic Vitalis: Life, Works and Interpretations*, ed. by Charles C. Rozier et al. (Woodbridge: Boydell, 2016), pp. 385–98.

Weston, Jenny, 'Manuscripts and Book Production at Le Bec', in *A Companion to the Abbey of Le Bec in the Central Middle Ages (11th–13th Centuries)*, ed. by Benjamin Pohl and Laura L. Gathagan (Leiden: Brill, 2017), pp. 144–70.

Weston, Lisa M., 'Conceiving the Word(s): Habits of Literacy Among Earlier Anglo-Saxon Monastic Women', in *Nuns' Literacies in Medieval Europe: The Hull Dialogue*, ed. by Virginia Blanton et el. (Turnhout: Brepols, 2013), pp. 149–67.

White, Stephen D., 'Locating Harold's Oath and Tracing His Itinerary', in Elizabeth C. Pastan and Stephen D. White, *The Bayeux Tapestry and Its Contexts: A Reassessment* (Woodbridge: Boydell, 2014), pp. 105–25.

Wiech, Martina, *Das Amt des Abtes im Konflikt: Studien zu den Auseinandersetzungen um Äbte früh- und hochmittelalterlicher Klöster unter besonderer Berücksichtigung des Bodenseegebiets* (Siegburg: Schmitt, 1999).

Wieland, Michael, 'Das Schottenkloster St. Jakob in Würzburg', *Archiv des historischen Vereins für Unterfranken und Aschaffenburg* 16 (1863), 1–183.

Wijsman, Hanno, *Luxury Bound: Illustrated Manuscript Production and Noble and Princely Book Ownership in the Burgundian Netherlands (1400–1550)* (Turnhout: Brepols, 2010).

Wilson, Katharina M., 'Introduction', in *Medieval Women Writers*, ed. by Katharina M. Wilson (Athens, GA: University of Georgia Press, 1984), pp. vii–xxix.

Winkler, Emily A. and Emily Dolmans, 'Discovering William of Malmesbury: The Man and His Works', in *Discovering William of Malmesbury*, ed. by Rodney M. Thomson et al. (Woodbridge: Boydell, 2019), pp. 1–11.

Winterer, Christoph, *Das Evangeliar der Äbtissin Hitda: Eine ottonische Prachthandschrift aus Köln: Miniaturen, Bilder und Zierseiten aus der Handschrift 1640 der Universitäts- und Landesbibliothek Darmstadt* (Darmstadt: Wissenschaftliche Buchgesellschaft, 2016).

Witten, Bärbel, *Die Vita der Heiligen Lioba: Eine angelsächsische Äbtissin im Karolingerreich* (Hamburg: Kovač, 2012).

Wogan-Browne, Jocelyn, 'Barking and the Historiography of Female Community', in *Barking Abbey and Medieval Literary Culture: Authorship and Authority in a Female Community*, ed. by Jennifer N. Brown and Donna A. Bussell (Woodbridge: Boydell, 2012), pp. 283–96.

——, 'Dead to the World? Death and the Maiden Revisited in Medieval Women's Convent Culture', in *Guidance for Women in Twelfth-Century Convents*, ed./tr. by Vera Morton and Jocelyn Wogan-Browne (Cambridge: Brewer, 2003), pp. 157–80.

Wolf, Gerhard and Norbert H. Ott, eds., *Handbuch Chroniken des Mittelalters* (Berlin: De Gruyter, 2016).

Wolff, Karl, 'Johannes Trithemius und die älteste Geschichte des Klosters Hirsau', *Württembergische Jahrbücher für Statistik und Landeskunde*, no volume number (1863), 229–81.

Wollasch, Joachim, '"Benedictus abbas Romensis": Das römische Element in der frühen benediktinischen Tradition', in *Tradition als historische Kraft: Interdisziplinäre Forschungen zur Geschichte des früheren Mittelalters*, ed. by Norbert Kamp and Joachim Wollasch (Berlin: De Gruyter, 1982), pp. 119–37.

Wolter, Hans, *Ordericus Vitalis: Ein Beitrag zur kluniazensischen Geschichtsschreibung* (Wiesbaden: Steiner, 1955), pp. 106–8.

Wood, Ian N., 'Roman Barbarians in the Burgundian Province', in *Transformations of Romanness: Early Medieval Regions and Identities*, ed. by Walter Pohl et al. (Berlin: De Gruyter, 2018), pp. 275–88.

——, 'Saint-Wandrille and Its Hagiography', in *Church and Chronicle in the Middle Ages: Essays Presented to John Taylor*, ed. by Ian N. Wood and Graham A. Loud (London: Bloomsbury Academic, 2003), pp. 1–14.

Wood, Jamie, 'Isidore of Seville as an Historian', in *A Companion to Isidore of Seville*, ed. by Andrew T. Fear and Jamie Wood (Leiden: Brill, 2019), pp. 153–81.

Woodford, Charlotte, *Nuns as Historians in Early Modern Germany* (Oxford: Oxford University Press, 2002).

Woodman, Francis, 'The Waterworks Drawings of the Eadwine Psalter', in *The Eadwine Psalter: Text, Image, and Monastic Culture in Twelfth-Century Canterbury*, ed. by Margaret Gibson et al. (London: MHRA, 1992), pp. 168–77.

Worstbrock, Franz J. 'Konrad von Scheyern', in *Die deutsche Literatur des Mittelalters-Verfasserlexikon*, ed. by Burghart Wachinger et al., 2nd rev. ed., 14 vols. (Berlin: De Gruyter, 1977–2008), V, 252–4.

——, 'Wolfger von Prüfening', in *Die deutsche Literatur des Mittelalters-Verfasserlexikon*, ed. by Burghart Wachinger et al., 2nd rev. ed., 14 vols. (Berlin: De Gruyter, 1977–2008), X, 1352–60.

Yardley, Anne B., 'Liturgy as the Site of Creative Engagement: Contributions of the Nuns of Barking', in *Barking Abbey and Medieval Literary Culture: Authorship and Authority in a Female Community*, ed. by Jennifer N. Brown and Donna A. Bussell (Woodbridge: Boydell, 2012), pp. 267–82.

Zapke, Susana, ed., *Hispania Vetus: Musical-Liturgical Manuscripts from Visigothic Origins to the Franco-Roman Transition (9th–12th Centuries)* (Bilbao: Fundación BBVA, 2007).

Zelzer, Klaus, *Ambrosius, Benedikt, Gregor: Philologisch-literarisch-historische Studien* (Vienna: LIT, 2015).

Zemler-Cizewski, Wanda, 'Guibert of Nogent's *How to Preach a Sermon*', *Theological Studies* 59 (1998), 406–19.

Zettler, Alfons, 'Spaces for Servants and *provendarii* in Early Medieval Monasteries: The Example of the Virtual Monastery on the Plan of Saint Gall', *Bulletin du centre d'études médiévales d'Auxerre* 8 (2015), 1–17.

——, 'Überlegungen zu den karolingerzeitlichen Herrscherbesuchen in den Bodenseeklöstern', in *Pfalz–Kloster–Klosterpfalz: Historische und archäologische Fragen*, ed. by Hans R. Sennhauser (Zurich: Hochschulverlag, 2009), pp. 105–20.

Ziegler, Hans U., 'Das Ebersberger Urkundenbuch–Ein Großprojekt historischer Forschung im Landkreis Ebersberg', *Land um den Ebersberger Forst* 4 (2001), 8–37.

——, 'Das historische Gesamtwerk des Abtes Williram von Ebersberg (1048–1085)', in *Kloster Ebersberg: Prägekraft christlich-abendländischer Kultur im Herzen Altbayerns*, ed. by Bernhard Schäfer (Ebersberg: Garnies, 2002), pp 161–84.

Ziegler, Walter, 'Die Bursfelder Kongregation', in *Die Reformverbände und Kongregationen der Benediktiner im deutschen Sprachraum*, ed. by Ulrich Faust and Franz Quartal (St Ottilien: Eos, 1999), pp. 315–407.

Zur Nieden, Andrea, *Der Alltag der Mönche: Studien zum Klosterplan von St. Gallen*. (Hamburg: Diplomatica, 2008).

Unpublished Literature

'Illuminated: Manuscripts in the Making' (online exhibition), https://www.fitzmuseum. cam.ac.uk/illuminated/manuscript/discover/the-peterborough-psalter/section/theme/folio/ folio-139v.

Coutant, Coraline, 'Le cartulaire de l'abbaye du Mont-Saint-Michel et ses additions (XIIe– XIVe siècles): Étude et édition critique', 2 vols. (Thèse diplôme d'archiviste-paléographe, École nationale des chartes, 2009).

Dutton, Anne M., 'Women's Use of Religious Literature in Medieval England' (unpublished PhD dissertation, University of York, 1995).

Freeman, James, 'The Lacock Cartularies' (2014), https://blogs.bl.uk/digitisedmanuscripts/ 2014/08/the-lacock-abbey-cartularies.html.

Freise, Eckhard, 'Die Anfänge der Geschichtsschreibung im Kloster Fulda' (unpublished PhD dissertation, University of Münster, 1979).

Gerzaguet, Jean-Pierre, 'Les communautés religieuses bénédictines de la vallée de la Scarpe (Saint-Vaast, Anchin, Marchiennes, Hasnon, Saint-Amand) du XIe au début du XIVe siècle: Travaux, recherches, perspectives' (unpublished habilitation, University of Lille, 2001).

Gometz, Abigail K., 'Eugippius of Lucullanum: A Biography' (unpublished PhD dissertation, University of Leeds, 2008).

Jackson, Eleanor, 'The St Albans *Benefactors' Book*: Precious Gifts and Colourful Characters', *British Library Medieval Manuscripts Blog*, https://blogs.bl.uk/digitisedmanuscripts/2020/ 05/the-st-albans-benefactors-book.html.

Johnston, Nick, '*Vexatio Falsorum Fratrum*: The Medieval Laybrother in the Order of Sempringham in Context' (unpublished PhD dissertation, University of Toronto, 2017).

Lecouteux, Stéphane, 'Les Annales de Flodoard de Reims (919–966) dans la tradition historiographique du Moyen Âge: Travail de l'annaliste et de l'historien, perception et maîtrise du temps (VIIIe–XIIe siècles)' (unpublished Master's thesis, École Pratique des Hautes Études, 2010–11).

McCaffray, Edmund M., 'The Culture of Literate Power at Cluny, 910–1156 CE' (unpublished PhD dissertation, Arizona State University, 2015).

McCann, Allison, 'Women's Books? Gendered Piety and Patronage in Late Medieval Bohemian Illuminated Codices' (unpublished PhD dissertation, University of Pittsburgh, 2019).

Niblaeus, Erik, 'German Influence on Religious Practice in Scandinavia, c.1050–1150' (unpublished PhD dissertation, King's College, London, 2010).

Parsons, Simon T., 'The Use of *Chanson de Geste* Motifs in the Latin Texts of the First Crusade, c.1095–1145' (unpublished PhD dissertation, Royal Holloway, University of London, 2015).

Raaijmakers, Janneke, 'Sacred Time, Sacred Space: History and Identity in the Monastery of Fulda (744–856)' (unpublished PhD dissertation, University of Amsterdam, 2003).

Turnock, Jonathan, 'Landscapes of Patronage, Power and Salvation: A Contextual Study of Architectural Stone Sculpture in Northern England, c.1070–c.1155', 2 vols. (unpublished PhD dissertation, Durham University, 2018).

Vlček Schurr, Jennifer S., 'The Passional of Abbess Cunegund: Protagonists, Production and a Question of Identity' (unpublished MPhil dissertation, University of Glasgow, 2009).

Ward, Elizabeth F., 'The Career of the Empress Judith, 819–843' (unpublished PhD dissertation, King's College, University of London, 2002).

Webber, Teresa, 'Reading in the Refectory: Monastic Practice in England, c.1000–c.1300', Annual John Coffin Memorial Palaeography Lecture 2010 (rev. 2013), https://www.academia.edu/9489001/Reading_in_the_Refectory_Monastic_Practice_in_England_c_1000_c_1300.

Westgard, Joshua A., 'Dissemination and Reception of Bede's *Historia ecclesiastica gentis Anglorum* in Germany, c.731–1500: The Manuscript Evidence' (unpublished PhD dissertation, University of North Carolina at Chapel Hill, 2005).

Winzer, Ulrich, 'Studien zum Kalender Hugos von Flavigny' (unpublished PhD dissertation, University of Münster, 1979).

Index

Note: Figures are indicated by an italic "*f*", following the page number.

For the benefit of digital users, indexed terms that span two pages (e.g., 52–3) may, on occasion, appear on only one of those pages.

Index nominum et locorum

Ægelric II, abbot of Crowland 181–2
Ælberht, archbishop of York 298–9
Ælfflæd, abbess of Whitby 129–30
Ælfgyva, abbess of Barking 136–7, 161–2
Ælfric, abbot of Eynsham 130–1
Ælfric, abbot of St Albans 201n.144
Ælred, abbot of Rievaulx, *see* Ælred of Rievaulx
Ælred of Rievaulx 127–30, 233–4
   De quodam miraculo mirabilia 127–9
   De sanctis ecclesiae Haugustaldensis 127–9
   Eulogium Davidis regis Scotorum 127–9
   Genealogia regum Anglorum 127–9
   Relatio de standardo 67–8, 127–9
   Vita Edwardi regis et confessoris 127–9, 233–4
   Vita Niniani 127–9
Æthelburh, abbess of Barking 135–7
Æthelred I, king of Wessex 130–1
Æthelweard, ealdorman 130–1, 133–4, 233–4
   Chronicon 130–1, 233–4, 321–2
Æthelwulf, king of Wessex 130–1
Abingdon
   Abbey 221–3
   De obedientiariis abbatiae Abbedonensis 221–3
   Historia ecclesie Abbendonensis 221–3
   Liber terrarium 223
Absalon, abbot of Saint-Amand 232–3
Adalard, abbot of Corbie, *see* Adalard, abbot of Corvey
Adalard, abbot of Corvey 106–7
Adalbero, archbishop of Reims 291
Adalbero, bishop of Laon 60, 140–1
Adalbert, abbot of Flavigny 52n.118, 325–9
Adalbert, abbot of Hornbach 210–11
Adalbert, provost of Corvey 272–3
Adalbert I of Ostrevent 119–21
Adalgar, abbot of Flavigny, *see* Adalgar, bishop of Autun
Adalgar, bishop of Autun 325–9
Adalolf, abbot of Saint-Bertin 68–70

Adam, abbot of Dryburgh, *see* Adam of Dryburgh
Adam, abbot of Evesham 218–19
Adam, abbot of Saint-Denis 149–51
Adam, *amanuensis* 36*f*, 309–13
Adam I, abbot of Casauria 98n.35
Adam II, abbot of Casauria 98n.35
Adam III, abbot of Casauria 98n.35
Adam de Damerham 302–4
   Historia de rebus gestis Glastoniensibus 302–4
Adam of Dryburgh 105–6
   Liber de quadripartito exercitio cellae 105–6
Adela, countess of Blois 25–6
Adelheid, empress 23–4, 131–2
Adelheid I, abbess of Quedlinburg 131–2
Adelheid II, abbess of Quedlinburg 131–2
Adelheid III, abbess of Quedlinburg 132n.167
Adelhelm, abbot of Bamberg/Michelsberg 204n.150
Adgar/William 135–6
   Le Gracial 135–6
Adomnán, abbot of Iona 16n.6
Adrald, provost of Flavigny 325–9
Adrevald, abbot of Flavigny 325–9
Adrian IV, pope 98, 99*f*
Adso, abbot of Montier-en-Der 290–1
Aduard, abbey 17n.10
Agnes, abbess of Nivelles 137–8
Agnes, abbess of Poitiers 264–6
Agnès de Thieuville, abbess of Caen 81–2, 86–7, 305
Agnes III, abbess of Quedlinburg 132n.167
Aichard, abbot of Jumièges 298–9
Aiglerius, archbishop of Naples 297–8
Aimeric, abbot of Casauria 98n.35
Aimoin of Fleury 285–6
Alan, Count of Brittany 65–7
Alan de Nesse, abbot of York 110–12, 111*f*
Alan Strayler 201–3
Alavicus, abbot of Pfäfers 178–9
Alberic, abbot of Casauria 98n.35

Alberic of Coucy 60
Albert, abbot of Stade 24-5
    Annales Stadenses 24-5
Albert II of Lauterbeck, abbot of Admont 192-4
Albinus, abbot of Canterbury 92-4, 233-4
Alcuin, abbot of Flavigny 325-9
Alcuin of York 107-8, 298-9
    Vitae 298-9
Aldhelm, abbot of Malmesbury 135-6
    De virginitate 135-6
Alexander III, pope 98, 218-19, 226-7
Alexandria 188-9
Albert II, bishop of Passau 199-200
Albert von Schmidmüln, abbot of St Emmeram 302-4
Albrecht Dürer 263-4
Alfanus, archbishop of Salerno 189-90
    Carmen acrostichum 189-90
Alferius, abbot of Cava 62-3
Alfred, king of the English 130-1
Algar, prior of Durham 94-5
Alparius, abbot of Casauria 98n.35
Altmann, abbot of Tegernsee 182-3
Altsig, abbot of York(?) 235-6
Amadeus, abbot of Flavigny 325-9
Amulricus, prior of Saint-Amand 229
Anastasius 190
    Historia tripertita 190
Andreas, *capellanus* 78-9
    Vita Roberti 78-9
Andreas Lang, abbot of Bamberg/Michelsberg 5, 14-15, 32-3, 162-3, 164f, 199-200, 203-4, 212-15, 287-90
    Catalogus abbatum 14-15, 32-3, 162-3, 199-200, 288
    Catalogus Bambergensis ecclesiae pontificum 14-15
    Catalogus sanctorum ordinis sancti Benedicti 14-15
    Chronica episcoporum Babenbergensium 14-15, 288
    Fasciculus abbatum 14-15, 32-3, 162-3, 164f, 199-200, 203-4, 212-15, 214f, 215f, 289-90
    Vitae Ottonis 14-15, 288
Andreas of Marchiennes 122-6
    Chronicon Marchianense 121-6, 161-2
    Historia succincta de gestis et successione regum Francorum 122-6
Andres, abbey 21-3
Angelus de Clavasio 282-3
    Summa angelica 282-3
Angelus Manse, abbot of Rein 274-7
    Series abbatum Runensium 274-7

Anna Maria von Mellin, abbess of Himmelpforten 82-3
Anonymus Beccensis, see Maurice of Le Bec
Ansbert, abbot of Saint-Wandrille 91-2, 293-4, 294f
    Vita Ansberti 293-4
Ansegis, abbot of Saint-Wandrille 91-2, 183-4, 227-8
Anselm, abbot of Le Bec, *see* Anselm of Canterbury
Anselm, archbishop of Canterbury, *see* Anselm of Canterbury
Anselm, prior of Le Bec, *see* Anselm of Canterbury
Anselm of Canterbury 112-16, 240-3
Anstrudis, abbess of Laon 137-8
Antoninus of Florence 285-6
Apollinaris, abbot of Flavigny 325-9
Aquinus, provost of Flavigny 325-9
Arnaud, abbot of Sens 198-9
    Chronicon sancti Petri Vivi 198-9
Arnold, abbot of Lübeck 18-20
    Chronica Slavorum 18-20
    Translation of *Gregorius* 18-20
Arnulf of Carinthia 300-1
Arnsburg
    Abbey 247-8
    Liber actorum 247-8
Attalanus, abbot of Bobbio 292-3
Augsburg
    Abbey 244-5
    Catalogus abbatum 248-9, 286-7
Augustine 211-12, 230-1, 259-60, 292-3, 298-9
Austreberta, abbess of Pavilly 137-8
Avitus of Vienne 298-9
    De spiritualis historiae gestis 298-9
Aymo, abbot of Flavigny 325-9
Azelinus, abbot of Blaubeuren 180-1
Azenaire, abbot of Reims 147

Baldric, abbot of Bourgueil, *see* Baldric of Bourgueil
Baldric, bishop of Noyon/Tournai 230-1
Baldric of Bourgueil 25-6, 78-9
    Vita Roberti 78-9
Balduin, abbot of Beaumont 302-4
Baldwin, abbot of Bury St Edmunds 179-80
Bamberg/Michelsberg 21-3, 203-4, 212-15
Barbara Lutzin, prioress of Würzburg 82-3
Barking
    Abbey 134-5, 158-9
    Liber 135-6
    Vie d'Edouard 134-5

Bartholomaeus Anglicus 248–9
    De proprietatibus rerum 248–9
Bartholomew, bishop of Laon 61–2
Battle of Hastings 298–9
Battle of Lechfeld 133–4
Baudonivia, nun of Poitiers 137–8
    Vita Radegundis 137–8
Baugulf, abbot of Fulda 20–1, 151–3, 299–300
Bayeux
    Bayeux Tapestry 165–7
    Cathedral 165–7
Beate, abbess of Derneburg 248–9
Beatrice, abbess of Überwasser 79–80, 86–7
Beatrice of Kent, abbess of Lacock 277–9
Beatrix I, abbess of Quedlinburg 131–2
Beatus, abbot of Casauria 98n.35
Bede 92–4, 177–8, 233–6, 243, 285–6
    *Chronica maiora/De temporum
        ratione* 301–2
    De natura rerum 301–2
    De temporibus 240–1, 301–2
    De VIII quaestionibus 92–4
    Historia abbatum 153–4, 177–8, 298–9
    Historia ecclesiastica gentis Anglorum 92–4,
        129–30, 135–6, 185–6, 298–9
    In regum librum XXX quaestiones 92–4
Benedict 96–7, 164–5, 189–90, 191f
Benedict, abbot of Canterbury, *see* Benedict
    Biscop
Benedict, abbot of Peterborough 205–6
Benedict, abbot of Wearmouth-Jarrow, *see*
    Benedict Biscop
Benedict Biscop 177–8, 298–9
Benedict VI, pope 325–9
Benedictus Levita 200–1
    *Capitularia Caroli magni et Ludovici
        pii* 200–1
Benediktbeuern
    Abbey 182–3
    Breviarium 182–3
Beneš, *scriptor* 208–10
Benzo of Alba 285–6
Berard, abbot of Casauria 98n.35
Berengar, abbot of Montier-en-Der 291
Beringer, abbot of Weingaten 196–8
Bern, abbot of Reichenau 21–3
Bernard, abbot of Admont 274–7
Bernard, abbot of Clairvaux, *see* Bernard of
    Clairvaux
Bernard, abbot of Cluny 175–6
Bernard, abbot of Marmoutier 145–7
Bernard, abbot of Mont-Saint-Michel 309–11
Bernard, abbot of Rein 273–4
Bernard of Clairvaux 312–13

Bernhelm, abbot of Sponheim 164–5, 262–3
Berthold, abbot of Weingarten 195–8, 197f,
    198f
    Berthold Sacramentary 195–6
Berthold, abbot of Zwiefalten 24–5
    *Libellus de constructione monasterii
        Zwivildensis* 24–5
Bertila, abbess of Chelles 234–5
    Vita Bertilae abbatissae Calensis 234–5
Bertradis I, abbess of Quedlinburg 132n.167
Bertradis II, abbess of Quedlinburg 132n.167
Blanche d'Auberville, abbess of Caen 81–2
Blasius, abbot of Hirsau 21–3, 127, 253–5
Bloemkamp, abbey 17n.10
Bobulenus, abbot of Bobbio 292–3
Boccaccio 268–9
    Decameron 268–9
Boethius 182–3, 232–3
    De consolatione philosophiae 232–3, 244–5
Boniface, bishop of Mainz 20–1, 154–8, 234–5,
    281–2
Boreas 189–90
Bors, Sir 268–9
Bovo, abbot of Saint-Bertin 69–71
Bovo II, abbot of Saint-Amand 229–31
Bristol, abbey 267–8
Brun Candidus 20–1, 153–7, 160–1
    Vita Aegil 20–1, 158–9
    Vita Baugulphi 153–7
Bruno, abbot of Hirsau 180–1
Burchard, abbot of Reims 146–9
Burchard, *armarius* 199–200
Burchard of Ursperg 285–6
Bursfelde
    Abbey 1–2, 175–6, 246, 305
    Caeremoniae Bursfeldenses 79–80, 175–6
    Congregation 1–2, 4–5, 21–3, 79–80,
        127, 305
    General Chapter 1–5, 14–15, 255–6

Cædmon 129–30
Caelius Sedulius 182–3, 290–1
Caen
    Abbey of La Trinité 86–7, 305–7
    Abbey of Saint-Étienne 240–1
Caesaria II, abbess of Arles 252–3
Caesarius, prior of Heisterbach, *see* Caesarius of
    Heisterbach
Caesarius of Heisterbach 101–2
    Continuation of *Catalogus archiepiscoporum
        Coloniensium* 101–2
    Dialogus miraculorum 101–2, 122
Calixtus II, pope 146–7
Campsey, abbey 161–2

Canterbury
    Abbey 136–7, 165–7, 192–4, 297–8
    Cathedral Priory 94–5, 116, 240–1, 289–90
    General Chapter 110–12
Caritas Pirckheimer, abbess of Nuremberg 80–1, 86–7
Casauria
    Abbey 97, 99
    Chronicon Casauriense/Liber instrumentorum seu chronicorum 97, 151–3, 321–2
Cassiodorus 231–2, 298–9
    Historia tripartita 231–2, 237, 298–9
Catherine Ire de Blangy de Saint-Hilaire, abbess of Caen 81–2
Celsa, abbess of Arles 137–8
Celsus, *praepositus* of Casauria 98
Ceolwulf, king of Northumbria 92–4
Charlemagne, emperor 77–8, 107–8, 183–4, 325–9
Charles the Bald, king of the Franks 140–1
Charles the Simple, king of the Franks 325–9
Chesthunt, abbey 305
Chilperic, king of the Franks 325–9
Christ 210–11, 217
Cicero 224–5, 273–4, 290–1
Clemence, nun of Barking 134–5, 161–2
Clothar III, king of Neustria 293–4
Clotsinda, abbess of Marchiennes 119–21
Clovis, king of the Franks 325–9
Cluny
    Abbey 21–3, 176–7, 244–5
    Consuetudines Cluniacenses 175–6
Colda, *scriptor* 208–10
Conrad, abbot of Scheyern 217–18, 227–8
    Chronicon Schirense 217–18
    Series abbatum Schirensium 217–18
Conrad, abbot of Tegernsee 182–3
Conrad I, abbot of Augsburg 248–9
Conrad I of Wagenbach, abbot of Weingarten 196–8
Conrad III, king of Germany 272–3
Conrad of Scheyern 217–18, 227–8
Constable, abbot of Cava 62–3
Corbie, abbey 21–3
Cornelia Melyn, abbess of Antwerp 82–3
Corvey
    Abbey 272–4
    Catalogus abbatum 273–4
Cosmas of Prague 256–8
    Chronica Bohemorum 256–8
Council of Paris 246–7
Council of Poitiers 50–1
Council of Valence 50–1

Crowland
    Abbey 181–2
    Historia Croylandensis 181–2
Cuthswith, abbess of Inkberrow 281–2

Dargun, abbey 219–20
Darius Phrygius 185–6, 301–2
    De origine Troianorum 185–6, 301–2
    De excidio Troiae 185–6
David Juyner, abbot of Cleeve 279
Dedimia, abbess of Chelles 137–8
Desiderius, abbot of Montecassino 95–6, 189–90, 191*f*
Deutz, abbey 21–3
Dietrich, abbot of Petershausen 178–9
Dijon, abbey 43–4, 47–8
Dominic, abbot of Casauria 98n.35
Dudo of Saint-Quentin 140–1
    Historia Normannorum 140–1
Duraclusius, monk of Würzburg 256, 258–9
Durham, cathedral priory 94–5

Eadburga, abbess of Minster-in-Thanet/ Wimbourne 234–5, 281–2
Eadmer of Canterbury 112–16
    Historia novorum in Anglia 112–14
    Vita Anselmi 112–14
Eadric, abbot of St Albans 201n.144
Eadwine, *scriptor* 253
Eadwulf, abbot of Malmesbury 145
Ealdred, abbot of St Albans 201n.144
Eberhard, abbot of Prüfening 216–17
Eberhard, abbot of Reichenau 248–9
Eberhard, abbot of Tours 118, 233–4
Eberhard III, abbot of Bamberg/ Michelsberg 204n.150, 289–90
Eburnant, *scriptor* 210–11
Edith of England 130–1
Edmund Horde, prior of Hinton 305–7
Edward the Confessor, king of England 127–9
    Vita Ædwardi 127–9
Edward the Elder, king of the English 130–1
Egbert, abbot of Tegernsee 182–3
Egmond, abbey 17n.10
Egwin, monk of St Albans 249–50
Eigil, abbot of Flavigny 325–9
Eigil, abbot of Fulda 16n.6, 20–1, 107–8, 151–61, 267–8
    Vita Sturmi 20–1, 153–5, 157–8, 160–1, 163
Einhard 91–2, 185–6, 285–6, 301–2
    Vita Karoli 185–6, 301–2
Einhard, abbot of Seligenstadt 235–6
Einhard, lay abbot of Saint-Wandrille, see Einhard

Einsiedeln, abbey 178-9
Ekkehard, abbot of Aura, *see* Ekkehard of Aura
Ekkehard of Aura 24-5, 285-6, 288
Ekkehard of St Gall 64-5
　Continuation of *Casus sancti Galli* 64-5
Ela, abbess of Lacock 277-9
Elinand, bishop of Laon 60-2
Elisabeth Herold, abbess of
　Oberschönenfeld 82-3
Elisabeth I, abbess of Quedlinburg 132n.167
Elisabeth Kempf, prioress of Unterlinden 81-2
　Translation of *Vitae sororum* 81-2
Ellinger, abbot of Benediktbeuern, *see* Ellinger of
　Tegernsee
Ellinger, abbot of Tegernsee, *see* Ellinger of
　Tegernsee
Ellinger of Tegernsee 182-5, 244-5
Elmuin, abbot of Flavigny 52-4, 325-9
Emo, abbot of Wittewierum 256-8
　Chronicon abbatum in Werum 256-8
Empress Matilda, *see* Matilda, empress
Enguerrand, bishop of Laon 61-2
Enguerrand I of Boves, lord of Coucy 61-2
Eoban, *presbyter* 234-5
Erbo, abbot of Prüfening 139-40, 216-17
Erchempert of Montecassino 190
　Historia Langobardorum Beneventanorum
　　degentium 190
Erfurt, abbey 1-2, 5, 305
Erhard, abbot of Würzburg 284
Erlebald, abbot of Reichenau 184-6
Etto, abbot of Reichenau 184-5
Eudes Rigaud, archbishop of Rouen 269-70
Eugippius, abbot of Castellum
　Lucullanum 15n.5, 321-2
　Vita Severini 321-2
Eusebius 33-4, 35f, 185-7
Eutyches 290-1
Evesham
　Abbey 218-19, 267-8
　Chronicon/Historia abbatiae de
　　Evesham 218-19

Falco, abbot of Cava 62-3
Farfa
　Abbey 21-3, 176-7
　Liber tramitis 105-6, 108, 175-6, 243-4
Faritius, abbot of Abingdon 221-3,
　224f
Fécamp, abbey 237-8
Ferréol of Uzès 172
Flavigny
　Abbey 325-9
　Series abbatum Flaviniacensium 325-9

Flavius Josephus 185-6, 285-6
　Antiquitates Iudaicae/Historiae
　　antiquitatum 185-7
　De bello Iudaico 185-7, 190
Florentius of Tricastina 137-8
Floricus, prior of Saint-Amand 229
Folcuin of Saint-Bertin 68-9, 187-8
　Chronicon Sithiense/Gesta abbatum
　　Sithiensium 187-8
Fontevraud, abbey 25-6
Franco, abbot of Casauria 98n.35
Freculf, bishop of Lisieux 140-1, 290-1
　Historiarum libri XII 140-1, 290-1
Frederick, abbot of Hildesheim 178-9
Frederick, abbot of Hirsau 180-5, 252-3
Fridebold, abbot of Augsburg 21-3
Frithric, abbot of St Albans 201n.144
Fromund of Tegernsee 244-5
Frontinus 245-6
　Strategemata 245-6
Frowin, abbot of Engelberg 211-12, 213f
Frutolf of Michelsberg 24-5, 288
　Chronica 288
Fulcard, abbot of Marchiennes 119-21
Fulcher, abbot of Flavigny 325-9
Fulcuin, prior of Saint-Amand 229, 232-3
Fulda
　Abbey 151-61, 165-7, 185-6, 235-6
　Annales Fuldenses antiquissimi 151-3
　Annales necrologici 151-3
　Cadmug Codex 300-1
　Catalogus abbatum Fuldensium 153-4
　Codices Bonifatiani 300-1
　Recension of *Chronicon Laurissense*
　　breve 151-3
　St Michael's Church 157-9, 158f, 159f
　Supplex libellus 154-5
　Vita Ratgarii 153-4

Galahad, Sir 268-9
Gallus Öhem 184-6
Gandersheim, abbey 131-2
Garnier, abbot of Saint-Germer-de-Fly 42-3,
　114-16
Garnier de Pont-Saint-Maxence 134-7, 144-5,
　161-2
　Vie de saint Thomas le martyr 134-5
Gaudry, bishop of Laon 61-2
Gébuin, bishop of Laon 60
Gebhard, abbot of Regensburg 194-5
Gellius 245-6
　Attic Nights 245-6
Geoffrey, abbot of Mont-Saint-Michel 309-11
Geoffrey d'Orleans, abbot of Crowland 181-2

Geoffrey de Gorham, abbot of St Albans 221
Geoffrey I, abbot of Vendôme 31-2, 194
  Annales Vindocinenses 31-2
Geoffrey of Breteuil/Saint-Victor 169-70, 172-3
Geoffrey of Monmouth 29-30, 285-6
  Historia regum Britanniae/De gestis
    Brittonum 29-30, 37
Geoffrey of Viterbo 285-6
George I, abbot of Bamberg/
    Michelsberg 204n.150
George Sarens, abbot of Saint Trond 187-8
Gerard, abbot of Dryburgh 105-6
Gerard, abbot of Flavigny 325-9
Gerard, bishop of Autun 325-9
Gerard, prior of Flavigny 49-51
Gerberga II, abbess of Gandersheim 133-4
Gerbert, abbot of Bobbio, see Sylvester II, pope
Gerbert of Aurillac, see Sylvester II, pope
Gertrude, abbess of Nivelles 137-8, 234-5
Gertrude, abbess of Quedlinburg 132n.167
Geruin, abbot of Flavigny 52n.118, 325-9
Gervase, abbot of Westminster 219-20
Gervase of Canterbury 308-9
Gervase of Chichester 309-11
Gervold, abbot of Saint-Wandrille 91-2, 183-4
Gerwin, abbot of Saint-Riquier 187-8
Gest of Robyn Hode 67-8
Gesta Alexandri Magni 186-7, 231-2, 287-8
Gesta ducis Ernesti 287-8
Gesta Francorum 148-9
Gesta Romanorum 279
Geylo, (abbot) of Flavigny 325-9
Giacomo Filippo Foresti 285-6
Gilbert, abbot of Gloucester 308-9
Gilbert, *magister* 229-30
Giovanni Berardo, prior of Casauria 97
Girfred, provost of Flavigny 325-9
Gisela, abbess of Chelles 77-8, 137-8
Giselbert, abbot of Casauria 98n.35
Giso, abbot of Casauria 98n.35
Gloucester
  Abbey 307-9
  *Historia monasterii sancti Petri
    Gloucestriae* 307-8
Godefrid, abbot of Prüfening 216
Godescalc, abbot of Saint-Bertin 187-8
Godfrey, abbot of Malmesbury 142-3
Godfrey, abbot of Nogent-sous-Coucy 61-2
Goscelin of Saint-Bertin 136-7, 144-5
  Vitae 136-7
Goszer, abbot of Flavigny 325-9
Gothelm, abbot of Benediktbeuern 182-3
Gottschalk of Benediktbeuern 182-3
Gozbert, abbot of St Gall 186-7, 266-7

Gozbert, abbot of Tegernsee 237
Gregory I, pope 106-7, 129-30, 154-5, 299-300, 325-9
Gregory of Tours 185-6, 285-6
  Historia Francorum 185-6, 190
Gregory the Great, *see* Gregory I, pope
Gregory VII, pope 47-8, 54-5, 146-7
Grimald, abbot of St Gall 186-7, 266-7, 301-2
Grimoald I, abbot of Casauria 98n.35
Grimoald II, abbot of Casauria 98n.35
Gumpold, abbot of Bamberg/
    Michelsberg 204n.150, 288
Gundela/Joyce Rowse, abbess of Romsey 270-1
Gunther, prior of Saint-Amand 229, 232-3
Gunther of Nordhausen, abbot of Erfurt 1-6, 14, 18-20, 119-21, 255-6, 271-2, 321-2
  De historiae studio et utilitate 1-5, 7-8, 14-15, 127, 322-3
Guibert, abbot of Nogent-sous-Coucy, *see*
    Guibert of Nogent
Guibert of Nogent 42-4, 56-62, 79-80, 114-16, 145-6
  Gesta Dei per Francos 56-7, 114-15
  Monodiae 56-8, 62, 114-15
  Moralia Geneseos 61-2, 114-15
  Tropologia in Osee 42-3
Guido, abbot of Nonantola 221-3
Guillaume Caoursin 285-6
Guy, abbot of Saint-Germain d'Auxerre 24-5

Hagano, bishop of Autun 48-9, 54-5
Haito, abbot of Reichenau 184-6
Halberstadt, abbey 3
Hamelin, abbot of Gloucester 307-9, 308f
Hariulf, abbot of Oudenburg, *see* Hariulf of
    Saint-Riquier
Hariulf of Saint-Riquier 187-8
  Chronicon Centulense 187-8
Hartmann, abbot of Pfäfers 178-9
Hartmut, abbot of St Gall 186-7, 266-7, 301-2
Hartung, abbot of St Emmeram 244-5
Hartung II, abbot of Bamberg/
    Michelsberg 204n.150
Hartwig, archbishop of Bremen 273-4, 304
Hatto, *armarius* 224-5
Hatto I, abbot of Fulda 139-40, 158-9, 300-1
Heilwig, abbess of Chelles 77-8, 321-2
  Continuation of *Annales Mettenses
    priores* 77-8
Heinrich Bullinger 271-2
Heldric, abbot of Flavigny 325-9
Hellin, abbot of Mont d'Hor 229-30, 232-3
Hellin, prior of Saint-Amand, *see* Hellin, abbot of
    Mont d'Hor

Helmeric, abbot of Bamberg/
   Michelsberg 204n.150
Heloïse, nun of Argenteuil 87–8
Hemfrid, abbot of Saint-Bertin 68–9
Henning Kalberg, abbot of Hildesheim 178–9
Henry, abbot of Bamberg/Michelsberg 204n.150
Henry, abbot of Kamp 302–4
Henry, abbot of Pfäfers 178–9
Henry, abbot of Scheyern 217–18
Henry, abbot of Waverley 127–9
Henry, bishop of Trient 247–8
Henry Berengar 272–3
Henry I, abbot of Reims 146–7
Henry I, king of England 103, 309–11
Henry I, king of France 325–9
Henry II, emperor 131–6
Henry II, king of England 267–8, 307–8, 308f, 309–12
Henry IV, emperor 47–8, 54–5
Henry of Blois, abbot of Glastonbury 45–6
Henry of Huntingdon 2n.11, 36f
   Historia Anglorum 37
Henry of Segusio 297–8
Henry VIII, king of England 267–8, 279, 305–7
Heribert, abbot of Saint-Bertin 70–1
Herluin, abbot of Le Bec 241–2
Herman, abbot of Bamberg/
   Michelsberg 199–200, 204n.150, 288
Herman, abbot of Tournai 24–5, 256–8
   Liber de restauratione monasterii sancti Martini Tornacensis 24–5, 252–3
Hermuin, abbot of Sens 198–9
Herold, abbot of Bamberg/
   Michelsberg 204n.150
Herrand, abbot of Tegernsee 182–3
Hervé, abbot of Flavigny 325–9
Hesso, abbot of Pfäfers 178–9
Hilarius 292–3
Hilda, abbes of Whitby 129–30
Hildebert II, abbot of Saint-Wandrille 91–2
Hildebrand, abbot of Saint-Bertin 68–9
Hildegard, abbess of Disibodenberg, *see* Hildegard of Bingen
Hildegard, abbess of Eibingen, *see* Hildegard of Bingen
Hildegard, abbess of Rupertsberg, *see* Hildegard of Bingen
Hildegard of Bingen 31–3, 34f, 87–8
   Liber divinorum operum 31–2
   Liber vitae meritorum 31–2
   Scivias 31–3
Hildelith, abbess of Barking 135–7
Hildemar of Corbie 96–7, 172
   Expositio regulae Benedicti 172

Hilgod, abbot of Marmoutier 147
Hincmar, archbishop of Reims 243
Hirsau
   Abbey 5, 127, 164–5, 176–7, 180–1
   Codex Hirsaugiensis 180–1
   Constitutiones Hirsaugienses 105–6, 108, 175–6
Historia Troianorum 287–8
Hitda, abbess of Meschede 206–8, 207f
   Hitda Codex 206–8, 207f, 210–11
Hornbach
   Abbey 210–11
   Hornbach Sacramentary 210–12
Hrotsvita of Gandersheim 133–4
   Gesta Ottonis 133–4
   Primordia coenobii Gandersheimensis 133–4
Hucbald of St Amand 119–21, 229–30
Hugh, abbot of Cluny 325–9
Hugh, abbot of Corbie 226–7
Hugh (I), abbot of Flavigny 325–9
Hugh (II), abbot of Flavigny, *see* Hugh of Flavigny
Hugh, abbot of Revesby 127–9
Hugh, archbishop of Lyon 48–9
Hugh, bishop of Die, *see* Hugh, archbishop of Lyon
Hugh I, abbot of Saint-Amand 229
Hugh II, abbot of Saint-Amand 297–8
Hugh of Cyfeiliog, earl of Chester 304
Hugh of Flavigny 43–4, 46–56, 55f, 79–80
   Chronicon 43–4, 46–56, 60
   Series abbatum Flaviniacensium 52–4
Huoggi, abbot of Fulda 300–1

Idung of Prufening 139–40
   Dialogus duorum monachorum Cisterciensis et Cluniacensis 139–40
Ilderic, abbot of Casauria 98n.35
Ingulf, abbot of Crowland 181–2
Innocent II, pope 218–19
Innocent III, pope 218–19
Institutiones beati Gilberti et successorum eius 109–10
Isidore of Seville 7–8, 316–17
   Etymologiae 7–8, 56–7, 69–70, 182–3, 316
Itto, abbot of Casauria 98n.35
Ivo I, abbot of Cluny 286–7

Jacob, abbot of Kastl 244–5
Jacqueline Bouette de Blémur, prioress of Caen 305–7
Jakob Wipfeling 283–4
Jarento, abbot of Dijon 43–4, 47–52, 54–6

Jean de Joceval, abbot of Saint-Germain d'Auxerre 24–5
Jerome 33–4, 35f, 172–3, 185–7, 235–6, 259–60
Jerome, abbot of Pomposa 192–4, 258–9
Jerome, abbot of St Eutychius 194
Jerusalem 291, 325–9
Johann Kolenhausen, abbot of Sponheim 164–5, 263–4
Johannes Centurianus 256, 259–60
Johannes Legatius 178–9
   Chronicon coenobii sancti Godehardi 178–9
Johannes Rode, abbot of Trier 274–7
Johannes Trithemius
   Abbot of Sponheim 5–6, 14–15, 21–3, 127, 164–5, 255–62, 283–4, 321–2
   Abbot of Würzburg 14–15, 21–3, 253–5, 260–4, 283–4
   Annales Hirsaugienses 14–15, 21–3, 127, 164–5, 253–5, 261–2
   Chronicon Hirsaugiense 14–15, 127
   Chronicon Sponheimense 14–15, 164–5
   Compendium... monasterii sancti Iacobi in suburbio Herbipolensi 14–15
   De duodecim excidiis observantiae regularis 5, 14–15
   De laude scriptorum 5, 259–60, 285–6
John, abbot of Arnsburg 247–8
John, abbot of Corbie 226–7
John, abbot of Fécamp 237–8
John, abbot of Glastonbury 302–4
John, abbot of Hirsau 21–3, 127, 253–5
John, abbot of Loccum 248–9
John, abbot of Malmesbury 145
John, abbot of Saint-Bertin 70–1
John de Cella, abbot of St Albans 201n.144
John de Gamage, abbot of Gloucester 307–8
John de Gilling, abbot of York 110–12
John I, abbot of Casauria 98n.35
John I, abbot of Montecassino 96–7
John II, abbot of Casauria 98n.35
John III, abbot of Bamberg/Michelsberg 204n.150
John III, abbot of Casauria 98n.35
John IV, abbot of Bamberg/Michelsberg 204n.150
John of Brinkley, abbot of Bury St Edmunds 302–4
John of Salerno 256–8
John of Salisbury 94–5
   Historia pontificalis 94–5
John of Wheathampstead, abbot of St Albans 201–3, 267–8, 280
John of Worcester 94–5, 308–9
   Chronicon ex chronicis 308–9

John Peckham, archbishop of Canterbury 270–1
John the Archchanter 177–8
John V, abbot of Subiaco 296–7
John VIII, pope 325–9
John XXIII, (anti-)pope 281–2
Jonas/Jonatus, abbot of Marchiennes 119–21
Jordan, abbot of Mont-Saint-Michel 297n.202
Jordanes 190
   De origine actibusque Getarum 190
Judith, abbess of Marchiennes 120n.123
Judith, empress 77–8
Julia, abbess of Pavilly 137–8
Julius Caesar 285–6, 291, 301–2
   Bellum Gallicum 291
   Cosmographia 301–2
Justinus 190, 285–6
   Epitome of *Historiae Philippicae* 190, 298–9
Jutta, abbess of Quedlinburg 132n.167
Juvenal 244–5

Kaiserchronik 288
Kamp
   Abbey 17n.10, 302–4
   Chronicon monasterii Campensis 302–4
Katharina of Gebersweiler, prioress of Unterlinden 81–2
   Vitae sororum 81–2
Katherine de Sutton, abbess of Barking 270–1
Kunigunde, abbess of Prague 208–10, 209f, 282–3
   Kunigunde Passional 208–10, 209f, 282–3
Kunigunde, abbess of Quedlinburg 132n.167
Kunigunde, abbess of Regensburg 139–40
Kunigunde, empress 131–2
Kunigunde of Bohemia, *see* Kunigunde, abbess of Prague
Kuno, bishop of Regensburg 37–41

L'abbesse qui fu grosse 268–9
Lacock
   Abbey 277–9
   Book of Lacock 278–9
   Lacock Annals 278–9
Lactantius 292–3
Lambert/Lantpert, abbot of Liège 24–5
Lambert, abbot of Saint-Bertin, *see* Lambert of Saint-Bertin
Lambert, monk of Reims 146–7
Lambert of Reninghelst 304
Lambert of Saint-Bertin 68–73, 187–8, 304
Lampert of Hersfeld 24–5, 285–6
   Annales 24–5

Libellus de institutione Hersveldensis ecclesiae 24–5
Vita Lulli archiepiscopi Moguntiacensis 24–5
Lancelot, Sir 268–9
Lanfranc, abbot of Caen, *see* Lanfranc of Canterbury
Lanfranc, archbishop of Canterbury, *see* Lanfranc of Canterbury
Lanfranc, prior of Le Bec, *see* Lanfranc of Canterbury
Lanfranc of Canterbury 240–2
Lantram, *amanuensis* 235–6
Lastingham, abbey 65–7
Laurence, abbot of Westminster 127–30, 233–4
Laurence de Budot, abbess of Caen 305–7
Leduin, abbot of Marchiennes, *see* Leduin, abbot of Saint-Vaast
Leduin, abbot of Saint-Vaast 119–21
Leo, abbot of Saint-Bertin 71–2
Leo IV, pope 300–1
Leo IX, pope 325–9
Le Bec, abbey 28–31, 37, 237–41
Leo I, abbot of Cava 62–3
Leo Marsicanus 95–6
  Chronica monasterii Casinensis 95–6
Leo of Ostia, *see* Leo Marsicanus
Leonas, abbot of Casauria 97–8, 99f, 151–3, 321–2
Letardus, abbot of Le Bec 30–1
Liber pontificalis 91–2, 153–4, 185–6
Liétry, bishop of Laon 60
Lionel, Sir 268–9
Liutprand of Cremona 285–6
Livy 285–6
Lobbes, abbey 21–3
Lorsch, abbey 185–6
Lothar III, emperor 272–3
Louis II, emperor 325–9
Louis VII, king of France 224–5
Louis the Pious, king of the Franks 77–8, 183–4, 325–9
Luitgard, abbess of Quedlinburg 132n.167
Lupus, abbot of Casauria 98n.35
Lupus, abbot of Ferrières, *see* Lupus of Ferrières
Lupus of Ferrières 235–6, 243

Macharius, abbot of Fleury 224–5
Madonna Usimbalda 268–9
Magdalena, abbess of Frauen-Chiemsee 80–1
Magna Carta 307
Magoald, abbot of Flavigny 51–4, 325–9
Majolus, abbot of Cluny 23–4, 243n.308, 286–7
Malmesbury, abbey 94–5
Manasses, abbot of Flavigny 52n.118, 325–9
Manasses I, archbishop of Reims 146–7

Manasses II, archbishop of Reims 146–7
Manegold, abbot of Hirsau 180–1
Marchiennes
  Abbey 119–22, 161–2
  Poleticum Marceniensis cenobii 122–3, 125–6
Marcus Sabellicus 285–6
Marcward, abbot of Prüm 235–6
Margarete, abbess of Frauental 221–3
Marianus, abbot of Flavigny 325–9
Marianus Scotus, abbot of Regensburg 256–8
Marie de Pontécoulant, abbess of Caen 305–7
Marinus, abbot of Cava 62–3
Marquard, abbot of Augsburg 248–9
Marquard, abbot of Deutz 37–41
Martianus Capella 232–3, 290–1
  De nuptiis Philologiae et Mercurii 232–3
Martin, abbot of Bamberg/Michelsberg 204n.150
Martin of Troppau 287–8
  Chronicon pontificum et imperatorum 287–8
Martin of Weißenburg, abbot of Reichenau 184–5
Mary 196–8
Mary, abbess of Barking 134–5
Matilda, abbess of Barking 135–6
Matilda, abbess of Essen 130–1, 133–4, 233–4, 321–2
Matilda, abbess of Quedlinburg 131–2, 138–40
Matilda, empress 144–5
Matilda of Ringelheim 131–4
Matilda of Scotland 141–2
Matilda of Tuscany 258–9
Matthew Paris 161–2
Matthias Dietrich, abbot of Würzburg 283–4
Maurice, emperor 325–9
Maurice of Le Bec 240–1
Maurus Servius Honoratus 290–1
Maximilian I, emperor 14–15
Maximus, bishop of Mainz 262
Meaux, abbey 21–3
Melchior, abbot of Augsburg 286–7
Melk
  Abbey 21–3
  Reform 21–3
Menendo, abbot of León 255n.12
Menko, abbot of Wittewierum 256–8
Mette, abbess of Wöltingerode 248–9
Metz, abbey 21–3
Michael of Mentmore, abbot of St Albans 280, 296–7
Milo, abbot of Flavigny 325–9
Mont-Saint-Michel
  Abbey 28–30, 33–4, 165–7, 237–40, 309–13
  Guanandrier 311–12
  Livre blanc 311–12

Montecassino
    Abbey 189–90, 299–300
    Chronica monasterii sancti Benedicti Casinensis 96–7, 189–90

Nennius
    Historia Brittonum 67–8
Nicholas, *amanuensis* 312–13
Niederaltaich, abbey 21–3
Nogbert the Brave, *see* Tether, Leah
Nonnosus, *amanuensis* 32–3, 162–3, 212–15, 215f, 288
Nordhausen
    Abbey 131–2
    Gunther of, *see* Gunther of Nordhausen, abbot of Erfurt
    Vitae Mathildis reginae 131–4
Norgaud, bishop of Autun 46–52, 54–5
Nothelm, *presbyter* 92–4, 233–4

Odalrichus, abbot of Pfäfers 178–9
Odbert, abbot of Saint-Bertin 69–70
Oderisius I, abbot of Montecassino 95–6, 190
Odilo, abbot of Cluny 23–4, 105–6
    Vita domni Willelmi abbatis 23–4
Odilo, abbot of La Croix-Saint-Leufroy 241–2
Odo, abbot of Cluny 256–8
Odo, bishop of Bayeux 165–7
Odo, prior of Canterbury 134–5
Odo I, abbot of Flavigny 325–9
Odo II, abbot of Flavigny 325–9
Olbert, abbot of Gembloux 188–9
Oldrius, abbot of Casauria 98n.35
Oliba, abbot of Ripoll 243–4
Oliba, bishop of Vic, *see* Oliba, abbot of Ripoll
Oliva/Gdańsk, abbey 21–3
Orderic Vitalis 94–5, 103–4, 138–9, 141–2, 144–5, 169, 252–3
    Historia ecclesiastica 103–4, 169
Origen 245–6, 259–60
Orosius 190
    Historiae adversus paganos 190
Osbert de Clare
    Vita beati Eadwardi regis Anglorum 127–9
Osterlinde, abbess of Quedlinburg 132n.167
Oswiu, king of Northumbria 129–30
Otbert, provost of Flavigny 325–9
Otto, abbot of Garsten 199–200
Otto, bishop of Bamberg 14–15, 217
Otto I, duke of Swabia 130–1
Otto I, emperor 130–4
Otto II, emperor 118–19, 133–4

Otto of Freising 274–7, 285–6
    Gesta Friderici 274–7
Oudenburg, abbey 21–3

Palladius 172–3
Pascal II, pope 49–50
Paul of Caen, abbot of St Albans 201n.144, 220–1
Paul the Deacon 106–8, 122–3, 149
    Historia Langobardorum 106–7, 190
    Historia Romana 106–7
Paulinus of Nola 298–9
    Carmina 298–9
Persius 244–5
Peter 210–11
Peter, abbot of Casauria 98n.35
Peter, abbot of Gloucester 307–8
Peter, abbot of Micy 204–5
Peter, abbot of Reims 94–5
Peter, bishop of Arras 122–3
Peterborough
    Abbey 204–5
    Peterborough Psalter 204–6, 205f
Peter Abelard 149–50
    Historia calamitatum 149–50
Peter Aldus, abbot of Bobbio 118–19
Peter I, abbot of Cava 62–4
Peter II, abbot of Venosa 62–4
    Vitae quatuor primorum abbatum Cavensium 62–4
Peter Lombard 239–40
    Libri quattuor sententiarum 239–40
Peter Mangot 169–70, 172–3
Peter Moraunt, abbot of Malmesbury 145
Peter the Venerable, abbot of Cluny 172, 244–5
Petershausen, abbey 178–9
Petronilla de Chemillé, abbess of Fontevraud 25–6, 78–9, 86–7, 94–5, 321–2
    Continuation of *Statuta* 78–9
Pfäfers
    Abbey 178–9
    Liber confraternitatis 178–9
Philip de Harcourt, bishop of Bayeux 239–40
Philip I, king of France 61–2
Phocas, emperor 325–9
Pierre le Duc, abbot of Saint-Victor 174–5
Pierre Le Roy, abbot of Mont-Saint-Michel 311–12
Pippin, king of the Franks 325–9
Pirminius, abbot of Reichenau 184–6
Pliny the Elder 298–9
    Historia naturalis 298–9

Pompeius Trogus 186–7
   Historiae Philippicae 186–7
Pontius, monk of Ripoll 243–4
Ponzius, abbot of Casauria 98n.35
Poppo, abbot of Oberaltaich 192–4
Poppo, abbot of Saint-Vaast 120n.125
Prosper of Aquitaine 182–3
Prüfening
   Abbey 139–40, 216
   Prüfening Isidore 216
Ptolemy II Philadelphus 188–9

Quedlinburg
   Abbey 131–2
   Annales Quedlinburgenses 131–2
Queen Matilda, *see* Matilda of Ringelheim *or* Matilda of Scotland
Quintilian 224–5, 235–6

Rabanus Maurus 20–1, 107–8, 262
   Abbot of Fulda 20–1, 139–40
   Archbishop of Mainz 139–40
   Liber de laudibus sanctae crucis 139–40
Radegund, queen of the Franks 264–6
Rainald, abbot of Flavigny 54–5, 325–9
Rainald of Dassel, archbishop of Cologne 245–6
Rainard, monk of Bobbio 118–19
Raingus, provost of Flavigny 325–9
Raino, abbot of Flavigny 325–9
Ralph, abbot of Battle 242–3
Ralph d'Escures, archbishop of Canterbury 112–14
Ralph of Diceto/Diss 26–7
Ramwold, abbot of St Emmeram 194–5, 237
Randulf, abbot of Evesham 218–19
Ranulf, abbot of Saint-Évroult 104
Ranulf, prior of Mont-Saint-Michel 309–11
Ranulf Flambard 94–5
Ranulf Flambard, bishop of Durham, *see* Ranulf Flambard
Raoul de Villedieu, abbot of Mont-Saint-Michel 297n.202
Raphael de Marcatellis, abbot of Ghent 285–6
Ratger, abbot of Fulda 20–1, 107–8, 154–7, 299–300
Ratlegius, abbot of Seligenstadt 235–6
Ratpert of St Gall 64–5, 266–7, 301–2
   Casus sancti Galli 64–5, 186–7, 266–7, 301–2
Ravenna 237–8
Reginald, abbot of Evesham 218–19
Reginbert, *armarius* 185–6
Reginbold, abbot of Muri 178–9
Regino of Prüm 285–6
   Chronicon 67–8

Regula Augustini 109–10, 171–3
Regula Benedicti 37–41, 63–4, 67–8, 96–7, 99–100, 102–3, 109–10, 154–5, 160–1, 171–2, 175–6, 223
Regula Ferrioli 162n.303, 172
Regula Magistri 171–2, 175–6
Regula Pachomii 171–3
Regularis concordia 240–1
Reichenau
   Abbey 184–5
   Cronick des gotzhuses Rychenowe 184–6
Reinhardsbrunn, abbey 5, 14–15
Reinher, *amanuensis* 32–3, 162–3, 212–15, 214*f*
Richard, abbot of Saint-Évroult 104
Richard, abbot of Saint-Vanne 69–70
Richard, abbot of Westminster 281–2
Richard d'Aubigny, abbot of St Albans 201–3, 201n.144, 221
Richard de Ware, abbot of Westminster 108
Richard Guthrie, abbot of Arbroath 302–4
Richard I, duke of Normandy 140–1
Richard II, duke of Normandy 140–1
Richard of Hexham
   Continuation of *Historia regum* 67–8
   De gestis regis Stephani 67–8
Richard of Wallingford, abbot of St Albans 280, 296–7
Richard of Warwick, abbot of Bristol 267–8
Richburga, abbess of Nordhausen 133–4
Richene, *scriptor* 211–12, 213*f*
Richolfus, abbot of Arnstein 302–4
Rictrude, abbess of Marchiennes 119–23
Rievaulx, abbey 129–30
Robert, abbot of Evesham 267–8
Robert, abbot of Flavigny 325–9
Robert, abbot of Vendôme 226–7
Robert, monk of Reims 146–7
Robert d'Arbrissel 78–9
Robert de Courçon 246–7
Robert de Gorham, abbot of St Albans 201n.144, 221
Robert de Lindsey, abbot of Peterborough 204–6, 205*f*
Robert Gaguin 285–6
Robert I, abbot of Chester 304
Robert Jolivet, abbot of Mont-Saint-Michel 26–7
Robert of Torigni, abbot of Mont-Saint-Michel 26–30, 33–4, 36*f*, 37, 86–7, 200–1, 237–40, 253, 254*f*, 309–13, 321–2
   Chronica 26–31, 33–7, 237–8, 312–13
   Continuation of *Gesta Normannorum ducum* 28–31

Robert the Monk 145-9
  Historia Iherosolimitana 145-9
Robert Wyvil, bishop of Salisbury 278
Roderic, abbot of Saint-Bertin 68-72
Rodulf, abbot of Nonantola 192-4
Rodulf, abbot of Saint-Vanne 43-4, 47-8, 51-2, 54-5
Rodulf, abbot of Tournai 252-3
Rodulfus Glaber 23-4
  Historiarum libri quinque 23-4
Roger, abbot of Evesham 218-19
Roger, abbot of Le Bec 30-1
Roger, abbot of Saint-Évroult 103, 138-9
Roger, bishop of Salisbury 142-3
Roger de Norton, abbot of St Albans 201-3, 201n.144
Romanus, abbot of Casauria 98n.35
Rome 37, 92-4, 154-7, 177-8, 192-4, 233-5, 298-9, 325-9
  Basilica sancti Petri 155-7
Rotmund, abbot of Flavigny 325-9
Ruadhelm, abbot of Reichenau 184-6
Rudolf, abbot of Saint Trond 187-8
  Gesta abbatum Trudonensium 187-8, 264-6
Rule of Pachomius, see *Regula Pachomii*
Rule of St Augustine, see *Regula Augustini*
Rule of St Benedict, see *Regula Benedicti*
Rule of the Master, see *Regula Magistri*
Ruotpert, abbot of Bamberg/Michelsberg 204n.150
Rupert, abbot of Deutz, *see* Rupert of Deutz
Rupert of Deutz 37-41, 40f, 41f, 272-3
  Continuation of *Vita sancti Heriberti archiepiscopi* 37-41
  Libellus 37-41
  Liber de Divinis officiis 37-41
  Vita Cunonis abbatis Sigebergensis 37-41
Rusticula, abbess of Arles 137-8

Sabinian, pope 325-9
Sadalberga, abbess of Laon 137-8
Saint-Amand
  Abbey 228-30
  Liber privilegiorum 231-2
Saint-Bénigne de Dijon, see Dijon, Abbey
Saint-Denis, abbey 21-3, 179-80
Saint-Évroult, abbey 103, 138-9
Saint-Germain d'Auxerre, abbey 23-5
Saint-Vanne, abbey 43-4
Saint-Victor
  Abbey 174-7
  Liber ordinis 174-5
Saint-Wandrille
  Abbey 91-2

Gesta abbatum Fontanellensium 91-2, 153-4, 183-4, 187-8, 227-8, 293-4, 321-2
  Maius chronicon Fontanellense 293-4
Saint Trond, abbey 21-3, 187-8
Salimbene di Adam 221-3
Salomon, *amanuensis* 243-4
Sarulf, abbot of Flavigny 325-9
Saxo Grammaticus 285-6
Scheyern
  Abbey 21-3
  Scheyerer Matutinalbuch 227-8
Scholastica 96-7
Scolland, abbot of Canterbury 165-7
Sénuc, priory 146-7
Secundius, archbishop of Lyon 325-9
Seiwold, abbot of Bath 298-300
Sergius, *armarius* 63-4
Serlo, abbot of Gloucester 307-8
Serlo of Wilton 67-8
Sibyl de Felton, abbess of Barking 281-2
Siegfried, abbot of Schaffhausen 192-4
Siegfried, abbot of Tegernsee 182-3
Sigard, abbot of Flavigny 325-9
Sigebert of Gembloux 26-8, 33-7, 188-9, 285-6
  Chronica 28
  Gesta abbatum Gemblacensium 188-9
Sigismund, archduke of Austria 287-8
Simon, abbot of Auchy-lès-Hesdin, *see* Simon, abbot of Saint-Bertin
Simon, abbot of Marchiennes 119-27, 161-2
Simon, abbot of Saint-Bertin 24-5, 68-73
  Continuation of *Chronicon Sithiense*/*Gesta abbatum Sithiensium* 24-5, 68-73, 187-8
Simon, abbot of St Albans 200-1, 201n.144, 221, 294-7, 295f, 312-13
Siward, abbot of Rastede 179-80
Smaragdus, abbot of Saint-Mihiel 172
Sophia Dobbers, abbess of Überwasser 79-80
Sophia of Stolberg, abbess of Helfta 3-6, 87-8, 321-2
  Libellus de fundatione monasterii in Helfta 3-5, 87-8
Sponheim, abbey 127, 164-5
St Albans
  Abbey 21-3, 267-8, 294-6
  Gesta abbatum 200-4, 219-20, 249-50, 296-7, 312-13
  Liber benefactorum 201-4
St Emmeram, abbey 133-4
St Gall
  Abbey 186-7
  Plan of St Gall 266-7
St Olaf's Church, York 65-7
Stephanus, *amanuensis* 37-41, 40f

Stephen, abbot of Casauria 98n.35
Stephen, abbot of Marchiennes 123–4
Stephen, abbot of Saint-Airy 37, 38*f*
   Vita sancti Agerici 37
Stephen of Lexington, abbot of
   Savigny 132n.167
Stephen of Ripon 296–7
Stephen of Whitby, abbot of York 64–8, 110–12
   Historia fundationis abbatiae sanctae Mariae Eboracensis 64–5, 67–8
Stephen V, pope 325–9
Sturmius, abbot of Fulda 20–1, 151–8
Suetonius 235–6
   De vita Caesarum 235–6
Suger, abbot of Saint-Denis, *see* Suger of Saint-Denis
Suger of Saint-Denis 45–6, 149–51
   De administratione 45–6
Swicher, *scriptor* 216
Swicher of Prüfening, *see* Swicher, *scriptor*
Sylvester II, pope 118–19, 233–4, 256–8, 291
Symeon of Durham 94–5, 144–5
   Historia regum 67–8
   Libellus de exordio 94–5

Tacitus 190, 285–6
   Annales 190
   Historiae 190
Terence 290–1
Tetbaldus, bishop of Langres 325–9
Tether, Leah, *see* Nogbert the Brave
Theobald, abbot of Le Bec, *see* Theobald, archbishop of Canterbury
Theobald, archbishop of Canterbury 30–1
Theodemar, abbot of Montecassino 106–7, 122–3, 149, 189–90
Theoderic, bishop of Verdun 47–8
Theoderic, king of the Franks 325–9
Theoderic of Homborch, abbot of Bursfelde 1–2
Thiemo, abbot of Bamberg/Michelsberg 204n.150, 288
Thierry de Mathonville, abbot of Saint-Évroult 252–3
Thomas Arundel 305–7
Thomas Cromwell 305–7
Thomas de la Mare, abbot of St Albans 201–3, 280
Thomas Findon, abbot of Canterbury 192–4
Thomas le Roy 311n.265
Thomas Malory, Sir 268–9
   Morte Darthur 268–9
Thomas Marle, lord of Coucy 61–2
Thomas of Marlborough, abbot of Evesham 218–19

Thomas Sam, abbot of Cerne 281–2
Thomas Walsingham 201–3
Thucydides 285–6
Tournai, abbey 21–3
Trasaire, abbot of Saint-Wandrille 91–2
Trasemund, abbot of Casauria 98n.35
Turgot, prior of Durham 94–5
Turnei von dem zers, der 268–9

Udalric II, abbot of Bamberg/Michelsberg 204n.150
Udalric III, abbot of Bamberg/Michelsberg 204n.150
Udalrich I, abbot of Tegernsee 182–3
Udo, abbot of Chartres 225–6
Ulrich, abbot of Bamberg/Michelsberg 289–90
Ulrich Tinkler, abbot of Kappel 271–2
Ulrich von Richenthal 285–6
Uppsala 179–80
Urban II, pope 147
Ursinus, monk of Cava 63–4
Ursula Pfaffinger, abbess of Frauen-Chiemsee 80–1, 321–2
   Continuation of *Gschicht Büech* 80–1, 86–7
Uto I, abbot of Bamberg/Michelsberg 204n.150
Uto II, abbot of Bamberg/Michelsberg 204n.150

Vabres, abbey 21–3
Valerius Maximus 285–6
Vendôme, abbey 31–2
Victor III, pope, *see* Desiderius, abbot of Montecassino
Vigilius, abbot of Flavigny 325–9
Villarceaux, priory 269–70
Vincent of Beauvais 287–8
   Speculum historiale 287–8
Volcold, abbot of Bamberg/Michelsberg 204n.150
Volmar, abbot of Hirsau 180–1
Volmar, *amanuensis* 31–3, 34*f*
   Disibodenberg Chronicle 31–2
Vorgust, abbot of Bobbio 292–3
Vornbach
   Abbey 21–3
Vulfald, abbot of Flavigny 325–9

Walafrid, abbot of Reichenau, *see* Walafrid of Strabo
Walafrid of Strabo 246
Waldo, abbot of Reichenau 184–6
Walo, abbot of Flavigny, *see* Walo, bishop of Autun

Walo, bishop of Autun 325–9
Walter, abbot of Bamberg/Michelsberg 204n.150
Walter, abbot of Flavigny 325–9
Walter, abbot of Tournai 229–30
Walter, bishop of Autun 325–9
Walter, prior of Saint-Amand, *see* Walter, abbot of Tournai
Walter Daniel, monk of Rievaulx 127–9
Walter Frocester, abbot of Gloucester 307–9
Walter Hungerford, Sir 305–7
Walter I, abbot of Saint-Amand 229–33
Waltram, abbot of Fischingen 178–9
Wando, abbot of Saint-Wandrille 183–4
Wandregisel, abbot of Saint-Wandrille 293–4
Warin, abbot of Saint-Évroult 103, 138–40
Warin, abbot of St Albans 201, 202*f*
Warin, (quasi-)abbot of Flavigny 325–9
Wearmouth-Jarrow
  Abbey 92–4, 233–4
  Vita Ceolfridi 153–4
Werner Rolevinck 285–8
  Fasciculus temporum 287–8
Westminster, abbey 108, 127–30, 219–20
Whitby, abbey 65–6
Wibald, abbot of Corvey 245–6, 272–4, 275*f*, 304
Wibert, prior of Canterbury 289–90
Wichard, abbot of Flavigny 325–9
Widerard, abbot of Flavigny 52n.118, 325–9
Wido, abbot of Casauria 98n.35
Widukind of Corvey 131–2, 138–9, 285–6
  Res gestae Saxonicae sive annalium libri tres 131–4, 190
Wigand, abbot of Hirsau 5–6
Wilfrid, (arch)bishop of York 296–7
William, abbot of Andres, *see* William of Andres
William, abbot of Hirsau 180–1
William, abbot of Marmoutier 147
William, *capellanus* 280, 304
William, monk of Tournai 115–16, 117*f*
William de Percy, baron 65–7
William I, abbot of Caen 241–3
William I, king of England, *see* William the Conqueror
William II, duke of Normandy, *see* William the Conqueror
William II, king of England 65–6, 94–5
William III, landgrave of Thuringia 287–8
William Malvern/Parker, abbot of Gloucester 25–6, 308–9
William of Andres 25–6, 123–4

William of Bernham, abbot of Bury St Edmunds 302–4
William of Brussels, abbot of Saint Trond 187–8
William of Dijon, *see* William of Volpiano
William of Jumièges 28, 285–6
  Gesta Normannorum ducum 28
William of Malmesbury 45–6, 141–5
  De antiquitate Glastoniensis ecclesiae 45–6, 141–2, 144–5
  Gesta pontificum Anglorum 141–2
  Gesta regum Anglorum 67–8, 141–5
William of Saint-Thierry 274–7
  Vita prima Bernardi 274–7
William of Trumpington, abbot of St Albans 201n.144
William of Tyre 287–8
  Historia Ierosolymitana 287–8
William of Volpiano 23–4, 237–8
William the Conqueror 65–7, 165–7
William the Subdeacon, *amanuensis* 42–4
Williram, abbot of Ebersberg 247–8
  Catalogus abbatum Eberspergensium 247–8
  Chronicon Eberspergense 247–8
Wiric, abbot of Saint Trond 187–8, 264–6
Witham, abbey 105–6
Wolfgang I, abbot of Bamberg/Michelsberg 204n.150
Wolfgang II, abbot of Bamberg/Michelsberg 204n.150
Wolfgang Joner, abbot of Kappel 271–2
Wolfger, *armarius* 217
Wolfhard, abbot of Flavigny 325–9
Wolfram I, abbot of Bamberg/Michelsberg 199–200
Wolfram II, abbot of Bamberg/Michelsberg 204n.150
Worcester, cathedral priory 94–5
Würzburg
  Abbey 253–5
  Cathedral 153–4
Wulfhild, abbess of Barking 136–7
Wulfstan II, bishop of Worcester 94–5
Wulnoth, abbot of St Albans 201n.144, 249–50
Wulsic, abbot of St Albans 201n.144

York, abbey 64–8, 110–12

Zacho, abbot of Flavigny 51–2, 325–9
Żagań
  Abbey 21–3, 219–20
  Consuetudines 219–20
Zbraslav, abbey 21–3
Zwettl, abbey 282–3

Index manuscriptorum

Arras, Bibliothèque municipale
   MS 294 (849) 299n.211
   MS 364 (453) 123–4
   MS 573 (462) 299n.211
   MS 849 (539) 298–9
   MS 1029 (812) 298–9
   MS 1071 (274) 299n.211
Augsburg, Archiv des Bistums, MS 78
   248–9, 286–7
Austin, TX, Harry Ransom Center, MS 29
   182–3
Auxerre, Bibliothèque municipale, MS 212
   198n.132
Avranches, Bibliothèque patrimoniale
   MS 145 200–1
   MS 149 297n.202
   MS 159 28, 30n.58, 33–4, 35*f*, 36*f*, 237–8, 239n.287
   MS 210 309–11

Bamberg, Staatsarchiv
   Rep. 29 no. 9 199n.137, 287n.166
   Rep. 187 no. 3030 199n.137, 287n.166
Bamberg, Staatsbibliothek
   MS Misc. 182.1–2 287n.167
   MS Msc. Hist. 146 81n.226
   MS Msc. Hist. 147 81n.226
   MS RB Msc. 48 162–3
   MS RB Msc. 49 162–3, 163n.305, 204n.150, 212–15, 214*f*, 215*f*, 287n.167, 288n.171, 289nn.172,175, 290nn.176–178
Basel, Universitätsbibliothek, MS F III 42 154n.264
Berlin, Staatsbibliothek zu Berlin–Preußischer Kulturbesitz
   MS lat. fol. 252 273–4, 275*f*
   MS Phill. 1870 46n.88, 52n.118, 55*f*, 325–9
Boulogne-sur-Mer, Bibliothèque municipale
   MS 146 304n.236
   MS 146A 304n.236
Bruges, Rijksarchief, S. Bertijns Poperinge 3 304
Brussels, Koninklijke Bibliotheek van België, MS 9850–52 298–9

Cambridge, Corpus Christi College
   MS 51 34n.75
   MS 77 280n.132
   MS 92 281n.133
   MS 139 64–5
Cambridge, Fitzwilliam Museum, MS 12 204–5, 205*f*

Cambridge, Gonville and Caius College, MS 391/611 26n.45, 309n.255
Cambridge, Jesus College, MS 18 281n.133, 302–4
Cambridge, St John's College
   MS D.6 204n.154
   MS D.27 277n.116
   MS G.15 (183) 200n.140
Cambridge, Trinity College
   MS B.14.36 280n.132
   MS R.5.33 302–4
   MS R.17.1 289n.173
Cambridge, University Library
   MS Ee.4.20 280
   MS Ee.4.23 281–2
   MS Gg.4.11 280n.132
   MS Ll.1.10 281n.134
Canterbury, Cathedral Archives and Library
   DCC/ChAnt/A/66C 297–8
   DCC/ChAnt/Z/141 281n.133
   DCC/LitMS/C/11 281n.133
Cardiff, Public Library, MS 1.381 161–2
Charleville-Mézières, Bibliothèque municipale–Médiathèque Voyelles, MS 25 302–4

Darmstadt, Universitäts- und Landesbibliothek
   MS 1640 206–8, 207*f*
   MS 1948 206n.160
Dijon, Bibliothèque municipale, MS 448 52–4
Douai, Bibliothèque Marceline Desbordes-Valmore, MS 850 123–5, 124n.137
Dublin, Trinity College
   MS 57 (A.4.5) 255n.12
   MS 444 280n.132

Engelberg, Stiftsbibliothek
   MS Cod. 4 211–12
   MS Cod. 5 211–12, 213*f*
   MS Cod. 23 211n.177
   MS Cod. 47 211n.177
   MS Cod. 88 211–12
Erlangen, Universitätsbibliothek, MS 136 222n.213
Evreux, Bibliothèque municipale, MS Lat. 46 170n.4

Florence, Biblioteca Medicea Laurenziana
   MS Plut. 66.21 190
   MS Plut. 68.2 190
Frankfurt, Universitätsbibliothek, MS Barth. 104 31–2
Freiburg i. Br., Universitätsbibliothek, MS 15 184–5

Fulda, Hochschul- und Landesbibliothek
  MS B1 153n.262
  MS B3 300-1

Gloucester, Cathedral Library
  Frocester Register 1397 (*olim* Reg. A)
    307n.249
  MS 34 307n.247

Hanover, Niedersächsisches Landesarchiv
  Cal. Or. 100 Loccum, Urkunde 842 248-9
  Dep. 76, C 113 3n.13
Heidelberg, Universitätsbibliothek
  MS Cod. Sal. IX 42a 178-9
  MS Cod. Sal. X.16 32-3, 34*f*
Hildesheim, Dombibliothek
  MS 313b 285n.156
  MS 785 285n.156

Kew, National Archives, C 150/1 307-8, 308*f*

Laon, Archives départementales de l'Aisne,
  H 325 60n.154, 61n.155
Le Havre, Bibliothèque municipale Armand
  Salacrou, MS 332 293-4, 294*f*
Leiden, Universiteitsbibliotheek
  MS Scaliger 49 154n.264
  MS Voss. Lat. Q. 110 204n.151
Leipzig, Universitätsbibliothek, MS Rep. II. 69
  188n.101
León, Biblioteca de la Real Colegiata de San
  Isidoro, MS Cod. I 3 255n.12
Lich, Fürst zu Solms-Hohensolms-Lich'sches
  Archiv, Liber actorum Arnsburg 247-8
Liège, Archives de l'État, Abbaye impériale de
  Stavelot, MS I 341 272-3
Lille, Archives départementales du Nord, 12 H 1,
  no. 38 231n.254
London, British Library
  MS Add. 38816 67n.184
  MS Add. 40007 26-7
  MS Add. 59678 269n.76
  MS Add. 70513 161-2
  MS Add. 88973 278-9
  MS Add. 88974 278-9
  MS Arundel 34 267-8, 280n.126
  MS Cotton Claudius C IX 223, 224*f*
  MS Cotton Claudius E III 26-7
  MS Cotton Claudius E IV 201, 202*f*, 294-6,
    295*f*
  MS Cotton Domitian A VIII
    307nn.247-248,250, 308n.251
  MS Cotton Julius A XI 206n.158
  MS Cotton Julius D III 313n.272
  MS Cotton Nero D VII 201-3, 203*f*
  MS Cotton Otho B. IV 280n.126
  MS Cotton Otho C. XI 108
  MS Cotton Vitellius A XIII 222n.214
  MS Cotton Vitellius A VIII 278-9
  MS Cotton Vitellius C VI 297-8
  MS Harley 3045 302-4
  MS Harley 3661 81-2
  MS Harley 5019 278-9
  MS Harley 5765 281-2
  MS Royal 8 G I 280n.132
  MS Royal 9 C X 280n.132
  MS Royal 10 D III 280n.132
  MS Royal 13 D IV 296-7
London, Society of Antiquaries, MS 59 204n.154
Lucca, Biblioteca Statale, MS 1942 32-3

Manchester, University Library–John Rylands
  Library, Rylands Charter 1436 304n.237
Marburg, Universitätsbibliothek, MS 75 246
Melk, Stiftsbibliothek, MS 20 1n.4
Milan, Biblioteca Ambrosiana, MS S 45
  sup. 292-3
Modena, Biblioteca Estense Universitaria, MS
  Lat. 390 (*a*.H.4.6; *olim* VI.F.5) 193n.113,
  258-9
Montecassino, Archivio dell'Abbazia–Biblioteca
  Statale del Monumento Nazionale
  MS Casin. 175 96-7
  MS 6 190
  MS 275 190
  MS 298 190
Montpellier, Bibliothèque
  interuniversitaire–Bibliothèque
  universitaire historique de médecine,
  MS H 151 37n.77, 43-4
Munich, Bayerische Staatsbibliothek
  MS Clm. 703 15n.2, 21-3, 253-5
  MS Clm. 704 15n.2, 21-3, 253-5, 256n.17
  MS Clm. 1072 183n.76
  MS Clm. 1925 282-3
  MS Clm. 4623 96n.25
  MS Clm. 6911 258n.23
  MS Clm. 9540 192-4
  MS Clm. 13002 216, 217n.189
  MS Clm. 13031 216
  MS Clm. 14222 194-5
  MS Clm. 14355 37-41, 40*f*, 41*f*
  MS Clm. 14361 216n.184
  MS Clm. 14398 212n.180
  MS Clm. 14437 255n.12
  MS Clm. 14641 152n.256
  MS Clm. 14958 244n.313
  MS Clm. 17142 170n.3

MS Clm. 17401 227-8
MS Clm. 17403 217n.192
MS Clm. 18192 182-3
MS Clm. 18571 182-3
MS Clm. 19411 237n.277
MS Clm. 19412 237nn.276-277
MS Clm. 19472 274n.107
MS Clm. 21521 277n.116
Munich, Bayerisches Hauptstaatsarchiv
  Kloster Benediktbeuern, Amtsbücher und
    Akten 1 182-3
  Kloster Ebersberg, KL 2 247-8, 248n.326
  Kloster Prüfening, KL 2 217
  Kloster St. Emmeram, Regensburg Urkunden
    526 302-4
Münster, Landesarchiv Nordrhein-
    Westfalen-Staatsarchiv
  MS I 133 273-4
  MS I 243 273-4

New York, NY, Pierpont Morgan Library
  MS M.710 195-6
  MS M.826 298-9

Oldenburg, Landesbibliothek, MS 99i 5n.19
Oldenburg, Staatsarchiv, Bestd. 23,1, No. 3
    179n.58
Oxford, Bodleian Library
  MS Bodley 39 110-12, 111f
  MS Bodley 292 280n.132
  MS Bodley 309 31-2
  MS Digby 86 255n.12
  MS Douce 136 109-10
  MS Laud Lat. 114 279n.123
  MS Laud Misc. 126 154n.265
  MS Laud Misc. 264 280n.132
  MS Laud Misc. 279 277n.116
Oxford, University College, MS 169 281-2

Paris, Bibliothèque nationale de France
  Coll. Picardie 233 60n.154
  Coll. Picardie 268 60n.154
  Coll. Picardie 291 61n.155
  MS Baluze 42 59, 60n.150
  MS fr. 10468 26-7
  MS fr. 13513 134-5
  MS Lat. 529 116n.111
  MS Lat. 1245 269-70
  MS Lat. 1820 204n.151
  MS Lat. 1847 232nn.256,258
  MS Lat. 1850 228-9, 231n.250, 298n.205
  MS Lat. 1862 204n.151
  MS Lat. 1918 230n.245
  MS Lat. 2012 230-1

MS Lat. 2502 42-3
MS Lat. 2858 243-4
MS Lat. 5411 97, 98nn.34,37, 99f
MS Lat. 5547 290-1
MS Lat. 7696 224-5
MS Lat. 10912 23-4
MS Lat. 10938 286n.163
MS Lat. 11757 37n.77
MS Lat. 12681 60n.154, 61nn.155-156
MS Lat. 14651 37n.77
MS Lat. 17545 28n.53
MS Lat. 17767 227n.233
MS Lat. 17768 227n.233
MS Lat. 17770 227n.233
MS Lat. 17775 61n.155
MS Moreau 42 231n.254
MS Nouv. acq. lat. 1219 231n.254
Paris, Institut de France-Bibliothèque Mazarine
  MS 753 115-16, 117f
  MS 2013 151
Pommersfelden, Gräflich Schönbornsche
    Schloßbibliothek, Cod. 340 (olim
    2821) 194-5
Prague, National Library of the Czech Republic
  MS VII G 17/d 209n.167
  MS XII D 10 209n.167
  MS XII D 11 209-10nn.167-168
  MS XII D 12 209n.167
  MS XII D 13 209-10nn.167-168
  MS XII D 8a 209n.167
  MS XII D 8b 209n.167
  MS XII D 9 209n.167
  MS XII E 14c. 209-10nn.167-168
  MS XIV A 17 208-10, 209f, 282-3
  MS XIV D 13 209n.167
  MS XIV E 10 209-10nn.167-168

Rein, Stiftsarchiv, MS D 274-7
Rome, Biblioteca Nazionale Centrale di Roma
  MS Sess. 44 (1473) 192n.112
  MS Sess. 45 (1364) 192n.112
Rudolstadt, Historische Bibliothek,
  2° Ink 3 282-3

Saint-Lô, Archives départementales de la
    Manche
  1 H 13 310n.258
  15 Fi 13 310n.258
San Marino, CA, Huntington Library, MS
    27187 280n.132
Schaffhausen, Ministerialbibliothek,
  MS 17 192-4
Solothurn, Sankt-Ursen-Kathedrale,
  MS U1 210-11

St-Omer, Bibliothèque d'Agglomération,
    MS 815 72-3
St Gall, Stiftsarchiv, Cod. Fab. 1 178-9
St Gall, Stiftsbibliothek
    MS Cod. Sang. 267, 614 186-7, 301-2
    MS Cod. Sang. 614 187n.94
    MS Cod. Sang. 1092 266-7
Stuttgart, Landesarchiv Baden-
        Württemberg-Hauptstaatsarchiv
    A 478 Bü 16 (*olim* Rep. Blaubeuren B.
        16) 180-1
    MS B 515 2a 196n.131
    MS HB I 240 195-6, 197*f*, 198*f*

Thurgau, Gemeindearchiv, KKG 16, B 6.2.01/1
    (*olim* B.VIII 1c/C.XV 13, no. 13) 178-9
Turin, Archivio Di Stato, MS IB.II.27 292-3

Valenciennes, Bibliothèque
        municipale-Médiathèque Simone Veil
    MS 39 (*olim* 33) 228n.239
    MS 50 (*olim* 43) 232n.259
    MS 60 (*olim* 53) 232n.256
    MS 65 (*olim* 58) 232n.256
    MS 66 (*olim* 59) 232n.256
    MS 156 (*olim* 148) 232n.256
    MS 298 (*olim* 288) 232n.258
    MS 498 (*olim* 458) 230n.246, 232n.256
    MS 546 (*olim* 500) 230n.246
Vatican, Biblioteca Apostolica Vaticana
    MS Pal. lat. 929 15n.2
    MS Pal. lat. 1877 299-300

MS Reg. lat. 12 179-80
MS Reg. lat. 95 204n.152
MS Reg. lat. 124 139-40
MS Reg. lat. 339 301-2
MS Vat. lat. 1202 189-90, 191*f*
MS Vat. lat. 3340 190
MS Vat. lat. 5758 292-3
MS Vat. lat. 11051 283n.148
Vendôme, Bibliothèque
        municipale-Médiathèque Parc Ronsard,
    MS 26 194n.123
Verdun, Bibliothèque d'étude du Grand Verdun,
    MS 8 37, 38*f*
Vienna, Österreichische Nationabibliothek, MS
    Cod. 460 152n.256

Wiesbaden, Hochschul- und Landesbibliothek
        RheinMain, MS 1 32-3
Wolfenbüttel, Herzog August
        Bibliothek
    MS Cod. 164.1 Extrav. 81-2
    MS Cod. Astron. 13.4 285n.156
    MS Cod. Guelf. 143.1 Extrav. 164-5
    MS Cod. Guelf. 265.4 Extrav. 283-4
Würzburg, Universitätsbibliothek
    MS ch. f. 126 15n.2, 164-5
    MS ch. f. 340 262
    MS p. th. q. 2 281-2
    MS p. th. q. 13 153n.262, 154-5
    MS p. th. q. 22 160-1

Zwettl, Stiftsbibliothek, MS 22 282-3